THE METAPHYSICS OF CREATION

THE METAPHYSICS
OF CREATION

Aquinas's Natural Theology
in Summa contra gentiles *II*

NORMAN KRETZMANN

CLARENDON PRESS · OXFORD

*This book has been printed digitally and produced in a standard specification
in order to ensure its continuing availability*

OXFORD
UNIVERSITY PRESS

Great Clarendon Street, Oxford OX2 6DP

Oxford University Press is a department of the University of Oxford.
It furthers the University's objective of excellence in research, scholarship,
and education by publishing worldwide in

Oxford New York

Auckland Cape Town Dar es Salaam Hong Kong Karachi
Kuala Lumpur Madrid Melbourne Mexico City Nairobi
New Delhi Shanghai Taipei Toronto
With offices in
Argentina Austria Brazil Chile Czech Republic France Greece
Guatemala Hungary Italy Japan South Korea Poland Portugal
Singapore Switzerland Thailand Turkey Ukraine Vietnam

Oxford is a registered trade mark of Oxford University Press
in the UK and in certain other countries

Published in the United States
by Oxford University Press Inc., New York

ISBN 0-19-823787-1

080081

To my friends

PREFACE

In January 1997 the Clarendon Press published my book *The Meta-physics of Theism: Aquinas's Natural Theology in* Summa contra gentiles *I.* In the present volume I continue my study of what I take to be the fullest and most promising natural theology ever produced, and I hope to be able to complete this project with a book devoted to Aquinas's *Summa contra gentiles* III.

Although this is a sequel to *The Metaphysics of Theism*, and although Aquinas conceives of his enterprise in *Summa contra gentiles* I–III as rigorously continuous, most of the topics covered in *The Metaphysics of Creation* can be considered on their own—especially those having to do with philosophy of mind, which occupy more than half the 101 chapters of Aquinas's Book II.

Philosophy and philosophical scholarship thrive on criticism. In writing *The Metaphysics of Theism*, I benefited from thought-provoking questions raised by members of graduate seminars and lecture audiences, and from the even more valuable detailed written criticisms faithfully provided by the best readers I could have wished for, all of whom I'm happy to count as friends of mine. Because I wrote *The Metaphysics of Creation* without nearly as much opportunity to try it out in lectures and seminars, I've been even more dependent on written criticisms I received on various drafts, especially on those I received on every chapter's first draft from my faithful friend and first reader, Eleonore Stump. William Rowe and Zoltán Szabó gave me helpful comments on some of these chapters, Anthony Kenny and Scott MacDonald on most of them, and William Alston on absolutely all of them. Once again I've had the best readers imaginable, for whose hard work and unstinting friendship I'm very grateful.

I've been able to work on these two books during the past six years largely because of the good offices of William S. Tyler, MD, whose humane, judicious treatment and character have left me grateful not only to have been his patient but also to have come to know him. And everything I've tried to do during these years and very many before them has been made much easier for me by Barbara's loving-kindness and by the loving cheer our family provides us with. I couldn't have done any of it nearly so happily without her and all of them.

The decision to dedicate this book to my friends seemed the least unsatisfactory way out of an embarrassment of gratitude and affection. I wanted to acknowledge many of my colleagues, near and far, some of whom have been my friends for almost half a century; and I wanted to recognize in the same way the many former students of mine whom I'm very glad to count among my friends. After discarding some worrisomely short and clumsy long lists of names, and realizing that I might not have another dedication to offer, I've dedicated this book to all of them. The dedicatees will recognize themselves under that description. And I hope I'll have let them know, in other ways as well, how much they've meant to me.

NORMAN KRETZMANN

January 1998

CONTENTS

Abbreviations   xiii

One. Nature from the Top Down   1

   1. The aims of the book   1
   2. Aquinas's natural theology   2
   3. SCG II as the thematic continuation of SCG I   8
   4. 'Divine truth'   10
   5. God's immanent and transeunt activity   14
   6. The positive results of meditating on creation 18
   7. The corrective results of meditating on creation 23
   8. How philosophy and the faith are taught   25
   9. Aquinas's plan for SCG II   28

Two. From God to Everything Else   30

   1. SCG II as the logical continuation of SCG I   30
   2. Considering the source   33
   3. The *actus purus* argument   36
   4. God's active power   41
   5. How to attribute power to God   44
   6. How to attribute relations to God   47
   7. God as the source of everything else   53
   8. Argument E/U   56

Three. Creation as Doubly Universal Production   70

   1. For all things the cause of being   70
   2. Out of no antecedent matter   73
   3. Not even prime matter   78
   4. Not through movement or change   81
   5. Something out of nothing   85
   6. Movement and change considered more closely   87
   7. No successiveness in creating   91
   8. No body can create   98
   9. Creating belongs to God alone   99

Four. Creation's Modalities   101

    1. Why would God create?   101
    2. The scope of God's creative power   103
    3. Separated substances as counter-instances to the
       single-effect account of creation   107
    4. Corporeal matter as a counter-instance to the
       single-effect account of creation   110
    5. Omnipotence and absolute possibility   113
    6. The modality of creative action   120
    7. The modalities of intellection and volition   126
    8. Justice, goodness, and God's plan as possible grounds
       for obligatory creation   130
    9. Kinds of necessity in created things   137

Five. Could the Created World have Existed for Ever?   142

    1. 'The eternity of the world'   142
    2. The modalities of beginningless creation   148
    3. The created world need not have existed for ever   152
    4. Beginninglessness based on considerations of God   159
    5. Beginninglessness based on considerations of created
       things   167
    6. Beginninglessness based on considerations of the
       making of things   172
    7. Purported proofs that the world must have begun
       to exist   175
    8. Aquinas's probable argument for the greater
       goodness of a temporally finite world   182

Six. The Origin of Species   183

    1. From producing to distinguishing   183
    2. Distinguishing and furnishing   186
    3. Aquinas's non-creationist reading of Genesis 1   190
    4. Distinguishing distinguished, broadly   193
    5. The complex product of an absolutely simple
       producer   196
    6. Distinguishing distinguished, more narrowly   198
    7. A mind behind the scenes   203
    8. Not by chance   205
    9. Not by matter alone   211
   10. Manifold manifestation   216
   11. God's choice of this world   224

Seven. Intellects 228

   1. Considering created things themselves 228
   2. Considering intellective creatures only 230
   3. Reasons why creation includes intellective substances 235
   4. Intellects and wills 240
   5. Will and freedom 244
   6. What intellective creatures could not be 251
   7. The metaphysical complexity of the simplest possible
      creatures 256
   8. The two species of potentiality–actuality composition 263
   9. Incorruptibility 268

Eight. Metaphysical Hybrids 270

   1. Intellective substances and corporeal substances 270
   2. Inapplicable modes of union 273
   3. Power contact 278
   4. Unconditional union 284
   5. Aquinas's unreasonable hypothesis 290
   6. The very nature of a human being 294
   7. Soul as the first principle of life 296
   8. Body and soul 299
   9. Body and souls? 307
  10. The peculiar character of the human soul 313

Nine. The Soul's Anatomy 323

   1. Aquinas's philosophy of mind in SCG II 323
   2. Special features of the soul's union with the body 325
   3. Aquinas's agenda in SCG II.73–78 337
   4. Parts of the soul 342
   5. The sensory part 345
   6. Sense in intellect's service 350
   7. Intellective cognition 357
   8. Organlessness 364

Ten. Souls before Birth and at Death 369

   1. The rest of Book II 369
   2. Reproduction, embryology, science, and metaphysics 373
   3. Aquinas's basic argument regarding the origin of an
      individual human being 376
   4. Particular creation as the source of a human soul's
      existence 384

5. Other naturalistic explanations of the origin of a
   human soul   387
6. The argument from the substantial unity of the
   human soul   396
7. Arguing for the incorruptibility of intellective souls 403
8. Arguing against arguments for the corruptibility of
   intellective souls   412

Appendix I: A Chronology of Aquinas's Life and Works   419
Appendix II: A Table Indicating the Correspondence
   between Sections of Chapters of SCG II in the Pera
   (Marietti) Edition and the Anderson Translation   427
Appendix III: In Sent. I.44.1.2: Could God Make a Better
   Universe?   436

References   440

Index locorum   451

General index   467

ABBREVIATIONS

CT	*Compendium theologiae*
DAM	*De aeternitate mundi, contra murmurantes*
DEE	*De ente et essentia*
DSS	*De substantiis separatis*
In BDH	*Expositio super librum Boethii De hebdomadibus*
In BDT	*Expositio super librum Boethii De trinitate*
In DA	*Sententia super De anima*
In DDN	*Expositio super librum Dionysii De divinis nominibus*
In EN	*Sententia libri Ethicorum*
In Met.	*Sententia super Metaphysicam*
In PA	*Sententia super Posteriora analytica*
In PH	*Sententia super Peri hermenias*
In Phys.	*Sententia super Physicam*
In Sent.	*Scriptum super libros Sententiarum*
QDA	*Quaestio disputata de anima*
QDP	*Quaestiones disputatae de potentia*
QDSC	*Quaestio disputata de spiritualibus creaturis*
QDV	*Quaestiones disputatae de veritate*
QQ	*Quaestiones quodlibetales*
SCG	*Summa contra gentiles*
ST	*Summa theologiae*

ONE

NATURE FROM THE TOP DOWN

1. The aims of the book

This book is the second in a projected series of three volumes. My book *The Metaphysics of Theism* (1997) is related to Book I of Thomas Aquinas's *Summa contra gentiles* (SCG) as this book is to Book II, and I hope to complete the series with *The Metaphysics of Providence*, corresponding to Book III.

'Aquinas's Natural Theology', a subtitle these three volumes share, identifies what I take to have been developed and presented in SCG I–III.[1] The subtitle may also suggest that the series of volumes is intended primarily as a project in philosophical scholarship, presenting a historical account and critical exposition of Aquinas's thirteenth-century achievement.[2] It's certainly true that one reason I've had for undertaking this study is my conviction that

---

[1] Very near the beginning of SCG, in his general introduction to the entire work, Aquinas says, 'It is difficult to argue against mistaken views associated with particular people, . . . because some of them—Muhammadans and pagans, for instance— do not agree with us about the authority of any scripture on the basis of which they can be refuted. . . . And so it is necessary to have recourse to natural reason, to which everybody is compelled to assent, even though natural reason cannot do the whole job of dealing with divine matters'—i.e. with God and with everything else as related to God (I.2.10–11). (For the interpretation of references in this form, see n. 7 below.) In the first three of SCG's four books Aquinas takes natural reason to be a sufficient basis on which to do a very large part of the whole job—from establishing the existence of God to working out details of human morality. It's for that reason that I am treating SCG I–III as the paradigm of a fully developed natural theology. (Aquinas does not, however, use the Latin equivalent of 'natural theology' to designate this undertaking. On the history of natural theology see esp. Webb 1915 and Gerson 1990.) The insufficiency of natural reason which Aquinas mentions at the end of the quoted passage accounts for SCG's fourth and last book, in which, beginning again with God and working his way down through rational creatures, he addresses in particular just those few, distinctively Christian doctrinal propositions to which reason would have no initial access without the revelation he accepts— propositions such as the doctrines of the Trinity, the Incarnation, and the resurrection of the body. He does this, he says, with the aim of showing that even those propositions 'are *not opposed* to natural reason' (IV.1.3348).

[2] By far the best available historical account of SCG is in Gauthier 1993.

Aquinas's systematic natural theology constitutes a philosophically interesting historical subject that has been generally neglected, misunderstood, or simply unrecognized for what it is. So my plan for these three volumes includes trying to present, explain, and evaluate the treatments of several essential topics in each of the three parts of his natural theology. In this way, I hope that these books will make a contribution to medieval philosophical scholarship.[3]

But other considerations have also motivated me, considerations that make Aquinas's natural theology philosophically important, I think, as well as interesting. They have led me to approach it not merely as the monumental achievement it already was when Aquinas completed it in 1265,[4] but also as the classic version of an ambitious theory that invites extrapolation and sometimes needs correcting in its details. Viewed in that way, this natural theology is a continuing enterprise for which Aquinas's work has provided rich material developed in promising patterns. So in this book, as in *The Metaphysics of Theism* (TMOT), I mean also to engage in that enterprise in ways that will, I hope, encourage the critical co-operation of others in pursuing the development of a wide-ranging natural theology along the lines Aquinas drew.

2. Aquinas's natural theology

In my view, a great deal—not all—of theology's traditional subject-matter is really continuous with philosophy's subject-matter, and ought to be integrated with it in practice. Most philosophers who lived before the twentieth century would share this view, and no substantive developments in the last hundred years should have obscured it. In the first three-quarters of the twentieth century it surely was obscured, but we have recently been witnessing a devel-

---

[3] Just after I delivered the series of lectures that prefigured the first of these three volumes, I was surprised to hear a friendly reviewer describe the lectures as 'a commentary on the first book of Aquinas's *Summa contra gentiles*'. I didn't then, and don't now, intend anything so comprehensive and detailed as a commentary would have to be. My aim is rather to produce a selective, critical analysis of Aquinas's natural theology, occasionally extrapolating from it in ways that strike me as consonant with the already impressively wide-ranging theistic metaphysics he developed in SCG I–III.

[4] See Appendix I below, 'A Chronology of Aquinas's Life and Works'.

opment in which that view is no longer so hard to find among philosophers: as late twentieth-century theologians have been moving away from their traditional subject-matter, philosophers have been moving in.[5] And natural theology, a branch of philosophy, interests me especially, because it provides the traditional, and still central, means of integrating (some of) theology with philosophy.

I presented my conception of natural theology in detail in TMOT's Chapter One, and the details do not need rehearsing here. But for a concise, general account of natural theology's nature and status, independent of any particular concern with Aquinas's work, I couldn't do better than to offer William Alston's view of the discipline in the following passage:

Natural theology is the enterprise of providing support for religious beliefs by starting from premises that neither are nor presuppose any religious beliefs. We begin from the mere existence of the world, or the teleological order of the world, or the concept of God, and we try to show that when we think through the implications of our starting point we are led to recognize the existence of a being that possesses attributes sufficient to identify Him as God. Once we get that foothold we may seek to show that a being could not have the initial attributes without also possessing certain others; in this manner we try to go as far as we can in building up a picture of God without relying on any supposed experience of God or communication from God, or on any religious authority. (Alston 1991: 289)

The view which Alston takes in this passage is broad by comparison with the more familiar notion of natural theology, which limits it to attempts to argue for (or against) the existence of God.[6] His view here could serve well as a sketch of Aquinas's undertaking in SCG I, which Aquinas himself describes as covering 'matters associated with God considered in himself' (I.9.57[7])—i.e. the subject-matter of

---

[5] Perhaps the fullest, clearest evidence of this development can be found in the thriving journal *Faith and Philosophy*, founded in 1984 and associated with the Society of Christian Philosophers.

[6] See e.g. Alvin Plantinga's discussion of natural theology in Plantinga 1983, which begins by identifying it as 'the attempt to prove or demonstrate the existence of God' (p. 63).

[7] My many references to SCG are in this form. The initial roman numeral indicates a book of SCG: I, II, III, or IV. (Since the vast majority of my references in this volume are to SCG II, the roman numeral will often be omitted.) The two subsequent arabic numerals, preceded by full points, designate the chapter and section as numbered in the edition of the Latin text that is best for practical purposes: *S. Thomae Aquinatis, Doctoris Angelici, Liber de Veritate Catholicae Fidei contra*

what might fairly be called classical natural theology: the existence of something whose inferred nature constitutes a prima-facie basis for identifying it as God and the further aspects of God's nature that can be inferred in working out the implications of that starting-point.

But an even broader view of natural theology is called for if it is to include the topics which Aquinas goes on to develop in SCG II and III—a view almost as broad as the one that Alston takes up soon after presenting the one we've been considering:

> This characterization of natural theology [the one quoted above] sticks closely to the classically recognized 'arguments for the existence of God', but it need not be construed that narrowly. It also includes attempts to show that we can attain the best understanding of this or that area of our experience or sphere of concern—morality, human life, society, human wickedness, science, art, mathematics, or whatever—if we look at it from the standpoint of a theistic ... metaphysics. (Alston 1991: 289)

The idea of a natural theology that goes far beyond arguments for God's existence is one which Alston shares with Aquinas, as can be seen in detail in SCG II and III. I think it's quite likely that Aquinas believes, too, that the explanatory capacity of natural theology is in theory universal, as Alston suggests with his 'or whatever'. But the idea Aquinas puts into practice in SCG is less broad than the one Alston outlines here. Aquinas does take up some of the broad topics which Alston lists, and a few more besides. But he expressly excludes the concerns of natural science from the scope of the project in which he is engaging, as we'll see, and he shows no signs of having ever thought about including art or mathematics. Still, Alston's implied characterization of natural theology as theistic metaphysics is very like what Aquinas seems to have had in mind generally—as the titles of these books of mine are meant to suggest, and as their contents show.

In TMOT I dealt only with the topics of SCG I: 'matters associ-

errores Infidelium seu 'Summa contra Gentiles', Textus Leoninus diligenter recognitus, ed. C. Pera, OP, with the assistance of P. Marc, OSB, and P. Caramello, OSB (3 vols., Turin and Rome: Marietti, 1961–7). In this book all quotations from Aquinas in English are my translations, and those taken from SCG are based on the Marietti edn. Appendix II below provides a complete table of parallel references in SCG II for readers who want to consult the only complete published English translation currently in print, in which the sections of the chapters are numbered differently. The translation of SCG II is contained in the second volume—Anderson 1975—of that 5-vol. complete translation.

ated with God considered in himself'. In this volume I deal with the topics of Book II, which Aquinas describes as 'the emergence of created things from him', and I hope to be able to go on in a third volume to deal with the topics of Book III, 'the ordering and directing of created things toward [God] as their goal' (I.9.57). As even Aquinas's short descriptions of the three parts of his natural theology may suggest, it is intended to integrate a great many topics that would ordinarily be treated separately, and differently, in other branches of philosophy—branches recognizable both in the Aristotelian philosophy he knew best and in the philosophy of the late twentieth century—including metaphysics, philosophy of mind, epistemology, and ethics.[8] Integrating all those topics by means of natural theology involves developing within this particular branch of philosophy some of the subject-matter specifically associated with theology as it developed outside philosophy in the three great monotheisms, in the form of 'revealed' or 'dogmatic' theology, based on Scriptural exegesis. That, of course, is what makes this branch of philosophy natural *theology*: investigating, by means of analysis and argument, at least the existence and nature of God and, in this fuller development, the relation of everything else—but especially of human nature and behaviour—to God considered as reality's first principle.

But developing parts of that subject-matter within philosophy of course requires forgoing appeals to any putative revelation or religious experience as evidence for the truth of propositions, and taking for granted only those few naturally evident considerations that traditionally constitute data acceptable to philosophers generally.[9] That's what makes it *natural* theology.

[8] 'For human philosophy considers them [i.e. natural things] in their own right' rather than as advancing and enhancing natural theology's investigation of God, 'which is why we find different parts of philosophy corresponding to different kinds of things' (II.4.871).

[9] Throughout SCG Aquinas freely introduces as premises of his arguments not only propositions he has argued for earlier, but also many propositions which he treats as *principles*, as needing no support within this project itself. As might be expected, Aquinas gets these principles almost entirely from Aristotle. No doubt he takes some of them to be self-evidently true, and surely he is sometimes within his rights to do so—e.g. 'A conditional proposition with an impossible antecedent can be true,' or 'Substance does not depend on accident, although accident depends on substance.' I believe that he takes all the others to have been successfully argued for by Aristotle. For instance, when he invokes the Aristotelian thesis of the incorporeality of the human intellect, something he hasn't even discussed in the preceding chapters of SCG I, he justifies doing so by pointing out that '*it has been proved*

Aquinas's natural theology does, however, make a restricted, philosophically tolerable use of propositions he considers to have been divinely revealed. Often at the end of a chapter in SCG I–III, after having argued for some proposition in several different ways, each of which scrupulously omits any reference to revelation, he will cite Scripture by way of showing that what has just been established by unaided reason agrees with what he takes to be revealed truth.[10] (For example, in Book I, chapter 20, after having presented ten arguments to show that God is not in any way corporeal, he observes that 'divine authority concurs with this demonstrated truth', citing three biblical passages, including John 4: 24: 'God is a spirit . . .' (188).) On those occasions he certainly does not take himself to be introducing a revealed text in order to remove doubts about natural theology's results; they are, after all, the results of 'natural reason, to which *everybody* is *compelled* to assent' (I.2.11). 'Divine authority' is not invoked as *support* for propositions occurring as premises or conclusions in the logical structure of SCG I–III.[11]

that intellect is not a corporeal power' (I.20.183)—which must be an allusion to Aristotle's own arguments to that effect in *De anima* III (an allusion of a sort that his thirteenth-century academic contemporaries would have had no trouble picking up). Since the natural theology which Aquinas is developing evidently has, by his own lights, the status of a science subordinate to metaphysics proper, to *Aristotelian* metaphysics, there is every reason why he should—indeed, must—help himself to Aristotelian first principles and argued theses in developing his subordinate science. (On natural theology's status as a subordinate science in this sense, see TMOT, Ch. One, sects. 5 and 6.)

[10] In this context, '*unaided* reason' is intended as short for 'reason guided but unsupported by revelation', or 'reason which revelation has provided with topics but not with premisses'.

[11] James F. Anderson gives a different, and misleading, impression in the introduction to Anderson 1975: 'Assuredly, there is a metaphysics—a straight philosophy—of creation contained in Book II of the *Summa Contra Gentiles*, but the Book is not merely a metaphysics of creation. . . . St. Thomas uses arguments purely natural in character, *as well as arguments appealing to the revealed word of God*' (p. 13; emphasis added). Although Anderson gives no example of the latter sort of argument at that point, the only such example he does give, later in the introduction, is clearly not what he thinks it is: 'St. Thomas, as we shall see, does not limit himself to the so-called purely rational order. He proceeds to argue [in II.92], on Scriptural as well as rational grounds, that such substances are exceedingly numerous . . . Scripture itself bears witness not only to the existence but to the very great number of separate substances: "Thousands of thousands ministered to Him, and ten thousand times a hundred thousand stood before him" (Dan. 7: 10). Certainly there are rational and natural considerations. . . . But it is the Word of God which is fully conclusive in this matter' (p. 19). In fact, Aquinas introduces the passage from the book of Daniel only at the end of the chapter, after having

Scripture's systematic contribution to Aquinas's natural theology may be construed as primarily an aid to navigation, showing him his destinations and practicable routes to them in a rational progression. From any one of the propositions previously argued for in the systematic development of his natural theology, reason could, in theory, validly derive infinitely many further propositions. But Aquinas's systematic natural theology, like the presentation of any well-defined subject-matter in a series of connected arguments, is more expository than exploratory.[12] It is designed to show, primarily, that reason *unsupported* by revelation could have come up with many—not all—of just those propositions that constitute the established subject-matter of what he takes to be revealed theology. But that design requires that reason be *guided* by what he takes to be revelation. Whatever may be said of natural theology generally, Aquinas's version of it certainly is, as Alston puts it, 'the enterprise of providing support *for religious beliefs* by starting from premises that neither are nor presuppose any religious beliefs'.[13] So Aquinas needs Scripture in these circumstances to provide a chart to guide his choice of propositions to argue for, as well as a list of specifications that can be consulted to see, first, that it is indeed one and the same 'truth that faith professes and reason investigates' (I.9.55) and, second, '*how* the demonstrative truth is in harmony with the faith of the Christian religion' (I.2.12). But his distinctive, primary aim in the first three books of SCG is the systematic development of that demonstrative truth, *up to* the point at which the theism being argued for begins to rely on propositions that are

produced all his non-Scriptural arguments for the chapter's thesis, in just the way he handles biblical passages generally in his natural theology: 'Now Sacred Scripture bears witness (*attestatur*) to these things, for in Daniel 7[: 10] it says . . .' (92.1794). Bearing witness to, or confirming the conclusions already argued for is very different from being 'fully conclusive in this matter'.

[12] In this respect, as in others, it seems likely to have been intended to approximate the idea of an Aristotelian science. 'Aristotle does not pretend to be offering guidance to the scientist—or, for that matter, to the historian or the philosopher—on how best to pursue his researches or how most efficiently to uncover new truths. . . . Rather, it [Book A of the *Posterior Analytics*] is concerned with the organization and presentation of the results of research: its aim is to say how we may collect into an intelligible whole the scientist's various discoveries—how we may so arrange the facts that their interrelations, and in particular their explanations, may best be revealed and grasped. In short, the primary purpose of [Aristotelian] demonstration is to expound and render intelligible what is already discovered, not to discover what is still unknown' (Barnes 1975: pp. x–xi).

[13] Alston 1991: 289, quoted more fully above; emphasis added here.

initially accessible to reason only via revelation and becomes *distinctively* Christian.

As I see it, then, SCG I–III is Aquinas's most unified, systematic contribution to the project of arriving at a thoroughly rational confirmation of perfect-being theism generally, of showing the extent to which what had been revealed might have been discovered, the extent to which 'the invisible things of God from the creation of the world' might be 'clearly seen, being understood by the things that are made' (Rom. 1: 20). As such, it is addressed to every open-minded, reasoning person.[14]

3. SCG II as the thematic continuation of SCG I

The fuller development of Aquinas's natural theology, in which he moves beyond matters associated directly with God considered in himself, begins where SCG II begins. His introduction to the new material occupies Book II's first five chapters. The titles of chapters in SCG are not always Aquinas's own,[15] but the wording of the title presumably supplied by some medieval scribe for chapter 1 strikes just the right note, introducing the investigations to be carried out in Book II as the 'continuation' of those carried out in Book I. For what SCG II.1 goes on to show is not just what one might reasonably have expected—the relevance of Book II's new study of creation to Book I's just-completed study of God—but rather the indispensability of Book II's contribution to the *continuing* study of God. In Aquinas's view, it is not as if in Book I he develops a rational investigation of God, and then in Book II shifts his focus and investigates creation in the same way. Instead, this natural-theological study of God's creation is a further study of God, intended to enhance and extend the results of the initial study of God, considered *in himself*. And that strong continuity is just what

[14] For what clearly deserves to be the last nail in the coffin of the stubborn tradition that Aquinas wrote SCG as a manual for Dominican missionaries to Jews and Arabs, see Gauthier's 'Appendice: La Légende "Missionaire"', in Gauthier 1993: 165–76.

[15] In SCG II the titles of only the following chapters can be found in the autograph, the surviving part of the original MS in Aquinas's own handwriting: 11–13&14, 15, 18–28, 30–1, 34–5, 39–44, 47–8, and 50–60. (See the eds.' n. 1 on p. 114 in vol. ii of the Marietti edn.) Among the lost parts of the autograph is the one that contained SCG II.61–III.43 (see Gauthier 1993: 8–10).

should have been expected from Aquinas's original plan for SCG I–III: 'So, for us, intending to pursue by way of reason those things *about God* that human reason can investigate, the first considera-tion is of matters associated with *God considered in himself*; second, of the emergence of created things *from him*; third, of the ordering and directing of created things *toward him* as their goal' (I.9.57). Creation and providence, then, the topics of Books II and III, are included among the things *about God* that unaided human reason can investigate.

That single, fixed focus of all three parts of his investigation is what Aquinas's general conception of theology, whether natural or revealed, would also lead us to expect: 'the discussion carried on in this science is *about God*, for it is called *"theo-logia"*, which means the same as "discourse about God". Therefore, *God* is the subject of this science' (ST Ia.1.7, sc[16]). And in this first chapter of SCG II the goal which Aquinas outlines for Books II and III, founded on Book I's accomplishments, is 'the filled-out (*completam*) consideration of divine truth'—i.e. the truth *about God* (II.1.856).[17]

Exclusive concern with God or the truth about God might seem too narrow for the broad conception of natural theology I've attrib-uted to Aquinas and adopted myself, a conception that I described in TMOT as a sort of Grandest Unified Theory, with the capacity of being ultimately explanatory of absolutely everything. But that misgiving should be dispelled when we find out what Aquinas

[16] My references to ST will be in this form, beginning with the traditional desig-nation for the Part (*Pars*)—Ia (*Prima*), IaIIae (*Prima secundae*), IIaIIae (*Secunda secundae*), or IIIa (*Tertia*). The first arabic numeral following any one of those designations indicates the Question in that Part, and the next arabic numeral, following a full point, indicates the Article belonging to that Question. A 'c' imme-diately following the second arabic numeral indicates that the passage belongs to Aquinas's reply in that Article (the 'body' (*corpus*) of the Article); 'obj. 1', 'obj. 2', etc., indicates one of the 'objections' (opposing arguments); 'sc' indicates the 'sed contra' (the citation of an authority or generally acceptable consideration contrary to the line taken in the Objections), and 'ad 1', 'ad 2', etc., indicates one of Aquinas's rejoinders to the objections.

[17] The term 'divine truth' presents a minor problem, discussed in sect. 4 below. I translate *completam* here as 'filled-out' rather than 'complete', mainly because of Aquinas's careful disclaimer about the possibility of acquiring complete knowledge of God by the methods of his natural theology (or, indeed, by any means available to human beings). Even the 'consideration focused on God's substance', which makes up most of SCG I (chs. 28–102), 'will not be complete (*perfecta*), however, because there will not be cognition of *what he is in himself*'—i.e. we cannot on that basis provide a complete account of God's essence (I.14.118). See also n. 28 below and SCG I.30.278, quoted in sect. 5 below.

thinks is included in the truth about God. Theology, he says, has as its 'main aim . . . to transmit a cognition of God, and not only as he is in himself, but also as he is the source of [all] things, and their goal—especially of the rational creature' (ST Ia.2, intro.). So the subject-matter of theology is the truth about *everything*, with two provisos: first, it is about God *and* about everything other than God, but *only* as everything other than God relates to God as its source and its goal; second, it is about everything other than God as related to God in those ways, but *especially* about human beings (for reasons that will become clear, if they aren't already). Theology is about God considered in himself and considered in the fundamentally explanatory source-and-goal relationships—primarily the relationships of efficient and final causation—to everything else, especially to the rational creature. It is in this way that the business of theology is the single ultimate explanation of everything, the Grandest Unified Theory; and it is for this reason that Aquinas describes its practitioner as one 'whom all the other arts diligently serve' (IaIIae.7.2, ad 3).[18] And, he insists, universal scope is just what one should expect in a rational investigation of the truth about God: 'All things are considered in theology (*sacra doctrina*[19]) under the concept of God, either because they *are* God, or because they have an ordered relationship *to* God as to their source and goal. It follows from this that the subject of this science is really God' (Ia.1.7c), even though the intended explanatory scope of the fully developed science is universal, as it can be only because its primary subject is God, the absolutely first principle.[20]

4. 'Divine truth'

Since what we believe is what we believe to be the truth, it is only natural that Aquinas, like anyone else presenting an argued confir-

[18] See also the discussion of SCG II.4 in sect. 8 below.

[19] For a discussion of the special sense of *sacra doctrina*, see TMOT, Ch. One, sects. 5 and 6.

[20] As Anthony Kenny has pointed out to me, Aquinas's natural theology seen in this way reveals its close association with Aristotle's first philosophy, which looks like ontology when Aristotle describes it as the science of being *qua* being, and like theology when he describes it as the science of being *qua* divine. The unity of the two descriptions can be seen when 'being *qua* being' is understood as what first philosophy is intended to investigate and explain, and 'being *qua* divine' is understood as the ultimate explanation resulting from that investigation.

mation of his beliefs about anything, should describe the subject-matter of SCG generally as the truth. And since he thinks that all the truth about God that is available to us, whether through reason or through revelation, coincides or at least coheres with Christian doctrine in the form in which he accepts it, he can describe SCG's subject-matter more narrowly as 'the truth that the Catholic faith professes' (I.2.9). His intention in SCG, he says, is to make that truth clear, to the best of his ability (ibid.). Of course, the truth that the Catholic faith professes is based on revelation, and one can try to clarify it simply by expounding that revealed truth, as is done in dogmatic theology. But Aquinas carefully spells out a quite different programme for SCG:

> We will aim first [in Books I–III] at making clear the truth that faith professes and reason investigates, bringing in both demonstrative and probable arguments, some of which we have gathered from the books of the philosophers and of the saints—arguments on the basis of which the truth will be confirmed and its adversary overcome. Next, in order to proceed from things that are clearer to those that are less clear, we will move on [in Book IV] to the clarification of the truth that surpasses reason, dismantling the arguments of its adversaries, and elucidating the truth of the faith by means of probable and authoritative arguments, as far as God grants it. (I.9.55–6)[21]

In his general introduction to SCG he bases the division between the philosophical theology of SCG IV[22] and the natural theology of SCG I–III on a division between 'two modes' (*duplex modus*) of that one truth that faith professes and reason investigates: 'Now there are two modes of truth in connection with the things we [Christians] confess about God [in our creeds]. For [1] there are

---

[21] Notice the broad but crucial methodological division between SCG I–III and SCG IV: the devices of natural theology are 'demonstrative and probable arguments'—the sorts of arguments characteristic of philosophy generally—whereas those of the last book's philosophical theology are 'probable and *authoritative* arguments', the latter involving direct appeals to Scripture or to doctrines that rest on ecclesiastical authority.

[22] Dogmatic theology's processing of the raw data of revelation gives rise, traditionally, to 'philosophical' theology, the analytical and argumentative clarification, extension, and defence of the articles of faith. Philosophical theology is what was produced by most medieval theologians, whether or not they would have been happy with that designation for it, and what is being produced by many philosophers of religion now. Technically and traditionally, philosophical theology should be classified as a part of revealed theology rather than of philosophy, just because it includes putatively revealed propositions among its starting-points. On philosophical theology, see Kenny 1964 and MacDonald 1996.

some truths about God that surpass every faculty of human reason—e.g. that God is three and one—but [2] there are others that even natural reason can attain to—e.g. that God exists, that God is one, and others of that sort—which philosophers, too, led by the light of natural reason, have demonstratively proved about God' (I.3.14). The small number of distinctively Christian, mode-1 truths comprise 'the mysteries' of the faith, the doctrinal propositions that are initially available to human beings via revelation alone.[23] They are reserved for treatment in SCG IV, where Aquinas undertakes to show that 'natural reason *cannot* be *contrary* to the truth of the faith' (I.9.52), even when the propositions composing that part of the truth of the faith are such that natural reason left to itself would not have arrived at them.

The many more mode-2 truths about God, the propositions comprising perfect-being theism, that part of the truth of the faith to which natural reason unaided by revelation *does* have initial access, are the subject-matter of SCG I–III. Aquinas elsewhere calls them '*preambles* to the articles of faith' (ST Ia.2.2, ad 1), not because they are not themselves included among the articles of faith,[24] but because they can also be arrived at as conclusions of arguments that include no articles of faith among their premisses. However, his development of this subject-matter in his natural theology goes far beyond merely supplying argumentative confirmation for revealed propositions included in the original stock of mode-2 truths. This application of natural reason aims also to disclose via argumentation certain theoretical propositions that are included among those truths only implicitly—e.g. that God could not be composite in any way (I.18), or specified by differentiae (I.24), or the subject of an a priori demonstration (I.25).[25]

At the outset of ST Aquinas presents his view of the relationship between these two modes of the truth about God and the reason why even the mode-2 truths have been revealed:

[23] As William Alston has pointed out to me, this number is small only if we restrict our consideration to such fundamental Christian doctrines as the Trinity and the Incarnation, but not if we take into account the details of salvation history—which might be construed as the historical details of the Incarnation. Aquinas omits most of those details from consideration in SCG IV.

[24] See e.g. I.4.21: 'Therefore, because there are two truths having to do with divine matters that can be intellectively cognized—the one that reason's inquiry can attain to, and the other, which rises above every ability of human reason—it is appropriate that both of them are divinely set before human beings to be believed.'

[25] On the derivation of all these negative characterizations and several more besides, see TMOT, Ch. Four.

It was necessary that human beings be instructed by divine revelation even as regards the things about God that [unaided] human reason can explore. For the truth about God investigated by a few on the basis of reason [without relying on revelation] would emerge for people [only] after a long time and tainted with many mistakes. And yet all human well-being, which has to do with God, depends on the cognition of that truth. Therefore, it was necessary for human beings to be instructed about divine matters through divine revelation so that [the nature of human] well-being might emerge for people more conveniently and with greater certainty. (Ia.1.1c)

However, at least one detail of SCG II.1 might seem to blur the clear, practical division which we have been noting. We have seen Aquinas describe Book II as required for 'the filled-out consideration of divine truth' (II.1.856). But 'divine truth' (*divina veritas*) is a term that has a semi-technical sense in Book I, especially in chapter 62, where it is used throughout as the designation for the all-inclusive truth that may conveniently be thought of as the total content of God's omniscience, the *divina veritas* that is among truths 'the first and highest' (I.62.515–18) or 'the first, highest, and absolutely perfect', the truth by which any 'truth possessed by any intellect must be measured' (519). And because Aquinas has argued in Book I for God's absolute simplicity,[26] in accordance with which that divine truth simply *is* God himself, no distinction between modes of truth can apply to 'divine truth' in this special sense: 'I speak of two truths of divine matters not in connection with God himself—who *is* truth, one and simple—but in connection with our cognition, which is related in different ways to the divine matters about which we are to attain cognition' (I.9.51).[27] And, of course, the divine truth referred to in II.1.856, which is to be 'filled out' in Books II and III, cannot be God himself or the content of God's omniscience. Is Aquinas, then, simply using *divina veritas* in a non-technical sense here at the beginning of Book II to mean something as broad as Book I's 'truths about God' (*vera . . . de Deo*) (I.3.14)? I think so. But, as we've been seeing, the infinitely many truths about God that unaided reason might investigate must, for practical purposes, be restricted to the ones

---

[26] See esp. I.18. See also Stump and Kretzmann 1982.

[27] See also I.1.7, quoted in sect. 6 below. Sometimes, as in I.4.21 (quoted in n. 24 above) or in 9.51, Aquinas uses what appears to be language stronger than 'the two modes of truth'—viz. 'the two truths [or 'the double truth'] of divine matters (*duplicem veritatem divinorum*)'. But the context shows that he means by it no more than the practical division we are discussing.

that comprise 'the truth that the faith professes' (I.9.55), explicitly or implicitly.

5. *God's immanent and transeunt activity*

The status of Book II as Book I's continuation, required for a fuller understanding of God's nature, is brought out concisely and convincingly in the argument with which II.1 begins. Our effort to fill out our cognition of the nature of *anything* must include the attempt to acquire some cognition of the thing's *powers*, those aspects of its nature that explain its characteristic *activities*; 'for any thing is suited to act [in certain ways] on the basis of its actually having such and such a *nature*' (1.852). But we can draw inferences regarding the (intrinsic) powers which a thing must have only on the basis of what we can learn about its (extrinsic) activities. So the further development of natural theology's investigation of God requires us to attend to what can be identified as God's activities: 'One cannot have a complete (*perfecta*) cognition of any thing at all unless one has cognition of its activity (*operatio*), for the measure and the quality of a thing's power are evaluated by the mode and type of its activity; but a thing's power reveals its nature' (ibid.).[28]

This programme for Aquinas's project in Book II may seem surprising, since he has already devoted almost all of Book I (chs. 14–102) to an investigation of God's nature, after having established the existence of God as the necessitated explanation of certain undoubted features of ordinary reality.[29] The first stage of

---

[28] A *complete* cognition of even ordinary things is in Aquinas's view an ideal that can only be approximated in varying degrees. See e.g. In DA I: L1.15: 'the essential principles of things are unknown to us'; *Collationes super Credo*, preface: 'our cognition is so feeble that no philosopher has ever been able to investigate completely the nature of a fly'; also QDV 4.1, ad 8; 6.1, ad 8; 10.1c; 10.1, ad 6; QDSC 11, ad 3; SCG I.3.18; ST IIaIIae.8.1c; In PA I: L4.43; II: L13.533.

[29] What he actually accomplishes in this line, and the ways in which he accomplishes it, are examined in detail in TMOT, esp. Chs. Two–Five. Alston's description of natural theology, formulated with no particular attention to Aquinas, turns out to provide a reasonably good synopsis of the development in SCG I: 'We begin from the mere existence of the world, or the teleological order of the world, or the concept of God'—Aquinas argues that this *third* (Anselmian) starting-point is *not* really available to us (I.10–11)—'and we try to show that when we think through the implications of our starting point we are led to recognize the existence of a being that possesses attributes sufficient to identify Him as God. Once we get that foothold we may seek to show that a being could not have the initial attributes without also possessing certain others' (Alston 1991: 289; quoted more fully above).

that investigation proceeded by what he calls the eliminative method, which is designed to start us finding out about God's nature by discovering what such an absolutely necessary, ultimately explanatory being could not be: 'we come closer to the knowledge of it to the extent to which we can through our intellect *eliminate* more [characteristics] from it; for the more fully we discern anything's differences from other things, the more completely do we discern it' (I.14.117). The investigation's second stage, based on the eliminative method's distinctions between God and everything else, systematically derives *affirmative* predications by considering characteristics of ordinary natural things and inferring some of what must be positively attributed to the entity that is ultimately explanatory of the existence and essential characteristics of such things. The transition to the new, more direct method begins in I.28, with Aquinas's linked arguments *against* every *imperfection* in the first source of being and *for* its *universal perfection*. As a consequence of I.28's arguments for the necessary elimination of all imperfection from God, Aquinas thereafter often refers to divine attributes generally as perfections.[30]

Within the limits of natural theology there are, he observes, only two sorts of bases on which we can justifiably ascribe perfections to God: either '[1] through *negation*, as when we call God eternal [i.e. beginningless, endless, timeless] or infinite [i.e. limitless]; or also [2] through a *relation* he has to other things, as when he is called the first cause, or the highest good. For as regards God we cannot grasp what he is, but rather [1] what he is not, and [2] how other things are disposed relative to him' (I.30.278). Having used the first of these two bases for the eliminative method, he then develops the second as the basis for the more elaborately justified of his two specific methods for natural theology. This relational method governed most of Aquinas's philosophical account of God's nature in SCG I (the material developed in chs. 37–102), enabling him to introduce those divine attributes or perfections that can be inferred from what we know about the ordinary things of which that nature is, one way or another, the ultimate explanation.[31] And, since (if we set aside ontological arguments, as Aquinas does) *any* philosophical account

---

[30] On this transition and the new method see TMOT, Ch. Five.

[31] The relational method is essential also in Aquinas's systematic development of revealed theology. See e.g. ST Ia.13.2. For a very helpful survey of Aquinas's methods in theology generally, see Wippel 1992.

of God's existence and nature must be based on inferences from the natures and modal statuses of things other than God, something more or less like Aquinas's relational method will have to be used by anyone attempting to develop a natural theology.

Among the divine perfections which Aquinas argued for by his relational method are intellect and will, to which he devoted 53 of Book I's 102 chapters.[32] And intellect and will are *powers*, whose primary *activities* are intellection (or intellective cognition) and volition (within which Aquinas includes divine joy and love). Consequently, Book I already involved considerable attention to activity in God. But all the intellective and volitional activities with which Book I was concerned belong to the first of activity's two species: to God's intrinsic, 'immanent' activity, the kind that Aquinas considers to be the paradigm of activity (or action) generally, partly because it is 'a completing [or perfecting, or actualizing] of the active thing itself' (II.1.853). This is the species of activity that is justifiably ascribed to God 'in that he has intellective cognition, wills, enjoys, and loves' (854); and Book I has argued that all these must be true of God.[33] Any being characterized by intellect and will is completed, perfected, or actualized in those respects only to the extent to which its intellective and volitional powers are in action; and God is entirely, eternally active (I.16). And any intellective, volitional being that is also perfectly good—as SCG I.37–41 has argued God must be[34]—must also be characterized by joy and love (I.90–1).

Book II's continuity with Book I is borne out by its pursuing the investigation of activity in this logically natural progression, moving from the first to the second species of activity: from God's immanent activity to his extrinsic, 'transeunt' activity, his effecting and affecting things other than himself.[35] Transeunt activity in

---

[32] The arguments for and about intellect in God occupy chs. 44–71, and chs. 72–96 have to do with will in God (72–88 more obviously, 89–96 a little less so).

[33] These immanent divine activities and Aquinas's arguments in support of ascribing them to God are considered in detail in TMOT, Chs. Six, Seven, and Eight.

[34] On Aquinas's account of God's perfect goodness see also Stump and Kretzmann 1988.

[35] 'Transeunt' in this connection is of course just the antonym of 'immanent', adopted in order to avoid the misleading connotations of the more familiar 'transient', which is roughly synonymous with 'transitory' or 'ephemeral'. As Aquinas points out (II.1.853), the distinction between immanent and transeunt activity is found in Aristotle (*Metaphysics* VIII 8, 1050a23–b2); but neither Aquinas nor Aristotle has technical terms for these two kinds of activity.

intellective-volitional agents (the only sort at issue here) depends on immanent activity, the paradigm of activity. Any transeunt activity that can be strictly ascribed to an agent must stem from some immanent intellective and volitional activity on the agent's part, which is prior to the transeunt activity 'naturally' or, as we would say, logically (though it may be simultaneous with it temporally): 'the first kind of activity must be the basis (*ratio*) of the second and precede it naturally, as cause precedes effect. This appears clearly in human affairs, of course; for an artisan's considering and willing is the source and basis of [the artisan's] building' (1.854). But, of course, not all immanent activity need result in transeunt activity. A transeunt activity that expresses some immanent activity on the agent's part—your picking up the telephone, having decided to call your friend—should, Aquinas thinks, be called 'making' (*facere*) more strictly than 'acting' (*agere*). This making, this transeunt activity, completes or perfects not the *agent*, but 'the result that is set up (*constituitur*) through that very [immanent] activity' (853). Your deciding actualizes *you* as your picking up the phone does not: your ability to use a telephone is not an essential aspect of your rational animality, as your decision-making capacity is. And any external *result* (*factum*) that is 'set up' through an agent's immanent action is construed as, ideally, an external *manifestation* of that immanent action, the action strictly so-called (1.854–5).[36]

But while this logical transition between topics shows the continuity of the investigation across the division between the first two books of SCG, it is the quite different character of this second species of activity that also makes such a division at this point natural. For if God is absolutely perfect, and intellect and will are powers entailed by that perfection, and God is entirely, eternally active, then all God's *immanent* activity of perfect intellection and

---

[36] Of course, all the a posteriori reasoning in SCG I about God's existence and nature is fundamentally dependent on starting with what turn out to be divine *facta*. So Aquinas has to that extent *already* been investigating God's transeunt activity without identifying it as such. Has he, then, been illegitimately anticipating results which he is now supposed to be setting out to obtain? I don't think so. In Book I he was just reasoning from *explanandum* to *explanans*, where the *explanandum* was not the bare existence but the nature of ordinary things. In doing so, he was not identifying the *explanandum* as creation or making specific claims about the origin of its existence. But now, in Book II, he will try to make that identification, and he will be making such claims. In Book II he will be looking into the causal mechanism of the relationship that justifies the kind of a posteriori reasoning that constitutes Book I.

volition is *necessary* to him—as Aquinas argues at length in Book I.[37] But, since intellection and volition *need not* concern anything outside the agent, it seems that no *transeunt* activity at all—and certainly no *particular* transeunt activity—is necessary to God. So it looks as if the transition from Book I to Book II might well be from considering divine necessity—what God could not not be or not do—to considering divine contingency—what God might very well not have done.[38]

Aquinas introduces the new consideration by ascribing transeunt activity to God 'in that he [1] brings things into existence, [2] preserves, and [3] rules them' (1.854). I think that this catalogue of divine transeunt activity—(1) creation, (2) conservation, (3) providence—is intended to be complete, at least for purposes of natural theology.[39] Understandably, most of the discussion in this short introductory chapter of the book on creation centres on (1), and (2) gets mentioned only this once (although conservation might well be considered to be an aspect of creation[40]). Thus we are told that 'for the filled-out consideration of divine truth we still have to investigate the second kind of activity—the one through which things are [1] produced and [3] governed by God' (856).

6. *The positive results of meditating on creation*

At the very beginning of SCG Aquinas introduced a biblical passage as an epigraph, apparently for the whole work, but perhaps also especially for Book I: 'My mouth will meditate on the truth, and my lips will abominate wickedness' (Prov. 8: 7). He artfully uses Scripture to develop the theme further in the epigraph he places at the beginning of Book II: 'I have meditated on all your activities, and I was meditating on the works of your hands' (Ps. 142/3: 5).

---

[37] See TMOT, Chs. Six and Seven.

[38] See Ch. Four below and, more particularly, SCG II.30.1076c–e.

[39] Even a divine transeunt activity such as redemption might well be included under providence, even though, considered just as such, it lies outside the scope of natural theology.

[40] See e.g. II.25.1027; also Ch. Two below, sect. 8. Being brought into existence only for a durationless instant—if that is conceivable—could not count as more than a limiting case of having been created; and any utterly dependent, creaturely existence that is more than instantaneous would have to involve its creator's conserving it.

In twentieth-century English, 'meditating' is associated almost exclusively with a non-intellectual or even anti-intellectual religious or quasi-religious exercise of some sort, as sharp a contrast with natural theology as might be found. But the Latin verb and noun which Aquinas uses in this connection—*meditor, meditatio*—have a much broader meaning, covering any sort of intense thought, reflection, or consideration (as in Descartes's *Meditationes de prima philosophia*). Aquinas, describing himself as intending in SCG 'to take up the role of a wise person, though that may exceed my powers' (I.2.9), expressly identifies meditating as the primary phase of the highly intellectualized, argumentative, co-operative activity proper to wisdom: 'the role of the wise person is to meditate on the truth, especially the truth regarding the first principle, and to discuss it with others, but also to fight against the falsity that is its contrary' (I.1.6). (And, of course, as Book I develops, the truth regarding the first principle turns out to be the truth about God.)

When in Book I Aquinas explained his choice of the epigraph from Proverbs, he pointed out its appropriateness to the philosophical task which he was undertaking in SCG:

In the words set out [at the very beginning of the work], the mouth of Wisdom aptly portrays the two aspects of the wise person's role: that he plainly express the divine truth (which is, antonomastically, 'the truth') on which he has meditated—which the passage touches on when it says 'My mouth will meditate on the truth'—and that he fight against error, the contrary of the truth—which the passage touches on when it says 'and my lips will abominate wickedness', by which is meant the falsity that is contrary to the divine truth. (I.1.7)

Aquinas finds the same sort of appropriateness in the epigraph he draws from Psalms for Book II. In chapter 1, after he has developed the distinction between immanent and transeunt divine activity, pointed out the relevance of the artisan analogy, and explained why he is taking up transeunt activity after having considered immanent activity (in Book I), he says: 'In fact, we can derive this ordering from the words set down [in the epigraph] above, for the passage puts meditating on the first kind of activity first when it says "I have meditated on *all* your activities", in such a way that "activity" is associated with divine intellecting and willing,' since all other activities stem from intellection and volition. 'But it adds something regarding meditating on *making* [i.e. on transeunt activity] when it says "and I was meditating on the works of your hands", in such a way that by the works of his hands we understand the heaven and the earth and all the things that come into existence from God as handiwork comes from an artisan' (II.1.857).

Aquinas begins the second chapter of Book II with a variation on that theme: 'This sort of meditating on divine works is of course necessary for teaching human faith about God (*ad fidem humanam instruendam de Deo*)' (2.858). Before seeing why he thinks so, we might just note a couple of puzzling features of this passage.

First, it seems oddly redundant to specify '*human* faith'; but perhaps that phrase is used here only to provide a rhetorical contrast with '*divine* works'. Second, and more important, if *instruendam* here really does mean the same as 'teaching', as it probably does, then there seems to be something inappropriate about characterizing the work of unaided reason in SCG I–III as teaching *faith*—unless, as seems most likely, what it is supposed to teach is just the doctrinal propositions that are the objects of faith (propositions that are supported here on argumentative, non-authoritative grounds), without also advocating the authoritative, non-philosophical basis on which those propositions are accepted in faith as 'faith' is ordinarily understood.[41]

But there is also a further possibility: *instruendam* can mean not only teaching, but also building, constructing, organizing, equipping, furnishing. It's tempting to think that those less specified senses of Aquinas's Latin word contribute to the shaping of his thought here: i.e. this sort of meditating, the sort that infers conclusions about God's nature from an investigation of God's works, is needed in order to *equip* or *furnish* (the propositions of) the faith with the support of natural-theological (philosophical) analysis and argumentation.[42] If SCG has a practical purpose for those who already have this faith—and, as we'll soon see more clearly,

---

[41] If it weren't for the unusual expression 'human faith' (*fidem humanam*), it would be more natural to read *fidem* here as 'the faith', an expression that is easily interpreted as a designation for the propositions believed. In any case, this way of reading the phrase seems to be in keeping with the less problematic use of the related expression 'the teaching of the truth' at the beginning of ch. 3 (864). See sect. 7 below.

[42] I'm suggesting that his thought here may well have been in the spirit of 1 Pet. 3: 15: 'be ready always to give an answer to every man that asks you a reason of the hope that is in you'.

Aquinas must have thought it had to have one—that is its purpose. *Fides quaerit, intellectus invenit.*[43]

In explaining his claim that the work of Book II is necessary for the teaching or equipping of the faith, Aquinas first (in ch. 2) spells out four positive results of meditating on divine works and then (in ch. 3) shows how the proper consideration of created things avoids four mistaken views about God. These introductory chapters, not yet under the regimen of natural theology, are everywhere replete with biblical passages (as chapters in the body of Book II cannot be) and rhetorical flourishes of a sort usually absent from Aquinas's writing. I will just briefly survey their conclusions.

Of the four positive results of meditating on divine works, the first is that 'we can in one way or another admire and consider divine *wisdom*. For things that are made by means of an art are representative of the art itself . . . But God has brought things into existence by his wisdom . . . And so we can infer divine wisdom from a consideration of [divine] works' (2.859). 'In the second place, this consideration leads to admiration of God's unsurpassable *power*,' a claim in support of which Aquinas quotes Romans 1: 20: 'The invisible things of God are clearly seen, understood through the things that have been made: even his everlasting power, and his divinity' (2.860). 'In the third place, this consideration kindles human souls into love of divine *goodness*. For, whatever goodness and perfection has been distributed among the various created things considered in particular, the whole of it is united universally in him, as in the source of all goodness (as was shown in Book I [chs. 28 and 40])' (2.861).[44]

It is hardly surprising that the consideration of created things is expected to lead to a special recognition of these three standard divine attributes in particular: wisdom, power, and goodness. But before looking at the fourth positive result, which is quite different from these three, I want to say just a little about the way in which

---

[43] 'Faith seeks, understanding finds.' For a detailed discussion of the significance of this Augustinian maxim, see Kretzmann 1990.

[44] These passages on seeing evidence of divine attributes in created things suggest what we are in any case entitled to assume: that Aquinas in Book II is continuing to employ the relational method he introduced in Book I (see sect. 5 above). The suggestion is confirmed in his summary of the results of ch. 2 as showing the importance of 'created things in so far as a kind of likeness of God is reflected (*resultat*) in them' (4.871).

Aquinas presents them here. For although there is plenty of plainly epistemic talk about these attributes in this introductory survey, it certainly has overtones of worship as well. We are expected not only to 'consider', 'cognize', and 'infer' but also to 'admire' divine wisdom; there is to be not only intellective cognition (or understanding) of God's power, but also 'admiration' which leads to 'fear of God' and 'reverence'; and the language used here regarding God's goodness is altogether emotive and worshipful. These are not the tones characteristic of natural theology, Aquinas's included. But some of the emotive, worshipful language which Aquinas uses here is pretty clearly just echoing that sort of language in the biblical passages that proliferate in this unregimented introductory material. And perhaps there is no compelling reason to consider such language and the attitudes it expresses as out of place in previewing the results of natural theology's sober argumentation. After all, natural scientists, too—even those who are not theists—are occasionally moved, awed, overwhelmed, by reflecting on their science's discoveries regarding what Aquinas takes to be God's works.

If Aquinas's catalogue of four positive results is thought of, not unreasonably, as intended to motivate the reader to press on into Book II, then he seems to have saved the best for last:

In the fourth place, this consideration [of God's works] endows human beings with a kind of likeness of divine perfection. For in Book I [chs. 49 ff.] it was shown that in cognizing himself God regards (*intuetur*) all other things within himself.[45] Therefore, since the Christian faith principally teaches (*instruit*) a human being about God, and through the light of divine revelation makes the human being one who cognizes created things, a kind of likeness of divine wisdom is brought about in the human being. (2.862)

This particular inducement to meditating on God's works seems exaggerated, however, since the promised 'kind of likeness of divine perfection' consists only in acquiring 'a kind of likeness of divine wisdom'—just one aspect of that absolute perfection—and since even that kind of limited likeness seems purely formal. The kind of likeness of divine wisdom—God's perfectly cognizing all things in perfectly cognizing himself—that is to be brought about in

---

[45] For a critical exposition of the apparently altogether introspective character of divine omniscience, see Stump and Kretzmann 1995.

the human being is a necessarily imperfect cognition of created things that is based merely inferentially on a necessarily very imperfect cognition of God.[46]

The passage also contains some puzzling features. '*This* consideration', the one we're about to take up in Book II, is explicitly *not* one in which 'the Christian faith . . . teaches . . . *through the light of divine revelation*'. Notice, too, that here in 2.862, unlike 2.858 (discussed above), the Christian faith is not being taught, but is itself doing the teaching. Furthermore, although it's obvious why Aquinas would say that the Christian faith operates generally through the light of divine revelation, how is it supposed by that means to make the human being a being who cognizes created things? Does this mean something like 'makes the human being a being who cognizes himself and the things around him *as* created things'—i.e. as things that are entirely dependent on a creator for their existence and nature? Does it perhaps connect with the final clause of the Ecclesiasticus passage (42: 15) which Aquinas cites at the very end of the chapter (863): 'in the words of the Lord are his works'—i.e. it is in Scripture that one ordinarily learns that all these things *are* his works? Even so, it is not *exclusively* in Scripture that one learns it, since Aquinas devotes II.15 to *arguing* that 'God is for all things the cause of their being'.[47] I don't have satisfactory answers to these questions, but I'm inclined to think that puzzles of this sort in the introductory material needn't detain us.

7. The corrective results of meditating on creation

In chapter 3 Aquinas completes his account of the benefits to be gained from meditating on creation, moving from explaining its utility 'for the teaching of the truth' (*ad veritatis instructionem*) (864) to showing how considering created things in the right way helps to do away with four mistaken views about God.

Aquinas sees all four of the mistakes catalogued here as made by people who *start* with a consideration of created things[48] rather than moving to it from a consideration of God in himself, as he is

---

[46] See also II.4.876, discussed in sect. 8 below.

[47] For discussions of this thesis, see Chs. Two and Three below.

[48] This seems to be what Aquinas thinks the pre-Socratic practitioners of 'physical theology' did; see TMOT, Ch. One, sect. 6.

doing in moving to it from Book I. Anyone who does begin in this misleading way, and who is 'thinking of nothing beyond created things that are *seen*', might infer that the first principle of such wholly corporeal things must *itself* be 'some sort of body', despite the fact that a body is obviously the sort of thing 'that can exist only on the basis of something else' (865)—e.g. some other body or bodies—and is therefore incapable of being the first principle. This mistake—of ascribing to the creator what can be ascribed only to a created thing—is the most primitive sort of error about God that stems from meditating on creation the wrong way around.

But, second, even people who think also of created things that are *not* seen, if they are 'ignorant of the nature of a created thing', might very well be led into the mirror image of the first sort of mistake—ascribing 'to certain created things that which is God's alone' (866). Aquinas doesn't expressly say that such people take incorporeal beings into account, but he does say that they ascribe 'to causes other than God' such activities as 'creating things, knowing future events, or working miracles' (866); and he himself would never consider ascribing such activities to bodies considered just as such, bodies devoid of invisible, incorporeal intellect and will. And surely the worshippers of the 'stones and pieces of wood' he mentions in this connection must have thought them to be more than ordinary stones and pieces of wood in just such respects.

Third, some people think of God's will and God's nature as alternative ultimate explanatory principles, and maintain that 'things come from God not on the basis of divine volition but on the basis of the necessity of nature', while others 'remove all or some things from divine providence, or deny that it could operate outside the ordinary course [of nature]' (867). It's clear why Aquinas says that people of these sorts 'belittle divine power', which he of course associates with divine will. It might seem that the nature being talked about here is neither God's nature nor nature conceived of as God's creation, since these people are said to 'assign *two* sources of things'. But it will become clear, I think, that the nature being talked about *is* God's nature, and that the intended contrast is between 'non-necessitarian' and 'necessitarian' accounts of creation—based, respectively, on considerations of God's free choice and on considerations of what God's nature necessitates where created things are concerned (see Ch. Four below, sect. 6).

Aquinas's fourth and last sort of catalogued mistake about created things is a cluster of wrong views about the human creature specifically, and about its elevated place in the scheme of things. These are wrong views about God only implicitly. For instance, a person who takes astrology seriously in a certain respect, one of 'those who subject the wills of human beings to the stars', thinks of himself as 'subjected to certain created things to which he is [in fact] superior' (868), in the only relevant respects of having intellect and will. People who think that their souls are not created by God himself but 'that angels are the creators of souls, that human souls are mortal, and, in general, those who detract from human dignity in similar ways' (ibid.) are also misled along such lines.

8. How philosophy and the faith are taught

In chapter 4, the last substantive piece of his introduction to Book II, Aquinas shows plainly what his several allusions in these intro-ductory chapters have already been suggesting: the practical purpose of SCG is pedagogical. And, not forgetting everything Aquinas seems to have been saying about its subject-matter, we seem to be entitled to say that what SCG teaches is, in a word, theism. In Book IV, of course, this turns out to be Christian theism; but there is nothing distinctively Christian about Books I–III. Nevertheless, Aquinas himself seems to identify SCG's purpose *generally* as 'the teaching [*instructio* or *doctrina*] of the Christian faith'[49]—which, of course, is the purpose of the *whole* work, taking all four of its books into account. And in chapter 4 he identifies the person who engages in teaching Christian theism in the natural-theological style of SCG as 'the believer'. This believer—paradigmatically, Aquinas himself—argues just as a philosopher ordinarily does, except, Aquinas says, that a philosopher present-ing his view regarding created things of some sort 'draws his argu-ment from the proper [immediate, natural] causes of the things, while the believer draws his argument [regarding the same things] from the *first* cause' (4.873)—not, it should be noted once again, from revelation.

[49] See e.g. II.2.863: *ad instructionem fidei Christianae*, and 4.871: *doctrina fidei Christianae*.

Just because these passages occur in the introduction to his systematic, natural-theological consideration of created things in
Book II, the philosophy with which he is contrasting his approach
is mainly *natural* philosophy (or what we would call 'natural science'), as is clear from his examples. The central examples are
different accounts of fire that might be given by a (natural) philosopher and by 'the believer', and the broad aim of those passages is to
explain that it is no shortcoming in this teaching of the faith that it
does not provide detailed, systematic accounts of, for example,
astronomy and mechanics. And in that connection Aquinas
appears to put 'the teaching of the faith' on a par with natural
philosophy and geometry in respect of their being three legitimate
but very different ways of considering nature: 'For that reason
the teaching of the faith must not be charged with incompleteness
if it makes no mention of many properties of things—the configuration of the sky, for instance, and the quality of motion. For
in the same way, the natural philosopher does not consider the
characteristics of a line that the geometer considers, but only
those that are associated with it in so far as it is the limit of a natural
body' (872). Here Aquinas, the one engaged in the teaching of
the faith, is to the natural philosopher as the natural philosopher
is to the geometer. Contrasts of that sort do not at all set 'the
teaching of the faith' apart from philosophy as twentieth-century
philosophers conceive of philosophy. We are as little likely as
Aquinas is to think that our metaphysical accounts are inadequate
because they don't explain 'fire's being carried upward, for example' (872).

The philosopher considers nature from the bottom up, while
Aquinas's believer looks at it from the top down. That's because
the believer 'considers only those aspects of created things that are
associated with them in so far as they are traced back to God—that
they have been created by God, that they are subject to God, and
things of that sort' (872). On the basis of that description of the
believer's work, Aquinas shows that it is the very sort of work he
envisaged for himself at the beginning of SCG, when he portrayed
himself as essaying the role of a wise person: i.e. the enterprise of
'considering the highest causes' (I.1.3). He points out that because
the argumentation employed in this teaching of Christian theism is
orientated as it is, particularly in Book II, 'it must be called the

greatest wisdom, as considering the absolutely highest cause' (4.874).[50]

His description of his undertaking in these terms might throw some doubt on my characterization of it as philosophical, as developing the metaphysics of theism, of creation, and of providence. But doubt of that sort should be dispelled when we look more carefully at what Aquinas himself says about his purpose in writing SCG.

A wise person, he says, is one of those 'who give things an appropriate order and direction and govern them well' (I.1.2). Obviously, such a person has to be concerned with purposes and causes, goals and sources; so the wisest person will be 'one whose attention is turned toward the universal goal, which is also the universal source' (I.1.3). Therefore, wisdom's concern must be the highest, most universal, explanatory truth. So anyone aspiring to wisdom will attend to metaphysics, since, Aquinas reports, Aristotle rightly identified metaphysics as 'the science of truth— not of just any truth, but of the truth that is the origin of all truth, the truth that pertains to the first principle of being for all things' (I.1.5). The explanatory truth associated here with metaphysics is, as we've already seen, the truth associated also with theology. So Aquinas is speaking as both a metaphysician and a theologian when he describes himself as intending in SCG 'to take up the role of a wise person, though that may exceed my powers', in order 'to clarify, to the best of my ability, the truth that the Catholic faith professes, by getting rid of mistakes that are contrary to it' (I.2.9).[51]

The last of the contrasts which Aquinas draws between 'the two kinds of teaching' is just what we should expect on the basis of what else he has said about them. He portrays his project in Book II, his metaphysics of creation, as orientated in the direction opposite to the one taken in Aristotelian natural philosophy and metaphysics: 'the two kinds of teaching do not proceed in the same order', he says.

---

[50] Deut. 4: 6, which Aquinas quotes immediately after this passage, is particularly apt if the referent of its first word is nature itself: 'This'—the world of created things we are now considering—'is your wisdom and understanding *in the sight of the nations.*'

[51] '. . . ce que saint Thomas se propose en écrivant la *Somme contre les Gentils*, c'est tout simplement de faire son métier de sage' (Gauthier 1961: 88).

For in teaching philosophy (*doctrina philosophiae*), which first considers created things in their own right and leads on from them to a cognition of God, the consideration of created things is first, and the consideration of God is last. On the other hand, in teaching the faith (*doctrina fidei*), which considers created things only in their systematic relationship to God, the consideration of God comes first, the consideration of created things afterwards.[52] And in this way it is more perfect, as being more like God's cognition, who observes [all] other things in cognizing himself. (II.4.876)[53]

Some of what philosophy's teaching covers in its own way, from the bottom up, is being covered here by 'the teaching of the faith' in *its* own way, from the top down. But in Book I Aquinas arrived at that diametrically opposed starting-point for the teaching of the faith by *arguing* for it, largely on the basis of lines of argument he found in Aristotle's *Physics* and *Metaphysics*.[54] For, he explains here, his project is orientated in such a way that 'human philosophy is in its service, as if [the teaching of the faith] were its overseer (*principali*). And therefore divine wisdom sometimes proceeds from human philosophy's starting-points' (II.4.875).[55]

9. Aquinas's plan for SCG II

The fifth and last chapter of Aquinas's introduction to Book II is a very brief, very broad outline of the three large-scale tasks that he plans to accomplish in it. He will begin by dealing with 'the production of things as regards their being' (877), in chapters 6–38.[56]

---

[52] So this 'human philosophy' is itself ultimately theistic—like Aristotle's metaphysics. And it seems that Aristotle's philosophy is indeed Aquinas's paradigm of 'human philosophy', as SCG is the paradigm of 'the teaching of the faith'. Notice that the contrasting order of the two kinds of teaching is not precise. In Aquinas's project the consideration of created things comes not last—like the consideration of God in human philosophy—but just later. What comes last in Aquinas's project is the consideration of the truths about God to which reason has access only via revelation. See also n. 54 below.

[53] See n. 45 above.

[54] Since Aquinas's arguments for the existence of God in I.13 (and 15; see TMOT, Chs. Two and Three) are all a posteriori, there is a sense in which at least a brief consideration of created things comes at the very beginning of his project in SCG.

[55] 'Divine wisdom' here is of course Aquinas's project in SCG, not an attribute of God. See sect. 4 above.

[56] The Latin here—*de productione rerum in esse*—would in other circumstances be more naturally translated as 'the bringing of things into existence'. But, for

There is reassurance in that announcement, since the tone and even much of the terminology of chapters 1–4 can sometimes be taken as suggesting that Aquinas is considering God's having created the world to be an obvious, if not expressly derived, consequence of Book I. Instead, arguing specifically and carefully for divine creation will be the first task he takes up in his systematic, natural-theological work in Book II, especially in chapters 6–15. He will then undertake, in chapters 39–45, to explain the fact of nature's prolific diversity, which is at least prima facie not what might be expected as the result of an absolutely perfect, absolutely simple being's transeunt activity.

Those first two tasks, which will occupy him for less than half of Book II, provide the basis for its principal undertaking, the one that figures so prominently in his introduction to the book: dealing with 'the nature of the things themselves that have been produced and distinguished [from one another], in so far as it pertains to the truth of the faith' (877). Chapters 46–101, then, are devoted to the enterprise of considering the results of God's transeunt activity, sharply focused on the aspect of those results that Aquinas considers most promising for his purposes: the existence of intellects in nature.

In the chapters of this book I will be examining all three of those aspects of Aquinas's metaphysics of creation, sometimes criticizing or extending various features of them. Chapters Two–Five below are devoted to the first part (II.6–38), Chapter Six to the second part (II.39–45), and Chapters Seven–Ten to the third part (II.46–101).

reasons that will emerge in Chs. Two and Three below, I want the translation here and elsewhere in the early chapters of Book II to bring out the fact that Aquinas's account of creation presents it as a species of production.

TWO

FROM GOD TO
EVERYTHING ELSE

1. SCG II as the logical continuation of SCG I

Aquinas begins the real work of Book II in chapter 6. The transition from the introductory material of the first five chapters to this resumption of the systematic development of his natural theology, which he began in Book I, is marked by two prominent stylistic changes. One is the reappearance of a format already familiar from the systematic chapters of Book I. The arrangement of Book II's chapter 6 provides a handy paradigm. It has three parts: (1) an opening statement of the chapter's thesis (878), (2) arguments supporting the thesis (879–84), and finally (3) citation of a biblical passage selected to show that the thesis argued for by means available to unaided reason agrees with what Aquinas takes to be revealed truth (885). This is the format he uses, with minor variations, in almost every chapter of SCG I–III in which he is furthering the development of his natural theology.[1]

The second of those notable stylistic changes is that in chapter 6 Aquinas begins regularly to refer to results that were already established in the arguments of Book I, because he is relying on those results as bases for the new ones he is out to establish in the arguments of Book II. In the five chapters that make up Aquinas's introduction to Book II there are a few explicit references to Book I—one in chapter 1 and four in chapter 2—and they do help to

---

[1] In the later chapters of Book II there are some interesting variations in format; see e.g. Ch. Eight below, sect. 6. But in the standard format it is the form of the third of those three parts that is most subject to variation. Sometimes, as in II.15, it is supplemented by an indication of philosophical or theological positions that are ruled out by the results of the chapter's arguments. But when the chapter's thesis presents a theoretical consequence for which Aquinas sees no direct Scriptural backing, that third part is simply omitted—as e.g. in II.8–14.

show the continuity between the two books.[2] But when the work of
Book II begins in earnest, the references to Book I take on a role
that is indispensable to the fundamental logical structure of the
enterprise: they locate the support for many of the premisses of
Book II's arguments, claiming again and again that the truth of this
or that premiss, which is not expressly supported by considerations
introduced in an argument of Book II, 'was shown in the first book'.
For example, in the forty-one arguments in chapters 6–15, there are
thirty-one explicit references of this kind to results that were argued for in Book I.[3] Such retro-references, essential to the cogency
of Aquinas's natural theology, show that the continuity between
Books I and II is not merely thematic but also, and much more
importantly, logical.[4] The opening words of chapter 6 present
Aquinas's view of this logical structure: 'Therefore, taking for
granted (supponentes) the things that have been shown in the preceding [arguments] (superioribus), let us now show that . . .' (878);
and all six of the chapter's arguments do take for granted premisses
that were argued for in Book I—the first five of them explicitly, the
sixth implicitly (as we'll see). As is only to be expected in the
development of an Aristotelian (subsidiary) science, the work that
its practitioner is about to take up depends logically on the work
that he has already successfully completed.[5] And, naturally, that

---

[2] There is a reference to I.44–96 in 1.856; to I.28, I.40, and I.38 in 2.861; to I.49 ff.
in 2.862. The very broad reference in ch. 1 is only by way of showing that God's
immanent activities were already discussed in Book I, but those in ch. 2 indicate
where the support is to be found for claims being made in argumentative passages
of the chapter.

[3] Besides the explicit references, there are also places in which Aquinas's argument clearly does depend on a result achieved in Book I that he neglects to cite,
even though he can't have failed to recognize it. Such cases should be considered
implicit references. After ch. 6, there are, naturally, also increasingly many explicit
references to results achieved in earlier systematic chapters of Book II. The form of
Aquinas's explicit references is, I think, never more precise than 'in the first book',
and is often as vague as 'above'. The eds. of the Leonine and Marietti edns. have
contributed a great deal toward identifying the references, which are not always
unmistakable. But a good deal of work remains to be done, perhaps especially as
regards the editors' many non-specific identifications of references to I.13, the long
chapter that includes SCG's explicit arguments for the existence of God. A complete, precise catalogue of all the retro-references in SCG, implicit as well as explicit, would enable us not only to see its logical form more clearly, but also to assess
the structural importance of previously established results, some of which are cited
over and over, while others are never used at all.

[4] On the thematic continuity, see Ch. One above, sect. 3.

[5] As I make clear in TMOT, I don't think that all of Aquinas's arguments in SCG
I succeed. In particular, much of TMOT's Ch. Two is devoted to a detailed

logical dependence is to be seen not only in the systematic relation-ship between *books* of SCG; very many of its chapters, too, begin with the words 'Now on that basis' (*Ex hoc autem*), which introduce the new chapter's thesis as partially supported by results achieved in the preceding chapter's arguments.[6]

What Aquinas envisages the work of Book II to be, we have already seen in very broad outline in the prospectus he provides in chapter 5, where he identifies his first large-scale topic in the new book as 'the producing of things as regards their being' (877).[7] He explicitly completes his consideration of that first topic by the end of chapter 38.[8] But, of course, there are subdivisions to be drawn within that broad topic, especially when examined by a mind as superbly orderly as Aquinas's is.[9]

Production always involves a source (the producer), a terminus (the product), and the producing itself. So Aquinas takes up, first, the source of the production of things, in chapters 6–14, and then its terminus, in chapter 15. The essence of the producing itself occu-pies him in chapters 16–21, and he takes up the special characteris-tics of God's producing of things (and some problems associated with it) in chapters 22–38.

In this chapter I focus on developments that take place in Aquinas's chapters 6–14 and chapter 15. The first nine of those ten chapters may be analysed more precisely into the one that consid-ers the source itself (II.6), those that consider the source's power

examination of a large-scale failure of that sort. But in dealing with arguments in SCG II that depend on arguments in SCG I (or on earlier arguments in SCG II), I will of course avoid using any results that I believe are unacceptable. It is an advantage of Aquinas's flurry-of-arguments approach in SCG I–III that one is seldom if ever faced with an announced result for which he has provided no defensible argument.

    [6] In chs. 6–15, e.g., this very formula introduces chs. 7, 8, and 9, and chs. 10 and 11 begin with more elaborate versions of it. Ch. 15 begins by announcing its depend-ence on a result already achieved, apparently in ch. 6.

    [7] See Ch. One above, n. 56.

    [8] See Ch. One above, sect. 9. The explicit transition from the first large-scale task to the second appears in the opening words of ch. 39: 'Now, however, having dealt with matters that pertain to the production of things, it remains for us to deal with . . .' (1151).

    [9] The eds. of the Marietti edn. provide a detailed and generally very intelligent outline of SCG, chapter by chapter, based directly on the outline developed by Francis Sylvester (1474–1528) in his commentary on it. Anyone who reads SCG closely is bound to find reasons to amend some details of that standard outline, but it still provides a good first approximation, and I will sometimes adapt it to my purposes here. Sylvester's commentary is printed together with the text of SCG in the Leonine edn.

(II.7–10), and those that consider relations between the products and their source (II.11–14).

2. *Considering the source*

Aquinas's very first move in undertaking the systematic work of Book II may seem unnecessarily cautious: 'Therefore, taking for granted things that were shown in the preceding [arguments], let us now show that it is appropriate for God (*competit Deo*) to be the source (*principium*) and cause of being for other things' (6.878). After all, those preceding arguments of Book I very often reasoned to the existence and the nature of God from the existence and the natures of other things, and many of them did so on the basis of just such a causal relationship between God and other things.[10] So, since Aquinas is taking the results of those same arguments for granted now, why doesn't he begin by simply announcing that it has already been shown that God *is* the source and cause of being for other things, and then go on at once to examine just exactly how that well-established causal relationship is to be understood?

The answer to that question depends on clearly recognizing the location of Book II's starting-point within the systematic development of Aquinas's natural theology. In beginning by taking for granted what was achieved in Book I's characterization of God considered in himself, we are indeed beginning with a detailed, reasoned, theoretical account of God's existence and nature. But that account as developed so far has not explicitly attended to the question of how the transeunt activity involved in producing other things is compatible with what has already been established about God's nature: 'We have, of course, spoken of God's *first* sort of activity in the preceding book, where divine cognition and volition were dealt with. And so, for a filled-out consideration of divine truth [i.e. the truth about God[11]] we have *still* to investigate the *second* kind of activity—the one through which things are produced and governed by God' (1.856). Moreover, as Aquinas also made clear in the introductory chapters of Book II, it is essential to his overall plan that he move *to* this consideration of natural things

---

[10] For a perfectly clear and clearly relevant example of this sort of argumentation, see the discussion of I.13.113 later in this section.

[11] See Ch. One above, sect. 4.

from that consideration of God in himself; that he look at creation from the top down, considering 'only those aspects of created things that are associated with them in so far as they are traced back to God' (4.872). When we recognize God's producing of other things as the first transeunt activity to be considered for inclusion in this ongoing account of God's nature, it's clear that it is precisely the propriety of that inclusion that needs to be established first.

In support of his thesis that producing other things is suited to the nature of God as understood so far, Aquinas offers six arguments, the last four of which (881–4) are worded in ways that show them, more or less clearly, to be yielding just that conclusion. The third argument, for instance, concludes that 'it is appropriate for God to bring about something actually existent, for which he is the cause of its being' (881). But the first and second of the chapter's six arguments may raise further questions about Aquinas's opening move, because what they expressly conclude is not that it is *appropriate* for God to be the source of production, but simply that God *is* or *must be* 'the cause of being for other things' (879, 880).[12] Here, for instance, is the first argument: 'For it was shown above [I.13.113], on the basis of Aristotle's demonstration, that there is a first efficient cause, which we call God. But an efficient cause brings its effects into being (*effectus ad esse conducit*). Therefore, God exists as the cause of being for other things' (879).

Suppose, for the sake of this argument, that it was indeed shown above that there must be a first efficient cause, and that it is justifiably identified as God.[13] In that case Aquinas is reminding us that one of the arguments by which his natural theology first established

---

[12] In the rest of this discussion I will ignore the second argument of ch. 6, partly because it is founded on G2, the fatally flawed existence argument in SCG I.13 that I considered in detail in TMOT, 60–83.

[13] The existence argument that Aquinas is referring to here reads this way in SCG I.13.113: 'In all ordered [series of] efficient causes, the first is the cause of the intermediate [cause], and the intermediate is the cause of the last [effect], whether there is one or more than one intermediate [cause]. But when a cause has been removed, that of which it is the cause is removed. Therefore, if the first were removed, the intermediate could not be a cause. But if one goes on *ad infinitum* where efficient causes are concerned, none of the causes will be first. Therefore, all the others, which are intermediate, are deleted. But this is obviously false [since effects of the relevant sort obviously do exist]. Therefore, one must posit that there is a first efficient cause—which is God.' In a couple of introductory sentences Aquinas attributes this argument to Aristotle in *Metaphysics* II 2, 994a1–19. Its

the existence of some being that counted as God served also to establish implicitly the status of efficient cause as one aspect of that being's nature. Although nothing was made of that aspect in developing the characterization of God's nature in Book I after God's existence was established in the early chapters, it remained on the record, to be taken into account when it became relevant. And just now, when Aquinas is beginning his inquiry into divine transeunt activity, it does become relevant for the first time. The nature of an efficient cause considered just as such—and most obviously the nature of an efficient cause whose existence is inferred on the basis of existing effects—*is* the nature of that which produces something else.[14] The being that was initially shown to exist 'as the cause of being for other things' (879) must therefore be—whatever else it may turn out to be—a being for which 'it is appropriate . . . to be the source and cause of being for other things' (878). So, although I think that Aquinas could have spelled out the relevance of his first two arguments in chapter 6 more perspicuously, they do in fact support the chapter's thesis of propriety.[15]

We have already seen Aquinas introducing the work of Book II by remarking that our effort to fill out our cognition of the nature of anything must include an attempt to acquire some cognition of the thing's powers, those aspects of its nature that directly explain

cogency depends on interpreting the series of efficient causes at issue as 'essentially' ordered—i.e. ordered in the way a hand, a stick, and a stone are ordered when the hand is moving the stick, which is moving the stone—rather than inessentially ('accidentally') ordered, in the way the series consisting of a woman, her daughter, and her daughter's daughter is ordered. See sect. 8 below.

[14] The characteristic that standardly distinguishes efficient causes from formal, final, and material causes is the production of something else—as in the case of the stick's motion and the stone's motion, where the productive cause is also the sustaining cause, or in the case of the woman and her daughter, where it isn't.

[15] The first argument of ch. 6, based on God's established status as first efficient cause, can be read by Aquinas's own lights as supporting not only the appropriateness of God's *producing* but also the appropriateness of his producing *something else*. See e.g. DEE 4.27: 'Now whatever belongs to something is either caused by principles of its nature—e.g. the capacity for laughter in a human being [a capacity caused by rationality]—or comes to it from some extrinsic principle—e.g. light in the air from the sun's influence. But it cannot be the case that being itself is caused by the very [substantial] form or quiddity [or nature] of a thing—I mean, as by an efficient cause. For in that case some thing would be the cause of itself, and some thing would bring itself into being—which is impossible. Therefore, every thing such that its being is other than its nature has being from something else.' For a very helpful discussion of the longer argument of which this passage is a part, see MacDonald 1984.

its characteristic activities (1.852). And when he makes that remark in connection with turning his attention to God's transeunt activity, it looks as if that investigation will begin with observations regarding some evident divine transeunt activity, proceed inferentially from that activity to the requisite power, and then from that power to the relevant aspect of the agent's nature: 'We cannot have a complete cognition of any thing at all unless we have cognition of its activity, since the measure and the quality of a thing's power are evaluated by the mode and type of its activity; but a thing's power reveals its nature' (ibid.).[16]

But the structure of chapter 6 and the arrangement of chapters 7–15 (as we'll see) show that the pattern of reasoning is, instead, to begin with a consideration of some established aspect of the agent's nature which shows the propriety of the agent's transeunt activity of producing other things (II.6), to proceed inferentially to consider what must on that basis be true of the agent's power (II.7–10), then to consider what must on that basis be true of relations between the agent and its products (II.11–14), then to identify the products (II.15), and, finally, to investigate the activity itself (II.16–38). That is, the reasoning is to proceed *from* God *to* everything else. In reasoning to the *propriety* of God's producing other things, Aquinas is laying the foundation for the claim that the nature for which that activity is appropriate must somehow involve the *power* requisite for it. And in every such argument in chapter 6 he reasons in that way from some aspect of God's *nature* (as established in Book I): 879, first efficient cause; 880, immovable first mover; 881, (fully) actual being (*ens actu*); 882, supreme perfection; 883, perfection of will; 884, pure actuality (*actus purus*).

3. The actus purus *argument*

The propriety of God's producing other things is, I think, established even by the simple, first argument we've already looked at. But, before going on from chapter 6, I want to look at its last and most complex argument, especially because it introduces several elements of Aquinas's natural theology that are fundamental to what follows.

---

[16] See Ch. One above, sect. 5.

The more perfect the source of an action is, the more it can extend its action into more things, and into more remote things. (For if a fire is weak, it warms only the things near it; but if it is strong, it warms remote things, too.) Now pure actuality (*actus purus*), which God is, is more perfect than actuality mixed together with potentiality, as it is in 5 us. And actuality is the source of action. Therefore, since on the basis of the actuality there is in us we can perform not only actions that remain in us—such as intellection and volition—but also actions that extend into external things, through which we produce some external results (*aliqua facta*), much more can God, in virtue of being in actu- 10 ality, not only act intellectively and volitionally, but also produce an effect. And in this way he can be for other things the cause of their being. (884)

Notice, first, that the argument's conclusion, in lines 12–13, is just what's wanted in support of the chapter's thesis of propriety: 'in this way he *can* . . .'. On analogy with the claim in lines 6–10 that we human beings *can* do the sorts of things we undoubtedly do, the conclusion means not merely that it is possible that God produce other things, but that his actually doing so is appropriate for him, entirely compatible with what else has been shown about his nature.

The heart of the argument is in the two sentences in lines 4–6, which contain four claims important to Aquinas's metaphysics of creation: (1) actuality is the source of action; (2) pure actuality is more perfect than actuality mixed together with potentiality; (3) actuality in us is mixed together with potentiality; (4) God is pure actuality. Aquinas's presentation of claim (4) is one of the not-so-rare passages in SCG I–III where he neglects to refer to an earlier result when he could and should have done so: he argued for God's status as *actus purus* in I.16, most explicitly in 16.131.[17] The meaning of claim (4) will be easier to see after we have looked at claim (2).

In describing pure actuality as more perfect than actuality mixed together with potentiality, Aquinas does of course mean to be

---

[17] Here is the argument, offered in support of the thesis that 'in God there is no passive potentiality': 'Again, anything whatever acts in so far as it is in actuality. Therefore, what is not in actuality entirely (*totus actus*) acts not with its whole self (*toto se*) but with something belonging to itself (*aliquo sui*). But what does not act with its whole self is not the first agent, since it acts by means of participation in something (*alicuius participatione*), not through its own essence. Therefore, the first agent, which is God [see I.13.113, discussed in sect. 2 above], has no admixture of potentiality but is pure actuality (*actus purus*).'

valuing the former more highly than the latter. But, in addition to its more familiar evaluative aspect, perfection has a metaphysical aspect that is crucial to his frequent use of the concept, a metaphysical aspect on which its evaluative aspect supervenes, one that no writer of Latin could fail to recognize. Aquinas knows that his word *perfectum* is just an adjectival use of the perfect passive participle of a Latin verb meaning to do thoroughly—to fulfil, finish, achieve, complete, accomplish.[18] Consequently, 'anything is perfect [or complete] in so far as it is actualized [and] imperfect in so far as it is in a state of potentiality, lacking actuality. Therefore, that which is in no way in a state of potentiality but is pure actuality must be most perfect. But that is what God is. Therefore, he is most perfect' (I.28.264). And, on the basis of this same argument, God, who is most perfect, must, strictly speaking, be pure actuality (rather than merely fully actualized)—claim (4).[19]

So claim (2) is the plainest possible instance of comparative perfection, directly evaluating nothing but degrees of actuality and potentiality.[20] And on this basis it is easy to see why a human

[18] The fact that the word's fundamental sense has to do with the culmination of a process leads him to warn in another context that 'perfection (*perfectio*) cannot appropriately be attributed to God if we pay attention to the signification of the noun from the standpoint of its derivation, for what is not *done* (*factum*) [at all] cannot be called *thoroughly done* (*per-fectum*). But everything that gets done (*fit*) is brought from potentiality to actuality, and from not-being to being, when it has been done (*factum est*); so it is correctly said to be *per-fectum*—as if to say "totally done" (*totaliter factum*)—when the potentiality has been totally brought down to actuality so that it retains no not-being but has complete being' (I.28.268). So immutability and pure actuality in God make the attribution of perfection to him misleading etymologically. But, as Aquinas observes, 'through a kind of extension of the [adjectival] name, not only that which *achieves* complete actuality *through* getting done (*fiendo*), but also that which *is in* complete actuality *without* any doing or bringing about (*factione*), is called *per-fectum*. And it is in *this* way that we say that God is perfect' (ibid.).

[19] See also II.8.893: 'God is actuality itself, not a being that is in actuality as a consequence of some act that is not what he himself is.' For a fuller consideration of Aquinas's account of God's perfection in SCG I, see TMOT, Chs. Four and Five.

[20] The abstractness of such considerations may make the metaphysical aspect of perfection seem remote from its familiar evaluative aspect; but everything Aquinas says about the metaphysical aspect—being fully actualized, in no respect incomplete—helps to show how it provides the basis for the ordinary use of 'perfect' as the term of highest praise. A thing is perfect of its kind in the laudatory sense to the extent to which it is a whole, complete specimen, free from relevant defect; to the extent to which it is fully realized or developed; to the extent to which the potentialities definitive of its kind—its specifying potentialities—are actualized. So, as Aquinas puts it elsewhere (ST Ia.5.1c), a thing is perfect and hence desirable (good of its kind) to the extent to which it is in being. For a fuller discussion of the

being's actuality must be described, in claim (3), as 'mixed together with potentiality'. The mere fact that human existence is temporal rather than eternal already entails that the actual existence of any human being at any time is mixed together with countless unactualized potentialities, some of which, such as your being sound asleep later today, are theoretically actualizable, while others, such as your being sound asleep right now, are theoretically unactualizable. Since, as Aquinas has argued (in I.15), God's mode of existence must be eternity rather than time,[21] such a purely time-dependent admixture of potentiality is impossible in the unique case of divine actuality.[22]

The fact that a temporal being cannot exercise all its capacities at once is enough to show that its actuality is mixed together with potentiality; but it is not the most important consideration of that sort, because it considers only 'second actuality': 'Now there are two levels of actuality (*Actus autem est duplex*): first and second. A thing's first actuality, of course, is its form and wholeness (*integritas*), but its activity (*operatio*) is its second actuality' (ST Ia.48.5c). If you're actually reading English now, you can't also be actually reading Arabic now, even if you can read Arabic, even if an ability to read Arabic is part of your first actuality. But if, like me, you can't read Arabic, then you have left unactualized a potentiality that is part of your nature as a rational animal. And, of course, it is the evitable and inevitable gaps of that sort in one's *first* actuality that constitute one's imperfections in a more than technical sense. Human nature and the finiteness of human existence make it necessary that any human being will leave some natural potentialities unactualized. Full, metaphysical perfection is theoretically unattainable for a human being. Other things being equal, human being B is metaphysically less fully perfected than human being A to the extent to which B, unlike A, has left some natural rational capacity undeveloped, left his or her distinctively human, first actuality more mixed with potentiality than in theory it might have been—e.g. by not having learned to read Arabic. What's

connection between metaphysical and evaluative considerations in Aquinas's thought, see Stump and Kretzmann 1988.

[21] For Aquinas on God's eternity see TMOT, 116–17; also Stump and Kretzmann 1981, 1987, 1991, 1992.

[22] The admixture of potentiality also has deeper metaphysical consequences, as Aquinas sees it: 'everything that has potentiality mixed into its substance can, to the extent to which it has potentiality, not exist' (I.16.128).

more, even A, who has learned to read Arabic, has thereby re-placed the corresponding potentiality with what is, most of the time, only *first* actuality, a developed *ability*. It is just when A is actually reading Arabic that that original potentiality in her is replaced by *second*, fully-fledged actuality. And, obviously, 'second actuality is more perfect than first actuality' (I.45.385), at least metaphysically. Activity (or operation) is the further, culminating actualization of the agent's original potentiality. So, if the distinc-tion between first and second actuality could be applied to God at all (in the absence of all potentiality), God's *pure* actuality would have to be conceived of as *second* actuality, the actuality of which it makes sense to claim, even in connection with human beings, that (1) actuality is the source of action[23]—the immediate source of action, as first actuality is the more remote source of action.[24]

It is for that reason that Aquinas is entitled to infer that 'since on the basis of the [*im*pure, *im*perfect] actuality there is in us *we* can perform not only actions that remain in us—such as intellectively

---

[23] *Actus actionis principium est.* Aquinas has already invoked this plainly Aristo-telian principle often in SCG, usually in a form more nearly resembling the one he uses a little earlier in this same ch. 6: *unumquodque agens secundum hoc agit quod in actu est* ('Any agent acts in so far as it is in a state of actuality') (881). See e.g. I.16.131, 132, 133—i.e. in three of the arguments of his chapter on the absence of passive potentiality in God—also I.28.265, 29.270, 37.307, 50.420, 73.630. I have made no systematic search for Aquinas's uses of it, but in those which I have noticed, he does not argue for it. Of course he could, with some justification, be taking it to be a self-evident principle—a thing acts only in so far as it actually exists and actualizes the power it has that is a source of the act it performs. Alternatively, he could be taking it to be one of Aristotle's first principles or a proposition for which Aristotle has successfully argued, although in such cases he typically gives a reference, at least on some occasions of invoking it. But I haven't seen such a reference, whether by him or by his editors. It seems to me that there is relevant material in e.g. *Metaphysics* IX 3 and 6, and XII 6; *De anima* III 7 (431a3); *De generatione animalium* II 6 (743a23); and *Physics* II 3 (195b28). (I owe the last of these references to Terry Irwin.)

[24] Aquinas sometimes refers to God as the uniquely first actuality in this different sense: 'the first actuality (*primus actus*) is the universal source of all acts, since it is infinite, having, in respect of its power, all things within itself before they exist (*virtualiter in se omnia praehabens*), as Dionysius says [*De divinis nominibus* 5]' (ST Ia.75.5, ad 1). See also QDP 1.1c: 'It is suited to God to be pure and *first* actuality. That's why it is especially suited to him to act and to diffuse his likeness into other things. So active power is especially suited to him, for power is called active in so far as it is the source of action.' I think it's because Aquinas in this passage is working toward making sense of attributing power to God *as* the source of God's action that he emphasizes the suitability of attributing *first* actuality to God. In SCG II, as we'll see, he argues that power should *not* be attributed to God as the source of God's action. On first and second actuality generally see also e.g. Ch. Six below, sect. 6.

cognizing and willing—but also actions that extend into external things, through which we produce some external results, much *more* can *God*, in virtue of being in [pure, perfect, second] actuality, not only intellectively cognize and will but also produce an effect' (lines 6–12).

4. God's active power

In keeping with the pattern of reasoning that I sketched in section 2 above, Aquinas, having argued in chapter 6 from several established aspects of God's nature to the propriety of God's producing other things, moves on in chapter 7 to argue on the basis of that result that the *power* of producing other things is appropriately attributed to God. It is appropriate for God to do X; therefore, it is appropriate for God to have the power to do X. Obviously, no great logical distance needs to be covered here; accordingly, chapter 7's four arguments are short and simple. But the chapter's thesis may seem to be unnecessarily complicated and cautious: 'on that basis [i.e. the result of ch. 6] it is apparent that God has *power*, and that *active* power is appropriately attributed to him' (886).

I think that this cautious complexity is a consequence of the facts that the last argument of chapter 6, the *actus purus* argument considered in section 3 above, made its point by stressing the *absence* of *potentiality* in God, and that the same Latin word, *potentia*, is used both for potentiality and for power.[25] In those circumstances it makes sense to assure the reader that nothing said in the *actus purus* argument precludes what would otherwise seem to be an obvious corollary of its being appropriate to attribute to God the *activity* of producing other things. So we might think of the thesis of chapter 7 as tacitly prefaced in this way: Although, as we have just seen, God's pure actuality is utterly unmixed with potentiality (*potentia*), it is apparent none the less, '[1] that God has *power* [or is powerful] (*est potens*[26]), and [2] that *active* power (*potentia activa*) is appropriately attributed to him'.

[25] *Potestas* and *virtus* are more particularly associated with power, and Aquinas sometimes uses one of them rather than (or together with) *potentia* when he means power rather than potentiality more broadly considered.

[26] *Potens*, from which *potentia* derives, is the present participle of the verb *possum* ('can', 'be able'), here used adjectivally, in the sense of 'powerful'.

Naturally, 'active power' is used primarily in contrast with 'passive power', as the conclusion of chapter 7's last argument makes plain: 'active, but not passive, power is appropriately ascribed to God' (890). Elsewhere Aquinas helpfully associates the distinction between active and passive power with the distinction between second and first actuality:

> [W]e speak of *potentia* on the basis of actuality. For actuality is of two sorts—first actuality, which is form; and second actuality, which is activity. . . . That's why there are likewise two *potentiae*: one that is active, to which the actuality that is activity corresponds (and it is to this that the name 'potentia' seems to have been given first); and another that is passive *potentia*, to which first actuality, which is form, corresponds (to which, likewise, the name 'potentia' seems to have been passed on secondarily). For just as nothing undergoes anything except because of passive *potentia*, so nothing acts except because of first actuality, which is form. (QDP 1.1c)[27]

Passive power, then, is the power that gets actualized in first actuality—acquiring an 'accidental' form or inessential characteristic, as in learning to read Arabic. Active power, on the other hand, gets actualized in second actuality—actually reading Arabic.[28]

The first and simplest of Aquinas's arguments for the thesis of chapter 7 is also the best of them for my purposes here: 'Active power is the source of acting on something else in so far as it is something else, and [by II.6] it belongs to God (*Deo . . . convenit*) to be the source of being for other things. Therefore, [(2) active power belongs to him; and, therefore, (1)] having power belongs to him' (887). Acting on something else in so far as it is something else is a fair description of transeunt activity, and it may look as if the

---

[27] Aquinas's way of putting the distinction is sometimes oversimplified: 'Just as anything whatever is naturally suited to act in so far as it is in a state of actuality (*est actu*)'—see n. 23 above—'so is it naturally suited to be affected in so far as it is in a state of *potentia*' (I.16.132). But when he draws the conclusion to the argument of which that sentence is a part, he seems to remember the need to be more precise about *potentia*: 'God, therefore, has no *potentia* at all—passive, that is (*Nihil ergo habet de potentia, scilicet passiva*)' (ibid.).

[28] Of course, the process of learning a language involves a great deal of activity, but anyone who has learned a language has thereby actualized a passive potentiality. There seems to be no neat correlation between Aquinas's usage and ours. In non-technical twentieth-century English, 'power' will, in different contexts, mean what Aquinas means by 'active power', by 'first actuality', or even by 'second actuality'; 'potentiality', on the other hand, will cover approximately the same ground as 'passive power', 'active power', and 'first actuality'.

first of this argument's two premisses is identifying active power as the source of transeunt activity. But, of course, the power you have of (immanently) thinking about the letter you plan to write tomorrow is just as *active* (rather than passive) as is the power you have of (transeuntly) writing the letter. That first premiss must mean— and for the sake of the argument need mean—only that transeunt activity provides particularly clear evidence of the presence of active (rather than passive) power in its agent.[29]

But I think that there is, or ought to be, more than that to the notion of active power as it is used here: that Aquinas means, or should mean, more by 'active' here than simply not passive. For, as we saw in considering the *actus purus* argument, in terms of the distinction between first and second actuality, God's pure actuality must be understood as pure *second* actuality. Consequently, the power associated with any divine action, immanent or transeunt, must be power *in action*. We attribute to the weight-lifter the power to lift 300 pounds, and we attribute it to him when he's resting as well as when he's in the act of successfully lifting that weight. But there is something distinctive about our attributing the power to him when he's in the act, because his actually doing it (as distinct from his actually having acquired the power to do it) is the *culminating* actualization—the *perfecting*—of that power of his and, thereby, of an aspect of himself.[30] And we already have good grounds for recognizing that all attributions of power to God are best understood in terms of that distinction, since all of God's power must be power *in action*—second actuality.[31]

Having argued for the propriety of attributing to God the power to produce other things, Aquinas does as he so often does when introducing a conceptually distinguishable aspect of God's nature: he pauses to argue that God's absolute simplicity is in no way compromised by that introduction.[32] That is what he does here in two chapters, first in what might be thought of as an inner-directed identification—II.8: 'God's power *is* his substance'—and then in an outer-directed identification—II.9: 'God's power *is* his action.' For

---

[29] See also 10.903: 'active power is a source of acting on something else, as is clear from what the Philosopher says in *Metaphysics* V [12, 1019a15–20; 1020a1–2, 5–6]'.

[30] See Aristotle, *Nicomachean Ethics* IX 7, 1168a5–9.

[31] See also QDP 1.1c: 'we attribute activity to God because of [its nature as] the final completing [of actuality], not because of that into which the activity passes over'.

[32] On absolute simplicity see TMOT, 121–9; also Stump and Kretzmann 1982.

absolute simplicity precludes any sort of compositeness, thereby entailing the elimination of any real components, and thus the elimination of all real distinctions within God's nature. All talk of God's power or, for that matter, God's action is justified only to the extent to which it aids our attempt to acquire some provisional, analogical understanding of the absolutely simple nature that we cannot understand as such. Ontologically speaking, God's power, like any other conceptually distinguishable aspect of God's nature, must be really identical with God's substance (or essence), since 'in things whose powers are not their substances, the powers themselves are in the categories of accident (*sunt accidentia*). (That's why natural power is placed in the second species of quality.[33]) But in God there cannot be anything belonging to the categories of accident (*aliquod accidens*), as was shown in the first book [in ch. 23]. God, therefore, *is* his power' (8.896).[34] Similarly, 'an action that is not the agent's substance is in the agent the way something belonging to the categories of accident is in its subject. (That is why action is counted among the nine categories of accident.[35]) But in God there cannot be anything by way of an accidental characteristic. In God, therefore, his action is not other than his substance [II.8] and his power' (9.902).[36]

5. How to attribute power to God

We have already seen that the combination of Aquinas's conception of God as pure (second) actuality together with his different

[33] Quality, one of the nine Aristotelian categories of accident, is itself divided into four kinds, the second of which includes natural powers, both active and passive. See Aristotle, *Categories* 8, 9a14–27.

[34] I'm paraphrasing rather than simply translating most occurrences of *accidens* in this passage and the next one, in order to bring out the technical points which Aquinas obviously intends to be making, and in order to avoid the misunderstandings to which plain 'accident' might give rise.

[35] See Aristotle, *Categories* 9, 11b1–14.

[36] Here Aquinas is simply registering, rather than examining, the claim that God's power *is* God's action, but the claim does raise a problem: *Can* God do (or *could* God have done) *more* things than he does, or things *other* than those he does? Suppose that the only doing at issue is the producing of other things. It's clear that not all really possible creatures have been or can be—now or hereafter—produced: e.g. my non-existent twin brother, or nineteenth-century land animals as big as the biggest dinosaurs. But surely these are things which an omnipotent God *could have* produced. If that's so, then isn't his power different from his action, after all? If not, is he omnipotent? Aquinas will discuss this issue in II.23 and 25–7; see Ch. Four below.

uses of the single word *potentia* creates problems for any attribution of *potentia* to God. It's not surprising, then, that he devotes a chapter to explaining just how *potentia* is to be attributed to God. The thesis of this chapter 10 is made up of two claims: 'power is attributed to God (a) not as the source of the *action*, but (b) as the source of the external *result* (*facti*)' (903).

Aquinas's relational method, which he introduced in Book I and uses everywhere in his natural and philosophical theology, entitles its practitioner to apply certain ordinary terms to God as long as, roughly speaking, the practitioner strips from the standard definition of the term anything that ties it to imperfection of any sort, even of a sort that would among created things count only as an ineluctable feature of natural existence. Any imperfection implied in a term's definition of course renders the term inapplicable to God in true, non-metaphorical propositions.[37] Here, for instance, is the way he adapts the term 'substance' to God: ' "substance" signifies something subsistent but subject to something else. So we do use "substance" . . . in connection with God, but because of subsistence, not because of standing-under' or subjection (QDP 1.1c). In the same way, claim (a) in the thesis of chapter 10 rules out part of the standard definition of 'power' when 'power' is applied to God. As Aquinas explains elsewhere, 'we attribute power [to God] because of [i] its being *permanent* [i.e. present all at once rather than successively] and [ii] its being a *source*, *not* because of [iii] its being brought to completion through activity' (QDP 1.1c). The attribution of power to God in respect [iii] would carry incompleteness (or imperfection) with it. As for [ii], power's being a *source*, we would ordinarily recognize the weight-lifter's power as the source either of his *action* of lifting the weight or of its *effect*—his holding 300 pounds above his head. Claim (b) in the thesis of chapter 10 is plainly intended to preserve [ii] as an aspect of the power attributed to God, but only as regards its being a source of the effect. As Aquinas puts it in another place, 'in the case of God, the defining characteristic (*ratio*) of power is preserved in so far as it is the source of the *effect*, but not in so far as it is the source of the *action*, which is the divine essence' and which, therefore, cannot have any source (ST Ia.25.1, ad 3).

Claim (a) in the thesis of chapter 10 is expressly supported by a simple argument based on chapter 9: since nothing is the source of

---

[37] See TMOT, 139–44.

itself,[38] and God's power *is* God's action, God's power is not the source of God's action (903). In that respect, of course, God's power and action are related to each other very differently from yours or mine. As I produce this written sentence, my power to write English (and to move my fingers) is the source of my activity of writing the sentence (by moving my fingers on the keys). The immediate source of the existence of the written English sentence is that activity of mine engaging with this electronic equipment, and its more remote source is my power to do that sort of thing. But since in God there is no real (but only a conceptual) distinction between his power (to produce other things) and his activity (of producing other things), power is attributable to him not as the immediate source of his activity (and thereby the more remote source of its effects) but simply as the source of the effects—hence claim (b) of the thesis.

Now this line of thought may seem not so much to explain how power is to be attributed to God as to show how the attribution of divine power might be dispensed with altogether. For in us, of course, the immediate source of effects is *activity*, second actuality. And God *is* pure (second) actuality. So, why shouldn't God's activity be identified—altogether naturally—as the source of the external result? In that case, power would be attributed to God *neither* as the source of his action *nor* as the source of what is brought about by that action. Then Aquinas could simply note that although at a pre-theoretic level we find it natural to draw the conceptual distinction between God's power and God's action, reflection shows us that it is unnecessary, not particularly illuminating, and possibly misleading.

Much of what is said in chapter 10 can be read as supporting this radical view. For example, power 'is not said to be in God in respect of action except in accordance with [our] mode of understanding, in so far as our intellect considers the two of them under different concepts: divine power and God's action. So if some actions that belong to God do not pass over into any external result but remain in the agent, in respect of them power will be said to be in God only in connection with [our] mode of understanding, not in reality. But intellection and volition are actions of that sort.... Intellect and

---

[38] See e.g. DEE 4.27, quoted in n. 15 above; also SCG I.22.207, which argues in more detail against the possibility of anything being the efficient cause of its own existence.

will, therefore, are in God not as powers [as they are in us] but solely as actions' (903). And indeed, as long as we consider God's action itself, whether transeunt or immanent, the radical view is the right one: 'power implies a relationship, in the nature of a source, to something else' (ibid.); and the action of an agent who is himself conceived of as pure (second) actuality leaves no real role for power to play. In this context, it is only when the effects of God's transeunt activity are taken into account that attributing power to God becomes more than a conceptual possibility that might better be left unrealized. Because 'active power is the source of acting on something else, . . . it is clear that [active] power is attributed to God in respect of external results [not merely conceptually but] in reality (*secundum rei veritatem*). . . . Therefore, God's power, strictly speaking, has to do not with such actions but with effects only' (903). It's all right to attribute (active) power to God as long as we realize that what can be represented in our case as

$$power \rightarrow activity \rightarrow effect$$

is less misleadingly represented in God's case as

$$power/activity \rightarrow effect.$$

And one reason for retaining the conceptual distinction between power and activity in the case of God's *transeunt* activities may be that those activities have external effects that are themselves temporal or otherwise subject to considerations of real potentiality, both passive and active. We'll see. In any case, no such considerations are relevant in the case of God's immanent activities, with respect to which the notion of power has no application at all.[39]

6. How to attribute relations to God

As Aquinas has been arguing, attributing power to God differs in several respects from attributing power to human beings, most notably because power in God should not be identified as the source of God's *acting*—claim (a) in the thesis of chapter 10: 'power is attributed to God *not* as the source of the *action*' (903). But, as

---

[39] QDP 1.1*c*, 'Is there power (*potentia*) in God?', quoted more than once in this section, is particularly helpful in this connection. See also e.g. ST Ia.25.1.

the relational method requires, there is also an important respect in which the attribution of power to God does correspond to ordinary attributions of power, those in which we recognize a person's power to do something as the source of the outward *effect* of her actually doing it—claim (b): 'power *is* attributed to God . . . as the source of the external *result*' (903). Then, since being a source is one part of the defining characteristic of power that warrants attributing power to God, and since characterizing something as a source cannot be understood except 'in relation to that of which it is the source, it's clear that something relational can be said of God, in respect of his effects' (11.905). And this relational term 'source' is the very term that links the discussion of power in chapters 7–10 to the new discussion of relations in God. Chapter 11 briefly catalogues several other divine attributes that were argued for in Book I and that, we are now reminded, involve saying something relational of God—e.g. God *knows* things other than himself (908) and *moves* things other than himself (909). Aquinas of course recognizes that picking out the various ways in which created things are *like* God—the foundation of his relational method—also involves saying something relational of God (907). All these relational terms—'knows', 'moves', 'is like'—involve true two-place predications in which a created thing is one *relatum* and God is the other: 'one thing cannot be understood to be spoken of in relation to another unless the latter would be spoken of conversely in relation to the former. But other things are spoken of in relation to God. For instance, as regards their being (which they have from God, as was shown [in II.6]), they are said to be *dependent on* him. God, therefore, will be spoken of conversely in relation to created things'—e.g. as that on which they depend for their being (906).

By the end of chapter 11, then, we have been given good reasons to think that there are several true two-place predications in which God and created things are the *relata*, and we have not yet been given any reasons to suppose that those predications do not apply in just the same way to those two *relata*, despite the acknowledged, radical, metaphysical differences between God and everything else. But the very title of the very next chapter shows that, as we should have expected, this sameness is only apparent: chapter 12, 'The relations said of God with reference to created things are not in

God really'—though, as we've already been seeing, they are in created things really.[40]

There are just two ways in which any characteristic can be in any thing really: either essentially, as an aspect of the thing's nature or substance, or inessentially ('accidentally'); and, as we've been reminded more than once, there can be no accidental characteristics in God. If any relations are in God really, they must be aspects of his substance, like everything else that is in God really. But Aquinas argues that relations to created things cannot be aspects of God's substance, basing his argument on Aristotle's definition of *relata*, or 'relatives', as 'things that in their very being pertain in some way *to something else*' (12.913).[41] If such relations were aspects of God's substance, then God's substance would be really a *relatum* in a relation to a created thing, and so 'would have to be said to be the very thing that is *to something else*. But that which is said to be *to something else* depends on it in a way, since it can neither be nor be understood without it. Therefore, God's substance would have to be dependent on something else, extrinsic to it' (913). Although Aquinas's first argument for the thesis of chapter 12 doesn't end there, this much of it may fairly be described as a complete *reductio ad absurdum* in its support. I want to look at it before considering the rest of his argument and its final conclusion.

The middle sentence of this part of the argument contains a crucial claim, which I think can be filled out in this way: If anything is correctly called an A, and on that basis alone is correctly understood as related to an A', then A depends on A', since in that case A can neither be nor be understood without A'. Because this claim includes no restrictions to certain kinds of relations, it is very strong—so strong that it may look implausible. If A is an artisan, then it is an artisan of some artefact, and in that case A' is an artefact. It's obvious that an artefact, considered just as such, can

---

[40] The titles of chs. 11, 12, 13&14, and 15 are among the few in Book II that we can be sure were written by Aquinas himself (see Ch. One above, n. 15). Aquinas does recognize real relations in God, but only those that hold between the persons of the Trinity (see e.g. QDP 1.1, ad 1), which are therefore outside the scope of the natural theology of SCG I–III, where the only relevant divine relations are those said of God 'with reference to created things'.

[41] *Cum enim relativa sint quae secundum suum esse ad aliud quodammodo se habent*; see *Categories* 7, 6a36–7, b6–8.

neither come to be without an artisan nor be understood, considered just as such, unless its causal dependence on an artisan is understood. In the argument, however, it's not this reciprocal dependence of A' on A that is supposed to concern us, but only the dependence of A on A'. We can, of course, acknowledge that an artisan considered just as such cannot be or be understood without an artefact. Is that enough to show the dependence of A on A'? Well, yes, but with a difference. The dependence of an artefact on an artisan is an aspect of every artefact's substance. Every artisan is human, but because being an artisan is not essential to being human, not an aspect of any human being's substance, even a human being who happens to be an artisan could, considered just as human, be or be understood without an artefact. So the acknowledged dependence of A on A' in this case is not an aspect of the substance of any A. It is, therefore, conceptual, rather than real, dependence.

For the sake of the argument we're examining, and for the sake of simplicity, suppose that we temporarily consider being the producer of things as the *only* relation said of God with reference to created things. Obviously, the producer, considered just as such, can neither be nor be understood without things he produces. And then the issue in this argument is whether or not being the producer of created things is essential to being God, an aspect of God's substance. If being the creator is an aspect of God's substance, then God could not be without being the creator, or be understood without being understood as the creator. But if God's substance does include God's being the creator, then, since God's being the creator obviously does depend on there being created things, 'God's substance would have to be dependent on something else, extrinsic to it'—dependent on there being something or other besides God—which is absurd.

To drive home the absurdity of that sub-conclusion, Aquinas goes on to conclude this argument by referring to a part of what I consider to be the strongest argument for God's existence in Book I: 'And in that case God's substance would not be necessary being through itself (*per seipsum necesse esse*), as it was shown to be in the first book [in 15.124].[42] Therefore, relations of this sort are not in God really' (913).

[42] I provide a detailed discussion of the argument in I.15.124 in TMOT, 95–112, where it is labelled 'G6'. See also sect. 8 below.

I think that this argument in 913 does establish chapter 12's thesis. But the three further arguments in the chapter make some special contributions of their own, such as providing examples of familiar relations that have formal features of the sort that Aquinas needs if he is to predicate relations of God without entailing that God's existence or nature is in any way dependent on being a *relatum* in any of those relations. Thus he argues that God is related to created things as something that can be known is related to someone's knowledge of it: 'although what is knowable is spoken of in relation to the knowledge, in reality the relation is not in what is knowable but only in the knowledge', Aristotle having said of the knowable[43] just what Aquinas needs to say here of God: 'what is knowable is spoken of in relational terms *not* because it *itself* is related [to anything else], but because something *else* is related to it' (914). Again, 'some relations are said of God for the first time— e.g. that he is lord or governor of this thing that [now] begins to exist for the first time. Therefore, if any [such] relation were predicated of God as actually existing in him, it would follow that something would happen to God for the first time, and that he would in that way be changed' (916)—which cannot be true of a being that has been shown to be eternal (I.15) and devoid of passive potentiality (I.16). Aquinas might have helped his case here by pointing to ordinary instances: no real change occurs in X simply as a consequence of X's first becoming the younger Y's second cousin twice removed, or merely because Z has just become X's secret admirer.

But what may look like the most interesting of these three arguments is, I think, a tactical mistake on Aquinas's part. The heart of this third argument is the thesis that 'there are no real relations of that which is actual to that which is not actual but potential' (915). Since A's having a real relation to B is equivalent to A's being metaphysically dependent on B, then if A is actual and B is only potential, A cannot have a real relation to B: what is actual cannot depend for its existence on what is only potential and does not itself actually exist. What makes the thesis particularly relevant is Aquinas's observation that God has knowledge not only of things that actually exist but also of things that could but don't actually exist: knowledge is 'said of God not only in respect of things that

---

[43] *Metaphysics* V 15, 1021a29–30.

are in actuality but [also] in respect of those that are in potentiality, since he has knowledge of them as well' (915). The trouble with these considerations is that they present God as the one *actual relatum* in this epistemic relation with merely potential things, and so as the only *relatum* in which this relation between God and the merely potential *relata could* be a real relation. And it *must* be a real relation, as is clear even from the immediately preceding argument, in which, as we've seen, Aquinas observes that 'although what is knowable is spoken of in relation to knowledge, *in reality* the relation is not in what is knowable but only in the knowledge' (914).[44] So in my view, chapter 12 would have been better if it had not included this third argument. It doesn't destroy the main point, but it does detract from it.

In discussing Aquinas's chapter 12, which he devotes solely to arguing for the negative claim that God's relations to created things cannot be in God really, I've already been interpolating his positive account of such relations as attributable to God only conceptually, drawing on other texts of his and also on his immediately preceding explanation of attributions of power to God. Aquinas himself, however, postpones his positive account of relational attributions to chapter 13&14,[45] 'How those relations *are* said of God', where he says what I've already been saying on his behalf: the relations whereby God is related to creatures 'are attributed to him solely in keeping with our mode of understanding, based on the fact that other things are referred to him' (919*b*).[46] But even though rela-

---

[44] See also e.g. QDV 4.5c: 'Whenever any two things are related to each other in such a way that the one depends on the other but not vice versa, then the relation is real in the one that depends on the other, but in the one on which it depends the relation is conceptual only. For example, we cannot understand anything to be referred to something else without also understanding the opposing relation from the standpoint of that other thing, as is clear in the case of knowledge, which depends on what is knowable, and not vice versa. And so, since all created things depend on God, but not vice versa, there are in created things real relations by which they are referred to God, but the opposing relations are in God conceptually only.' For relevant special features of Aquinas's account of God's knowledge, see Stump and Kretzmann 1995.

[45] In the autograph there is no title for a ch. 14 and no division at all in the text, but a reasonable tradition assigns the designation 'Chapter 13' to sects. 917–20 in the Marietti edn. of the text and 'Chapter 14' to sect. 921. See the eds.' n. 1*a* on p. 114.

[46] Even here Aquinas deals first with one more untenable account—viz. that 'the relations we have been discussing are externally *existent* as, so to speak, real things (*res aliquae*) outside God' (917). His infinite regress argument against this possibility strikes me as decisive: 'one would have to consider God's relations also to those relations, which are real things. And if *these* [relations of God to *those* relations] are

tions to created things are predicated of God 'only in a conceptual way (*secundum modum intelligendi*), all the same, [our] intellect is not mistaken' in framing such predications (920)—as long as we don't drift into thinking of the relations as in God *really*. Analogously, there's nothing wrong in thinking relationally of Caesar's assassination as an object of your knowledge as long as you acknowledge that 'we understand and talk in relational terms about what is knowable [only] because the *knowledge* is referred to it' (920).[47]

7. God as the source of everything else

Of the thirty-three chapters (6–38) which Aquinas devotes to 'the producing of things as regards their being', the first of his large-scale topics in Book II, the last twenty-three are concerned with

again real things, one will, again, have to find *third* relations—and so on *ad infinitum*. Therefore, the relations by which God is referred to other things are not real things existing outside God' (918). See also QDP 3.3c, which contains an argument against the reality of relations on their own that is ingenious, even though it depends on a premiss that has not yet been argued for at this stage of SCG II: 'Some people have said that creation is something in reality, midway between creator and created thing. And because what is in the middle is neither of the extremes, it followed that creation would be neither the creator nor the created thing. But this has been judged an error by the masters, since every thing existing in any way has its being only from God.' So creation thought of in this way would be simply another created thing.

[47] In 921 Aquinas provides familiar reassurances about the preservation of divine simplicity despite the many relations to created things that are correctly predicated of God, reassurances that are hardly needed here, where the multiplicity has already been shown to be only conceptual. But he also introduces the dubious principle that 'anything's power is greater, and it is the source of more things, to the extent to which it is simpler; and it is on that basis understood as related in many more ways. A point, for example, is the source of more things than a line is, and a line than a surface.' First, he must mean to rank a point as greatest in power only among the members of its species: geometrical entities. Second, he must mean that its power is greatest only because as the projective source of infinitely many lines, each of which is in turn the source of infinitely many surfaces, the point is the primary source of every surface of which every one of those lines is projectively a source, and of every volume of which every one of those surfaces is a source. Whether or not this principle can be exported beyond geometry, it seems to be false in general: an earthworm is an animal much simpler, and much *less* powerful (in the relevant sense), than a chimpanzee. But perhaps we needn't be concerned with the dubious principle that 'the simpler anything is, the more powerful it is', since Aquinas introduces this material here only in order to provide further, unneeded support for *simplicity*: 'Therefore, the very fact that many things are said of God relationally attests to his supreme simplicity' (921).

precisely that: the *producing* of things, how the producer produces natural things. What he has to say in a preliminary way about the producer, considered just as such, and the things produced, he says in chapters 6–15, the material I'm focusing on in this chapter. Having argued that being the productive source of things is suited to God's nature (II.6), as long as certain special considerations regarding God's power (II.7–10) and God's relations to those things (II.11–14) are taken into account, Aquinas devotes just one chapter to considering the things themselves. This allocation of space seems drastically unbalanced until we see that in this preliminary consideration of the things produced Aquinas is interested primarily in showing that the things produced by God are *all* the natural things there are.[48]

The chapter in which he argues this is another of the few that were titled by Aquinas himself—chapter 15: 'God is for *all* things the cause of being'. That the emphasis in the title is intended to fall on 'all' is clear from the first sentence of the chapter, which presents its thesis: 'Now since it has been shown that God is the source of being for *some* things, it must be shown, further, that *everything* besides him derives its being from him' (922). So Aquinas is introducing his arguments for this universal thesis by announcing that he has already argued for a particular version (or particular versions) of it. Where has he done that? The absence of any reference here to 'the first book' weakly suggests that he has in mind some preceding chapter of Book II;[49] the Leonine editors identify it as II.6. I think the editors are right to try to locate the passage referred to as near to chapter 15 as possible, and among the preceding chapters of Book II there is no other plausible candidate. But it would be surprising if Aquinas were to refer to chapter 6 as a place where he has shown that God is the source of being for *some* things.[50]

[48] He is also interested here in making another important, general point about God's production of things, but I'm postponing consideration of it (see Ch. Three below, sect. 1). This global consideration of the things produced is preliminary to the detailed investigation of 'the nature of those things' (877), the last and longest of the three principal tasks he sets himself in Book II, to which he devotes chs. 46–101.

[49] The form of the reference does not restrict it to Book II. See n. 52 below for an example of a reference in Book II in which 'as shown above' must mean as shown in Book I.

[50] In his Commentary on the *Sentences*, particular and universal versions of this thesis are clearly distinguished, and are given widely separated treatments. In Sent. II.1.1.2 addresses the question 'Can *anything* come from God via creation?', and

It's true that his aim in chapter 6 is expressly limited, as I noted when discussing it in section 2 above, but the limitation that is explicit in the chapter and perfectly suited to it has to do with arguing not that God is the source of being for *some* other things, but rather that it is *appropriate* for God to be the source of being for other things (*Deo competit ut sit aliis principium essendi*). There is no real difficulty in construing chapter 6 as arguing not merely the propriety but also the actuality of God's being the source. We've already seen that the first two of chapter 6's arguments simply bypass propriety to conclude straightforwardly that God *is*, or *must be*, 'the cause of being for other things' (879, 880), and it's not hard to read the conclusions of the other four arguments as providing explanations of the propriety of God's actual transeunt activity.[51] But can the chapter's six arguments be read as supporting only *particular* conclusions?

The conclusions of some of the arguments in II.6 do seem to be expressly stopping short of universality: 'God must be the cause of being for *many* things' (880); 'it is appropriate for God to bring about *something* actually existent, for which he is the cause of its existing' (881); 'it is appropriate for God to make *some* being like himself actual' (882); 'since the divine will is perfect, it will not lack the power of sharing its being with *something* by way of likeness' (883). The *actus purus* argument in 884 concludes, as we've seen, that 'in virtue of being in actuality God [can] not only intellectively cognize, and will, but also produce an effect. And in this way he can be for other things the cause of their being.' While that conclusion isn't expressly particular, it is obviously too weak to be itself taken as a universal conclusion or to entail one. And even the conclusion of the first-efficient-cause argument in 879, although not expressly particular, is not expressly universal either: 'God exists as the cause of being for other things.' Aquinas could without much effort have revised at least some, perhaps all, of the arguments of chapter 6 in ways that would have enabled them to support universal

II.37.1.2 begins 'Is *every* being from God?' Similarly, ST Ia.44.1: 'Must *every* being have been caused by God?', and 45.2: 'Can God create *anything*?'

[51] See also Aquinas's first argument in II.7, which takes ch. 6 to have shown that 'it belongs to God to be the source of being for other things' (887), as we saw in sect. 4 above. See too the discussion of II.11 in sect. 6 above, where Aquinas is pretty plainly referring to ch. 6 as providing evidence of the actuality of God's producing other things: 'other things are spoken of in relation to God. For instance, as regards their being (which they have from God, as was shown)' (906).

conclusions.[52] It seems likely that he deliberately avoided doing so just because his plan included arguing separately for the universality of God's producing of things.

The thesis that God is for all things the cause of their being is of course centrally important for Aquinas's theology, natural or revealed. So it is hardly surprising that near relatives of most of the seven arguments he produces in support of various versions of the thesis in chapter 15 can also be found elsewhere in his writings.[53] Some of those more familiar arguments are especially powerful, and invite further attention.[54] I haven't seen Aquinas using either the fifth or the sixth of these arguments for this purpose anywhere else, but each of them is closely related to an important argument developed in Book I, and they have some connection with each other. For reasons that will emerge, it seems particularly appropriate to focus on the fifth of these arguments.

8. Argument E/U

Chapter 15's fifth argument for the universality of God's production is a reworking of an argument Aquinas introduced in Book I to support God's eternality. I'll refer to it as the E/U argument.

Everything regarding which it is possible that it be and that it not be has a cause. For considered on its own it is disposed to either, and so

---

[52] Notice e.g. that the argument for the universal conclusion in 15.925 relies on the premiss 'God is the first cause, as was shown above', where the reference must be to the existence argument based on efficient causation in I.13.113. (See n. 13 above.) But that is the very argument he invokes in 6.879 as support for the weak, non-universal conclusion.

[53] For the first argument (923), see also e.g. DEE 4.27; In Sent. II.37.1.2, sc 2; QDP 3.5 (third argument). For the second (924), In Sent. II.1.1.2c; ST Ia.44.1c?; CT I.68.116. For the third (925), QDP 3.5 (first argument). For the fourth (926), In Sent. II.37.1.2c; ST Ia.44.1c; CT I.68.117; QDP 3.5 (second argument). For the seventh (929), In Sent. II.1.1.2c?; QDP 3.5 (second argument?).

[54] This is especially true, I think, of the first of them (923). The version of the thesis it argues for looks too strong: 'everything that is *in any way at all* (*quocumque modo*) derives its being from God'. On its most natural interpretation that claim would be denied by Aquinas. Sin, for instance, which in his view qualifies as something that is in some way—even something that is as 'a sort of substance or nature'—does not, he argues, derive its being from God. (See e.g. In Sent. II.37.1.1 and 37.1.2.) But, as the eds. of the Marietti edn. of ST point out in n. 2 to Ia.44.1c, which presents a near relative of the first argument in ch. 15, the *quocumque modo* phrase here must mean no more than every (natural) being of any kind at all.

there must be something else that determines it to just one. So, since this cannot go on *ad infinitum*, there must be something necessary that is the cause of all the things that can be and can also not be. Now there   5
is a *kind* of necessary thing that has a *cause* of its necessity. In this connection, too, one cannot go on *ad infinitum*. And so we must arrive at something that is necessary being *per se*. But there can be only one such thing, as was shown in the first book [in ch. 42], and that is God. Therefore, everything other than he must be traced back to him as to   10
the cause of its being. (927)

It's not hard to say, very broadly, how this E/U argument is intended to show that God is the universal producer. Every existent being is either contingent or necessary; the ultimate source of the existence of contingent beings is itself non-contingent, or necessary; every necessary being is either caused or uncaused; the ultimate source of the existence of caused necessary beings (and thereby of contingent beings) is itself an uncaused necessary being; there can be only one such being; and that is God. But what's most interesting about this argument isn't apparent in that broad outline.

The core of the E/U argument, from line 1 through the sentence ending in line 8, is formally the same as the core of the argument for God's eternality in SCG I.15.124. In TMOT, Chapter Three (sect. 6), I extracted the core of that eternality argument, and presented it as a successful argument for the existence of an ultimately explanatory being. I labelled that existence argument 'G6'. Because the line of reasoning that leads to 'something that is necessary being *per se*' here in E/U is spelled out in a little more detail in G6, I'll try to clarify E/U by drawing on G6. (I will, in the process, also have to draw on my discussion of G6 in the earlier volume, tailoring the explanations to present purposes.)

The things at issue in lines 1–5 are natural contingent beings, contrasted with the necessary beings at issue in lines 5–8. The identification of them as natural contingent beings is clearer in the portion of G6 corresponding to the first sentence of E/U: 'We see things in the world regarding which it is possible that they be and that they not be—I mean those that can be generated and can be destroyed. Now everything regarding which it is possible that it be [and not be] has a cause.'[55]

---

[55] My translation of I.15.124 here is slightly different from the one I offer in TMOT, 95. I'm modifying it here to bring out the similarities between the two arguments more clearly.

The respect in which E/U claims that every natural contingent being has a cause is brought out in its second sentence (lines 2–3), but too vaguely. It is of course only *existent* natural contingent beings that are at issue in an argument designed to show that all the things brought into existence depend on God as the source of their existence. This restriction is implied in the opening words of G6, quoted just above: 'We see things in the world . . .'. It is also clearer in the sentence of G6 that corresponds to the second sentence of E/U: 'For since on its own it is disposed indifferently to those two— being and not being—*if being is its status*, this must be on the basis of some cause.' Aquinas thinks that an ordinary contingent (produced) being's present existence is dependent in two respects. First, it depends on something else for having come into existence.[56] Second, it depends on something else for continuing to exist, 'something else that determines it to just one', because it has no intrinsic tendency to exist: 'considered on its own it is disposed to either' existing or not existing (lines 2–3). The purpose to be served by E/U in the context of II.15 might seem to warrant our ignoring sustaining causes and limiting our attention to the causes that bring natural contingent things into existence; but we'll find that that restriction is unwarranted.

The natural sciences provide answers to questions about the causes that are productive of very many sorts of natural contingent (dependently existing) things, and those answers are in terms of other dependently existing things. But, of course, such questions can and, at least from the standpoint of metaphysics, should be asked again about each dependent entity referred to in such explanatory answers, no matter what level of generality they're formulated at, no matter how pervasive or simple may be the dependent things, events, or states of affairs they refer to. And the crux of Aquinas's line of reasoning in E/U is his claim that it is theoretically impossible to trace back explanatory beings *ad infinitum*, leading to his claim that 'there must be something *necessary* that is the cause [of the existence] of all the [existent] things that can be and can also not be' (lines 4–5). Especially given the purpose that E/U is designed to serve, it looks as if, by denying the

---

[56] Certainly most, perhaps all, contingent things come into existence, begin to exist. But what is essential to the notion of contingent existence or existence as produced is *dependence on something else* for existence, even if that existence is beginningless. See Ch. Five below.

possibility of an infinite regress here, Aquinas means that it is theoretically impossible for the series of dependent explanatory beings to be beginningless, theoretically impossible for the question 'And what produced *that*?' to be correctly answered again and again in terms of produced productive causes that 'go on *ad infinitum*' into a beginningless past time. However, that can't be what he means.

As we'll see, when (in II.31–8) he takes up the problem known to the medievals as 'the eternity of the world', he argues that the infinite temporal and causal regress entailed by the notion of our world's having existed always is *not* a theoretical impossibility.[57] In making that sort of argument, there and elsewhere, he sometimes expressly supports the theoretical possibility of a regress that is infinite, as he says, only accidentally (*per accidens*). For instance,

in connection with efficient causes a regress that is infinite *accidentally* is *not* considered impossible—if, that is, all the infinitely many causes have the order of only one cause, but their being many is accidental. A carpenter, for example, acts by means of accidentally many hammers because one after another of them breaks; and so it is an accidental characteristic of this hammer that it acts after the action of another hammer. Similarly, it is an accidental characteristic of this man, in so far as he begets, that he has been begotten by another; for he begets in so far as he is a man and not in so far as he is the son of another man, since all men considered as begetters have a single status among efficient causes, the status of a particular begetter. And so it is not impossible that a man be begotten by a man, *ad infinitum*. (ST Ia.46.2, ad 7)

For many things to 'have the order of only one cause' or to 'have a single status among efficient causes' is for their plurality to be irrelevant to the causal activity of any one of them, whether or not they are elements in a single causal series. The many hammers successively owned and used by the carpenter, one at a time, are not elements in a single causal series, but are altogether causally independent of one another: each of them does its hammering without in any way depending on its predecessors. On the other hand, each human begetter in a single line of biological descent is causally dependent on his immediate predecessor in that causal series in one respect—for his having been begotten. But, even so, each of them does his begetting without depending on any of his

---

[57] See Ch. Five below.

predecessors in *that* respect. A father's begetting, considered just as such, is no more dependent on his father's begetting him than this hammer's hammering is dependent on the most recently discarded hammer's hammering. Since the plurality of these independently operating causes is entirely accidental to the causality of any one of them, there is in theory no reason why the series of hammers, or even the series of begetters, should not have been beginningless, should not constitute a temporally infinite regress.

So, when Aquinas says in line 4 of E/U that 'this cannot go on *ad infinitum*', we're bound to suppose that he doesn't mean that if we start with any existing natural contingent thing, we can't in theory correctly answer infinitely many regressive questions about its causal origin in terms of a beginningless series of productive causes—an infinite regress of dependently existent, dependently operating explanatory beings.

Aquinas is occasionally willing to adopt the hypothesis of this world's beginninglessness for the sake of argument. Quite rightly, he takes an argument for the existence of a *first* cause for natural contingent beings to be strengthened by the inclusion of that hypothesis just because it poses a stiffer challenge to such an argument.[58] So suppose, for the sake of argument E/U, that for each and every thing that comes into existence a correct explanation of its having come into existence can be given in terms of the causality of at least one earlier dependent being. In other words, suppose that there actually is a beginningless series of dependent beings all of which are brought into existence by earlier dependent beings. Call that series S. Theories of biological, geological, and cosmological evolution have given us good reasons to think that the uncountably many concurrent productively causal series of dependent beings tend to converge as they are traced back in time, that these series branch only in one 'direction'—from past to future. For simplicity's sake I will suppose that we're dealing with just one many-branched causal series S in which can be found the answer to 'What brought *that* into existence?' for any and every dependently existent thing to which the question applies. Series S contains the hypothetically beginningless history of the natural world, 'all the [actual] things that can be and can also not be' (E/U, line 5). So the nature of God's role as the universal source and cause of being may be

---

[58] See TMOT, Ch. Two, sects. 3 and 7.

construed in terms of the ultimate explanation of the existence of series S.

But such an explanation obviously can't be elicited by asking 'What brought *that* into existence?' about the series S itself, be-cause, by hypothesis, S never began to exist. If S itself is in some respect a dependently existent being, it isn't a dependently existent being in that respect: nothing *could* have brought S into existence. But if all the natural, dependent productive causes of 'all the things that can be and can also not be' are included within S, then identi-fying '*the cause* of all the things that can be and can also not be' must be identifying the cause of S. As we've seen, it is impossible that S have a producer that brings it into existence, but that doesn't preclude its depending on something else for its existing and con-tinuing to function as the natural causal series it is.

The dependence of ordinary contingent things on sustaining causes is beyond dispute. But does series S itself need sustaining? Does it make sense to ask what explains S's sempiternality, its beginningless, continuous, operational ongoingness? Well, *is* series S a dependently existent thing in the sense of requiring a sustaining cause? Is it a thing at all? Since S's existence is successive, since there is no time at which all its members exist together, we might feel uncomfortable about regarding S as a thing in its own right.[59] I don't think worries of that sort are justified, but the issue doesn't have to be settled here. In asking about the explanation of S's going on right now, we're asking about the explanation of S's now having any members rather than none at all. So in this case we're asking not for an explanation of S as a beginningless, diachronic whole, but rather for an explanation of its instantaneous, synchronic, present phase, which I'll label Sn. Unlike S itself, Sn is not at all successive; all of Sn's members exist at once. And since each of Sn's members is, by hypothesis, a being that depends for its existing on the present operation of sustaining causes, the explanation of Sn can be construed as simply the sum of all the explanations of the existing of the dependent beings that are Sn's members. If such a construal makes sense, then the sum of all those particular explana-tions would explain S's now having not merely any elements at all but even the very elements it now has.

---

[59] This sort of question has been admirably dealt with in Rowe's analysis and appraisal of the metaphysical status of a beginningless causal series, Rowe 1975*a* and esp. Rowe 1975*c*, and my discussion here owes something to his.

Such an explanation of S's going on right now in terms of explaining Sn would be enormously more complex than is needed for purposes of argument E/U. Besides, it may seem that all those particular explanations are too disparate to be summed into an explanation of Sn. After all, beings that depend on other beings for their existing have very different necessary conditions. Your presently existing needs the earth's atmosphere as part of its explanation; a mountain's or a star's presently existing does not. But Sn converges when traced up its chain of continuating causes as S converges when traced backwards in time. Moving up several levels in the explanation of your continuing to exist, the existing of the earth's atmosphere requires earth's gravity, and so does the mountain's continuing to exist—though not the star's. And moving up many more levels of explanation all at once, the continuing existence of earth's gravity, and of the star, and of every other natural contingent being has the continuing existence (or obtaining) of natural laws as a necessary condition. For my immediate purposes, I can pause there, at the level of explanation at which a general reference to natural laws is the most (or the only) appropriate move to make. And, naturally, part of any generally correct answer to the question of what keeps the world going, what explains the producing of things over time, will have to be that natural laws continue to obtain.[60]

So I maintain that an explanation in terms of sustaining causation does apply to S in virtue of applying to Sn, and that it applies to Sn in virtue of applying to each of Sn's members in such a way as to lead, through repeated applications, to an identifiable single condition necessary for S's going on right now: the persisting efficacy of natural laws. I am definitely not maintaining that the persistence of natural laws needs no explaining, that natural laws themselves are the 'something necessary that is the cause of all the things that can be and can also not be' (E/U lines 4–5). (I'll return to this point below.) Here I want only to claim that in E/U Aquinas's first denial of the theoretical possibility of going on *ad infinitum* can and should be construed as applying also to explaining S's presently continuing. But how, exactly?

As we've seen (in n. 13 above), Aquinas thinks that a causally

---

[60] By 'natural laws' here I mean nature's actual governing regularities, of course, not anybody's up-to-the-minute codified best estimate of what those regularities might be.

linked series of efficient causes does not admit of an infinite regress just in case, for each cause in the series, its causally operating is required for its immediate successor's causally operating, so that the effect is not achieved unless all the causes in the series are operating simultaneously: 'in connection with efficient causes a regress that is infinite *essentially* (*per se*) is *impossible*—if, that is, the causes that are essentially required for some effect were infinitely many. For example, if a stone were moved by a stick, the stick by a hand, and so on *ad infinitum*' (ST Ia.46.2, ad 7). If we picture S as a horizontal series of productive causes, stretching back infinitely into the past, then the series of sustaining causes we're considering in connection with Sn should be pictured as vertical, the series of causes all of which must be operating at once, right now, in order to explain the present existing of anything that is 'considered on its own . . . disposed to either' being or not being (E/U, line 2).

E/U's claim that an infinite regress in the explanation of the existence of natural contingent things is theoretically impossible is paralleled in G6 by a passage in which Aquinas says that the impossibility 'was proved above on the basis of Aristotle's reasoning'. In the context of G6 he is clearly alluding to this argument: 'That which is moved instrumentally cannot move anything unless there is something that moves it initially (*principaliter*). But if one goes on *ad infinitum* as regards movers and things moved, all of them will be moving instrumentally, so to speak, because they are posited as moved movers; but nothing will be [operating] as the initial mover. Therefore, nothing will be moved' (SCG I.13.95).[61]

Like the Aristotelian example of the hand, the stick, and the stone, this argument has to do with causes of motion rather than with sustaining causes as such. But the relevant sort of causes of motion, considered just as such, obviously is a species of sustaining cause: the stone stops moving as soon as the stick stops moving, and the stick stops moving as soon as the hand stops moving. In such a synchronic causal series all the intermediate causes, however many they may be, must be merely *instrumental*, dependent for their causal operation on the causally prior, but temporally simultaneous, operation of some cause that is causally first in that series. So

---

[61] Aquinas finds this argument in Aristotle, *Physics* VIII 5, 256a21–b3.

this inferred first cause cannot itself be an instrumental cause in the series, but must instead be the originally operative cause relative to which all the others in the causal series are instrumental. Aquinas does not, and need not, concern himself with how many intermediate instrumental causes may be involved in explaining a dependent being's presently existing. When he says that 'this cannot go on *ad infinitum*', he means that each such being's present existence must be traceable to a first (or ultimate) cause, even if the causal distance between the first cause and the sustaining of the dependent being were *infinitely* divisible into simultaneously operating intermediaries.

But what entitles Aquinas to deny the possibility of going on *ad infinitum* in such a causal series? The most fully satisfactory answer I know is the one developed by Rowe. Suppose that A is a dependent being whose existing right now is explained by B's current sustaining activity, and that B's sustaining of A is explained by reference to C. 'Can we now say', Rowe asks, 'that the explanation for the fact that the causal activity of causing A to exist is now going on might be found in B? It seems clear we cannot' (1975*a*: 33).[62] In keeping with a later medieval tradition, Rowe calls a causal series of this sort 'essentially ordered'.

Now if C is causing B to be causing A to exist, then since we are operating within an essentially ordered series it also will be true that C is now causing A to exist. C, therefore, will be exhibiting that very sort of causal activity we are trying to explain. And if C is the first member of the series, we might be able to explain why the causal activity *causing-A-to-be-now-existing* is now going on by reference to C. However, if C is an intermediate cause, if some other thing is now causing C to be causing A to exist, then we cannot find the explanation for the fact that this activity is going on by reference to C. What then if the series progresses to infinity? Each member of the series will be right now exhibiting the causal activity we are trying to explain. It will be true that every member of the series is exhibiting the causal activity in question and also true that the fact that the causal activity is going on cannot be explained by any member of the series. For any member we select, it will be true that it is caused to exhibit the activity in question by some other member and, therefore, true that we cannot explain the fact that this sort of causal activity is going on in the universe by reference to that member. . . . [I]f the series proceeds to infinity there will

---

[62] In these passages Rowe is in fact developing an interpretation of one of Aquinas's attempts to block an infinite regress.

be no explanation of the fact that a certain sort of causal activity[—causing A to be now existing—] . . . is going on in the world. (ibid. 34–5)

And, therefore, I would add, there could not in that case be a philosophically satisfactory, metaphysical explanation of the fact that A—or S—is now continuing to exist.[63] A's—and, therefore, S's—existing now would be a brute fact, theoretically inexplicable, 'if the essentially ordered series of causes resulting in A's present existence proceeds to infinity, lacks a first member' (ibid. 35–6).

Aquinas doesn't take the brute-fact alternative seriously, in E/U, in G6, or anywhere else. As Rowe quite rightly observes (ibid. 36–7), that fact about Aquinas shows that he assumes, or considers self-evident, some form of 'the Principle of Sufficient Reason [PSR], a principle that in its strongest form maintains that no thing can exist and no fact can obtain without there being an explanation for that thing's existence or for that fact's obtaining' (ibid. 37). Rowe argues convincingly (in 1975b) that PSR is untenable in its strongest form, and I agree. But I also agree with his claim that 'no one has put forth any convincing argument for the falsity of PSR$_2$', this weaker form of PSR: '*Every existing thing has a reason for its existence either in the necessity of its own nature or in the causal efficacy of some other beings*' (1975a: 261). I subscribe to PSR$_2$, interpreting the expression 'a reason for its existence' in the sense of a reason for its presently existing. Not only the history of science, but even a fundamentally rational attitude towards ordinary reality, presupposes PSR$_2$. And since there is no ordinary existing thing about which we could tolerate the blithe announcement that there simply is *no* reason for its existence, rationality

---

[63] Rowe carefully distinguishes between 'two different items: *i. the fact that A now exists*, and *ii. the fact that a certain sort of causal activity (causing A to exist) is now going on*' (1975a: 33). His apparent reason for doing so is that 'Someone might argue that, even though B is not the first member, we can still explain item (i) by reference to B and B's causal activity vis-à-vis A. I do not wish to dispute this point. To say that we have not really "explained" the present existence of A until we explain why B is causing A to exist, tracing each step backward until we arrive at an ultimate first cause, may be nothing more than a confusion as to the nature of explanation' (ibid.; see also the sentence on pp. 34–5). But the situation that Aquinas is concerned to characterize as no explanation at all is not one in which an ordinarily adequate sort of first-level explanation has been captiously rejected as insufficient. It is, instead, one in which the first-level explanation is in terms of something that is itself theoretically inexplicable. In such a situation, no one with a philosophical interest in understanding A's presently existing could consider its being referred to B's causal activity to constitute any explanation at all.

forbids our abandoning the principle when the existing thing in question is extraordinary or all-pervasive—a thing such as the universe, or matter.

It may already be apparent, but it will become clearer, that the form of PSR required for E/U is PSR_2. Even at this point it should be clear at least that in E/U Aquinas is assuming that *every existing thing* that considered on its own is disposed to either existing or not existing *has a reason for its existence . . . in the causal efficacy of some other beings.*

It seems to me, then, that argument E/U is acceptable through the sentence ending in line 5. In any essentially ordered series of causes invoked to explain the presently continuing existence of any and every dependent being there must be something that serves as a first, non-contingent, non-instrumental, independently existing, independently operating cause.

Could that something be the natural laws themselves? Their persistence is a universal necessary condition for the existing and operating of all the dependent beings we've been considering, but the persistence of the laws—or, more precisely, of the governing regularities represented in them—certainly isn't self-explanatory. The necessity that has sometimes been ascribed to them isn't *logical* necessity, but rather a kind of conditional necessity. Nor do the laws themselves, even sublimated and unified in the Theory of Everything, or the Final Theory, constitute a plausible candidate for the role of first, non-instrumental, independently operating cause. Anything that could count as the source and cause of the production of all things must, obviously, have some intimate sort of relationship with natural laws, but identity goes too far.[64] Pointing to the laws counts as indicating part of the answer to the big question, 'Why is there this sort of world rather than another sort, or nothing at all?', but only the part that has to do with there being this sort of world rather than another, and not at all with the part that has to do with there being something rather than nothing.

Now, what about the sub-conclusion in lines 4–5 of argument E/U? It infers that 'there must be something necessary that is the cause [of the existing] of all the [existent] things that can be and can also not be'. Something necessary is something that is and cannot not be. But in Aquinas's view 'there is a *kind* of necessary thing that

---

[64] The picture of creation that begins to be discernible in argument E/U resembles that of Davies 1983. See TMOT, Ch. Three, n. 30.

has a *cause* of its necessity' (lines 5–6). In his Aristotelian view of nature, some actually existent things—the sun, for instance—exist necessarily in the special, narrow sense of not being subject to any natural processes of beginning and ceasing to exist—they are neither 'generable' nor 'corruptible'—and yet they exist dependently. A dependently *necessary* being is independent of all natural originating and sustaining causes. But the sun's nature doesn't entail its existence any more than the nature of the carrot I'm about to eat entails its existence. The (Aristotelian) sun's existing independently of natural generation and corruption warrants its being described as necessary in this special sense, while the fact that its nature does not entail its existence dictates its being described in the corresponding passage of G6 as having 'the cause of its necessity *in something else*'—something else that sustains it in an existence that is not subject to the vicissitudes of nature.[65]

Argument E/U aims at showing that 'we must arrive at something that is necessary being *per se*' (lines 7–8). But since Aquinas and his contemporaries believed in *necessary* beings that have the cause of their necessity *in something else*, he has first to rule out those lesser necessary beings. He does so by denying the possibility of an infinite regress of dependently necessary beings (in lines 6–7). That denial must be analysed along the lines of the analysis already provided for the analogous denial in line 4.

Whatever ultimately explains the present continuing of S, the beginningless series of dependent productive causes and their effects, and thereby the coming into existence of members of S, must itself exist necessarily *per se*: beginninglessly, endlessly, and altogether independently. The universal producer considered simply in its explanatory relationship to S can't depend on anything else for its existing, because it has been identified as the requisite first cause in the essentially ordered series of causes that explains Sn's existing and thus S's going on right now.

In this analysis of E/U, such a first cause was shown to be required by the nature of an essentially ordered series of causes and PSR_2. Invoking PSR_2 in order to get to the *per se* necessary

---

[65] As we'll see, human souls and angels are among the things that Aquinas thinks exist necessarily in this sense, because he takes them to involve no matter, and therefore to be incorruptible—invulnerable to natural disintegration. But since their natures do not entail their existence, they, too, exist dependently. For a helpful critical survey of Aquinas's views on this topic, see Brown 1964. For more on the incorruptibility of human souls, see Ch. Ten below, sects. 7 and 8.

universal producer and then discarding the principle would be unjustifiable, and Aquinas has no inclination to declare its *per se* necessary existence inexplicable. All necessary existence is explicable, either on the basis of extrinsic necessitation—having 'a *cause* of its necessity'—or on the basis of intrinsic necessitation—'something that is necessary being *per se*' (lines 6–8). And the necessary existence that must belong to the *universal* producer must of course be explained intrinsically. Putting it in terms of PSR$_2$, the universal producer must have *a reason for its existence*, and cannot have it *in the causal efficacy of some other beings*, and so must have it *in the necessity of its own nature.*[66]

Summing up, let A be some existing natural thing that can also not exist—you, or this planet, or this galaxy, or all the galaxies taken together—something that does actually exist but that, considered on its own, in its own nature, is disposed indifferently to either existence or non-existence. And suppose that A is a present member of a beginningless series of dependent productive causes and their effects. Then, since *every existing thing has a reason for its existence either in the necessity of its own nature or in the causal efficacy of some other beings*, there must be some reason for A's existing. That reason cannot be in the necessity of A's own nature, since A considered on its own is related indifferently to existence; so the reason for A's existing must be in the causal efficacy of other beings. However many other beings may in their causal efficacy be contributing instrumentally to A's existing now, their operating causally would not constitute the reason for A's existing now if there were not some first cause at the head of that essentially ordered series of causes, something such that everything other than it must be traced back to it as to the cause of its being (lines 10–11). Therefore, since A does exist, such an absolutely universal first producer must exist. As such, it must be not an instrumental but an altogether independent cause, dependent on absolutely nothing else for its present causal operation that actualizes simultaneously the causal efficacy of all the instrumental causes in the series. What makes the first sustainer of S also the universal producer is that its sustaining of nature (involving all the natural laws) is what makes possible all the natural changes that occur when and as they do

---

[66] In lines 8–9 of argument E/U Aquinas rightly offers evidence for the uniqueness of anything correctly characterizable as 'necessary being *per se*', evidence developed at length in I.42 (discussed in TMOT, Ch. Five, sect. 9).

because of the natures of things. The existential status of the first sustaining cause, the universal producer, must be 'necessary being *per se*'. It must be necessary through itself—i.e. it must be altogether independent, in the sense that its existing and operating are to be explained solely on the basis of its own nature. Its existing and operating, then, are obviously independent of natural laws. But since those laws are inevitably referred to at some relatively elevated stage in the explanation of any dependent being's existing, natural laws must be intimately related to the nature of the universal producer in some way. Aquinas has already provided the basis for that relationship in his investigation of God's intellect in SCG I.44–71,[67] and we'll be seeing other aspects of it in our further consideration of the metaphysics of creation.

[67] Discussed in TMOT, Ch. Six.

THREE

CREATION AS DOUBLY UNIVERSAL PRODUCTION

1. For all things the cause of being

Very broadly speaking, the topic of both SCG II and SCG III is God's transeunt action. As we've seen Aquinas explain at the beginning of Book II, in his investigation in Book I of matters concerning God considered in himself, the only divine action he investigated was the immanent action of intellection and volition. Consequently, 'for the complete consideration of divine truth we still have to investigate the second [i.e. transeunt] kind of activity— the one through which God produces things [Book II] and governs them [Book III]' (II.1.856). The producing of things, the only divine transeunt activity we're considering now, has been investigated so far as regards its source in God (II.6–14) and its terminus in everything else (II.15). Consequently, Aquinas is ready to undertake the direct examination of the activity itself, a project to which he devotes the next six chapters (II.16–21).

He begins by delineating this divine activity as a species of production, which is itself a species of transeunt action (II.16). Delineating a species, or constructing a real definition, involves identifying its differentia, the characteristic or set of characteristics that differentiates that species from all others in its genus. The differentia which Aquinas identifies for God's universal production reveals that this activity can correctly be classified as production, or even as transeunt action, only on the basis of Aquinas's relational method for adapting ordinary terms to the purposes of making true statements about God.[1] In this case the method prescribes omitting from the definition of God's universal production some elements of the standard definitions of production and of transeunt action—

---

[1] On the relational method, see TMOT, Ch. Five, sects. 1–5. See also Ch. Two above, sect. 5.

those elements that are incompatible with absolute perfection. In chapters 17–19 Aquinas examines more closely the omission of one particularly important set of those elements. Having in this way delineated the peculiar character of this activity, he reasons from it to the sort of agent it entails (II.20–1), concluding that universal production must be the action of God alone.

(I'm postponing regular use of the established, familiar name for God's universal production only because in Book II Aquinas himself seems careful to avoid using the verb *creare* (or the noun *creatio*) until the very end of chapter 16, where he introduces it in special circumstances which we'll be looking at. Nowhere in chapters 6–15 does he speak explicitly of 'creating' or of 'creation'. Even in the introductory chapters 1–5 there is only one stray occurrence of the verb, and that one is in an example.[2] And although in chapters 1–16 he often uses the associated noun *creatura* (which I'm almost always translating as 'created thing', at least to begin with), he is plainly treating it not as a technical term, but just as a generic designation for any natural thing considered in the way required by his purposes in Book II—i.e. in its relation to God.[3] As he says elsewhere, 'every being that is not God is a created thing (*creatura*) . . .' (ST Ia.5.3, sc).)

That God is the producer of everything else was established in chapter 15, which Aquinas himself entitled 'God is for all things the cause of being'. When I discussed it in sections 7 and 8 of Chapter Two above, I focused exclusively on Aquinas's arguing for this distributive universality of God's production because it has an indispensable role to play in developments after chapter 15, and because arguing for it seems to be his principal aim there. However, even the title of the chapter shows that distributive universality isn't all that's at issue. The causal claim isn't merely 'God is for all things the cause'. If it were, there would be no good reason not to read it simply and broadly as 'God is the cause of all things'. That God is for all things the cause of being is a narrower, and immeasurably stronger, claim.

When you make a salad, you are the (efficient) cause of the salad. And since without you that particular salad would not have been, it

---

[2] 'But the believer considers only those aspects of created things that are associated with them in so far as they are traced back to God—that they have been created by God, that they are subject to God, and things of that sort' (4.872a).

[3] On the general purpose of Book II, see Ch. One above, sect. 1.

might seem right, if a little stilted, to say that you are for that salad the cause of being. But putting it that way exaggerates your role, which might be described more accurately as your being for that salad *a* cause of being.[4] In the case of an artificial thing, such as a salad, characterizing you as a cause of being for it means simply that without you there would not have been that result of your altering and moving natural things: in this case, (leaves of) lettuce, (slices of) tomato, (shreds of) carrot, etc. You've given certain natural things a new inessential (accidental) form: what were unassociated, particular, whole vegetables have been transformed into a new artificial particular thing that didn't exist before. You might even have been the gardener who grew those vegetables from seed, in which case it would be right to say that you are for that head of lettuce (and the rest) a cause of being. If you had left that seed unplanted, that head of lettuce wouldn't exist at all. But neither you nor any other ordinary individual agent is for *lettuce* the cause of being. All ordinary artificial production can be analysed along the same lines, in terms of altering and moving pre-existing stuff that is ultimately natural.

The pattern of this analysis can be obscured in cases where the strata of artifice are many and go deep. When you compose a poem, you're making English sentences that have never been made before; you are for those sentences and for that poem a cause of being, through giving their constituent words a new arrangement. Now the making of the poem is unlike the making of the salad, because the things that you the poet are combining in novel ways— the words—are themselves not natural but artificial. And even the particular, mostly complex vocal sounds that long ago became words of English also originated in deliberate human actions. None the less, neither you nor the first speakers of English nor the first users of language are for *sound* (or even for *human vocal* sound) the cause of being. All the strata of artifice, however many there may be, are always supported on the bedrock of nature.

Ordinary production that is artificial—i.e. that at some stage involves human intellect and will—makes up only a tiny fraction of ordinary production, of course. A seed's production of a plant, the plant's production of a flower, the flower's production of a fruit, the fruit's production of a seed—all of those, like countless other,

---

[4] Alternatively, in terms of a distinction Aquinas will apply in this connection, you might be described as the *per se* cause of that *salad* and the *per accidens* cause of its *being*. See Ch. Four below, sect. 5.

widely divergent processes, are instances of ordinary *natural* production. And, again, while that flower on this plant can be correctly described as for this fruit a cause of being, neither it nor any other ordinary producer can be identified as for *fruit* the cause of being.

No one should imagine—looking ahead just a little—that considerations of these sorts will be called on to support a hypothesis of some extraordinary individual producer that is for sound or for fruit the direct cause of being. The natural sciences have given us good reasons to believe that variously linked cosmological, physical, chemical, biological evolutionary processes operating within the stuff of the universe in accordance with natural laws can account for the being of hydrogen, helium, and uranium; of light, heat, and sound; of galaxies, stars, and planets; of viruses, plants, and animals. If in that context we take seriously the thesis that God is for *all* things the cause of *being*, that God's productive action is the ultimate explanation of the existence of whatever else exists, artificial as well as natural, then we are supposing that God's productive action is the cause of being for (at least) all the primordial stuff of the universe and the dispositions natural to that stuff (the natural laws), and that God is in that way (at least) the cause of being for *everything* other than God. 'Everything there is besides God is from God as its *first* source' (ST Ia.7.2, sc).

And now, looking back once more to chapter 15, we can see that in it Aquinas is explicitly out to show both that God's production is distributively universal, and that God's production is absolutely fundamental, or *intrinsically* universal in the sense that it presupposes nothing. I think that the second of those two claims is less effectively argued in chapter 15 than the first.[5] In chapter 16, however, intrinsic universality emerges more clearly and is argued effectively.

2. Out of no antecedent matter

The thesis of chapter 16 is contained in its first sentence, which deserves to be examined as a whole: 'Now on that basis it is

---

[5] All seven of the chapter's arguments are unmistakably intended to show distributive universality, that God is for *all* things the cause of being. The first four of them (15.923–6) are, I think, directed more clearly than the last three (927–9) at showing also that God's universal production is absolutely fundamental, that God is for all things *the cause of being*.

apparent that God has produced things as regards their being out of no pre-existing [subject], as out of matter (*Ex hoc autem apparet quod Deus res in esse produxit ex nullo praeexistente sicut ex materia*)' (932).

The first words of the sentence, 'Now on that basis it is apparent that . . .', show that Aquinas takes this thesis to follow readily from the result of chapter 15, as it surely does. Besides God himself, there can't be anything at all that exists *before* 'God is for *all* things the cause of being', any pre-existing stuff *out of* which God produces *all* things as regards their being (as you produce things out of vegetables or out of words, the matter of your salad or of your poem). The fact that Aquinas none the less provides eleven arguments in support of the chapter's thesis suggests that he wants to accomplish more here than simply to establish that 'God has produced things as regards their being out of no pre-existing [subject], as out of matter'. We'll be looking at additional results of this sort in some of those arguments.

The first part of chapter 16's thesis, 'God has produced things as regards their being', is clearly intended to be a version of the thesis established in chapter 15. And so, I think, it can justifiably be emended to read '. . . has produced *all* things . . .'. With that emendation, chapter 16's thesis is, of course, even more apparent on the basis of chapter 15. But the version of chapter 15's thesis embedded here—'God has produced [all] things as regards their being'—is more awkward than the original: 'God is for all things the cause of being.'[6] That's because Aquinas in this thesis is expressly refining the notion of God's 'producing' everything else, which has been his explicit topic in Book II so far.

The refining consists in bringing out the provenance of this production, in the last words of the thesis: '. . . out of no pre-existing [subject], as out of matter'. Anyone who has any acquaintance with the concept of divine creation will recognize this as a wordy surrogate for the familiar, elegant 'out of nothing' (*ex nihilo*). Even the medieval scribe responsible for giving chapter 16 its title reverts to that simple formula: *Quod Deus ex nihilo produxit res in esse.* Aquinas himself, however, studiously avoids it throughout the chapter, always using a more detailed expression, like the one he

---

[6] Some of the awkwardness is a consequence of my translating *in esse produxit* so as to bring out the fact that Aquinas's account of creation presents it as a species of production. See Ch. One above, n. 56.

uses here, in the first statement of the thesis.[7] Since in those expressions he is presenting what he takes to be the differentia that specifies creation within the genus of production, it is only sensible to stay with his less elegant, more careful formulations in our investigation of chapter 16.

Besides, these more complicated formulations suggest that Aquinas has some particular purpose for using them here, since he is in general certainly not opposed to characterizing creation as *ex nihilo*. On the contrary, 'it must be firmly maintained that God can, and does, make something out of nothing (*ex nihilo*)', as he insists in a later work (QDP 3.1c). And in his Commentary on the *Sentences*, written before SCG, he distinguished three ways in which 'the thing that is said to be created' can rightly be said to be 'out of nothing': (1) 'because it is not out of anything pre-existing'; (2) because in the case of any created thing not-being is '*naturally* prior' to being, by which he means that 'the thing has being only from the influence of a higher cause' and 'if left to itself' reverts to not-being; (3) because in the case of any created thing not-being is not just naturally (or logically) but also *temporally* prior to being, 'so that it is said to be out of nothing because it is temporally after nothing' (In Sent. II.1.1.2c). Regarding (3), Aquinas says that 'in *that* way creation cannot be demonstrated, nor is it granted by philosophers. It is, however, supposed through faith' (ibid.).[8] So it can't be in this third way that creation could be said to be *ex nihilo* in Aquinas's natural theology in SCG II, in which he is out to argue for creation in a way that will be acceptable to philosophers. Of (1) and (2), on the other hand, Aquinas says that 'if these two suffice for the defining characteristic (*ratio*) of creation, then in that way creation can be demonstrated. And it is in that way that philoso-

---

[7] 'God in producing his effects does not need antecedent matter from which to work' (933); 'in his action he requires no antecedent matter' (934); 'it is not impossible to bring things into existence without antecedent matter' (935); 'it is not suited to God to need pre-existing matter in order to make something' (936); 'God does not require antecedent matter for his action' (937); 'he does not require antecedent matter in order to produce an effect' (938); 'God does not require antecedent matter from which he acts of necessity' (939); 'he does not require matter of necessity' (940); 'if any matter is found proportioned to divine action, God himself is the cause of it' (941); 'matter is not presupposed of necessity for his action' (942); 'divine action does not require a pre-existing nature' (943).

[8] For an investigation of this claim regarding the indemonstrability of the world's temporal beginning, see Ch. Five below.

phers have posited creation' (ibid.).[9] Sense (2) does have relevance here, perhaps especially in light of considerations like those brought out in our examination of argument E/U,[10] which show that God's role as first cause has as much to do with sustaining as with bringing into existence, as much to do with explaining the continuing existence of things as with explaining their coming into existence. However, the formulations which Aquinas uses in SCG II.16 clearly show that it is only (1) that is explicitly at issue in this chapter. And perhaps it is just because he is concerned here with only one of the three senses he had already distinguished for *ex nihilo* that he prefers to avoid that expression in favour of less familiar, unambiguous formulations.

At the end of section 1 above I referred to the 'absolutely fundamental, or *intrinsically* universal' character of God's production. I mean that in this species of production the producer is not merely a cause of the product that results from the producer's engaging in a process of moving and changing pre-existing stuff, as in all other, ordinary species of production. Instead, God is for any created thing considered just as such the ultimate cause of its being *at all*. On the basis of even these preliminary considerations of chapter 16's thesis we are entitled to conclude that this characterization of God's production is entailed by the production's being absolutely independent of antecedent matter (and, therefore, devoid of any operation on any pre-existing stuff). The no-antecedent-matter differentia also tends to support the claim that God is the ultimate producer of everything else, since the species of production that depends on nothing will be what produces the stuff for all ordinary species of production (unless there is some basic cosmic matter that is entirely unproduced, existing independently[11]). Ordinary production, all of which does depend on antecedent matter, is neither universal in this way—distributively—nor, of course, can it ever be universal intrinsically, in the sense that it accounts for the *whole* product. This intrinsic universality of God's production of things depends even more clearly on the no-antecedent-matter differentia. Aquinas brings out this consequence in replying elsewhere to

---

[9] That is, there are philosophical grounds for dependent existence and for the natural priority of not-being, but not for the temporal priority of not-being. For a more detailed account of the way 'philosophers grant that things have been created and made by God', see In Sent. II.1.1.5, ad sc 2.

[10] In Ch. Two above, sect. 8.   [11] See sect. 3 below.

the question 'Is creating making something out of nothing (*ex nihilo*)?':

We have to consider not only the emanation of a particular being from a particular agent, but also the emanation of the whole of being (*totius entis*) from the universal cause, which is God. And it is this emanation that we designate by the name 'creation'. . . . [S]o if we are considering the emanation of the universal whole of being (*totius entis universalis*) from the first source, it is impossible that any being be presupposed for that emanation. But 'nothing' is the same as 'no being'. Therefore, . . . creation, which is the emanation of the whole of being (*totius esse*), is out of the non-being that is nothing. (ST Ia.45.1c)

As it has emerged so far, then, the no-antecedent-matter differentia of this species of production seems to have several interrelated consequences; but they can conveniently be reduced to these two: God's production of things is (A) distributively universal and (B) intrinsically universal. God is (A) for *all* things (B) the cause of *being*.

And, as I suggested earlier, what differentiates divine production also distinguishes it from all ordinary transeunt activity, especially because of (B). Even Aquinas's introduction of the notion of transeunt activity indicates this, when he describes it at the very beginning of Book II as activity 'that goes over into an external thing (*in exteriorem rem transit*)—e.g. heating, cutting, and building—and is a completing of the result that is established (*constituitur*) through that very [first kind of] activity'—i.e. immanent activity (1.853).[12] His careful formulation—'goes over into an external thing'—leaves room for characterizing God's doubly universal production of things out of no antecedent matter as transeunt activity. But, as his (Aristotelian) examples show, all ordinary transeunt action must be action on some pre-existing stuff. So, in ascribing transeunt action to God, the natural theologian using the relational method will have to omit transeunt action's dependence on antecedent matter, because dependence on anything indicates something less than absolute perfection in the agent. God's productive transeunt action is like the ordinary kind in that the agent causes the existence of some other thing, and different from the ordinary kind in that the agent achieves that result absolutely independently of any pre-existing stuff. If, as we

---

[12] See Ch. One above, sect. 5.

already have some reason to think, for God to produce something is simply to will its existence,[13] then this transeunt action of God's will turn out to be a special case of his immanent action of intellection and volition.[14]

3. Not even prime matter

The eleven arguments of chapter 16 present an embarrassment of riches.[15] Since, as we've been seeing, the chapter's thesis really is apparent on the basis of chapter 15's result, these arguments are less important as providing support for the no-antecedent-matter differentia than for their exploration of some of its ramifications. Several of the arguments are worth investigating; I will take up just two of them. These two are, I think, especially clear in themselves, they focus on concepts central to Aquinas's theoretical account, and they involve no technicalities extraneous to our considerations here.

The argument I want to consider first focuses on *prime* matter, the only element of Aquinas's account of nature that even a friendly critic might well suppose could not be included within the distributive universality of divine production.[16] One could argue for its exclusion along these lines, for instance: 'Some actuality is the terminus of every action, just as the action also proceeds from some actuality; for every agent acts in so far as it is in actuality, and every

---

[13] See SCG I.75: 'God in willing himself also wills other things', and 76: 'God wills himself and other things in a single act of will', discussed in TMOT, Ch. Seven, sect. 7.

[14] See Ch. Four below.

[15] One of those arguments is misprinted in the Marietti edn. The phrase *non potest esse effectus materiae*, which appears on p. 300, col. b, lines 2–3, of the Leonine edn. of II.16, has been omitted from line 13 of 16.941 (the ninth argument) in the Marietti edn.

[16] In Aquinas's Aristotelian metaphysics, prime matter is an essential theoretical component of all material things, one that seems easiest to identify retrospectively as the terminus of a thorough analysis of any material thing: this page is the result of the imposition of certain forms on ink and paper; this paper is the result of the imposition of a certain form on cellulose; that cellulose is the result of the imposition of certain forms on carbon, hydrogen, and oxygen; . . . is the result of the imposition of a certain form on pure potentiality. 'Matter' as it's been used earlier in this chapter means not prime matter, but absolutely any antecedent, pre-existing thing or stuff considered as receptive of any substantial or accidental form—matter considered relatively rather than absolutely (as in 'prime matter'). All physical matter, right down to quarks and even beyond, is matter considered relatively.

agent does something like itself in nature. But *prime matter is pure potentiality*. Therefore, the action of creating cannot terminate in it. And so not all things are created by God' (QDP 3.5, obj. 3). Everything that is taken for granted in this objection is a principle or definition that is basic to Aquinas's own (Aristotelian) metaphysics, including the crucial definition of prime matter as pure potentiality.[17] So this is a formidable argument against including prime matter within the otherwise universal scope of God's production. How could even an omnipotent agent produce pure potentiality? It's true that producing the world's primordial stuff with all its built-in, natural dispositions would necessarily involve producing natural potentialities also. But not even those distinguishable, natural potentialities—such as liquid water's potentialities to be converted into steam or ice—are produced in their own right or numbered among existent things.

In his rejoinder to the objection against including prime matter within the ranks of created things, Aquinas acknowledges that it's true that pure potentiality, considered just as such, really cannot be created: 'That argument does prove that prime matter is not created *per se*. But from this it does not follow that it is not created *under a form*; for it is in that way that prime matter has being in actuality' (QDP 3.5, ad 3). 'For that reason',[18] as he helpfully puts it elsewhere, 'it is more *con*created than created' (ST Ia.7.2, ad 3)—i.e. it is created only as a theoretically necessitated metaphysical element of the created thing whose existence gives it actuality.[19]

Even these brief introductory remarks provide enough background against which to assess this eleventh argument of chapter 16, which I'll label 'PM' for its use of the notion of prime matter.

[17] See e.g. ST Ia.115.1, ad 2: 'But this is prime matter, which is pure potentiality just as God is pure actuality'; also QDSC 1c: 'that is commonly named prime matter which is in the genus of substance as a kind of understood potentiality, beyond every species and form, and even beyond privation, [but] which is none the less capable of taking on both forms and privations [of forms]'.

[18] The reason provided in the immediately preceding sentence is that 'Prime matter does not exist in nature on its own (*per seipsam*), since it is a being not in actuality but only in potentiality'.

[19] See also ST Ia.84.3, ad 2: 'Prime matter has substantial being through a form, and so it must be the case that it would be created under some form. Otherwise it would not be in actuality. However, while existing under one form, it is in potentiality to others.'

Prime matter *is*, in a way, since it is being in potentiality (*ens in potentia*). But God is the cause of *all* that are (*omnium quae sunt*), as was shown above [in II.15]. Therefore, God is the cause of prime matter. *No* [matter] is pre-existing [matter] for *it*. Therefore, divine action does not require a pre-existing nature. (943)   5

What I've been saying about prime matter so far has certainly not cleared up all the difficulties in the notion, but nothing about it could be clearer than the crucial claim in PM's line 4: there *couldn't* be any pre-existing matter out of which *prime* matter could be produced. So if the claim that 'God is the cause of prime matter' is justified, it will indeed follow that 'divine action does not require a pre-existing nature' out of which to produce its products, since the production of prime matter, at least, cannot require any pre-existing nature. However, the justification offered in argument PM itself for that causal claim in lines 3–4 strikes me as dubious and unnecessarily weak, partly because of the overly generous existential claim with which PM begins, but even more because Aquinas then cites the *distributive* universality of divine production (in lines 2–3), where an appeal to its *intrinsic* universality would have done the job more effectively. He shows this, I think, in a parallel discussion in ST: 'Therefore, that which is the cause of things *in so far as they are beings* must be the cause of things not only in so far as they are *thus-and-so* through accidental forms, or in so far as they are *these* [things] through substantial forms, but also as regards *all that pertains to the being of those things in any way at all*. And it is on that basis that we have to posit even prime matter as created by the universal cause of beings' (Ia.44.2c). How exactly prime matter does pertain to the being of things will be explored by Aquinas in later chapters of Book II—e.g. 39–45.[20] For present purposes it seems enough to recognize that Aquinas can justify his claim that even prime matter must be included among the products, or among at least the by-products, of God's universal production, although the justification he offers in argument PM is not the strongest sort available to him. We can also see that, as argument PM claims, the production (or by-production) of prime matter is paradigmatically production out of no antecedent matter.

[20] See Ch. Six below.

4. Not through movement or change

Chapter 16's fourth argument is the other one I want to consider. I'll call it 'MC', for its rejection of 'movement and change' as features of God's universal production.[21]

Acting only through movement and change is inappropriate for the universal cause of being, for it is not through movement and change that a being is made out of *absolute* non-being. On the contrary, [the result of acting through movement and change is just that] a being that is *this* is made out of a being that was *not this*.[22] But God is the   5
universal source of being, as has been shown [in II.15]. Therefore, it is not appropriate for God that he act only through movement or through change. Neither, therefore, is it appropriate for God to need pre-existing matter in order to make something. (936)

Part of the description of ordinary production in argument MC (lines 3–5) is perfectly obvious. Since all ordinary production is out of antecedent matter, all ordinary producing must involve doing something to that stuff: moving or changing it in some way—either substantially (as in generation and corruption) or accidentally (as in artificial production). As Aquinas observes in the immediately preceding argument, 'everything that cannot produce things as regards their being (*producere res in esse*) except out of antecedent matter acts only by moving and transmuting (*transmutando*), for making something out of matter occurs through some kind of movement or change (*mutationem*)' of that matter (935).[23]

But ordinary production is also described (in lines 4–5) as making 'a being that is *this* . . . out of a being that was *not this*'. Of course, in ordinary production the being that was *not* this, the antecedent matter that the ordinary producer moves or changes in order to make the being that *is* this, is more readily recognized as some other, pre-existing *being* or *beings*. The antecedent matter

---

[21] Aquinas doesn't ordinarily refer to movement and change together as he does here. I think he wants to make it clear that what is being ruled out is the whole range of Aristotelian movement/change: local motion, alteration, augmentation/diminution, generation/corruption.

[22] *sed ens hoc ex non ente hoc.* I owe my understanding of this passage to Anthony Kenny's insightful criticism of my earlier translation of it.

[23] 'Transmuting' can mean changing in a particularly thoroughgoing way (see e.g. ST IaIIae.18.2, ad 3), but here it seems interchangeable with 'changing'.

out of which you make an omelette is ordinarily thought of as eggs rather than as just not-that-omelette, though it can be thought of in that way, too—with a little effort. Aquinas is thinking of it in that way here, because he is contrasting ordinary production in this respect with God's universal production 'out of *absolute* non-being (*ex non ente simpliciter*)' (line 3). Anyone who does think of creating as involving change will take it to involve the change from non-being to being, and will liken it in that respect to ordinary production, which involves a change from what was not X to what is X. But in the unique case of creating, there is nothing at all, not even prime matter, that can be identified as not-X. Every *change* is a move from that to this, or has two extremes. Creating, though, has only one.[24]

Argument MC's descriptions of God as 'the universal cause of being' (lines 1–2) and 'the universal source of being' (lines 5–6) are plainly to be interpreted here as picking out *intrinsic* universality. What's at issue in MC isn't that *every* thing owes its being to God, but that everything owes to God the fact that it is *at all*. It's only on that basis that Aquinas can argue (as he does in lines 1–3) that 'Acting only through movement and change is inappropriate for the universal cause of being' just because 'it is not through movement and change that a being is made out of *absolute* non-being'.

Notice, however, that what is 'inappropriate for the universal cause of being' is 'acting *only* through movement and change' (line 1), and that 'it is not appropriate for God that he act *only* through movement or through change' (lines 6–8). Moreover, MC's conclusion is that it is not 'appropriate for God to *need* pre-existing matter in order to make something' (lines 8–9). (The conclusions of all the other arguments of chapter 16 are relevantly like this one, as can be seen in n. 7 above.) The plain implication is that although God's doubly universal production necessarily involves no pre-existing matter, and thus no movement or change, there may be *other* divine transeunt action that *does* involve the moving or changing of pre-existing matter. For instance, a miracle, conceived of as a divine intervention in natural processes, would presumably qualify

---

[24] In ch. 19, however, Aquinas does acknowledge that 'being and non-being . . . are, *so to speak*, the extremes of creation (*Inter esse autem et non esse, quae sunt quasi extrema creationis, non potest esse aliquid medium*)' (957). See also sect. 6 below.

as transeunt action of that sort—e.g. the parting of the Red Sea. But miracles are no part of Aquinas's concern here, where he is developing his natural theology, detached from the data of revelation. More relevantly, since in Aquinas's usage every particular natural thing is a 'created thing' (*creatura*), a divinely produced thing, there must be perpetual, ubiquitous transeunt action in which God does act through moving or changing pre-existing matter. If there is some sense in which God is the producer of the maple tree now growing in my garden, then he has produced it not out of nothing, but out of pre-existing matter: a maple seed, dirt, water, air, sunlight, etc. And if all the galaxies are results of the Big Bang, then they, too, are things God produces out of antecedent matter through movement and change. If God's production of things is distributively universal in the sense that every natural particular is one of its products, then it will have to involve all the innumerable modes of natural generation actually going on in the universe. But, of course, in none of those modes will natural generation be production out of no antecedent matter. That sort of doubly universal production—creating—must be distinguished, strictly speaking, from natural generation, as Aquinas will explain later in Book II.[25]

This emerging picture of a perpetually busy divine producer occupied with unimaginably many, unimaginably tiny details of natural production is by no means the only one discernible here, however. On the basis of what Aquinas has been arguing for so far, it is also possible, and in some respects more attractive, to view the entire primordial universe—all the stuff there was at the beginning, along with all its natural dispositions—as the sole immediate product of God's doubly universal production out of absolute non-being. As argument E/U in Chapter Two above suggests, one way of combining the distributive and intrinsic universality of God's production of things is to view the primordial universe, the-whole-of-what-there-was-to-begin-with-other-than-God, as its single immediate effect. On this holistic interpretation of God's doubly

---

[25] See e.g. II.42.1189: 'there are many things that cannot come into being except through creation—e.g. all those that are not composed of form and matter that is subject to contrariety. For things of that sort must be incapable of being generated, since all generation is from what is a contrary [of what is generated], and out of matter. . . . Therefore, we have to maintain that all *such* things have acquired the beginning (*principium*) of their being from God *directly* (*immediate*).' See also II.22.982, discussed in Ch. Four below, sect. 3.

universal production of everything else, everything in the universe, down to each particular generated in keeping with its natural laws, will then be viewed as entirely and ultimately dependent on God for its being at all, for its coming into being and for its remaining in being as long as it does. In producing the universe out of no pre-existing matter, and so without engaging in any movement or change, God is ultimately the producer also of this maple tree. And this maple tree counts as a created thing—as a thing for which God is the cause of being—even though it is rightly viewed as directly produced out of antecedent matter through a process of movement and change in accordance with natural laws.[26]

This holistic interpretation is not the whole story; but it is the crucial beginning of it, the part that most clearly manifests the intrinsic universality of God's production of things in a way that can be read as implying also its distributive universality. Perhaps this interpretation is adumbrated already in the first chapter of Book II. There, as we've seen, Aquinas says that by the phrase 'the works of your hands' in the passage 'I have meditated on all your activities, and I was meditating on the works of your hands' (Psalms 142/3: 5), 'we understand the heaven and the earth, and all the things that come into existence from God as handiwork comes from an artisan' (857). '[T]he heaven and the earth' is plausibly interpreted as the universe, and 'all the things that come into existence from God as handiwork comes from an artisan' is plausibly interpreted as the natural particulars that are produced immediately out of antecedent matter through a process of movement or change in accordance with natural laws. So his choice of that passage from Psalms as the epigraph for Book II suggests the interpretation I'm proposing.

In chapter 16 itself, the passage that most dramatically suggests the holistic interpretation is also focused on a verse of Scripture, Genesis 1: 1, the only verse that Aquinas quotes as confirmation of his claims in this chapter: 'Now Holy Scripture confirms this truth, saying "In the beginning God created the heaven and the earth."' Aquinas then takes this verse, with its use of the verb 'create', to provide him with the occasion on which, finally, to introduce the technical term he will freely use from this point onward in Book II:

[26] The two views contrasted here are just the extremes of a continuum of accounts of creation, most of which would involve less post-creational direct intervention than the first, hyperactive interpretation, but more than the holistic interpretation.

'For *to create* is nothing other than to produce something as regards its being without antecedent matter' (944). All that warrants his reading this verse as depicting producing something as regards its being without antecedent matter is the phrase 'In the beginning'; but taking the very first words of Scripture strictly enough to provide that warrant is not unreasonable. And the something that is produced in that way is 'the heaven and the earth', which, as is especially clear regarding the very beginning, is the-whole-of-what-there-was-to-begin-with-other-than-God.

5. *Something out of nothing*

Besides the confirming allusion to Genesis 1: 1, the postscript to chapter 16 contains Aquinas's correction of what he characterizes as an ancient philosophical mistake.

Now on this basis [i.e. ch. 16's establishing no-antecedent-matter as the differentia for creation] we refute the mistake of the ancient philosophers who claimed that there is absolutely no cause for matter. [They claimed this] because they observed that there is always something antecedent to action where the actions of particular agents are concerned. From that observation they derived the opinion, common to all, that nothing is made or comes about out of nothing (*ex nihilo nihil fit*). As regards *particular* agents that is of course *true*. But they had not yet arrived at a cognition of the *universal* agent, which is productive (*activum*) of the *whole* of being, [the agent] for whose action it is necessary to presuppose *nothing*. (945)

The 'opinion, common to all' that is at issue here—*ex nihilo nihil fit* (ENNF)—is powerful and broad enough to look like a universal first principle.[27] In acknowledging its truth as regards particular agents, Aquinas is indeed accepting ENNF as a universal first principle *of nature*, which applies correctly to the productive activity, natural or artificial, of any and every created thing. The ancient philosophers' mistake is not their having adopted ENNF, which they correctly derived from their observation of particular agents,

---

[27] See e.g. ST Ia.45.2, obj. 1: 'According to the Philosopher in *Physics* I [4, 187a26–9], ancient philosophers accepted as a common conception of the mind that nothing is made or comes about out of nothing. But God's power does not extend to the contraries of first principles—e.g. [it is impossible] that God bring it about that a whole not be greater than its part, or that an affirmation and its negation be true at the same time. Therefore, God cannot make something out of nothing, or create.'

but their having maintained on the basis of ENNF that 'there is absolutely no cause for matter'. For that reason Aquinas will, later in Book II, recognize ENNF as a principle indispensable to the work of the natural philosopher, rather than as just a superseded stage in the history of philosophy.[28] And it is, after all, natural philosophers to whom Aristotle attributed ENNF.[29] But Aquinas's present concern is not with nature, but with the metaphysics of creation. And creation, the intrinsically universal production of things that here constitutes the sole exception to ENNF, is the business not of the natural philosopher, but of 'the metaphysician, who considers universal being, and things that exist or occur apart from movement (*philosophum primum, qui considerat ens commune et ea quae sunt separata a motu*)' (II.37.1130e).

However, Aquinas's account of creation as it has been developed so far may seem to be compatible with ENNF. Although creation is production out of no antecedent matter, it is also an act of God's intellect and will. For just that reason it may seem drastically misleading to consider it as the unique counter-instance to ENNF, as the unique instance of production out of *nothing*.

I think we're inclined to read ENNF simply as 'nothing from nothing', and when it's read that way, it seems not at all to conflict with creation *ex nihilo*, just because although what is created is *something*, it's *from God*. As Aquinas reads ENNF, however, in Latin, it does look incompatible with creation *ex nihilo*. Interpreted most strictly, the combination of the verb *fit* and the preposition *ex* in *ex nihilo nihil fit* means 'is made out of', or 'is produced out of'; and the account of creation that Aquinas is arguing for could be summarized in this way: the universe *is produced* by God *out of* nothing. And the universe is not nothing. So he does have to treat creation out of no antecedent matter as the exception to ENNF: 'nothing is produced out of nothing'.[30]

---

[28] See II.37.1130e, quoted in part just below, and Ch. Five below, sect. 6.

[29] Aristotle describes ENNF as 'the common opinion of the natural philosophers' (*Physics* I 4, 187a26–9).

[30] Could God's 'ideas' be considered as something out of which God creates? After all, Aquinas's account of God's intellect presents God's knowledge as causative and God's ideas as the patterns of divine production. But, of course, the divine ideas are the *formal*, not the *material* cause, of created things. And they're not like our ideas, or even Aristotle's or Shakespeare's ideas, because all human ideas arise out of experience. See TMOT, Ch. Six, sects. 5 and 6; also Stump and Kretzmann 1995: esp. 115–17.

Taking ENNF to be a universal first principle of nature, as Aquinas does, means taking seriously the possibility that from the special standpoint of natural philosophy the existence of the natural world entails beginningless matter, an infinite regress of natural causes, or both. Aquinas will consider this possibility in detail in chapters 31–8 of Book II.[31]

6. Movement and change considered more closely

Once Aquinas has explicitly introduced the notion of creation, at the end of chapter 16, he uses its terminology freely. Even the titles of chapters 17–21 all contain either the noun 'creation' or the verb 'create'.[32] In the first three of those chapters Aquinas examines more closely one set of elements found in the standard definitions of production and of transeunt action but omitted from his account of creation because they are incompatible with absolute perfection. Chapters 17–19 variously emphasize and refine Aquinas's denial that creating, God's doubly universal production of things, could be characterized as some sort of movement or change—a denial which we have already seen him develop and defend in chapter 16's argument MC (16.936). This particularly close dependence of the new material on (one of) the results of chapter 16 warrants his introducing chapter 17 by remarking that its thesis is '*obvious*, once *that* has been shown'.

In chapter 17 Aquinas is out to show that 'the action of God's that is without antecedent matter and that is called creating is neither movement nor change, strictly speaking' (946). The only features of this thesis that we haven't seen before seem not to mark a clear advance over chapter 16. First, Aquinas notes that the technical term 'creating' is now in use. Second, and more interestingly, he seems to be softening the denial that creating is either movement or change, by suggesting that the denial applies only in a strict sense. But that suggestion isn't developed in the arguments of chapter 17, which bear on it merely by sharpening the concepts of movement and change, thereby delineating the strict sense. It isn't until chapter 18, as we'll see, that Aquinas introduces the

---

[31] See Ch. Five below.   [32] The titles of chs. 18–28 are Aquinas's own.

broader sense in which creating might, after all, be considered movement or change.

If, then, we appropriate the first and temporarily ignore the second new feature of chapter 17's thesis, and if we leave to one side the by now well-established no-antecedent-matter differentia, we're left with a simple claim that seems to add nothing but the term 'creating' to the results of chapter 16, or even just to the results of argument MC: the action of God's that is called creating is neither movement nor change. After all, MC already contains the claim that 'it is not through movement and change that a being is made out of absolute non-being', and making a being out of absolute non-being is what creating is. Nor does the fact that the thesis focuses on creating as an *action* of God's count as a novel contribution, for MC already contains the premiss '*acting* only through movement and change is inappropriate for the universal cause of being' and the sub-conclusion 'it is not appropriate for God that he *act* only through movement or through change'. Those propositions from MC, with their talk of its being *inappropriate* for God to act *only* through movement and change, may look weaker than the thesis of chapter 17. But, as we've seen, that appearance is a consequence of MC's leaving room for divine transeunt action *other than* creating, and the thesis of chapter 17 is expressly concerned just with creating.[33]

Still, there is an aspect of God's action in creating that hasn't yet been examined, and that might well seem to raise new questions about change. For in cases of ordinary production the movement to which the matter is subjected and the change effected in the matter begin as some sort of movement or change *in the agent*—e.g. deciding to make an omelette now—and it may not be obvious that

---

[33] In the Leonine and Marietti edns. the first sentence of ch. 17 reads: *Hoc autem ostenso, manifestum est quod Dei actio, quae est absque materia praeiacente et creatio vocatur, non sit motus neque mutatio, proprie loquendo.* The punctuation of this passage, like the punctuation found in printed medieval texts generally, has been added by the eds. But reading this passage with the eds.' second and third commas converts what should be a modifying clause into a clause in apposition, which requires the thesis to be read this way: 'God's action, which is without antecedent matter and is called creating, is neither movement nor change, strictly speaking.' (Anderson's translation reads this way (1975: 54).) But the arguments of ch. 16 make it very clear that creating is not God's only (transeunt) action, and that God's transeunt action other than creation may indeed involve antecedent matter, movement, and change. And so, it seems to me, the relative clause must be read as modifying *Dei actio*, and the eds.' second and third commas must be deleted.

God's creating out of no antecedent matter is compatible with God's absolute immutability, even if God's creating X involves no more activity on his part than his merely willing (efficaciously) that X be now. But, although some of what chapter 17 accomplishes is relevant to such considerations, Aquinas doesn't mention them anywhere in the chapter.[34]

So it isn't easy to say just how chapter 17 advances the discussion. As far as I can see, the particular contributions of chapter 17 to the investigation of creating are that it focuses tightly on the nature of the action itself, leaving aside any considerations of the agent (such as shape the conclusions of all the arguments of ch. 16[35]), and that it sharpens one's understanding of what is involved in the omission of movement and change. Both these contributions appear plainly in all four of chapter 17's arguments, but especially in the last one, which I'll call MT, for its attention to movements and their termini.

A movement or change must durationally precede that which is brought about through the change or movement, since [its] having been brought about is the beginning of rest and the end of the movement. That's why every change must be a movement or the terminus of a movement, which is successive. And, for that reason, what is being brought about *is* not. For as long as the movement lasts, something is being brought about and *is* not; while at the very end of the movement, at which rest begins, something is already not *being* brought about but *has been* brought about. In connection with creating, however, this cannot be the case. For if the very act of creating (*creatio ipsa*) preceded [its result], like movement or change, some subject would have to be established prior to it—which is contrary to the defining characteristic of creating. Creating, therefore, is neither movement nor change. (950)

We can think of the change involved in the building of a barn either as (M) the process—the barn's being built—or as (T) the final result—the new barn's having been built: 'every change must be [M] a movement or [T] the terminus of a movement' (lines 4–5). And, of course, the change in the M-sense must precede, be earlier

---

[34] Strictly speaking, his account of God's atemporal eternality of course excuses him from taking such worries seriously (see e.g. TMOT, Ch. Five, sect. 10; also Stump and Kretzmann 1981). But in such situations he ordinarily introduces at least a reference to relevant earlier results of that sort.

[35] See n. 7 above.

than, the change in the T-sense (lines 1–4). As long as the barn is still being built, it isn't yet built—i.e. the new barn as yet is not (lines 5–7). The instant at which the last nail has been hammered home is the first instant of the barn's existence (lines 7–9).[36] And the same analysis applies in all cases of ordinary production, even when the process is so fast that it's ordinarily not noticed, as in turning on a flashlight: the light's having been turned on is preceded by the pressing of the button and the consequent activating of the current, first in the batteries, then in the bulb.

'In connection with creating, however, this cannot be the case' (lines 9–10). For if the distinction between (M) the process and (T) the result were applicable to creating, in *what* could the movement or change associated with the process occur? Not in God, who is absolutely immutable. Not in the universe, which doesn't exist *before* it exists, so as to be changed by *beginning* to exist: 'when the whole substance of a thing is produced as regards its being, there cannot be any same thing that is first one way, then another, because that would be not produced but rather presupposed by the production' (949). And so argument MT shows how the no-antecedent-matter differentia rules out the possibility of a process of creating.

It looks as if a contemporary controversy may have led Aquinas to emphasize that movement and change are entirely absent from creating.[37] He devotes chapter 18 to explaining how to reply to those who, taking creating to be a kind of change, 'attack creating [as Aquinas conceives of it] with arguments drawn from the nature of movement or change' (951). And, as he has argued in chapters 16 and 17, creating cannot involve movement or change. 'None the less,' he must admit, 'from a purely conceptual standpoint creating does *seem* to be some sort of change—I mean, in so far as our intellect takes one and the same thing as first not existing and afterwards existing' (953), although, of course, there can't really *be* one and the same thing first not existing and then existing.[38] That's evidently why the thesis of chapter 17 claims that 'creating is

---

[36] On the medieval analysis of change in terms of first and last instants, see Kretzmann 1976.

[37] Hayes 1964 provides surveys of the accounts of creation put forward by several philosopher-theologians of the thirteenth century, including Aquinas, but I haven't found any evidence of such a controversy in the discussion of the relevant material on pp. 102–5.

[38] See also n. 24 above.

neither movement nor change, *strictly speaking*' (946). But, as Aquinas explained in chapter 17, 'in every change or movement there must be something that is one way now and another way earlier, for this is what the very name "change" indicates' (949), and this is precisely what is ruled out by the no-antecedent-matter differentia.

So, appearances to the contrary notwithstanding, 'creating is *not* change but, rather, the very dependence of created being on the source by which it is established' (18.952). In making this pronouncement, Aquinas intends to be re-establishing creation in the category of *relation*, which, as we've seen, is what he thinks it must be classified as in reality. But what he says here also suggests the absence of any fundamental natural distinction between creation and conservation. The kind of dependence relation on which argument E/U is based, for example, is most naturally thought of as the total dependence of the universe on God for its continuing to exist; but on this interpretation of creation, that total dependence looks like creation.

7. *No successiveness in creating*

Chapter 19 is the third in the trio of chapters that seem designed to drive home the general point argued for in chapter 16's argument MC, and to explore the ramifications of Aquinas's denial that creating could involve movement or change. Chapter 19's thesis— 'all creating is without successiveness'—can be established very easily on the basis of MC and the material in the two immediately preceding chapters, especially chapter 17's argument MT. It really needs no more additional support than Aquinas provides for it in chapter 19's first, very short argument: 'For successiveness is proper to movement. But creating is not movement, nor is it the terminus of movement, like a change.[39] Therefore, there is no successiveness involved in it' (956). In the strict usage developed by thirteenth-century logicians in their analysis of the concepts of beginning and ceasing, *successive* things or states are those that can exist or occur as such only over a temporal interval, not at a single instant.[40] Local motion is, naturally, the paradigm of a successive

---

[39] See 17.950—i.e. argument MT, quoted and discussed in sect. 6 above.
[40] See Kretzmann 1976: esp. 110.

state, but the claim that 'successiveness is proper to movement' applies much more widely. It means that successiveness and movement (or change) of any kind are essentially linked together. Any single instant within the interval during which a body is moving from one place to another is, of course, an instant of the body's local motion; but at that instant the body can only be located at a point. And, for all that the instantaneous location indicates, that point could quite as well be a point at which the body is at rest. So local motion, like every other sort of movement, occurs as such only during a temporal interval, not at a single instant.

But Aquinas here in chapter 19's first argument characterizes as successive not only the process of a thing's changing, but also its acquisition of the changed state, as he did in the earlier argument MT: 'That's why every change must be a movement or the terminus of a movement, which is successive' (17.950). Medieval logicians tended to classify the *terminus* of a movement, the *acquisition* of a changed state, not as successive but as *instantaneous*: a state that could occur only at an instant (and that was therefore not to be confused with the *persistence* of that state). No matter how long it takes X to get from A to B, and however long X remains at B, X's arriving at B occurs at an instant.[41] By the principle of the excluded middle, there can't be any time during which X has neither arrived nor not arrived, and, by the principle of non-contradiction, there can't be any time during which X has both arrived and not arrived.

Still, I think Aquinas is right to see the *terminus* of a movement as successive, too—not physically or logically, but as regards our comprehension of such an instant. The instant at which X arrives at B has to be understood as an instant immediately *before* which X's state was not what it is at that instant *for the first time*. So, in terminology allowable outside the logical analysis of successiveness as a feature of extra-mental reality, both the movement and its terminus, the acquisition of the changed state, can helpfully be viewed as successive. And so, since 'creating is not movement, nor is it the terminus of movement, like a change . . . there is no successiveness involved in it' (956).[42]

---

[41] A and B can, of course, be states as well as locations; X's getting from A to B can be a leaf's turning from green to not-green as well as its falling from the twig to the ground.

[42] Even stronger versions of this conclusion (the thesis of ch. 19) are drawn in other arguments in the chapter—e.g. 'It is, therefore, impossible that there be

Aquinas's Scriptural confirmation of chapter 19's thesis in the chapter's last paragraph depends on a very stringent interpretation of Genesis 1: 1: 'And that is why divine Scripture declares the creating[43] of things to have been effected at an indivisible [instant],[44] saying "In the beginning God created the heaven and the earth". Indeed, Basil explained this beginning as the beginning of time, which, as is proved in *Physics* VI [3, 233b33–5], must be an indivisible [instant]' (961). The Latin *In principio* may invite this interpretation more than 'In the beginning' seems to do, because it can be read (and by a thirteenth-century Aristotelian would be read) as '*At* the beginning'.[45] And since Aquinas here is making use of the (unsurprising) Basilian line about this beginning's being also the beginning of *time*,[46] and since the very beginning of any temporal interval, including all of time, must itself be not a (divisible) temporal interval (which must have its own beginning) but an absolutely indivisible instant, the first two words of the Vulgate text of Genesis 1: 1 *can* be read as strong support for the view that the creating of the heaven and the earth was *durationless, instantaneous*—utterly without successiveness.

But would that be enough to show that '*all* creating is without successiveness'? The rest of the first chapter of Genesis provides the account of what is ordinarily referred to as 'the six days of creation', an account that certainly appears to involve *successiveness*, however those 'days' are interpreted. Of course, Aquinas won't be taking them into account here in SCG, where he's doing natural theology. He needn't even mention them in this context, since the story of the six days is a particularly clear instance of revealed rather than natural theology, in Aquinas's view as well as ours. But, as we've seen, developing a natural theology that will be *compatible* with revelation is essential to his project in SCG I–III. How, if at all, is his account of creation without successiveness compatible with the rest of Genesis 1?

successiveness in creating' (958); 'It remains, therefore, that creating takes place at an instant. And so anything *while being* created *has been* created, just as anything while being illuminated has also been illuminated' (960).

[43] The Marietti edn. has *creatione* in line 42, where it should have *creationem*.

[44] The nominalized adjective *indivisibile* is often used by medieval philosophers to mean either an instant or a point, depending on the context.

[45] See also ST Ia.74.1, ad 1. *In* is the Latin preposition used by logicians and other medieval philosophers to indicate temporal location *at* a durationless instant (*in instanti*), or spatial location *at* a dimensionless point (*in puncto*), contexts in which the use of the English preposition 'in' would be mistaken.

[46] See also e.g. ST Ia.46.3c; 66.4, ad 4.

Chapter 19 itself provides a part of the answer to that question, though not the most important part. Even if there were successive acts of creating, one after another, *each one* of them would have to be without any successiveness within the act itself. And in that respect—in the intrinsic universality of the creative act—each successive act of creating would be different from ordinary productive acts.[47] To set the stage for displaying this part of the answer, the original statement of the chapter's thesis—*omnis creatio . . .*— could be read, a little less naturally, as '*every* creating is without successiveness', instead of as '*all* creating is without successiveness'. Against that background, this part of the answer is presented especially clearly in the chapter's fourth argument: 'there can be successiveness in movement, or in any making, in so far as that in association with which the movement occurs is divisible, either quantitatively (as in local motion and augmentation), or in terms of [qualitative] intensification and diminution (as in alteration). . . . However, the very substantial being of a created thing is not divisible in the way just mentioned, because substance does not admit of more and less [*Categories* 5, 3b33–4]. . . . It remains, therefore, that there cannot be any successiveness involved in creating' (959)—because, as we've seen, creation's product must be 'the very substantial being of a created thing', the *whole* being of the brand new thing.[48] In this way Aquinas's denial of successiveness in creating does rule out the possibility of successiveness in any one act of creation, and in this way that denial is entirely compatible with the story of the six days.

But it seems to be Aquinas's considered view that the work of the six days, as revealed in Genesis, is *not* creation, strictly speaking. I take his considered view on this topic to be the one he develops in ST Ia.65–74, a set of ten questions sometimes called 'The Treatise on the Work of the Six Days'.[49] In his preface to this

---

[47] As can be seen in 19.960, quoted in n. 42 above, Aquinas takes the ordinary act of illuminating to involve no successiveness, but that's only because he, like all his contemporaries, takes the propagation of light to be instantaneous; see e.g. ST Ia.67.2c, *Secundo . . .* He also maintains, plausibly enough, that thinking something and having that thought are simultaneous: *simul formatur verbum in corde et formatum est* (Ia.45.2, ad 3).

[48] See also In Sent. II.1.1.2, ad 3 (and Baldner and Carroll 1997); ST Ia.45.2, ad 3.

[49] That Aquinas considers the doctrine of the six days to be a part of revealed theology only is shown by several features of this treatise, among them the fact that many of the passages introduced *sed contra* in its twenty-nine Articles are simply citations of the relevant passages in Genesis and, in five cases, no more than this

treatise he says that, in connection with the production of corporeal created things, the first chapter of Genesis 'mentions *three* works: the work of *creating* (when it says, "In the beginning God created the heaven and the earth", etc.), the work of *distinguishing* (when it says, [1: 4] "God divided the light from the darkness" and [1: 7] "divided the waters which were under the firmament from the waters which were above the firmament" [etc.]), and the work of *furnishing* (when it says, [1: 14] "Let there be lights in the firmament", etc.).' Strictly speaking, then, he takes the creating of the heaven and the earth to occur, utterly without successiveness, *before* the first of the six days. The work of distinguishing he assigns to the first three days,[50] and the work of furnishing to the last three.[51]

I am not now interested in defending the details of Aquinas's account of the work of the six days. Although I think there's something to be said in support, or at least in appreciation, of 'distinguishing' and 'furnishing' and of their relation to each other in the development of the physical universe, what's important here is the fact that those post-creational operations *are* instances of the movement and change of antecedent matter, even if their agent is God himself.[52] This fundamental division between instantaneous creating to begin with, and successive distinguishing and furnishing thereafter, is an essential and attractive feature of Aquinas's account of the beginning and the early development of the universe. The distinguishing and furnishing that give rise to the physical universe as we experience it are only the development of what is already entirely available in potentiality at the first instant. For creating is, as we've been seeing, not only intrinsically but also distributively universal, as can be seen again in 21.979*a*, where

general observation: 'The authoritative passage of Scripture to the contrary suffices.'

[50] See e.g. ST Ia.67, preface: 'Next we have to consider the work of distinguishing in its own right: first, the work of the first day; second, the work of the second day; third, the work of the third day.' For further consideration of distinguishing, see Ch. Six below.

[51] See e.g. ST Ia.70, preface: 'Next we have to consider the work of furnishing: first, as regards the individual days in themselves; second, as regards all six days in general. In connection with the first of these two, we have to consider, first, the work of the fourth day; second, the work of the fifth day; third, the work of the sixth day . . .'. Aquinas provides a helpful survey of creating, distinguishing, and furnishing in Ia.70.1c.

[52] See e.g. Ia.70.1c.

Aquinas once more cites only the very first verse of Genesis as providing Scriptural confirmation of God's having created *'all things'*, again (of course) leaving the six days entirely out of account. And even in ST, where he *is* developing a detailed account of the work of the six days, he is careful to say: 'Therefore, in order to show that *all* bodies were created by God *immediately*, Moses said, "In the beginning God created *the heaven and the earth"'* (Ia.65.3c).[53] None the less, 'the *forming* of corporeal created things was effected through the work of *distinguishing*. But confusion is opposed to distinguishing, just as formlessness is opposed to forming. Therefore, if formlessness temporally preceded the forming of matter, it follows that at the beginning there was a *confusion* of corporeal created things, the confusion that the ancients called "chaos"' (Ia.66.1, sc).[54] Distinguishing, then, is the successive process of sorting out the product of the primordial, instantaneous creating of the heaven and the earth, the product in which elements, species, and individuals exist *potentially*.[55]

Although Scripture assigns the work of the six days directly to God, there seems to be no reason in principle why 'distinguishing' and 'furnishing' could not be natural processes, the divinely overseen development of dispositions built into the instantaneously created heaven and earth: 'Nature produces an effect in actuality from a being in potentiality, and so in the working of nature a potentiality must temporally precede the actuality, and formlessness must temporally precede forming. God, however, produces a being in actuality out of nothing [i.e. in creating], and so he can [in that way] produce a complete thing at once, in keeping with the magnitude of his power' (Ia.66.1, ad 2).

[53] See also Ia.65.3, sc; 68.1, ad 1; 73.1, ad 3.
[54] See also Ia.66.1c for a full and very useful discussion of the creation of matter and the imposition of forms; also Ia.68.1c: 'the production of *the substance* of the firmament belongs to the work of *creation*, but some *forming* of it belongs to the work of the second day'; and Ch. Six below.
[55] See e.g. Ia.74.1, ad 1: 'it can be said that the work of distinguishing and furnishing implies some changing of what is created (*creaturae*), which is measured by time. The work of creating, on the other hand, consists in the unique divine action of producing the substance of things at an instant. And that is why each work of distinguishing and furnishing is said to be carried out *in a day*, while creating is said to be carried out *at the beginning*, which means something indivisible.' Also Ia.74.2, ad 1: '[when] God created the heaven and the earth, he also created every plant of the field—not *actually*, but "before it grew in the earth" [Gen. 2: 5], i.e. *potentially*'; also ad 2 and ad 4.

Taking alternative hypotheses of this sort seriously is not out of keeping with Aquinas's own approach, even within the bounds of revealed theology. It requires observing the relevant Augustinian rules which Aquinas applies when the story of the six days strikes him as presenting very difficult claims, as in its account of the work of the second day:

In connection with questions of this sort [i.e. Was the firmament made on the second day?] two [rules] must be observed, as Augustine teaches [*De Genesi ad litteram* I, chs. 18, 19, 21]. First, of course, that Scripture's truth be maintained unwaveringly. Second, since divine Scripture can be interpreted in many ways, [the other rule to be observed is] that a person should not adhere to any interpretation so absolutely that, [even] if it is established by undoubted reason that what he believed to be the meaning of Scripture is false, he may be so presumptuous as to assert it anyway. [This second rule should be observed] so that Scripture may not be made the laughing-stock of unbelievers, and so that the way of believing should not be closed off to them. (Ia.68.1c)[56]

[56] In the Leonine and Marietti edns., the third sentence of this passage reads this way: *Secundo, cum Scriptura divina multipliciter exponi possit, quod nulli expositioni aliquis ita praecise inhaereat quod, si certa ratione constiterit hoc esse falsum, quod aliquis sensum Scripturae esse asserere praesumat* . . . The Leonine eds. ordinarily register few variants, but they list many for this sentence. The fathers of the English Dominican Province, who can usually be counted on for a literal translation, seem to have given up on this text, presenting what they take to be its sense in words that do not match the text: 'The second is that since Holy Scripture can be explained in a multiplicity of senses, one should adhere to a particular explanation, only in such measure as to be ready to abandon it, if it be proved with certainty to be false.' The most significant of the variants listed by the Leonine eds. they attribute to *Editiones aliquae*, one of which is the Migne edn. (1860): *Secundo, cum Scriptura . . . ut si certa ratione constiterit hoc esse falsum quod aliquis sensum Scripturae esse credebat, id nihilominus asserere praesumat* . . . (I'm grateful to Winthrop Wetherbee for calling my attention to the Migne text.) This edn. of course has no authority as a source for the text, but its sensible wording clearly brings out the evident sense of the corrupt passage, and my translation of it here follows this Migne text.
    Here are some of the relevant passages in Augustine on which Aquinas is drawing: 'In matters that are obscure and far beyond our vision, even in such as we may find treated in Holy Scripture, different interpretations are sometimes possible without prejudice to the faith we have received. In such a case we should not rush in headlong and so firmly take our stand on one side that, if further progress in the search of truth justly undermines this position, we too fall with it. That would be to battle not for the teaching of Holy Scripture but for our own, wishing its teaching to conform to ours, whereas we ought to wish ours to conform to that of Sacred Scripture' (*De Gen. ad litt.* I.18.37; Taylor 1982: i. 41). 'Now it is a disgraceful and dangerous thing for an unbeliever to hear a Christian, presumably giving the meaning of Holy Scripture, talking nonsense on these topics. . . . The shame is not so much that an ignorant individual is derided, but that people outside the household of faith think our sacred writers held such opinions' (ibid. I.19.39).

A Christian is bound to maintain Scripture's *truth*, but just because 'Scripture can be interpreted in many ways', it will not always be obvious which among the many possible interpretations conveys the truth. Moreover, some of the possible interpretations may be proved false. So, observing the first of these two rules requires the responsible open-mindedness enjoined in the second rule. Abandoning Scripture's truth is ruled out. But it is important to see that insisting on interpreting Scripture in a way that seemed right but turns out to be incompatible with what has been irrefutably (*certa ratione*) shown to be true independent of revelation is one way of abandoning Scripture's truth.

8. No body can create

The thesis of chapter 20, that 'no *body* can produce anything by way of creating', is so obvious at this point in the development of the notion of creation that it seems to need no special support. In fact, as we've seen, the possibility that the original source of corporeal things must *itself* be 'some sort of body' is one of the ancient mistakes which Aquinas dismissed at the outset of Book II, rejecting this one in particular on the adequate grounds that a body is obviously the sort of thing 'that can exist only on the basis of something else' (3.865)—e.g. some other body or bodies—and is therefore incapable of being a *first* principle of anything. Nor does this thesis acquire any special interest in virtue of its apparent association with *natural* explanations of the origin of the universe, since no one contemplating such an explanation would dream of employing the technical notion of *creation* as the causal mechanism at the heart of the explanation. But every one of chapter 20's five arguments in support of its negative thesis depends on taking 'creation' in the strict sense that has been developed for it in the immediately preceding chapters.[57]

I think Aquinas's reason for including this apparently unnecessary denial at this advanced stage in his development of the concept

[57] While all five arguments serve their common purpose well enough, the fourth of them may be the most important in the grand scheme of Aquinas's natural theology, since it picks up the argument for the infinity of God's power that Aquinas developed in detail in I.43 (see TMOT, Ch. Five, sect. 10), and shows (again) how the capacity to produce something on the basis of absolutely nothing is what defines infinite power.

of creation shows up in the chapter's final paragraph, where we're told that what has prompted this explicit, argued denial is a later, more detailed version of the simple, ancient mistake he has already dismissed—viz. 'the falsity of the position of some who say that the substance of the heavenly bodies is the cause of the matter of the elements. For since matter is the *first* subject of movement and of change, matter cannot have a cause except that which acts by creating' (20.968).

9. *Creating belongs to God alone*

In several respects, chapter 21 is like chapter 20. First, its thesis seems to be already well established by this stage of the investigation: 'creating is an action proper to God, and creating belongs to him alone' (969). So it seems not to need anything like as much support as Aquinas supplies for it in the chapter's nine arguments. Some of those arguments are just as short and familiar as we might expect—e.g. 'Again, that God creates things has been shown on this basis, that there can be nothing besides him that is not caused by him. But that can belong to no other, since nothing else is the universal cause of being. Therefore, creating is appropriate for God alone, as his proper action' (971).

Second, chapter 21 is also motivated by Aquinas's recognition of a prevalent mistake that needs correcting, one that emerges in the chapter's final paragraphs, where 979 presents, with Aquinas's approval, John Damascene's rejection of the theory of creation by angels, which was almost certainly an outgrowth of the Neoplatonist emanationism which Aquinas rejects in 980. It is clearly the existence of such competing *theistic* theories, rather than any competition from a *naturalistic* cosmogony, that drives him to include this elaborate, otherwise unnecessary chapter. But because those competing theories introduce the notion of subsidiary, instrumental agents of creation, chapter 21 also includes more complex arguments that do add something to the concept of creation—e.g. 'An instrument is applied because of its appropriateness for what is caused [by means of its application], so that it is a medium between the primary cause and what is caused, and is in touch with both of them. And in that way the [causal] influence of the first reaches what is caused by means of the instrument. For that reason, in that which is caused by means of the instrument there must be something that receives the [causal] influence of the first. This is contrary to the defining characteristic of creation, for it presupposes *nothing*. It remains, therefore, that nothing else besides God can create, neither as the principal agent nor as an instrument' (974).[58]

[58] The account of primary and instrumental agent causes in this (fifth) argument is developed further in the fourth and sixth arguments (973 and 975).

FOUR

CREATION'S MODALITIES

1. Why would God create?

Creating has been investigated so far as regards its source in God (II.6–14); its terminus in everything else (II.15); its essential nature—i.e. producing the universe out of no antecedent matter (II.16);[1] its consequent lack of all movement or change, and of all successiveness (II.17–19); and the impossibility of ascribing creating, so understood, to any cause other than God (II.20–1). Although almost everything Aquinas has argued for in his treatment of creation in those sixteen chapters has had to do with the creator and creating rather than with the created things themselves, he still isn't ready to move on from his consideration of the agent's acting. He has yet to examine the modal character of several aspects of God's act of creating.

Is the act of creating free in every respect? Is God free to choose whether or not to create, or does the nature of the absolutely perfect being somehow entail creating something or other? And is God bound to create one sort of world rather than another? Anyone who has wondered why an absolutely perfect being would create anything at all will acknowledge the importance of such questions. Since there can be only one absolutely perfect being, any other being must, at its best, be less than absolutely perfect.[2] So the existence of the absolutely perfect being and absolutely nothing else must constitute the only absolutely perfect state of affairs, which seems, on the face of it, to be the best of all possible worlds. So why would an absolutely perfect being create anything

---

[1] Or, as I put it in Ch. Three above, creating is God's distributively and intrinsically universal production of things: God is for *all* things the cause of *being*.

[2] In SCG I.42 Aquinas argues convincingly that the absolutely perfect being, which must be characterized by existing necessarily through itself, must therefore also be unique. See TMOT, Ch. Five, sect. 9. See also II.25.1026, where he argues that God, although omnipotent, cannot make anything equal to himself.

at all?[3] In the context that Aquinas has established in Book II so far, the answer to this question about what explains the creator's creating—if it admits of an answer—would have to provide the ultimate explanation of the existence of whatever there is besides God. If 'God is for all things the cause of being', then the reason why God acts in such a way as to warrant that description will have to be the terminus of explanations of the existence of anything other than God. And any putative answer supplying such a reason must lie along either one of two divergent lines, the starting-points of which can be represented in two rudimentary responses to the question. The response 'Because producing things other than himself is a necessary consequence of God's nature' begins what I call the necessitarian line of explanation. The second rudimentary response, 'Because God chooses to produce things other than himself and could equally well have chosen to produce nothing at all', is the starting-point of the non-necessitarian line.

Explanations lying along the necessitarian line try to show that an absolutely perfect being must be *essentially* productive. So the necessitarian line entails that the state of affairs consisting of the absolutely perfect being's existing all by itself is impossible, that the existence of the absolutely perfect being and absolutely nothing else doesn't constitute a possible world after all. On the other hand, non-necessitarian explanations deny that God is essentially productive (as he is, for instance, essentially intellective, or essentially good), and insist that God could be absolutely perfect without being a creator. And, as we'll see, non-necessitarian explanations divide into those that do and those that don't tolerate attempts to say *why* God freely chooses to create.

Aquinas is a non-necessitarian regarding God's act of creation, as is already clear in Book I, particularly in chapters 81, 'God does not will things other than himself necessarily', and 88, 'There is free decision in God'.[4] He is, furthermore, a non-necessitarian who

---

[3] I've considered this question in TMOT, Ch. Seven, sect. 8, and in more detail in Kretzmann 1991*a*. I draw on both those sources in dealing with this question here. See also Peghaire 1932, Kremer 1965, Kretzmann 1991*b*.

[4] In I.88 Aquinas expressly associates God's libertarian freedom exclusively with his actions regarding created things: 'in respect of himself he has *only* volition, but in respect of other things he has *choice* (*electionem*). Now choice is always accomplished by means of free decision (*liberum arbitrium*). Free decision, therefore, is attributable to God' (88.732). See TMOT, Ch. Seven, sect. 8. *Liberum arbitrium* is sometimes translated 'free choice', but there are several reasons for preferring 'free decision', reserving 'choice' for *electio* (see Ch. Seven below, sect. 5).

argues for the possibility of discerning God's motive in creating, as is clear in chapter 86, 'A reason can be assigned for divine volition'. But the details of his position regarding God's freedom to create emerge in the chapters of Book II that we're about to consider. In these chapters Aquinas deals with questions about the modalities of the creator's creating; and he does so in ways that lead him naturally to begin to consider created things themselves more closely, starting with the relation between the creator's choice and the modal status of the things produced as a consequence of that choice. In this chapter I focus on that transitional investigation, first of non-necessitated choice in the act of creating, and then of contingency and absolute necessity in created things.

Aquinas begins the investigation by returning to the topic of God's power (which he has already discussed in II.7–10[5]) and providing a more detailed account of it, one that is particularly concerned with the scope of God's power in creating (II.22). He then goes on to argue in detail that creating cannot be necessitated by any aspect of God's nature or by any obligation on God's part (II.23–9). Finally, he undertakes to show how not merely conditional but even absolute necessity characterizes certain aspects of the created world, despite his conviction that its original production is entirely free (II.28–30).[6]

2. The scope of God's creative power

The claim 'God can do all things (*Quod Deus omnia possit*)', which Aquinas uses as his title for chapter 22, is potentially misleading. It looks as if it might very well be introducing a chapter whose arguments are designed to support the thesis that God is omnipotent. But why should Aquinas think that there was any need for further argument in support of omnipotence after I.43's support for attributing infinity to God, which includes (in 43.368) a convincing argument to show that God's power must be considered infinite?[7] If

---

[5] See Ch. Two above, sects. 4 and 5. It may be worth recalling that 'admiration of God's unsurpassable power' is one of the four positive results of meditating on divine works which Aquinas promised in II.2.

[6] The oddly overlapping references here are a consequence of the fact that the undivided ch. 28&29 straddles these last two topical divisions. See sects. 8 and 9 below.

[7] See TMOT, Ch. Five, sect. 10; also Ch. Three above, n. 57.

Aquinas wanted now to reaffirm that God can do all things, in the
sense that there can be no limits to the power of an absolutely
perfect being, he could simply have alluded to his earlier arguments
for infinite power, in keeping with his identification elsewhere of
infinite power as the *cause* of omnipotence: 'Some people have said
that God is omnipotent because he has infinite power. They are
talking not about the definition (*rationem*) of omnipotence, but
about its [formal] cause—just as the rational soul is the [formal]
cause of the human being, although not its definition' (QDP 1.7c).
But, it turns out, the title of chapter 22 is *not* announcing the
chapter's thesis. Aquinas is less concerned here with showing that
God is omnipotent than with saying just what omnipotence must
amount to, besides infinite power.[8]

It makes sense that he should want to examine the notion of
omnipotence. Everyone who has thought about omnipotence even
a little recognizes that it can't be precisely expressed in the simple
formula that serves as the title of chapter 22. As Aquinas himself
acknowledges elsewhere, 'when one says that God can do *all*
things, there can be uncertainty about what is included under that
distribution'; consequently, 'it is difficult to assign a definition
(*rationem*) to omnipotence' (ST Ia.25.3c). In that same article of ST
he argues that *not* all otherwise readily doable things are things that
God can do.[9] Sins, for example, are things that God is incapable of.
Aquinas even argues that omnipotence itself rules out the possibility of sinning: 'To sin is to fall short of a perfect action. Thus, to be
able to sin is to be able to fall short as regards acting, which is
incompatible with omnipotence. And for that reason God, who is
omnipotent, cannot sin' (ad 2).[10]

This line of argument may well seem inadequate. It offers no
reason for supposing that omnipotence, considered just as such, is
the capacity to perform all and only *perfect* actions. For all that's
presented in this argument, why shouldn't omnipotence include the
ability 'to fall short as regards acting' if that's what the omnipotent

---

[8] But, once he has said what it must mean to be able to do all things, he isn't
entirely unconcerned with showing that the chapter's title expresses a truth, as can
be seen from his general conclusion at the end of the chapter's arguments: 'It
remains, therefore, that divine power is not limited to some effect but is capable of
absolutely (*simpliciter*) all things—i.e. that God is omnipotent' (986e).

[9] He also devotes SCG II.25 to cataloguing things which 'God is said to be unable
to do even though he is omnipotent' (1009a); see sect. 7 below.

[10] See also e.g. In Sent. I.42.2.2c, where this line of argument is adumbrated.

being chooses to do? What's more, later in ST Aquinas sensibly (and relevantly) observes that 'what is good about the products of an art is not a good that has to do with the [artisan's] human appetite. And so an art'—or a power—'does not presuppose a [morally] right appetite' in the artisan or the one exercising the power, where volition is included under 'appetite'. 'Thus an artisan who does something wrong (*peccat*) voluntarily gets more praise than one who does something wrong involuntarily' (ST IaIIae.57.4c).[11] None the less, a being that chooses to fall short, to fail (*deficere*), in an action the perfection of which is within its power, is a being that chooses to divest itself of some power, even if only momentarily; and that sort of choice *is* incompatible with omnipotence.[12]

Aquinas argues otherwise against omnipotent God's sinning when he says, a little later in the same rejoinder, that of course 'God *can* do wicked things if he *wills* them; for nothing prevents a conditional with an impossible antecedent (and consequent) from being true' (ad 2). And, pretty clearly, the impossibility of the conditional's consequent—'God *can* do wicked things'—depends entirely on the impossibility of its antecedent—'God *wills* to do wicked things'.[13]

That it is not Aquinas's primary intention in chapter 22 to argue that God can do all things is clear from the chapter's thesis, which is quite different from its title, and which appears to be explicitly claiming for God no more than *pluri*potence: 'divine power is not limited (*determinatur*) to some single effect' (22.981). As the wording of this thesis suggests, what matters most to Aquinas here is fending off restrictions on God's power—i.e. preserving the most fundamental of creation's modalities. We can more clearly identify this as his main concern when at the end of the chapter we find out one of the reasons why he has chosen to argue in particular against

---

[11] I'm grateful to Scott MacDonald for helping me find this passage again.

[12] Choosing to fail is not to be confused with pretending to fail. A pianist who chooses not to practice although she knows that a good performance of her scheduled programme requires practice is choosing to fail; but if, as a teacher, she deliberately misplays a passage as an illustration for her student, she is of course not divesting herself of any power.

[13] See also II.25, where in his catalogue of things which omnipotent God is incapable of doing he says, 'Again, because God is an agent acting through will [see sect. 6 below], he cannot do things that he cannot will. . . . [But] it was shown above [I.95] that God cannot will anything evil. And so it is clear that God cannot sin' (1028 and 1030).

this narrowest possible restriction of God's power to a capacity for producing (or, presumably, refraining from producing) just one effect.[14] He intends this chapter to address specifically the mistaken view of 'certain philosophers who claimed that only a single effect was produced by God immediately—as if his power were limited to the production of it[15]—and that God can bring about something other [than that single immediate effect] only in so far as the course of nature allows' (22.988).[16] Since it is only what God directly creates out of nothing that is 'produced by God immediately', the restriction at issue here applies only to God's *creative* power. As we saw in Chapter Three above, if *all* things other than God are products of God's action, then the overwhelming majority of them, considered individually, will turn out to be things that God does bring about 'only in so far as the course of nature allows'—i.e. in keeping with the natural order divinely instituted, however inchoately, at the instant of the creation of the universe. So neither Aquinas nor these opponents of his would reject the idea that God can and does in that way bring about 'created' things other than whatever he directly creates out of nothing. The only view that Aquinas is opposing here is the single-effect account of creation properly so-called, the idea that there is just one thing that God could (and did) directly create out of nothing, the idea that everything else (other than artificial productions by creatures) must be divinely produced in ways that we ordinarily recognize as natural.[17]

---

[14] A second, more important reason for this choice becomes clear in ch. 23. See sect. 6 below.

[15] The philosophers' claim that 'only a single effect was produced by God immediately (*immediate*)' might mean no more than that God freely chose to create only one thing. But, as this clause indicates, Aquinas interprets it as a claim that that was all that God *could* have done. See also the 'can' in the next clause of the passage.

[16] The Leonine eds. cite Avicenna as one of those (Neoplatonist) philosophers who put forward this single-effect account of creation. In his *Liber de philosophia prima*, tr. IX, cap. iv, Avicenna claims that 'the things that are from him first of all— and those are the created things—cannot be many, whether numerically or as regards the division into matter and form; for that which follows from him is from his essence, not from anything else' (479.92–4). Also, 'It is clear, therefore, that the first of the things that are [caused] by the first cause is numerically one, and that its essence and its quiddity are unity, not in matter' (479.4–6). (Trans. from the medieval Latin version (van Riet 1980).) Although Avicenna says 'and these are the created things', what he's describing here is really the emanation of other things from God—their following from his essence—rather than his creating them. See sect. 6 below.

[17] Aquinas's own analysis of creation as developed through the immediately preceding chapters could look as if it, too, accommodated the single-effect account,

3. *Separated substances as counter-instances to the single-effect account of creation*

The first of Aquinas's five arguments in chapter 22 is the one that is most precisely designed to support the chapter's explicit thesis, and it is worth considering seriously for other reasons as well. I'll call it SE, for its pointed opposition to the single-effect account of creation.

> If creating belongs to God alone, then whatever things can be produced by their cause only by way of creation must have been produced by him immediately. But all separated substances, which are not compounded of matter and form, are of that sort—let their existence be supposed for now—and, likewise, all corporeal matter. There-   5
> fore, these existents, so diverse,[18] are an immediate effect of the power we're talking about. But no power that produces more than one effect immediately, not out of matter, is limited to a single effect. I say 'immediately', because if [the power] were to produce through intermediaries, then the diversity could arise from the intermediate causes.   10
> And I say 'not out of matter', because in virtue of a diversity of matter one and the same agent causes diverse effects, even by the same action—e.g. the heat of a fire, which hardens clay and melts wax.
> Therefore, God's power is not limited to a single effect. (982)

Argument SE is concerned only with God's power to create, as its first sentence indicates; so 'the power we're talking about' (lines 6–7) is creative power. If SE succeeds in showing that God's *creative* power is not limited to a single effect, it will of course have justified the argument's general conclusion about God's power (line 14), although in a way that would have been expressed more clearly in a conclusion that was specifically about God's creative power. As we've seen, the single-effect account against which Aquinas is arguing is clearly not intended to apply to God's power generally.

SE begins with a conditional sentence whose antecedent—'creating belongs to God alone' (line 1)—is the well-supported thesis of the immediately preceding chapter (II.21) and can be taken for granted here. So, since God is the ultimate cause of being for *all* things, if there exists any thing that could not have been produced through moving or changing pre-existing stuff, either by divinely ordered natural processes or artificially by creatures, it must have

---

as my 'holistic interpretation' of his view was meant to suggest (in Ch. Three above, sect. 4).

[18] On a difficulty in the text at this point see the Marietti edn.: 132 n. 2.

been directly created by God, 'produced by him immediately' (lines 2–3), or 'immediately, not out of matter' (line 8). And if there is more than one such thing, then the single-effect account of creation is plainly false. To complete his case against the single-effect account as he develops it in SE, then, Aquinas needs only to present at least two things that are (a) undoubtedly existent and (b) incapable of having been produced in any natural or creaturely artificial way.

Of course, he has already presented one such thing. The directly created thing that is at the heart of his analysis of creation as developed so far is, naturally, the single universe,[19] the-heaven-and-the-earth that, according to Genesis, God brought into being at the beginning, instantaneously. And the universe is one thing that clearly does satisfy criteria (a) and (b). Although from the instant of its creation it contained *potentially* all the natural kinds of things we know about and unimaginably more besides,[20] Aquinas plainly and rightly considers it to be a single effect of God's creative power. So, to refute the single-effect account along the line he takes in SE, he needs at least one more instance of an existing thing that couldn't have come into existence otherwise than by being directly created. Needless to say, such instances aren't easy to find. It's much easier to grant that the whole universe must have been produced out of nothing at the beginning than to identify anything *within* the universe that clearly could not be the actualization of some potentiality built into the newly created universe, and that therefore must *itself* have been directly produced out of nothing.

In argument SE Aquinas supplies two examples that are supposed to fill the bill: (1) 'all separated substances, which are not compounded of matter and form', and (2) 'all corporeal matter' (lines 3–5). He needs only one example besides the universe itself, but he has special reasons for introducing both these two. Since (1) is itself a plurality of species, it will overwhelmingly complete his case against the single-effect account if separated substances meet the criteria of being (a) undoubtedly existent and (b) incapable of having been produced in any natural or creaturely artificial way. So for in Book II, separated substances haven't even been discussed,

---

[19] For Aquinas's argument that the universe is unique, see ST Ia.47.3.

[20] See the discussion of 'distinguishing' in Ch. Three above, sect. 7, and esp. in Ch. Six below.

so they plainly can't at this stage satisfy criterion (a). But Aquinas asks us to *suppose* for now that they exist (lines 4–5), and it's not unreasonable for us to adopt that hypothesis for the sake of argument SE, because he's going to devote several later chapters to considering separated substances generically, beginning with chapter 46, where he argues that any universe God could have created would have to include such things. In those chapters he will speak more often of 'intellective substances', which, as we'll see, include separated substances as he conceives of them. Some intellective substances are called separated because they are said to exist altogether separately from matter, as forms only; and they're called substances because they are said to subsist, to exist on their own, separately, and not, like other (material) forms, only in something else that is their subject.[21] 'Separated' should not be taken to imply that all of them *have been separated* from the matter in which they once existed.[22] According to Aquinas's account of intellective substances, most of them are never enmattered; so 'separated substances' is not a perfectly unambiguous designation for such entities. But 'separate substances', the perhaps more familiar translation of *substantiae separatae*, is even worse, since it applies equally well to all ordinary, hylomorphic substances—like you, or this planet—which exist separately, but *are* 'compounded of matter and form'.

If, for the sake of the argument, we agree to suppose for now that separated substances are (a) undoubtedly existent, then we are at this stage of Book II in no position to raise any principled objection against the claim that they are (b) incapable of having been produced in any natural or creaturely artificial way.[23] If there really are separately subsisting forms in the universe, then it seems eminently plausible that they would have had to be created directly—produced out of nothing—whether later or at the beginning, simultaneously with the creation of the universe. At any rate, forms

[21] Since Aquinas gets his impression of Plato's views almost entirely from Aristotle's account of them, it isn't surprising that he interprets Plato's theory of Forms as claiming that the species of sense objects—e.g. tiger or topaz—are separated substances, a claim that he of course rejects. See e.g. ST Ia.50.3c.

[22] However, as we'll see (in Ch. Ten below, sects. 7 and 8), Aquinas thinks that that is the condition of an intellective substance that is a human soul and that has been separated from the corporeal matter of a human body at the time of a human being's death.

[23] Aquinas is clearly within his rights when he observes, in this same chapter, that 'corporeal active power cannot produce a separated substance' (986*b*).

existing on their own, 'which are not compounded of matter and form', obviously could not be the result of any process of production, natural or artificial, that consists in moving or changing antecedent matter.[24] So separated substances, Aquinas's first example, seem very likely to give him just what he would need to refute the single-effect account in this way, *if* they can be shown to exist—something I'll postpone considering until we reach the point in Book II at which Aquinas takes it up. At this point, however, in argument SE itself, our hypothetical acceptance of existent separated substances as a counter-instance couldn't by itself support the categorical refutation of the single-effect account of creation that Aquinas puts forward in the argument's conclusion.

4. Corporeal matter as a counter-instance to the single-effect account of creation

This result of our consideration of Aquinas's first counter-instance in SE might suggest that we would have done better to focus instead on (2), corporeal matter. Corporeal matter is not, like prime matter, a theoretical entity the existence of which can hardly be considered undoubted. Corporeal matter as Aquinas ordinarily conceives of it seems clearly to be proximate matter, the relativistically, retrospectively identified antecedent stuff of ordinary artificial and natural production—the thread out of which cloth is made, the cloth out of which a shirt is made, the quarks that make up a proton that is one of the constituents of the nucleus of an atom of helium. If that's what corporeal matter is, then, unlike separated substances, corporeal matter is (a) undoubtedly existent.

The words with which Aquinas introduces this second counter-instance to the single-effect account of creation show us what attracts him to it. He intends to present two kinds of things (besides the universe itself) that 'can be produced by their cause only by way

---

[24] See also this passage from later in Book II: 'there are many things that cannot come into being except through creation—e.g. all those that are not composed of form and matter that is subject to contrariety. For things of that sort must be incapable of being generated, since all generation is from what is a contrary [of what is generated], and out of matter. . . . Therefore, we have to maintain that all such things have acquired the beginning (*principium*) of their being from God immediately' (42.1189).

of creation' (lines 1–2). Having pointed out that the first kind—separated substances—'are not compounded of matter and form', he introduces the second kind by saying 'and, likewise, all corporeal matter', where the 'likewise' seems clearly intended to point out that corporeal matter, too, is not compounded of matter and form. 'Therefore, these existents, so diverse'—matterless forms and formless matter—'are an *immediate* effect of the power we're talking about' (lines 5–7).

If, on the other hand, corporeal matter is *not* formless, if cloth and protons really are examples of it, then it has no claim to be (b) incapable of having been produced in any natural or creaturely artificial way. And, in fact, Aquinas's own discussions of *materia corporalis* indicate that he recognizes that it is not pure potentiality (like prime matter) but, of course, distinctively *corporeal* potentiality, as when he remarks that 'sensible matter [i.e. matter that can be experienced by human senses] is called corporeal matter in so far as it is subject to sensible qualities such as hot and cold, hard and soft' (ST Ia.85.1, ad 2). More explicitly, he remarks that 'as long as we live in this life, our soul has its existence in corporeal matter'—i.e. in the human body (ST Ia.12.11c). He also describes semen as corporeal matter.[25] If examples such as these illustrate what Aquinas means by 'corporeal matter' in argument SE, it becomes very hard to imagine why he would have tried to present it as a counter-instance to the single-effect account. And if he's using the expression here in some other, apter way, he ought to have made that clear.

Perhaps he supposes that the context makes his meaning clear. For Aquinas does sometimes use 'corporeal matter' in another way that is at least more appropriately indefinite than any of the examples I've just cited; and, like argument SE, this other use occurs in the context of considering creation: 'But some people have said that corporeal things were created by God by means of spiritual creatures. In order to rule this out, "*In the beginning* God created the heaven and the earth" is expounded as "*Before all things* . . .". For four things are taken to have been created together and at once: the empyrean heaven, corporeal matter (which is what "the earth" is understood to mean), time, and angelic nature' (ST Ia.46.3c). Aquinas is reporting rather than arguing for this

---

[25] See e.g. SCG III.102.2771; QDP 3.11, ad 8; but esp. Ch. Ten below, sects. 2–6.

exposition, but he plainly approves of it. The third of the 'four things', time, can readily be thought of as implicit in 'In the beginning', as we've already seen him observe.[26] And the inclusion of 'angelic nature' shows that this particular exposition of Genesis 1: 1 contains the claim that separated substances were created simultaneously with the creation of the heaven and the earth, and separately—not as mere potentialities implicit in the structure of the universe.[27] Finally, the first two items in this list of the 'four things' are obviously expositions of 'the heaven' and 'the earth', respectively. Only the second of them concerns us here.[28]

This exposition of 'the earth' in Genesis 1: 1 as corporeal matter strikes me as very well suited to Aquinas's account of the creation of the universe. We might think of it as the most fundamental component(s) of physical reality, whatever it (or they) might be, or as whatever it was that the Big Bang began the expansion of. And in that case it seems that we could very reasonably say of corporeal matter that it satisfies *both* the criteria for entities that can serve as counter-instances to the single-effect account of creation. None the less, corporeal matter on this otherwise promising interpretation of it will not give Aquinas what he needs for purposes of argument SE. What he needs is a clear case of something *other* than the universe itself that must be produced by its cause 'only by way of creation', 'immediately'. And on this interpretation of corporeal matter, its creation is just one (very important) aspect of the creation of the universe itself. In fact, from the point of view that most late twentieth-century educated people are likely to find most congenial, the beginning of corporeal matter's existence is tantamount to the beginning of the existence of the universe itself.

So, neither of the two examples which Aquinas supplies in SE is a convincing counter-instance to the single-effect account of creation. The argument supports, at best, only this conditional conclusion: If separated substances do undoubtedly exist, then God's creative power is not limited to a single effect.

As I remarked in section 3 above, the innumerable, incredibly diverse effects of God's power when it is exercised in nature

[26] SCG II.19.961; see Ch. Three above, sect. 7.

[27] If they were taken to be so, they couldn't qualify as things that 'can be produced by their cause only by way of creation' (argument SE, lines 1–2).

[28] In Aquinas's thirteenth-century Aristotelian astronomy, 'the heaven, since it is by its nature incorruptible, has matter that cannot be under any other form'—i.e. not corporeal matter (ST Ia.68.1c).

through intermediary causes, on matter, are not at issue here. In the rest of argument SE (lines 8–14) Aquinas shows that he recognizes that *that* undoubted plurality of effects cannot supply counter-instances to the single-effect account of *creation*.

In SE Aquinas takes an appealing a posteriori approach to refuting the single-effect account. The heart of this approach is his observation that 'no power that produces more than one effect immediately, not out of matter, is limited to a single effect' (lines 7–8). If we set aside the words 'immediately, not out of matter', which again show that 'the power we're talking about' (lines 6–7) is creative power, we can see how incontrovertibly sound the heart of SE is: 'no power that produces more than one effect . . . is limited to a single effect'. For any power P, if we can just identify more than one existent effect that has undoubtedly been produced by P, we are certainly entitled to conclude that P is not limited to a single effect. P's range may be enormous, but all we need for purposes of refuting a single-effect account of any power P along this a posteriori line is just two existent things that are undoubtedly effects of P. That transparent simplicity is what's appealing about this approach. But, as we've just been finding out, it turns out to be not at all easy to identify two such things when P is God's creative power—at least, not at this stage of Book II.

5. Omnipotence and absolute possibility

The other four arguments of chapter 22 are like one another, and unlike SE in at least two respects. First, they take not an a posteriori but an a priori approach to supporting the chapter's thesis that 'divine power is not limited to some single effect' (22.981). Second, their conclusions are formulated not as specific refutations of the single-effect account, but as general claims about God's power. The second of these two differences seems to be a natural consequence of the first. In this context, an a priori argument that is based not on counter-instances to an opposing thesis, but rather on an understanding of the essential nature of divine power, is headed toward a general conclusion about that power. Because the four arguments are general in that way, they contribute to clarifying the concept of omnipotence, as argument SE does not. I want to examine just one of the remaining arguments, which

I'll call 'NB', for its special attention to not-being in its account of omnipotence.

> Every perfect power extends to all the things to which the effect that belongs to it *per se* and is proper to it can extend. (For example, the power to build, if it is perfect, extends to all things that can have the defining characteristic (*rationem*) of a building.) Now the divine power is *per se* the cause of being, and being is its proper effect (as is   5
> clear from things that have been said). Therefore, it extends to all things that are not incompatible with the defining characteristic of being. For if God's power could result in only a certain sort of effect, it would not be *per se* the cause of a being considered just as a being, but rather the cause of *this* being [considered just as such]. Now what   10
> is incompatible with the defining characteristic of being is the opposite of being: not-being. Therefore, God can do all things that do not include within themselves the defining characteristic of not-being. But those are the things that involve (*implicant*) a contradiction. There-
> fore, we are left with the conclusion that God can do whatever does   15
> not involve a contradiction. (983)

NB's conclusion claims an enormous range for God's power, and the general formula in which it does so is, of course, familiar from standard accounts of omnipotence: 'God can do whatever does not involve a contradiction' (lines 15–16). None the less, this argument, too, is dependent on considerations of God's creative power, as we'll see. Moreover, its negative bearing on the single-effect account is not left implicit, but is brought out in lines 7–10.

In section 2 above I quoted Aquinas's observation that although infinite power is the cause of omnipotence, it can't count as its defining characteristic. Later in that same quoted passage (QDP 1.7c) he explains that this is because the notion of omnipotence isn't as simple as the notion of limitless power, because 'omnipotence involves the relations (*rationes*) of operations to their objects'. Anyone who wants to understand what it really means to say that God can do *all* things has to clear up the natural 'uncertainty about what is included under that distribution' (ST Ia.25.3c). And doing so requires careful consideration of exactly what sorts of things can be the objects and effects of God's infinite power, now that the notion has been refined by considering what it means to say that God is for all things the cause of being.[29]

Argument NB plainly does take that tack, approaching an understanding of God's productive power via a consideration of the

---

[29] See Ch. Three above, sect. 1.

nature of 'the effect that belongs to [a productive power] *per se* and is proper to it' (lines 1–2). (There is a technical distinction between *per se* and 'proper' effects,[30] but I don't think it's essential for purposes of NB; in this discussion I will refer simply to a power's *per se* (and *per accidens*) effects.) Every productive power has precisely one *per se* (sort of) effect, and productive powers are classified on the basis of their *per se* effects. For instance, the *per se* effect of the power to build is anything 'that can have the defining characteristic of a building' (lines 3–4). Whenever that power is effectively exercised, what actually gets built is, of course, that skyscraper, this barn, or a particular building of some other sort. But this barn, considered just as a barn, is a *per accidens* effect of the power to build. The power's *per se* effect extends to the actual barn only in so far as it is considered just as a building.[31] If P is classified as the power to produce an X, then for any actual effect E of P, E instantiates the *per se* effect of P (or the *per se* effect of P extends to E) in all and only those respects in which E is an X, considered just as such. To say that the power P is perfect is to say that P can produce as an actual effect absolutely anything that can instantiate P's *per se* effect: 'the power to build, if it is *perfect*, extends to *all* things that can have the defining characteristic of a building' (lines 2–4).[32] God's power, of course, is perfect. And the *per se* effect of God's power is being, 'as is clear from things that have been said' (lines 5–6) in the immediately preceding chapter,

[30] An effect is *proper* to a cause if it can be produced by that cause only. (See e.g. SCG II.15.925; 35.1114; 43.1200.) When the arresting officer inks the culprit's thumb and presses it on to the fingerprint record, the officer's movement is not the proper but rather an extraneous cause of the thumb-print, which is the proper effect of the pressure of the culprit's inked thumb. (Cf. 21.971, quoted in Ch. Three above, sect. 9, where creating is identified as 'God's proper action', implying that whatever is created is a proper effect of God's power.) Something is a *per se* effect of a power if it is the very sort of thing that is essentially produced by that power, which is partially definitive of its cause's nature. A building, considered just as such, is the *per se* effect of the power that makes a builder a builder; but a building's non-essential characteristics, such as its particular dimensions, are *per accidens* effects of that same cause. (See e.g. In Sent. IV.5.2.2.3c; QDP 3.6, ad 6; ST IaIIae.85.5c.)

[31] This distinction is brought out well regarding God's power, though not explicitly in terms of *per se* and *per accidens*, in ST Ia.44.2c: 'that which is the cause of things *in so far as they are beings* must be the cause of things not only in so far as they are *thus-and-so* through accidental forms, or in so far as they are *these* [things] through substantial forms, but also as regards *all that pertains to the being of those things in any way at all*'.

[32] Compare the first premiss of the *actus purus* argument considered in Ch. Two above, sect. 3: 'the more perfect the source of an action is, the more it can extend its action into more things, and into more remote things' (6.884).

II.21, where Aquinas argued that being is both the proper and the *per se* effect of God's power.[33] Therefore, God's productive power extends to all things that *can* have the defining characteristic of being—i.e. 'to all things that are *not incompatible* with the defining characteristic of being' (lines 6–7).

Although argument NB's conclusion concerns God's power generally, the argument turns on the defining characteristic of *creative* power. As NB suggests, productive powers are sorted out on the basis of their *per se* effects. Anything that exists now and didn't exist before is an effect of a productive power. But considering that thing itself isn't always enough to determine its status as a *per se* effect. Suppose that the new thing under consideration is a mudball. Then just considering that thing's nature won't in theory enable us to determine whether it is (a) the *per se* effect of a very limited power to make balls of mud or (b) a *per se* effect of the divine power to produce a being, considered just as such. What is both necessary and sufficient for making that determination is knowing the provenance of the new thing.

In determining a new thing's status as a *per se* effect, the crucial question is what exactly has begun to exist; and the answer to that question partly depends on knowing what, if anything, it has come from. When a child makes a ball out of pre-existent mud, what begins to exist, what is made *per se*, is only the newly shaped old stuff—this rounded mud, considered just as such. In that case, even if the one making a ball out of pre-existent mud were God himself, the maker's power is 'the *per accidens* cause of the being [considered just as such], and the *per se* cause of the being of *this* [sort of] thing' (21.978). If it's the imposition of such a form on such matter that is the *per se* effect, then the power that produced it has the *being* of the mud-ball as its *per accidens* effect. If it's the *being* of the mud-ball that is the *per se* effect, then that matter formed in that way is a *per accidens* effect of the power that produced it. It is only when the new thing's provenance is nothing at all besides the

---

[33] 'Being is what is caused first, as is apparent because of its commonness. Therefore, the proper cause of being is the first and universal agent, which is God' (972). 'Therefore, when something is made entirely from not-being, being *per se* is made. It must, therefore, [be made] by that which is the *per se* cause of being, for effects are traced back to their causes proportionally. But that is only the first being, which is the cause of a being considered just as such. Other things, however, are the *per accidens* cause of the being [considered just as such], and the *per se* cause of the being of *this* [sort of] thing' (978).

productive power itself that the *per se* effect of the productive power is the *being*, considered just as such. So it is only in the exercise of *creative* power, only 'when something is made entirely from not-being', that 'being *per se* is made' (ibid.), even if the thing made entirely from not-being were a mud-ball. And if the directly created thing is the universe itself, then in that case, too, 'if God's power could [result] in only a certain sort of effect'—if it were a power whose *per se* effect was only whatever can have the defining characteristic of a universe—'it would not be *per se* the cause of a being considered just as a being, but rather the cause of *this* being [considered just as such]' (NB, lines 8–10).[34]

Since being is the *per se* effect of God's power, and since absolutely every possible effect is a being (although that can't be the complete description of any effect), God's power has the widest possible range, extending to all things that can have the defining characteristic of a being. For practical purposes, the most convenient delineation of this vast range is negative: God's power extends to 'all things that do not include within themselves the defining characteristic of not-being. But those are the things that involve a contradiction' (lines 12–14). The defining characteristic of not-being is logical impossibility, and a thing that involves a contradiction is one whose full description violates the principle of non-contradiction.[35] In some such cases the violation is perfectly

---

[34] My power to make this sentence, or to make anything else I can make, is the *per se* cause of *this* being, considered just as such, and not the *per se* cause of its being, considered just as such. Even though in marvelling at creation we typically marvel at the forms/ideas that are given being—at galaxies and DNA molecules—it's the *being* that *should* stagger us. And sometimes it does, as when we ask the big question, the question that leads to cosmological arguments: Why is there something rather than nothing?

[35] See also 25.1018–21: 'God must be said to be unable to do whatever is contrary to the defining characteristic of being (in so far as it is being), or of a being that is made (in so far as it is made). But we have to find out what things of that sort are. First, therefore, whatever removes the defining characteristic of being is of course contrary to it. But the defining characteristic of being is destroyed through its opposite (just as the defining characteristic of human being is destroyed by things opposed to it or to its particulars); and the opposite of being is not-being. Therefore, God cannot make one and the same thing both be and not be at once—which is [to bring it about that] contradictories be at once. Further, contraries and privative opposites include contradiction. (For it follows that if there is white and black, there is white and not-white; and if there is sighted and blind, there is sighted and not-sighted.) And so for the same reason God cannot make [contraries and privative] opposites be in the same thing at the same time in the same respect. Moreover, the removal of the thing itself follows [logically] the removal of any essential principle

apparent in even a superficial description. Thus omnipotent God cannot produce anything that is both red and not-red at the same time and in the same respect. Such a thing is logically impossible, just because it would include within itself the defining characteristic of not-being. But a more detailed analysis of the thing that lies beyond omnipotence is required in order to show that omnipotent God cannot construct a rectilinear triangle whose interior angles do not equal two right angles, or change the past.[36]

Of course, delineating the range of omnipotence in that negative way provides the basis for a positive account as well, as Aquinas sometimes shows (although not in ch. 22). For example, 'power is spoken of in relation to things that are possible',[37] and so 'when God is described as being able to do all things, there is no more correct understanding of it than that he can do all *possible* things. And let him be called omnipotent for that reason' (ST Ia.25.3c). But then it is important to see that the possibility at issue in this account of omnipotence is not merely relative. 'Possible' here cannot mean merely possible 'with respect to some power', even with respect to God's power. For 'if anyone were to say that God is omnipotent because he can do all the things that are possible for his power, the explanation of omnipotence would be circular, since that would be saying nothing more than that God is omnipotent because he can do all the things that he can do' (ibid.).

The non-relative, 'absolute' possibility that Aquinas requires for his account of omnipotence is logical possibility: 'Therefore, we are

---

[of it]. Therefore, if God cannot make a thing be and not be at once, neither can he bring it about even that one of the thing's essential principles be lacking while the thing itself remains—as, for instance, that a human being not have a soul.'

[36] See 25.1022–3: 'Since the principles of certain sciences, such as logic, geometry, and arithmetic, are derived exclusively from the formal principles of things, on which the essence of a thing depends, it follows that God cannot bring about the contraries of those principles—e.g. that a genus not be predicable of its species, or that lines drawn from the centre of a circle to its circumference not be equal, or that a rectilinear triangle not have three angles equal to two right angles. On this basis it is also clear that God cannot make the past not to have been, for that, too, includes a contradiction; for the same necessity attaches to something's being while it is and to something's having been while it has been.'

[37] See also In Sent. I.42.2.2c: 'Power (*posse*) implies a relation between what has the power and what is possible, just as knowing implies a relation between what has the knowledge and what is knowable.'

left with the conclusion that God is called omnipotent because he
can do all things that are *absolutely* possible (*omnia possibilia
absolute*)[38] . . . Now something is said to be absolutely possible or
[absolutely] impossible on the basis of the relationship of terms:
[absolutely] possible because the predicate is not incompatible with
the subject—as in Socrates' being seated—but absolutely impossible because the predicate is incompatible with the subject—as in a
human being's being a donkey' (ST Ia.25.3c).[39] 'Socrates is seated'
is obviously a logically possible proposition. At the risk of explaining what is almost as obvious, the proposition 'A human being is a
donkey' is logically impossible, because the differentia of the
human species of animal is *rational*, but every donkey is a member
of one and the same species of *non-rational* animals; so this proposition is an instance of 'Something is both rational and non-rational
at the same time and in the same respect'. Therefore, not even
omnipotent God can produce a human being that is a donkey.
'[W]hat is incompatible with the defining characteristic of the absolutely possible (which is what is subject to divine omnipotence) is
what involves within itself being and not-being at once. For it is not
subject to omnipotence—not because of a defect in the divine
power, but because it cannot have the defining characteristic of
what is doable or possible. . . . And so it makes more sense to say
that such things cannot be done than that God cannot do them'
(ibid.).[40]

[38] Sometimes he calls such things 'possible in themselves (*secundum se*)'; see e.g.
QDP 1.7c. And cf. QDP 1.7, ad 4: 'it must be said that God is called omnipotent
because he can do all things that are absolutely possible (*omnia possibilia absolute*)'.
[39] See also e.g. ST Ia.19.3.
[40] A survey of Aquinas's positive account of omnipotence would be incomplete
without at least a reminder that he bases his explanation of God's productive power
on his account of God's intellective cognition, in which all absolutely possible things
are included virtually, as divine ideas that can be actualized: 'Now the defining
characteristic of divine power is based on divine being, which is infinite, not limited
to any natural kind (*genus*) of being but prepossessing within itself the perfection of
all being. Thus whatever can have the defining characteristic of being is included
within absolutely possible things, in respect of which God is called omnipotent' (ST
Ia.25.3c). See also TMOT, Ch. Six, sects. 4–6.
   Defining God's omnipotence in terms of what is absolutely or logically possible
requires special care. It is logically possible that some human being always freely do
what is right, but 'God *causes* someone always *freely* to do what is right' is contradictory. Therefore, not even omnipotent God can actualize every logical possibility.
An argument of this sort is at the core of Plantinga's well-known freewill defence
against the argument from evil. See e.g. Plantinga 1974.

6. The modality of creative action

In section 1 above I said that Aquinas is a non-necessitarian regarding God's act of creating, and in section 2 I claimed that what matters most to Aquinas in the chapters we're now considering is fending off restrictions on God's power and denying any sort of constraint on God's transeunt action—i.e. preserving what he considers to be the most fundamental of creation's modalities, the creator's freedom of choice regarding whether or not to create. This aim and Aquinas's non-necessitarianism are brought out in the thesis of chapter 23: 'where created things are concerned, God acts not through the necessity of [his] nature (*necessitatem naturae*) but through the decision of [his] will (*arbitrium voluntatis*)' (989).[41] Near the beginning of Book II we saw Aquinas highlight the negation of this thesis as one of four important mistakes that would be avoided or corrected as a result of his account of creation: 'in virtue of being ignorant of the nature of a created thing, a person takes something away from the divine power [considered as] operative where created things are concerned. This is clear in the case of people who assign two sources of things, and who claim that things come from God not on the basis of divine volition but on the basis of the necessity of [his] nature' (3.867).[42] In talking about the way 'things come from God', the only conceivable plurality of sources or principles will have to derive from conceptually distinct aspects of God's nature, those that underlie the fundamentally distinct explanations of God as the source of everything else—i.e. either because his very nature gives rise to such production without volition (emanationism), or because he wills to create: either because

---

[41] My first addition of 'his' in this passage is significant, because the interpretation of the phrase *necessitatem naturae*, considered on its own, is not obviously the one imposed by my addition. That this is the interpretation Aquinas has in mind becomes clear in II.23 itself, but evidence for it is also available elsewhere—e.g. ST IIIa.14.2c: 'There are two kinds of necessity. One, of course, [is the necessity] of *coercion*, which is brought about by an extrinsic agent. And this kind of necessity is of course contrary both to nature and to will, each of which is an intrinsic source. But the second kind is *natural* necessity, which is a consequence of natural sources, such as form (e.g. it is necessary that fire give heat) or matter (e.g. it is necessary that a body made up of contraries disintegrate).' Necessity of coercion may be thought of as having to do with efficient causation; necessity of nature (or natural necessity), with formal or material causation. Of the two intrinsic sources (or principles), nature and will, nature necessitates as will does not. See also e.g. Ia.19.4c; 82.1c; and TMOT, Ch. Seven, sect. 5.

[42] Discussed in Ch. One above, sect. 7.

his very nature necessitates such willing (the necessitarian account of creation), or because he freely decides to do what he could equally well have refrained from doing (the non-necessitarian account).

The non-necessitarian thesis of chapter 23, like chapter 22's opposition to the single-effect account of creation, is directed against 'a mistake made by certain philosophers', this time against the mistake of those 'who said that God acts through the necessity of [his] nature' (23.1001). As the Leonine editors point out, Avicenna, identified as a proponent of the single-effect account, fits this description, too, and on the basis of the same passage: 'that which follows from him [God] is from his essence, not from anything else'.[43] What's more, Avicenna introduces this position as the *basis* for his single-effect account of creation: 'the things that are from him first of all—and those are the created things—cannot be many, whether numerically or as regards the division into matter and form; for that which follows from him is from his essence, not from anything else' (479.92–4).[44] One reason why chapter 23 contains so many arguments devoted to refuting the premiss which Avicenna uses in this reasoning is that Aquinas, too, accepts the validity of this inference: if God's creating follows from his essence, Aquinas thinks, then the single-effect account of creation must be true. He shows this most clearly in the first of the chapter's arguments:

For the power of anything that acts through the necessity of [its] nature is limited to a determinate single effect. And that is why all natural things, events, or states of affairs (*naturalia*) always come about in the same way (unless there is an impediment). But it is not that way with things, events, or states of affairs that are volitional (*voluntaria*). Now the divine power is not disposed to only a single effect (as was shown above [in II.22]). Therefore, God acts not through the necessity of [his] nature, but through [his] will. (990)[45]

---

[43] *Liber de philosophia prima*, tr. IX, cap. iv, 479.94; see also n. 16 above.

[44] Avicenna's way of expressing his position here is pretty clearly more restrictive than a necessitarian account of God's act of creation, maintaining not merely that in creating God *acts* in virtue of the necessity of his nature but, rather, that all things other than God emanate from God, willy-nilly. Strictly speaking, emanationism is not an alternative to non-necessitarianism as an account of *creation*.

[45] See also e.g. ST Ia.19.4c, *Secundo*. Aquinas of course recognizes the difficulty of supporting the contrast in this thesis in view of God's absolute simplicity. His attempts to draw the relevant distinction are not obviously successful. For instance, 'Just as will, essence, and wisdom in God are the same really, [but] distinguished conceptually, so, too are [God's] activities distinguished on the basis of the defining

It seems clear retrospectively, then, that chapter 22's most important contribution to the logical structure of Aquinas's account of creation is its establishing this basis for his rejection of necessitarianism in chapter 23.

Some of his nine arguments against necessitarianism illuminate large-scale topics that have already been developed in SCG. For instance, the third argument derives the chapter's thesis from reflections on Book I's establishment of the causal role of God's intellect, on the artisan analogy:[46] 'a likeness of his effect must be in him in an intelligible mode. Therefore, he acts through intellect. But intellect actualizes (agit) an effect only by means of will, whose object is a good intellectively cognized, which moves the agent as an end. Therefore, God acts through [his] will, not through the necessity of [his] nature' (992).[47]

In the fourth argument, reflections on such observations about the intellective/volitional character of God's activity lead Aquinas to say quite clearly what was already adumbrated in his discussions of divine immanent and transeunt activity earlier in Book II. At that point it might have seemed that, in moving from considering God himself (in Book I) to considering God's creating, we were indeed going to focus on transeunt *rather than* immanent divine activity: 'for the complete consideration of divine truth we still have to investigate the second [transeunt] kind of activity—the one through which things are produced and governed by God' (1.856). But, of course, a little reflection shows that creating, producing

characteristics of various attributes even though there is just one activity of his, which is his essence. And so because the creating of things, even though it is an activity of his essence, [is so] not only in so far as it is the essence but also in so far as it is wisdom and will, it follows the condition of knowledge and will. And because will is free, God is said to make things on the basis of the freedom of [his] will and not on the basis of the necessity of [his] nature' (In Sent. I.43.2.1, ad 2); 'Whatever is in God is his essence and so is as a whole eternal, uncreated, and necessary. None the less, however, the effect that proceeds from his activity does not proceed necessarily. For it proceeds from the activity in so far as it is from will; and so [God] produced the effect in accordance with freedom of will' (ibid., ad 3); 'An effect follows from an action in accordance with the principle of the acting. Thus, since the divine will, which has no necessary relation to a created thing, is considered to be the principle of divine action (as regards our way of understanding), a created thing need not proceed from God through the necessity of [his] nature, even though the action itself is God's essence or nature' (QDP 3.15, ad 18).

[46] Cf. II.24.1006: 'Therefore, all created things are related to God as the products of an art are related to the artisan.'

[47] Cf. QDP 3.15c, *Tertia ratio*; ST Ia.19.4c, *Tertio*; also Ia.14.8. See TMOT, Chs. Six and Seven; also n. 41 above. SCG II.24.1006 is also broadly relevant.

things *out of nothing*, really could not involve any extrinsic activity: 'divine activity cannot belong to the [transeunt] kind of activities that are not in the agent, since his activity is his substance (as was shown above [in II.9]). Therefore, it must belong to the [immanent] kind of activities that are in the agent and are, so to speak, the perfecting of the agent. But activities of that sort belong only to what has cognition and appetite. Therefore, God operates by cognizing and willing; not, therefore, through the necessity of [his] nature, but through the decision of [his] will' (993).

God's cognizing and willing regarding things other than himself can and should be considered transeunt rather than immanent just because its *effect*—not the activity itself—is extrinsic to him. Aquinas's way of handling this distinction might raise questions simply because it has no application in our own case. When you mentally plan the garden you mean to plant, all your intellective/ volitional activity is immanent. But if you *could* cause those plants to appear in your garden simply by willing that they do so, that activity of yours, altogether immanent in itself, would deserve to be specified further as transeunt just because, unlike all the immanent activity we actually engage in, it would have an immediate extrinsic *effect*. In God's case, as we've seen, even power is attributed to him, strictly speaking, 'not as the source of the action, but as the source of the result' (10.903).[48] It is because there is only a conceptual distinction between God's power to create and his actually creating, that power is attributable to God not as the immediate source of his activity (and thereby the more remote source of its effects)— as in our own case—but simply as the source of the effect. We also saw that power 'is not said to be in God in respect of action except in accordance with [our] mode of understanding, in so far as our intellect considers the two of them under different concepts: divine power and God's action. And so if some actions that belong to God do not pass over into any [external] result, but remain in the agent, in respect of them power will be said to be in God only in connection with [our] mode of understanding, not in reality. But intellection and volition are actions of that sort. . . . Intellect and will, therefore, are in God not as powers [as they are in us] but solely as actions' (10.903). And we are now in a position to see that the

---

[48] See also ST Ia.25.1, ad 3: 'in the case of God, the defining characteristic of power is preserved in so far as it is the source of the *effect*, but not in so far as it is the source of the *action*, which is the divine essence'; also Ch. Two above, sect. 5.

conceptual distinction between power and activity is applicable
even to God's intellection and volition when they do pass over into
an external result, as in creating.[49]

If that were not the case, there would be no explaining the fact
that countless logical possibilities remain unactualized by God's
will, a fact Aquinas appeals to in chapter 23's second argument:

[W]hatever does not involve a contradiction is subject to divine power (as
has been shown [in II.22]). But many things do not exist among created
things that would, none the less, not involve a contradiction if they did
exist. This is especially clear as regards the number, the sizes, and the
distances between stars and other bodies, in connection with which no
contradiction would be involved if the arrangement of things were otherwise. Therefore, many things are subject to the divine power that are not
found in nature. But whoever makes some of the things he can make and
does not make others acts through the choice (*electionem*) of [his] will and
not through the necessity of [his] nature.[50] Therefore, God acts not through
the necessity of [his] nature, but through [his] will. (991)[51]

There's more than one reason why you or I leave undone things we
could do: some of them we decide not to do, but very many others
we don't get around to doing, or don't even recognize as possible
for us. Only the first of those explanations can apply in the case of
omniscient, omnipotent God: every for-ever-unactualized logical
possibility that is subject to God's will alone (and not also to some
creature's will) must be actively willed against by God, so that there
are no unactualized potentialities in his will.[52] If that were not the

---

[49] See QDP 3.15c, *Quarta ratio*: 'It is, therefore, through God's intellection and
volition that he does whatever he does that is extrinsic to himself.'

[50] This generalized claim is too strong. Ordinary free, productive agents are
constrained by considerations of time, energy, interest, etc.; thus, not 'whoever'. But
since this premiss need apply only to God, its unwarranted universality doesn't
affect the argument.

[51] See also e.g. QDP 1.5; ST Ia.25.5. It may be clearer in those parallel discussions
than it is here in II.23 that arguing on this basis for the voluntariness of creation has
more to do with *what* to create than with *whether* to create. In TMOT, Ch. Seven,
sect. 9, and Kretzmann 1991*a* and 1991*b*, I argue for a non-necessitarian line regarding what to create, agreeing with Aquinas in that respect, and for a necessitarian line
regarding whether to create. I also try to show that there is a good deal of evidence
that Aquinas himself was strongly attracted to the latter position, despite his official,
explicit rejection of it.

[52] Cf. QDP 3.15, ad 11: 'As regards what has to do with God himself, no possibility can be assigned, but only natural and absolute necessity. In respect of a created
thing, however, one can consider possibility in connection with God—not as regards
passive potentiality but as regards active power, which is not limited to a single
effect.'

case, there would be a sense in which the thesis of II.9, 'God's power is not other than his activity', would be false.

The conclusions of all but one of chapter 23's arguments contrast God's acting through the necessity of his nature with his acting through his will. But those two descriptions are certainly not incompatible in Aquinas's own view of them, as he showed quite clearly in Book I. For example, 'The principal object of the divine will, therefore, is the divine essence. However, since the divine essence is God's intellection and everything else that is said to be in him, it is clear, further, that in the same way [as he wills his essence] he principally wills his intellection, his volition, his being one, and whatever else is of that sort' (I.74.637–8); 'God necessarily wills his being and his goodness, and he cannot will the contrary' (I.80.676). At the core of divine volition, in what is principally willed by God, God's acting through his will must be the same as his acting through the necessity of his nature, and must, therefore, involve no free decision or choice among real alternatives.[53]

However, the thesis of chapter 23 (989) and the conclusion of its fourth argument (993) contrast God's acting through the necessity of his nature with his acting through the decision (*arbitrium*) of his will; the second argument (991) speaks of the choice (*electio*) of his will; and the sixth (995) focuses on an agent's being in control of its own action (*sui actus dominus*). These three descriptions, especially the first two of them, are inapplicable to acting through the necessity of one's own nature if decision or choice entails real alternatives. But, as I suggested in TMOT,[54] many an essential aspect of even an imperfect being can be recognized as at least *counterfactually* chosen, as something the willer necessarily has or is but would choose to have or to be if, *per impossibile*, an occasion for choosing it were to arise. And it seems clear that in the case of an absolutely perfect being its every essential aspect would be counterfactually chosen by it: 'in respect of its principal object, which is God's own goodness, the divine will does have necessity— not, of course, the necessity of coercion but, rather, the necessity of natural order, which is not incompatible with freedom. . . . For God cannot will that he not be good and, consequently, that he not be intellective, or powerful, or any of those things that the essential nature of his goodness includes' (QDV 23.4c).[55] I think that

---

[53] See also e.g. ST Ia.19.3; QDV 23.4.   [54] Ch. Seven, sect. 6.

[55] See also e.g. SCG I.80, 'God necessarily wills his being and his goodness'.

counterfactual choice is what characterizes this freedom compatible with natural order, and that all essential aspects of an absolutely perfect being are paradigmatically objects of counterfactual choice.

Now, of course, what's at issue in chapter 23 is not God's willing of himself, but his willing of other things. All the same, Aquinas's own presentation of God's willing of other things, particularly in Book I,[56] and his acceptance of the Dionysian principle ('Goodness is by its very nature diffusive of itself and [thereby] of being') commit him to a necessitarian explanation of God's willing things other than himself.[57] I favour such an explanation, which sees God's creating as his (freely) acting through the necessity of his nature (considered as perfect goodness), and which confines the creator's free choice among alternatives to the selection of which ones to actualize for purposes of manifesting the goodness that is identical with his being. As I see it, God does (freely) create through the necessity of his nature, and freely chooses among alternatives in deciding what to create.

7. The modalities of intellection and volition

Having shown unmistakably through the nine arguments of chapter 23 that he is a non-necessitarian regarding God's volition to create, Aquinas is careful in the very next chapter to remind us that his non-necessitarianism is not voluntarism, according to which the fullest possible 'explanation' of any divine action consists in nothing more than 'God wills it'. In chapter 24 Aquinas repudiates voluntarism, 'the mistake of certain people who said that all things depend on the simple will of God, *without any reason*' (24.1008), as he has already done briefly in Book I (87.727), and will do again at the end of II.28&29.

Given Aquinas's standard, well-established account of the relations between will and intellect, which he introduced appropriately in chapter 23's third argument (992; see sect. 6 above), it comes as

---

[56] See e.g. I.75.643: 'In willing himself, therefore, God also wills other things'; 76.647: 'God wills himself and other things in a single act of will'; and 81.682: God 'wills all other things in willing his goodness'.

[57] As I argue at length in TMOT, Ch. Seven, sects. 7–9, and elsewhere (see n. 51 above).

no surprise that he finds the reasons for God's willing in God's intellect, again employing the artisan analogy (24.1006). The only addition to the expected explanation is that he here focuses on wisdom, an 'intellectual virtue', as the aspect of intellect in accordance with which 'God produces his effects'.[58]

In general, Aquinas takes the three virtues of theoretical intellect to be *understanding* (in the technical, restricted sense of grasping self-evident first principles, the starting-points of theoretical cognition), *scientia* (in the sense of possessing the fully worked-out, demonstratively organized system of cognition regarding some specific body of knowledge), and *wisdom* (the full cognition of ultimate, universal explanations, which are of course unified in God, so that wisdom involves full cognition of God and of everything that that entails).[59] That's not all Aquinas means by 'wisdom',[60] but it seems to be all that's needed here. For if God himself is the primary object of God's perfect intellective cognition, then God's cognition simply *is* wisdom.[61] 'For will is moved to acting as the result of some sort of apprehending, since will's object is an apprehended good. But God is an agent through [his] will (as has been shown [in II.23]). Therefore, since in God there is only intellective apprehending, and since he apprehends anything only by apprehending himself [I.46], and since intellectively apprehending him is what it is to be wise, we are left with the conclusion that God operates [i.e. "produces his effects" (1002)] in accordance with his wisdom' (1003). This outcome clearly is not to be confused with God's simply willing, 'without any reason'.

Chapter 25 provides a *catalogue raisonné* of ways in which 'God is said to be unable to do some things even though he is omnipotent' (1009a). Several of its observations were particularly relevant at earlier stages of our investigation of omnipotence in this chapter, and I've already introduced them there.[62] Aquinas evidently

[58] Cf. In Sent. I.43.2.1, ad 2, quoted in n. 45 above.

[59] See e.g. ST IaIIae.57.2.

[60] For an illuminating, fuller account, see Stump, forthcoming *b*. See also TMOT, Ch. One, sects. 7 and 9.

[61] See SCG I.94.792: 'For if wisdom consists in the cognition of the highest, deepest causes (as the Philosopher maintains at the beginning of the *Metaphysics* [I 2, 982b9–10]), and God especially has cognition of himself and cognizes anything only by cognizing himself (as has been proved [I.46–9]), then it is obvious that wisdom must be ascribed to him most especially. . . . The Philosopher also says at the beginning of the *Metaphysics* [I 2, 982b28–30; 983a5–10] that wisdom is a divine, not a human, possession.'   [62] See nn. 2, 9, 13, 35, and 36 above.

wanted to postpone explaining each of these merely apparent exceptions to omnipotence until he had presented *all* the logical bases
for his explanations—from I.16's arguments against passive potentiality in God (cited in 1009*b*) through II.24's retrospective
arguments that God acts through intellect and will (in 1033). Consequently, most of what Aquinas has to say in this helpful compendium is familiar.

But one of his observations introduces a modal notion that is
new to Book II and worth noting:

Likewise, it was shown above [in I.82] that God's will cannot be mutable.
In this way, therefore, he cannot bring it about that what is willed by him
not be fulfilled. But it is important to know that the sense in which he is
said to be unable to do this is different from that which applies in the
preceding cases. For in those cases God unconditionally (*simpliciter*) can
neither will nor bring it about.[63] In a case of this sort, however, God can
indeed either bring it about or will it if we consider his will or power
absolutely, but not if we consider it under the presupposition that he has
willed the opposite. For in respect of created things the divine will has
necessity only *ex hypothesi* (as was shown in the first book [in chs. 81–3]).
(1031–2*a*)[64]

Propositions expressing modalities *ex hypothesi* are often open
to more than one interpretation. Aquinas draws on a medieval
logical distinction to dispel this sort of technical ambiguity: 'all
these statements [such as] "God cannot do the contrary of the
things he has decided to do" (and any that are similarly expressed)
are [to be] interpreted in the compounded sense; for in that way
they imply the supposition of a divine volition of the opposite. If,
however, they are interpreted in the divided sense, they are false;
because [in that case] they have to do with God's power and will
considered absolutely' (1032*b–c*). In an Aristotelian-medieval

[63] e.g. God 'cannot be a body' (1010), 'can neither repent nor become angry or
sad' (1017), 'cannot do things that he cannot will' (1028).

[64] There is a good deal of relevant material in I.81–3, but the following passage is
perhaps most directly relevant to the point Aquinas is making here: 'although where
things caused [by God] are concerned God wills nothing absolutely necessarily, he
does will something necessarily *ex hypothesi*. For it has been shown [in I.82] that the
divine will is immutable. Now as regards anything immutable, if it once is something,
it cannot afterwards not be that; for of anything that is different now and earlier, we
say that it is moved [or changed]. Therefore, if the divine will is immutable, then,
supposing that God does will something, it is necessary *ex hypothesi* that he will it'
(83.701–2).

paradigm, the ambiguous statement 'This seated man can stand' is standardly sorted into its false compounded sense—'That this seated man is standing is possible'—and its true divided sense— 'Regarding this seated man, it is possible that he stand'—which present the modality *de dicto* and *de re*, respectively.[65] Analogously, the true, compounded interpretation of Aquinas's example here is 'That God do the contrary of something he has decided to do is impossible', while its false, divided interpretation is 'Regarding X, something that God has decided to do, it is impossible that he do the contrary of X'.[66]

In the next two chapters Aquinas undertakes to show the acceptability of two theses that a less fastidious arguer might justifiably have viewed as already established: that neither God's intellect (II.26) nor God's will (II.27) is restricted to certain determined effects. For instance, in argument NB, considered in section 5 above, Aquinas concludes that 'God can do whatever does not involve a contradiction', and he gets to that conclusion by way of the familiar artisan analogy, which implies that the effects that are in God's intellect virtually (i.e. in respect of God's power to bring them about) must include whatever does not involve a contradiction. None the less, the fifth and last of his arguments in chapter 26 is a recasting of argument NB, making explicit what was pretty transparently implicit in NB itself.[67] And since will gets its objects from intellect, the absence of restrictions on God's will is a corollary of the absence of restrictions on God's intellect (as can be seen plainly in II.27.1044)—unless, of course, some *moral* restriction applies to the will of the creator.

---

[65] For further technical and historical information see Kretzmann 1981, Knuuttila 1982, and esp. Knuuttila 1993.

[66] For a relevant, fuller account of this distinction by Aquinas himself, see e.g. QDV 2.12, ad 4.

[67] II. 26.1039: 'The divine knowledge is related to the things produced by it as an artisan's knowledge is related to the things made by his art. But any art covers all the things that can be contained under the genus that is the subject of that art—e.g. the builder's art covers all buildings. But the genus that is subject to the divine art is being, since through God's intellect he is the universal source of being (as has been shown [in II.15 and 22–4]). Therefore, the divine intellect extends its causality to all things with which the defining characteristic of being is not incompatible; for all things of that sort considered in themselves are naturally suited to be contained under being. Therefore, the divine intellect is not confined to certain determined effects.'

8. Justice, goodness, and God's plan as possible grounds for obligatory creation

Aquinas considers that possibility in the next chapter, which presents a minor but difficult textual problem, one that has led to its being referred to as II.28&29 (Marietti sects. 1046–62). For although Aquinas himself entitled chapters 28 and 30, he neither titled chapter 29, nor indicated where it begins. There are two obvious possibilities, each of which has some support in the manuscript tradition. The Leonine and Marietti editors locate the beginning of chapter 29 in 1058, and it's clear that the topic Aquinas begins to discuss there differs significantly from the topics he discusses in 1046–57. But there is also a significant shift in topics beginning in 1053, and, what's more, the two immediately preceding sections contain the sorts of things that so often form the end-matter of a chapter in SCG: Scriptural confirmations of the results of the preceding arguments (1051) and indications of mistakes ruled out by those results (1052). It's almost as if we had not just two but three chapters run together here. In light of this confusion, my references to material in II.28&29 will use the numbers of its Marietti sections: 1046–62.

The first broad topical division is contained in 1046–52. There Aquinas provides four arguments in support of the thesis that 'God has not operated out of necessity in the creation of things as [he would have done] if he had produced things as regards their being out of an obligation (*debito*) of justice' (1046).[68] This thesis isn't hard to prove. If there is any moral constraint on the volition to create, the source of it obviously could not be God's perfect *justice*,[69] because of considerations introduced most plainly in Aquinas's second argument: 'since the act of justice is to render to each whatever is his own, an act by which something is made someone's own [necessarily] precedes [any] act of justice.... Therefore, the act by which something is made someone's own for the first time cannot be an act of justice. But it is through creation that a created thing begins for the first time to have any-

---

[68] The verb *debeo* and its perfect passive participle *debitum* (often nominalized, as in this sentence) play very prominent roles in II.28&29, where they are not always easy to interpret. I'll indicate their occurrence whenever I think the reader needs reminding of the various senses in which Aquinas seems to be using these words here.

[69] On justice in God see esp. ST Ia.21.1.

thing of its own. Therefore, creation does not proceed out of an obligation of justice' (1048). It really is inconceivable that creating is morally necessitated by God's having an obligation to possible created things. The appropriate analogy would be an obligation based on your relation to characters in a novel you might conceivably write, not on your relation to your possible great-great-grandchildren.

A more challenging possibility, which I've already examined or alluded to several times, is taken up by Aquinas in 1053–7, which constitute the second broad topical division. Could it be that God's perfect *goodness* necessitates, morally or otherwise, his creating something? I'm convinced that God's perfect goodness does necessitate, not morally but metaphysically, God's creating something.[70] But, as I've been saying, and as we'll now see, Aquinas rejects any necessitation stemming from God's goodness.

Having shown that creation could not be necessitated by an obligation of justice on God's part to non-existent, logically possible things, Aquinas looks in the other direction: 'although the universal production of things is preceded by nothing *created* to which there can be any obligation, it is preceded by something uncreated, which is the source of creation' (1053a). Of course, nothing but God himself is uncreated as that word is used here, but Aquinas is expressing himself obliquely, because he wants to call attention to three divine attributes, aspects of the uncreated: 'divine goodness itself precedes [creation] as the end and the primary motive for creating, according to Augustine, who says "Because God is good, we exist" [*De doctrina christiana* I.32]. God's knowledge and will, on the other hand, precede [creation] as those [aspects of God] by which things are produced as regards their being' (1053b–c). If any conceptually distinguishable aspect of God's nature could necessitate God's creating, it would be one of these three, which play the only causal roles discernible in creation: divine goodness, the final cause; divine intellect, the formal cause; and divine will, the efficient cause.

Although Aquinas argued just a little earlier against necessitation in God's intellect or will where created things are concerned (in II.26 and 27), there is a relation between the formal and the efficient cause of creation that still needs to be investigated in

---

[70] See TMOT, Ch. Seven, sects. 7–9; also n. 51 above.

this connection: 'if we consider the divine plan (*dispositionem*) by which God planned to produce things as regards their being by his intellect and will, then in that way the producing of things did proceed out of the necessity of the divine plan. For it cannot be that God plans to make something that he afterwards does not make; otherwise his plan would be either mutable or weak. Therefore, it is of necessity owed (*debetur*) to his plan that it be fulfilled' (1057*a*). Of course, the necessity which Aquinas acknowledges here is *ex hypothesi*, and so poses no threat to his account of creation, since he has already argued that 'in respect of created things the divine will has necessity only *ex hypothesi*' (1032*a*; see sect. 7 above). Still, he is concerned to avoid leaving an impression that the relation between God's producing and God's plan might, after all, inject considerations of justice into creation: 'None the less, this indebtedness (*debitum*) is not a sufficient condition for [associating] the defining characteristic of justice strictly so-called with the creation of things' (1057*b*). As Aquinas has just explained, 'justice strictly so-called requires an obligation of necessity (*debitum necessitatis*); for what is rendered to someone out of justice is owed to him out of necessity of right' (1056*a*). 'And, as is clear from what the Philosopher says in *Ethics* V [11, 1138a4–5, b4–14], there is no justice strictly so-called between a person and himself. Therefore, it cannot be said, strictly, that God has produced things as regards their being out of an obligation of justice in virtue of his having planned to produce them through [his] knowledge and will' (1057*b*). The basis for Aquinas's denial of an obligation of justice in this connection is obviously quite different from the one he used in 1046–52 (discussed above); but here, too, the denial is well founded.

I am naturally most concerned, however, with his denial of any necessitation of creation stemming from God's perfect goodness, which, as we've seen, he introduces in this context as 'the end and the primary motive for creating' (1053*b*). He begins his investigation of it as a possible source of obligation by stating what looks like a conclusion: 'Therefore, if we consider divine goodness absolutely, we find no obligation where the creation of things is concerned' (1053*d*). His beginning in this way may seem unwarranted, since the only available basis for drawing a conclusion about divine goodness here is his remark in 1053*b* about its causal and motivational role in creation. But it isn't really as unwarranted as it may seem. As he argues convincingly elsewhere, the sort of necessitation that stems from a final cause is compatible with choice.[71] More importantly, he seems simply to have inverted the argument, since he goes on at once to offer two kinds of support for this conclusion.

As I've been saying, I think that God's perfect goodness does necessitate God's creating something, and that this necessitation is metaphysical, not moral. So the fact that Aquinas is here focusing on the possibility that God might be *obligated* to create may give the impression that my opposition is simply irrelevant to this aspect of his account of creation. That impression is certainly strengthened by the first sort of support he provides for his conclusion that 'if we consider divine goodness absolutely, we find no obligation (*debitum*) where the creation of things is concerned' (1053*d*). The question, as Aquinas sees it, is whether God's goodness somehow obligates him to create something, and the first kind of obligation he considers in this connection is what we've just seen him calling an obligation of right, associated with 'justice properly so-called'.[72] Since the paradigm he offers is that 'it is owed to a benefactor that he be thanked for benefits inasmuch as the one who received the benefit owes this to him' (1053*e*), it looks as if the kind of obligation that Aquinas is considering here might be conceived of more narrowly as what he sometimes calls an obligation of gratitude.[73] But we hardly need to be told that 'this sort of obligation has no place where the creation of things is concerned' (ibid.). Neither in these ways nor in any other does God's justice morally obligate him to create.

The second sort of support which Aquinas provides for his conclusion that 'if we consider divine goodness absolutely, we find no obligation where the creation of things is concerned' brings him very near to considering the necessitation/obligation that I think we do find where the creation of things is concerned. 'In a second way something is said to be owed to someone or something considered just as such. For whatever is required for the completing (*perfectionem*) of anything is owed to it of necessity' (1053*f*).[74] I'm

---

[71] See e.g. ST Ia.82.1.   [72] See 1056*a*, quoted above.

[73] See e.g. ST IIaIIae.107.1, ad 3.

[74] Cf. I.93.784: 'It was shown above [in 83.705] that on the hypothesis that God wills something, he wills the things and conditions (*illa*) that are required for it. But whatever is required for the completion (*perfectionem*) of something is owed

interrupting Aquinas's presentation of this second kind of support in order to observe that what he's described so far looks like metaphysical necessity, despite the use of 'owed'. Aquinas sometimes does express metaphysical necessity in terms of obligation, as when he identifies an obligation deriving from the kind of nature a thing has—*debitum secundum conditionem naturae*: 'for instance, if we say that it is owed to a human being that it have reason and the other things that pertain to human nature' (ST IaIIae.111.1, ad 2).

If this is what he's introducing here, then it seems to me that it provides good grounds for inferring that in *this* way it *is* owed to God's perfect goodness that it have productivity and the other things that pertain to the nature of goodness. For, according to the Dionysian principle, which Aquinas often appeals to in other contexts,[75] goodness is by its very nature diffusive of itself and (thereby) of being. The principle expresses an important truth about goodness, most obviously about the goodness of agents— goodness essentially associated with volitional action informed by intellect—which is the only kind at issue here. There is no obvious inconsistency in the notion of knowledge that is for ever unexpressed, never shared by the agent who has it, even if the agent is omnipotent; but there is inconsistency in the notion of goodness that is for ever unmanifested, never shared by the perfectly good, omnipotent agent.

Sometimes Aquinas does present God's goodness in that light, as in this passage from SCG I: 'The sharing of being and goodness proceeds from goodness. This is indeed evident both from the very nature of the good and from its defining characteristic. . . . But that diffusion is appropriate for God, since he is the cause of being for other things' (37.307); or in this one from ST: 'every agent, to the extent to which it is in actuality and perfect, makes or does (*facit*) something like itself. That's why it also pertains to the defining characteristic of will that the good that anyone has he shares with others as much as possible. And it pertains above all to the divine will, from which every perfection is derived in virtue of a kind of

---

(*debitum*) to each [such thing]. Therefore, in God there is justice, the nature of which is to distribute to each its own.'

[75] See the list in Peghaire 1932: 19* nn. 45 and 46.

likeness' (Ia.19.2c). If perfect goodness is an aspect of God's essence, and self-diffusiveness is essential to goodness, it looks as if God's willing the production of things as regards their being is a metaphysical necessity.[76]

But it's not clear that Aquinas intends this second sort of support for his conclusion in a sense as strong as the one I've just been suggesting for it. He continues his presentation of it by offering an example that seems notably weaker than his example of its being 'owed to a human being that it have reason and the other things that pertain to human nature' (ST IaIIae.111.1, ad 2), which I cited above in connection with proposing an interpretation in terms of metaphysical necessity. Here's how he proceeds in the argument we're examining: 'For example, it is owed to a human being that it have hands, or strength,[77] because without these it cannot be complete. But divine goodness needs nothing external (exteriori) to it for its completeness. Therefore, the production of creatures is not owed to it by way of necessity' (1053f).

So the way in which something is necessary for a thing's completeness seems to fall short of metaphysical necessity. A human being without hands or strength is certainly incomplete, but one can be human without them, as one can't without 'reason and the other things that pertain to human nature'.[78] All the same, even if we assess the claim about divine goodness in accordance with this

[76] Unless the diffusion of goodness can somehow be completely accounted for within the divine essence. In almost all the passages in which Aquinas relies on the Dionysian principle he speaks of God's sharing goodness with other things; but in In Sent. I.2.1.4, sc, he argues that it is only among the Persons of the Trinity that perfect goodness can be completely shared. This Trinitarian application of the principle deserves consideration within philosophical theology, which is informed by revelation; but it can play no role here, in Aquinas's natural theology. Besides, it is God, not some one divine Person, whom Aquinas identifies as 'goodness itself, not merely good' (SCG I.38.310). Consequently, no matter what role might be assigned to the principle within the plurality of divine Persons, the essential self-diffusiveness of goodness as an aspect of the essence of God remains in force, necessitating external, volitional diffusion—i.e. creation as I see it and as I think Aquinas is sometimes strongly inclined to see it (e.g. in SCG I.75.644). See also Kretzmann 1991a.

[77] Virtutem, the word Aquinas uses here, can, of course, also mean virtue; and there are reasons for taking that possibility seriously. Not much turns on the choice, as far as I can see, but I think 'strength' is more plausible in this context. (Both of the complete published English translations have 'strength'.)

[78] Cf. ST Ia.21.1, ad 3, which is relevantly instructive in more than one respect.

weaker sense of what is owed to it, Aquinas's crucial premiss seems false: like any agent's goodness, divine goodness must, for its completeness, manifest itself by bringing about something external to it. If, as I've been saying, the perpetually unmanifested goodness of an omnipotent agent is inconceivable, then such goodness is, *a fortiori*, also incomplete. No attribute of an absolutely perfect being could need the *acquisition* of anything external to it for its completeness; but creating as the metaphysically necessitated manifestation of perfect goodness is not the acquiring of created things for the completion of goodness that would otherwise be imperfect. And, of course, the Dionysian line is that goodness *entails* its own manifestation in bringing about goodness and, consequently, being. A being that is good (and not relevantly powerless) *simply is* a being productive of good things external to it. The external things it produces in manifesting its goodness are dependent on *it*, not vice versa.

Aquinas offers two more arguments intended to show that there is no mode of necessity in which it is owed to divine goodness that God create anything. Neither of them is nearly as interesting or challenging as the one (in 1053) we've been considering, and the second of them (1055) is particularly weak. But having concluded, finally, that 'there is no kind of necessity in which it is owed to divine goodness that things be produced as regards their being' (1055), Aquinas offers a diluted concession, after reviewing his case against considering God's creating as obligated by God's goodness: 'just as the production of created things cannot be said to have occurred out of an obligation of justice by which God is obligated to a created thing [1046–50], so neither can it be said to have occurred out of an obligation of justice by which he is obligated to his own goodness, if "justice" is taken strictly' (1056). As I've been saying, I think Aquinas is right about that, because I think God's creating is necessitated by God's goodness metaphysically, not morally. But Aquinas uses this result here as a springboard for his concession: 'None the less, if "justice" is taken *broadly*, then it *can* be said that there is justice in the creation of things, in so far as it is *suited* to (*condecet*) divine goodness' (ibid.). In that case, 'creating can be said to be owed to God's own goodness by way of some sort of suitability' (ibid.)—but only, I think, in the misleading way in which thinking can be said to be owed to a human being's rationality by way of some sort of suitability.

9. Kinds of necessity in created things

In 1058–60, but especially in 1060, Aquinas develops an account of ways in which it might seem, after all, that God is obligated where created things are concerned. What is at issue here, however, is not the possibility of God's being obligated to create at all, but rather of his being obligated to create *that* sort of thing because of creating *this* sort of thing. In this connection, Aquinas admits, God's production of things as regards their being *is* necessitated. The necessity involved here 'is not absolute but, rather, conditional necessity: if *this* is to be made (*debeat fieri*), it is necessary that *that* be prior to it' (1060a).[79] In keeping with this conditional necessity, he says, 'we find three kinds of [conditional] obligation in the production of creatures' (ibid.): (1) the obligation to make certain things that are necessary for the existence of the planned universe as a whole— e.g. stars;[80] (2) the obligation to make certain things that are necessary for the existence of other kinds of things within the universe—e.g., as Aquinas says, plants and animals; (3) the obligation to bring into existence the 'parts, properties, and accidents on which a [kind of] created thing depends as regards either its being or some perfection [naturally] belonging to it. For instance, on the hypothesis that God willed to make a human being, there was an obligation *ex hypothesi* that he should conjoin a body and a soul in it, and that he should provide senses for it and other such aids, both intrinsic and extrinsic' (1060b–d). Aquinas can admit all these divine conditional obligations quite readily because, as he correctly observes, 'In all these cases, if they are rightly considered, God is said to be obligated, not to a created thing, but to the fulfilment of his own plan' (1060e), an observation for which he prepared the ground in his discussion of God's plan in 1057.

Turning, finally, from his consideration of ways in which God can and cannot be said to be necessitated as regards creating itself and as regards created things, Aquinas focuses on necessitation within the realm of nature itself—*in rerum natura*—where he finds not only conditional but also *absolute* necessity. He identifies two bases for absolute necessity in nature: (1) the essential principles of

---

[79] Conditional necessity (*necessitas conditionalis*) seems to be the same as necessity *ex hypothesi* (*necessitas ex suppositione*).

[80] Aquinas's examples are the sun and the moon, which strike me as too particular and too parochial.

natural things—matter and form (or the material and formal causes of things); (2) the efficient causes of natural things (1061*a*).

Although almost all efficient causes of natural things are themselves natural, *some* natural things were supernaturally produced 'in the first creation of things', where type-2 absolute necessity couldn't apply: 'For in that creation God alone was the efficient cause (as was shown above [in II.21]), and in creating, God operates not by the necessity of [his] nature but by [his] will (as was shown above [in II.23]). But things that are made by will can have no necessity other than on the sole basis of the hypothesis of an end. In accordance with that hypothesis, the obligatoriness (*debitum*) is associated with the end, in such a way that the things through which that end is achieved should exist' (1061*b*).[81] But since many of the things produced in the first creation of things were constituted of matter and form,[82] type-1 absolute necessity applies even to them. Aquinas's examples are expressed in terms of antiquated natural science (1061*c*), but he expressly picks out the conformity of created things to mathematical laws as one sort of type-1 absolute necessity, and I see no reason why we couldn't, or shouldn't, identify their conformity to natural laws as another.

As for type-2 absolute necessity, after the first creation of things, it applies universally within the realm of nature (leaving unpredictable divine intervention out of account, as natural theology is bound to do). 'But when a created thing is already an efficient cause in the propagation of things, there can be an absolute necessity [stemming] from the created efficient cause. For example, terrestrial (*inferiora*) bodies are changed necessarily by the movement of the sun' (1061*d*).

Although Aquinas argues in these ways in II.28&29 for absolute necessity's obtaining in nature, he devotes a long chapter 30 to considering '*How* there can be absolute necessity in created things'. He begins by revealing his primary reason for taking up this question. He has been arguing that 'all things depend on God's will as their first cause', and that necessity *ex hypothesi* is the only sort of

---

[81] As we've seen (in sect. 8 above), when Aquinas introduces divine goodness in this context, he identifies it as 'the end and the primary motive for creating' (1053*b*). One way of bringing out the difference between the account of creation which Aquinas gives and the one I think he should have given is to say that he thinks that perfect goodness, God's primary motive for creating, does not necessitate God's creating anything, while I think that it does so, absolutely.

[82] See sects. 3 and 4 above for putative exceptions.

necessity applicable to God's volition.[83] Against that background, it might look as if he has 'to grant (*fateri*) that all things are contingent. Someone could think so, in virtue of the fact that things have flowed from their cause without absolute necessity, since, ordinarily, an effect that proceeds from its cause without necessity is contingent in connection with things, events, or states of affairs' (30.1063*a*).[84] This relationship that obtains 'ordinarily' between non-necessitated efficient causation and contingent effects obtains, pretty clearly, throughout nature after the first creation of things. None the less, 'among created things there are some regarding which it is unconditionally (*simpliciter*) and absolutely necessary that they be' (1063*b*), things that have in their nature no potentiality for not being. Most created things are not like that, just 'because the matter in them is in potentiality to another form' (1064), and so they are naturally susceptible to the kind of radical alteration that constitutes disintegration, or 'corruption'. Consequently, unconditionally and absolutely necessary created things are 'those in which either there is no matter or, if there is, it is not susceptible (*possibilis*) to another form' (ibid.). Separated substances belong to the first group (see sect. 3 above); Aquinas's Aristotelian astronomy mistakenly puts heavenly bodies in the second group, where, I imagine, twentieth-century physics might locate some subatomic particles.[85]

Aquinas concludes his full survey of creation's modalities by showing how each kind of cause—material, formal, efficient, and final—gives rise to absolute necessity in nature. The first two he treats together, as a thing's 'essential principles': 'a thing cannot be without its essential principles, which are matter and form, and so whatever belongs to a thing because of its essential principles must have absolute necessity in all cases' (30.1070). We've already seen examples of ways in which a natural thing can be absolutely necessary in virtue of the relation of its matter and form to its being, and

---

[83] See also 30.1069.
[84] See also 30.1066: 'From the fact that created things come into being from the divine will, they must be such as God wills them to be. But the fact that God is said to have produced things as regards their being through will, not through necessity, does not rule out his having willed that there be some things that are necessarily and some that are contingently, so that there may be an ordered diversity in things. Therefore, nothing prevents some things produced by the divine will from being necessary.'
[85] See n. 28 above; also 30.1073*a*.

Aquinas discusses such examples in more detail in 1071–3. Most things in nature have matter and form that are themselves not simple. For instance, 'the matter proper to a human being is a body' that is chemically, physiologically, and anatomically complex.[86] So 'it is absolutely necessary that a human being have in itself each of the elements, humours, and principal organs' proper to a human body. 'Likewise, if a human being is a mortal rational animal, and if that is a human being's nature or form, then it is necessary that the human being be both animal and rational' (1074). Furthermore, some of a thing's characteristics, often called *propria*, are neither accidental to it (in the ordinary sense of 'accidental') nor part of its matter or form, but are nevertheless entailed by its essential principles, and so absolutely necessary to it—such as a human being's capacity to learn, or to laugh (1075).

Aquinas's analysis of absolute necessity stemming from efficient causation (30.1076–78) is worth studying in detail, but my present purposes are best served, I think, by bringing out the points he makes in summing up:

[I]n some cases the necessity that comes from an agent cause depends on the disposition of the agent only, but in others on the disposition of both the agent and the patient. Therefore, if such a disposition in accordance with which the effect follows of necessity is absolutely necessary in both the agent and the patient, there will be absolute necessity in the agent cause, as in things that act [as they do] necessarily and always. If such a disposition is not absolutely necessary, however, but capable of being eliminated, then there will be necessity from the agent cause only on the hypothesis that both [the agent and the patient happen to] have the disposition required for the acting—as in connection with those [sorts of] things that are sometimes hindered in their operation, either because of a lack of power or because of the violence of something contrary to them. (That's why they do not act always, but [only] for the most part). (1078*a–c*)

As Aquinas sees it, absolute necessity stems from a final cause only in connection with natural agents and not in connection with volitional agents, which is what we might have expected. And where natural agents are concerned, the absolute necessity stemming from a final cause is hard to distinguish from the sort that stems from a formal cause: 'in the case of natural things an intention of the end belongs to the agent in keeping with its form,

---

[86] Or, as Aquinas puts it, 'that is mixed, complicated (*complexionatum*), and equipped with organs (*organizatum*)'.

through which the end is suited to it. That's why a natural thing tends toward an end in keeping with the power associated with its form—the way a heavy body tends toward the centre [of the earth] in accordance with its weight' (1079b).[87]

---

[87] The Aristotelian account of falling bodies, famously refuted by Galileo at Pisa.

FIVE

COULD THE CREATED WORLD HAVE EXISTED FOR EVER?

1. 'The eternity of the world'

In SCG II.31–8 Aquinas presents what is probably the most fully developed of his many contributions to the medieval debate concerning 'the eternity of the world'.[1] Before considering his work in those eight chapters, I'll sketch the character of the debate.

Obviously, the physical universe—matter itself and everything material—either began to exist or has existed for ever. Can either of those alternatives be proved, or disproved? Kant's first antinomy gave those questions a place in modern philosophy. But much earlier, during the high Middle Ages, they had already prompted an intense and occasionally deep philosophical discussion under the designation *de aeternitate mundi*, 'on the eternity of the world'.[2]

Despite that designation, the medieval debate was not seriously concerned with a hypothesis that the world's mode of existence might be eternity in the strict sense of the word—i.e. the same as God's atemporal mode of existence, discussed by Aquinas and others in terms of Boethius's definition: 'the complete possession all at once of illimitable life'.[3] What prompted the debate was a

---

[1] See also e.g. In Sent. II.1.1.5 (also Baldner and Carroll 1997); CT I.98–9; QDP 3.14, 3.17; ST Ia.46.1, 46.2; QQ III.14.2, XII.6.1; In Phys. VIII: L2.986; DAM; In Met. XII: L5.2496–7; DSS 9.99–100; *Collationes super Credo in Deum* 1.880.

[2] For a survey of most of Aquinas's relevant texts and a discussion linking Kant's famous treatment of the issue with the medieval debate, see Antweiler 1961. For the history of the medieval discussion and its ancient sources, see e.g. Vollert *et al.* 1964; Behler 1965; van Steenberghen 1974: 512–30; Sorabji 1983: chs. 13–15, 17, and 1987; Davidson 1987; Wippel 1987; Dales 1990; Dales and Argerami 1991; Brown 1991; Hoenen 1992; Kretzmann and Pasnau 1992. On Aquinas's position in particular, see e.g. Vollert *et al.* 1964; Brady 1974; Wallace 1974; Weisheipl 1983; Wippel 1984; Wissink 1990; Bukowski 1979 and 1991; MacIntosh 1994; Baldner and Carroll 1997.

[3] *The Consolation of Philosophy* V, pr. 6; see Stump and Kretzmann 1981. Participants in the debate occasionally brought up the notion that the issue might be whether the world could be eternal in the strict sense, but only in order to dismiss

hypothesis that was only confusedly associated with eternity—the hypothesis that the world's indubitably temporal existence was illimitable as regards the past: i.e. beginningless, and in just that sense infinite. Even the further hypothesis that its temporal existence might also be endless was seldom considered in detail, and was in any case not really at issue. And, of course, no one would have taken seriously any suggestion that the world's existence might be characterized as life, or as atemporal (complete all at once). But even though medieval philosophers sometimes expressly noted that the use of 'eternity' or 'eternal' in a hypothesis about the world's existence was confused, the terminology seems to have been universal. For instance, all participants in the debate addressed some form of the question of whether the world could have existed *ab aeterno*, a phrase that is standardly translated as 'from eternity'. That expression, if it makes any sense at all, is even more misleading than 'the eternity of the world'. *Ab aeterno* really means no more than 'always' or 'for ever' as regards the past, or, more precisely, 'beginninglessly'.[4]

However, the immediate concern for the medievals, as for Kant, was not the beginningless-world hypothesis itself, but rather the *provability* either of the world's having begun to exist or of its having existed for ever. Among the ancients, it was Aristotle who had most famously argued that the world must have existed for ever.[5] Of course, most Christian philosopher-theologians of the high Middle Ages took Aristotle's arguments on any topic very

it. Aquinas did so, for instance, in QDP 3.14, ad sc 1: 'according to Boethius at the end of *The Consolation of Philosophy*, even if the world had existed for ever, it would not be coeternal with God because its duration would not be all at once, which is required for the defining characteristic of eternity. For eternity is "the complete possession all at once of illimitable life", as is said in that same place. The successiveness of time, on the other hand, is caused by movement (as is clear from what the Philosopher says [in *Physics* IV 11]). And so whatever is subject to mutability, even if it exists for ever, cannot be eternal.' Cf. QDP 3.14, ad sc 3: 'variability by its very nature rules out eternity, but not infinite duration'; also In Sent. II.1.1.5, ad sc 7.

[4] In this chapter I'll avoid using the misleading terminology myself, but I will translate it literally when quoting from Aquinas or from other medieval texts.

[5] See e.g. *Physics* I 9, 192a25–34; VIII 1, 251a9–b28; *De caelo* I 3, 270a12–22; 12, 282a21–b1; II 1, 283b26–284a2; *Metaphysics* XII 6, 1071b3–11; 7, 1072a21–6. That the world must be beginningless was also the view of almost all other ancient philosophers besides Plato (see e.g. *Timaeus* 29E–30B). 'Did the universe have a beginning? With only a very few possible exceptions, such a view was denied by everybody in European antiquity outside the Judaeo-Christian tradition' (Sorabji 1983: 193).

seriously, even if only as requiring refutation. So the mere fact that he had argued for a beginningless universe might well have been enough to start them thinking hard about the cogency of those arguments.[6] Moreover, most of those who expressed themselves on the issue understandably supposed that the proposition 'The world was created' entails 'The world began to exist', and is therefore incompatible with 'The world has existed for ever'.[7] So the additional fact that they were all doctrinally committed to God's having created the world ensured their worrying about the Aristotelian arguments.

A medieval thinker who, like Aquinas, was committed to the project of assimilating Aristotle's philosophy to Christian theology, would of course be especially concerned to deal carefully with this apparent obstacle to the project, in order to show, if possible, that the obstacle was only apparent. The most direct way of doing so would be to produce a disarming interpretation of what Aristotle had had to say about beginninglessness, one that would convince critics that he didn't really mean what almost everyone took him to have said. Aquinas, the consummate Christian Aristotelian, did just that during the earlier part of his career. He offered evidence that Aristotle not only intended none of those arguments of his as proofs of the beginningless-world hypothesis, but also believed that the issue of the world's either having begun to exist or having existed for ever could not be resolved by argument at all.[8] But

[6] Dales claims that, contrary to what he and others writing on the controversy *de aeternitate mundi* used to believe, 'It was not the reacquisition of Aristotle's natural philosophy which occasioned disputations about the eternity of the world; rather it was Lombard's *Sententiae*, whose sources were patristic, not Aristotelian' (Dales 1990: 259). Even if Dales is right about that in general, Aquinas, as we'll see, pretty clearly takes Aristotle, along with Avicenna and Averroës, to be the most formidable source of the beginningless-world cosmology.

[7] In his late treatise *On the Eternity of the World, Against Grumblers* (DAM), Aquinas identifies the heart of the debate as the issue concerning the logical relation between these propositions: 'So the whole question comes to this, whether or not [*a*] something's having been created by God as regards its entire substance and [*b*] its not having a beginning of its duration are incompatible.' He goes on at once to argue that *a* and *b* are *not* incompatible (DAM 298).

[8] See In Sent. II.1.1.5c: 'Therefore, I maintain that there are no demonstrations for either side of the question but, rather, probable or sophistical arguments for each side. And that is what is meant by the Philosopher's words when he says [*Topics* I 11, 104b12–17] that there are certain problems regarding which we do not have an argument, such as whether the world is eternal—which is why he himself never intends to demonstrate [i.e. to prove] this, as is clear from the way he proceeds. For whenever he treats this question thoroughly, he always adds some persuasive con-

eventually, acknowledging that Aristotle really did think he had proved that the world must have existed for ever, Aquinas repudiated such an attempt at a disarming interpretation as silly, and as having been undertaken in vain.[9] How he managed, none the less, to avoid acknowledging an unbridgeable gap between Aristotelianism and Christian orthodoxy remains to be seen; but I hope it will be seen in the remainder of this chapter.

We can begin sorting out the main positions taken by medieval Christian philosophers and theologians who worried about the Aristotelian view by noting the extent to which their attitudes were unanimous regarding the propositions (B) 'The world began to exist' and (not-B) 'The world has existed for ever'. Everyone involved in the debate would have agreed that B is known to be true on the basis of divine revelation (if in no other way), and that not-B is known to be false in virtue of its incompatibility with B (if for no other reason). They were, then, agreed on the substantive issue: the hypothesis of a beginningless world is false.

What primarily divided medieval thinkers in the debate stemming from this issue is their radically opposed assessments of the grounds available for denying not-B and affirming B, their views regarding the disprovability of not-B and the provability of B.

What I'll call the *audacious* assessment of those grounds is the view that there are metaphysical or empirical, as well as doctrinal, grounds on which to reject not-B, grounds on which to reject it as

sideration based on a view that many people share, or on their approval of arguments—things that a person offering demonstrations avoids entirely.' Aquinas presents a more cautious version of this disarming interpretation again in ST Ia.46.1c. For a helpful critical account of his developing views on the issue, along with a wealth of pertinent bibliographical information, see Wippel 1984. See also Baldner and Carroll 1997.

  [9] See esp. In Phys. VIII: L2.986: 'However, some people, trying in vain (*frustra*) to show that Aristotle did not speak against the faith, have said that in this passage Aristotle does not intend to *prove* that motion is perpetual, as something that is *true*, but rather to introduce an argument on each side, as [one does with] an issue that is in doubt. Given the very way he proceeds [here], that looks silly (*frivolum*). Furthermore, he uses the perpetuity of time and motion as a principle on the basis of which to prove that there is a first source—both here in *Physics* VIII and in *Metaphysics* XII. So it is clear that he relies on this as something that has been proved.' Aquinas seems to have changed his mind about Aristotle's intentions sometime between 1266, when he is likely to have written ST Ia.46 (see n. 8 above), and 1269, the probable date of his commenting on *Physics* VIII. His commentary on the *Metaphysics*, written around 1272, appears to combine elements of the views he expresses in ST and in In Phys.; see In Met. XII: L5.2495–9. For the chronology of these writings see Appendix I below.

not merely false but impossible. The audacious assessment, then, is the view that it can be, and indeed has been, demonstratively proved that the world could not have existed for ever. And, since not-B is contrary to B, such a disproof of not-B would, given that the world exists, also constitute a proof of B—a proof that the world must have begun to exist.

On the other side of the debate is the *judicious* assessment of the available grounds on which to deny not-B and affirm B. Since its adherents, too, are committed to the truth of B, they, like their opponents, criticize the Aristotelian account, and set out to refute Aristotelian arguments and any others that purport to prove not-B. They are, however, also critical of the various sorts of arguments offered by adherents of the audacious assessment, denying that such purported demonstrations really do disprove not-B (or prove B). Their rejection of the so-called proofs on both sides of the issue wouldn't by itself constitute a position on the possibility or impossibility of not-B; but some adherents of the judicious assessment do claim that not-B is possible, and that it is only on doctrinal grounds that not-B may be cogently denied and B affirmed. At least one of those medieval adherents explicitly distinguished three degrees of strength in their opposition to the audacious assessment, from the weakest claim (i), that the impossibility of not-B has not been demonstrated in any of the available arguments; through (ii), that the impossibility of not-B cannot be demonstrated; to the strongest claim (iii), that not-B, though false, is possible.[10] Since they were all committed to the doctrine of divine creation, those who went so far as to claim that not-B is possible had also to maintain that 'The world was created' does not entail B, and is therefore not incompatible with not-B. So adherents of the judicious assessment, who at the very least rejected all known attempts at demonstrative arguments in support of B (or against not-B), tended to rely on merely authoritative arguments in B's support, arguments based on Genesis 1: 1.

It's probably not surprising that their opponents, who subscribed to the audacious assessment and believed that the beginningless-world cosmology had been disproved, formed a powerful majority among medieval philosopher-theologians. So although the members of the judicious minority were cautious in their assessment of

---

[10] The distinction was drawn by Giles of Rome (1243/7–1316), *In secundum librum Sententiarum* 1.1.4.2. See Wippel 1984: 193; also Bukowski 1991.

not-B's dialectical status, their argumentative stance was really daring. It required them to oppose most of their fellow Christians, who had every right to think of themselves as philosophically defending the faith on this issue.

The fact that adherents of the audacious assessment looked like defenders of the faith wasn't their only initial advantage in the debate. The unimaginability of an infinite past conferred an additional psychological advantage on their doctrinally unimpeachable position. Analogies can help to give some sense to the mind-blurring billions in terms of which twentieth-century cosmologists have presented their best inferences regarding the age of the universe since its beginning in the Big Bang.[11] But no imagery can provide a reassuring orientation within what Shakespeare calls 'the dark backward and abysm of time',[12] on the brink of which we must be living and back into which we have to look when we consider our world as being not ten, or fifteen, or twenty billion years old, but *infinitely* old. Ten billion is represented by a 1 followed by ten zeros. A 1 followed by a *hundred* zeros has been called a googol, and a googolplex is a 1 followed by a *googol* zeros. Yet, of course, even a googolplex-year-old world would be no more *nearly* infinitely old than is old Archbishop Ussher's six-thousand-year-old world. A googolplex is no nearer infinity than is 6,000 or, for that matter, 1.

The medievals who adhered to the audacious assessment and argued against the possibility of the world's being infinitely old naturally traded on some of the counter-intuitive aspects of infinite past time, thereby appearing to ally themselves with common sense as well as with orthodoxy. Rejecting their arguments and opposing their position on provability required not only intellectual courage, but also dialectical ingenuity on the part of their very few judicious opponents.

In Aquinas's day, the most prominent and influential of those who subscribed to the audacious assessment, and developed detailed arguments for the impossibility of a beginningless world, was Bonaventure (*c.*1217–74).[13] Aquinas, Bonaventure's younger

---

[11] See e.g. Sagan 1977: ch. 1.   [12] *The Tempest* I. ii. 50.

[13] On Bonaventure's position and his contributions to the debate, see e.g. Vollert *et al.* 1964: 100–17; Bonansea 1974*a*, 1974*b*; Kovach 1974; Baldner 1989; and van Veldhuijsen 1990a. Other well-known medieval philosophers who also subscribed to the audacious assessment include Anselm, Richard of St Victor, Robert Grosseteste, Alexander of Hales, Thomas of York, Roger Bacon, Henry of Ghent,

contemporary, is the most important medieval representative of the much less popular judicious assessment.[14]

2. The modalities of beginningless creation

Aquinas uses the chapter's thesis as the title of the first of his eight chapters on 'the eternity of the world' in SCG II: 'It is not necessary that created things have existed for ever.' He's using 'created things' here broadly enough to include the whole spectrum from a single creature to the created world considered as a whole, as is clear from the very beginning of the chapter's first argument: 'For if it is necessary that *the universe* of created things, or *any one* created thing, exist . . .' (31.1081). The thesis of chapter 31 denies specifically that the *created* world must have existed for ever, a proposition that, presumably, never even crossed Aristotle's mind.

John Pecham, Matthew of Aquasparta, Richard of Middleton, Henry of Harclay, Thomas of Wilton, and William Alnwick. See e.g. Hoenen 1990, van Veldhuijsen 1990*b*, and Thijssen 1990. The views of Albert the Great, Aquinas's teacher and senior partner in the assimilation of Aristotle to Christian theology, appear to have changed during his career, ending in a position that resembles Aquinas's; see Snyder 1991. Many of the arguments associated with the audacious assessment in the Middle Ages originated in the work of John Philoponus, a Christian philosopher of the late fifth and early sixth centuries; see Wildberg 1987.

[14] In fact, he is, as far as I know, the *only* person during his lifetime (the second and third quarters of the thirteenth century) who adopted the judicious assessment in its strongest form without compromising his Christian orthodoxy to any degree. He (i) undertook to refute every argument he encountered on both sides of the substantive issue; he (ii) argued that neither side *could* be proved; and he (iii) was committed to the possibility of a beginningless *created* world. (See Wippel 1984.) The other most important medieval representatives of this under-represented position whom I know of are Godfrey of Fontaines (*c*.1250–*c*.1306) and Giles of Rome (*c*.1245–1316)—both very likely to have been Aquinas's students—and William Ockham (*c*.1295–1349). The 'Latin Averroists' Siger of Brabant (*c*.1240–84) and Boethius of Dacia (*fl.* 1275) might also be considered adherents of the judicious assessment, although their initially more radically Aristotelian positions seem to have become more judicious as a result of the criticism they encountered from theologians at Paris. On Godfrey, see Wippel 1980: 159–69; on Giles, see Wippel 1984: 193; on Ockham, see Kretzmann 1985; on Siger, see van Steenberghen 1977 and Wippel 1980: 156–8; on Boethius, see Wippel 1987. Duns Scotus's position on the issue has been thought ambiguous, but he, too, seems to have been an adherent of the judicious assessment; see Dumont, forthcoming. See also van Veldhuijsen 1990*a*: 23: 'there have always been Christian thinkers until the very beginning of the 13th century, albeit only a small minority, who did advocate the idea of an eternally created world. Boethius, for example, Philoponus in his first period, John Scotus Eriugena, some platonists from the 12th century' (end-note references omitted).

So it may look as if this thesis can't count as a denial of the Aristotelian claim that the world must have existed for ever. But since in Book II Aquinas has been arguing at length that the only world there is must be a created world, at this stage of his treatise on creation the thesis of chapter 31 really does count as his denial of Aristotle's claim.

Most people, then and now, think that 'The world was created' entails B, 'The world began to exist'.[15] Consequently, Aquinas's thesis is also likely to look absurdly weak. If having been created does entail having begun to exist, then it's flatly *impossible* that created things have existed for ever; so arguing merely that it's *not necessary* looks like wasted effort.

None the less, Aquinas appears to think that in the context of SCG II it is important to begin by arguing for just that thesis. He opens this chapter by announcing that it is 'on the basis of things that have already been established' in his own account of creation up to and including chapter 30 that 'it remains to be shown that it is not necessary that created things have existed from eternity' (31.1080). Those introductory remarks suggest that he thinks that what he's said about creation so far might very well have led someone to think that it *is* necessary that created things have existed for ever. Could anyone be excused for thinking so on that basis?

As evidence that someone might be, consider the following facts. Aquinas has long since argued that God, the creator, exists beginninglessly (I.15.122). He has also argued, more recently, that the creator is omnipotent, capable of bringing about anything that does not involve a contradiction (II.22), and it is already pretty clear that he does not share the common view that having been created entails having begun to exist. We have seen him arguing

---

[15] Bonaventure is prominent among such people. He treats the alleged incompatibility between 'created' and 'beginningless' as the corner-stone of his opposition to the possibility of beginningless creation. He makes this declaration: that God created the world 'from eternity . . . I believe to be absolutely impossible, since it entails a contradiction. For from the fact that the world is taken to be made, it is taken to have a beginning (*principium*); but from the fact that it is taken to be eternal, it is taken not to have a beginning' (*In Sent.* I.44.1.4c). Moreover, 'to claim that the world is eternal, or eternally produced, on the basis of claiming that all things have been produced out of nothing is altogether against truth and reason. And it is *so* contrary to reason that I don't believe that any philosopher, no matter how puny his intellect, has supposed it, since it entails a manifest contradiction' (*In Sent.* II.1.1.1.2.6c).

that creation is neither movement nor change (II.17), 'but, rather, the very dependence of created being on the source by which it is established' (18.952). And, as he expressly says later in this discussion, only agents that produce their effects through movement must temporally precede their effects (38.1143). So, as he puts it elsewhere, 'having been made and existing for ever are *not* incompatible considered in themselves' (QDP 3.14, ad 8). He has thus already suggested in SCG that the *essential* relation of the created world to the omnipotent, beginningless creator is that of total existential dependence, not that of having been brought into existence for the first time, even if the created world was in fact brought into existence for the first time a finite number of years ago. On this basis alone, then, it seems clear that in Aquinas's view it is not impossible—though of course it is in fact false—that the world, the *created* world, has existed for ever in total, beginningless existential dependence on omnipotent God.[16] So here, in chapter 31, Aquinas begins this one of his many contributions to the medieval debate by suggesting what a reader of SCG might already have inferred: that he does not see a *beginningless* existence of *created* things as impossible.[17] For just that reason it is especially important for him to open this discussion by expressly denying that his account of creation so far commits him, further, to the *necessity* of a beginningless existence for the created world.

And we need not describe his position only in guarded negatives. That he sees the beginningless existence of created things as possible is entailed by his claim that a *per accidens* infinite regress of generative causes is not impossible.[18] If, as he argues in that connection, 'it is not impossible that a man be begotten by a man *ad*

---

[16] See Ch. Three above, sect. 6.

[17] See also I.43.368: 'But this argument [for the infinity of God's power (discussed in TMOT, Ch. Five, sect. 10)] works as a proof of the infinity of divine power even for those who posit the eternity of the world. They say that eternal God is the cause of the sempiternal world as a foot would from eternity have been the cause of a footprint if from eternity it had been pressed into some dust. Once that assumption has been made, it none the less follows according to the argument we are discussing that God's power is infinite. For whether he produced in time (*ex tempore*) (according to us) or from eternity (according to them), there can be nothing in reality that he did not produce, since he is the universal source of being.' As a Christian, he of course rejects as false the beginningless-world hypothesis put forward by 'them' (certain Platonists, including Porphyry; see van Veldhuijsen 1990a: 21). Still, in this passage he treats it as an alternative possibility. See also QDP 3.14, obj. 7 and ad 7; DSS 9.99–100.

[18] For an important use he makes of this claim, see Ch. Two above, sect. 8.

infinitum', then it is not impossible that created things have existed for ever.[19] And if it is neither impossible nor necessary that created things have existed for ever, then a beginningless created world is possible.

Before looking at any details of chapter 31, it will be helpful to get an overview of the structure of the discussion as Aquinas develops it through the series of eight chapters beginning with II.31. In that chapter he argues, on the basis of what he's already established, against the necessity of 'Created things have existed for ever'. There is no explicit corresponding argument anywhere in these eight chapters against the impossibility of that proposition, just Aquinas's refutations (in II.38) of arguments which he has come across that have been designed to prove its impossibility. Such an approach is what should be expected dialectically, since the claim that the proposition is impossible is just an overly strong version of the claim that it is false, which, as we've seen, Aquinas accepts on Scriptural and doctrinal authority (and, as we'll see,[20] also as the conclusion of a probable—less than demonstrative—argument). On the other hand, the claim that it is necessary is of course incompatible with his position, so must be refuted explicitly.

[19] See esp. In Sent. II.1.1.5, sc 5: 'If the world has existed from eternity, then generation, too, has occurred from eternity, of human beings as well as of animals. But all generation involves what generates and what is generated, and what generates is the efficient cause of what is generated. And so one must go back *ad infinitum* as regards efficient causes, which is impossible (as is proved in *Metaphysics* II [2, 994a1–8]). Therefore, it is impossible that there have been generation always—and the world, too.' Aquinas's rejoinder (ad sc 5): 'It is impossible that one and the same effect be preceded by infinitely many causes *per se*, or essentially. Accidentally, however, it is possible. That is to say, it is impossible that there be an effect whose defining characteristic it is to proceed from infinitely many causes. However, as regards causes the multiplication of which makes no difference to the effect, there can be infinitely many of them for the effect. For example, several *per se* moving causes are required for the existence of a knife—such as a smith and a tool—and it is impossible that these be infinitely many, because it would follow that there would be infinitely many things in actuality at once. But it is *per accidens* that a knife made by an old smith who has many times gone through new tools comes after a successive multitude of tools. And nothing prevents there being *infinitely* many tools preceding this knife, if the smith were to exist from eternity. It is like this as regards the generation of animals, too . . . And in that same way infinitely many days can have preceded this day, since, according to them, the substance of the sun is from eternity and each rotation of it is finite. (And the Commentator introduces this argument in [commenting on] *Physics* VIII.)' For all the In Sent. passages cited in this chapter see Baldner and Carroll 1997. See also ST Ia.46.2, ad 7.

[20] In sects. 4 and 8 below.

In chapters 32–4 Aquinas presents three sets of arguments whereby 'many people' have intended to prove not-B, and in the corresponding chapters 35–7 he offers three sets of rejoinders to all those arguments: 'However, because many people have taken the position that the world has existed for ever and of necessity, and have tried to demonstrate it, we still have to present their arguments in order to show that they do *not* of necessity support the conclusion of the world's sempiternity' (32.1086). So chapters 35–7 are devoted to showing that not-B has not been proved, despite all the arguments supporting it in chapters 32–4. Finally, chapter 38 is devoted to setting aside arguments designed 'to *prove* that the world has *not* existed for ever' (38.1135), and to showing thereby that not-B has not been philosophically disproved any more than it has been proved.[21]

3. The created world need not have existed for ever

In chapter 31 Aquinas offers five arguments to show that the created world need not have existed for ever. The first four of them depend explicitly on his having already established that (as he puts it in the second argument) 'God brings created things into existence not in virtue of the necessity of [his] nature but in virtue of [his] volition (as has been proved [in II.23]); nor is it of necessity that he wills that created things exist (as was shown in Book I [ch. 81])' (31.1082).[22] I'll draw on those four arguments in order to present an overview of his main line in support of the chapter's thesis.

Since what is at issue here is the necessity of the *created* world's beginninglessness, it's clear that no such necessity could be inherent in the nature of that world itself. As created, it is utterly dependent for its existing *at all*, and 'it is impossible that what does not have *existence* by reason of itself have *necessity* of existence by reason of itself' (1081b).

Well, then, could a created thing's existence be necessarily beginningless as a consequence of its being absolutely necessary in

---

[21] As Eleonore Stump pointed out to me, chs. 31–8 have the look of a disputed question in an unusual arrangement: objections, 32–4; *sed contras*, 38.1135–41; reply, 31; rejoinders to objections, 35–7; rejoinders to *sed contras*, 38.1142–8.

[22] See Ch. Four above, sect. 6.

one of the ways that Aquinas has just finished laying out for created things? In 29.1061 and throughout chapter 30 he argued for 'absolute necessity' within creation on the basis of each of the four causes.[23] Any created thing's material and formal causes, its essential principles, clearly do give rise to a kind of absolute necessity. For instance, it is absolutely necessary that any human being be constituted of flesh and bone as its matter and an intellective soul as its form: 'a thing cannot be without its essential principles, which are matter and form, and so whatever belongs to a thing because of its essential principles must have absolute necessity in all cases' (30.1070). However, it couldn't be on the basis of its matter and form, its *intrinsic* causes, that a created thing might have necessarily beginningless existence, 'because whatever is understood as *intrinsic* to a *created* thing has being from something else' (1081c). That's what it *is* to be a created thing. And, as Aquinas has just argued, what does not have *existence* by reason of itself cannot have *necessity* of existence by reason of itself. So the only remaining bases on which it might be thought necessary that a created thing have existed for ever are its two *extrinsic* causal relations, efficient and final causation.

According to Aquinas, the efficient cause of a created thing is God's unnecessitated volition. And so 'it is not necessary that God will that a created thing have existed for ever, since it is not even necessary that God will that a created thing exist at all (as was shown in Book I [ch. 81][24])' (31.1083). Plainer reasoning is hard to find, but, as I've said more than once, I think that by Aquinas's own lights it *is* necessary that God will that a created thing exist. God's willing the external manifestation of his goodness is an intrinsic, essential aspect of his goodness, not a contingent effect of it. Consequently, I can't accept this bit of plain reasoning. Perhaps the basis on which I reject its premiss can be illuminated against the background of what Aquinas says here about the notion that a beginningless existence of created things might somehow be necessitated by *final* causation. The only way in which created things could conceivably acquire necessity in this way is as things whose beginningless existence makes some sort of indispensable, extrinsic contribution to the end that motivates God's volition to create. But

---

[23] See Ch. Four above, sect. 9.   [24] See also II.27.

things that are directed toward an end do not acquire necessity from the end except in so far as the end either cannot be [at all] without them (e.g. the preservation of life without food) or cannot be as good [without them] (e.g. a journey without a horse). Now the end for the divine volition from which things have come into being cannot be anything other than God's own goodness (as was shown in Book I [chs. 74–84]). God's goodness, of course, does not depend on created things, whether for being, since it is necessary being *per se* (*per se necesse esse*), or for being as good as it can be (*quantum ad bene esse*), since it is absolutely perfect in itself. (1081e)[25]

This unimpeachable conclusion rules out the possibility that God's necessary, perfect goodness depends on anything extrinsic to it for being at all or for being perfect. But, as I see it, in the light of the Dionysian principle, externally manifesting goodness is to being good as heating is to being hot. Neither involves dependence on anything extrinsic.

I can bring out my objection a little more fully in a form directly relevant to Aquinas's aims in chapter 31 by considering its fourth argument, which I'll call the 'sempiternity argument': 'Nothing proceeds necessarily from a volitional agent except by reason of some obligation (*debitum*). But God produces a created thing out of no obligation, if the universal production of a created thing is considered absolutely (as was shown above [in II.28]).[26] Therefore, it is not out of necessity that God produces a created thing. Neither, therefore, is it necessary, if God is sempiternal, that he has produced a created thing from eternity' (31.1084).

The conclusion of this sempiternity argument is oddly worded. What is meant by 'if God is sempiternal (*si Deus sempiternus est*)'? Strictly speaking, sempiternal existence is beginningless and endless temporal existence, not 'the complete possession all at once of illimitable life' that Aquinas takes God's atemporal mode of existence to be.[27] None the less, even in the chapter of Book I that he devotes to showing that 'God is eternal' (I.15), Aquinas sometimes uses 'eternal' where only 'sempiternal' (beginningless and endless) is really justified (15.121 and 123), and in 15.125 God is not called

---

[25] These very strong claims about God's goodness, that it is *per se necesse esse* and *secundum se perfecta simpliciter*—claims that Aquinas ordinarily makes only about God himself—must of course be read in the light of God's absolute simplicity, according to which God *is* goodness itself.

[26] See Ch. Four above, sect. 8.

[27] See n. 3 above; also e.g. ST Ia.10.

eternal at all, but only sempiternal.[28] In the context of the sempiternity argument, it is appropriate and justifiable to read 'God is sempiternal' as 'God exists beginninglessly and endlessly'. And since Aquinas sees that this claim is implicit in the thesis that God's mode of existence is 'the complete possession all at once of *illimitable* life', I think we can and should take 'God exists beginninglessly (and endlessly)' as an established premiss of the sempiternity argument.

But then why does he say '*if* God is sempiternal'? Latin (like English) allows the use of *si* ('if') to introduce clauses expressing a known fact; still, I think it's quite possible that the *si* here is a slip for *etsi* ('although').[29] In any case, I think the point of this oddly worded conclusion is plain: God's (necessarily) existing beginninglessly does not necessitate his having created beginninglessly.

The argument supports that conclusion on the basis of the premisses that God's creating is (a) volitional and (b) unnecessitated, which, Aquinas says, have already been established. Premiss (a) is implicit, and premiss (b) is spelled out in the first two sentences of the sempiternity argument: 'Nothing proceeds necessarily from a volitional agent except by reason of some obligation. But God produces a created thing out of no obligation, if the universal production of a created thing is considered absolutely (as was shown above [in II.28]).'

However, from the position I've already argued for,[30] it follows that Aquinas has provided good support for (a), but not for (b), since God's perfect goodness does metaphysically necessitate God's productivity. And, as we've seen, Aquinas does sometimes present metaphysical (absolute) necessity in terms of indebtedness or obligation, as when he identifies an obligation to X that derives from the very nature of X—'an obligation (*debitum*) deriving from the circumstances of [a thing's] nature': 'for instance, if we say that it is owed to a human being that it have reason and the other things that pertain to human nature' (ST IaIIae.111.1, ad 2). It is in *this* way, I think, that it *is* owed to God's perfect goodness that it

[28] The use of 'sempiternal' in its strict sense is appropriate for that argument. Only in 15.122 is there an argument explicitly and unmistakably for God's atemporality: 'He is, therefore, beginningless and endless, possessing the totality of his being all at once—which is what the defining characteristic of eternity consists in.' See also n. 3 above and TMOT, Ch. Three, sect. 5.

[29] The Leonine edn. lists no variants here.

[30] In Ch. Four above, sect. 8.

have productivity and the other things that pertain to the nature of goodness. For, as I've said before, according to the Dionysian principle (which Aquinas himself often appeals to in other contexts), goodness is *by its very nature* diffusive of itself and (thereby) of being. So, in just that way, it is owed to perfect goodness—an aspect of God himself—that it (or God himself) be productive of goodness and being. Since perfect goodness is an aspect of God's essence, and since self-diffusiveness is essential to goodness, it seems clear that God's willing the bringing of things into existence *is* necessitated—not morally, but metaphysically.

Since the other three of the first four arguments of chapter 31 also depend explicitly on Aquinas's denial that God's volition to create is in any way necessitated,[31] I don't find any of those arguments offering convincing support for the chapter's thesis: that it is not necessary that created things have existed for ever. I want, therefore, to consider the fifth and last of the chapter's arguments, the only one that does not explicitly invoke God's unnecessitated volition. I'll call it the necessity argument.

It was shown above [in II.29.1061 and II.30] that absolute necessity in connection with created things results not from their ordered relation to the first source, which is necessary being *per se*—God—but from their ordered relation to other causes, which are not necessary being *per se*. But the necessity of an ordered relation to that which is not   5
necessary being *per se* does not compel anything to have existed for ever. For this follows: if something is running, it is moving; none the less, it is not necessary that it have been moving for ever, since that it is running is not necessary *per se*. Therefore, nothing requires created things to have existed for ever. (31.1085)   10

The only sort of things about which it makes sense to suppose that their having existed *for ever* might be necessary is the sort of things whose existing *at all* is absolutely necessary. In the chapters immediately preceding this one Aquinas has argued that many things, events, or states of affairs in creation do exist, occur, or obtain with absolute necessity. This absolute necessity in creation can't result directly from the causal relationship of created things

---

[31] First argument: 'God does not act out of any necessity to produce created things' (1081*d*); second: 'Nor is it of necessity that he wills that created things exist' (1082); third: 'it is not even necessary that God will that a created thing exist at all' (1083).

to God's unnecessitated volition. As we've seen Aquinas observing, 'ordinarily, an effect that proceeds from its cause without necessity is contingent' (30.1063*a*). None the less, 'the fact that God is said to have brought things into existence through will, not through necessity, does not rule out his having willed that there be some things that exist necessarily and some that exist contingently. . . . Therefore, nothing prevents some things produced by the divine will from being necessary' (30.1066). The first sentence (lines 1–5) of the necessity argument reviews that result: 'absolute necessity in connection with created things results not from their ordered relation to the first source . . .—God—but from their ordered relation to other [i.e. created] causes'. And, as we've just been seeing, efficient causation is the ordered (causal) relation likely to provide the most relevant sort of absolute necessity: 'when a created thing is already an efficient cause in the propagation of things, there can be an absolute necessity [stemming] from the created efficient cause. For example, terrestrial (*inferiora*) bodies are changed necessarily by the movement of the sun' (29.1061*d*).

However, in his summary account of absolute necessity in nature at the beginning of the necessity argument, Aquinas adds explicitly what would otherwise go without saying. The causal operations of created things, such as 'the movement of the sun', that account for absolute necessity in nature are themselves '*not* necessary being *per se*' (lines 4–5). So he might have developed the necessity argument naturally along this familiar, purely causal line by going on at once to observe (1) that for any thing, event, or state of affairs that is not necessary being *per se*, it is not necessary that it have been for ever; and (2) that for any effect it is necessary that it have been for ever only if it is necessary that its cause have been for ever.

Instead, he widens the focus of the necessity argument beyond causal necessitation of the sorts that are essential to the account of absolute necessity in chapters 29 and 30. The 'ordered relation' at issue here is not just causal, but also logical, necessitation. The crux of Aquinas's argument is his treatment of the example in lines 7–10, which depends on familiar modal distinctions that Aquinas himself laid out earlier in SCG, when he was developing his account of God's atemporal cognition of temporal things by analogy with our present visual experience.

If any thing is cognized by God as presently seen, then what God cognizes
will be necessary in the way it is necessary that Socrates be seated in virtue
of the fact that he is seen to be seated. This, however, is not *absolutely*
necessary—or, as some say, [necessary] with the necessity of the *consequent*—but, rather, [necessary] *under a condition*, or with the necessity of
the *consequence*. For the conditional proposition 'if he is seen to be seated,
he is seated' is necessary. And so if the conditional is transformed into a
categorical proposition, so that one says 'whatever is seen to be seated is
necessarily seated (*quod videtur sedere necesse est sedere*)', that is clearly
true, understood *de dicto* and in the compounded sense [i.e. 'it is necessary
that whatever is seen to be seated is seated']; and it is false understood *de
re* and in the divided sense [i.e. 'regarding whatever is seen to be seated,
it is necessary that it be seated']. (I.67.565)[32]

In the necessity argument the conditional proposition 'if something is running, it is moving' is necessary with the necessity of the
consequence (*necessitas consequentiae*): necessarily, if X is running,
X is moving. But, of course, one cannot validly infer from the
necessity of the consequence the necessity of the consequent
(*necessitas consequentis*): necessarily, if X is running, X is moving;
X is running; therefore, X is moving necessarily. The inference is
fallacious, because the antecedent of the necessary conditional
proposition is itself contingent: 'that it is running is not necessary
per se' (lines 8–9). If X's running *were* necessary *per se*, then X's
running *for ever* would be necessary, and so X's *moving* for ever
would be necessary, too. But, since 'the necessity of an ordered
[*logical*] relation to that which is not necessary being *per se* does not
compel anything to have been for ever' (lines 5–7), *a fortiori* the
same is true regarding an ordered *causal* relation between created
things. And since no created cause is necessary being *per se*, no
absolutely necessitated effect of such a cause need have existed for
ever because of that necessitation. The necessity argument succeeds, but only in ruling out a special account of necessitated
beginninglessness that couldn't be taken very seriously to begin
with, just because it confines its attention to necessitation within
creation, and leaves God's creative volition out of account.

In view of my claiming that beginningless God's perfect goodness necessitates his creating something or other, how can I join
Aquinas in denying that it is necessary that created things have

---

[32] See also II.29.1060–1; also Ch. Four above, sect. 7. For more on the distinction
between the compounded and divided senses, see Kretzmann 1981.

existed beginninglessly? By taking seriously God's atemporality, which entails that all temporal things, events, and states of affairs are present to God's cognition and power timelessly at once— 'cognized by God as presently seen'—whether any of them or the whole world made up of them has existed for ever or began to exist. If any things besides God exist at all, for ever or for only a day, atemporal God isn't alone at all. So I agree with Aquinas: it is not necessary that created things have existed for ever. Given the existence and nature of God as Aquinas has argued for it, it is merely necessary that eternal God's atemporal volition regarding the temporal location and duration of created things be carried out.

Aquinas himself comes very close to saying just that in his treatise *De substantiis separatis* (DSS 10.100):

For even though the origin of created things is without motion [and] from an immovable source, it is not necessary that their existence be sempiternal. For an effect proceeds from any agent in accordance with the agent's mode of being; but the being of [the agent that is] the first source is his intellection and volition. Therefore, the universe of things proceeds from the first source as from an [agent that acts by] intellection and volition. Now it belongs to an [agent that acts by] intellection and volition to produce something not, indeed, necessarily, as [the agent] itself is, but rather as [the agent] engages in volition and also in intellection. But every mode of being and every measure . . . of duration is included within the intellect of the first intellectively active [agent]. Therefore, just as he did not bestow on things the same mode of being with which he exists, . . . so also he gave to things such a measure of duration as he willed, not such as he himself has. Therefore, . . . a determinate measure of duration follows from the first agent's action out of the divine intellect's prescribing it. It is not as if he himself is subject to successive duration, so that now he wills or does something that earlier he willed against, but because the whole duration of things is enclosed under his intellect and power, so that from eternity he determined for things the measure of duration that he wills.[33]

4. Beginninglessness based on considerations of God

As we've seen, Aquinas eventually acknowledged that Aristotle did think that he had proved that the world must have existed for

---

[33] See also e.g. 35.1113–15, rejoinders to three arguments in II.32 purporting 'to prove the eternity of the world on the basis of considerations of God', discussed in sect. 4 just below.

ever. But when Aquinas takes up purported proofs of that sort in order to refute them, the set of arguments he begins with, in chapter 32, have a distinctly un-Aristotelian look about them. All of them are based on attributes of God the creator, and so they are expressly concerned to show only the *created* world's beginninglessness. In one respect this approach is just what is to be expected, however. If Aquinas has accomplished what he set out to accomplish in chapters 1–30, then he has already shown that the world which Aristotle was contemplating is really the world created by the God whose existence and nature have already been argued for in SCG. Accordingly, chapter 32's 'arguments of people who want to prove the eternity of the world on the basis of considerations of God'[34] all rely on aspects of God's nature and activity that Aquinas himself has already argued for.

Aquinas doesn't tell us in chapter 32 itself who those people might have been. However, three of this chapter's arguments have parallels in his earliest investigation of the beginningless world hypothesis (In Sent. II.1.1.5), where he does identify all his sources. The sources named there for arguments corresponding to these three are Avicenna, Averroës, and Aristotle.[35] Of course, he hadn't found in Aristotle an argument for the world's beginninglessness based on considerations of the nature of the creator. The Aristotelian connections he cites are tenuous, consisting in Aristotle's views on the nature of the first mover and his analysis of volitional action.

But in any case, identifying extrinsic sources for chapter 32's seven arguments strikes me as less important than recognizing that all the attributes of God on which these arguments are founded have been established in some form or other in Aquinas's own natural theology as he has developed it to this point. So each of chapter 32's arguments can be viewed as an attempt to show that, despite chapter 31's conclusion to the contrary, Aquinas's own

[34] Of the titles of chs. 31–8, only those of 31, 34, and 35 are Aquinas's own.
[35] The first and second arguments (32.1088 and 1089) parallel In Sent. II.1.1.5, obj. 11, about which Aquinas says: 'this argument can be extracted from the Philosopher's words in *Physics* VIII [1, 251b19–28, a8–28]'. The fourth argument (in 1091) parallels objs. 12–14. Regarding obj. 12 Aquinas says: 'this argument belongs in common to the Philosopher in *Physics* VIII [1, 251a28–b5, 252a5–b6], and to Avicenna [*Metaphysics* IX 1], and to the Commentator [Averroës]'. He describes obj. 13 as 'the Commentator's argument in [commenting on] *Physics* VIII' and obi. 14 as 'the Commentator's argument in the same place'.

account of the creator in SCG so far *can*, after all, be shown to entail that created things *must* have existed for ever. Even if he did find versions of some of these arguments in other authors, his presentation of them here looks like part of an ongoing effort to examine his own system, to make sure that it doesn't support unwanted conclusions. In three of chapter 32's arguments for beginninglessness, the premisses that introduce the relevant considerations of God are expressly identified as having already been supported in SCG.[36] But the four arguments that lack explicit references of this sort are also plainly dependent on considerations of God that Aquinas has already argued for in Books I and II.[37]

Broadly speaking, the first five of these arguments intended to show that God's nature entails that his creation must have been beginningless are founded on considerations of the creator's absolute simplicity, immovability, and eternality. Since creating is an act of God's will, and since an absolutely simple, immovable, eternal creator could not have *begun* to will the existence of other things, could not will it after not willing it, the world could not have begun to exist, but must have existed for ever.[38]

Aquinas's rejoinders to these arguments (in chapter 35) quite rightly draw a distinction that applies to ordinary human willing as well as to God's creative volition, the distinction between (a) beginning to will at time *t* that certain things begin to exist then, and (b) changelessly willing that they begin to exist at *t*.[39] For instance,

---

[36] First argument (1088): 'God is moved neither *per se* nor *per accidens*, as was proved in Book I [ch. 13]'; fourth argument (1091): 'nothing other than God himself is uncreated, as was shown above [in II.15]'; fifth argument (1092): 'besides the whole universe of created things there is nothing but God's eternity . . . the whole of which is uniform and simple, as was shown in Book I [ch. 15]'.

[37] Second argument (1089): 'Otherwise God would become an agent in actuality from being an agent in potentiality, and he would have to be brought to actuality by some prior agent, which is impossible' (see e.g. I.16); third argument (1090): 'Otherwise God would not *be* the cause but would rather be in a state of potentiality for being the cause . . .—which is plainly impossible' (see e.g. I.16); sixth argument (1093): 'Now the end for created things that proceed from the divine will is the divine goodness, which alone can be the end of the divine will' (see e.g. II.29); seventh argument (1094): 'Now divine goodness is infinite' (see e.g. I.37–41).

[38] See also, for the first (1088), In Sent. II.1.1.5, obj. 11; QDP 3.17, objs. 6, 12, 26; ST Ia.46.1, obj. 6; for the second (1089), In Sent. II.1.1.5, obj. 11; QDP 3.17, objs. 12, 26; ST Ia.46.1, objs. 6, 10; for the third (1090), QDP 3.17, obj. 4; ST Ia.46.1, obj. 9; for the fourth (1091), In Sent. II.1.1.5, objs. 12(?), 13(?), 14; CT I.98; QDP 3.17, objs. 9, 13; ST Ia.46, obj. 6; for the fifth (1092), CT I.98.

[39] e.g. in ordinary human terms, (a) deciding now to turn on the light now; (b) having the alarm clock always set so that it rings at 6.

'nothing prevents our saying that God's acting [volitionally as the creator] has been from eternity, even though the effect has existed not from eternity, but rather *then*—[viz.] when God has from eternity arranged [that it begin to exist]' (35.1113); 'in order for a volition to be a sufficient cause, the effect need not be when the volition is, but rather when the volition has arranged for the effect to be' (1114); 'what is willed—that a created thing exist at a certain time—is not delayed, for the created thing began to exist *then*—[viz.] when God has from eternity arranged [that it begin to exist]' (1115). Those first five arguments for the created world's beginninglessness strike me as exposing one or another more or less natural misunderstandings of Aquinas's account of God in SCG, especially as regards God's eternal willing. His rejoinders to them are all aimed, naturally, at clearing up the misunderstandings; and they achieve that aim.[40]

None the less, one issue raised by those arguments, taken singly or together, remains unresolved in Aquinas's rejoinders to them. The fifth argument and its rejoinder bring out the issue most clearly. Suppose that the world did begin to exist. In that case, its beginning must have occurred some definite number of years ago— n, let's call it. But why should God have created the world n years ago rather than earlier or later? That altogether natural question motivates the fifth argument, which I'll call the 'why-then? argument'. It begins by pointing out that 'an intellective agent' such as God the creator 'chooses one thing over another only because of the one's being better than the other. But where there is no difference, there can be no being better.' Now what in God's view could make n years ago better for creating the universe than $n - x$ or $n + x$? God's view is eternal, and there can't be any difference at all *within* 'eternity, the whole of which is uniform and simple (as was shown in Book I [ch. 15])'. That is, God's causing the world to begin to exist n years ago couldn't be a consequence of his having then finally made up his mind to create. So God's choice of n must be motivated by his eternal recognition of some respect in which n is better for the beginning than $n - x$ or $n + x$. But all three of those

---

[40] For parallels to Aquinas's rejoinders to the first five arguments in II.32, see his rejoinders to the parallel arguments listed in n. 38 above. (Since the same information applies, *mutatis mutandis*, regarding parallels to his rejoinders generally in these chapters, I won't repeat it in the remainder of Ch. Five.) For some discussion of the eternal willing of temporally definite events, see Stump and Kretzmann 1981.

possible beginnings would, it seems, have to be moments in empty time, and 'no differences of moments can be assigned in connection with *nothing*, in the sense that something must come to be at one of those moments rather than another'. This absence of relevant differences in empty time means that God's volition to create at n could no more have been motivated by n's being better than $n - x$ and $n + x$ than by some (inconceivable) change in eternity. 'Therefore, we are left with the conclusion that throughout all eternity God's will is equally disposed to producing created things. Therefore, it is his will either [1] that a created thing should *never* or [2] that a created thing should *for ever* be established under his eternity.' Since [1] is obviously not the case, 'we are, it seems, left necessarily with the conclusion that [2] a created thing has existed for ever' (32.1092).

Aquinas's rejoinder to this why-then? argument (35.1116) is marked by a good deal of agreement with its premises. He accepts the argument's account of an intellective agent's basis for choosing among alternatives, and he of course endorses its account of eternity: 'God's duration, which is eternity, has no parts but is altogether simple, having neither before nor after, since God is immovable (as was shown in Book I [ch. 13]).' Moreover, he seems to accept the argument's dismissal of the possibility of relevant differences among moments of empty time: 'no distinctness of parts in any duration prior to the beginning of the whole of creation (*totius creaturae*) is to be admitted'. But in that apparent acceptance he is really rejecting the argument's assumption regarding empty time as a locus of possible differences, because he finds a vitiating confusion in the very notion of time 'prior to the beginning of the whole of creation': 'for *nothingness* has *no* measure or duration'. Empty *time* before n is inconceivable, because 'God brought into being both the created thing and time at once'. Time is the measure and duration of motion, and motion is a feature of created things only.[41] 'Therefore, the beginning of the whole of creation is not to be associated with any distinct designated dividers (*aliqua diversa signata*) in any pre-existing measure, . . . in such a way that there must be a reason in the agent why he brought a created thing

---

[41] See e.g. 33.1101: 'time is the measure of motion [*Physics* IV 11, 219b1]'; and 1102: 'time is an accidental characteristic, and there cannot be an accidental characteristic without a subject. Its subject is not God, however, since he is altogether immovable.' This second passage is quoted more fully in sect. 5 below.

into being at *this* designated divider of that duration and not at another one, earlier or later. (Such a reason *would* of course be required if there were *in addition to* the totality of what is created a duration divisible into parts—as happens in connection with particular agents that produce an effect in time, but not time itself.)'

Aquinas's implicit answer to the question underlying the why-then? argument is simply that there is no *then* about which to ask the question. But in offering that answer he expressly raises another question, which he leaves unanswered: 'as regards the production of the whole of creation, outside of which there is no time and together with which time is produced at once, we do not have to concern ourselves with the reason why [it is done] *then* and not before, with the result that we are led to grant an infinity of time. Instead, [we need ask] only *why not for ever?*' A proponent of the why-then? argument might well be encouraged by this rejoinder to bring the challenge in his argument down to Aquinas's own remaining question: All right, why not for ever?

Aquinas's earlier rejoinders to the second, third, and fourth arguments have some bearing on an answer to that question. In them, as we've already seen, he explains more than once, in slightly different ways, that there is no inconsistency in supposing that eternal God's beginningless, changeless volition to create includes his willing that the world begin to exist n years before you read this sentence. So God's eternal, unchanging volition to create does not provide a basis on which to argue cogently that the world must have existed for ever. That's right. But we are still entitled to ask, and Aquinas himself encourages us to ask, what could have motivated the creator to will that the world *begin* to exist—regardless of when—*rather than* exist for ever?

The most promising place to look for his answer to this question with regard to the present set of arguments is in his treatment of the last two of them, the sixth and seventh—and not only because they're the only ones left. To begin with, they have to do with God's goodness, which Aquinas has already established as the only conceivable motivation for God's creative action.[42] Even more pertinently, he opens his rejoinder to the first of these two arguments for beginninglessness based on God's goodness by describing that

---

[42] See e.g. 29.1053b, discussed in Ch. Four above, sect. 8.

argument as having been introduced 'in order to inquire into this'—i.e. in order to seek an answer to the question with which he ended the immediately preceding rejoinder, 'Why not for ever?'

The gist of the sixth argument is the presentation of considerations that are by now familiar: 'things that are directed toward an end have necessity from the end, and especially in connection with those that are done volitionally. Therefore, as long as the end is the same way, the things directed toward the end must be, or be produced, in the same way ... Now the end of created things that proceed from the divine will is the divine goodness ... Therefore, since in all eternity the divine goodness is the same way in itself and in relation to the divine will, it is evident that created things are produced by the divine will in the same way in all eternity' (32.1093).[43]

Aquinas's rejoinder also strikes a familiar note. God's goodness motivates him to create only 'in so far as he produces the effect for [its] participation in the end. Therefore, in connection with producing things for the sake of the end in this way, the uniform relation of the end to the agent is not to be considered a reason for a sempiternal product. Instead, we should pay attention to the relation of the end to the effect that is brought about on account of the end in order that the effect may be produced in such a way as to be more appropriately directed (*ordinetur*) toward the end' (35.1117). In other words, considerations of God's motivating goodness will lead to an answer to the question 'Why not for ever?' only if we can identify some way in which God's goodness may in some respect be manifested better in his causing the world to begin to exist than in his supporting its existence beginninglessly.

That's not an implausible line to take, but Aquinas takes it no further in his rejoinder to the sixth argument, reserving the end of the story for his rejoinder to the seventh and last argument, which draws on what he regards as an over-interpretation of the Dionysian principle.

Since divine goodness is absolutely perfect, when we say that all things have proceeded from God because of his goodness, we do not mean that anything was added to him from created things. Instead, we mean that [this comes about] because it belongs to goodness to share itself as much as

---

[43] I haven't identified a parallel to this sixth argument elsewhere in Aquinas's writings.

possible (*prout possibile est*), in which [sharing] goodness itself is manifested. Now since all things participate in God's goodness in so far as they
have being, the longer-lasting they are, the more they participate in God's
goodness. . . . But the divine goodness is infinite. Therefore, it belongs to
the divine goodness to share itself *ad infinitum*, not merely for some
determinate time. Therefore, it evidently pertains to the divine goodness
that some created things have existed from eternity. (32.1094)[44]

Aquinas in his rejoinder to that argument (35.1118) leaves the
Dionysian principle itself unchallenged, and concentrates on cir-
cumventing the argument's over-interpretation of it by identifying
a way in which God, and especially God's perfect goodness, would
be manifested better, more accurately, in a world that began to
exist than in a beginningless world. The world, he says, 'is *more*
appropriately directed to the end [of manifesting God's goodness]
in virtue of *not* having existed for ever'. The purpose of creation
is 'for the divine will to produce a created thing for participation
in God's own goodness in such a way that it would represent the
divine goodness by its likeness. Now there cannot be *that* sort of
representation by way of *equality*, in the way a univocal effect
represents its cause.'[45] If there could be, then someone might suppose that the world's beginninglessness would be required as representing one aspect of that equality, 'so that in this way eternal
effects would have to be produced by infinite goodness'. Instead,
the representation that there is in creation, the most faithful representation possible in the circumstances, is one in which 'the tran-
scendent is represented by that which is transcended. Now the
transcendence of a created thing by the divine goodness is expressed especially well by the created thing's *not* having existed for
ever. For from that circumstance it is plainly apparent [1] that all
things besides God have him as the author of their being, and [2]
that his power is not bound to produce effects of that sort (as
nature is bound to produce natural effects), and, consequently, [3]
that he is a volitional and intellective agent.' Of course, (1)–(3)
would no less *be the case* if the world had existed for ever. God's
goodness is specially manifested in his bringing the world into
existence n years ago, just because in that way (1)–(3) are made
'*plainly apparent*' to such creatures as can reason from phenomena

---

[44] See also QDP 3.17, objs. 1, 7, 8, 14.

[45] Biological reproduction is a paradigm of univocal causation, on which see
TMOT, Ch. Five, sect. 5; also Ch. Ten below, sects. 2–6.

to their causes. And, of course, Aquinas definitely does not intend his argument for the greater goodness of a temporally finite world as a proof that the created world could not have existed for ever, but only as a way of showing that the world would 'more appropriately' manifest its creator and his goodness 'in virtue of not having existed for ever'.[46] I think he achieves just what he intends to achieve here.

5. Beginninglessness based on considerations of created things

Aquinas's second set of purported proofs that the world must have existed for ever, presented in chapter 33, consists of 'arguments of people who want to prove the eternity of the world on the basis of considerations of created things'. As Aquinas presents them, then, these arguments, too, are supporting the beginninglessness of the *created* world. But since Aristotle's arguments for beginninglessness are based on considerations of natural things, and since natural things can be considered without being recognized as created things, Aristotle's arguments are more likely to be found in this set of seven than among those based on considerations of God. And in his earlier discussion of arguments like these Aquinas does attribute five of them to Aristotle.[47] Of the remaining two, one strikes me as negligible.[48] The other, the seventh and last

[46] See also 38.1149, discussed in sect. 8 below. In my presentation of Aquinas's rejoinder here it may seem that either I am or he is treating what seems to be a metaphysical issue regarding manifestation—does X manifest Y better than X' does?—as if it were epistemological. I think that manifestation or representation is a three-place relation, that 'X represents Y' is always short for 'X represents Y to Z', where Z is some interpreter (see Kretzmann 1991*b*). And I think that in this passage and elsewhere Aquinas shows signs of interpreting these relations in that way, too. I develop this point further in Ch. Seven below, sect. 3.

[47] The first argument (33.1097) is paralleled by In Sent. II.1.1.5, objs. 2 and 3, each of which is said to be 'the Philosopher's argument in *De caelo et mundo* I [obj. 2: 3, 270a12–22; obj. 3: 12, 281b18–282a4]'. Just the same is true of the second argument (1098). The third argument (1099) is paralleled by obj. 8—'this is the Philosopher's argument in *Physics* VIII [1, 251b5–10]'—and obj. 9—'this is the Commentator's argument in [commenting on] *Physics* VIII [1, 251b5–10]. The same can also be extracted from the Philosopher's words. The Commentator also introduces this argument in [commenting on] *Metaphysics* VII.' The fifth argument (1101) is paralleled by obj. 5—'this is the Philosopher's argument in *Physics* VIII [1, 251b10–28]'— and obj. 6—'this is the Commentator's argument in [commenting on] the same passage'. The sixth argument, like the fifth, is paralleled by obj. 5.

[48] The fourth argument (33.1100): 'Every agent that generates something like itself intends to preserve in the species the perpetual being that cannot be

of these arguments (33.1103), strikes an Augustinian note: 'Many propositions are such that whoever denies them must presuppose them. For instance, anyone who denies that there is truth presupposes that there is truth; for he presupposes that the negative proposition he utters is true.'[49] And the argument goes on to make the same point regarding the principle of non-contradiction. 'Therefore, if anything the presupposing of which follows from its denial must be for ever (as has been proved [in the sixth argument (1102)[50]]), it follows that the propositions we have been mentioning and all those that follow from them are sempiternal. Now those propositions are not God. Therefore, something besides God must be eternal.'[51] Aquinas's succinct rejoinder (36.1127) to this ingenious but not very formidable argument is decisive: 'the truth of propositions that has to be granted even by someone denying the propositions . . . has the necessity associated with a predicate's ordered relationship to a subject'—i.e. logical necessity. 'For that reason it does not require that any thing exist for ever—except, perhaps, the divine intellect, in which is the basis of all truth (as was shown in Book I [ch. 62]).'

The five remaining arguments, all recognizably Aristotelian, fall into three groups. The first and second arguments depend on considerations of certain natural things that Aristotle (and Aquinas) thought existed without any natural potentiality for non-existence; the third argument depends on considerations of motion; and the fifth and sixth depend on considerations of the nature of time. Because these arguments are all presented here against the background of Aquinas's account of the world as created, his appraisal of them is bound to be different from what it would be if he assessed them in a purely Aristotelian context.[52]

---

perpetually preserved in the individual. But it is impossible that an appetite of nature be to no purpose (*vanum*). Therefore, the species of generable things must be perpetual.' I have found no parallels to this argument elsewhere in Aquinas's writings. It deserves his dismissive rejoinder (36.1124): 'this argument applies only to natural things that have already been brought into existence; it has no relevance to the question of their being brought into existence, however'.

[49] See e.g. *Soliloquies* II.ii.2; also Anselm, *Monologion* 18 and *De veritate* 1.

[50] 'One must either affirm or deny. Therefore, if the presupposing of something follows from the denial of it, then it must be for ever.'

[51] See also QDP 3.17, objs. 27 and 28.

[52] See e.g. In Phys. VIII: L2, where Aquinas defends Aristotle's arguments for the beginninglessness of motion against Averroës's misappropriating them, in order to argue against the possibility of creation *ex nihilo*.

Chapter 33's first and second arguments (1097 and 1098[53]) both point to certain 'created things . . . in which there is no potentiality for non-existence' (1097). In his rejoinders to them (36.1121 and 1122) Aquinas accepts that characterization of heavenly bodies and intellective substances, the examples provided in the two arguments. But the first, stronger argument infers regarding such created things that 'it is impossible that they not exist. Therefore, it is necessary that they exist for ever.'[54] And, as Aquinas points out (1121), that inference is founded on a misunderstanding of the nature of the absolute necessity which he has argued for in created things:[55] 'the necessity of existence that is found among created things . . . is the necessity of an ordered relationship (*necessitas ordinis*) (as was shown in preceding discussions [in II.30]). But the necessity of an ordered relationship does not compel a thing in which such necessity obtains to have existed for ever (as was shown above [in II.31]).' As regards a created thing that is necessary in this way, 'such a necessity does introduce an impossibility of non-existence *once its substance has already been brought into existence. But it does not make it impossible that* [e.g.] the heavens not exist if we take into account the production of its very substance,' since the necessity of existence that characterizes it 'is a consequence of its substance', which depends on creation for existing at all.

Chapter 33's third argument (1099[56]) is a version of what is perhaps Aristotle's strongest, best-known argument for a beginningless world:

[W]henever something begins to be moved for the first time, either the mover, or what is moved, or both must be disposed otherwise now, when the motion is going on, than earlier when there was no motion. . . . However, anything that is disposed differently now and earlier is moved. Therefore, before a motion that begins for the first time there must be some other motion preceding it, either in the thing that can be moved or in the mover. Therefore, every motion either is eternal or has another motion before it. Therefore, there has been motion for ever and,

---

[53] See also, for the first argument (1097), In Sent. II.1.1.5, objs. 2, 3; QDP 3.17, objs. 2, 3; ST Ia.46.1, obj. 2; for the second (1098), In Sent. II.1.1.5, objs. 2, 3; QDP 3.17, obj. 2; ST Ia.46.1, obj. 2.

[54] Regarding heavenly bodies and intellective substances the second, weaker argument (1098) concludes only that 'it is appropriate (*competit*) for them to exist for ever; but whatever begins to exist does not exist for ever. Therefore, it is not appropriate for them to begin to exist.'

[55] See Ch. Four above, sect. 9.

[56] See also In Sent. II.1.1.5, objs. 8, 9; QDP 3.17, obj. 20; ST Ia.46.1, obj. 5.

consequently, things that can be moved. And in that case—since God is altogether immovable (as was shown in Book I [ch. 13])—created things have existed for ever.

However, the strength which this argument has on the assumption of a purely mechanistic cosmos is completely dissipated within the context established by Aquinas's natural theology to this point, as his rejoinder to it (36.1123) easily shows. This third argument 'does not compel us to posit the sempiternality of motion. For it is already clear [from the rejoinders to the arguments based on considerations of God[57]] that without any change in God, the agent, he can do something for the first time, something not sempiternal. But if it is possible that something be done by him for the first time, then it is clear [that it is possible] also that [something] be moved [by him for the first time]; for newness of motion follows from a determination of the eternal will regarding motion's not occurring for ever.'

The two remaining Aristotelian arguments in chapter 33 are based on considerations of the nature of time, so Aquinas might have dismissed them on grounds of having already shown that it is possible—even probable—that the created world began to exist, and that time began with it. But he takes them more seriously than that, basing his rejoinders to them on further considerations of the nature of time. The fifth argument (33.1101):

If time is perpetual, there must be perpetual motion, since time is the measure of motion [*Physics* IV 11, 219b1]. And, consequently, there must be perpetual things that can be moved, since motion is the actualizing of what can be moved [*Physics* III 2, 202a15]. But time *must* be perpetual. For it is inconceivable that there be time without there being a now [i.e. a present instant], just as a line is inconceivable without a point. But a now is always the end of the past and the beginning of the future, for that is the definition of the now [*Physics* IV 13, 222b1]. And so each given now has earlier time before it and later time [after it], and so none of them can be the first or the last. We are, therefore, left with the conclusion that things that can be moved, which are created substances, exist from eternity.[58]

In his rejoinder to this argument (36.1125) Aquinas rejects it because it 'assumes rather than proves the eternity of motion'. He

---

[57] See sect. 4 above.
[58] See also In Sent. II.1.1.5, objs. 5, 6; QDP 3.17, objs. 15–18, 24, 25; ST Ia.46.1, obj. 7.

whole-heartedly subscribes to the argument's Aristotelian account of time in terms of motion: 'the before and after of time and its continuity follow the before and after of motion and its continuity, as Aristotle teaches [*Physics* IV 11, 219a12–13, 17–19]'. And on that basis he accepts some of what the argument claims regarding 'the now': 'it is clear that the same instant is both the beginning of the future and the end of the past, because any designated divider in a motion is both the beginning and the end of different parts of the motion'. The single instant of noon is both the end of a.m. and the beginning of p.m. just because it (theoretically) marks both the end of the sun's movement across the eastern half of the sky and the beginning of its movement across the western half. But, must *every* instant of time be both the beginning of the future and the end of the past? Not 'unless every divider in *time* is taken as midway between a before and after in *motion*'. But to suppose that this is the case 'is to *assume* semipiternal motion'. So 'anyone who', like Aquinas, 'supposes that motion is *not* semipiternal can say that the first instant of time'—i.e. the very first instant of motion—'is the beginning of the future and the end of no past'.

The sixth argument (33.1102) might be viewed as a second, slighter attempt to prove the fifth argument's claim that 'time must be perpetual':

[I]f there has not been time for ever, we have to acknowledge its not-being before its being . . . But there can be *before* . . . in terms of duration only if there is time, for time is the measure of before and after [*Physics* IV 11, 202a25]. And in that case there will have to have been time before it began . . . Time, therefore, must be eternal. But time is an accidental characteristic, and there cannot be an accidental characteristic without a subject. Its subject is not God, however, since he is altogether immovable (as was proved in Book I [ch. 13]). Therefore, we are left with the conclusion that some created substance is eternal.[59]

We find it convenient, perhaps indispensable, to use ordinary temporal and spatial terms on the rare occasions when we talk about the limits of time and space. And the trouble with this argument, Aquinas observes (36.1126), is that it takes that convenient way of speaking as the basis for an inference about the nature of reality:

---

[59] See also In Sent. II.1.1.5, obj. 5; QDP 3.17, obj. 20; ST Ia.46.1, obj. 7.

[T]he 'before' that we use in saying 'before time was' does not presuppose a part of time in reality, but only in imagination. For when we say that time has being after not-being, we mean that there was *no* part of time before that designated [first] now. Analogously, when we say that there is nothing above the heavens, we don't mean that there is some place [where nothing is] that can be said to be higher relative to the heavens, but that there is *no* place higher than it. In either case the imagination can apply some measure to the existent reality. And just as its doing so [in the case of the heavens] is no reason for supposing infinite quantity in a body (as is said in *Physics* III [6, 206b24–5]), so neither is it any reason for supposing time to be eternal.

Aquinas has already made this sort of observation in developing his account of creation.[60] For although creation *ex nihilo* cannot involve movement or change 'strictly speaking' (as he argued in chs. 16 and 17), he acknowledges that 'from a purely conceptual standpoint creation does *seem* to be some sort of change—I mean, in so far as our intellect takes one and the same thing as first not existing and afterwards existing' (18.953).

6. Beginninglessness based on considerations of the making of things

In presenting his third and last set of purported proofs that the created world must have existed for ever, 'arguments drawn from the *making* of things', Aquinas seems primarily to be concerned with reviewing reasons he has already developed for denying that creating is to be construed as a kind of making at all, and warning against the kinds of misleading inferences that construing it in that way can give rise to.

The first and most formidable of these four arguments based on the nature of making (34.1106) draws on what I've labelled the ENNF principle,[61] 'the view common to all philosophers, that nothing is made out of nothing (*ex nihilo nihil fieri*)', and concludes on that basis that 'that out of which all things were made at first must be sempiternal. But that is not God, because he cannot be the matter of any thing (as was proved in Book I [ch. 17]). We are, therefore, left with the conclusion that something outside God is

---

[60] See Ch. Three above, sect. 6.   [61] See Ch. Three above, sect. 5.

eternal—viz. prime matter.'[62] But, as Aquinas has already observed in showing just how and why ENNF cannot be applied to creation, the ancient philosophers who formulated it 'had not yet arrived at a cognition of the *universal* agent, which is productive of the *whole* of being, [the agent] for whose action it is necessary to presuppose *nothing*' (16.945). As for prime matter's claim to be the sempiternal world stuff, Aquinas has already argued convincingly against it.[63]

His rejoinder to this first argument (37.1130) is elaborate, because it includes his (creditable) synopsis of the development of ancient philosophical accounts of making, both particular and universal. But in this context its most important feature is his reiterated claim that creating really is *not* a kind of making, even though 'we do, all the same, figuratively apply the word "making" to that originating, under a sort of likeness' (1130*f*). It isn't really making, because '"making" implies movement or change, but one cannot interpret this originating of the whole of being from a single first being as the transformation of one being into another (as has been shown [in II.17])' (1130*e*). Again, 'in this procession of all being from God it is not possible that anything be made out of something else antecedent to it; for that would not be the "making" of the *whole* of created being' (1130*d*).

The second of the four arguments which Aquinas presents in chapter 34 relies on that same appearance of change I remarked on at the end of section 5 above, an appearance that is hard to dispel from any hypothesis of the world's having begun to exist (34.1107):

But nothing that begins to exist for the first time is disposed in the same way now [when it begins to exist] and before. Therefore, that must happen through some movement or change. But every movement or change is in some subject . . . Now since a movement is prior to whatever is made through the movement (for the movement terminates in that), some subject that can be moved must exist *before* anything that is made. And since it is not possible to go on *ad infinitum* in this way, one must arrive at some first subject that does not begin [to exist] for the first time but is existent for ever.[64]

---

[62] See also In Sent. II.1.1.5, obj. 1 (which Aquinas identifies as 'Aristotle's argument in *Physics* I [9, 192a25–34]'); CT I.99 (first argument); ST Ia.46.1, obj. 1.

[63] In the PM argument (16.943), discussed in Ch. Three above, sect. 3.

[64] See also In Sent. II.1.1.5, obj. 8 (which Aquinas describes as 'the Philosopher's argument in *Physics* VIII [1, 251b5–10]'); CT I.99 (first argument).

Aquinas's rejoinder (37.1131) picks up on his earlier observation, argued at length in II.17, that 'creation cannot be called change except metaphorically, in so far as what is created is considered as having existence after non-existence'. He then summarily dismisses this line of argument: 'Since what does not exist in any way is not in *any* state', nothing in the argument 'enables one to conclude that [what has not been in existence] is in *different* states now, when it begins to exist, and before'.

The third argument (34.1108) attempts to argue for beginninglessness on the basis of an Aristotelian application of the notion of passive potentiality: 'As regards everything that begins to exist for the first time, before it existed it was possible that it exist. ... But anything of which it is possible that it exist is a subject that is potentially a being [cf. *Metaphysics* VII 2]. Therefore, before anything that begins to exist for the first time, there must pre-exist a subject that is potentially a being. And since one cannot go on *ad infinitum* in this way, one must posit some first subject that did not begin to exist for the first time', but existed beginninglessly.[65]

This is another case of treating creation as if it involved movement and change. For, as Aquinas points out in his rejoinder (37.1132), antecedent passive potentiality '*is* necessary in connection with things that acquire the beginning of their existence through movement, since movement is the actualizing of what is potentially existent [*Physics* III 1, 201a10]'. And he notes that 'in *Metaphysics* VII [7, 1032a12] the Philosopher uses this argument in connection with such things'. In the case of a *created* thing, however, if it did begin to exist, then before it began to exist, out of *no* antecedent matter, 'it was through *the power of the agent* possible that it exist', since that is the sole 'power through which it also began to exist'. The only other way in which to make sense of antecedent possibility in the case of a created thing is to assign that possibility to 'the relation of terms in which no incompatibility is found—which is indeed called possibility without any potentiality (as is clear from what the Philosopher says in *Metaphysics* V [12, 1019b12, 21–7]). For the predicate *existent* is not incompatible with the subject *world* or *human being* (as *commensurable* is incompatible with *diagonal*[66]).' And, as we've seen, it is in terms of this

---

[65] See also CT I.99 (second argument); QDP 3.17, objs. 10, 11; ST Ia.46.1, obj. 1.
[66] That is, the diagonal of a square is incommensurable with its side.

logical compatibility or possibility that Aquinas develops his account of 'the power of the agent', God's omnipotence.[67] 'And so it follows that before [the world] exists ... it is possible that it exist, even in the absence of all potentiality.'

The fourth, last, and least of chapter 34's arguments (1109) is of interest only because it affords Aquinas one more opportunity to drive home the difference between making and creating. As regards an ordinary product of ordinary making, 'while it is being made, there must be something that is the subject of the making; for there can be no making without a subject, since making is an accidental characteristic. Therefore, everything that is made has some pre-existing subject. And since one cannot go on *ad infinitum* in this way, there will follow a first subject that was not made but is sempiternal. From this it follows further that something besides God is eternal, since he cannot be a subject of making or of movement.'[68] The problem with these unimpeachable observations about making is that they can't apply to creating, which, as Aquinas's rejoinder (37.1133) reminds us, has been shown to involve no movement or successiveness of any kind (in chs. 17 and 19). And so if in connection with creating we tolerate figurative talk of making at all, we will have to say that in that case alone 'being-made is *not* prior to being'.

7. Purported proofs that the world must have begun to exist

In these eight chapters devoted to an elaborate examination of arguments *de aeternitate mundi*, the final, and by far the boldest, task that Aquinas takes on is the rejection of arguments on his own side of the issue, 'arguments by means of which certain people try to show that the world is not eternal'. Chapter 38 is devoted to very brief presentations of six such arguments[69] followed by Aquinas's very brief rejoinders. Although he says regarding the rejoinders that 'it seems appropriate to show how people who have asserted

[67] In ch. 22; see Ch. Four above, sect. 5.
[68] I haven't found a parallel to this argument elsewhere in Aquinas's writings.
[69] 'Now since these arguments do not support their conclusions with necessity, although they do have probability, it is enough just to touch on them, so that the Catholic faith may not seem to be based on empty arguments rather than on God's firmest teaching' (38.1142).

the eternity of the world oppose these arguments' (1142), all but the last of them show at least as clearly how Aquinas himself opposes them. Before writing SCG, Aquinas had already provided fuller versions of the arguments and the rejoinders, in the same order, in his treatment of these issues in his Commentary on the *Sentences*, and I'll draw on those fuller versions in discussing chapter 38.[70]

The first argument (38.1136) is especially short and peculiarly unimpressive: 'It has been demonstrated that God is the cause of all things. But a cause must durationally precede the things that are made through its action.' So the world cannot have existed for ever.[71] Aquinas's rejoinder (1143) is strong enough to do the job: an agent's preceding its effect 'is not necessary as regards those agents that act instantaneously', as he has shown the creator must do (in chs. 17 and 19). It is disappointing, though, that he leaves it at that, when it seems that he should make the more fundamental point which he brings out in his earlier rejection of such an argument: where God is the agent, it does not follow that the agent precedes its effect durationally, because God 'is giving existence not through motion but through eternal influence, in that his knowledge [and volition] is the cause of things' (In Sent. II.1.1.5, ad sc 1).

The second argument (38.1137) is based on a misunderstanding of *ex nihilo* that is familiar by this stage of Aquinas's account of creation.[72] 'Since the whole of being has been created by God, it cannot be said to have been made out of any being. So we are left with the conclusion that it has been made out of nothing, and, consequently, that it has being after not-being', and, consequently, that it cannot have existed for ever.[73] Aquinas's rejoinder here (1144) is again perfunctory, reduced in this case to a simple logical point: 'If "From *something* something is made" is not granted, the contradictory that must be provided is "It is not the case that from something something is made", not "From *nothing* something is made" (unless that's taken in the sense of the former). From this one cannot conclude that it is made after not being.' As a rejoinder,

---

[70] See In Sent. II.1.1.5, where each of the six arguments of ch. 38 is paralleled by a *sed contra* (sc). The first argument is paralleled by both the first and the ninth (last) sc; each of the others is paralleled, in order, by just one. Aquinas's rejoinders there (ad sc) parallel his rejoinders in ch. 38 in the same way.

[71] See also ST Ia.46.2, obj. 1.

[72] See Ch. Three above, sect. 5.

[73] See also ST Ia.46.2, obj. 2.

this is enough, barely; but the corresponding earlier version is more illuminating.[74]

From a modern, secular point of view, the most interesting medieval arguments for the impossibility of a beginningless world are found among those based on considerations of infinity. All four remaining arguments of Aquinas's chapter 38 draw on infinity one way or another; but the most formidable of them is the chapter's third argument (1138), which presents a line of reasoning from which Kant drew the proof of his First Antinomy's thesis, and which is still under discussion.[75] It claims that the world must have begun to exist 'because infinitely many things cannot be gone through.[76] But if the world has existed for ever, then [per impossibile] infinitely many things have already been gone through. For what is past has been gone through, but there are infinitely many past days (or revolutions of the sun) if the world has existed for ever.'[77] Simple as it is, this may well be the most formidable and

---

[74] In Sent. II.1.1.5, ad sc 2: 'Avicenna replies to the second [sed contra] in his Metaphysics [VI 1 and 2; IX 4]. For he says that all things have been created by God and that creation is from nothing, or of that which has being after not-being. But this can be understood in two ways: either [1] in such a way that an order of duration is designated—in which case it is false, according to him—or [2] in such a way that an order of nature is designated, in which case it is true. For that which belongs to a thing from itself is naturally prior, for anything, to that which belongs to it from something else. But each thing besides God has being from something else. Therefore, as regards its own nature it would be a non-being if it did not have being from God—as Gregory also says [Moralia in Iob XVI 37], viz. that all things would fall away into nothing if the hand of the omnipotent were not holding them together. And so the not-being that a thing has naturally, on its own, is prior to the being that it has from another, although not durationally. And it is in this way that philosophers grant that things have been created and made by God.'

[75] See e.g. the six essays submitted as entries in a competition on 'The Age of the Universe' and published under that title in the British Journal for the Philosophy of Science, 5 (1954–5), esp. Scriven 1954–5; also Wallace 1968; Huby 1971 and 1973; and the exchange between Whitrow (1978) and Popper (1978) on the impossibility of an infinite past. For an extended exchange that is in several respects analogous to the medieval dispute de aeternitate mundi, see Craig and Smith 1993.

[76] One of Aristotle's principles regarding infinity is that it is impossible for infinitely many things to have been actually gone through (Physics III 5, 204b7–10; VIII 8, 263b3–6; Metaphysics XI 10, 1066a35–b1). Sorabji has shown (1983: 214–24) that the three types of infinity arguments represented here by the third, fourth, and fifth arguments of ch. 38 stem from the sixth-century Greek Christian philosopher Philoponus. And since in this species of infinity argument Philoponus draws on an Aristotelian principle in order to argue against the possibility of a beginningless world, Sorabji aptly titles the introductory section of his discussion 'Philoponus turns Aristotle against himself' (p. 214).

[77] Cf. In Sent. II.1.1.5, sc 3: 'If the world has existed from eternity, then infinitely many days have preceded this day. But infinitely many cannot be gone

intriguing argument ever offered against the possibility of a beginningless world. If its attractiveness for the audacious party in the medieval debate isn't immediately obvious, just think about correlating each negative integer with one past day and counting *all* the negative integers, ending with -3, -2, -1.[78]

Anyone who, like Bonaventure, takes that line of argument to provide a proof that the world must have begun to exist,[79] would be unlikely to back down in the face of Aquinas's brief rejoinder (38.1145) to this third argument: '[A]lthough what is infinite does not occur all at once in actuality, it can none the less occur in succession, since any infinite taken in that way is finite. Therefore, each of the preceding days[80] could be gone through, because it was finite. However, as regards all of them taken together, if the world had existed for ever, one could not admit a first [day]. And so neither [could one admit that all the days were to have been] gone through,[81] which always requires two extremes.' This elegant refutation is too compressed for its own good,[82] but it makes the right point, which is spelled out more fully in Aquinas's earlier version of it: 'going through can be understood only as from one determinate [terminus] to another determinate [terminus]. And so, take any determinate [point in past] time at all: from that time to this is always a finite time. And in that way one must arrive at the present time' (In Sent. II.1.1.5, ad sc 3).

The idea behind the third argument, the source of its illusory strength, is the undeniable truth that an infinity that *is to be* gone through cannot ever *have been* gone through. And the source of that idea, here applied to the past, is likely to be reflections on the

---

through. Therefore, this day would never have been arrived at—which is false. Therefore, etc.' See also ST Ia.46.2, obj. 6.

[78] See Wallace 1968.

[79] Bonaventure's version (with 'days' replacing his 'revolutions of the celestial spheres'): 'It is impossible that infinitely many things have been gone through. But if the world did not begin, there have been infinitely many days. Therefore, it is impossible to go through them. Therefore, it was impossible to get to *this* day' (*In Sent.* II.1.1.1.2).

[80] For the sake of convenience, I'm replacing Aquinas's 'revolutions' with 'days'.

[81] This crucial clause—*Et ita nec transitum*—is so terse as to invite misunderstanding. It could just as easily be read as: 'And so neither [could one admit that all the days have been] gone through', which would spoil the argument as well as be blatantly false.

[82] This rejoinder and Aquinas's other versions of it have sometimes been radically misinterpreted, most notably in van Steenberghen 1980, and have seldom been fully appreciated. For a well-informed, helpful discussion see MacIntosh 1994.

future. For suppose that the world will never end. In that case there will be infinitely many days after today. And, of course, in that case all those future days can never *have been* gone through, because that would be to get to the last day, and *ex hypothesi* there can't be a last day. Paraphrasing Aquinas's observation, having been gone through can be understood only as *from* one determinate (spatial or) temporal terminus *to* another. In terms of his rejoinder to the third argument, each of the supposedly infinitely many days before today had a beginning and an end. At the beginning of any and every one of them, it is a finite time that *is to be* gone through; at the end of each of those infinitely many days, it is a time that *has been* gone through. 'However, as regards all [of them] taken together, if the world has existed for ever, one could not admit a first [day].' That is, there couldn't be anything in the supposedly infinite past taken as a whole that would correspond to the beginning of any one of its infinitely many days; there couldn't be any temporal location that would have been to the supposedly infinite past as today is to the hypothetically infinite future; there couldn't be any instant from which that infinite past *was to be* gone through. So, Aquinas says, pick any day you like from among the infinitely many past days: from that day to this 'is always a finite time', which can therefore *have been* gone through (and, of course, *must* have been gone through). Of course, any such day will have been preceded by infinitely many finite times that had *already* been gone through. The genuine impossibility of getting from today to the end of an infinite future has its analogue not in the alleged impossibility of having got to today out of an infinite past, but in having got to today from the (impossible) *first* day of the infinitely many past days, from the *beginning* of a beginningless past.[83]

Chapter 38's fourth argument (1139) relies on the naïve but initially plausible notion that an infinite set cannot have an infinite proper subset. If the world has existed for ever, 'it follows that [*per impossibile*] an addition is made to what is infinite, since every day something new is added to the past days (or revolutions)'. Again, Aquinas's rejoinder in chapter 38 (1146) is less satisfactory than it might have been: 'nothing prevents an addition's being made to what is infinite on the side on which it is finite. But from the

---

[83] I've discussed some of these points more fully in Kretzmann 1985, as developed not in Aquinas, but in Bonaventure and especially in Ockham, who is on Aquinas's side of this issue.

hypothesis that time is eternal it follows that it is infinite *before* but finite *after*; for the present is the terminus of the past.' We can find him making the fundamental point against this argument in his rejoinder to this earlier version of it: 'anything to which an addition can be made is something than which there can be something greater or smaller. But there can be an addition of days to the days that have preceded [today]. Therefore, past time can be greater than it is. But there is nothing greater than what is infinite, nor can there be. Therefore, past time is not infinite' (In Sent. II.1.1.5, sc 4).[84] In the middle of his lengthy rejoinder to it, Aquinas says, quite rightly, 'It's clear that this argument is sophistical, because it even rules out the infinite in the addition of numbers, as if to say: There are some species of numbers greater than ten that are not greater than one hundred; therefore, there are more species of number that are greater than ten than there are species of number that are greater than one hundred; and so, since infinitely many are greater than one hundred, there will be something greater than infinity' (In Sent. II.1.1.5, ad sc 4).[85]

The fifth of these attempted disproofs of the beginningless-world hypothesis (38.1140) takes a line that is familiar by now: 'there is [*per impossibile*] an infinite regress of efficient causes if there has been generation for ever, which must be said if the world exists for ever; for the cause of a son is a father, and the cause of him is another, and so on *ad infinitum*'.[86] We've already seen Aquinas's rejection of this sort of infinite regress argument more than once,[87] but his clear, concise rejoinder (1147) to this particular version of it is worth noting:

According to the philosophers, an infinite regress of agent causes is impossible in cases where causes act together, since the effect must depend on infinitely many actions taking place at once. And causes that are *per se* infinitely many are of that sort, because the infinity of them is required for the thing that is caused. On the other hand, where causes that do not act at once are concerned, this is *not* impossible, according to people who posit perpetual generation. But this infinity is accidental to the causes; for it is accidental to Socrates' father [considered just as such] that he is or is not another man's son. It is, however, not accidental to a stick that is moved by

[84] I haven't found any other parallels to this argument elsewhere in Aquinas's writings.

[85] By 'a species of number' Aquinas means what we mean by just 'a number'.

[86] See also ST Ia.46.2, obj. 7.

[87] Most relevantly in n. 19 above.

a hand in so far as the stick moves a stone; for it moves in so far as it is moved.

Because Aquinas accepts (a) Aristotle's rejection of the possibility of an actual infinity[88] and (b) the immortality of individual human souls, he finds the sixth and last argument (1141) the most challenging of all. If the world has existed for ever, 'it will follow that there are [*per impossibile*] infinitely many things—viz. the immortal souls of infinitely many past human beings'.[89] Aquinas's rejoinder (1148) avoids a direct attack, showing instead that this line of argument can succeed only *ad hominem*:

[W]hat is said about souls is more difficult. But, none the less, the argument is not much use, since it presupposes many things.[90] For some people who maintain the eternity of the world have also claimed that human souls do not exist after the body. Others, however, claimed that of all the souls there remains only a [unique] separated intellect—either an agent intellect, according to some, or a possible intellect as well, according to others.[91] But others maintained a cycling of souls, claiming that after some ages the same souls go back into bodies. And others say that there is no absurdity in there actually being infinitely many things that are not in an ordered relation to one another.

And, obviously, anyone belonging to any of those four groups of people would greet this so-called proof with derision. But since Aquinas himself definitely does not belong to any of the first three groups, he is either tacitly leaving open the possibility of an actual infinity of 'things that are not in an ordered relation to one another', or he is not even suggesting an effective rejoinder to this argument—which, like all the others in this chapter, he has characterized as probable.[92]

---

[88] See e.g. *Metaphysics* XI 10, 1066b11–12.

[89] See also ST Ia.46.2, obj. 8.

[90] See also II.81.1622.

[91] On 'agent intellect', 'possible intellect', and these views regarding them, see Chs. Eight and Nine below.

[92] One effective rejoinder, plausible from Aquinas's point of view as well as ours, is that human beings need not have existed as long as the world has existed. In his short polemical treatise on the eternity of the world, written after SCG, he still characterizes this argument as more challenging than some others. But he also dismisses it as simply 'not to the point, since God could have made a world without human beings and souls, or he could have made a human being when he did in fact make one even if all the rest of the world had been made from eternity' (DAM 310). For an excellent, thorough analysis of Aquinas's position, see Cartwright 1997.

8. *Aquinas's probable argument for the greater goodness of a temporally finite world*

By the end of chapter 38, Aquinas has rejected every one of these purported proofs that the world must have begun to exist, just because they 'do not support their conclusions with necessity (although they do have probability)', and 'so that the Catholic faith may not seem based on empty arguments rather than on God's firmest teaching' (1142). However, having undermined all those attempts to *demonstrate* the proposition that he accepts on Scriptural authority, he concludes this detailed examination of arguments for and against 'the eternity of the world' by reiterating his own creditable argument in support of the created world's having begun to exist, one that he must think has *more* probability than those he has just been rejecting.

However, as was mentioned above,[93] one can proceed to show this more efficaciously on the basis of the divine will's end. For, in connection with the production of things, the end of the divine will is God's goodness in so far as it is manifested by the things caused. But the divine power and goodness is manifested most forcefully in that things other than God have not existed for ever. For on that basis it is clearly shown that things other than he have their being from him, just because they have not existed for ever. It is also shown that he does not act through the necessity of [his] nature, and that his power in acting is infinite. This, therefore, was most appropriate for the divine goodness: that God should give to created things a beginning of their duration. (38.1149)

---

[93] In 35.1118; see sect. 4 above.

SIX

THE ORIGIN OF SPECIES

1. From producing to distinguishing

The second of the three big topics which Aquinas takes up in his natural theology, the one to which he devotes SCG II generally, is creation in its broadest sense, 'the emergence of created things from God' (I.9.57). But, as we've seen, his treatment of creation broadly conceived of is itself also organized into three parts.[1] Our consideration of the first of those three parts (chs. 6–38), the one he devotes to considering creation more narrowly conceived of, God's 'producing things as regards their being' (II.5.877), ended with our investigating his assessments of arguments for and against the possibility of the created world's having existed for ever. In terms of what I've been calling the big question—'Why is there this sort of world rather than another sort, or nothing at all?'—Aquinas's work in Book II so far, then, may be seen as having been focused on explaining only why there is something rather than nothing.

But now, in the second of those three parts (chs. 39–45), he undertakes to explain in broad terms why there is what there is rather than something else, why and how God produced *this* world. He thinks of this second, much shorter, part of his account of the emergence of things from God as dealing with 'the distinguishing of things'. And he clearly marks the transition between these two parts in the opening sentence of chapter 39: 'However, now that we have cleared up matters that pertain to the *producing* of things, we have next to proceed with those that must be considered in connection with the *distinguishing* of things (*rerum distinctione*)' (1151).

Nowhere in II.39–45 does Aquinas say plainly just what he means by 'the distinguishing of things'. In the seven chapters that make up the second part of his treatment of creation, he is mainly

---

[1] Ch. One above, sect. 9.

addressing theories of distinguishing put forward by others and
questions that might be raised by his own account of it. The details
of his conception of distinguishing will emerge as we go on in
this chapter. But it will turn out to be broadly correct to describe
it as his understanding of the origin of species, his explanation
of the fact that the complex world produced by God consists in
an ordered arrangement of all sorts of natural kinds, which we
would characterize as not just biological species, but also physical,
chemical, astronomical, and geological species of things. Plants
and animals, oceans and stars, the elements, and the basic potentialities and relationships expressed in natural laws are among the
features of reality that Aquinas thinks are to be explained fundamentally in terms of the distinguishing of things.

Consequently, it's in this phase of Aquinas's natural theology
that we are for the first time likely to be confronting not just
internal but also external difficulties, in the form of specific conflicts between Aquinas's explanations and natural science as it has
developed since his time. Science has nothing authoritative to say
about the existence and nature of God (the topics of Book I), or
about why there is something rather than nothing at all, or about
whether the world began to exist or has always existed[2] (the topics
of Book II so far). But, by contrast, the question of why the world
is as it is might fairly be said to be the question addressed by the
natural sciences generally, the question to which the sciences have
developed innumerable well-substantiated partial answers. And, as
I've already suggested, when we see more plainly what Aquinas
means by 'the distinguishing of things', we'll also see that it's scientific theories of evolution—cosmological, geological, or biological
evolution—with which his account of distinguishing may seem to
conflict most directly.

As we acquire a clearer idea of this second part of Aquinas's
account of creation, and resolve some of the difficulties internal to
it, we'll also be taking account of some of those external difficulties.
Apparent conflicts of this sort are obviously relevant to my project.
I've been maintaining that Aquinas's natural theology is of more
than historical interest, that intelligent, educated, late twentieth-

---

[2] I'm not suggesting that there's nothing authoritative about the Big Bang
hypothesis, for instance, but even it is about the beginning of the universe as we
know it from something else—something that could even be the result of a big
crunch of the matter making up the immediately preceding universe. And so it isn't
a claim that the world—all there is or ever has been besides God—began to exist.

century people can take it seriously as a theistic account of what
there is. And I'm assuming that part of what characterizes most
such people is their acceptance, at least on a lay level, of at least the
broad outlines of well-supported evolutionary theories that offer
some explanation of the way the natural world is. Claims of the sort
I've been making, then, will be weakened if there are unresolved
genuine conflicts between theories of evolution and Aquinas's
theistic account of the distinguishing of things.

It's not clear why Aquinas doesn't define the distinguishing of
things in the second part of Book II, which he devotes entirely to
arguments about it. Often when he begins to consider a concept in
detail, he does define it, even when it's a concept that was quite
familiar to his contemporaries. Conceivably, he sees no need to
reintroduce the topic here because he has more than once alluded
to distinguishing in earlier chapters of SCG. We'll be looking
at some of those passages.[3] But in fact none of them contains a
full definition of the concept he's working with in this part of his
natural-theological account of creation. It might seem that another
reason for his not providing a definition of distinguishing is that it's
too simple and familiar a notion to need defining. To begin with a
plain, generic truth, 'those things are distinct of which one is not the
other' (I.71.605), and nobody needs to be told that the natural
world is made up of things of which one is not the other. But the
notion of distinguishing with which Aquinas is concerned in II.39–
45 turns out to be nothing like so simple as that plain truth, and I
haven't found a single passage anywhere in Aquinas that presents
this notion of distinguishing clearly and completely.[4]

I'll begin the process of clarifying it by drawing on what might
reasonably be thought to be his fullest, definitive account of distinguishing—the one he develops in his 'Treatise on the Six Days' (ST
Ia.65–74), which I've already touched on.[5] Of course, nothing said
in Genesis about the creating or distinguishing of things can

[3] Probably the most important of those earlier passages is I.50.421, in which
Aquinas provides what turns out to be a synopsis of several features of his account
of distinguishing in II.39–45.

[4] However, one Article of his commentary on the *Sentences* provides a fairly full
analysis that will be especially helpful. See sect. 6 below.

[5] In Ch. Three above, sect. 7. In fact, Aquinas's treatment of distinguishing in
connection with Genesis 1 seems freer and more suggestive in his early Commentary on the *Sentences* than in ST's 'Treatise on the Six Days' (see sect. 3 below). ST's
status as a textbook for beginners in theology and Aquinas's sense of his pedagogical obligations may have dictated a more traditional approach in that later
treatment.

provide any premisses for the arguments by means of which he develops his natural-theological account in SCG II; nor can details of Aquinas's ST treatise that depend on data found in Scripture alone play any integral part in SCG I–III. But at least one important feature of the discussion in II.39–45 can be illuminated most clearly against the background of his analysis of Genesis 1's story of the six days in the ST treatise.

2. Distinguishing and furnishing

In his general introduction to the treatise (Ia.65, preface), Aquinas interprets the first chapter of Genesis as depicting '*three* works: the work of *creating* [Gen. 1: 1] . . ., the work of *distinguishing* [1: 2–13, the first three days] . . ., and the work of *furnishing*[6] [1: 14–31, the last three days]'. Two features of this traditional interpretation are relevant to my purposes here.

First, according to the story in Genesis 1, the various kinds of heavenly bodies and all animal species (including fish, birds, and human beings) originate during the last three days, and so the producing of them belongs not to distinguishing, but to furnishing. But, second, furnishing is never even mentioned in SCG II or, for that matter, anywhere else in SCG. So, if 'distinguishing' in II.39–45 designates Aquinas's explanation of the origin of *all* species, as I've claimed it does, then in SCG 'distinguishing' covers also what is carefully separated off as the work of furnishing not only in ST, written after SCG, but also in Aquinas's earlier Commentary on the *Sentences*.[7] The fact that the gist of the distinguishing/furnishing division was found in Peter Lombard's *Sentences* gave it an authori-

---

[6] *Ornatus*, which can also be translated 'adorning', or 'ornamentation'.

[7] See e.g. In Sent. II.13.1.1; 14.1.5; 15.1.1; 15.2.2; 17.2.2, obj. 3 and ad 3. In CT, written soon after SCG, Aquinas doesn't mention furnishing at all in his treatments of distinguishing (I.71–4 and 102, which also omit any reference to the six days), but only in connection with what he has to say about the *end* of the world, and then only twice, in the same passage (I.170.336): 'Now the essential parts of the universe are the heavenly bodies and the elements, since the entire structure (*machina*) of the world is constituted out of them. But other things seem to pertain not to the fundamental wholeness (*integritatem*) of the physical universe but rather to a sort of furnishing and decorating (*ornatum et decorem*) of it . . . the animals, the plants, and the mineral bodies. In the condition of [the world's] final consummation, however, another furnishing will be provided for the elements.' (CT I.161.323 contains one other, irrelevant use of *ornatum* in connection with human hair.)

tative status.[8] It had to be taken seriously, not only in commentaries on the *Sentences*, but also in other thirteenth-century works of dogmatic theology, such as ST. And the division does have some utility, if 'distinguishing' is thought of as the designation for sorting out the infrastructure of the universe, and 'furnishing' as having to do with the formation of its more apparent features.

But any advantage there may be in the distinguishing/furnishing division is at least diminished outside the context of interpreting Genesis 1. If authoritative creation stories are left out of account, speculative or scientific explanations of the way the world is

[8] *Sententiae* II.14.9 (which is the beginning of II.15 in the text Aquinas was using). The text of that chapter of the *Sentences* is based largely on two chapters in the *De sacramentis* of Hugh of St Victor (c.1096–1141). I.1.24: '*On these [first] three days the arrangement (dispositio) of things was carried out.* Behold, these are the works of the three days, before the sun and the other light-givers had been made. In those first three days the structure (*machina*) of this universe was set in order (*disposita est*) and distributed to its parts, with the firmament having been spread out from above. Next, once the earth had been revealed, residing below and balanced in its weight, and the masses of the waters had been collected within their receptacles, and the air had been cleared, the four elements of the world were distinguished and arranged (*distincta et ordinata sunt*) in their places' (PL 176, col. 202D). I.1.25: '*How the world was furnished (ornatus est) in the following three days.* Next followed their furnishing; and this, again, was done in the following three days. On the fourth (which was the first of the three), the firmament was furnished with sun, moon, and stars. On the fifth day (which was the second of the three), the air received furnishings of birds, and the water of fish. On the sixth day (which was the third of the three), the earth received wild beasts, cattle, reptiles, and the other animals that move on the earth. Now the human being was made on the last day: [made] of earth and on earth, but not for earth or for the sake of earth, but for heaven and for the sake of him who made earth and heaven. Therefore, the human being was made not as a furnishing of the earth but as its master and owner, so that the making (*conditio*) of the one for whose sake the earth was made is not to be traced back to the earth' (PL 176, col. 203A–B).

The tradition regarding 'furnishing' had an even older, more authoritative root in Augustine, *De Genesi ad litteram* II.13. He used the Old Latin translation of Genesis (from the Greek of the Septuagint), in which Gen. 1: 15 reads *Et sint in splendorem in firmamento coeli, ut luceant super terram* ('And let them be for an ornament in the firmament of heaven to shine upon the earth') instead of the Vulgate's drabber *Ut luceant in firmamento caeli et illuminent terram* ('So that they may shine in the firmament of heaven and light the earth'). In commenting on this passage, Augustine makes an apparently casual use of words related to the Latin verb *orno*, perhaps prompted by the occurrence of *splendorem* in his Old Latin text. II.13.26: 'For we cannot say that certain better things were chosen by which the series of days might be distinguished in such a way that the end and the middle [of the series] should stand out more ornately (*ornatius*).' And in II.13.27 he says, 'And because the heaven was made first, so it must be the first to be furnished (*ornandum*) with its parts of this kind'—i.e. visible, moving parts (PL 34, col. 274). Hugh may well have developed his more precise allocation of 'distinguishing' and 'furnishing' from these Augustinian hints.

naturally tend to suppose that the sorting and forming of it constitute one continuous process. Moreover, within the Scriptural context, where it is most at home, the division generates a special (if
artificial) interpretative problem for the traditional assignment of
distinguishing to the first three days and furnishing to the last three.
The description of the work of the third day (in Gen. 1: 9–13)
begins with the account of the separating of land from water (9–10),
which seems, intuitively, to count as a clear instance of the 'distinguishing' that is supposed to constitute the work of the first three
days. And that part of the description of the third day ends with the
formula 'and God saw that it was good' (10). But then, in verses 11–
12, the description of that same third day continues with the account of the origin of plants, which closely resembles the accounts
of the origins of fish, birds, and other animals, which are typical of
the 'furnishing' that is supposed to be the work of the last three
days. Moreover, the second part of the description of the third day
is followed, in verse 12, by *another* 'and God saw that it was good',
strengthening the impression that the description of the third day
covers two developments quite different in kind.

Aquinas takes up this interpretative problem in ST Ia.69.2 ('Is
the production of the plants appropriately assigned to the third
day?'), where he confronts this objection: 'Plants have life, as animals do. However, the production of the animals is not included
among the works of *distinguishing*, but pertains to the work of
furnishing. Therefore, neither should the production of the plants
be recorded on the third day, which pertains to the work of distinguishing' (obj. 1).[9] Elsewhere Aquinas himself seems casually to
include the production of the plants under decorating or furnishing.[10] None the less, when he is discussing the six days in ST and in
his Commentary on the *Sentences*, he dutifully tries to resolve this

[9] See also In Sent. II.14.5 ('Was the work of the third day appropriately described?'), esp. obj. 6: 'Plants evidently pertain to the *furnishing* of the earth. But the
last three days are assigned to furnishing. Therefore, no mention should have been
made of the production of the plants in connection with the work of the third day.'

[10] See e.g. ST Ia.66.1c: 'But two sorts of beauty were missing from the
earth: . . . [I]t has the second sort in virtue of being furnished (*ornata*) with herbs and
plants. And so it says [in Gen. 1: 2] that it was empty (or, according to another text,
disordered [*incomposita*]—i.e. not furnished)'; also Ia.69.2c: 'But two kinds of formlessness were ascribed to the earth: . . . second, that it was disordered and empty—
i.e. without having appropriate decoration (*debitum decorem*), which is acquired for
the earth from the plants, which in a certain sense clothe it'; also CT I.170.336,
quoted in n. 7 above.

interpretative problem by arguing that the origin of plants really does count as an aspect of distinguishing, unlike the origins of the heavenly bodies, the fish, the birds, and the land animals, all of which count as furnishing.[11] His arguments are resourceful, if unconvincing, and some of what he has to say in the course of them is interesting for other reasons, as we'll see. But they can scarcely be expected to succeed in defending the traditional division between distinguishing and furnishing in the face of the awkward fact of the description of the third day in Genesis 1. It's hard not to think that Aquinas is relieved by not having to deal with 'furnishing' in SCG, where the six days cannot be taken into account.

Aquinas's use of distinguishing alone in SCG II, with no reference to furnishing, does not constitute a departure from established usage, however. It even has its own authoritative backing, as can be seen most easily in his Commentary on the *Sentences*. In Sent. II.13.1.1 ('Was the work of distinguishing necessary after the work of creating?') includes this objection: 'In [Lombard's] text of Distinction 12 above [II.12.5.4 and II.12.6], it was said that God distinguished created things through species in the six days. Therefore, it seems that the *whole* work of the six days pertains to distinguishing. And so furnishing seems not to differ from the work of distinguishing' (obj. 5). In his rejoinder to this objection Aquinas attributes to Lombard a broad, inclusive sense of 'distinguishing' in addition to the sense in which it contrasts with 'furnishing': 'earlier [in Lombard's Distinction 12] "the work of distinguishing" was taken *generally*, in so far as it indicates the separating [of things] on the basis of any difference of power; and [taken] in that sense it does include furnishing as well.[12] However, [taken] in another sense it

---

[11] See e.g. ST Ia.69.2, ad 1: 'In reply to the first objection [quoted above], we have to say, then, that in plants life is hidden, because they lack local motion and sensation, the characteristics by which what is animate is most of all distinguished from what is inanimate. And so, because they immovably inhere in the earth, the producing of them is treated as a kind of forming of the earth'—just as the separating of the land from the water is a kind of forming of the earth and so counts as an instance of distinguishing.

[12] 'Distinguishing' in a broader sense is the topic also of a Question of ST that occurs well before the 'Treatise on the Six Days' in Ia.65–74—viz. Ia.47 ('The distinguishing of things generally'), the Preface to which begins by echoing the opening sentence of SCG II.39 (quoted in sect. 1 above): 'After [considering] the producing of things as regards their being, we have to consider the distinguishing of them.' Ia.48 ('The distinguishing of things specifically') is altogether concerned with the distinction between good and bad. Furnishing isn't mentioned anywhere in the nine Articles making up those two Questions.

differs from furnishing, as has been said. And that difference can be inferred (*sumi*) from Scripture's own mode of expression, which hints at some sort of division of three days as regards the works' (ad 5). This passage contains the germ of the notion of distinguishing that will concern us in SCG II.39–45, and we'll be looking more closely at its passing allusion to general distinguishing as the separating of things on the basis of any difference of power.[13]

3. Aquinas's non-creationist reading of Genesis 1

The passage quoted just above also suggests something we've already noticed: that the distinguishing/furnishing division arises more naturally in connection with interpreting the story of the six days than in simply reflecting, without recourse to Scripture, on why the world is as it is. For that reason I want to move toward an understanding of the relevant concept of distinguishing by considering first some observations which Aquinas makes about the interpretation of Scripture in general and of Genesis 1 in particular.

I also have another, more broadly important reason for making this detour. From the seventeenth century onwards, Scripture's account of the beginning of the world and the origin of species has often been waved as a banner on one side of the fiercest warfare between religion and science, and held up to ridicule on the other. Aquinas, of course, had no inkling of any scientific evidence that might prompt an attempt to provide a non-literal interpretation of the biblical account. But the very wording of the first chapter of Genesis, and his idea of the level of sophistication in the audience for whom it was originally intended, led him to join Augustine in taking a remarkably enlightened view of the way to read the story of the six days—a view that would, I think, have equipped Augustine and Aquinas to appreciate judiciously, rather than denounce, scientific accounts of evolution.[14]

And, as it happens, Aquinas states this view of his most perti-

---

[13] See sect. 6 below.

[14] 'We have had to look at early Christian views to avoid a fundamental historical error: the mistake of thinking that a literal reading . . . of *Genesis* has always been, for Christian theorists, a complete account of origins and species. . . . A brief examination of Augustine's and Thomas' accounts of creation will confirm this observation' (Hodge 1991: 566). See also McMullin 1985*a* and van Inwagen 1993.

nently in connection with his earliest account of distinguishing,[15] where he sets the stage for his Augustinian interpretation by discriminating between two sorts of 'matters that pertain to the faith': (1) those, such as the doctrine of the Trinity, that are '*per se* the substance of the faith', and (2) those that, like 'many historical details', belong to the faith 'only *per accidens*—that is, in so far as they are handed down in Scripture, which the faith claims was promulgated at the dictation of the Holy Spirit'. Among Christians, matters of type 1 are those 'in connection with which no one is permitted to think otherwise'. Matters of type 2, on the other hand, 'can of course be safely unknown by people who are not bound to know the Scriptures. And about those matters even the saints [i.e. the Church Fathers] have differing views, expounding divine Scripture in different ways.'

In particular, the subject with which we're concerned now includes matters of both those sorts: 'as regards the beginning of the world, there is something that [1] pertains to the substance of the faith—viz. that the created world began [to exist],[16] on which all the saints agree. However, [2] as regards *the way* and *the order* in which the world was made, such matters do not pertain to the faith except *per accidens*, in so far as they are handed down in Scripture. The saints have handed down various [views regarding such matters], preserving Scripture's truth in a varied exposition.'

Having declared the legitimacy of differing interpretations of Genesis 1, Aquinas provides two examples, drawn from 'the saints'. He expounds Augustine's reading in some detail, showing its relevance to the title question of In Sent. II.12.1.2, whether creating and distinguishing occur simultaneously. The answer he derives from Augustine is 'yes and no'. According to Aquinas, Augustine 'maintains that at the very beginning of creation *some* things were distinguished through their species in their own nature—e.g. the elements, the heavenly bodies, and the spiritual substances. But *other* things [were distinguished then] only in their specifying seminal natures (*in rationibus seminalibus*)[17]—e.g. animals, plants, and

---

[15] In Sent. II.12.1.2: 'Was it at one and the same time that all things were created and also distinguished through species?'

[16] On the status of this proposition, see Ch. Five above, sect. 2.

[17] *Ratio seminalis*, an important term in Augustine's writings, is sometimes translated as 'seminal reason', sometimes as 'seed-principle'. 'Specifying seminal nature' strikes me as coming closer to conveying what Augustine has in mind, although I'm also attracted by the less clumsy 'genetic pattern', which Anthony Kenny suggested

human beings. All those things were produced in their own natures later, in that work by which God, after the sixth day, guides (*administrat*) nature, which was previously established.' Notice that in Aquinas's Augustinian account biological species are not part of the original creation except as primordial natural potentialities in elemental earth, air, or water—'specifying seminal natures'— which get actualized 'later', under God's guidance (naturally), but as aspects of 'previously established' nature. And that's only the beginning of this non-literal interpretation, which, as we'll see, Aquinas declares to be more reasonable and thus more defensible than the literal reading.

Aquinas reports Augustine as claiming further 'that in connection with the distinguishing of things [as described in Genesis 1] we are to think not of a temporal order, but rather of the order of nature and of pedagogy (*doctrinae*)'. And he explains the difference between the natural and the temporal orders by observing that, for example, 'the sound is prior to the song *naturally*'—or, as we might say, logically—'but not temporally'. As for the order of pedagogy, the order followed by good teaching, it conforms to the order of nature in cases in which there is one to conform to. 'And so [in Genesis] things that are *naturally* prior are recounted *first*— e.g. earth is [naturally] prior to animals, water to fish, and so on as regards other things', such as plants to animals. But we can't validly infer any *temporal* order from that pedagogically ordered recounting. Good teaching may also give the impression of temporal ordering in the absence of even any *natural* ordering, 'as is clear in the case of people who teach geometry. For the parts of a figure constitute the figure without any temporal ordering', even though in *that* respect the figure does present the natural, non-temporal ordering of parts to whole, 'and yet geometry teaches that the construction of the figure is brought about by drawing one line after another'. The good teacher, observing the pedagogical order, has to intro-

---

to me. An acorn itself would not count as an instance of a *ratio seminalis*, but perhaps the-nature-of-an-oak-tree-as-contained-in-the-nature-of-an-acorn—which is clearly not an oak-tree 'in its own nature'—provides a reasonably good example of a *ratio seminalis* of an oak-tree. See e.g. Augustine's *De Genesi ad litteram* (PL 34, cols. 245–486; trans. Taylor 1982) II.15.30; III.12.18–19; IV.33.51–2; V.4.7–11, 23.44– 6; VI.1.1–2, 4.5–6.11, 10.17–11.19, 14.25–16.27; VII.24.35; IX.17.32. In the passage of Aquinas's In Sent. II.12.1.2c that I'm examining here, he seems to be drawing on more than one of those passages in Augustine. See also Taylor 1982: i. 252–4 n. 67. For more on *ratio seminalis*, see sect. 6 below.

duce a temporal order in the drawing of the lines, although they haven't even a natural order among themselves. In doing so, the teacher may, of course, inadvertently give the unwary student the idea that e.g. the base of a triangle comes into being before either of its sides. 'So, too, Moses, teaching an unsophisticated people about the creation of the world, divided into parts [in a pedagogical order] things that were done simultaneously', thereby inadvertently and perhaps unavoidably giving the unwary reader the idea that all those things were carried out in the sequence in which they were recounted.

Aquinas introduces his second example of biblical interpretations by acknowledging that, in contrast to Augustine, 'Ambrose and other saints claim that a temporal order *is* preserved in the distinguishing of things [as recounted in Genesis 1]. This view is, to be sure, more widespread, and it appears to be more in agreement with the *surface* of the text.' 'But', he says, Augustine's non-literal interpretation 'is the more reasonable one, and defends Holy Scripture better against unbelievers' ridicule.' So it's not surprising that Aquinas concludes this survey by declaring, 'And, indeed, this [Augustinian] position pleases me more' than the superficial, literal reading.[18] As he says later in this same Article of his *Sentences* Commentary, 'the authority of Scripture is in no way lessened when it is expounded variously while the faith is none the less preserved, because the Holy Spirit made Scripture bountiful, with a truth greater than any human being can find out' (ad 7).

4. Distinguishing distinguished, broadly

Clarifying the notion of distinguishing that is operative in chapters 39–45 requires drawing more than one terminological distinction. The broadest of them is one we've already encountered in passing.

---

[18] Aquinas quotes a sentence from Augustine's *De Genesi ad litteram* I.19 here, but the whole chapter is relevant and should be read in this connection, along with I.18.37. See Taylor 1982: i. 42–3. See also Ch. Three above, sect. 7, esp. n. 55. Peter van Inwagen's bold and otherwise admirable article 'Genesis and Evolution' (1993) misleadingly contrasts Augustine's non-literal interpretation with Aquinas's: 'Non-literalism was, of course, *rejected* by many important authorities in the Western Church. St. Thomas Aquinas, for example, was a literalist who explicitly stated that the Creation took place over a period of six successive twenty-four-hour days' (p. 100).

Although Aquinas has no need to introduce it explicitly into his natural theology, noting this broadest distinction now will set the stage for more fine-grained distinctions in what follows. It will also provide the basis for appreciating an apparent difficulty that Aquinas faces in connection with having even to acknowledge distinctions in created nature.

Since his investigation of distinguishing in SCG omits any consideration of furnishing, we have good grounds for supposing that his topic here is distinguishing 'taken *generally*'.[19] And, as we saw in looking at that passage earlier, taking distinguishing generally means taking it to *include* an account of the origins of species that were traditionally assigned to 'furnishing'. So, the investigation of *general* distinguishing is Aquinas's attempt to uncover the fundamental, metaphysical explanation(s) for all the natural world's complexity. The only universe that would not be characterized by distinctions at all would be absolutely unified and absolutely simple—a universe that could not be physical, a universe very hard even to imagine. As for the real, physical world which we inhabit and observe, which swarms with things of which one is not the other, Aquinas begins to sort it out by recognizing that there is one, and only one, respect in which *none* of those things is distinct from any other: 'Things are *not* distinguished from one another in respect of having *being*, since in that respect they all agree' (I.26.239). The broadest, most important respect in which natural things *are* distinct from one another is in the forms or natures that specify their being, at various levels of generality—e.g. inanimate/animate; non-sensitive animate/sensitive animate:[20] 'distinction, of course, has to do with the fact that one of them is not another, [a relation] they have not because of anything's having been added to them, but because of their own forms' (QDP 9.7c). 'Therefore, if things differ from one another, it must be . . . because being itself is suited to various natures in accordance with species [i.e. all sorts of natural kinds]. . . . [T]hings differ because they have various natures for which being is acquired in different ways' (I.26.239).

[19] In Sent. II.13.1.1, ad 5; quoted in sect. 2 above.
[20] In Aquinas's usage, 'genus' and 'species' are relative terms: e.g. *animate* is a species of *corporeal* but a genus of *sensitive animate* substance. A genus that is not a species of any other genus is a 'highest genus' (e.g. substance); a species that is not a genus of any other species is a 'lowest species' (e.g. human being); all others, between highest genera and lowest species, are 'subaltern' genera and species.

In Aquinas's technical usage, things are said to *differ* from one another only in case they are also recognized as *agreeing* somehow. And it is whatever essentially distinguishes one natural kind from another that counts as the paradigm of difference strictly so-called: '*Difference*, then, is to be looked for in those things that agree in some respect; for we must ascribe to them something on the basis of which they differ. For instance, two species agree in respect of a genus. That's why species [of the same genus] must be distinguished [from one another] by differentiae' (I.17.140*b*). So 'a differentia implies a distinction of form' against the background of a broader, more general unity of form (ST Ia.31.2, ad 2).[21] But, of course, a pigeon is distinct not only from a penguin but also from every other pigeon: 'those things are distinct of which one is not the other'. Accordingly, Aquinas recognizes that 'two kinds of distinction are found in things: one *formal* (in those that differ in species) but the other *material* (in those that differ only in number)'; and, naturally, 'the formal [specifying] distinction is more fundamental than the material [individuating] one' (ST Ia.47.2c).[22] Not only is every individual a member of some species, but also it is the various species—all the natural kinds of things there are—that in their interrelatedness constitute the form or structure of the universe, that taken together make this the kind of world it is. And since creating a world entails creating a world of *some* kind, it may seem that the distinguishing of natural things is just an aspect of the producing of them and hardly a subject in its own right. To some extent, that impression will turn out to be correct.

But Aquinas has reason to be especially careful in his approach to the distinguishing of things and its relation to creation proper— God's producing something or other out of nothing—because conclusions he has already argued for, together with principles he is firmly committed to, may seem to entail that the nature he has

[21] The Latin word *differentia* is often best translated as 'difference'—e.g. at the beginning of the quotation from I.17.140*b* just above. But when *differentia*, or its plural *differentiae*, is used to pick out the characteristic or characteristics that form part of the definition of a species, carving the species out of its genus and essentially distinguishing it from other species in that genus, I use 'differentia' or 'differentiae' as a technical term in English.

[22] See also e.g. In Sent. I.13.1.2c; 26.2.2c; 29.1.3c; SCG IV.24; ST Ia.36.2c; 50.3; 59.2, ad 2; 75.7c; and esp. SCG II.44.1211: 'All distinguishing is either in accordance with a division of quantity, which occurs in bodies only [i.e. material distinguishing, or individuation], . . . or in accordance with a formal division, which . . . is traced back to privation and form.'

argued must be God's could not be the nature of this world's producer.

5. The complex product of an absolutely simple producer

We've seen that such a consideration was perhaps the principal motivation for Aquinas's detailed analysis (in II.31–8) of the possibility of a beginningless world.[23] For although there are several other good reasons why he considers it in detail, the structure of his natural theology alone would compel him to take it up in the absence of all those other reasons, because the combination of one of his previous results and one of his favourite Aristotelian principles can be taken to imply that the created world must have existed for ever. The relevant principle is that every agent produces something somehow like itself; and the relevant previous result, argued for in I.15, is that God, the creator, is himself beginningless. In order to resolve this internal difficulty, Aquinas had to show that there is some respect in which a world that does begin to exist manifests God's nature more fully or more efficaciously than a beginningless world would do. And he showed it in his argument that 'the divine power and goodness is manifested *most* forcefully in that things other than God have *not* existed for ever', and that it is '*most* appropriate for the divine goodness that God should give to created things a *beginning* of their duration' (38.1149).[24]

Analogously, Aquinas is compelled to take up the topic of the distinguishing of things, and to view its inclusion in his natural theology as at least apparently problematic, because the combination of that same principle—that every agent produces something somehow like itself[25]—and his previously argued theses that God is

[23] See Ch. Five above, sects. 2 and 4.

[24] See Ch. Five above, sect. 8; also 35.1118, discussed in Ch. Five, sect. 4.

[25] See e.g. Aristotle, *De generatione et corruptione* I 7, 324a9–12; *De anima* II 4, 415a26–b2; *Metaphysics* VII 8, 1033b29–32. The Marietti eds. list thirty-one passages of SCG in which Aquinas uses this principle (see ii. 11 n. 3). A rough estimate of the principle's importance to Aquinas's discussion of distinguishing can be arrived at by noting that six of those passages occur in II.39–45, which are only seven of SCG's 463 chapters. The only passage that makes use of the principle in II.31–8 occurs in an argument whose conclusion is relevant to our consideration of distinguishing: 'the species of generable things must be perpetual' (33.1100)—which, of course, Aquinas argues against (in 36.1124).

absolutely simple (I.25) and absolutely one (I.42) might be taken
to imply that God's creation must be utterly unified and utterly
simple.[26] This problem is in fact more obvious than the previous
one, regarding the created world's having had a beginning, because
the only evidence Aquinas recognizes as conclusive in that case is
the authority of Scripture. By contrast, nobody needs *any* authority—or, for that matter, any argumentation—to see that the world
is neither absolutely unified nor absolutely simple.

Moreover, this problem is one we've encountered before, in
a less pointed version, when we considered the single-effect account of creation, associated especially with Avicenna.[27] His
emanationism stems from his convictions that God's essence is one
and simple, and that 'that which follows from him is from his
essence, not from anything else', so that 'the things that are from
him first of all—and those are the created things—cannot be many,
whether numerically or as regards the division into matter and
form'. 'It is clear, therefore, that the first of the things that are
[caused] by the first cause is numerically one, and that its essence
and its quiddity are unity, not in matter.'[28] Aquinas's earlier
concern with the single-effect account (in II.22) was prompted
by his recognition that it could be interpreted as a limitation
on God's power, which was the topic he was directly concerned
with then. But the single-effect account and the emanationism
associated with it are even more unmistakably incompatible with
the view that God is the immediate agent of the complexity and
multiplicity of nature; so, as we'll see, Aquinas is even more
directly concerned with those rival accounts in his investigation of
distinguishing.[29]

---

[26] See e.g. I.26.239, where Aquinas explains that 'if the divine being were the
formal being of all things, all things would have to be simply, absolutely one'; also
I.54.446: 'it can seem difficult to someone—or impossible—that one and the same
simple [being], such as the divine essence, should be the proper *ratio*, or [even] a
likeness, of different things'; also QDP 3.16, which is expressly concerned with
showing how the complexity and multiplicity of the world is compatible with its
creator's simplicity and unity.

[27] See Ch. Four above, sect. 6, and esp. n. 16.

[28] Both of these two passages are from Avicenna's *Liber de philosophia prima*,
tr. IX, cap. iv; the first is 479.92–4, the second 479.4–6. On the importance of
this kind of issue in thirteenth-century thought generally, see Hayes 1964:
ch. 2, §2.

[29] See also II.42, 'The first cause of the distinguishing of things is not an order of
secondary agents', esp. 1181 and 1191.

6. Distinguishing distinguished, more narrowly

However, as I've been saying, we need a fuller, clearer conception of the nature of distinguishing in order to assess Aquinas's investigation in those chapters. One Article of his Commentary on the *Sentences* is more illuminating and provides more relevant detail than any other single passage I've seen in his discussions of distinguishing. That Article, In Sent. II.13.1.1 ('Was the work of distinguishing necessary after the work of creating?'), is expressly associated with the story of the six days, but I think that its analysis of distinguishing provides the core of the concept which Aquinas has in mind in the natural-theological investigations he carries out in SCG II.39–45. We've seen one hint of this analysis already (in sect. 2 above) in a rejoinder extracted from that same Article, in which he identifies distinguishing 'taken generally' as 'the separating [of things] on the basis of any difference of power' (ad 5). What he means by explaining distinguishing in terms of power is made clear in the rest of the Article, which precedes that rejoinder.

The objections with which the Article begins are based on naïve, intuitive notions of distinguishing that Aquinas sets aside in the body of the Article and in his rejoinders to the objections. The first objection, for instance, assumes that all distinguishing must involve material separation, presumably by means of local motion:[30] 'There is no distinguishing except of things that were mingled and mixed together earlier. Therefore, if the distinguishing of things was carried out after creation, then the created things must have been mixed together earlier' (obj. 1).[31] In his rejoinder to this objection, Aquinas says nothing about the objection's assumption that creating is temporally as well as naturally prior to distinguishing. But the rest of his treatment of creating and distinguishing in this Article shows that he thinks of some distinguishing as necessarily simultaneous with creating, as an aspect of it, and of other distinguishing as necessarily later than creating. His rejoinder here focuses on replacing this intuitive interpretation of general distinguishing in terms of matter with his preferred interpretation in terms of form: 'The distinguishing of the world's parts is to be understood *not* as a

---

[30] See also obj. 3: 'Distinguishing has to do with things that can be mixed together and mingled as regards location.'

[31] See also Ch. Three above, sect. 7.

material extraction from some mixture but, rather, *formally*, as the conferring of various powers on various things' (ad 1). What powers, on what things? And just how does the conferring of powers constitute distinguishing?

The context in which Aquinas answers such questions is, as I've said, ostensibly associated with the story of the six days. But I think it's clear that this association in no way affects the substance of the analysis he develops here, so I'm going to set aside his few explicit references to the story, and focus exclusively on what he has to say in the Article about creating and distinguishing.

After the instant at which the universe began to exist,[32] 'nature was organized (*instituta*) in such a way [1] that the principles of nature'—viz. the elements[33]—'that were established (*condita*) then subsisted in themselves, and [2] that from them other things could be propagated as a result of correlated (*mutuam*) activity and passivity. And so [1] being had to be conferred on them [the elements] then, as well as [2] active and passive powers (which Augustine calls specifying seminal natures (*rationes seminales*)), by means of which consequent effects were produced out of them' (II.13.1.1c).

The numerals I've introduced into this passage are intended to sort out its two closely associated main topics, the first of which is creating: 'Therefore, as regards [1] the being of these principles themselves, we understand the work of *creating*, through which the substance of the elements of the world has been produced as regards its being' (ibid.). The several elements could be created, and they could then subsist in themselves, only if they were created distinct from one another in their essential natures: '*through* the work of creating, the principles of the world were *distinguished* as regards first being, which is [effected] through substantial forms' (ad 2). The substantial form of element X may be thought of as

---

[32] Aquinas begins this sentence with these words: 'in the works of the six days nature was organized'. Since he is talking here not about what happened 'in the beginning', but rather about the six days, taking this analysis to apply to a period after the beginning of the universe is in keeping with his own views. On the difference between the works of the six days and the instantaneous beginning of the universe, see Ch. Three above, sect. 7.

[33] For this identification, see the first sentence quoted in the next paragraph. In the natural science of Aquinas's time, the elements were identified as earth, air, fire, and water. None the less, much of what he has to say about the elements here can be understood as applying quite generally to *whichever* natural kinds are identified as the elements—e.g. hydrogen, helium, and the rest.

the physical constitution that makes X actual in circumstances in which it had been only potential, conferring on the sheer potentiality that is prime matter the first being (or first actuality) that is X,[34] considered just as such, thereby making X the element it is and not another one.[35] So *some* distinguishing is entailed by, and necessarily simultaneous with, any specifically plural creating; even the creating of more than one element involves some distinguishing. And this is *general* distinguishing, which we've seen Aquinas identify as 'the separating [of things]'—of the *elements*, in this case—'on the basis of *any* difference of power (*quamcumque virtutis differentiam*)' (ad 5).

The substantial form of element X, like every other substantial form, includes [2] certain specifying potentialities, certain 'active and passive powers', the actualizing of which at any time constitutes X's *second* actuality—i.e. the element's actually producing the kinds of immediate effects that are specifically characteristic of it in various circumstances.[36] The conferring of these specifying powers on the elements is an aspect of general distinguishing: 'through the work of distinguishing, general active and passive powers have been assigned to created things' (II.13.1.1c). '[T]he work of distinguishing had to occur so that they [the principles of the world] could also be distinguished as regards activity and passivity in accordance with the various powers conferred on things' (ad 2). Of course, powers of this sort associated with one element will differ from those associated with any other, and the active

[34] 'A substantial form brings about being absolutely, and its subject'—i.e. whatever the substantial form becomes the form of—'is a being only potentially' (ST Ia.77.6c). 'Actuality is twofold: first and second. First actuality is the form and fundamental wholeness (*integritas*) of a thing; second actuality is the activity' characteristic of that form and dependent on that fundamental wholeness (ST Ia.48.5c).

[35] See e.g. ST Ia.23.5, ad 3: 'Since prime matter is as a whole uniform in itself, where natural things are concerned a reason can be given why in the beginning God established one part of it under the form of fire and another under the form of earth—viz. so that there might be a diversity of species in natural things. But the reason why this part of matter is under this form, and that part under another form, depends on God's simple volition, just as it depends on the simple volition of the artisan that this stone is in this part of the wall, and that one in another part, even though the nature of his art demands that some stones be in this part and some in that part.'

[36] These powers or potentialities are among those that are codified in natural laws. Notice also that Aquinas identifies these powers with Augustine's *rationes seminales* (see sect. 3 above). On the difference between first and second actuality generally, see also e.g. Ch. Two above, sect. 3.

powers of one may complement the passive powers of another, giving rise to '*correlated* activity and passivity' among the elements. As a result, 'other things could be propagated' from the elements, for it is these 'active and passive powers . . . by means of which consequent effects were produced out of them [the elements]', and it is the '*general* active and passive powers' that Aquinas describes as 'moving them [the elements] toward *every* species' (ibid.).[37] As Aquinas sees it, the origin of species less fundamental than the elements themselves is a consequence of the correlated activity and passivity of the elements, stemming from the active and passive powers which God conferred on them in his general distinguishing of them, and governed thereafter by God's providence.

Aquinas's identifications of elemental general powers are drawn from thirteenth-century natural science, but they can be thought of as standing in for the improved identifications of such powers in more recent science. These are powers (and correlations) of a sort that, then as now, would be codified in principles of natural philosophy, or natural laws. '[T]here is a kind of diversity in those distinctions', because among the powers 'conferred on the elements are qualities that are principles of alteration[38] (e.g. the hot, the cold, and the like[39]) and also [qualities that are] principles of local motion (e.g. heaviness and lightness[40])' (ad 3).

Aquinas recognizes another, subsequent kind of distinguishing: a *determinate* distinguishing that is applicable to at least *biological*

---

[37] Notice how well this account complements the one in In Sent. II.12.1.2, which we looked at in sect. 3 above: 'at the very beginning of creation *some* things were distinguished through their species in their own nature—e.g. the elements . . . But *other* things [were distinguished then] only in their specifying seminal natures—e.g. animals, plants, and human beings. All those things were produced in their own natures later, in that work by which God . . . guides nature, which was previously established.'

[38] Aquinas shows that he associates all natural corporeal beginnings and ceasings with alteration when, later in this same Article, he speaks of 'the movement of alteration, in accordance with which generation and corruption occurs'.

[39] In the natural science which Aquinas is relying on, it isn't subatomic particles that in various combinations underlie the characteristics of the elements—e.g. one proton plus one electron for hydrogen. Instead, the hot and the cold, the wet and the dry, are the sub-elemental principles that in their various combinations underlie the characteristics of the elements—e.g. the cold and the dry for earth.

[40] These, too, are of course outmoded principles. But replacing them with references to the forces in terms of which local motion is now explained would not, I think, alter any aspects of this thirteenth-century account that are essential to Aquinas's purposes here.

species once the species have been formed. For 'some of the active and passive powers are [powers] that move (*sunt moventes*) [the elements] toward *determinate* species—e.g. the power that is in the semen of a lion, or of a horse' (II.13.1.1c).[41]

Distinguishing, then, is the process whereby the something that was created instantaneously out of nothing takes on the features of the natural world—the elemental features at once, as aspects of creating itself; the rest afterwards. So distinguishing provides the fundamental metaphysical framework for scientific theories intended to explain the development of this world's natural kinds, or species. The framework suggested in Aquinas's account of distinguishing appears to involve two explanatory components: (1) the principles of nature, or the elements, the substantial forms of which include active and passive powers that partially explain the development of the natural kinds that are more complex than one or another element alone and that have specifying powers of their own; and (2) the causal agency that interacts with those natural powers in such a way as to complete the explanation of the fact that the created world is characterized by *these* natural kinds rather than others. In the second of the three parts of his metaphysics of creation, in chapters 39–45, the issue for Aquinas is to establish the identity of (2).

His main strategic aims in those seven chapters, then, are to show, first, that, despite any appearances to the contrary within his own natural theology, the distinguishing of things can and must be ascribed to God, that God is the causal agent who not only confers but also governs those natural powers; and, second, that this ascription, correctly understood, enhances, rather than threatens, the account of God's nature which Aquinas has already argued for. The first six of those chapters are designed to achieve the first aim indirectly, by arguing against alternative explanations of the world's complexity and multiplicity. The last of them, chapter 45, is intended to achieve the second aim.

---

[41] In the context of the story of the six days, what I'm calling determinate distinguishing is associated by Aquinas with furnishing: 'Therefore, through the work of distinguishing, general active and passive powers have been assigned to created things, moving them to every species. But through the work of furnishing, powers moving toward determinate species have been conferred on things' (II.13.1.1c).

7. A mind behind the scenes

Some of the alternative explanations of distinguishing which Aquinas was faced with and had to try to refute are unlikely to strike any modern reader as plausible, never mind appealing; so I'll spend no more time on them than it takes to identify them, though I will often draw on them for explanatory material.[42] But the first alternative Aquinas deals with—chance—is a rival to his theistic explanation that has only gained in importance since the Middle Ages.[43] On at least one plausible notion of chance—as the unplanned convergence of two or more previously independent series of causes[44]—modern theories of evolution, biological and otherwise, might seem to be asserting what Aquinas is denying in the thesis of chapter 39: 'The distinguishing of things is not by chance' (1151).[45] Chance mutations (or chance events generally) together with natural selection constitute the causal agency identified in such theories. It is, of course, important to find out what Aquinas means by 'chance'; but we can be reasonably sure beforehand that no discovery along that line alone is going to reconcile theism and Darwinism as ordinarily understood.

However, the standpoint provided by the development of all of Aquinas's natural theology in Book I and the first part of Book II

[42] The alternatives that strike me as less important are presented in four chapters of the seven that make up this second part: 41, 'The distinguishing of things is not a consequence of contrary [primary] agents'—i.e. against Manichaeism, with its good agent and evil agent (see also Hayes 1964: ch. 1, §3: 'Dualism and the Problem of Evil'); 42, 'An ordering of secondary agents is not the first cause of the distinguishing of things'—i.e. against emanationism, and the view that not God but angels brought the physical world into existence; 43, 'The distinguishing of things is not the result of any secondary agent's introducing various forms into matter'; 44, 'The distinguishing of things did not stem from a diversity of merits or demerits'—i.e. against Origen's theory that 'God, from his goodness alone, at first produced all creatures equal, and all of them spiritual and rational. They were moved in different ways through free decision—some adhering more or less to God, others pulling away from him more or less. As a result of this, various grades were established among spiritual substances on the basis of divine justice' (1203), some of them being justly punished by being made to inhere in bodies.

[43] For an excellent recent study see van Inwagen 1995.

[44] See e.g. 41.1168; also 42.1182: 'things, events, or states of affairs that come out of a concurrence of various causes and not from one determinate cause are the ones that we say are by chance'; and 44.1205: 'what comes from a concurrence of various causes none of which depends on another is by chance'.

[45] The thesis is also the chapter's title; and the titles of chs. 39–44 are Aquinas's own.

does offer a view of these competing explanations of development that makes them look much less inimical, much more capable of contributing, to a co-operative explanation. In terms of the classification we've become familiar with in this chapter, scientific theories of evolution are theories of the distinguishing of things that are not accompanied by any theory of the producing of things as regards their being; they are accounts of the origin of species unconnected with any attempt at an account of the origin of the stuff out of which the species evolved. As answers to the big question, they are at least radically incomplete, having nothing to say about why there is something rather than nothing at all. By contrast, Aquinas's theory of the distinguishing of things is preceded by, and based on, his theory of the origin of the stuff that gets distinguished: God's producing something out of nothing. If, as I'm inclined to do, we take Aquinas's argument E/U to have already established the fact of God's creating,[46] the fact that 'everything other than God must be traced back to him as to the cause of its being' (as E/U concludes), then Aquinas approaches his theory of the origin of species equipped with a closely related theory of the origin of everything.

Besides, that more basic theory of his establishes the existence of a mind behind the scenes of nature, and that makes all the difference. If creation is a fact, then there is an all-knowing, all-powerful mind behind the scenes. And in that case it is at least highly implausible that the creating intellect and will should play no part in governing and guiding the development of its creation. Scientific theories of evolution provide explanatory accounts of what goes on in the scenes of nature, and they provide their explanations by applying scientific principles to data surviving from earlier scenes. No such accounts or explanations, considered just as such, are incompatible with, or even threatening to, the theistic account Aquinas is developing. Good explanations of Hamlet's behaviour in later scenes of the play can be developed by applying psychological principles to data gathered from earlier scenes without ever considering what Shakespeare may have had in mind, without even acknowledging that there is a playwright's mind behind those scenes. But, in general, good explanations of that sort are obviously compatible with explanations in terms of what the playwright may

---

[46] See Ch. Two above, sect. 8.

have meant in building these or those developments into the play, and there is reason to suppose that each sort of explanation might enhance the other.

Of course, because Aquinas identifies the mind behind the scenes of nature as the mind of omniscient, omnipotent, perfectly good God, attentive to and concerned with his creation, some of what goes on in those scenes can indeed look threatening to, and even incompatible with, theism.[47] But all that's important for now is that we've so far seen no reason in principle why theories of evolution couldn't be grafted on to Aquinas's theory of creating and considered as theories that fit the framework provided by his metaphysical, theistic account of distinguishing and extend it with a well-established physical account of distinguishing.

8. Not by chance

Given what I've just been saying about the starting-point of Aquinas's argumentation in defence of a theistic account of distinguishing, it might be expected that any argument of his against taking the world's natural kinds to have arisen by chance would be based on simply pointing out that no distinguishing effected by an absolutely perfect intellective-volitional being could be by chance. One of the senses in which he uses the word 'chance' would be likely to strengthen that expectation: 'what comes from an agent's action apart from (*praeter*) the agent's intention is said to happen by chance or fortune' (SCG III.3.1886);[48] for surely nothing that comes from an omniscient, omnipotent agent's action does so apart from the agent's intention—*if* by that is meant only what would be contrary to, or fall short of, the agent's intention.

However, just one of Aquinas's six arguments in chapter 39 takes that expected line:

[47] As I remarked in TMOT, 54, I consider the argument from evil the most powerful objection to theism, but one that has recently given rise to rejoinders that are at least as powerful. See e.g. Stump 1985, Adams and Adams 1991, Peterson 1992, Howard-Snyder 1995. And it's worth noting that van Inwagen presents his discussion of chance as 'a prolegomenon to a discussion of the problem of evil' (1995: 42).

[48] See also e.g. In Sent. I.13.2.1c; ST IIaIIae.64.8c; SCG II.39.1156, quoted just below; and 41.1174: 'What is brought about apart from an agent's intention does not have a cause *per se* but happens *per accidens*—as when someone who is digging in order to plant something finds a treasure.'

The form of any and every thing that proceeds from an agent acting through intellect and will was intended by the agent. But this very universe of created things has as its originator God, who is an agent acting through intellect and will (as is clear on the basis of things established earlier [in II.23–4]). Nor can any defect be found in his power, so that he might in that way fail to realize his intention; for his power is infinite (as was shown above [in I.43]). Therefore, the form of the universe must be intended and willed by God. Therefore, it is not by chance; for we say that things are by chance that are apart from an agent's intention. Now the form of the universe consists in the distinguishing and ordering of its parts. Therefore, the distinguishing of things is not by chance. (1156)

What makes this argument noteworthy is not its use of the ex-pected line, but what it has to say about form. It's the *form* of the universe that 'must be intended and willed by God', and so it's the form of the universe that can't be by chance. And 'the form of the universe consists in the distinguishing and ordering of its parts'—i.e. the natural kinds in their synchronic and diachronic interrelations. What's more, as Aquinas says in the next argument, 'what is good and best about the universe consists in the ordering of its parts relative to one another, which cannot occur without distin-guishing. For it is through that ordering that the universe is consti-tuted in its totality, which is what is best about it. Therefore, the ordering of the parts of the universe and the distinguishing of them are the end for which the universe is produced' (1157).[49] *Formal* distinguishing, the only kind that's at issue here, gives rise to the natural kinds, the parts of the universe. And the parts are what get ordered in the structure of the universe; and all this taken together is the form of the universe, the best thing about

[49] See also e.g. 42.1183: 'what is best in connection with all caused things is the order of the universe, in which the good of the universe consists'; 1184: 'what is best in connection with caused things is the distinguishing and ordering of them'; 1185: 'if there are any secondary causes in the production of things, their ends and actions must be for the sake of the first cause's end, which is the ultimate end where caused things are concerned. But that is the distinguishing and ordering of the parts of the universe, which is, so to speak, the ultimate form.' Also 44.1204: 'what is best in connection with created things is the perfection of the universe, which consists in the ordering of things that have been distinguished. For in all cases the perfection of the whole outranks the perfection of the individual parts.' As Aquinas observes here (in 1157), distinguishing, which accounts for the universe's having the parts it has, is a necessary condition of the ordering of the parts, but distinguishing is surely only *logically* prior to ordering. And, as these several passages suggest, the 'parts' of the universe and their 'order' turn out to be the essential components of his detailed account of the goodness of creation. See sect. 10 below.

it.[50] Although the form of the universe isn't the *ultimate* end for which the universe is produced, it is, as we'll see, the immediately subsidiary end that most evidently serves the ultimate end, which is the manifesting of God's goodness.

The most convincing and instructive evidence which Aquinas offers against distinguishing's having occurred by chance is developed in the chapter's second argument (supplemented by bits of the third). It begins with his unimpeachable observation that chance necessarily presupposes contingency: 'chance occurs only in connection with things, events, or states of affairs that can be otherwise (*in possibilibus aliter se habere*)' (1153).[51] And it goes on to apply this association of chance with contingency to considerations of form and matter, the metaphysically fundamental constituents of physical nature.[52] Matter considered absolutely—prime matter—is nothing but potentiality, the locus of all alternative real (not merely logical) possibilities for physical nature.[53] Even matter considered relatively—e.g. carbon and oxygen considered as the proximate matter for one or another compound—is, taken in that way, a locus of a certain range of alternative real possibilities. Matter, then, a source of real contingency, admits of chance effects. Form, on the other hand, is precisely what 'determines the possibilities[54] in matter to just one of them'—e.g. when the correlative active and passive powers of carbon and oxygen interact so as to determine the possibilities in those elements to just carbon dioxide or, in another case, to just carbon monoxide. So, 'since the source of that sort of possibility is matter, but not form . . . things

---

[50] Aquinas has more pointed reasons for saying that the form of the universe is the best thing about it (brought out in sect. 10 below). But it seems undeniable on the face of it that what is best or most impressive about the universe is the co-ordinating constitution of its totality, which is what makes possible the flourishing of any particularly impressive smaller-scale component of it.

[51] See also 1152: 'there can be chance only in connection with things, events, or states of affairs that can be otherwise; for of those that are necessary (*ex necessitate*) and for ever we do not say that they are by chance'.

[52] As used by Aquinas and in my discussions of his work, 'form' and 'matter' are, of course, technical terms associated with metaphysical concepts. So 'matter' as I'm using it here is not to be understood quite as it would be in its scientific or ordinary uses in twentieth-century English, even though some of my uses of it overlap those contemporary uses. See sect. 9 below.

[53] See e.g. 43.1195: 'prime matter cannot pre-exist by itself before all formed bodies, since it is nothing but potentiality only; for every case of existing in actuality is from some form'; also Ch. Three above, sect. 3.

[54] Reading *possibilitates* for *possibilitatem*.

distinguished on the basis of *form* are *not* distinguished by chance. Now the distinguishing of *species* [from one another]'—e.g. CO_2 from CO—'is on the basis of form, while the distinguishing of *individuals of one and the same species* [from one another]'—this molecule of CO_2 from that one—'is on the basis of matter.[55] Therefore, the distinguishing of things as regards their species cannot be by chance. However, perhaps chance can be what distinguishes some individuals [from one another]' (1153).

Metaphysically speaking, the generating of this particular pigeon from two others is an instance of the sort of alteration that constitutes determinate distinguishing.[56] And in Aquinas's view, the existence of this particular pigeon, which differs only materially and accidentally from that one, may well be a chance effect: 'since matter is the source and cause of things, events, or states of affairs that are by chance (as has been shown), there can be chance in the making of those that are generated out of matter' (1154)—i.e. in the making of all corporeal things that are not directly created, produced out of nothing. But since 'the distinguishing of things as regards their *species* cannot be by chance', the fact that there are pigeons at all cannot be by chance.

What does Aquinas mean by saying that 'perhaps chance can be what distinguishes some individuals [from one another]' (1153), or that 'there can be chance in the making of those that are generated out of matter' (1154)? He certainly does not mean that there may be no causal explanation for the existence of the pigeon that's now pacing my windowsill. In a later argument in that same chapter he *defines* chance as a kind of *cause*—'a *per accidens* indeterminate cause' (1155). I think he intends that formula to encapsulate the Aristotelian conception of chance as the result of an unplanned convergence of two or more previously independent series of causes. Of course, there are causal series that explain this pigeon's existing. But because those series are independent of each other, this particular pigeon's existence is a chance state of affairs. Only some agent's intervention—e.g. a pigeon-fancier's deliberately breeding a particular pair of pigeons to produce one of this particular genetic make-up, or God's working a covert miracle by intervening in nature to assure the mating of just those two—would

---

[55] See also ST Ia.47.2c, quoted in sect. 4 above.
[56] See sect. 6 above, esp. n. 38.

make this particular pigeon's coming into existence other than a chance occurrence.[57]

When Aquinas associates material, individual distinguishing with chance, is he implying that the generating of this or that pigeon in the wild 'comes from' God's action (of formal, specific distinguishing) '*apart from*' God's intention?[58] As I've already observed, if 'apart from' (*praeter*) means just *contrary to*, or *falling short of*, the agent's intention, then nothing that comes from an omniscient, omnipotent agent's action does so apart from the agent's intention. But, of course, very many of the particular effects of an agent's action may have been *neither* intended by the agent, *nor* disappointing to the agent, *nor* contrary to the agent's intention; and I see no reason why that should not be true of the action and intention of even an omniscient, omnipotent agent. It is worth noting that Aquinas uses 'perhaps' and 'can' to hedge his association of chance with material distinguishing.[59] He could be expressing uncertainty, but I think it's more likely that he's carefully leaving room to deny later that the coming into existence of this or that *human* individual takes place apart from God's intention.[60] However, as regards the generating of particular astronomical or geological entities and the generating of individual members of species of plants or of non-human animals, I think Aquinas is suggesting that they may take place apart from, though of course not contrary to, the intention of the creator/distinguisher.

Aquinas's arguments for the unique status of human individuals can't be assessed until we come to them. But, with all consideration of that issue having been postponed for now, I don't see any reason why a Darwinian would want to quarrel with Aquinas over his view of the existential status of *individuals*—astronomical, chemical, geological, or biological. On the other hand, his denial that chance can account for the *species* there are may look like an irreconcilable difference with evolution—unless and until the particular mutations on which natural selection operates are characterized as occurring by chance only in the sense that they occur apart from God's intention, and unless and until there is agreement that

---

[57] And even in such a case, the fact that the pigeon's flesh includes this atom of oxygen rather than that one would remain a chance state of affairs.

[58] See SCG III.3.1886 and II.39.1156, both quoted above in this section.

[59] See 39.1153 and 1154, quoted in the immediately preceding paragraph.

[60] See Ch. Eight and esp. Ch. Ten below.

natural selection could be God's instrument for formal distinguishing, supervenient on nature's correlated active and passive powers.

In 39.1159 Aquinas looks at pre-Socratic accounts of distinguishing, which happen to be the nearest approximations to evolution he
could have known about. He first rejects 'the view of the ancient
natural philosophers who claimed that there was only one material
cause, out of which all things came to be by means of rarefaction
and condensation'.[61] It is because those pre-Socratics do not recognize 'any agent's ordering intention' as the source of 'the distinctions among the things that we see in the universe' that 'it is
necessary for them' to ascribe those distinctions to 'the fortuitous
movement of matter'. With no mind behind the scenes, the rarefy-
ing and condensing of the primordial stuff must be fortuitous, at
least in the sense of being ultimately inexplicable. In theories that
involve no mind behind the scenes, it is inevitable that the series of
such explanations will, sooner or later, break off with an allusion to
chance—*per accidens* indeterminate causation.

Aquinas also considers 'the view of Democritus and Leucippus',
who, unlike their predecessors, posited not one, but 'infinitely
many material principles—viz. indivisible bodies [or atoms] of the
same nature but differing in shapes, ordering, and position. They
claimed that the diversity among things arises out of the concourse
of those atoms (a concourse that had to be fortuitous, since they
denied an agent cause) as a result of the three differences among
the atoms that have already been mentioned. . . . And from this it
followed that the distinctions among things are fortuitous.'
Aquinas declares this position to be 'clearly false on the basis of the
things already established', among which he must mean to include
the existence of an intellective-volitional agent and the restriction
of chance to the distinguishing of individuals from one another.

In 39.1158 Aquinas cites what he considers to be evidence that
the line he has taken in his arguments is compatible with Scripture.
His confirmation for ascribing to God not only creating but also
distinguishing depends on a misquotation (or, at any rate, a para-
phrase), but one that's understandable and perhaps even excus-

---

[61] Rarefaction and condensation are the principles introduced by Anaximenes to
account for the distinguishing of elemental air, his 'one material cause'; but Aquinas
appears to be citing them here as paradigms for *any* motive principles, or causal
powers, that the early natural philosophers may have introduced into one or another
single basic matter in order to explain the origin of species.

able: 'Holy Scripture acknowledges this truth, as is clear in Genesis 1, where, when it says, first [v. 1], "In the beginning God created the heaven and the earth", it adds [v. 4], "God distinguished (*distinxit*) the light from the darkness", and so on regarding other things, so that not only the creating of things but also the distinguishing of things is shown to be by God.' In the Vulgate text used by Aquinas, the verb in verse 4 is *divisit* ('divided'), not *distinxit*; nor does any form of the verb *distinguo* appear in the description of the first three days (vv. 2–13).[62]

Since his evidence for locating distinguishing in the story of the six days will concern us much less than his reasons for saying that the form of the universe is the best thing about it, we might note that he ends 1158 by offering Scriptural confirmation for that superlative. In Genesis 1 the formula 'And God saw that it was good' typically marks the end of the description of the work of one day.[63] However, the text offers a different appraisal of *all* the work: God carries out the work of distinguishing 'not by chance, but as what is good and best for the universe—which is why Scripture adds [v. 31]: "God saw *all* the things that he had made, and they were *very* good."'

9. Not by matter alone

Aquinas's rejection of chance as the explanation of the distinguishing of species is followed immediately by his rejection of the possibility that all distinguishing might be accounted for on the basis of matter alone, in chapter 40, 'Matter is not the first cause of the distinguishing of things'. Since he has just recognized at least the possibility that matter has a causal role in the distinguishing of *individual* things, the negation he argues for in chapter 40 provides an essential explanatory supplement to chapter 39. And since scientific accounts of even the *specific* distinguishing of things evidently would identify matter as its first cause, this chapter seems also to present a particularly clear instance of an external difficulty for Aquinas's account.

In that connection, it's important to introduce explicitly some

[62] In vv. 6 and 7 God is also described as dividing rather than distinguishing things: v. 6, *dividat*; v. 7, *divisitque*.

[63] See also sect. 2 above.

terminological differences regarding 'matter' that ordinarily go without saying. To begin with, (1) the metaphysical concept of matter (hereafter, metaphysical matter) is different from (2) the physical concept of matter (hereafter, physical matter).[64]

(1) Metaphysical matter is arrived at by speculation and conceptual analysis, independently of precise observation and experimentation. Metaphysical matter, the 'hyle' in 'hylomorphism', is the inert substratum represented in the concept of the material cause, which is always the matter *for*, or *relative to*, something else. Electrons are proximate metaphysical matter relative to atoms, elements relative to compounds, water relative to coffee; words are metaphysical matter relative to sentences, books relative to libraries. 'Prime matter' is metaphysical matter considered absolutely— a theoretical terminus of matter–form analysis rather than an independently real component of nature, as physical matter is. It is metaphysical matter about which Aquinas says, later in Book II, that 'being itself is the proper actuality not of the matter, but rather of the whole substance; for being is the actuality of that about which we can say that it *is*, and that it is, is said not about the matter, but about the whole [matter–form composite]. And so we can't say that the matter *is*; instead, *the substance itself* is that which is' (54.1289).[65] However, all metaphysical matter other than prime matter—all proximate metaphysical matter—even when it is *considered* only as matter for some further form, or as the matter of some substance, does have a substantial form of its own,[66] along with the active and passive powers that go with that form. So proximate metaphysical matter must have some form with its own specifying active and passive powers, even though it can be considered as inert metaphysical matter for purposes of analysis. Considered in themselves, *physically*, the carbon atom and the oxygen atom in a molecule of carbon monoxide are of course matter, but we know now that they are physically not inert. Considered relatively, *metaphysically*, they are merely the theoretically inert proximate matter underlying the form that determines a molecule of

---

[64] See n. 52 above.   [65] See also e.g. 43.1196–7.

[66] See also e.g. 43.1197: 'matter cannot exist without any form at all, and so some form is presupposed in matter'. Also ST Ia.50.5c: 'Considered in itself, being is associated with form, since anything is a being in actuality in that it has form. Matter, indeed, is a being (*ens*) in actuality through form'; also Ia.76.6c: 'Matter . . . has being (*esse*) in actuality through substantial form.'

carbon monoxide. And if the molecule is the subject of matter–form analysis, then it alone is the formed matter that is properly said to exist, while its constituent atoms are said to exist only *as* that formed matter's material component.

And so (2) physical matter is often assigned the role of metaphysical matter in particular instances of matter–form analysis. Historically, physical matter occurs in two varieties: (a) *philosophical*—e.g. elemental matter identified speculatively before precise observational and experimental identification was available, and consequently now superseded, as in the case of elemental earth, air, fire, and water; (b) *scientific*—i.e. matter as now conceived of in chemistry and physics at the level of the elements or, more generally, at various subatomic levels.

Neither in modern science nor in Aquinas's pre-scientific, philosophical conception of it is physical matter physically inert. In modern physics, energy is an aspect of matter as essential to it as mass is. To put it more crudely, from a scientific standpoint, the fundamental stuff of nature, considered just as such, has been discovered to be essentially *active*. As for Aquinas, he couldn't ascribe any sort of distinguishing to matter (as he does) if it weren't for the correlated active and passive powers that he thinks characterize all actually existing, physical matter, beginning with elemental matter.

Now what, exactly, is he out to accomplish in chapter 40? The negative claim in the chapter's title is stated more precisely in its thesis: 'the distinguishing of things is not a consequence of *the diversity of* matter as its first cause' (1160).[67] In this context, his characterization of matter as diverse indicates that what's at issue is elemental matter in all its varieties, the result of the primordial formal distinguishing that is an aspect of creating.[68] Of course, if

---

[67] See also CT I.71, 'The diversity of matter is not the cause of the diversity in things'.

[68] See also In Met. XII: L2.2438: 'Now although generation takes place out of the [kind of] non-being there is in potentiality, still, it's not the case that anything whatever is made out of anything whatever. Instead, various things are made out of various (*diversis*) matters. For each and every generable thing has determinate matter from which it is made, since form must be proportioned to matter. For although *prime* matter is in potentiality to *all* forms, it takes them on in a certain order. For it is in potentiality to *elemental* forms first, and through the medium of them, in accordance with the various proportions of their combinations, it is in potentiality to various [further] forms. That's why it cannot be the case that anything whatever is made out of anything whatever—except, perhaps, as the result of an

'*first* cause' is taken strictly, in the sense of a cause whose existence and efficacy are self-explanatory, the thesis scarcely needs an argument.[69] Aquinas comes closest to taking that approach in the fourth of the chapter's five arguments:

Things that have a cause of their existence and are distinguished [from other things] have a cause of their distinctness. For anything is made a being [only] in so far as it is made *one*—[i.e.] undivided in itself and distinct from other things. But if matter in its diversity is the cause of the distinguishing of things, we have to posit matters that are distinct in themselves. It is certain, however, that any matter has its existence from something else, because (as was shown above [in II.15]) everything that is in any way at all has its existence from God. Therefore, something else is the cause of distinguishing where matters are concerned. Therefore, the diversity of matter cannot be the *first* cause of the distinguishing of things. (1164)[70]

In some of the other arguments, however, 'first cause' seems to be taken less strictly and to indicate only whatever is to be identified as the terminus of explanations of the *distinguishing* that is at issue. Here, for instance, is the chapter's second argument: 'Things that exist as a result of an agent's intention'—and, as we've seen, such things include all *species*—'do not exist on account of matter as their first cause. This is because matter becomes a cause in actuality only in so far as it is moved by an agent; and so an agent cause is causally prior to matter.' For reasons that will emerge, if they're not already plain, in this part of the argument Aquinas is

---

analysis into prime matter.' Cf. SCG II.40.1165: 'the distinguishing of species in things, which is in accordance with form, does not occur on account of matter. Instead, various matters were created (*materiae sunt creatae diversae*) in order that they might be suited for various forms.' See also nn. 33, 34, and 66 above.

[69] See e.g. ST Ia.47.1c: 'even matter was created by God. For that reason, distinguishing also, if any distinguishing does stem from matter (*si qua est ex parte materiae*), must trace back to a higher cause.'

[70] See also e.g. 41.1170: 'Things that have a cause of their distinctness cannot be the first cause of the distinctions among things.' Also In Met. XII: L2.2440: 'But this argument [in 2439] goes against Anaxagoras in so far as he claimed that intellect needs matter to make things. For if he were to posit as the first source of things an intellect that produces matter itself, then the first source of the variety (*diversitatis*) of things will be from the order apprehended by that intellect, which, in so far as it intended to produce various things, instituted various matters naturally suited to the variety of things.' Cf. SCG II.40.1166: 'Now on this basis [viz. the arguments of ch. 40] is ruled out the view of Anaxagoras, who supposed that there were infinitely many material principles that were from the beginning mixed together in one confused mass [out of] which intellect afterwards established the distinguishing of things by separating [it]. The views of any others who posit various material principles to cause the distinguishing of things [are] also [ruled out].'

talking about *metaphysical* matter. 'For that reason, if some effect is a consequence of the disposition of matter and an agent's intention, it is not a consequence of the matter as its *first* cause.' So the formal distinguishing of species on the basis of the dispositions of various matters has as its *first* cause the agent's intention. 'And that's why we see that things that *are* traced back to the matter as to their *first* cause are *apart from* the agent's intention—e.g. congenital deformities, and other cases of nature's shortcomings (*peccata*).' *Rana pipiens*, the bullfrog, is a species and so can't be traced back to matter as its first cause. And in the case of an individual deformed bullfrog, it's not its being a bullfrog that has the matter as its first cause, but rather its being *this* bullfrog and so its being deformed that *is* traced back to the matter as to its *first* cause.[71] The fact that there is this deformed bullfrog is a *chance* state of affairs,[72] to be explained on the basis of the unplanned convergence (apart from the agent's intention) of previously independent series of causes. An individual's natural failure to actualize fully the potentialities that characterize its species—thus one of nature's shortcomings—is apart from the agent's intention. This frog's deformity may be the chance result of industrial pollution, of the interaction of correlative active and passive powers in chemical waste and genetic material.

[71] 'The distinguishing of things can arise from matter only in connection with those that are made out of pre-existing matter' (1163).

[72] 'For nothing determinate can arise from matter except by chance ... especially in the absence of an agent's intention (*sublata intentione agentis*)' (1161). See also e.g. 41.1176: 'What is altogether non-existent is neither good nor bad; but whatever is, is good, in so far as it is (as has been shown [in 1171]). Therefore, it must be that anything is bad in so far as it is a non-being; but *that* is a being that is [to some extent] deprived of being (*hoc autem est ens privatum*). Therefore, what is bad, in so far as it is so, is a being that is deprived of being; and the badness itself is that very privation. Now privation has no *per se* agent cause, because every agent acts in so far as it has form; so the *per se* effect of an agent must be something having form, since an agent does something like itself (except *per accidens*). Therefore, we are left with the conclusion that what is bad does not have a *per se* agent cause but happens *per accidens* in connection with effects of *per se* agent causes.' (See also Stump and Kretzmann 1988.) Also CT I.102.199: 'things, events, or states of affairs that arise only from the necessity of matter are evidently by chance (*quae solum ex necessitate materiae proveniunt, casualia esse videntur*)'. Also QDP 3.16c: 'Some [pre-Socratic philosophers], who did not understand that God is the originator of the universe, posited self-existent (*non ab alio existentem*) matter and claimed that the diversity of things is produced out of its necessity.... according to them, it followed that the distinguishing and ordering of the parts of the universe would be by chance, since it was necessary that it be that way on account of the necessity of matter.'

Form, on the other hand, does result from an agent's intention. This is clear from the fact that an agent does something like itself in respect of form. And if this sometimes falls short (*deficiat*), then that is by chance, on account of the matter. Forms, therefore, are not consequences of the disposition of matter as their first cause. On the contrary, matters are instead disposed in such and such ways so that there may be such and such forms (*materiae sic disponuntur ut sint tales formae*). But the distinguishing of things as regards species is through forms. Therefore, the distinguishing of things [as regards species] is not a consequence of the diversity of matter as its first cause. (1162)

10. Manifold manifestation

Aquinas appears to have organized his investigation of distinguishing in such a way as to deal first with the two most fundamental alternatives to his own theistic account: chance and the diversity of matter. After ruling them out as ultimate explanations (in chs. 39 and 40), he takes up and rejects (in chs. 41–3) three alternative accounts that are like his own in identifying the cause of distinguishing as an intellective-volitional agent (or agents), but radically different from his in requiring that the agent (or agents) of distinguishing be other than God. Origen's theory, a fourth alternative, is expounded in chapter 44. It does identify God as the cause and, like Aquinas's own account, is expressly opposed to Manichaeism. But Aquinas rejects it in detail because Origen, unlike Aquinas, couldn't accept the variety of natural kinds in the physical universe as an aspect of God's original plan and felt 'compelled to suppose that every diversity found in things has stemmed from a diversity of merits, in accordance with God's justice' (1203).[73] Aquinas then concludes this second part of his account of creation by disclosing, in chapter 45, 'What is *in truth* the first cause of the distinguishing of things'—by which he means not primarily to declare that God is its first cause, something he's already been arguing in various ways throughout the six preceding chapters, but rather to say what motivates God's distinguishing of things. And to explain distinguishing in this way is to say why God produced *this* world, which is also to provide the ultimate answer to the question of why there is what there is rather than something else.

[73] See n. 42 above for a brief synopsis of chs. 41–4.

Expressing the topic of chapter 45 in those terms is bound to suggest other questions.[74] What is the status of this world among all possible worlds? Is it the best of them? If it isn't, then why would an absolutely perfect being create it? If it is, then the best possible world involves a great deal of evil and suffering; so, again, why would an absolutely perfect being create it?[75] These particular questions about creation are of course connected with the general question I've discussed earlier: why would God, the absolutely perfect being, create anything at all?[76] I've argued that God's goodness requires something other than itself (so other than God himself) as its manifestation, that God therefore necessarily (although freely) wills the creation of something or other, and that the *choice* involved in creating is confined to the selection of which possibilities to actualize for the purpose of manifesting goodness—i.e. to the distinguishing of things. So, although I disagree with Aquinas's claim that God is free to choose whether to create, I'm inclined to agree with him about God's being free to choose what to create. A passage I quoted earlier in this connection will set the stage for our appraisal of chapter 45 and the questions associated with it: 'Speaking absolutely, God of course does not will things [other than himself] necessarily . . . because his goodness has no need of things that stand in an ordered relationship to it, except for purposes of manifestation, which can be carried out appropriately in various ways. And so there remains for him a free choice for willing this one or that one, just as in our own case' (QDV 24.3c).[77]

Most philosophers who have considered the question of God's freedom regarding what to create have come down on the other side of the issue. The standard position seems to be that if the world is the creation of omniscient, omnipotent, perfectly good God, then it must be the best of all possible worlds. Such a creator is,

---

[74] The remainder of Ch. Six draws on Kretzmann 1991*b*.

[75] See n. 47 above. I'm not going to discuss the problem of evil here. But the line which Aquinas takes in ch. 45 in answering such questions as these points to a certain sort of solution to the problem.

[76] See Ch. Four above, sect. 1; also TMOT, Ch. Seven, sect. 8, and Kretzmann 1991*a*.

[77] There is a textual difficulty in this passage. See Kretzmann 1991*a*: 222 n. 48, where I reluctantly adopted a different reading. In that last phrase, 'just as in our own case', I take Aquinas to be saying that God's choice of what to create in order to achieve his end of manifesting his goodness is like our choice among various courses of action for the achieving of our happiness, which Aquinas takes to be our naturally necessitated end.

therefore, *not* free to choose what to create.[78] In chapter 45 Aquinas, too, says some things that, taken by themselves, might suggest that he's on his way to the standard position:

[S]ince every agent tends (*intendat*) to introduce its likeness into its effect to the extent to which the effect can take it on, the more perfect the agent is, the more perfectly does it do this. . . . But God is the most perfect agent. It pertained to God, therefore, to introduce his likeness among created things most perfectly, to the extent to which that is compatible with created nature. But created things cannot attain a perfect likeness of God on the basis of just one species of created thing because, since a cause surpasses its effect, what is in the cause simply and as one is found complexly and as many in the effect, unless the effect belongs to the species to which the cause belongs. . . . Therefore, in order that a perfect likeness of God might be found in created things in the way that pertains to a created thing, there had to be multiplicity and variety in them. (1220)[79]

So Aquinas's Aristotelian principle that every agent produces something somehow like itself[80] makes it look as if Aquinas's God does have to create the best of all possible worlds, and is therefore not free to choose what to create.

Because the absolutely independent, simple, eternal nature of God, who is being itself, is radically unlike the modes of being available to utterly dependent, composite, temporal things, it is impossible that the universe, understood as the manifold manifestation of that nature, be a precise manifestation of its first cause. On the other hand, because of God's status as the most perfect agent, it looks as if the manifestation must be as *nearly* precise as pos-

---

[78] For the earliest version of this standard position, see Plato, *Timaeus* 29E–30B. Those philosophers who, like Leibniz, have reasoned along these lines to the conclusion that the actual world must in fact be the best possible world have set themselves up as easy targets for mockery of the sort that begins with 'Just look around you!' But a line of reasoning like the one I've just sketched is of course more often used as a basis for *denying* that such a being could be the creator of *this* world—perhaps the blandest version of the argument from evil.

[79] See also 1221: 'there wouldn't be a perfect likeness of God in the universe if there were only one level of all beings. Therefore, there is distinguishing among created things in order that a likeness of God may be attained more perfectly through many than through one'; 1222: 'in order for there to be a perfect imitation of God in created things, it had to be the case that various levels would be found among them'; 1224: 'it pertains to the perfecting of the universe that there are not only many individuals but that there are also various species of things and, consequently, various levels among things'; 1226: 'a product made by a supremely good artisan must not lack the highest perfection'.

[80] See n. 25 above.

sible—as if God did have to create the best of all *possible* worlds. Here again, then, the combination of the agent's-likeness principle with one of Aquinas's previously argued theses—in this case, that God is absolutely perfect (I.28)—might be taken to imply a conclusion that Aquinas would disown—in this case, that God's creating this particular world is necessitated by his nature.[81]

However, despite occasional passages that suggest otherwise, Aquinas really has no use for the familiar notion of the best of all possible worlds—the notion of the world that is best in all possible respects—as can be seen in his analysis and appraisal of possible worlds in terms of their forms' created constituents: their 'parts' (or natural kinds) and the 'order' of those parts.[82] He recognizes two sorts of order: first, the synchronic and diachronic *organization* of the parts with respect to one another—the structure of the universe—and, second, their *directedness* toward their end, which is the purpose of creation.[83] Although the parts and order of any one possible world are in fact inseparable constituents of its form,[84] variations in parts and variations in order are conceptually distinct. Even though God's nature entails that any world God might create would have to be the best possible in respect of its *order*, no world *could* be the best possible in respect of its *parts*. 'In respect of the most appropriate *order* conferred on these things [i.e. the parts, the natural kinds] by God, in whom the good of the universe is founded, the universe—supposing these things [to be its parts]—*cannot* be better. If any one of these *things* were better, the proportion of the order would be destroyed, just as the tuning of a harp would be destroyed if one string were stretched more than it had to be. None the less, God could make *other* things, or *add* others to these things after they were made. And in that case that universe

---

[81] For two other problems of this sort, see sect. 5 above.

[82] See n. 49 above.

[83] The difference between these two kinds of order is not unimportant. As Aquinas says elsewhere, 'Similarly, in an army, too, there is an order of the parts of the army to one another in accordance with their various duties, and there is the order [of the whole army] to the leader's good, which is victory. And the latter order is the principal one, the one for the sake of which the former order exists' (In Sent. I.44.1.2; see Appendix III below). None the less, for most of my present purposes these two kinds can be treated together as 'order' as distinct from 'parts'.

[84] The intimate association of innumerable parts *and order* in the unifying form of any world God could create is what justifies the designation 'universe' (*universum*: turned-into-one), which Aquinas uses much more often than 'world' (*mundus*). It is in this respect that Aquinas's account preserves the unity expected in God's creation.

would be *better*' (ST Ia.25.6, ad 3). Aquinas is claiming that the order of the actual world, or of *any* possible world God might have actualized, is the *best* possible. In respect of its order, 'the universe . . . cannot be better'. Generically, of course, there is one best possible cosmic order, the organization of natural kinds that most efficaciously serves the directedness of the universe and thus achieves God's purpose in creating. But that generically best order will naturally vary in its details depending on the parts that are ordered in it: this universe cannot be better in respect of *its* order, 'supposing *these* things' to be its parts.

Imagine a world the parts of which are just **1**, **2**, and **3**; and suppose that 'the most appropriate order' for them is numerical. One reason why numerical order is the best possible order for that world is just the nature of those parts; it's the best possible order *for them*. So, although this or that part—**3**, let's say—could have been made better considered in itself, occurring as **3.5**, if *it* had been better in that way while the other parts remained as they are, then in the resultant world of **1**, **2**, and **3.5** 'the *proportion* of the order would be destroyed'. And so God would not create that world.

Still, God might create a whole matched set of better versions of those parts, appropriately ordered—**1.5**, **2.5**, **3.5**—in which case he would create an intensively better version of the **1–2–3** world. Or he might create additional, compatible parts—**1**, **2**, **3**, **4**, and **5**—in which case he would create an additively better version of the **1–2–3** world. Or he might create a universe of altogether different parts—**7**, **8**, **9**—each of which is intensively better than its counterpart in the **1–2–3** world, in which case he would create a different world that was intensively better than the **1–2–3** world.

In his most detailed analysis of the problem of this world's status,[85] Aquinas presents his view of all the respects in which it is possible and all the respects in which it is impossible for God to make this world better than it is or to make a different world that would be better than this one. Although some of these improvements are concerned with variations in *parts*, the whole analysis is organized around considerations of the possibility of improvement in *order*. I can introduce the analysis most efficiently in the form of an outline.

---

[85] In *Sent.* I.44.1.2, trans. in full in App. III below.

Cosmic order

{1} The order *of the parts to one another* (organization)
  {1.1} Considered in respect of the ordered *parts*
    {1.11} *Additive* improvement: **possible**[86]
    {1.12} *Intensive* improvement
      {1.121} *Partial*: **impossible**[87]
      {1.122} *Total*
        {1.1221} In respect of *accidental* goodness: **possible**[88]
        {1.1222} In respect of *essential* goodness: **possible**[89]
  {1.2} Considered in respect of the *order* of the parts
    {1.21} *Additive* improvement: **impossible**[90]
    {1.22} *Intensive* improvement
      {1.221} In the order associated with *accidental* goodness: **possible**[91]
      {1.222} In the order associated with *essential* goodness: **impossible**[92]

{2} The order *directed toward the end* (directedness)
  {2.1} Considered in respect of *the end*
    {2.11} Improvement: **impossible**[93]
  {2.2} Considered in respect of *the order*
    {2.21} Improvement: **possible**[94]

---

[86] e.g. **1–2–3** plus **4–5**, where the result is neither merely an improved version of the **1–2–3** world nor an altogether different better world.

[87] e.g. **1–2–3.5**, destructive of the **1–2–3** world's order.

[88] e.g. **1.5–2.5–3.5**, where the result is a better version of the **1–2–3** world, conceivably as a consequence of evolutionary improvements of species **1**, **2**, and **3**.

[89] e.g. the **7–8–9** world, different from and better than **1–2–3**.

[90] Because additive improvement in this respect presupposes previously unordered parts, a state of affairs impossible in any world created by God. But even a universe consisting of pervasively *ordered* species may not always look *orderly*, viewed synchronically. Its 'organization', the order among its parts, may emerge only in the long run—in the universe viewed diachronically.

[91] e.g. if some species were to get better at achieving their natural ends, where the result would be a better version of the world affected in this way. Improvement of this sort would very likely involve adjustments of relations between species ('organization'), and could involve extinction of one species by another. Consider e.g. the human species and the AIDS virus.

[92] Because this sort of improvement in order presupposes different parts.

[93] Because it presupposes for the universe an ultimate goal better than assimilation to the absolutely perfect being. See App. III, lines 94–6 and cf. lines 41–2.

[94] e.g. if some species were to get better at achieving their natural ends, which are subsidiary to God's purpose for the universe. The result would be a better version of the world affected in this way, analogous to {1.221}.

Aquinas develops this analysis in replying to the question 'whether God could make a better universe',[95] and one of the issues is whether certain kinds of improvements would result in this world's becoming better than it is or in its being replaced by a different better world. The analysis is intended to show that in respect of putative improvements {1.121}, {1.21}, {1.222}, and {2.11}, this world is as good as possible. However, in respect of improvements {1.11}, {1.1221}, {1.221}, and {2.21}, God could make this world better. And in respect of improvement {1.1222} God could make a different world that was better.[96] A closer look at some of these improvements, possible and impossible, will help to clarify Aquinas's position.

An *additive* improvement of the world's organization in respect of the parts themselves {1.11} is possible 'through the addition of more parts in such a way that many other species would be created and the many levels of goodness there can be would be increased . . . And in this way God could have made and could make a better universe. But that universe would be related to this one as whole to part, so it would be neither entirely the same nor entirely different.'[97]

As for *intensive* improvement of the world's organization in respect of its parts, we've already seen why a *partial* improvement of that sort {1.121} cannot be accomplished without a worsening of the world. *Total* intensive improvement in respect of *essential* goodness {1.1222} 'would be possible for God, who can establish infinitely many other [intensively better] species. In that case the parts would not be the same, however; and, consequently, neither would it be the same universe.'[98] The other sort of total intensive improvement {1.1221} *would* count as bettering the actual world—e.g. replacing every species there is with a better counterpart.

An *additive* improvement of the world's organization in respect of the order itself {1.21} would have to be an extension of order to some previously unordered parts, but 'unless an addition were

---

[95] I've included all of In Sent. I.44.1.2 in App. III because I can't discuss all of it here, although all of it is relevant to this discussion.

[96] There is a sense in which God could also make a different world better in respect of {1.222}, but only in making a different world better in respect of {1.1222}. And it seems to me possible, and possibly important, to recognize {1.221} and {2.21} as respects in which this world could *become* better.

[97] App. III, lines 54–60.   [98] App. III, lines 73–6.

made to the *parts* of the universe', this sort of improvement is impossible because 'in the universe there is nothing that has not been ordered'.[99] So in this respect the actual world is as good as any world could be.

Intensive improvement of the world's organization in so far as it has to do with *accidental* goodness {1.221} takes place whenever any part gets better at being the sort of thing it essentially is, since the order is better to the extent to which any species ordered in it better fulfils its role in the world's organization—for instance, human beings behaving more rationally. In at least some such cases, it seems, the world *becomes* better rather than being directly *made* better by God. But there could be no corresponding improvement having to do with *essential* goodness {1.222}—i.e. better *sorts* of things—'unless other parts and [thus] another universe were made'.[100]

As for {2} in the outline above, since the *directedness* of the actual world, like that of any world that might have been created by God, is its orientation toward God himself in manifesting God's goodness, there can be no improvement of this order in respect of the end itself {2.11}, since 'there can be nothing better than God'[101]—another respect in which this world is as good as any world could be. This is the broad sense of 'order' in which there *is* a single best cosmic order regardless of parts. However, given the absolute perfection of that unique, universal, ultimate end, and the high degree of disorientation within at least the essentially rational part of the actual world, 'the order directed toward the end could be improved in so far as the [accidental] goodness of the parts of the universe and their order to one another prospered (*cresceret*), because the more closely they were related to the end, the more they would approximate a likeness to the divine goodness, which is the end of all things'.[102]

So Aquinas's analysis of evaluative differences among possible worlds reveals four respects in which God could make this world better (two of which are also respects in which it could just become better, with God's help), one respect in which God could make a different better world, and four respects in which this world is as good as possible.

---

[99] App. III, lines 78–80.   [100] App. III, lines 85–6.
[101] App. III, lines 90–1.   [102] App. III, lines 92–6.

11. God's choice of this world

Many of the difficulties and suggestions in this analysis will have to
be left to one side for now, but I want to call attention to an
apparently incoherent conclusion that seems to follow from it: the
conclusion that omniscient, omnipotent, perfectly good God
chooses to create a world that is not in every respect the best of all
possible worlds.[103] Given Aquinas's account of God's nature, the
only way he can dispel the appearance of incoherence is to show
that God's choosing to create this world is *not* his choosing less than
the best, which he can do by showing that there is no possible world
that is best in all respects. But that is just what his analysis does
show.

As I've already argued,[104] the absolutely-perfect-being-and-noth-
ing-else state of affairs is impossible. So, since nothing besides God
is absolutely perfect, no possible world is absolutely perfect. But it
doesn't follow that emptier is better where worlds are concerned.
As Aquinas's analysis shows—e.g. in the discussion of {2.21}—any
world's degree of perfection is the degree to which God's goodness
is manifested in it, the degree to which it represents God. The
utterly pervasive, optimal organization and directedness of its species, whatever they may be, is one respect in which any world can
(and would) represent God in the highest degree possible for those
species. But 'between even the highest [possible] created thing and
God there is an infinite gap',[105] so there can't be an optimal *set* of
parts for a universe—a series of species than which no better species could be conceived of. The creator's nature entails that whatever world he chooses to actualize is optimally *ordered* in respect of
the essential aspects of the order itself, as in {1.21} and {2.11}. Any
improved version of the actual world, or even a different world
better than this one, would be just like this one in respect of the
essentials of its necessarily optimal organization and directedness.
Consequently, all possible improvements have to do with species
rather than with order as such.[106]

[103] For other treatments of this problem, see Adams 1972, Quinn 1982, Grover
1988, Howard-Snyder and Howard-Snyder 1994, Rowe 1994, Menssen and Sullivan
1995.

[104] See n. 74 above.

[105] App. III, lines 56–7.

[106] It also depends on species rather than on individuals considered as such: 'the
perfection of the universe depends essentially on the diversity of natures by which
the various levels of goodness are fulfilled, rather than on the multiplying of individuals within one nature' (App. III, lines 131–4).

Focusing on {1.11} as presenting a paradigm of an additive improvement to the organization of species considered in respect of the species in the organization, we can see that the series of possible worlds stemming from it is an infinite series, the member worlds of which are ranked in respect of the richness of their parts. This means that omniscient, omnipotent God can no more choose the additively optimal *set* of species than he can pick out the largest fraction between 0 and 1. God's inability to create a world than which no possible world is better in any respect is just another aspect of the logical character of omnipotence. The complaint that God is not omnipotent because he can't make the traditional best of all possible worlds would be even less intriguing than the old complaint that God isn't omnipotent because he can't make a rock so big that he can't lift it. It would be on a par with a complaint that God isn't omnipotent because he can't make a rock so big that he can't make a bigger rock.

If the relevant possible additive improvements consist in increasing multiplicity or complexity—having more species or more gradations of goodness among species—then it does seem that such improvements are illimitable simply on the basis of arithmetical considerations. In creating, God undertakes to represent simple, eternal, perfect goodness in a composite, temporal, necessarily imperfect medium. It's like undertaking to represent a geometer's straight line (which is continuous, infinite, and invisible) by nothing but pencilled dots. An *accurate* representation can be effected by means of only two dots, even though that would be as *imprecise* as an accurate, visible representation of a line could be. Preserving the perfection of the *order* of these elements would require that any additional representational dots occur in positions that preserve the representation of the line's one-dimensional straightness. The addition of dots to the representation in that way could be said to improve the dotty representation, to enhance its capacity for conveying the nature of the invisible, continuous, straight, one-dimensional thing (visibly, discontinuously, not *perfectly* straightly, in pencilled dots that have at least two dimensions apiece). But, of course, there can't be a theoretically *best* representation of that sort.

Even if such considerations convinced everyone of the absurdity of complaining that God didn't create the best of all possible worlds, since there is no such thing, it would still remain true on this view of the matter that God could have created a world better in

certain respects than this one—that omniscient, omnipotent, perfectly good God chooses to create a world that is in some respect(s)
less good than another he could create. But if God could do better,
how can he be perfectly good?

As Aquinas has argued (in II.25), the logical truth that God's
actions conform to the principle of non-contradiction (PNC) entails no limitation on his power. And if God's creating a world
better than any other world he could create would constitute a
violation of PNC, then *a fortiori* that logical truth that does not
diminish his power also leaves his *goodness* undiminished. God's
being that than which nothing better can be conceived of can't
entail his producing a world than which none better can be conceived of. No matter which possible world he actualizes, there must
be infinitely many possible worlds better than the actual world in
some respect or other.

All the same, these observations seem to make the creator's
choice of what to create a predicament, one that Aquinas portrays
in a word in chapter 45 when he observes that 'it is appropriate for
the highest good to make what is *better*' (1223).[107] I want to conclude this discussion by trying to dispel, or at least to mitigate, this
impression of a predicament for the creator.

I've been claiming that there couldn't be a theoretically best
dotty representation of a geometrical line. But even though any
such representation must fall infinitely short of the thing to be
represented, once a certain level of precision has been reached, no
representation would be *practically* better, better *as a representation*, even though there would still be infinitely many theoretically
better representations possible. Changing the analogy slightly, a
photocopy that could not be a more precise representation of a
printed page except in ways that lie beyond the threshold of per-
ceptibility is *practically*, although not theoretically, a perfect photocopy—perfect, considered as the sort of thing a photocopy is
intended to be: a representation for practical purposes. Suppose,
then, that the actual world considered as a representation of God is
as good as possible in the sense that any world better than this one

---

[107] It is worth noting that in Anderson 1975 this sentence—*Summo autem bono
competit facere quod melius est*—is translated 'Now, it befits the supreme good to
make what is *best*' (p. 138; emphasis added). In English Dominican Fathers 1923 this
sentence is likewise translated 'But it becomes the sovereign good to make what is
best' (p. 107).

in respect of improved precision of representation would be no better at all in its capacity to represent God to any possible created percipient. That is, suppose that the limitations essential to created intelligence are such that the actual world is as good a representation of God as there could be for created intelligences—where 'as good as there could be' need not mean 'as clear as there could be'.[108] Then it would be irrational for God to choose to create any world theoretically better than this one, and to act irrationally is not only out of the question for God, it is also incompatible with any full-fledged instance of free choice.

Even if I've made a hypothetical case for the rationality of God's choice of a world theoretically less good than another he could have chosen, have I made that case in such a way as to leave no alternatives, establishing the rationality at the expense of the choice? Not if there's more than one world that is as good as possible considered as a representation—which seems quite plausible, given the radical differences between the God to be represented and the medium of the representation.

But what could motivate the creator's choice of this world rather than another that would also do the representing job supremely well? Suppose that Cosmos and Mundus are worlds either of which would be supremely good as a representation. In that case God has a motive for choosing to create either Cosmos or Mundus. But a motive for choosing either of two is a motive for picking one of them.[109] God chooses to create this world as the manifold manifestation of his goodness; but, as Aquinas's analysis shows, he could equally well have picked another that was as good in that respect.

---

[108] Even created intelligences no better than ours crave and thrive on complexity and subtlety. The Cliffnotes for *Hamlet* are clearer and much less good than the play itself. And it's important to consider the human observer-understander of the universe not, of course, as any individual (however gifted), but as the human species considered diachronically throughout its existence, past, present, and future—not merely the species at its present state of developing its capacities to observe and understand the world. My supposition that the limitations essential to created intelligence are such that the actual world is as good a representation of God as there could be for created intelligences depends on distinguishing between essential limitations and those that are merely characteristic of a particular developmental stage of human observational and interpretative capacities.

[109] See ST Ia.23.5, ad 3, quoted in n. 35 above.

SEVEN

INTELLECTS

1. Considering created things themselves

At the very outset of his investigation of creation in Book II, Aquinas quotes Psalm 142/3: 5, in which he finds a suggestion of the plan he means to follow: 'I have meditated on all your activities, and I was meditating on the works of your hands' (1.851). In the first and second parts of Book II (chs. 6–38 and 39–45), he has developed his accounts of God's transeunt activities of producing and of distinguishing. So he's ready now to consider directly the results of those activities, the created things themselves: 'by "the works of his hands" we understand heaven and earth and all things that come into existence from God as handiwork comes from an artisan' (1.857). This third and final part of Aquinas's investigation of creation, then, has as its topic 'the nature of the things themselves that have been produced and distinguished' (5.877)—a topic that surely looks broad enough to warrant Aquinas's devoting to it all fifty-six remaining chapters of Book II, even though he at once introduces a restriction, noting that he will be concerned with the nature of created things themselves only 'in so far as it pertains to the truth of the faith'.

As we saw in Chapter One above, part of what's excluded by that restriction is the consideration of natural things 'in their own right', and of 'aspects that are associated with them in accordance with their own nature—fire's being carried upward, for example' (4.871–2a). Such considerations are the business of natural philosophy, which not only considers nature differently from the way Aquinas proposes to consider it here, but is also intended to consider *all* of it, including many features that he excludes from consideration in his natural theology: 'the configuration of the sky, for instance, and the quality of motion' (4.872b). Aquinas intends to take up 'only those aspects of created things that are associated with them in so far as they are traced back to God: that they have been created by

God, that they are subject to God, and things of that sort' (872*a*). Restrictions along those lines are only to be expected since, as we've seen, Aquinas envisages his natural-theological study of God's creation in Book II as a further study of God—God considered in his works—intended to enhance and extend the outcome of the study of 'God considered in himself' in Book I.[1] But even such restrictions appear to leave an enormous range of natural kinds of things to be considered in this concluding part of his treatment of creation.

Moreover, it's not just the range, but also the significance, of the consideration of created things that evidently justifies Aquinas's allocating to it more than half of Book II. The special importance he attaches to it is indicated by the amount of attention he pays to 'the consideration of created things' in Book II's introductory chapters (1–5)—far more than to God's activities of producing and distinguishing. Chapter 2 explains (1) the usefulness of this consideration for enhancing one's understanding of certain divine attributes, and chapter 3 shows (2) how 'views that are mistaken about created things sometimes lead a person away from the truth of the faith, to the extent to which they are incompatible with a true cognition of God' (864). Chapter 4, then, begins by summing up these purposes, explaining that Aquinas's project has a concern with 'the consideration of created things [1] in so far as some sort of likeness of God is reflected in them and [2] in so far as a mistaken view regarding them leads to a mistaken view regarding matters concerning God' (871).

So, even after we have in these ways taken account of the restriction 'in so far as it pertains to the truth of the faith', we still have reason to expect Aquinas's consideration of created things themselves to cover very many natural kinds, especially 'in so far as some sort of likeness of God is reflected in them'. For, as he explains in Book I,

[T]he divine essence comprehends within itself the excellences of *all* things ... the divine intellect can comprehend in its own essence that which is proper to each thing by having intellective cognition of [the respects] in which anything imitates its essence and in which the thing falls short of its own perfection. For instance, in having intellective cognition of its own essence as imitable by way of life without cognition, the divine

---

[1] See Ch. One above, sect. 3; also TMOT, Ch. One, sect. 8.

intellect takes up the form proper to *plant*; while if [it has intellective cognition of its own essence] as imitable by way of cognition without intellect, [it takes up] the form proper to [non-human] *animal*; and so on as regards other things. (54.451)[2]

And when Aquinas actually begins this third part of his account of creation, connecting it with the second part's investigation of God's distinguishing of species, he writes as if he might well be intending to consider at least representative species from all levels of nature: 'Therefore, that being the reason for the diversity among things'— i.e. the manifold manifestation of God's goodness—'it now remains for us to go forward regarding the things that have been distinguished, to the extent to which doing so pertains to the truth of the faith—which was the third topic we proposed [in II.5.877]' (46.1229).[3]

2. *Considering intellective creatures only*

So it could come as a surprise that Aquinas in fact devotes the entire third (last) part of Book II to considering, broadly speaking, only one kind of created thing: *intellects*—or, more precisely, only such kinds of created things as are essentially intellective in them-

---

[2] See also TMOT, Ch. Six, sect. 5c.
[3] See also some of the passages considered in Ch. Six above as explaining the manifoldness of God's manifestation of his goodness—e.g. 45.1220: 'since every agent tends (*intendat*) to introduce its likeness into its effect to the extent to which the effect can take it on, the more perfect the agent is, the more perfectly does it do this. . . . But God is the most perfect agent. It pertained to God, therefore, to introduce his likeness among created things most perfectly, to the extent to which that is compatible with created nature. But created things cannot attain a perfect likeness of God on the basis of just one species of created thing because, since a cause surpasses its effect, what is in the cause simply and as one is found complexly and as many in the effect, unless the effect belongs to the species to which the cause belongs. . . . Therefore, in order that a perfect likeness of God might be found in created things in the way that pertains to a created thing, there had to be multiplicity and variety in them'; 1221: 'there would not be a perfect likeness of God in the universe if there were only one level of all beings. Therefore, there is distinguishing among created things in order that a likeness of God may be attained more perfectly through many than through one'; 1222: 'in order for there to be a perfect imitation of God in created things, it had to be the case that various levels would be found among them'; 1224: 'it pertains to the perfecting of the universe that there are not only many individuals but that there are also various species of things and, consequently, various levels among things'; 1226: 'a product made by a supremely good artisan must not lack the highest perfection'.

selves—human minds, for instance. Does anything he's said so far about his aims justify or explain that very narrow focus? Well, as we've seen more than once, in his natural theology he's concerned with investigating creation not as the sciences investigate it, but just for what it can show us about the nature of its creator. That's why he's committed to approaching created things from the top down, since in the context established by his natural theology so far, a created thing's nearness to the top of creation depends on the degree of its likeness to God. And, among created things known to us, it is *intellective* beings that exhibit the highest degree of likeness to God.[4] It is at least in that sense that his turning now to directly considering natural kinds, 'the things that are distinguished', is governed by the degree to which such an investigation 'pertains to the truth of the faith'.

Furthermore, as we've seen in reviewing his general introduction to his account of creation, he views the account as concerned with 'the consideration of created things [1] in so far as a kind of likeness of God is reflected in them and [2] in so far as a mistaken view regarding them leads to a mistaken view regarding matters concerning God' (4.871). But (1) a kind of likeness of God is reflected in *intellective* creatures to a greater extent than in stars, or in trees, or in cats; and (2) our mistaken views regarding *intellective* creatures, such as ourselves, lead to more importantly mistaken views about God. These two assessments strike me as altogether plausible, but there's also evidence for both of them in the introductory chapters.

In the opening sentence of Book II, where Aquinas is connecting the account of creation he's about to begin with his completed account (in Book I) of God considered in himself, he notes that the fullest knowledge of God available to us must include some knowledge of God's activity (1.852). In Book I he has already shown, in great detail, that intellect and will must be ascribed to God.[5] And, as Book II develops, it becomes clear, even in the introductory chapters, that not only God's *immanent* activity, but also such

---

[4] ST Ia.27.1c: 'Now since God is above all things, things that are said in connection with God should be understood not by way of the lowest created things, which are bodies, but in terms of the likeness [to God] that belongs to the highest creatures, which are intellective substances ([although] a likeness drawn even from them falls short of a representation of divine matters).' See also SCG II.47.1238: 'intellective substances are first among created things'.

[5] Intellect: I.44–61; will: 62–102. See also TMOT, Chs. Six–Eight.

transeunt activities of his as producing and distinguishing, are fundamentally intellective and volitional.[6] In chapter 3, which explains the importance of dispelling mistaken views about the nature of created things, the only dangerous mistakes that are expressly associated with the nature of one created thing specifically are the mistakes we intellective creatures make about ourselves—about the independence of our wills, about the origin and immortality of our souls, about our relation to God, about 'human dignity'—mistakes a person makes 'because of ignorance of the natures of things and, consequently, of his standing in the ordering of the universe' (3.868). Someone victimized by such ignorance may, for instance, believe that he is '*subjected* to certain created things to which he is *superior*. This is clear in the case of those who subject the wills of human beings to the stars' (ibid.).[7] And human beings, absurdly inferior to stars in all obvious physical respects, are superior to them only metaphysically, as beings that are, unlike stars, essentially alive, essentially sensory, and essentially intellective.

So there clearly are good reasons why Aquinas's natural-theological consideration of creatures focuses on those that are intellective. Moreover, the nature of intellective beings turns out to be endlessly complex in itself, and so important to natural theology in various ways that Aquinas devotes to it, besides the fifty-six remaining chapters of Book II, almost all the discussion in the 163 chapters of Book III.[8] In other words, beginning with chapter 46 of Book II, all the rest of Aquinas's natural theology in SCG I–III—219 chapters out of a total of 366—is concerned in one way or another with intellective creatures.

The ten chapters II.46–55 form a general introduction to this detailed exploration of a strictly limited range of creatures.[9] But the first thing to be determined is just exactly what Aquinas intends to be exploring. I've been using the term 'intellective creature' as if

---

[6] See e.g. 1.854 and 856; 2.859 and 862; 4.876; also Ch. One above, sect. 5; Ch. Two above, sects. 2 and 4; Ch. Three above, sects. 1 and 2; also TMOT, Ch. Seven. See also Stump and Kretzmann 1995.

[7] See also Ch. One above, sect. 7.

[8] Of course, the general topic of Book III is God's providence. But it's no surprise that God's plan for, and governance of, the intellective parts of creation should be the most important aspects of providence as investigated by human intellect.

[9] Because 'creatures' in contemporary English ordinarily means living things, or even just animals, I've so far been translating Aquinas's word *creatura* broadly as 'created thing'. In discussions of *intellective* beings, however, 'creature' seems less inappropriate.

everybody knows what must be meant by it, and as if human beings obviously count as intellective creatures. But the actual situation is not quite so clear, as we can begin to appreciate by surveying Aquinas's terminology in these introductory chapters. The created things he's talking about here he calls 'intellective creatures',[10] 'intellectively active creatures',[11] 'intellective substances',[12] 'intellectively active substances',[13] 'intellective natures',[14] 'intellective [beings]',[15] 'intellectively active [beings]',[16] or just 'intellects'.[17] I think that in Aquinas's usage these various terms are roughly interchangeable, and I'll use more than one of them, following him in using 'intellective substance' most often. As for the applicability of these terms to human beings, it is of course quite right to describe human beings as intellective creatures, broadly speaking. In this context, however, it will turn out to be more precisely right to restrict the application of any of these terms to just the intellective aspect of human beings: their minds, or, more generally, their distinctively rational souls.[18] In these chapters, Aquinas doesn't use the word 'mind' for these beings at all.[19] But although 'soul' isn't one of his designations for the created things he's introducing here, it does occur more or less significantly several times in these

---

[10] *Creaturae intellectuales*, in 46.1229, 1231, 1234, 1235; also 'creatures intellective in their very nature' (*creaturae secundum suam naturam intellectuales*), in 46.1233.

[11] *Creaturae intelligentes*, in 46.1230, 1232.

[12] *Substantiae intellectuales*, in the titles of chs. 47, 48, 50, 51, and 55 (except for 46 and 49, all the titles of these chapters are Aquinas's own); in 47.1236, 1238, 1239, 1240; 48.1246; 49.1247, 1249, 1256; 50.1259; 52.1273; 54.1293; 55.1297, 1298, 1299, 1300, 1301, 1302, 1303, 1304, 1305, 1310, 1312; also 'created intellective substances' (*substantiae intellectuales creatae*), in the titles of chs. 52 and 53; in 47.1237, 1238; 53.1282, 1283.

[13] *Substantiae intelligentes*, in 49.1248, 1252, 1255; 50.1260, 1261, 1262, 1263, 1266; 55.1305, 1308, 1309.

[14] *Naturae intellectuales*, in 51.1268, 1269, 1270; 55.1302, 1310.

[15] *Intellectualia*, in 48.1243, 1244, 1245, 1246.

[16] *Intelligentes*, in 46.1235; 51.1270; 55.1305, 1309.

[17] *Intellectus*, in 49.1250, 1251, 1252, 1253, 1254, 1255; 50.1261, 1263, 1264, 1265, 1266; 51.1271, 1272; 55.1306, 1307.

[18] In Aquinas's relatively infrequent use of *mens* (mind), it is typically a synonym for *intellectus* (intellect), which is usually his name for just the distinctive *cognitive* faculty of the distinctively human rational soul (*anima rationalis*) and not also its distinctive *appetitive* faculty, will (*voluntas*). See e.g. ST Ia.75.2c, where he says that this principle (or source, or faculty) of cognition 'is called mind, or intellect'. But he sometimes also uses these terms very broadly—e.g. 'the human soul, which is called intellect, or mind' (ibid.). See also TMOT, 173.

[19] But see his closely associated use of 'mind' in 46.1233, quoted in sect. 3 below.

chapters.[20] And, as he says later in Book II, 'The soul of a human being is a kind of intellective substance' (79.1598).[21] So human minds, or rational souls, are certainly one kind of created intellective substances under discussion in very general terms in these chapters. Angels are the most important other kinds which Aquinas recognizes elsewhere, but it's important to notice that in these introductory chapters he is dealing with intellective substances generically, rather than focusing specifically on human souls, angels, or demons.[22]

Several considerations make that clear. First, '*separated* [intellective] substances', all the non-human sorts, are taken up in their own right in chapters 91–101. Second, in the first paragraph following these ten introductory chapters (56.1313), Aquinas introduces

---

[20] *Anima*, in 46.1233; 49.1257, 1258; 50.1263, 1264; 55.1308; also 'intellective soul' (*intellectiva anima*), in 55.1308.

[21] It's important to notice that it's *the soul* of a human being that is classified as a kind of intellective substance, and not the complex rational animal as a whole. See e.g. ST Ia.108.5c: 'If a thing is to be called by a name designating its proper nature (*proprietatem ipsius*), then it should not be named on the basis of anything it *incompletely* participates in or on the basis of what it has to an *exceptional* degree (*quod excedenter habet*) but, rather, on the basis of what is precisely matched (*coaequatum*) to it. For instance, if someone wants to name a human being properly, he will say that it is a *rational* substance, but not an *intellective* substance. The latter is a name proper to an angel, since pure intellectivity (*simplex intelligentia*) is associated with an angel in virtue of its proper nature, but with a human being in virtue of participation. Neither will he say that a human being is a *sensory* substance, which is a name proper to a non-human animal. For sensing is something less than that which is proper to a human being. Besides, it is associated with a human being to an exceptional degree, more than with other animals.' But see also SCG II.44.1206 (quoted in the next paragraph), where 'rational substance' is used as a generic term interchangeable with 'intellective substance'.

[22] Demons aren't mentioned here at all, and *angelus* is used only once, when Aquinas is reporting on Ps. 148/9: 1–6, which expressly mentions angels in v. 2 (55.1311). It may also be worth mentioning that in these chapters Aquinas never calls these created things by the names *intelligentia*, *substantia spiritualis*, or, more significantly, *substantia separata*. None the less, the Marietti eds. label II.46–55 as *De natura substantiae spiritualis* in their outline (ii. 166), and they index these chapters under *de substantiis separatis* (ii, p. lxxiv). For reasons that will emerge, 'spiritual substance' would probably not be out of place here, but 'separated substance' is certainly too narrow. The eds. are quite right, however, in their choice of a running head for chs. 46–55: *De substantiis intellectualibus in communi* ('On intellective substances in general'). In connection with these terminological concerns, it may also be worth noting that even if the human soul can correctly be called a spiritual substance, there may be some reason for avoiding calling it a spiritual creature: 'the reason why the human soul has such an abundance of different powers is that it exists *on the borderline between* spiritual and corporeal creatures' (ST Ia.77.2c). Cf. QDA 1c: 'the human soul . . . is established *on the borderline between* corporeal and separated substances'.

his account of the human soul, his first *specific* investigation of intellective substances, by asking 'whether *any* intellective substance can be united to a body', a question he answers affirmatively just because of his conception of the human soul.[23] Third, already in chapter 44, in reducing to an absurdity Origen's account of the distinguishing of created things, Aquinas argues that from that account 'it will follow that all created rational substances—angels, demons, human souls, and the souls of heavenly bodies (which Origen claimed were ensouled)—belong to a single species . . . which is absurd. We are left, therefore, with the conclusion that the diversity of intellective substances is not a consequence of a diversity of merits,' as Origen had maintained (1206).[24] Finally, there's confirmation in chapter 94, where Aquinas argues that separated substances and human souls do not belong to a single *species*, even though 'intellective activity is proper to both a separated substance and an intellective soul' (1805).

3. Reasons why creation includes intellective substances

The correct identification of the general topic of these chapters has an important effect on the interpretation of the first of them, chapter 46, which is concerned with explaining the fact that the universe contains intellective creatures. If the topic really were just such exotic specimens as angels or demons, Aquinas would have had to begin by arguing that those unfamiliar sorts of beings really do exist. But since he is in fact considering the existence of intellects quite generally, the question of whether or not such things exist could be settled at once by the most direct sort of *observation*—introspection—which would show any reader that there is at least one intellect. Aquinas doesn't explicitly make this move, but the nature of the arguments he offers strongly suggests that he's taking its result for granted. In chapter 46, then, instead of offering proofs for the existence of intellects, Aquinas is to be read as arguing that it shouldn't be surprising that the universe includes us (or creatures relevantly like us); that, in fact, any created universe would have to include such creatures. Instead of showing *that* there are intellective substances, he must (and does) try to show *why* there are such

---

[23] See Ch. Eight below, sect. 8.   [24] See also Ch. Six above, sect. 10.

things (II.46), and just *what* they are, in respect of powers other than intellective cognition (47–8), and in respect of their fundamental nature (49–55).

Aquinas begins the work of chapter 46 by laying out the formal basis on which he proposes to show why intellective creatures exist: 'And we will show, first, that as a result of the divine plan assigning to created things the perfection that is optimal in accordance with their mode [of being], it was a consequence that some intellective creatures would be made, established at the highest level of things' (1229). I find this prospectus obscure.[25] More importantly, I think it leaves out of account Aquinas's most general and most convincing explanation for the undoubted fact that the world has intellects in it. Still, some features of the passage seem clear, and clearly right. The 'divine plan' at the heart of this account would evidently shape *any* world God might create, and so 'some intellective creatures would be made' as a part of any created universe. Intellective creatures are 'established at the highest level of things' not in the sense that this world includes the best created beings there could be—we've seen that that description has no application[26]—but in the sense that intellectivity marks off, generically, all the highest species of created things. Extraterrestrial beings relevantly better than human beings, or possible creatures exhibiting a greater likeness to God than do any actual creatures in the real world, would have to have powers at least the equal of our powers of intellect, whatever other powers they might have. So it seems that this prospectus might be intended to say that any universe God might create will serve its purpose—fulfil the divine plan—only if it includes intellect (generically considered), and that therefore every possible created world includes intellect. In any case, it should say at least that. What isn't clear to me from this passage alone is just how Aquinas intends to justify this claim.

The rest of chapter 46 consists in six arguments for its thesis, which is variously expressed in them.[27] The statements of the thesis

---

[25] *Et ostendemus primo, quod ex divina dispositione perfectionem rebus creatis secundum suum modum optimam assignante, consequens fuit quod quaedam creaturae intellectuales fierent, in summo rerum vertice constitutae.*

[26] In Ch. Six above, sect. 10.

[27] '[I]t was necessary for the perfection of created things that there be some intellectively active creatures' (1230); 'the optimal perfection of the universe required the existence of some intellective creatures' (1231); 'the highest perfection of things required that there be some creatures that would ... be active intellectively

are potentially worrisome, and so is the general line taken in the arguments. What can be worrisome about those statements is their using what look like pleonastic superlatives in their characterizations of the condition that accounts for the existence of intellects. That condition is identified as the 'perfection' of the universe, and 'perfection' is enhanced by such modifiers as 'optimal' (1229), 'ultimate' (1230), 'consummate' (1231), or 'highest' (1232 and 1233). However, as we've already seen, Aquinas's word *perfectio* can, and often should, be read as 'completion' or 'completing'; and if it is read that way here, then these apparently super-superlative characterizations may come to not much more than 'final completion'. Thus, for instance, the conclusion of the chapter's second argument might well be read as claiming that 'the final completion' (rather than 'the optimal perfection') 'of the universe required the existence of some intellective creatures' (1231).

I think that this reading of the thesis is what's really called for here, and I also think that Aquinas has access to good grounds for its support; but only one of these six arguments comes even close to presenting those grounds. The line he takes here generally can be exemplified in the fourth argument:

[A]n agent does something like itself in respect of the form in accordance with which it acts. Now the form belonging to the agent is of course sometimes received in the effect in the same mode in which it is in the agent. (The form of a generated fire, for instance, has the same mode of being as the form of the fire from which it was generated.) At other times, however, it is received in another mode of being. (For instance, the form of a building, which is in the builder's mind *intelligibly*, is received *materially* in the building that is outside the soul.) Now the first [sort of] likeness is clearly more perfect than the second. But the perfection of the universe of created things consists in a likeness to God, just as the perfection of any effect consists in a likeness to its agent cause. Therefore, the highest perfection of the universe requires not only the *second* [sort of] assimilation of a created thing to God but [also] the *first*, to the extent to which that is possible. Now the form through which God actualizes a created thing is in him an intelligible form, since he is an agent through intellect (as was

and volitionally (*esse intelligentes et volentes*)' (1232); 'for the highest perfection of the universe there had to be some creatures ... that are intellective in nature' (1233); 'intellect alone can cognize the divine goodness. Therefore, there had to be intellective creatures' (1234); 'intellective creatures have been made in order that the imitation of God's containing' or comprehending all other things 'might not be lacking to created things' (1235).

shown above [in II.23–4]). Therefore, for the highest perfection of the universe there had to be some creatures in which the form of the divine intellect is expressed in accordance with intelligible being—i.e. there had to be creatures that are intellective in nature. (1233)

I'm not now concerned with the details of this argument, but only with its basic structure, in which it closely resembles the other five. The comparison central to the argument is easy to grant: assimilation in the *same* mode is 'more perfect' assimilation than assimilation in a *different* mode—e.g. Julia's identical twin would be assimilated to her more completely than any photograph of Julia could be. Comparisons of that sort are essential to all the chapter's arguments. They constitute the crucial premises in arguments that have this general form: A is more perfect than B, so the universe had to have A rather than B, or A in addition to B. But, of course, *any* created B will also manifest God's goodness to some degree in some respect or other; and for any A, no matter how impressive its likeness to God, there could always be some still loftier creature that would manifest God's goodness even more impressively than A does.[28] Because arguments of this sort are based on considerations of the degree of precision in the manifold manifestation, they can never be conclusive. We observe that the universe has us intellective substances among its parts, and we may say that this feature of created existence makes God's creation more like God than it would otherwise have been. That's true enough, but as an explanation it's weak and dangerous. It invites the observation that *other*, *better* intellective creatures would make creation even *more* like God, so why *these*? If A, why not A+? All the arguments in chapter 46 are like that third argument in focusing on the *quality* of the manifestation. What's wanted is at least one argument that makes the point that created intellect is a *necessary condition* of God's manifesting his goodness *at all* in the way Aquinas's account of creation has him doing.

The final cause, the purpose, of God's creating is God's manifold manifestation of his simple, eternal, perfect goodness.[29] '[A] likeness to the divine goodness . . . is the end of all things.'[30] But mani-

---

[28] See Ch. Six above, sects. 10 and 11.

[29] In this paragraph I'm drawing on Kretzmann 1991*b*: 242.

[30] In Sent. I.44.1.2 (in App. III below, lines 95–6). See also n. 3 above; also ST Ia.50.1c: 'that which God especially intends as regards created things is the good that consists in assimilation to God'.

festation, like any other sort of representation, is minimally a three-place relation, involving (1) what gets represented, (2) what does the representing, and (3) the one to whom it gets represented.[31] The movement of a prehistoric glacier is represented by grooves in the rock, but only if somebody—some intellective being—sees and understands them for what they are. The mere effects of the glacier's movement are not yet signs of it. So, too, 'The heavens declare the glory of God and the firmament showeth his handiwork' (Ps. 19: 1) only if they're seen and understood. In maintaining that creation is God's manifestation of his goodness, Aquinas must be prepared to say to or for *whom* it is so. Now, the representation that creation is could hardly be for God's own contemplation. Omniscient goodness needs no looking-glass, nor has Aquinas suggested even the possibility of any such explanation. The requisite observer-understander must be a part of the created world, must itself be a part of the purposive manifestation. In short, any created world that could fill the bill which Aquinas has drawn up would have to include intellective creatures. It's this line of reasoning that I think provides the best available explanation for the existence of created intellects.

The only one of the chapter's six arguments that comes close to presenting such an explanation is the fifth:

All that moves God to the producing of created things is his own goodness, which he willed to share with other things by way of assimilation to himself (as is clear from things that have been said [in I.74 ff.]). But a likeness of one thing is found in another in two different ways: in one way, in respect of the being of nature—the way a likeness of a fire's heat is in a thing heated by the fire; in the other way, in accordance with cognition—the way a likeness of the fire is in the sense of sight or of touch.[32] Therefore, in order that a likeness of God might be in things perfectly in such ways as are possible, the divine goodness had to be shared with things through a likeness that would be shared not only in being but [also] in cognizing. But intellect alone can cognize the divine goodness. Therefore, there had to be intellective creatures. (1234)

[31] Any effect potentially manifests its cause, but an effect is an actual manifestation of its cause only in case it is interpreted as such. Skin blemishes may be symptoms of the presence of disease; but unless the blemishes are seen as manifesting disease, they are blemishes without being symptoms.

[32] Given the purpose of this argument, it's a little odd that Aquinas uses an example of sensory rather than intellective cognition. Sight and touch can cognize a fire, but 'intellect alone can cognize the divine goodness'. Still, even this example brings out the generic distinction between the two kinds of likeness.

This two-kinds-of-likeness argument is structurally like all the others in the chapter: a manifestation involving both kinds manifests more perfectly than a manifestation involving only one; therefore, etc. But in its two final sentences Aquinas does clearly say what I think he should have said more clearly and more often in these arguments.[33] In examining the rest of his general account of intellective substances, I'll be supposing that we have that explanation of their existence available to us.

4. Intellects and wills

So, any created world must include intellect as one of its parts. And intellect must be associated with *will*, as Aquinas goes on at once to argue in chapter 47: 'it is necessary that these intellective substances be volitional (*volentes*)' (1236). The first of his four arguments for that thesis is very simple, consisting in little more than a terminological review. It can't be considered a convincing argument on its own. But it lays out, more clearly than any of the others, the ingredients for what I think is Aquinas's most effective line of reasoning from intellect to will. I'll take this first argument as a starting-point from which to trace that line, without suggesting that it is more than adumbrated in the argument itself, which reads as follows:

An appetite for good is in *all* things, since, as philosophers teach, the good is what all things have an appetite for. Now in things that lack cognition this sort of appetite is of course called *natural* appetite; a stone, for example, is said to have an appetite for being farther down than it is. But in things that have sensory cognition it is called *animal* appetite, which is divided into the concupiscible and the irascible [powers].[34] In those that have intellective cognition, however, it is called *intellective* or *rational* appetite, which is *will*.[35] Therefore, created intellective substances have will. (1237)

[33] See also In DDN 4: L3.318: Dionysius 'says that intellective beings, such as angels, and rational beings, such as human beings, desire the divine good *cognitively*; for they alone can cognize the good itself, which is God'.

[34] The concupiscible power is the natural inclination of any animal, non-human or human, to seek what is suitable for it and to flee what is harmful (pursuit/avoidance instincts); the irascible power is any animal's inclination to resist and overcome whatever deters its access to what is suitable or promotes what is harmful (competition/aggression/defence instincts). See Kretzmann 1993.

[35] Perhaps Aquinas's fullest account of these species of appetite for the good is the one he provides in QDV 23.1c.

The genus under which Aquinas locates will as a species is what he identifies as the appetite for what is good, an absolutely universal appetite, associated with all being—a set of tendencies that includes, for instance, the love of money, the heliotropism of (noncognitive) plants, and even the weight of (inanimate) stones.[36] In SCG I.37.306 Aquinas offers the following explanation of Aristotle's famous citation of that principle of universal appetite:

The good is what all things have an appetite for—which the Philosopher introduces in *Ethics* I [1, 1094a2–3] as having been very well said. But all things have an appetite for being actualized in their own way, as is clear from the fact that each thing in keeping with its own nature resists harm to itself (*repugnat corruptioni*). Therefore, being actualized constitutes the essential nature of what is good. And that's why a potentiality's being deprived of its actualization leads directly to the bad that is opposed to the good [associated with the actualization of that potentiality], as is clear from what the Philosopher says in *Metaphysics* IX [9, 1051a4–17].

Aquinas's interpretation of the universal appetite for good grows naturally out of his thesis that the terms 'being' (*ens*) and 'goodness' (*bonum*) are the same in reference and differ only in sense.[37] Part of what this means is that any thing is good of its kind to the extent to which it is a whole, complete specimen of that kind, free from relevant defect, to the extent to which it is fully realized or developed, to the extent to which its specifying potentialities are actualized.[38] So a thing is good of its kind to the extent to which it is in being as a thing of that kind. 'Now every appetite is only for what is good. The reason for this is that appetite is nothing other than some sort of inclination for something on the part of whatever has the appetite. But a thing is inclined only to something like [it] and appropriate [for it] (*aliquid simile et conveniens*). Therefore, since every thing is some sort of good to the extent to which it is a being and a substance, it is necessary that every inclination be toward what is good. And it is for this reason that the Philosopher says (in *Ethics* I) that the good is what all things have an appetite for' (ST IaIIae.8.1c).

[36] Of course, it's absurd to attribute 'appetite' in any ordinary sense of the word to inanimate objects, but any other single translation for the term *appetitus* in this technical usage would simply introduce other apparent absurdities. In the rest of sect. 4 I'm drawing on TMOT, Ch. Seven, sects. 2–4.

[37] See ST Ia.5.1. On this thesis and some of its consequences see Stump and Kretzmann 1988; also MacDonald 1991. On such 'transcendental' terms in Aquinas generally, see Aertsen 1996.

[38] See also TMOT, Ch. Five, sect. 7.

So, the single referent shared by the terms 'X's being' and 'X's goodness' is X's nature to the extent to which it has been realized in X. The difference in sense between those terms shows up plainly in the fact that 'X is a good φ' explicitly commends X, as 'X is a φ' does not. A thing's goodness is its capacity to elicit appetite, to operate as a final cause.[39] And in a being that has cognition—sensory or intellective (or both)—the being's cognition of something as good for itself (whether or not it has already attained that good) will elicit appetite for that, activating the being's innate inclination toward, and approval of, its own preservation and fulfilment. As Aquinas reads the Aristotelian principle of universal appetite as applied to created (imperfect, temporal) beings, then, it seems to be expressible as a plausible, useful principle of developmental inertia: a thing tends to actualize its specifying potentialities unless adversely acted upon.

Any appetite typically has as its specific object the good of the being that has the appetite, a good which is for just that reason rightly construed as including (if not always identical with) self-preservation and self-fulfilment.[40] In the case of a human being, a creature that is sensory as well as intellective, animal appetite also plays an indispensable part in the being's achieving to any extent its preservation and fulfilment. But the specific preservation and fulfilment of what is distinctively human about us—intellect, or rationality—depend on an appetite for goods that only intellect itself can discern: the sciences and the humanities, for instance. Such preservation and fulfilment therefore require an appetitive faculty beyond animal appetite, one whose proper objects are goods of a sort the senses can't discern.[41] And, as Aquinas points out in chapter

---

[39] As at least a *subsidiary* final cause, since it may elicit appetite because of its perceived utility as something directed toward an end the agent is already inclined to rather than as an end in its own right: 'Now the essential nature of what is good, which is the object of the will's power, is found not only in an end but also in things that are directed toward the end. . . . However, things that are directed toward an end are not good or willed for their own sakes, but rather in virtue of their ordered relationship to the end. And so will is drawn to them only in so far as it is drawn to the end' (ST IaIIae.8.2c).

[40] If the being has cognition, sensory or intellective, then of course its appetite will have as its specific object what the being *takes* to be good for it, whether or not it really is so.

[41] 'Now some things are inclined toward what is good along with a cognition on the basis of which they cognize the essential nature of good—a condition proper to intellect—and these things are the ones most fully (*perfectissime*) inclined toward what is good. [It is,] of course, not as if they were directed toward what is good [for

47's fourth and last argument, since created intellect's cognitive range is theoretically unlimited, so is will's appetitive scope:

[I]n things that have cognition, the apprehending [or cognitive] power is related to the appetitive power as a mover is related to what is movable [by it]; for what is apprehended through sense, imagination, or intellect moves the intellective or the animal appetite. Intellective apprehension, however, is not limited to certain things [as sensory apprehension is], but instead has to do with all things.[42] (That's why the Philosopher in *De anima* III [5, 430a14–15] says regarding the possible intellect that it is that by which [the soul] becomes all things.[43]) Therefore, the appetite belonging to an intellective substance is disposed to all things. But to be disposed to *all* things is a proprium of *will*. (It's for that reason that the Philosopher says (in *Ethics* III [4, 1111b20–4]) that will has to do with both possible and impossible things.) Therefore, intellective substances have will. (1240)

When will is viewed in this way, as the intellectively informed inclination of unlimited scope, then some sort of intimate association with will is a condition necessary for the preservation and fulfilment of intellect, considered just as such. So, when intellective being is considered on the basis of the principle of developmental inertia, the presence of intellect may be recognized as a sufficient condition for the presence of will, considered as an intellective being's essential tendency to actualize its specifying potentialities.[44]

them] only by something other than themselves, like things that lack cognition, or [inclined] toward what is good only in some particular way, like things that have only sensory cognition. Instead, they are as if inclined toward *goodness itself*, considered *universally*. And *that* inclination is called *will*' (ST Ia.59.1c). See also ST Ia.59.4c: 'the object of intellective appetite (which is called will) is what is good considered in connection with the universal essential nature of the good.... That's why appetite in the intellective part [of the soul] is not divided in accordance with a distinction of any particular goods, as the sensory appetite is divided [into the concupiscible and the irascible powers]. [The sensory appetite] is oriented (*respicit*) not toward good considered in connection with [its] universal essential nature but rather toward some sort of particular good.'

[42] See also 49.1252: 'intellect's power of cognition is, in a way, infinite. For it intellectively cognizes species of numbers *ad infinitum* by the process of addition, and likewise species of figures and proportions. It also cognizes what is universal, which is virtually infinite in its scope since it contains potentially infinitely many individuals.'

[43] See TMOT, Ch. Six, sect. 5*b*. On the possible intellect, see Chs. Eight and Nine below.

[44] See also ST Ia.19.1c: 'will is entailed by intellect (*intellectum consequitur*). For just as a natural thing has being in actuality through its form, so [is] intellect intellectively cognizant (*intelligens*) in actuality through an intelligible form belonging to it. Now each thing has such a relationship to its natural form that when it does

That's why 'it is necessary that these intellective substances be volitional' as well.

5. Will and freedom

It's not unreasonable to think that any creature that has will must also have freedom, in some respect and to some degree. Aquinas made that connection explicit in Book I, in an observation about ordinary usage: 'will is what primarily has freedom where acting is concerned, for a person is said to perform freely any action he performs to the extent to which he performs it voluntarily' (72.624).[45] So he seems to be within his rights when he introduces chapter 48 by announcing that 'on this basis'—viz. his just-completed arguments for ascribing will to intellective substances— 'it is *apparent* that the substances we have been discussing are characterized by free decision in respect of their activity' (1241).[46] What he means here by having free decision (*liberum arbitrium*) becomes clearer in the chapter's five arguments, but it's worth noting that on at least one (later) occasion, in answer to the ques-

---

not have the form, it tends toward it; and when it has it, it rests in it. And the same [is true] of each natural perfection, that it is what is good for [that] nature. (In things that lack cognition this relationship to what is good is called natural appetite.) That's why an intellective nature, too, has a similar relationship to a good apprehended through an intelligible form—viz. that when it has it, it rests in it; but when it does not have it, it seeks it. And both [of those states] pertain to will. So in anything that has intellect there is will, just as in anything having sensation there is animal appetite.' See also SCG IV.19.3558: 'will must be found in each and every intellective nature. For intellect, in so far as it is intellectively active, is actualized through an intelligible form, just as a natural thing is actualized in respect of natural being through the form proper to it. Now a natural thing has an inclination, through the form by which it is perfected in respect of its species, toward the activities proper to it and the end proper to it, which it pursues through those activities. For any thing's activities conform to the sort of thing it is, and it tends toward things that are suitable for it. For that reason, furthermore, where an intellectively active being is concerned, an inclination toward the activities proper to it and the end proper to it must follow from an intelligible form. In the case of an intellective nature, however, that inclination is will, which is the source of the activities that are in us—activities by which an intellectively active being acts for the sake of the end. For will's object is the end and the good. Therefore, in any and every intellectively active being, will must be found as well.'

[45] See TMOT, Ch. Seven, sect. 5.

[46] As regards intellective creatures that are also human, 'the very fact that the human being is rational necessitates its being characterized by free decision' (ST Ia.83.1c). See also QDV 24.1.

tion 'Is free decision a power other than will?', he simply identifies having the power of free decision with having the power of will: 'will and free decision are not two powers, but one' (ST Ia.83.4c). Moreover, one of chapter 47's arguments for an intellective being's having will proceeds in such a way as to be also an argument for its being in certain senses free: 'Now among created substances we find some that do not activate (*agant*) themselves to their activities but are instead activated by a force of nature—e.g. inanimate things, plants, and non-human animals—for to-act-or-not-to-act (*agere et non agere*) is not in them. . . . Intellective substances, on the other hand . . . do activate themselves to their activities. But that is a proprium of *will*, through which a substance is in control of its action (*est domina sui actus*), since to-act-or-not-to-act is in it' (1238). If will is a power to act or not to act and a power through which a being is in control of its action, then it does look as if any being that has a will is, for just that reason, free in very important respects.[47]

However, in chapter 48, instead of simply alluding to these close conceptual connections in which having will (in virtue of having intellect) looks like a sufficient condition for having freedom, Aquinas offers detailed, instructive arguments in support of ascribing free decision to intellective, volitional substances. In the first of them (1242), he begins by arguing that *decision* is to be ascribed to intellective substances, and then goes on to show that that decision of theirs must be *free*.[48] He argues along these lines. Intellective substances have intellective cognition; nothing about them could be clearer than that. Furthermore (as we've just seen Aquinas arguing in 47.1238), in virtue of having will, intellective beings have control over their action. But any beings that have intellective cognition and control over their action must also have intellective *judgement* about activities to be carried out. It's only in virtue of passing judgement on various possible courses of action that an intellective being exercises control over its action, through its will's

---

[47] 'It is necessary that they [intellective substances] have freedom if they have control over their action' (48.1242); see the paragraph just below.

[48] 'It is clear that they act by decision in that through intellective cognition they have judgement regarding things to be done. But it is necessary that if they have control over their acting (as was shown [in 47.1238]), they have freedom. Therefore, the substances we have been talking about are characterized by free decision in their acting' (1242). My presentation of this argument immediately below involves some rearranging and supplementing of the materials Aquinas provides in it.

acting on the basis of its judgement. It's in just that way that its cognizing affects its willing. And in this context judgement (*iudicium*) is decision (*arbitrium*).[49] Necessarily, if any agent has control over its action, it has freedom.[50] Therefore, intellective substances are characterized by free decision in respect of their acting.

That first argument provides indispensable orientation, but for several reasons it's not so thorough and convincing as one might want—e.g. in its dependence on the casual association of will with control in 47.1238. The second argument is more satisfactory, in part because it offers some analysis of the concept of freedom.

'What is free is what is because of itself' [*Metaphysics* I 2, 982b26].[51] Therefore, what is not the cause of its own acting is not free in respect of its acting. But any things that are moved or that act only when moved by *other* things are not the cause of their own acting. There- fore, only *self*-movers have freedom in respect of acting, and only they   5 act on the basis of judgement. For a self-mover is divided into that which does the moving and that which is moved. But that which moves [any being] is appetite, [which is itself] moved by intellect, phantasia,[52] or the senses; and it is those [cognitive] faculties to which judging belongs. Therefore, among those [self-movers] the only ones that   10 judge freely are whichever ones move themselves as regards their judging. But a judging power moves itself to judging only in case it reflects on its own act; for if it activates itself to judging, it must cognize its own judgement—and that, of course, is a feature of intel- lect alone. Therefore, non-rational animals do indeed have free move-   15 ment or action, in a way, but not free *judgement*. Inanimate things, on the other hand, which are moved only by other things, do not have even free action or movement. Intellective beings, however, have not only free action but also free *judgement*—which is to have free decision. (48.1243)   20

[49] I've supplied this premiss here; it's explicit in the chapter's second argument (1243; see below).

[50] Moreover, 'We are in control of our actions to the extent to which we can choose this one or that one' (ST Ia.82.1, ad 3).

[51] The medieval Latin version of this Aristotelian passage is ambiguous in a way that is clarified in a note supplied by the Marietti eds. (ii. 87 n. 4). See also TMOT, 208 n. 15.

[52] Among the internal senses recognized by Aquinas, *phantasia* (or imagination) processes the raw data taken in through the external senses, producing and preserv- ing the 'phantasms', the sensory data that are indispensable to human intellect in its association with sensory cognition. See Chs. Eight and Nine below. See also Stump 1998.

From the Aristotelian definition with which he opens this self-mover argument, Aquinas immediately infers a conclusion (lines 2–3) that may be clearer when expressed affirmatively: a being is free in respect of its acting only if it is the cause of its own acting. So the freedom in respect of acting that concerns him here is not merely the negative variety that consists of your acting when your action is free from external control or coercion, but positive freedom, the sort of freedom you have only in case you yourself are *the source* of your doing what you do when and as you do it.[53] And, of course, any agent is the source of its own action only when its acting is not caused by something other than itself—i.e. only in case it is a *self-mover* (lines 3–6).[54] Any self-mover, X, is analysed into two (or three) components in terms of which X's self-moving may be analysed as follows: X_1, X's primary intrinsic mover, moves X_2, X's secondary intrinsic mover, which moves X itself. Aquinas's identification of these components (in lines 6–10) is less clear than it might be, but comes to this: X_1 is X's *cognitive* faculty—'intellect, phantasia, or the senses'—which moves X_2, X's *appetitive* faculty—intellective appetite (will), or sensory appetite—which moves X itself overtly. In terms of this analysis, Claudia's freely going to the library today is sorted out into her intellect's judging that, all things considered, going to the library today is the best thing for her to do and her will's consequently moving her limbs in the appropriate ways.[55] But her limbs are moved by her will, and her will is moved by her intellect. So answers to questions about the way in which, and the extent to which, Claudia is *free* in respect of her overt action of going to the library depend on answers to such questions not about the freedom of her overt movement or even about the freedom of her will, but rather about the freedom of her intellective act of judgement.

Every self-mover, considered just as such, must have as its primary intrinsic mover at least one sort of cognitive faculty, 'and it is those faculties to which judging belongs' (lines 9–10). Claudia's judgement, like any other of her actions, will be free only in case

---

[53] As further evidence of the close connection between an act's being voluntary and an act's being free, see ST IaIIae.6.2c: 'If an act is to be voluntary, its source must be within the agent.'

[54] On self-movers, see TMOT, Ch. Two, esp. 72–83.

[55] Of course, the terms of the analysis simply represent aspects of the agent herself, ways of usefully sorting out what is really *the agent's* judgement, volition, and overt action.

she herself is the source of it, only to the extent to which she moves
herself in respect of judging that it would be best, all things considered, to go to the library today (lines 10–12). And she will be able
to do that only in case she can be conscious of her judgement as
such and reflect on it (lines 12–14). Only cognitive created things
can be free in any sense, and all cognitive created things are free in
some sense (lines 15–16), as they can be only because all of them
have some sort of faculty of judgement. But not all of them have
free judgement. The instinctual faculty of judgement that is associated with sensory cognition alone—the faculty Aquinas calls 'the
estimative power'—lies below the level of self-reflection, and so
cannot be free: 'Some things lack freedom of judgement, either
because they have *no* judgement (as in the case of those that lack
cognition, such as stones and plants), or because they have a [kind
of] judgement that is determined by nature to one [outcome]—as in
the case of non-rational animals. For it is by the natural estimative
power that the sheep judges that the wolf is harmful to it, and it is
on the basis of that judgement that the sheep runs away from the
wolf' (48.1246). '[N]on-rational animals do indeed have free movement or action, in a way'—just because their action does have its
source within them, within their intrinsic, pre-programmed, instinctual judgement—'but not *free judgement*' (lines 15–16). Self-
reflective judgement, the only sort that can be free, 'is a feature of
intellect alone' (lines 14–15).[56] So 'Intellective beings . . . have not
only free action but also free judgement—which is to have free
decision' (lines 18–20).[57]

---

[56] See also 49.1254: 'Intellect . . . is reflexive in acting on itself, for intellect cognizes itself not only in respect of a part but in respect of the whole'; 1255: 'just as an
intellect cognizes a thing, so does it cognize itself cognizing, and so on *ad
infinitum*'—i.e. there is no *theoretical* limit to levels of reflexive cognition.

[57] See also the chapter's third argument, 48.1244: 'An apprehended form is a
source of movement to the extent to which it is apprehended under the aspect of
what is good, or appropriate. For in the case of self-movers, external movement
stems from a judgement by which something is judged good or appropriate through
the form already mentioned. Therefore, if the one doing the judging moves itself to
judging, it must be through some higher apprehended form that it moves itself to
judging. That [higher apprehended form] can, of course, be only the very aspect of
the good or the appropriate through which one judges regarding any determinate
good or appropriate thing. Therefore, the only beings that move themselves to
judging are those that apprehend the general nature of the good or the appropriate.
But those are only the intellective beings. Therefore, only intellective beings move
themselves not only to acting but also to judging. Therefore, they are the only ones
that are free as regards judging—which is to have free decision.'

Some important details of this account of freedom emerge only in Aquinas's account of providence in Book III.[58] But even for present purposes it is helpful to see more of what he means by claiming that intellective beings *decide* freely. If, as he often insists, it is part of intellect's nature to 'cognize the essential nature of good', as a consequence of which intellective substances 'are as if inclined toward goodness itself, considered universally',[59] then where in the relevant intellective cognition is there scope for *decision*? Decision, after all, entails at least two alternatives—contradictories (as in deciding whether or not to go to a library), or contraries (as in deciding which library to go to). Aquinas provides at least the beginning of an answer to this question in the fourth of chapter 48's five arguments (although this partial answer prompts further questions): 'Since movement and action have to do with *particulars*, movement and action do not follow from a universal conception except through the medium of a particular apprehension [or cognition]. But intellect naturally apprehends *universals*. Therefore, in order that movement or any sort of action may follow from intellect's apprehending, intellect's universal conception has to be applied to particulars.' For instance, Claudia's conviction that going to a library today would be the best thing to do will lead to movement and action only if she also knows where some particular library is, or how to find out where a library is. 'But a universal contains many particulars potentially. Therefore, an intellective conception can be applied to many and various things.' There may be more than one conveniently located library, and there will almost certainly be several different ways of finding out where a library is. 'Therefore, intellect's judgement regarding things that can be done is not determined to only one thing. Therefore, all intellective beings have free decision' (1245). So, as far as can be told from the arguments of chapter 48, the power of free decision that is a concomitant of being an intellective-volitional being may get exercised only in cases in which practical reasoning involves picking and choosing among a plurality of particulars all of which are covered by the relevant universal conception and judgement.

In the limiting case in which all those particulars are covered in just the same respect by an intellective judgement that can't be

---

[58] See e.g. SCG III.75, 85, 87–90.   [59] See n. 41 above.

made more specific in any relevant way, the faculty that carries out
the picking (which in such cases scarcely counts as choosing) is
simply the will associated with that intellect: 'it depends on the
simple volition (*ex simplici voluntate*) of the artisan that this stone
is in this part of the wall, and that one in another part, even though
the nature of his art demands that some stones be in this part and
some in that part' (ST Ia.23.5, ad 3). When the particular alternatives are all equally covered by the universal intellective conception
and judgement, all equally suitable in all relevant respects, then, if
free decision is a component of the process at all, it is exercised by
will alone, in an act of 'simple volition'.[60] But, of course, that
limiting case of strictly indifferent alternatives is rare.

Typically, the deciding in free decision will be exercised by intellect, and intellect's decision will be carried out by will: 'A judgement is, so to speak, the conclusion and determination of
deliberating. But, of course, deliberation is determined primarily
by reason's pronouncement (*sententia*), and secondarily by appetite's acceptance [of that pronouncement]. That's why the Philosopher says in *Ethics* III [5, 1113a9–12] that "judging *on the basis of*
deliberation, we desire *in accordance with* deliberation". And in
this way choice (*electio*) itself is called a kind of judgement, on the
basis of which it is named free decision' (ST Ia.83.3, ad 2).[61] This
linking of choice to judgement via decision indicates the intimate
relationship between will and intellect on which Aquinas's conception of freedom is based,[62] a relationship in which intellect naturally
takes the lead:[63] 'Will is the root of freedom considered as [free-
dom's] *subject*'—i.e. as the faculty through which freedom is finally
exercised.[64] 'Considered as [freedom's] *cause*, however, [the root of

---

[60] For the whole passage, see Ch. Six above, n. 35. It's in cases of this sort that
Aquinas's occasional identification of having free decision with having will seems
most obviously appropriate—e.g. ST Ia.83.4c: 'will and free decision are not two
powers, but one'.

[61] See also e.g. ST IaIIae.13.3c: 'Choice follows [intellect's] pronouncement or
judgement, which is a sort of reasoned conclusion about what is to be done.'

[62] See also ST IaIIae.1.1c: 'free decision is said to be a power of will and reason
[or intellect]'.

[63] 'An appetitive power [such as will] is a passive power that is naturally suited to
be moved by what is apprehended' by a cognitive power, such as intellect (ST
Ia.80.2c); 'an intellectively cognized good moves will' (ST Ia.82.3, ad 2). Aquinas
couldn't maintain that being intellective entails being volitional and having free
decision if he didn't also think that intellect was the dominant partner in the
intimate interaction of the two faculties.

[64] See also QDV 23.1, sc 4: 'will is the root of freedom'.

freedom] is reason [or intellect]. For will can be led freely to various things just because reason can have various conceptions of what is good. And so philosophers define free decision as the free judgement of reason (*liberum de ratione iudicium*), as if [to indicate that] reason is freedom's cause' (ST IaIIae.17.1, ad 2).[65]

6. What intellective creatures could not be

In arguing that beings that are intellectively active must also be volitional and exercise free decision, Aquinas has been explaining what such creatures must be like as regards other, appetitive faculties and operations essential to them in virtue of their distinctive cognitive faculties and operations. On the basis of this short, reasoned catalogue of their cognitive and appetitive aspects (in chs. 46–8), he intends to investigate the metaphysics of intellect, to show what must be the fundamental nature of intellective-volitional beings, considered just as such. Broadly speaking, we count as such beings, of course. However, at this stage of his investigation, Aquinas is concerned with the metaphysical status only of our intellective souls considered generically in themselves, as instances of created intellective being, and not with our status considered as human beings—i.e. rational (corporeal) animals.

He begins this phase of the investigation by clearing the ground: he devotes chapters 49–51 to ruling out some modes of being as incompatible with intellectivity.[66] An intellective substance cannot be a body—i.e. formed matter (II.49).[67] So, since Aquinas recognizes *only* corporeal matter, matter as a metaphysical component of nothing but various sorts of bodies,[68] an intellective substance

[65] There's a rapidly growing literature of very helpful, detailed philosophical and scholarly studies of Aquinas's conceptions of will, of will's relations with intellect, of the nature of free decision, and related topics. See e.g. Gallagher 1991 and 1994; Hause, forthcoming; MacDonald 1998; Stump 1997 and 1998.

[66] Although he has argued that having intellective cognitive faculties and operations entails having will and free decision, and although those latter characteristics seem also to provide grounds on which to argue against the modes of being he intends to rule out, in the arguments of these three chapters he appeals only to the *cognitive* aspect of intellective substances.

[67] '[A]nything that is composed of matter and form is a body' (50.1260). On matter in this metaphysical sense, see Ch. Six above, sect. 9.

[68] In this respect he differs significantly from many of his medieval predecessors and contemporaries, who were *universal* hylomorphists, metaphysically analysing *all* creatures as composites of matter and form, and thus committing themselves to

cannot be material *at all* (II.50).[69] In Aquinas's Aristotelian meta-physics, matter and form are the two metaphysical components of reality. Matter conceptually stripped of all form is *prime* matter, pure potentiality, which can't exist just as such, without any actual-izing form.[70] Certain forms devoid of all matter can, however, exist just as such. So, if intellective beings must be immaterial, then all the intellective beings there are must be forms. But most forms we're familiar with—forms such as star, tree, squirrel, and uni-corn—are parts of created reality only in so far as they do inform matter. Those ordinary forms *cannot* subsist—i.e. exist on their own, extra-materially and extra-mentally. So, if an intellective substance is to be identified as a form, it can't be one of those familiar '*material* forms' that depend for their real existence on being the forms of some matter (II.51). '[I]ntellective natures are *subsistent* forms rather than forms existing in matter as if their being depended on matter' (51.1268). In sum, no intellective substance could be a body, or material in any respect; every intellective substance must be an incorporeal, immaterial, subsist-ent form.[71]

Of course, these are radical claims. It would, and should, take quite a lot of ingenious argumentation to convince most people that among the things in the universe that exist on their own, there must be incorporeal, immaterial *forms*. Those of us who aren't scientists have been astonished again and again by new claims about what there is in more and more remote super-galactic and subatomic reaches of the world. But there are at least two respects in which all astonishing claims of those sorts should be recognized

accepting the doctrines of spiritual matter and the plurality of substantial forms. These issues and many others relevant to the subjects of this and following chapters in this book are explained in well-documented discussions in Pegis 1934.

[69] Obviously, then, he doesn't restrict 'substance' as he restricts 'matter'. This comes out plainly in 49.1257, where he explains 'a mistake of the ancient natural philosophers' on the grounds that they 'posited only *corporeal* substance'.

[70] See Ch. Three above, sect. 3; also Ch. Six above, sect. 9. See also e.g. CT I.74.128: 'And since a thing's being follows its form (*quia esse sequitur formam rei*), things of that sort [those that are subject to generation and corruption] of course exist when they have [their] form but cease existing when they are deprived of [their] form. Therefore, there must be in them something that can have a form at one time but be deprived of the form at another time—which is what we call matter.'

[71] As we've seen (in Ch. Six above, sects. 8 and 9), Aquinas takes matter to be the principle of individuation in created things. We can, therefore, anticipate a problem associated with the individuation of creatures that are in no way material. See e.g. II.92–3.

as less radical than the ones Aquinas is making here. In the first place, they all have to do with *physical* aspects of the world, with remote, unfamiliar, ordinarily inaccessible reaches of the familiar physical world, in some neighbourhoods of which we feel quite at home. But these claims of Aquinas's introduce into the created world non-physical, immaterial *spiritual* entities—definitely not included among the sorts of things we're sure we encounter every day.[72] In the second place, most—certainly not all—of those astonishing *scientific* claims are irrelevant to your conception of your own mind, the very aspect of reality you have some reason to say you know best, or at least most intimately. But Aquinas's claims here *are* claims about our intellects (whatever else they may be about), and most of us wouldn't unhesitatingly recognize our own familiar minds under his description of them as incorporeal, immaterial, subsistent forms.

To anyone who has been reading SCG I and II to this point, it's already obvious that Aquinas is not a materialist. From the early chapters of Book I onward it's been clear that God, the absolutely fundamental element of Aquinas's theory of everything, is in no way material. Still, it's not logically impossible that a god who is not at all material should create an altogether material world. And if Aquinas were claiming that the only exceptions to a material creation, the only immaterial creatures, were angels and demons, then we might be able to bracket our philosophical questions about created subsistent forms as having to do with a part of his theory that has little if any bearing on our ordinary experience of reality. But, of course, he seems to be claiming also that in one essential respect we ourselves are among those exceptions.

Considerations like those make it sensible to postpone appraising Aquinas's non-materialist account of intellect until we can see him arguing it in the specific context of an investigation of the human intellect, as we will do in the remaining chapters of this book. Aside from philosophy of religion, it's only in that context that non-materialism has any claim on contemporary philosophers' attention. So in that context we'll have a clearer idea of what's at

---

[72] Although Aquinas doesn't call these beings 'spiritual' or 'spirits' in any of the arguments of II.46–55, his review of pertinent biblical passages in 49.1256 shows that he considers such terms to be appropriate for them. See also IV.23.3592, where, after reviewing both etymology and authority, he says, 'And for that reason the sensory soul, the rational soul, angels, and God are called spirits.'

stake regarding our conception of ourselves, and we'll have better grounds on which to assess his premises when they have to do with our minds specifically, and not just with intellective beings generally.[73] Still, his denials here that intellects can be bodies, or material beings of any sort, or forms that depend on matter for their real existence, are naturally founded in part on positive claims about the nature and activity of intellects; so we shouldn't leave these three negative chapters behind without at least sampling those claims.

Aquinas's formulation of the thesis at the beginning of chapter 49 suits all three of these chapters: 'That no intellective substance is a body is shown on the basis of things already put forward (*ex praemissis*)' (1247). Of course, given the logical structure of Aquinas's natural theology,[74] this formulation should suit the presentation of every new thesis in every new chapter of it. So, for instance, chapter 51's denial that an intellective substance is a material form depends directly and almost entirely on the results of chapter 50, which denies that intellective substances are material at all. There can't be any doubt about the source of the previously introduced principles or conclusions on which chapter 51's arguments depend.[75] Chapters 49 and 50, however, present a special case, because Aquinas bases their negative conclusions on many claims about the nature and cognitive activity of intellect, most of which weren't already put forward in the near vicinity of these chapters.[76] The sources of those claims are more remote, and are occasionally obscure. Although he doesn't say so, Aquinas should be advancing them as having been previously shown in SCG, or as presenting Aristotelian or other philosophically authoritative principles that are explained and established elsewhere, or as obvious

---

[73] Chs. 46–55 might be viewed as Aquinas's general introduction to his development of philosophy of mind in chs. 56–90.

[74] See Ch. One above, sect. 2; also TMOT, Ch. Three, sect. 5.

[75] In the opening sentence of ch. 51, Aquinas says that its thesis 'is shown on the basis of *the same* considerations' (1268) as those that were appealed to or concluded in the immediately preceding chapter. Ch. 50, on the other hand, begins with the looser and much more familiar formula 'But on that basis it is apparent that (*Ex hoc autem apparet quod*)' (1259).

[76] But, as might be expected, some of them were put forward in the three preceding chapters on intellective substances: e.g. the claim that 'intellect's power of cognition is, in a way, infinite' (49.1252) might be traced to 47.1240; and the claim that 'the forms of things . . . [are not] in intellect materially, the way they are outside the soul' (50.1264) has a source in 46.1233.

from ordinary experience.[77] In any event, many of these claims about the cognitive aspect of intellective beings illuminate the topic of this third part of Book II, and prefigure parts of Aquinas's theory of human intellect, which we'll be examining in more detail in Chapters Eight and Nine below.

If we focus just on SCG prior to II.46, then the obvious place to look for 'things already put forward' as regards intellect generally is I.44–71, the chapters on God's intellect and cognition. And it seems to me that almost all of the fourteen (or more) general claims about intellect that Aquinas makes in II.49 and 50 (at least one in each of the arguments that make up those chapters[78]) do

---

[77] I haven't thoroughly searched the text of SCG and all other relevant literature, but the antecedents I've identified in many of these instances seem to constitute not so much solid bases for these claims about intellect as simply these claims themselves in other versions that have been 'already put forward'.

[78] 49.1248: 'Intellect . . . does not include an intellectively cognized thing through any quantitative commensuration. For by its whole self it cognizes and includes both the whole and a part, both quantitatively larger and quantitatively smaller things'; 1249: 'Intellect . . . is not corrupted but rather perfected by receiving the forms of all bodies. For it is perfected in intellectively cognizing, and it cognizes in so far as it has in itself forms of the intellectively cognized things'; 1250: 'If intellect were a body, the intelligible forms of things would be received in it only as individuated. However, intellect cognizes things through forms of them that it has in its possession. [If it is a body,] intellect, then, will cognize not universals but only particulars—which is clearly false'; 1251: 'We intellectively cognize many things that are not bodies'; 1252: 'Intellect's power of cognition is, in a way, infinite. For it intellectively cognizes species of numbers *ad infinitum* by the process of addition, and likewise species of figures and proportions. It also cognizes what is universal, which is virtually infinite in its scope since it contains potentially infinitely many individuals'; 1253: 'Two intellects contain and include each other whenever one of them intellectively cognizes the other'; 1254: 'Intellect . . . is reflexive in acting on itself, for intellect cognizes itself not only in respect of a part but in respect of the whole'; 1255: 'The action of an intellectively active substance . . . does terminate in the action. For just as an intellect cognizes a thing, so does it cognize itself cognizing, and so on *ad infinitum*'; 50.1261: 'The species of intellectively cognized things are made actually intelligible through being abstracted from individual matter. But in so far as they are actually intelligible, they become one with intellect'; 1262: 'If intellectively cognizing is the action of a composite, neither form nor matter will be cognized, but only the composite. But that is plainly false'; 1263: 'The forms of sensible things have being more perfectly in intellect than in the sensible things, for [in intellect] they are simpler and extend themselves to more things, since [for instance] intellect cognizes all human beings through the one form *human being*'; 1264: 'If intellect is composed of matter and form, the forms of things will be in intellect materially, the way they are outside the soul. Therefore, just as they are not actually intellectively cognizable outside the soul, so neither would they be so existing in intellect'; 1265: 'The forms of contraries are contrary in respect of the being they have in matter—which is why they exclude one another. As they are in intellect, however, they are *not* contrary. Instead, one of two contraries is an intelligible defining characteristic of the other,

have identifiable antecedents in the preceding chapters on intellect in Books I or II.[79] For instance, the claim that 'we intellectively cognize many things that are not bodies' (49.1251) could be supported on the basis of ordinary experience, but it also has antecedents in several previous arguments.[80] And the claim that 'the species of intellectively cognized things are made actually intelligible through being abstracted from individual matter' (50.1261) can be traced to arguments establishing the nature and activity of God's intellect, even though no such process of abstracting data from matter could characterize God's cognition itself.[81]

7. The metaphysical complexity of the simplest possible creatures

Aquinas's natural-theological commitment to approaching created things from the top down is what leads him to begin his consideration of the created world by focusing on intellective creatures generally, since 'among created things, intellective substances are first' in the only relevant respect: they exhibit the highest degree of likeness to God (47.1238). The most noticeable way in which such creatures, including us, exhibit likeness to God is by acting 'the way God acts . . . [viz.] through intellect and will' (46.1232). But in the three chapters with which Aquinas begins his investigation of the metaphysics of intellect (II.49–51), he has gone beneath that most apparent likeness, arguing that creatures that are intellective must, for just that reason, be like God also in more fundamental respects.

since the one is cognized through the other'; 1266: 'Intellect as a result of its receiving forms is not moved, but rather perfected; and it cognizes in a state of rest. What's more, in intellectively cognizing, it is hindered as a result of movement [*Physics* VII 3, 247b8 ff.].'

[79] The clearest and most notable exception, I think, is the claim about intellects in 49.1253, where the entire argument reads as follows: 'It is impossible that two bodies contain each other, since the one that contains exceeds the one that is contained. However, two intellects do contain and include (*comprehendunt*) each other whenever one of them intellectively cognizes (*intelligit*) the other. Therefore, an intellect is not a body.' I haven't identified any proposition already put forward in SCG on which this metaphorical claim about intellects might be based; nor do I know of any other source for it. (As Robert Pasnau suggested to me, it looks as if Aquinas may have meant to say 'whenever the two of them intellectively cognize each other'.)

[80] e.g. I.63.521; II.46.1234, 48.1244 and 1246.

[81] See e.g. I.44.376, 47.397, 53.443. See also TMOT, Ch. Seven; and Stump and Kretzmann 1995.

As part of the transition to the concluding half of his account of the
metaphysics of intellect (in II.52–4), Aquinas sums up those results:
like God, created 'intellective substances are not corporeal, or
composed of matter and form, or existing in matter as material
forms' (52.1273).[82] Of course, a good deal of what Aquinas thinks
he's entitled to conclude about God in his natural theology depends on his conviction that 'things that are said in connection with
God should be understood . . . in terms of the likeness [to God]
that belongs to the highest creatures, which are intellective substances' (ST Ia.27.1c). The likeness that Aquinas has invoked in
SCG so far has been the likeness in activity, the intellective-
volitional likeness. But now the arguments in II.49–51 that deny
that intellects are bodies, or matter–form composites, or material
forms, have greatly enhanced the likeness of intellects to God,
inferring those metaphysical likenesses from that likeness in activity. In the light of those results, it's beginning to be apparent that
intellects, the only created things that are immaterial, subsistent
forms, are as metaphysically *simple* as any creatures could be. So
Aquinas, the ever-vigilant champion of God's unique simplicity,
has to draw a line between God, the *absolutely* simple intellective
substance, and all created intellective substances. The structural
purpose of chapters 52–4 is to establish boundaries, first between
God and the creatures most like God, and then between those
immaterial creatures and all the others. In serving that purpose,
those chapters naturally constitute the most fundamentally metaphysical phase of his investigation of intellect generally.

He begins by drawing the line between God and the highest
creatures. Despite immaterial intellective substances' special metaphysical likeness to God, 'no one should think that they are therefore on a par with divine simplicity; for some composition is found
in them' (52.1273). And, as Aquinas argued at length in SCG I.21–
2 and 31, there can't be any sort of metaphysical components in
God. So, if *any* composition is found in those creatures, then they
aren't *absolutely* simple, as God is. Aquinas goes on at once to
identify the two components that make any and every existent
intellective substance a composite: its essence (*quod est*) and its
existing (*esse*). '[I]n their case, *esse* is *not* the same as *quod est*'

[82] For these points of resemblance, see e.g. SCG I.20: 'God is not a body'; 17:
'There is no matter in God'; 27: 'God is not the form of any body'. See also TMOT,
118–20.

(ibid.).[83] And *that* sort of metaphysical composition is the one whose absence is at the heart of the unique divine simplicity: God's being *is* the same as God's essence or nature.[84] Everything else in these three chapters is devoted to developing and explaining this non-simplicity, this compositeness, that distinguishes even the highest creatures from God.[85]

The components of the composition that Aquinas argues for in even the highest creatures can be readily recognized in connection with any contingent entity, although these components are so pervasive and so intimately associated that we wouldn't ordinarily distinguish between them.[86] For instance, if I want to know whether there is such a thing as a marsupial dog, I want to know whether or not anything with that essential nature exists, to know whether or not that nature is instantiated, or has being. I know, roughly, what *sort* of thing a marsupial dog would have to be, but I don't know

---

[83] The essence/existence distinction in Aquinas is well-researched and problematic; see e.g. Wippel 1984: esp. chs. 5 and 6; Kenny 1987*a*; and McInerny 1991. For present purposes, the controversies may be left to one side.

[84] For an account of Aquinas's identification of God's nature with God's being, see TMOT, Ch. Four, sects. 4–5. In considering existence and essence in SCG and other works, Aquinas almost always uses the nominalized infinitive *esse* for the first element. It's best translated in different ways in different places—as e.g. 'being', 'existing', or 'existence'. But he uses several words and expressions, perhaps not altogether synonymously, for what we usually call 'essence', including *essentia*, *natura*, *quidditas*, *quod quid est*, *quod quid erat esse*, and *substantia*, the last of which is his preferred term in these chapters of SCG II. Aquinas's occasional and unusual use of *quod est* for essence here may have been influenced by Boethius's usage in *De hebdomadibus*, on which Aquinas had been commenting around the time he began writing SCG (see App. I). That possibility is strengthened by terminological remarks he makes in 54.1295 and esp. 1294, where he says that the composition of '*substantia* and *esse* is called by some people a composition of *quod est* and *esse*, or of *quod est* and *quo est*'—i.e. that *by* which, or in accordance with which, a thing is. The latter pair are the terms favoured by Boethius. (See also QDSC 1, obj. 8 and ad 8; ST Ia.50.2, ad 3.) (MacDonald 1991 contains an excellent translation of the Boethius text; see also McInerny 1991 on Aquinas's commentary.) But there appears to be a special ambiguity in *quod est* in this context, as may be seen in this passage from CT I.11.20: 'For it is in virtue of its being (*esse*) that we say of anything *that* it is (*quod est*), but in virtue of its essence (*essentiam*) that we say of anything *what* it is (*quid sit*). It's for that reason, too, that a definition, signifying an essence, shows *what* the thing is (*quid est res*).'

[85] In this way the uniqueness, the sublimity, of what Aquinas calls the 'sublime truth' that God's being = God's essence is safeguarded (see SCG I.22.211 and TMOT, Ch. Four, sect. 5). The fact that II.52 ends with a citation of that sublime metaphysical truth is entirely appropriate: 'It's for this reason that in Exodus 3: 14 the name proper to God is put forward as THE ONE WHO IS (*QUI EST*), since it is proper to God alone that his substance is not other than his being' (1281).

[86] Some of this paragraph is drawn from TMOT, 122.

whether there *is* (or ever *was*) any thing of that sort; I don't know whether a marsupial dog has being, whether any creature is a composite of that nature and existence. And the same distinction characterizes every contingent natural thing: if and when the thing actually exists, it instantiates some essential nature that could also be uninstantiated, or that could be, and very often is, instantiated also by the existing of some other individual. We couldn't know that unicorns don't exist if we didn't know what sort of thing would count as a unicorn—which is to know, roughly, their essential nature. But the nature of unicorns doesn't entail their non-existence. We need to know a lot more than what sort of thing a unicorn would have to be in order to know that there aren't any. In short, the existing of a contingent thing is other than the nature of such a thing, as Aquinas argues in chapter 52, which he titles 'There is a difference between existence and essence (*quod est*) in created intellective substances'. The crucial word here is 'created'. Even God can be described as intellective substance (with some care to avoid misinterpretation);[87] and in God's case, of course, there is no such difference.

   None of chapter 52's seven arguments depends in any way on the nature of created intellective substances considered just as such. But that's only to be expected. Aquinas needed observations about the nature of intellectivity as bases for establishing the immateriality of such creatures, as we've seen. Once that's been argued for (in chs. 49–51), it's no longer the metaphysics of *intellect* that is directly at issue but, rather, the metaphysics of *immaterial substance*. Furthermore, most of those arguments offer only indirect support of the thesis stated in the chapter's title. What they're out to show directly is that *in God alone* is there *no* difference between being and essence. (Essence is referred to in these arguments either as *quod est* or as *substantia*.) For instance, 'nothing other than God can be its own being. Therefore, as regards every substance there is besides God, its being must be other than the substance itself' (1274). Only two of these arguments, 1277 and 1278, even take creatures as their main subject. The second of those two is instructive about more than the topic of chapter 52: 'The *substance* [or

---

[87] God cannot be metaphysically located in the Aristotelian *category* of substance (I.25.235–6). But for Aquinas's references to God's substance, or to God as substance, see e.g. 52.1274 (partially quoted in the next paragraph) or 1281 (in n. 85 above); also I.14.117–19 and 16.130.

essence] of each and every thing belongs to it in its own right (*per se*) and not as a consequence of something else (*per aliud*). (For that reason, being bright in actuality does not belong to the substance of the air, because it belongs to the air as a consequence of something else.) But the *existence* of every created thing does belong to it as a consequence of something else; otherwise a created thing would not be a caused thing. Therefore, no created substance's *existence* is its *substance*' (1278). Therefore, *every* created substance, material or immaterial, is composite in at least this respect, that that substance or essence itself must be instantiated, brought into existence, by something else. In the case of a created thing, what it is never entails that it is.

Since an X's substance is just what it is to be an X, there couldn't be anything about an X that would belong to it in its own right more intimately or more clearly than its substance does. Its substance couldn't belong to it as a consequence of something else. There are no conceivable circumstances in which anything—even God— could bestow on an X its substance, because any circumstances in which such bestowing might seem possible would include the utter metaphysical absence of an X, the only eligible recipient of it.[88] On the other hand, a contingent X's substance may or may not be instantiated in reality. An X's substance is the potentiality of which an existent X is an actualization. And if by this stage in our examination of this natural theology we're in a position to think of an X's substance as a species in the creator's intellect, then an X's substance may be thought of as a recipient of being in something like the way in which at sunrise the dark air is made bright. The substance of unicorn is what a unicorn is no less than the substance of squirrel is what a squirrel is; but, as a consequence of *something else*, being belongs to the latter substance and not to the former.

Part of what I've just been suggesting about essence–existence or substance–being (s–b) composition is brought out expressly by Aquinas in chapter 53, the thesis of which is that 'in created intellective substances there is composition of actuality and potential-

---

[88] So talking about a thing's substance as belonging to it is talking loosely, since without the substance there couldn't be a thing to which the substance could belong. As we'll see, this is one respect in which the composition of substance and being differs from the composition of matter and form.

ity' (1282). Here again the emphasis falls on 'created', since there's nothing in any of the chapter's four arguments that depends on the *intellectivity* of these substances. The logical relation between this thesis and its immediate predecessor in chapter 52 is that of genus to species. Potentiality–actuality (p–a) composition is the genus of which s–b composition is one of two species; so, necessarily, anything characterized by s–b is characterized by p–a as well. And, as we'll see, s–b is the only species of metaphysical composition that characterizes immaterial substances. So chapter 53 isn't introducing another kind of composition for intellective creatures in addition to the kind argued for in chapter 52.

This can be brought out especially clearly in connection with chapter 53's first argument, which begins with a general claim: 'In anything in which we find two [components], one of which is the complement of the other, the relationship (*proportio*) of one of them to the other is as the relationship of potentiality to actuality; for nothing is completed except through its own actuality.' Because this much of the argument is a claim about the generic p–a composition, it has two interpretations, corresponding to the two species of p–a. An artificial example may be the most efficient means of bringing out each of those two interpretations.

First, the letters o, p, s, t may be described as one component of several different words, the other component of each word being the arrangement of the letters. The relationship of those letters to one or another of those arrangements 'is as the relationship of potentiality to actuality'. Any of the arrangements that turn those letters into a word is for that word the complement of the letters, completing them by actualizing the word 'post', for instance. In this case, then, adding that arrangement to those letters constitutes a p–a composition in which the letters are the matter on which the form 'post' is imposed. Of course, the arrangement of letters that actualizes the word 'post' is an arrangement just *of letters*. Like any other material form, it can't occur without its matter. So the kind of p–a composition which this case exhibits is matter–form composition, the other species of p–a (besides s–b). Under a different form, that same matter could be actualized, or completed, in the word 'spot', for instance (and, obviously, those aren't the only possibilities). But, considered from the standpoint of words, that group of letters on its own is merely potential matter that requires

arrangements, or forms, as its complements in order to be actualized as a component of e.g. 'post'.[89]

The second interpretation of the general observation with which
Aquinas begins the argument shows up more clearly when he goes
on to apply it to the case at hand: 'But in a created intellective
substance we do find two [components]—viz. the substance itself
and its being, which, as was shown [in II.52], is not the substance
itself. Instead, being itself is what completes the *existing* substance
(*est complementum substantiae existentis*); for it's in virtue of having being that anything actually *is*. Therefore, we're left with the
conclusion that in each of the substances we've been discussing
there is composition of actuality and potentiality' (1278).[90] Because
an intellective substance must be immaterial, it can't have components analogous to those letters (matter) and that arrangement of
them (form). But our artificial example can also illuminate the
second interpretation required here. The word 'post'—as distinct
from this or any other particular printed instance of it, as distinct
from any token of that word-type—is the analogue of 'the substance itself', and its having been actually instantiated in this paragraph is analogous to the substance's having being. If I hadn't
written it into this paragraph, it would have remained a word that
was only potentially instantiated here. So, even if we set aside
entirely the m–f composition discernible in 'post' and treat it as a
whole that is unanalysable in terms of m–f—i.e. treat it as an
analogue of an immaterial substance—we can and should, none the
less, recognize the s–b compositeness of the word-token actually
appearing here in this paragraph. Obviously, I could have thought
of the word 'post' without having written it here, just as I did with
some of the other words that could have been formed from those
letters. The occurrence of that word here is the actualization of a
certain potentiality, the composition of that word's substance with

[89] Analogously, considered from the standpoint of chemical compounds, the
group of elements on its own is merely potential matter that requires arrangements,
or forms, as its complements in order to be actualized as a component of e.g.
CO_2.
[90] There's evidence for the generic character of p–a composition in the conclusions of the chapter's three remaining arguments, which ascribe p–a composition
not only to 'the [immaterial] substances we have been discussing' but also to material substances: 'in *each* created substance there is potentiality and actuality' (1284);
'*every* created substance is related to its being as potentiality to actuality' (1285); 'in
each created substance there is composition of actuality and potentiality' (1286).

being (as a consequence of something else—my action). So we can, and should, recognize s–b composition as another species of p–a composition.

Aquinas has argued, in II.52, that immaterial substances are characterized by s–b composition, and, in II.53, that s–b composition is p–a composition. The informed, observant reader of chapter 53, realizing that m–f composition, too, is p–a composition, might therefore wonder, retrospectively, about Aquinas's denials of materiality in chapters 49–51. In chapter 54, which Aquinas titles 'To be composed of substance and being is *not* the same as to be composed of matter and form', he therefore takes special care to explain just how m–f and s–b, the two species of p–a, differ from each other.

8. The two species of potentiality–actuality composition

He begins by making explicit what was pretty clearly implicit in the immediately preceding chapter: 'composition of matter and form [m–f] does not have the same defining characteristic as composition of substance and being [s–b], although each of them is composition of potentiality and actuality [p–a]' (1287). In the course of clarifying the likenesses and differences between m–f and s–b as the two species of p–a, he develops a detailed analysis that shows the interrelations of these basic metaphysical concepts of matter, form, substance, being, potentiality, and actuality.

In one respect, the matter in m–f composition corresponds to the substance in s–b composition: each of them is the potentiality component in the composition it's a part of. However, where m–f composite substances are concerned, 'the matter, of course, is not the very substance of the thing. . . . Instead, the matter is a *part* of the substance' (1288).[91] Where the thing is an atom of hydrogen, its substance has as its metaphysical parts (1) the matter that is a proton and an electron and (2) the form of a hydrogen atom. Harking back to our artificial example, the m–f composite

---

[91] The sentence I've omitted here as unnecessary for present purposes provides an interesting sidelight. If matter *were* the very substance of a thing, 'it would follow that *all* forms are accidents, as the ancient natural philosophers thought'. Instead, as Aquinas thinks, a single *substantial* form—e.g. the form of squirrel—actualizes some matter as a substance. All *other* forms of that substance—e.g. its colour—are accidental rather than essential/substantial.

substance is the word 'post', of which the letters are only a *part*. That's the first way in which m–f differs from s–b composition: in all material substances, the matter and the form are the metaphysical parts of the substance that is the potentiality component in s–b composition.

Second, the form in m–f composition corresponds, in one respect, to the being in s–b composition: each of them is the actuality component in the composition it's a part of. But these two actuality components are not to be confused with each other, 'because being itself [in s–b composition] is the actuality that is proper not to the *matter* [in an m–f composite substance] but to *the whole substance*. For being is the actuality of that about which we can say that it *is*. That it is, however, is said not about the matter [in an m–f composite], but about the whole [composite]. For that reason, the matter cannot be called that which is. Instead, the substance itself is that which is' (1289).[92]

The claim that 'being itself is the actuality that is proper not to the matter but to the whole substance' can be made intuitively plausible by reflecting again on our artificial example, this time thinking of o, p, s, and t as magnetized plastic letters. Of course, they don't cease to exist when they're arranged on the refrigerator in the form that results in 'post'. But when that word is actually formed there, it's the resultant whole thing about which we would recognize that it exists now. The undoubted fact that that (old) matter *goes on* existing, now as part of that newly existing word-token, would ordinarily be beneath our notice. Since any material substance is itself the result of an m–f composition, when the substance that is the potentiality component of an s–b composition is a material substance, the substance in that s–b composition is itself already an m–f composite. 'In the case of substances composed of matter and form there is a *double* composition of actuality and potentiality: first, of course, the composition of the substance itself, which is composed of matter and form; but, second, the composi-

---

[92] The final four sentences of my translation here correspond to these three Latin sentences: *Eius enim actus est esse de quo possumus dicere quod sit. Esse autem non dicitur de materia, sed de toto. Unde materia non potest dici quod est, sed ipsa substantia est id quod est.* The sense of the passage seems to require translating *quod sit* and *quod est* here as 'that it is' (and *id quod est* as 'that which is'). See n. 84 above. For the sake of clarity, I translate *esse* in the second of these sentences as 'that it is' rather than as 'being'—an unusual but not, I think, impossible reading.

tion of being and that very substance, already composed [of matter and form]' (1295).[93]

A third reason why m–f can't be equated with s–b composition is also drawn from the distinction between form and being, the actuality components. Since material forms don't exist really (as distinct from conceptually) unless they are actually informing matter, it's obvious that form is not being itself. 'Instead, form and being itself are an ordered pair (*se habent secundum ordinem*); for form is related to being itself as light is related to lighting, or whiteness to being white' (1290). To be white is to be, but whiteness has no real (as distinct from conceptual) being except as instantiated in some real thing's being white.[94] As for our artificial example, you can, of course, have in mind that arrangement of the letters—that formed matter—without actually instantiating it in writing, giving the word being here and now. The arrangement itself might be thought of as the formal cause of the word-token whose efficient cause might be your writing it down.

In his fourth and final observation, Aquinas brings out an aspect of the distinction between the actuality components in these two species of p–a composition that is particularly important for his purposes here: 'being itself is related as actuality even to form itself. For the reason why the form is said to be a source (*principium*) of being in things composed of matter and form is that the form is what completes the substance (*complementum substantiae*), the actuality of which is being itself' (1291). In other words, to say that the form is the actuality component in m–f composition is to say only that it is a necessary condition for the full-fledged actual existence of which the complete substance is the only proper subject—'just as transparency is a source of lighting for the air because it makes the air the proper subject of light' (ibid.). It's right to say that the form of squirrel exhibited in that organic matter over there is a source of that squirrel's existence, but only in

---

[93] For the sake of clarity, I've reversed the order of the conjuncts in the final clause: *secunda vero ex ipsa substantia iam composita et esse*. See also ST Ia.50.2, ad 3.

[94] See also In BDH: L2.22: 'Now we signify one thing in virtue of saying "being (*esse*)", and another in virtue of saying "that which is (*id quod est*)"—just as we also signify one thing when we say "running" (*currere*), and another in virtue of saying "the runner" (*currens*). For running and being are signified abstractly, just as whiteness is also. But what is (*quod est*)—i.e. the being (*ens*) and the runner—are signified concretely, as is white.'

the way in which, and to the extent to which, it's right to say that the transparency of the air is a source of this morning's bright sky. There couldn't be a squirrel if there weren't that form; there couldn't be a sunlit sky if the air weren't transparent. But in each case there's another necessary condition as well, an efficient cause, something else that accounts for this squirrel's existing, or for the sky's being bright now.

Having completed his elaborate distinguishing of m–f from s–b composition, Aquinas offers a synopsis of the results as they apply to the sorts of things we're most familiar with: 'Accordingly, as regards things composed of matter and form, neither the matter, nor the form, can be said to be that which is (*ipsum quod est*) or being itself. Still, the form can be said to be that *by* which the thing is (*quo est*), in so far as it is a source of being. But the whole substance itself is that which is. And being itself is that *by* which the substance is designated an entity (*ens*)' (1292).

Against that elaborate background, Aquinas can re-describe the compositeness of immaterial intellective substances, this time on the basis of his review of metaphysical fundamentals: 'On the other hand, in the case of intellective substances, which are *not* composed of matter and form (as was shown [in II.50 and 51])—instead, in their case form itself is the subsistent substance—the form is *what* is (*quod est*), while being itself is the actuality and that *by* which it is (*quo est*). And for that reason there is in their case only a single composition of actuality and potentiality, which is, namely, a composition of substance and being' (1293–4).[95]

This description certainly follows from the metaphysical fundamentals he has laid out here. But even if, like me, you find those fundamentals both plausible and attractive, we're not yet in a position to accept or reject the description. We're sure that there are

---

[95] See also QDSC 1, ad 8, and In BDH: L2.34: 'although something is called simple in virtue of the fact that it lacks composition, nothing prevents something that is not *altogether* simple from being simple *in a certain respect*, in so far as it lacks some [sort of] composition. . . . Therefore, if some forms are found [to be] not in matter, each of them is of course simple in so far as it lacks matter and, consequently, quantity, which is a disposition of matter. None the less, because each form is determinative of being itself, none of them *is* being itself, but is something possessing being. . . . Each of them, in so far as it is distinguished from another, is a certain specific form participating in being itself; and so none of them will be truly simple.'

intellects—at least the ones we have. But we've only previewed Aquinas's reasons for insisting that all intellects must be entirely immaterial substances simply in virtue of being intellective. So we'll have to postpone assessing this concluding description until we've examined (in Ch. Eight below) his arguments for the immaterial substantiality of human intellects.

Aquinas concludes here that intellective substances are not composites of matter and form, but simply forms. But his calling those immaterial forms themselves subsistent substances means only that they are eligible for being without the addition of any matter; it doesn't mean that those forms somehow entail their own existence. Any actual created intellect is a contingent composite of such a purely formal substance and the being bestowed on it, an s–b composite without any m–f composition. And although the forms that intellects are said to be aren't *material* forms, that doesn't mean that it's *impossible* for any of them to exist as forms of matter (as we'll see), but only that none of them *must* be enmattered in order to exist.

Having applied the results of his analysis of metaphysical composition to intellective substances specifically, he ends with a broader overview that turns out to have an immediate further consequence:

In this way, therefore, it is clear that there is composition of actuality and potentiality in more things than there is composition of form and matter. That's why matter and form divide [only] natural substance, while potentiality and actuality divide being in general.[96] And, for that reason, any states (*quaecumque*) that are indeed concomitants of (*consequuntur*) potentiality and actuality considered just as such are common to both material and immaterial created substances—e.g. receiving and being received, completing and being completed. On the other hand, any states that are proper to matter and form considered just as such—e.g. being generated and being corrupted, and others of that sort—are propria of material substances and in no way go together with created immaterial substances. (1296)

---

[96] It seems odd to describe components as dividing what they compose, but he pretty clearly means that every natural substance can be analysed/divided into matter and form, and that being in general can be analysed/divided into potentiality and actuality. By 'natural substance' here he must mean at least corporeal, but possibly also non-artificial, substance.

9. Incorruptibility

The concluding sentence of that overview plainly implies several propositions that might be worth investigating, but the most important of them is the one Aquinas immediately singles out as the thesis of chapter 55: 'every intellective substance is incorruptible' (1297). This general thesis is less interesting to us, or at least harder to evaluate, than the specific instance of it that Aquinas argues for later in Book II—that every human soul is incorruptible (chs. 79–81)—and so I'm postponing a careful consideration of the incorruptibility of intellects.[97] But Aquinas argues at length for the general thesis in the thirteen arguments of chapter 55, some of which make fundamental metaphysical points important for our present purposes. Others depend more on the nature of intellect—even human intellect—and so will be more relevant in subsequent chapters of this book.

The first of these incorruptibility arguments has nothing to do with intellectivity as such, but builds on the immateriality of intellective substance in ways that make it continuous with the arguments on the metaphysics of intellect, requiring only the addition of this definition of corruption: 'All corruption occurs through a separation of form from matter—*simple* corruption through the separation of the *substantial* form, of course, but corruption *in a certain respect* through the separation of an *accidental* form' (1298). Turning a tree into paper involves its simple corruption; spraying its green needles pink is the corruption of it only in a certain respect—unless the spraying kills the tree, in which case separating from it one of its accidental forms has led to the separation of its substantial form from the organic matter that used to be, but is then no longer a metaphysical part of a tree: a dead tree is no longer a tree. And since that's what Aquinas means by corruption, it's already clear that every immaterial substance must be incorruptible, as this argument goes on to spell out. 'For as long as a form remains, there must be a thing; for it is through form that a substance is made a proper subject (*susceptivum*) of that which is being. But where there is no composition of form and matter, there can be no separation of them; therefore, no corruption either. But it was shown [in II.50] that no intellective substance is composed of

---

[97] See Ch. Ten below, sects. 7 and 8.

matter and form. Therefore, no intellective substance is corruptible' (ibid.).[98]

As those observations about corruption imply, corruption is
natural or artificial destruction within created nature, and is not to
be confused with annihilation, replacing something with absolutely
nothing. 'In every case of corruption, when an actuality is removed,
a potentiality remains. For when something is corrupted, it is not
corrupted into utter non-being (just as something is not generated
from utter non-being)' (1300). Generation is no more to be confused with creation than corruption is with annihilation. 'But in the
case of intellective substances (as was shown [in II.53]), the actuality [in their species of p–a composition] is being itself, while the
substance is the potentiality, so to speak. Therefore, if an intellective substance were corrupted, it would remain after its corruption—which is completely impossible. Therefore, every intellective
substance is incorruptible' (ibid.).

We'll take a closer, more critical look at intellective incorruptibility in its species-specific form of human immortality in Chapter
Ten below.

---

[98] Or, to put it more succinctly, 'in corruptible substances themselves there is a
potentiality for not-being in the complete substance itself only because of the
matter. In intellective substances, on the other hand, there is no matter' (1301).

EIGHT

METAPHYSICAL HYBRIDS

1. Intellective substances and corporeal substances

Aquinas develops most of what I've been calling his metaphysics of
intellect in chapters 46–55. In the first three of them he lays out
some of what he takes to be the implications of intellective nature
in general. He argues that all species of created intellects, considered just as such, must be incorporeal, immaterial forms that are
subsistent, or capable of existing on their own. The term 'intellective substances', his preferred designation for them, seems intended to bring out their status as subsistent entities. Then, in
chapters 49–55, he shifts his focus from the intellectivity of intellective substances to various aspects of their metaphysical character,
which obviously must be very different from that of any other
created things.[1] For instance, he argues at length in chapter 55 that
one implication of their incorporeality is that created intellective
substances cannot be 'corrupted', or naturally destroyed.[2] He contrasts them in that respect with the corporeal substances that we're
more familiar with and understand better,[3] even if it does turn out
to be the case that our own minds are some sort of intellective
substances. Those investigations provide the general background
against which he very soon begins considering human intellects, or
'intellective souls', specifically. But, as we'll see, the transition to
his consideration of human beings occurs as part of an unusual
dialectical process he employs in exploring one last metaphysical
issue that has to do with intellective substances considered generically. In dealing with that issue, Aquinas moves away from his
standard procedure in SCG I–III, in which he organizes a chapter
around the statement of a thesis and the presentation of arguments

---

[1] See Ch. Seven above, sects. 6–8. [2] See Ch. Seven above, sect. 9.
[3] This contrast between intellective and corporeal substances is brought out
especially in 55.1304.

in its support.[4] Instead, in chapters 56–69 he develops a dialectically more complex investigation that calls for some detailed commentary.

As I've been saying, it's Aquinas's plan of considering created things from the top down that leads him to begin with intellective creatures.[5] And since he has already argued that such creatures, considered just as such, must be incorporeal substances, he has presented us with what looks like an exhaustive and exclusive division of created things into the higher, more God-like, incorporeal substances (or intellects) and the lower, corporeal substances (or bodies). The remaining issue at this general level, then, is whether or not that division of created things really is exhaustive and exclusive. Aquinas puts it this way: 'Now since it was shown above [in II.49] that an intellective substance is not a body, or [in 49.1252] a power dependent on a body, we must still investigate whether an intellective substance can be *united* with a body' (56.1313).

Anyone reading that sentence will be almost irresistibly tempted to think of this issue at once in terms of the relation between the human mind and the human body. For most of us there aren't any other terms in which it could be a real issue, and, of course, those are the terms in which the issue is familiar in the history of philosophy. Moreover, given all that Aquinas has been saying about intellective and corporeal substances, an attentive reader of SCG might very well also expect that Aquinas's account of the mind–body relationship will have to turn out to be a substance dualism of the sort Descartes's account is standardly taken to be.[6] All the same, we ought to resist such temptations and expectations. Here, at the beginning of chapter 56, Aquinas hasn't yet made the transition from a consideration of intellective substances generally to his specific consideration of the human intellective soul. At this point,

---

[4] For different reasons, some of which we'll be considering in Ch. Nine below, Aquinas appears to find that familiar format awkward or simply unusable as he moves into his account of intellective substances, and he departs from it in various ways as the investigation develops, beginning no later than II.49. See Ch. Seven above, sect. 6.

[5] And it's his plan of considering 'the nature of those produced and distinguished things'—i.e. creatures—'in so far as it pertains to the truth of the faith' (II.5.877) that leads him to *confine* his attention to intellective creatures. See Ch. Seven above, sect. 2.

[6] For a very helpful, detailed contrast of Descartes's and Aquinas's dualisms, see Stump 1995.

his concern with the possibility of a union between an intellective substance and a body still has to do with both of those components considered at the generic level. To interpret either component as specifically human here would be a mistake, giving Aquinas both more advantages and more problems than he deserves at this stage of the investigation.[7]

But if we are still dealing with the very broad considerations that characterized chapters 46–55, why should we suppose that the possibility of a union between an intellective substance and a body is something that 'we *must* still investigate' in that context? That human beings should feel a need to investigate the relations between their minds and bodies is only natural, but what considerations would demand the investigation which Aquinas says is needed here, at this much more abstruse, generic level?

In an investigation of this material as thoroughgoing as Aquinas's is, an abstract concern about its formal completeness might provide reason enough to press on in that direction even if the investigator did *not* have good reason to think that such a union really was a feature of the created world. The general inquiry which Aquinas began and almost completed in chapters 46–55 has provided a detailed metaphysical distinction between bodies and intellective substances. Bodies, all corporeal substances, have been analysed as composite in *two* respects—characterized essentially by *both* matter–form (m–f) composition *and* substance–being (s–b) composition—while intellective substances have been explained as *purely* s–b composites.[8] So Aquinas's analysis of corporeal and

---

[7] Theoretically, the issue at this stage should cover not just fundamental aspects of the familiar mind–body problem, but also such antique doctrines as an angel's (or an intellective soul's) being somehow 'united' with an otherwise inert celestial sphere as its mover (see II.70 and 90; also sect. 10 below). Aquinas is at least as likely as anyone else is to be particularly interested in getting on to the consideration of human beings in this connection, but he writes as if he wants to avoid introducing that specific topic until he has set up the general background. He omits any discussion of the human mind or soul from his discussion of intellective substances in II.46–55 (see n. 51 below). In fact, he never mentions human beings at all in those chapters, except incidentally in examples.

[8] See Ch. Seven above, sect. 7. The references supplied in my quotation of 56.1313 above indicate where in Book II Aquinas has argued against identifying an intellective substance with (1) a body or (2) a power dependent on a body. II.49 argues very fully and fairly convincingly against (1). In 55.1304 Aquinas treats (2) as having already been established. 49.1252 does argue for (2), but not very directly or very convincingly. And, of course, if we do (prematurely) think of the issue of II.56 in terms of the mind–body problem, (2) is a much more attractive hypothesis than

incorporeal substances has certainly left them looking like two mutually exclusive, jointly exhaustive genera of created things. And, of course, they must be exhaustive: whatever there is must be either corporeal or not corporeal. But are they necessarily exclusive? Or could there be another kind of created thing, a metaphysical hybrid whose nature shows that it exists on the borderline between those two kinds, a partly corporeal and partly incorporeal creature in which a body and an intellective substance are combined in such a way that the result would count as their having been *united*—made into one thing, a third kind of thing? I doubt very much whether this formal question would get raised at all if the human being raising it weren't thinking of human beings as at least very likely to turn out to be such hybrids. None the less, it is, on the face of it, just that abstruse, generic question (and not any question specifically about human beings) that is at issue in chapter 56. And the chapter's title, 'How an intellective substance *can* be united to a body', promises an affirmative answer to the question.[9]

2. Inapplicable modes of union

Aquinas takes a very broad approach in setting out to fulfil that promise. He begins by examining various circumstances in which we would ordinarily recognize that two or more things are united with one another. Because his survey leads him to conclude that an intellective substance and a body really *can* be united in one of the modes of union he looks at, he needn't examine all the real possibilities, and clearly he doesn't. But I think he does manage to consider the most obviously relevant possibilities of ordinary union, and perhaps one or two more besides.

Since Aquinas's method here consists in taking up and assessing the applicability of various modes of union, it's worth noticing that just before he begins the survey, in the opening sentence of chapter 56 (1313, quoted in sect. 1 above), he might be read as reminding us

(1). However, if we postpone thinking of the issue in those specific terms, as I think we must, we will have less stake in the immediate outcome and less reason to object at this stage to Aquinas's sharp distinction.

[9] The titles of chs. 56–60 are all Aquinas's own, the last ones in Book II of which this can be said with confidence. The folios containing II.61–III.43 have been lost from the manuscript of SCG written in Aquinas's own hand.

that, as it happens, two modes of union have already been ruled
out: an intellective substance is not (1) *the same thing as* a body; nor
is it (2) *a power dependent on* a body.[10] However, the absolute
identity dismissed in (1) may seem too strong to count as a mode of
union anyway, since it would involve no real plurality of things to
be really united—as in the absolute identity of the border between
New York and Vermont with the border between Vermont and
New York. Conversely, (2) might seem too weak to count as genuine union—as in the visual power's dependence on an eye.[11]

Aquinas begins his explicit survey by considering an ordinary
mode of union that looks especially strong: A is united with B if A
and B are *mixed together*. Mixing together a half-gallon of blue
paint and a half-gallon of yellow paint unites them. It makes what
were two quite distinct things into one thing: a gallon of green
paint. This sort of mixing together presents a paradigm case of
ordinary uniting, but Aquinas can't take it seriously for his present
purposes: 'it's clear, first of all, that an intellective substance *cannot*
be united with a body by way of *mixing*' (1314*a*). The inappropri-
ateness of mixing as a mode of union for this purpose begins to
emerge in his observations that A and B can be united in that way
only if (i) they are 'altered relative to one another' in the process,
and that the relevant sort of alteration 'can happen only in connection with [ii] things whose matter is the same [sort]', and that those
are (iii) 'things that can be [both] active and passive relative to one
another' (1314*b*). Where A and B are quantities of blue paint and
yellow paint, conditions (i) and (ii) are plainly satisfied. But what
about the less perspicuous (iii)? What Aquinas means by (iii) can
be seen more clearly in the passage from Aristotle's *De generatione
et corruptione* on which he's drawing here: 'some things—viz. those
that have the same [sort of] matter—*reciprocate*: i.e. they are such
as to act on one another and to undergo action from one another'

---

[10] If the opening sentence is given that interpretation, then it seems that its final
clause should be read like this: 'we must still investigate whether an intellective
substance can be united with a body [in some other way]', or, perhaps, just like this:
'we must still investigate whether an intellective substance *can* be united with a
body'.
[11] Moreover, it might seem to be obviously impossible that an intellective *substance* should turn out to be any sort of *power*, let alone a *dependent* power. (This
metaphysical issue is obviously quite distinct from what might be called a psychological question about the powers *belonging to* an intellective substance. See Ch.
Nine below.)

(I 10, 328b20). And it certainly does seem right to say that the blue paint does something to the yellow paint, and vice versa—most obviously in the superficial sense that the blue darkens the yellow and the yellow lightens the blue.

Now why, exactly, is it impossible that mixture, understood in this way, should be the mode of union for an intellective substance and a body? Notice that Aquinas introduces (ii) and (iii) as conditions necessary for (i), which is itself a necessary condition of things that are genuinely mixed together. So denying either (ii) or (iii) for any case will entail denying (i) for that case, which entails denying that it really is a case of mixture. Given that logical structure, Aquinas's line of argument against the possibility of mixture as an appropriate mode of union can be, and is, especially simple. Obviously, any two things that satisfy (ii) must both be material. But since an intellective substance isn't material at all, it can't satisfy (ii), so it can't satisfy (i), so it can't be an ingredient in a mixture at all, even one whose other ingredient is a body (and thus an m–f composite, and thus material).

It may be worth while pointing out two features of this line of argument, at least for future reference. First, in following this line, Aquinas avoids taking any account of the interesting-looking possibility that (iii) might hold of an intellective substance and a body, that they might turn out to be both active and passive relative to one another. Second, his rejection of mixture as a mode of union appropriate for an intellective substance and a body depends on taking 'mixture' very narrowly—in a way that would also rule out accurately describing anyone's character as 'a fatal mixture of weakness and temerity', for instance. But the fact that one of the ingredients at issue here must be corporeal may justify Aquinas's sticking with this stringently literal interpretation. At any rate, his ruling out literal, physical mixing as a mode of union appropriate for an intellective substance and a body is no indication that he couldn't in other circumstances recognize (non-literal) mixture as a mode of union for two incorporeal ingredients.

Although Aquinas certainly needs no further argument to show that physical mixture can't be the mode of union he's looking for here, the second argument he offers for that purpose does present some interesting observations: 'once a mixture has already been made, the things that are mixed together do not remain actually, but only virtually (*virtute*); for if they were to remain actually, it wouldn't be a mixture, but only a jumble (*confusio*). (That's why a body that is a *mixture* of elements *is* not any of those elements.[12]) But it is impossible that this happen to intellective substances, since they are incorruptible (as was shown [in II.55]). Therefore, an intellective substance cannot be united with a body by way of mixing' (1314c–d).

If you stir grains of barley into grains of wheat, you have only a jumble of grains of barley and grains of wheat.[13] The ingredients of the jumble remain unaltered themselves, and you could, in theory, separate them again into pure barley and pure wheat by no more than local motions. So a mere jumble is not a mixture or, presumably, a mode of union at all.[14] In the mixed green paint, however, the blue paint and the yellow paint are no longer present actually— at least, not in the sense that you could, even theoretically, simply remove the blue paint from the green, leaving only the yellow. But what's meant by the claim that the ingredients of a mixture do remain virtually—*virtute*, which might be spelled out as 'in respect of their power'? Well, when you say that you made the green paint by mixing together blue and yellow paint, you're saying that it has blue and yellow paint *in* it, in the sense that the actualizing of certain potentialities or powers of those two ingredients is what explains their green union. A true mixture's ingredients remain in it not actually but only 'virtually', just because (i) they are 'altered relative to one another' to such an extent that they cease to exist as what they were. So, in the generating of the green paint, the blue and the yellow paints are corrupted. And because an intellective substance *can't* be corrupted, it can't be an ingredient in a mixture.

So, it's an intellective substance's immateriality (in the first of these two arguments) and its incorruptibility (in the second argument) that rule out the possibility of its being united with a

---

[12] It seems clear that Aquinas would also recognize as mixtures what we think of as chemical compounds: table salt, a compound of sodium and chlorine, *is* neither sodium nor chlorine. See e.g. ST Ia.47.2c and 76.4, ad 4; but see also QDA 9, ad 10.

[13] Aristotle's example of this sort of thing, in *De generatione et corruptione* I 10, 328a1 ff.

[14] See also ST IIIa.2.1c, which is relevant in several respects, including a reference to 'some people who have claimed that there is union by way of a jumble'—e.g. 'as a heap is made of many stones brought together without any order but solely through being put together'—'or, alternatively, by way of being ordered together'— e.g. 'as a building is made of stones and beams arranged in a certain order'.

body in the mode of union that would consist in their being mixed together.

'But it's likewise clear', he says, 'that an intellective substance cannot be united with a body by way of *contact*, taken literally (*per modum contactus proprie sumpti*). For touching (*tactus*) [each other] is a feature only of bodies, since things that are touching each other are those whose extremities are together[15]—I mean, the points, lines, or surfaces that are the extremities of bodies. Therefore, an intellective substance cannot be united with a body by way of contact' (56.1315). And, of course, it is an intellective substance's incorporeality that renders it incapable of being united with a body by way of contact, which is, presumably, considered literally here for the same reason as mixture was: because we're beginning by examining ordinary, familiar modes of union.

However, as mixture is an especially strong mode of union, so contact seems especially, maybe even absurdly, weak. *Fastening*— as in stapling two sheets of paper together—might qualify as a universally recognized way of uniting two things by making the one touch the other. But if contact taken literally is itself a mode of union, then merely laying one piece of paper on top of another already unites them. In fact, any single sheet of paper lying on a table is thereby 'united' with the table below it and with the air above it. Moreover, viewed in that light, the stirred-together grains of barley and of wheat will constitute not just a jumble, but a kind of 'union'—a union of contact taken literally.[16] Why would Aquinas bother to consider what could at best count only as a limiting case among modes of union, a case that must be recognized instantly as obviously irrelevant to his purpose?

For two reasons, I think. First, he understands contact to be a necessary condition of three other modes of union, all of which are, therefore, ruled out when he shows the inapplicability of contact taken literally. These other modes are nothing like so weak as contact itself, especially *fastening* (*colligatio*) and *continuity*

---

[15] See Aristotle, *Physics* V 3, 227a21 ff.

[16] This mode of union may seem less blatantly irrelevant if it's taken to be instantiated in natural things, and especially in living things—e.g. the leaf's union with its tree, or the shell's union with its oyster. But the essential organic connections between the ingredients in such natural unions seem to render them instances of more than 'contact, taken literally', where the more seems to count as their 'being ordered together' (see n. 14 above).

(1316).[17] Fastening is so clearly restricted to bodies that it's not worth any further attention for Aquinas's purpose here. But continuity is certainly not always exclusively corporeal, in Aquinas's usage or in ours. The left half of a geometrical line segment is continuous with its right half at its mid-point; morning is continuous with afternoon at the instant of noon; and many a thought is temporally continuous with another thought. Still, if contact taken literally is to be understood as a necessary condition for the three other modes of union, then they, too, must be understood on that literal basis; and so the continuity considered here must be corporeal only—the way New York is continuous with Vermont at the state line. *Composition*, the third of these additional modes, may seem to pose a special problem, since 'composition' is the term which Aquinas used prominently in connection with intellective substances themselves in chapters 52–4 when he was explaining that they were not absolutely simple, just in virtue of their s–b composition.[18] But in this case, too, he must be read as ruling out only the corporeal sort of composition—physically putting together, com-positioning (or juxtaposing)—the sort for which contact taken literally is at least a necessary condition.

His other reason for considering contact seriously as a mode of union is, as we'll see, that he's going on to recognize another, non-literal kind of contact as an *appropriate* way of uniting an intellective substance with a body.

We've now seen all the kinds of union which Aquinas rules out as obviously unavailable for a union of an intellective substance with a body. He certainly hasn't considered all ordinarily recognized kinds of union. But if it's only possible unions of one incorporeal ingredient with one corporeal ingredient that he needs to take into account, his short list isn't too short for his purpose, especially because it prepares the way for his introduction of an ordinarily recognized mode that *isn't* inapplicable.

3. Power contact

Because one of the two ingredients in the sort of union Aquinas is looking for must be corporeal, it makes some sense for him to begin

---

[17] See also In Sent. III.27.1.1, ad 5: 'There are two kinds of union. One of them results in what is one [only] in a certain respect—e.g. a union of things collected together [and] superficially touching one another . . . the other kind is a union that results in what is unconditionally one—e.g. a union of continua, and of form and matter.' See also In Met. V: L7.   [18] See Ch. Seven above, sect. 7.'

his survey by considering mixture and contact—ordinary modes of union in which both ingredients are corporeal. But, since mixture involves the corrupting of both the ingredients in the union, no mode of union that could be literally described as a version of mixture is going to be available for uniting two ingredients of which one is *not* subject to corruption. That consideration doesn't eliminate *contact* taken literally, however, since none of the varieties of contact surveyed by Aquinas involves the corrupting of either ingredient. Of course, contact taken literally, purely corporeal contact considered just as such, couldn't itself be the mode of union Aquinas is looking for, in which one of the ingredients is *not* corporeal. 'However,' he says, 'there is, all the same, a *kind* of contact by which an intellective substance *can* be united with a body' (56.1317).

The way in which Aquinas announces this applicable mode of union strongly suggests that he's introducing something quite different from contact taken literally. And so he is, eventually. But, at least to begin with, he intends to be calling attention to a familiar aspect of ordinary, purely corporeal contact—contact between 'natural bodies'. He observes that 'in touching each other, natural bodies alter each other' (1317). He's no longer considering just the *fact* of corporeal touching, but now also an *effect* of it. Probably there can't really be any corporeal touching that doesn't involve some alteration, however slight or superficial, in one or both of the touching bodies; but Aquinas needn't, and apparently doesn't, take such a microscopic view of the relationship. He wants only to claim that physical contact is at least often accompanied by some sort of alteration, and that such concomitant alteration involves yet another mode of union. When the brush loaded with green paint touches the white wall, the brush and the wall 'are united with each other *not only* as regards their quantitative extremities *but also* as regards a qualitative or formal likeness, as long as the body doing the altering impresses its form on the body that is altered' (ibid.). And, in fact, the brush's impressing a qualitative or formal likeness of itself on the wall—altering as a concomitant of touching—does, intuitively, unite the two of them (in their shared greenness) much more than would their mere contact taken literally. Altering as a concomitant of contact is a mode of union stronger than contact considered just as such. Furthermore, although the wall is touching the brush no less than the brush is touching the wall, and although the wall is draining the paint out of the brush no less than the brush is laying the paint on the wall, there is a clear sense in which the brush is impressing its form on the wall, and not vice versa. The standard agent/patient distinction is natural and helpful in ordinary circumstances of this sort.

Aquinas, having called our attention to the agent–patient relationship in the altering that accompanies contact, shifts his focus from contact taken literally to the embedded agent–patient relationship itself. 'If one does pay attention to action and passion [in cases of contact], then some [bodies] will be found to be *only touching*, and others to be *only touched*' (1317). That description obviously demands a broader than literal sense of 'touch',[19] so my wall-painting example no longer fills the bill. But it's easy to find one that will. In the sense that interests Aquinas here, the sun's lighting a stone is a case of the sun's only touching the stone and the stone's being only touched by the sun. The sun touches the stone in so far as the sun alters the stone, but the sun isn't touched by the stone, because in that relationship the stone doesn't act on the sun.[20] And, in general, 'if there are any agents that do not touch [their objects] by their quantitative extremities, they will none the less be said to touch [them] in so far as they act [on them]' (ibid.). The non-literal sense of 'touch' he's introducing here seems just right for the sun-and-stone example, and the metaphor it involves is dead as a doornail—in scholastic Latin, I think, as well as in twentieth-century English. If we were watching the stone at sunrise, we would find it perfectly natural, and perfectly prosy, to describe the beginning of the sun's lighting the stone as the sun's first touching the stone.[21] So far, so good.

---

[19] As Aquinas recognizes in his observation that 'if only the quantitative extremities were considered, then the touching would have to be mutual in *all* cases' (ibid.).

[20] I'm paraphrasing here, because Aquinas's example involves antiquated natural science: 'heavenly bodies do of course touch elementary bodies in so far as they alter them; but the former are not touched by the latter, because they are not acted on by them' (1317).

[21] My simple sun-and-stone example strikes me as suiting Aquinas's purposes well, but he uses a very different sort of example here: 'as we say that a person who saddens us touches us'. He found it in Aristotle (*De generatione et corruptione* I 6, 323a32–3: 'And so if anything imparts motion without itself being moved, it may touch what is moved and yet itself be touched by nothing. For we sometimes say that a man who saddens us touches us, but not that we touch him'). It's true that a man who saddens us does 'touch' us without literally coming into contact with us, and in a way that makes him only touching and us only touched. To simplify the case, we can also suppose that his touching us in this way is altogether unintentional, like the sun's touching the stone. All the same, the example of our being touched by a man

But, having said no more than that about this mode of union, Aquinas is already prepared to draw the important conclusion that, 'as regards *this* mode of touching it *is* possible for an intellective substance to be united with a body through contact' taken non-literally, because, he says, 'intellective substances do act on bodies and move them, even though they are immaterial and exist in a higher state of actuality' (1317). This premiss about intellective substances acting on bodies is, of course, essential support for that conclusion of his. But, as a matter of fact, in his treatment of intellective substances in Book II so far, he hasn't even mentioned their acting on bodies or moving them.[22] So at this stage, as far as I can see, the possibility expressed in that conclusion can't be considered more than a bare logical possibility, and the crucial premiss about intellective substances acting on bodies must be considered to be without any support.

Those circumstances are disconcerting, especially as regards the systematic aspect of Aquinas's work in SCG I–III. Still, I think we can set aside this logical embarrassment if we step back for a moment to take a more generous, informal view of the situation. For although Aquinas isn't yet discussing human minds and bodies explicitly, he can't be blamed severely for anticipating things he'll need when he does come to develop his account of them. And, clearly, one such thing is some explanation of the kind of contact there obviously is between the human mind and the human body— just the sort of thing that might be broadly expressed to begin with by saying that a mind 'touches' the body it's associated with in the sense that it acts on and moves that body.

Aquinas strengthens this view when he goes on at once to emphasize what he has already clearly implied: 'this sort of

who makes us feel sad is inappropriately complicated. We couldn't be touched in that way at all if we weren't conscious and susceptible of emotion. This non-literal kind of contact is supposed to be under consideration as a possible mode of union between an intellective substance and a body, but there's nothing in the saddening person example that could be a plausible analogue for a merely corporeal substance.

[22] In 49.1249–50 he mentions intellect's being receptive to the forms of all bodies in cognition, which, of course, has nothing to do with intellect's acting on bodies. In 49.1251 he does talk about intellect's 'action' in connection with 'the order of bodies', but he identifies the action in question as intellective cognition, and he's interested simply in pointing out that 'we intellectively cognize many things that are not bodies'. All the other material on intellective substances in chs. 46–55 is even more clearly irrelevant to establishing the premiss at issue here.

touching'—the sort that he says *can* unite an intellective substance with a body—'has to do not with quantity but with *power*' (56.1318). The mode of union now under consideration is not contact taken literally, but *power* contact (*contactus virtutis*), the kind that unites an agent with its patient whether or not they are in corporeal contact.[23] But it's still just a possibility under consideration, not yet accepted as really doing the job of uniting intellective substances with bodies.

As a first move in considering this possibility, Aquinas distinguishes power contact from corporeal contact in three respects. The fundamental distinction is already clear: A is in power contact with B if and only if A is acting on B or being acted on by B, and A is in corporeal contact with B if and only if some quantitative extremity of A is together with some quantitative extremity of B. The point of Aquinas's further distinctions here is to bring out respects in which he thinks power contact is well suited to unite an intellective substance with a body.

First, 'an intellective substance, although it is indivisible'—not as a geometrical point is indivisible, but in the sense of not belonging to the category of quantity at all—'can touch a divisible quantity in so far as it acts on it' (1318*a*). Suppose that B is a body, a theoretically divisible quantity, and that A is acting on B without corporeally touching B, as the moon is acting on the earth gravitationally without corporeally touching it. Aquinas hasn't provided any example of that sort in which A itself is indivisible, and neither have I. Still, unless such circumstances *entail* that A, too, must be corporeal/divisible—and I don't see that they do—we can provisionally allow this possibility.[24] However, I think we can't be so generous as regards the second and third of these distinctions of his.

---

[23] Cf. ST Ia.75.1, ad 3: 'There are two sorts of contact: quantitative contact and power contact. In the first sort, a body is touched only by a body. In the second sort, a body can be touched by an incorporeal thing that moves the body.' See also Ia.105.2, ad 1.

[24] Aquinas's own presentation of this possibility strikes me as unclear and dubious, but in ways that seem not to affect the main issue as I've extracted it. For instance, although along the way he makes some standard observations about geometrical points—e.g. 'A point is indivisible, of course, as the terminus of a quantity; and so in a continuum it has a determinate location beyond which it cannot be extended'—he also says that 'the *only* thing that can be touched by a point is something indivisible'. But, of course, points in a continuum (such as a line) can no more be touching other points than there can be two cuts through a sausage without any sausage between them. The mid-point of a line touches only divisible one-dimensional quantity, as Aquinas himself recognizes elsewhere (see e.g. In Phys. V: L5.694).

'Second, . . . quantitative touching occurs only in respect of extremities, while the touching that has to do with power relates to *the whole thing* that is touched. For a thing is touched in this way in so far as it is acted on, and moved. Now that happens in so far as it is in a state of potentiality; but potentiality has to do with the whole, not [merely] with the extremities of the whole. And for that reason *the whole* of the thing is touched' in power contact (1318*b*). He's certainly right to say that quantitative/corporeal touching involves only extremities. But his argument for the contrasting character of power contact seems plainly unsound. Here are its premisses: (1) in power contact a thing is touched in so far as it is acted on; (2) a thing is acted on in so far as it is in a state of potentiality; (3) potentiality has to do with the whole of the thing that has it, not merely with its extremities. (1) and (2) seem uncontroversially acceptable, but (3) seems plainly false in general. My radio, I suppose, may be said to be touched in power contact by the radio station whose broadcast it's receiving, something it can do only in so far as it's in a state of potentiality to be acted on in just that way: it's a radio in good working order, tuned to that station, equipped with well-charged batteries, and turned on. But it could be acted on in just the same way even if some of its parts—such as the volume-control knob—were removed. Even then, the radio's relevant potentiality wouldn't have to do with the whole of what remained of it, since its outer case, for instance, couldn't be relevantly acted on in that power contact. In short, I don't see any grounds, much less any grounds Aquinas is offering, for supposing that power contact can't involve just some parts, or even just one part, of the whole thing that is acted on.[25] The sun's lighting a stone appears to be another clear, simple instance of power contact, and it's obviously only the surface of the stone, not the whole of it, that is touched in the relevant way.[26]

---

[25] Cf. Descartes's pineal-gland hypothesis: 'We need to recognize also that although the soul is joined to the whole body, nevertheless there is a certain part of the body where it exercises its functions more particularly than in all the others. . . . [T]he part of the body in which the soul directly exercises its functions . . . is a certain very small gland situated in the middle of the brain's substance' (*Passions of the Soul* 31, in Descartes 1988: 230). However mistaken this hypothesis may be, it could hardly have been ruled out simply on grounds of the necessarily global character of power contact.

[26] Again, it's plausible to suppose that he's anticipating features of his account of the human being. What he's presenting here is a picture of at least one respect in which the human soul appears to be in power contact with the human body—animating *the whole* body. But he has provided no argument for any such picture at this point.

As Aquinas observes, his third distinction depends on the second.[27] But the way it does so renders the third distinction unacceptable, too. 'In the case of quantitative touching, which takes place in respect of extremities, what does the touching must be extrinsic to what is touched and cannot go through it, but is impeded by it. On the other hand, *since* the kind of touching that has to do with power, the kind that is suited to intellective substances, extends to the innermost constituents of the thing (*sit ad intima*), it makes the substance that is doing the touching [1] be within that which is touched[28] and [2] go into it without any impediment' (1318c). Again, what he says about *quantitative* touching is unimpeachable. And the distinctions he wants to draw here aren't hard to accept in weaker versions. In *power* contact, A *needn't* be extrinsic to B, and A's power *might* be able to affect what is intrinsic to B, to go into, or even all through, B. But those intuitively acceptable characterizations are nothing like so strong as Aquinas's claims here: that in power contact A's power (its 'touching') does extend to B's innermost constituents—reiterating his second distinction—or that power contact involves (1) A's being *within* B, and (2) A's going into B *without any impediment*. If something like my sun-and-stone example, or even Aquinas's Aristotelian example of the saddening person, is supposed to guide us in acquiring the notion of power contact,[29] then all these claims about it seem plainly false. None the less, on the basis of those claims and others we've been examining, Aquinas draws a conclusion that may look as if he thinks he's already settled the matter: 'In this way, therefore, an intellective substance can be united with a body through power contact' (1319a).

4. Unconditional union

I've been arguing that Aquinas hasn't yet provided good grounds for accepting that conclusion, even if he means to stress the 'can' in it, concluding only that this sort of union is a real possibility. So we

---

[27] 'On that basis'—i.e. on the basis of the second distinction—'the third difference is clear' (1318c).

[28] The sense in which A is supposed to be within B here must obviously be very thoroughgoing: not merely the way wine is in a bottle (without permeating the very glass that forms the bottle). Perhaps the way electricity is in an uninsulated wire?

[29] See n. 21 above.

might be at least a little reassured by the fact that he goes on at once to indicate that, after all, union through power contact is not what he's been looking for, or, at any rate, not all that he's been looking for. His stated aim in chapter 56 has been to explain 'how an intellective substance can be united with a body', and his conclusion regarding power contact doesn't fully achieve that aim in his own view (as may be seen at least superficially from the fact that more than 40 per cent of the chapter *follows* his announcement of that conclusion). What leaves him unsatisfied is that 'things that are united through that sort of contact are not *unconditionally* one (*unum simpliciter*);[30] for they are one in respect of acting and being acted on, which is not to be one unconditionally' (1319a).[31] And the fact that he has this concern here shows that he is indeed looking for a mode of union stronger than power contact, a mode of union in which those two genera of ingredients can be combined in one other, unconditionally united, metaphysically hybrid *species* of creature, one whose nature establishes it on the borderline of creation's radical division between bodies without intellects and intellects without bodies.

(It may seem strange that Aquinas argues at length regarding power contact as a possible mode of union between an intellective substance and a body, and then, as soon as he concludes that it is so, begins backing away from it as not fully satisfactory because the union it can support doesn't result in something that is unconditionally one. But, again, I think that one explanation for this

---

[30] See also e.g. I.18.141b: 'In every composite, there must be actuality and potentiality, since more than one cannot be made unconditionally one except where something is an actuality and something else a potentiality. For things that exist in actuality [beforehand] are united only as fastened together (*colligata*), or juxtaposed (*congregata*)—which are not [ways of being] unconditionally one. [But] where such things are concerned, even the very parts that have been juxtaposed are a kind of potentiality (*sicut potentia*) in respect of the union, since they are united in actuality after having been unitable in potentiality.' In this earlier passage he is plainly claiming that a necessary condition for the unconditional unifying of two ingredients is an agent–patient relationship between the ingredients. But that it is not also a sufficient condition is clear from the way in which he goes on immediately in the passage now under consideration (1319a).

[31] I think the point is already clear on the basis of that simple observation, but the passage goes on in this way: 'For a thing is called one in the same way as it is called a being [see e.g. ST Ia.11.1; QDV 1.1]; but being an agent does not signify being unconditionally (*esse autem agens non significat esse simpliciter*), and so neither is being one in respect of acting [the same as] being one unconditionally.' This further explanation in terms of the transcendentals *being* and *one* strikes me as more obscure than what it's intended to explain.

surprising transition may well be that he knows that he will need the unity of power contact *too*, once he establishes *unconditional* unity in the result by some other means. And, as we'll see, he needs it also for his critical exposition of the Platonist account of human nature in chapters 57 and 58.)

According to Aquinas, 'there are three ways a thing is called one unconditionally: as *indivisible*, as *continuous*, or as *what is one in respect of a defining characteristic*' (1319*b*). He doesn't try to show that power contact alone can't make A indivisible from B or continuous with B, or make the two of them into something that is unconditionally one in that third respect. Presumably he thinks it's obvious that no two things that 'are one in respect of acting and being acted on' are, considered just as such, also one in any of those stronger respects. If that's what he thinks, I think he's plainly right. So the question is whether an intellective substance could be united with a body in any of those three stronger ways in addition to power contact.

He begins developing his answer to that question by rejecting the first two ways as inapplicable. Something that is unconditionally one in virtue of being '*indivisible* cannot be made from an intellective substance and a body, for that [one] would have to be compounded out of two' (1319*b*). But being compounded out of two ingredients surely can't be enough to rule out indivisibility. To take just one pertinent example, *mixtures* of two ingredients are indivisible in the relevant sense: the original ingredients can't be divided from each other, or recovered from the mixture (just because their being mixed together involves their corruption, as Aquinas himself observes).[32] Of course, mixture itself is no longer a live option as a mode of union that could unite a body with an intellective substance. Perhaps Aquinas is taking it for granted that all remaining real possibilities must be found among forms of *contact*. In that case I suppose it would be plausible to claim that no one thing can be theoretically indivisible if its unity consists simply in the fact that its ingredients are *in contact* with each other, whether in corporeal contact or in power contact. It wouldn't be unreasonable to suppose that theoretical indivisibility is a *necessary* condition of unconditional union; but since Aquinas goes on to investigate other ways in which an intellective substance and a body might be uncondi-

---

[32] See sect. 2 above.

tionally one, after denying that they could be indivisible from each other, he plainly takes indivisibility to be only a *sufficient* condition of the sort of union he's looking for.[33]

The fact that continuity, the second way in which two things can be made unconditionally one, has already been introduced as a mode of contact taken literally is some confirmation for the hypothesis that only modes of contact are under consideration here. But something that is unconditionally one in virtue of being continuous can't be made from an intellective substance and a body, since all 'the parts of a continuum are quantitative' (1319*b*); and although a body is quantitative, an intellective substance is not. Aquinas's earlier discounting of continuity seemed based on interpreting it too narrowly as an exclusively corporeal relationship,[34] but his restriction of it here to quantitative ingredients, presumably either spatial or temporal, is unobjectionable.

'Therefore, we are left with having to inquire whether a unit that is [unconditionally] one in respect of a defining characteristic (*ratione unum*) can be made from an intellective substance and a body' (1319*b*). This third way of being unconditionally one is the hardest to interpret; but it's also crucially important, because this is the one that Aquinas thinks will serve his present purposes.[35] Because of the notorious ambiguity of *ratio*, the crucial phrase *ratione unum* is ambiguous. One published English translation has 'the one in reason', and another has 'logically one'.[36] But even a rubbish heap can correctly be characterized as one in reason, or logically one, although certainly not as unconditionally one.[37] So those translations, plausible outside this context, are too weak here, as we'll see. For reasons that will emerge very soon, my translation picks up the sense of *ratio* as 'essence' or 'defining characteristic', another sense in which Aquinas of course uses the word very often.

Having eliminated indivisibility and continuity as ways of being unconditionally one that can't apply to an intellective substance

---

[33] Looking ahead once again, since Aquinas wants to leave open the possibility of a human soul's existing after death, apart from the human being's body, indivisibility is definitely not what he wants for the union of an intellective substance with a body.

[34] See sect. 2 above.

[35] So, again, since he's *accepting* one of the three possibilities he's examining, his survey of ways in which 'a thing is called one unconditionally' doesn't have to be exhaustive.

[36] Anderson 1975 and English Dominican Fathers 1923.   [37] See n. 14 above.

and a body, Aquinas expands on the remaining third way: 'Something that is [unconditionally] one in respect of a defining characteristic is made of two permanent entities only in the way [something is made] of a substantial form and matter. For what is one in respect of a defining characteristic is not made of a subject and an accident: *human being* and *white* [e.g.] do not have the same defining characteristic' (1319c). This important passage presents several problems.

The context shows that 'an intellective substance and a body' must count as 'two permanent entities'. What does Aquinas mean here by 'permanent entities (*permanentibus*)'? This designation has an established technical sense in medieval discussions of the logic of 'begins' and 'ceases', where a 'permanent' entity or state is one that can be said to exist as a whole at any instant of its duration—e.g. a cat, or being fully grown—and one that is 'successive' can exist as a whole only over an interval—a dance, or growing to a height of six feet.[38] An intellective substance and a body are permanent entities in that technical sense, but I think it's clear that Aquinas is using 'permanent' here in the less technical, more literal sense of lasting, remaining through[39]—just the sort of thing that might be appropriately said of substances, intellective and corporeal alike. And, since the formula 'an intellective substance and a body' certainly seems to be describing two substances, this passage taken in that way strengthens the impression that his account of the mind–body relationship will have to be a strong version of substance dualism.

However, he stipulates that this unconditional union of 'two permanent entities' can occur 'only in the way [something is made] of a substantial form and matter', thereby strongly suggesting that a substantial form and its matter can also qualify as two permanent entities, even though no ordinary substantial form or any form's matter could qualify as a substance in the fullest sense: I mean, as an individual in the Aristotelian category of substance, a natural primary substance, such as an amethyst, an oak, or a salamander. He also stipulates that the *result* must be something that is 'one in

---

[38] See Kretzmann 1976.

[39] See e.g. *Physics* I 7, 190a9–13, where the person 'is permanent' (*permanet*, in the Latin translation Aquinas used), and the person's states of being unmusical and being musical aren't. In his commentary on the passage, Aquinas puts it this way: *alterum istorum est permanens et alterum non permanens* (In Phys. I: L12.102).

respect of a defining characteristic', a paradigmatic instance of which is a natural primary substance. So, in spite of terminology that can hardly fail to lead a reader of Book II so far to think that an intellective substance is being presented as a natural primary substance,[40] Aquinas seems to be heading toward an account in which an intellective substance will be the substantial form for which a body will be the matter—an aim he expressly identifies just after this passage (in 1319d). But no natural primary substance could be the substantial form of any other natural primary substance. If Aquinas's account is going to turn out to be coherent, then some of these appearances will have to turn out to be deceiving.

Aquinas ends the passage we're examining by expressly rejecting a kind of union that might have seemed to be a pertinent, real alternative to m–f composition: the union of a *subject*—e.g. an m–f composite such as a human being—and an *accidental* form—such as that human being's whiteness. Such a union, he observes, is *not* one in respect of a defining characteristic, just because *human being* and *whiteness* do not have the same defining characteristic (nor is either of them part of the defining characteristic of the other). Aquinas, then, is rejecting subject–accident union considered only as another instance of union *in respect of a defining characteristic*, and he's undoubtedly right to do so. But it seems that subject–accident union should count as another way in which two ingredients could be made unconditionally one, a fourth way in addition to (1) indivisibility, (2) continuity, and (3) unity in respect of a defining characteristic. It can't be disqualified simply because a subject and its accident aren't theoretically indivisible from each other, because, as we've seen, he treats indivisibility as a condition that is sufficient, but not necessary, for unconditional union.

---

[40] Considered generically, an intellective substance itself is unconditionally one in respect of a defining characteristic, and it is, on its own, a composite entity with two components. (And in Aquinas's view any angel would count as a kind of intellective substance that is also a natural primary substance.) As we've seen, every incorporeal, immaterial, intellective substance is an s–b composite, a composition of substance (or essence) and being, and obviously not an m–f composite, a composition of matter and substantial form. All the same, its union of substance and being may count as having been made 'only *in the way* (*sicut*) [something is made] of a substantial form and matter'. See 54.1287: 'composition of matter and form [m–f] does not have the same defining characteristic as composition of substance and being [s–b], although *each of them is composition of potentiality and actuality* [p–a]'; also n. 30 above and Ch. Seven above, sects. 7 and 8.

Moreover, the combination of a subject and an accidental form might strike someone as a way of being unconditionally one that deserves to be considered in this context, in which it certainly seems to be a less implausible alternative than (2) continuity. So, I think, Aquinas ought to have said more about this kind of union before setting it aside.

In any event, he considers himself entitled to conclude on the basis of these two surveys—of modes of union and of ways of being unconditionally one—that 'we are left with having to inquire whether an intellective substance can be the substantial form of some body' (1319d). In his view, he has shown that that's the only conceivable way in which something that is unconditionally one might be made of two permanent entities, one of which is incorporeal and the other corporeal.

5. Aquinas's unreasonable hypothesis

Aquinas's investigation so far, then, has shown him that an intellective (incorporeal) substance *cannot* be united with a body by being mixed together with it or literally in contact with it, and that an intellective substance *can* be united with a body by being in power contact with it. But a union of two things in respect of power contact only—e.g. a compass needle and the magnetic pole—does not constitute something that is *unconditionally* one, which turns out to be what Aquinas was looking for. There are at least three ways in which two things *can* be unconditionally one.[41] But if those two things are an incorporeal substance and a corporeal substance, they *cannot* be unconditionally united as (1) *indivisible* from each other or as (2) *continuous* with each other. It is only (3) *in respect of a defining characteristic* that something that is unconditionally one could be made of two permanent entities of those two kinds. And the only way two permanent entities could be made unconditionally one in respect of a defining characteristic is for one of them to be the substantial form for which the other is the matter. (An accidental form and its subject are *not* one in respect of a defining characteristic.) Since an intellective substance is an immaterial,

---

[41] Although Aquinas doesn't say so, in this context it seems sensible to suppose that the things whose unconditional unity is under consideration should at least include, if not be confined to, things already united in power contact.

subsistent form, the only way an intellective substance might conceivably be united in the appropriate way with a body is for the former to be the form for which the latter is the matter. So, in answer to the question with which the chapter began—how an intellective substance can be united with a body—Aquinas has distilled out of all these considerations the following stringent hypothesis, which I'm labelling SFB: An intellective substance can be appropriately united with a body only by being the substantial form of that body.

So he might be expected to end the chapter at this point, perhaps expressing some sense of accomplishment. Instead, he says: 'However, to those who consider this [hypothesis SFB] *rationally*, it seems *impossible*' (56.1320). He then does go on to end the chapter, but with a series of five arguments of just the sort that such rationally considering people might bring against his hypothesis SFB to show that it is impossible—either in general, because it is impossible that an intellective substance and a body (or corporeal substance) be unconditionally united at all, or in particular, because it is impossible that they be united in the way specified in hypothesis SFB. To those five potentially devastating arguments Aquinas offers no rejoinders here or, indeed, anywhere else in the next twelve chapters.

It's true that he has arrived at hypothesis SFB only by critically evaluating and mostly eliminating various modes of union, a process that puts him in a position to conclude that nothing short of the kind of union stipulated in SFB would be a kind of union appropriate for a body and an intellective substance. He hasn't yet offered evidence that this kind of union of such ingredients is really possible. Before doing so, he evidently wants to examine various arguments for rejecting it as *im*possible. That's not a bad tactic for him to adopt, especially given SFB's initial implausibility. But it certainly looks peculiar for Aquinas to characterize such arguments as objections that occur to people who consider his hypothesis 'rationally' (*rationabiliter*), and then to leave the arguments standing with no further comment, without so much as a promissory note regarding rejoinders to them.[42] On the other hand, the painstaking critical review of other objections and contrary doctrines with which he fills the immediately following chapters is certainly the sort of thing

---

[42] In sect. 6 below I suggest a way of explaining, if not altogether dispelling, the peculiar appearance of this move.

he needs to do in order to undercut the natural assumption that there must be plausible alternatives to his unreasonable-looking hypothesis SFB. If he can succeed in clearing the ground in that way, he will have prepared the reader to take his positive evidence more seriously when he does finally offer it.

When, in chapter 69, Aquinas is finally ready to refute the five opposing arguments presented here at the end of chapter 56, he introduces his rejoinders by saying that 'it isn't hard to resolve' those five arguments 'now that these things have been considered' (69.1460). By 'these things' he seems most likely to mean all the many things he's considered in chapters 57–68. For that reason I want to postpone any evaluation of the arguments. Simply summarizing them will be enough for now.

The first argument (N1) takes for granted something that certainly seems to have been implied by developments in Aquinas's investigation so far: viz. that any union of an intellective substance with a body would have to be a union of two actually existing substances. And N1 reasons that 'nothing [that is unconditionally] one can be made of two actually existing substances' (56.1321).[43] Notice that N1 argues that Aquinas's SFB is impossible in general—just in virtue of considerations of (unconditional) union, leaving aside any consideration of the fact that, in the proposed union, one of these two actually existing substances is supposed to be the substantial form of the other. But it seems that this further feature of SFB could only strengthen argument N1's case against it. N1, then, can be construed as an argument anticipating and opposing the substance dualism that has seemed to be prefigured by Aquinas's general consideration of the union of an intellective substance with a body.

N2 is more specific and more technical than N1: it focuses exclusively on the purported matter–form relationship that N1 ignores. The argument is based on a principle that, as we'll see, Aquinas accepts: both the matter and the form of any m–f composite thing are included in one and the same genus. But, of course, an incorporeal substance and a corporeal substance belong to radically different genera.[44] 'Therefore', N2 concludes, 'it does not seem

---

[43] See also n. 30 above.

[44] *Corporeal* and *incorporeal* are the very first two (and thus the broadest) genera that divide the Aristotelian category *substance* in the standard Porphyrian Tree.

possible that the one be the form of the other' (1322); and, consequently, SFB does not seem possible.

N3 points out that 'if an intellective substance is the form of a
body, its being must be in corporeal matter' (1323), which is clearly
supported by Aquinas's own principles. N3 then claims that in an
m–f composite 'the being of the form is not over and above
(*praeter*) the being of the matter'. In fact, the substantial form in an
ordinary m–f composite is just what Aquinas calls a 'material form',
and he has devoted an entire chapter (II.51) to arguing that 'an
intellective substance is not a material form'.[45] So Aquinas's SFB
hypothesis is impossible—unless, of course, he were willing to give
up his already argued thesis that an intellective substance must be
immaterial.

N4 might be viewed as building on N3 by enlisting the aid of
'philosophers' who have shown that intellect is 'separate
from body', being 'neither a body nor a power in a body' (1324).
Everything we've seen so far strongly suggests that Aquinas
himself agrees with those philosophers.[46] But from his hypothesis
SFB it follows that an intellective substance would have its being
in a body, and 'it is impossible that anything the being of which
is in a body be separate from that body'. Therefore, SFB is
impossible.

Finally, argument N5's attack on SFB gains strength from
appearing to agree with Aquinas on other important points: 'something that is unconditionally one, one as regards its being, is made
of a form and matter' (1325). On that basis N5 argues that 'if an
intellective substance is the form of a body, its being must be
common to it and to the body', in which case 'its power will be a
power in a body'. But that outcome apparently conflicts with the
philosophers' view relied on in N4 and accepted by Aquinas.

So Aquinas's hypothesis SFB, his painstakingly developed answer to the question of how an intellective substance can be united
with a body, does indeed seem unreasonable. The opening sentence of the next chapter could have served equally well as the
concluding sentence of chapter 56: 'Moved by these [five negative

---

[45] See also 43.1197 and 52.1273. On the other hand, QDA 9c seems to say that 'the
rational soul is the most perfect of material forms (*formarum materialium*)', although in at least three manuscripts there is the more plausible variant reading
formarum naturalium ('natural forms'). See Robb 1968: 148.

[46] See e.g. 56.1313 and sects. 1 and 2 above.

arguments] and arguments like them, some people have said that no intellective substance can be the form of a body' (57.1326*a*).

6. *The very nature of a human being*

The chapter format of SCG is obviously unlike the scholastic disputational format that Aquinas uses more often in his writings, most famously in ST. The differences between them are more than stylistic. The two formats provide two methods of organizing thought. But in chapters 56–69 of Book II Aquinas organizes his thought in such a way that we can, and should, recognize in those fourteen chapters all the formal elements of an ordinary article of ST in their standard relations to one another.[47] Chapter 56 develops a 'title question', raised expressly in 1319*d*—Can an intellective substance be the substantial form of a body?—in response to which arguments N1–N5 constitute the 'objections', supporting a negative answer to the question. Chapters 57–68 constitute the reply ('the body of the article'), in which Aquinas first argues against other views (in 57–67), and finally, on that basis, restates his own (in 68).[48] Only then, in chapter 69, does he offer his rejoinders to the objections, arguments N1–N5. But, in keeping with the disputational format, between the objections and the reply we should expect to find a *sed contra*, a generally accepted authoritative pronouncement or a generally acknowledged matter of fact that appears to support the other side of the question (in this case, the affirmative side). What Aquinas provides at the appropriate juncture, in the second sentence of chapter 57, fills that bill precisely. 'However, since that position [that no intellective substance can be the form of a body] was evidently contradicted by the very nature of a human being, who does appear to be composed of an intellective soul and a body, those [same] people thought out certain ways in which they

[47] I think it's very likely that by the time Aquinas began to write SCG in 1259 he had acquired a disposition to organize his thoughts along those disputational lines. Much of his education and his teaching made use of 'the scholastic method', and he had already written five works in disputational format (including the very substantial In Sent. and QDV) before beginning SCG (see App. I below; also Ch. One above, n. 16). There are further dialectical complications within chs. 56–69, as we'll see, but their overarching structure exhibits the disputational format.

[48] Many of his more elaborate replies in ST and other works in the disputational format display this eminently sensible pattern.

might preserve the nature of a human being' (1326*b*)—despite their formal rejection of the possibility of such a union.[49]

Here, at last, is the anticipated transitional passage. Up to this point the consideration has been generic, investigating the possibility of an appropriate union of any sort of intellective substance with any sort of body. It has also been almost exclusively an a priori consideration. But now Aquinas shifts our attention from the general to the specific, and from the a priori to the a posteriori, to 'the very nature of a human being'—something to which we seem to have empirical access. And he does so just because—*sed contra*—a human being 'does appear to be composed of an intellective soul and a body'. That a human body is a body needs no argument. So, if a human being's intellective soul counts as a kind of intellective substance, and if this apparent composition turns out on examination to be a union in respect of a defining characteristic in which the intellective soul is the substantial form and the human body is the matter, then the apparent nature of a human being will be all the evidence that Aquinas's hypothesis SFB needs. If a human being is composed as Aquinas says it appears to be composed, then an intellective substance *is* united with a body; and the way in which it is so, if that can be determined, will show us in detail 'how an intellective substance *can be* united with a body'.

The grand strategy of Aquinas's argument in chapters 56–69 requires that the 'intellective soul' of a human being will turn out to qualify as one sort of intellective substance. At the conclusion of this long argument he says it in so many words: 'the human soul is an intellective substance' (68.1449).[50] At this point, however, he has said very little at all about souls, none of it systematic.[51] His account

---

[49] Someone who insists that no intellective substance can be the substantial form of a body could, of course, consistently agree that a human being appears to be, or even is, 'composed of an intellective soul and a body', only not in the way stipulated in Aquinas's hypothesis SFB. And, as we'll see, the opponents Aquinas deals with did take this line. The evident contradiction Aquinas is claiming here presumably depends on his having already argued that nothing weaker than SFB will do, that the requisite unconditional unity in respect of a defining characteristic can be achieved only in an m–f composition in which the body is the matter and the intellective substance is the substantial form.

[50] See also 79.1598: 'The soul of a human being is a kind of intellective substance.'

[51] See e.g. 46.1233, where 'soul' is used interchangeably with 'mind' in an example; 49.1257, in a reference to pre-Socratic views about the soul; 49.1258, regarding a heretical doctrine of the soul; 50.1263, regarding what Empedocles thought about the soul; 50.1264, where 'soul' is apparently interchangeable with 'intellect'; and the somewhat more interesting 55.1308: 'intellect is perfected not through movement,

of the human soul can and should be allowed to emerge from this long argument in chapters 56–69, but a summary of his general concept of soul will provide useful background for it.[52]

7. Soul as the first principle of life

Obviously, Aquinas is no materialist. As we've seen, the fundamental division in his classification of created things is between the corporeal and the incorporeal (or the spiritual)—an exhaustive division that turns out not to be perfectly exclusive, if the human soul is what he's going to argue it is.[53] But simply having a soul isn't enough to give a creature a spiritual component, since Aquinas uses 'soul' generically in a way that even many materialists could tolerate. Nobody objects to dividing physical objects into animate and inanimate things, and Aquinas's generic use of *anima*, his word for soul, treats the term as if it were merely a noun of convenience associated with 'animate' (*animata*), rather than a designation for an incorporeal substance: 'In order to inquire into the nature of soul, we have to presuppose that "soul" is what we call the first principle of life in things that live among us; for we call living things "animate" [or "ensouled"], but things that are devoid of life "inanimate" [or "not ensouled"]' (ST Ia.75.1c).[54] So not only we, but mosses and worms, too, have souls, although in Aquinas's view neither plants nor non-human animals are in any respect *spiritual* creatures. In ascribing souls to plants, he means only to be referring

but instead through its being outside movement. For as regards the intellective soul we are perfected by knowledge and prudence when both bodily changes and changes associated with the soul's passions are at rest.' See also Ch. Seven above, sect. 2.

[52] This summary is drawn from Kretzmann 1993: 128–31. For other accounts, see Kenny 1993: ch. 11 and Stump 1995.

[53] See e.g. 68.1453*b*: 'And that's why the intellective soul is said to be a kind of horizon and borderline between corporeal and incorporeal things, in so far as it is an incorporeal substance and yet also the form of a body.' See also QDA 1c: 'the human soul . . . is established on the borderline between corporeal and separated substances', and ST Ia.77.2c: 'the human soul . . . exists on the borderline between spiritual and corporeal creatures'.

[54] Notice that he intends his claim to cover only terrestrial, biologically living beings, those that 'live among us', not every being that can be said to be living—such as God, or angels. And he must intend to emphasize the 'in' when he describes soul as the first principle of life in terrestrial beings, since he of course takes God to be unconditionally (and extrinsically) the first principle of life for creatures.

to whatever it is in the essence of plants that accounts for their exhibiting a certain range of 'vegetative' or 'nutritive' potentialities and functions—such as growth and reproduction. Still, he emphatically denies that even the merely nutritive soul of a plant or the nutritive + sensory soul of a non-human animal can be simply identified with any of the living thing's bodily parts. He finds a basis for ruling out that possibility in what he uses as soul's defining formula: 'the first principle of life'.

From Aristotle, Aquinas had learned of pre-Socratic materialists who simply identified souls as bodies—bodily parts of living bodies. He saw those philosophers as having begun, quite sensibly, by considering what is most apparent about life: the presence in living things of certain distinctive activities that are called vital just because they naturally imply life (*vita*) at some level or other—e.g. reproducing, or talking. But in Aquinas's view those ancient reductive materialists, 'claiming that bodies alone are real things, and that what is not a body is nothing at all' (ST Ia.75.1c), confused the shorter-range project of identifying material sources or partial explanations (*principia*) of one or another vital activity with the search for the soul behind *all* of a plant's or animal's vital activities, the *first* principle, the *ultimate* intrinsic source or explanation of all of an animate thing's characteristic activities and mode of existence.

The confusion in pre-Socratic materialism regarding the soul can be shown in many ways, Aquinas thinks, as can be seen in considering his arguments against it in chapter 65. But none of those arguments in SCG II is as strong as the argument he develops later (in ST Ia.75.1c) against the possibility of reducing an animate being's soul to any of its bodily parts. In that anti-reductionist argument he invites us to consider a particular vital activity, such as seeing. Of course, eyes must be included in a correct explanation of vision—and, he might have said, skin in the explanation of touch, roots or stomachs in explanations of growth, and so on. That is, vital activities typically do have bodies—organs—among their principles. And since a principle of a particular *vital* activity may indeed be considered a principle of *life* (although only in that particular respect and to an appropriately restricted extent), it may be granted that some bodies—such as a living animal's normal eyes—are principles of life. It's in that special, limited sense that the ancient materialists were on the right track. But no one, Aquinas thinks, would call an eye (or a root, or a stomach) a *first* principle of life—i.e. a *soul*. So, he says, it's true that some principles of life are bodies, but those that are bodies clearly aren't souls.

Now there are other kinds of bodies—stones, for instance—that not only are not principles of life, but are even naturally, essentially lifeless at all times and in every respect. And the fact that there are naturally lifeless bodies shows that *no* body considered just as a body has life *essentially*. But a *first intrinsic principle* of life, which as such imbues everything else in an animate body with life, must have life essentially. If it didn't, its having life would have to be explained on the basis of something else intrinsic to that living body, and so it wouldn't be that body's *first* principle of life. Therefore, *no* soul, no *first* principle of life, is a body. If any sort of soul is in any respect corporeal—in its essential dependence on some bodily organ, for instance—it won't be in virtue of its corporeality that it animates the thing whose soul it is.

Furthermore, any vegetable or animal body has the life it has only in virtue of being a body organized in a way that confers on it natural potentialities for being in particular sorts of states and performing certain sorts of actions. And a body is organized in this or that way and has these or those potentialities only because of a certain principle that is called the body's *actus*, the substantial form that makes it actually be such a vegetable or animal body. Therefore, the *first* principle of life in a living body, its soul, is no bodily (or quantitative) part of that body, but rather its form, one of the two metaphysical parts of the m–f composite that absolutely every body is.[55]

This argument, which Aquinas applies to the explanation of life in any and every living corporeal thing, is compatible with some forms of materialism. Materialists who tolerate Aquinas's generic concept of soul, and who understand soul not simply as a bodily

---

[55] On metaphysical, as distinct from quantitative, parts, see e.g. 72.1485; also QDA 10c. As we've already seen more than once, *actus* is an important technical term for Aquinas. He uses it to mean both action and actuality, in ways that may be clarified along these lines. A thing *acts* only if, and only to the extent to which, it exists *actually* and not just potentially, and is a thing of such and such a sort. Consequently, whatever it is in virtue of which the thing acts in a certain way is identical with that in virtue of which it is a thing of that certain (appropriate) sort. Therefore, that in virtue of which *primarily* the thing acts (the primary intrinsic source or first intrinsic principle of its characteristic natural action) is identical with *the substantial form* of the thing. See also ST Ia.76.1c.

part of a living body, but as a function of a body, or as the effect of a configuration of physical components, could also tolerate the critical line taken in this anti-reductionist argument, however they might react to its conclusion identifying soul with form. We have yet to see whether Aquinas's account of the human soul in particular is entirely incompatible with materialist theories of living things.[56]

8. Body and soul

What I've picked out as Aquinas's *sed contra* in this context is, appropriately, a commonplace. There clearly are empirical grounds on which human beings have almost always been taken to be combinations of body and soul. And Aquinas tells us in chapter 57, not altogether plausibly, that it was just that commonplace that worried philosophers who would otherwise have had no qualms about dismissing hypothesis SFB as impossible (as in arguments N1–N5). In his critical survey of Greek and Muslim views opposed to his own view,[57] Aquinas suggests that the philosophers he criticizes began by rejecting the possibility that any sort of intellective substance could be the substantial form of any sort of body. Then, troubled by their realization that the human being may appear to be a real instance of that sort of union, they were motivated to develop alternative accounts of human nature. It seems much more likely that their positions developed simply *as* positions about the constitution of a human being; but there's a legitimate tactical advantage for Aquinas in retelling the story along this line, whatever the historical facts might be.

His ground-clearing review of his opposing predecessors, individually or in groups, is carefully structured in a way that can be appreciated against the background of the Aristotelian account he's putting forward in hypothesis SFB. As applied to the human

---

[56] Although I'm presenting this anti-reductionist argument from ST only as regards souls and bodies quite generally, in view of the evidence in SCG II.56 suggesting that Aquinas's account of human nature will have to be some version of substance dualism, it's worth noting that the soul–body relationship as delineated in this argument is not a radical substance dualism. See Stump 1995: esp. 520–3.

[57] He argues, especially against Averroës, Alexander, and Avicenna, that his view is Aristotle's view as well. See e.g. chs. 61, 62, 70, and 78.

soul specifically, SFB can be analysed for present purposes into the following claims:[58]

A The human being has an intellective soul.
B The intellective soul is an intellective substance.
C The intellective soul is in the human body.
D The intellective soul is closely connected with the human body.
E The intellective soul is united with the human body as its substantial form.

Of the eight opposing accounts which Aquinas considers in chapters 57–68, all share Aquinas's claims A and D. Claim C is accepted by all the opponents considered here except Averroës and Alexander of Aphrodisias. Claim B is fully accepted only by Plato, accepted by Averroës and Alexander as regards different aspects of the intellective soul, and rejected by all the others.[59] And it should come as no surprise to learn that none of the opponents accepts claim E. (It's only in that respect that they are all opponents.) Of the eight opposing accounts, then, Plato's comes closest to Aquinas's own in these respects, since only Plato, as Aquinas presents him, fully accepts claims A, B, C, and D. Consequently, Aquinas's careful critical analysis of what he takes to have been the position of Plato and his followers gives rise to important developments in his presentation of his own position on the nature of a human being, and is essential to an understanding of it.

In Aquinas's view, it is Plato's opposition to hypothesis SFB that accounts for the fact that he, 'and his followers as well, claimed that the intellective soul is united with the body *not* as a form is united with matter, but only as a mover is united with what is movable [by it], saying that the soul is in the body as a pilot is in a ship. And the union of the soul and the body, viewed in that way, would be [a

---

[58] The version of SFB specific to human beings appears e.g. as a summary statement which Aquinas feels entitled to make based on his rejections of all the opposed accounts: 'we are left with this: that the human soul is an intellective substance united with the body as a form' (68.1449). See sect. 10 below.

[59] For Averroës and Alexander, see sect. 9 below. Aquinas says that Galen characterized the human soul as a temperament (*complexio*) (II.63), that Empedocles characterized it as 'a harmony . . . of the contraries that [he and others] viewed as making up the animate body' (64.1422), that some ancient materialists characterized it as a body (a bodily part of the human body) (II.65), that other ancients identified it with the senses (II.66), and still others with the imagination (II.67). From our point of view, most of the opposing accounts can be safely ignored; they are either fantastic, or philosophically unedifying, or both. See 68.1449 for Aquinas's summary. See also Ch. Nine below, esp. sect. 3.

union] through power contact only' (57.1327).[60] As I've been saying, the historical accuracy of this account (or of any others that
Aquinas provides in chs. 57–68) is not at issue, especially because
his main purpose in criticizing his predecessors here is to refine and
defend hypothesis SFB as applied to the human soul. He implies
that Plato and the Platonists adopted their union-by-power-
contact-only theory because they felt compelled to reject SFB as
impossible. But what really matters here is what he says in criticizing the theory he ascribes to them.

In Aquinas's view, power contact is a mode of real union, and
one that really is suited to unite an intellective substance with a
body, as we've seen. Furthermore, power contact is a mode of
union—though not the only one—in which Aquinas, too, is going
to say that the human soul is united with the human body. So, the
Platonist theory presented here is, from Aquinas's own point of
view, partly right. It can't be more than partly right, of course,
because 'what results from that sort of contact is not something that
is *unconditionally* one, even though what results from the union of
soul and body is a human being. Therefore, [on the Platonist
theory] we are left with the conclusion that a human being is *not*
unconditionally one or, consequently, unconditionally a being but,
rather, a being [only] *per accidens*' (1328). That thing out there,
moving on the water—Maria in her kayak—is *one* thing, *a* being,
only *per accidens*. If that's the sort of thing a human being is, then
a human being as ordinarily understood, in terms of soul and body,
is not a natural substance, not really a being, at all.

As Aquinas tells the story, Plato saw the absurdity of this consequence—the being *per accidens* account of a human being—and in
order to avoid it took the drastic course of claiming 'that a human
being is *not* something composed of a soul and a body but, rather,
that the human being is *the soul itself, using a body*—just as Peter is
not something composed of a human being and clothes but, rather,
a human being using clothes' (1329). So the Platonist way of avoiding this absurd consequence is to adopt a radical, thoroughgoing,
substance dualism according to which a human being is really,

---

[60] I've substituted a pilot for the sailor in the familiar Aristotelian analogy—*sicut
nauta in navi* (*De anima* II 1, 413a8–9). An ordinary seaman couldn't have been
what the Platonists had in mind, because that image would leave the soul looking
like a mostly passive, subservient passenger. An even clearer nautical instance of
power contact might be someone's using a one-person kayak.

essentially, exclusively an incorporeal, immaterial intellective substance using a particular body of the sort we ordinarily call human,
through power contact with that body.[61]

Given Aquinas's approach so far in this investigation (chs. 46–
56), it wouldn't be unreasonable to expect him to be at least sympa-
thetic to what he presents as Plato's way out. After all, Aquinas,
too, appears to take the existence of an intellective substance as his
starting-point and then ask about the possibility of its being somehow united with some body. None the less, he firmly repudiates
Plato's way out as 'impossible', basing his rejection, to begin with,
on an altogether commonsensical observation: 'an animal and a
human being are certain sorts of sense-perceptible, natural things.
But that wouldn't be the case unless a body and its parts belonged
to *the essence* of a human being and of an animal, since a soul isn't
anything sense-perceptible or material.[62] But, according to the
[Platonist] position described above, the *whole* essence of a human
being and of an animal would be a soul. Therefore, it is impossible
that a human being or an animal be a soul using a body rather than
something composed of a body and a soul' (1330).[63]

But Aquinas has another, more technical basis on which he
rejects this particularly strong version of substance dualism more
effectively. The human soul and body as the Platonists conceive of

[61] As Stump points out (1995: 505), Aquinas's description of Plato's substance
dualism closely resembles at least one of Descartes's accounts of his own dualism:
'my essence consists solely in the fact that I am a thinking thing. It is true that I may
have (or, to anticipate, that I certainly have) a body that is very closely joined to me.
But nevertheless, on the one hand I have a clear and distinct idea of myself, in so far
as I am simply a thinking, non-extended thing; and on the other hand I have a
distinct idea of body, in so far as this is simply an extended, non-thinking thing. And
accordingly, it is certain that I am really distinct from my body, and can exist without
it' (Meditation VI, in Descartes 1988: 114–15).

[62] The basis formally available to Aquinas for this claim at this point seems to be
no more than his having occasionally mentioned souls in his treatment of intellective
substances in chs. 49–55, where he never expressly describes human souls as immaterial. See n. 51 above; but see also sect. 7 above.

[63] As Kenny puts it (1993: 139), 'According to St Thomas what I am, what you are,
what everyone else is is nothing less than a human being. He refuses to identify the
individual with the individual's soul, as Descartes was to do.' But is Aquinas playing
fair when he brings non-human animals into this criticism? *Would* a Platonist have
made the same claim about a cat—that Grizzy is really, essentially, only Grizzy's
soul? Still, perhaps that's part of Aquinas's point. If the Platonists say this about the
human being, they ought to be prepared to say it about any animate, ensouled
thing—which would be absurd. But why shouldn't the Platonists reply that they
were talking *only* about the distinctively human *intellective* soul, and not also about
nutritive and sensory souls? (See sect. 9 below.)

them are two radically different kinds of things. But 'it is impossible that [two] things that are disparate in respect of being should have one single operation. I'm calling an operation one not in virtue of [a] whatever the action terminates in [i.e. its effect], but as regards [b] that which emanates [immediately] from the agent [or agents]. For many men hauling a boat do perform an action that is one [a] as regards what gets done, which is one thing. None the less, [b] as regards those doing the hauling there are many actions, because there are the various [individual] efforts (*impetus*) at hauling' (1331). If Steve and Bob are both hauling the boat, their operations are essentially separate. The fact that those separate operations have a joint effect that neither of them could achieve alone requires a further explanation—e.g. an explanation in terms of power contact: Steve's regularly shouting 'Pull!' and Bob's complying. So co-operative boat hauling is *not* an operation that is one in the relevant sense, though it does seem to be an appropriate analogue for a Platonist account of any operation involving both the soul and the body, where the soul's power contact with the body appears to be the only available Platonist explanation of the co-operation.

Again, power contact is not enough to preserve Aquinas's strong sense of the unconditional unity of the human being. 'However, although there is an operation that is *proper* to the soul, an operation in which the body does *not* share—intellective cognition, for instance—there are also some operations that are *common* to soul and body—such as being afraid, getting angry, sensing, and the like. For these latter operations occur in accordance with some change in a determinate part of the body, from which it is clear that they are operations of soul and body together. Therefore, *one thing* must be made of soul and body, and soul and body must not be disparate in respect of being' (1331).[64]

Still, power contact does seem to explain quite a lot of what might otherwise look like 'operations of soul and body together'. A person's soul can reasonably be described as sometimes controlling the bodily manifestations of fear or of anger, or directing the sense-organs (to look, to turn away, to listen, etc.). 'It was in *that* way, therefore, that Plato claimed that the operations just mentioned

---

[64] The construction of this last sentence is a little unusual: *Oportet igitur ex anima et corpore unum fieri, et quod non sint secundum esse diversa.* But I think there can be no doubt about its interpretation.

are common to the soul and the body—viz. that they belong to the soul as to the mover, and to the body as to what is moved' (1332). But, however far the power-contact-only explanation of such operations might be extended, it couldn't do the whole job. Among 'the operations just mentioned', it's most obviously and most importantly sensing that can't be explained fully in that way.

Sensing occurs in respect of being moved by external sense objects. So a human being cannot have sensation in the absence of an external sense object, just as nothing can be moved in the absence of a mover. Therefore, in sensing, a sense-organ is moved and is acted on, but by an external sense object [rather than by the soul]. And that by means of which [the organ] is acted on is the sense, since things that lack sensation are not acted on by sense objects in that sort of undergoing (*passionis*). Therefore, the sense is a passive power belonging to the organ itself. Therefore, the sensory soul, in sensing, does not play the role of the mover and agent, but is rather that by means of which what is acted on is acted on—which in respect of being cannot be disparate from that which is acted on. Therefore, in respect of being, the sensory soul is not disparate from the body that is animated [by it]. (1333)[65]

This particular argument from the nature of sensation is dialectically crucial, as we'll see; but it is only the first of six arguments which Aquinas raises at this point against the radical Platonist dualism (57.1333–8). The vigorous thoroughness of his opposition to what might have seemed to be the account of human nature that he himself would have to give is interesting in its own right. Only one of those other arguments seems to make an important contribution to the dialectical development, however.

Suppose that the Platonists are right, he argues, and that the human soul is associated with the human body in power contact only, somewhat as the newscaster is associated with a portable radio that is broadcasting her words. But 'a thing that is movable [by something else] doesn't get its *species* from the thing that moves it. Therefore, if the soul is joined to the body only as a mover is joined to what is movable [by it], then the body and its parts do not derive their species from the soul. Therefore, in the absence of the soul, the body and its parts will still belong to the same species.' A

---

[65] Aquinas's detailed analysis in this passage of the roles of the external object, the organ, the sense, the sensory soul, and the body deserves a more careful treatment than I can or need to give it for my purposes. (For such a treatment of this material, see Stump, forthcoming *a*.)

radio that is turned off is still a radio. But since, as we've seen, a living thing's soul is the intrinsic first principle of its being alive, the absence of its soul is the absence of its nature.[66] So, if the Platonists are right, then a person's corpse, the exanimate body, is still a human body, with human organs and human limbs. 'But', says Aquinas, 'that is obviously false. For after the soul has left [the body], the flesh, a bone, a hand, and parts like them are called by those names only equivocally, because [then] none of them has its proper operation, which is a consequence of the species. Therefore, the soul is united with the body not only as a mover is united with what is movable by it, or as a man is united with his clothes' (1335). We do, of course, talk about dead bones (and the rest), but 'only equivocally', since the operations proper to bones include, for instance, the production of blood cells for the circulatory system of the body that is structured by those bones, an operation that naturally ceases at death.[67] All the bones in the churchyard, then, really are bones only in a manner of speaking. The conclusion which this argument leads right up to without expressing it is that the human body must derive its species from the human soul—which is of course to say that the human soul is the substantial form of the human body.

And, after three further arguments against the Platonists' power-contact-only theory, that is very nearly what Aquinas does expressly say, arguing for it directly in three arguments (1339–41) which he introduces by announcing that 'one proves in the following way that the soul *is* united with the body as the form that is proper to it'. The individual conclusions of those arguments are that 'the soul is the form of the animated body', 'the soul is the form of the body', and 'the soul is the form and *actus* of the body'.[68] His introductory announcement and those three conclusions all look like abbreviated versions of claim E—that the intellective soul is united with the human body as its substantial form—the most controversial element of hypothesis SFB applied to the human soul, and the only one rejected by the Platonists. So we might get

---

[66] See also 57.1336.

[67] The modern medical capability of transplanting organs from recently dead donors to living recipients who need replacements for damaged organs doesn't constitute an embarrassment to this rather stringent-sounding account of death, since the organs to be transplanted must be kept artificially viable. Only a *fully* human heart—i.e. one that is still living—will do the recipient any good.

[68] On *actus* see n. 55 above.

the impression that Aquinas thinks of his critical analysis of Platonist dualism so far as having already cleared the ground enough to warrant the introduction of arguments directly supporting his own final position. In view of the fact that most of the opposing views he recognizes have yet to be considered and rebutted, that would seem very unlikely.[69] In fact, he presents these arguments here in support of something like SFB only because of the dialectical role they play in his analysis of the Platonist account, as can be seen by the way chapter 58 begins, immediately following his presentation of them: 'But for present purposes the [three] arguments [just] above can be *resisted* in accordance with Plato's view' (1342). We'll see in a moment how he thinks the Platonist dualism can resist them. As for the arguments themselves, the first of them, based on Aquinas's conception of human development, may be the most important in the long run, since it comes closest to supporting hypothesis SFB itself.[70] For Aquinas's immediate purposes, however, it is less pertinent than the other two, both of which concern sensing, which Aquinas has already picked out as the paradigm of those 'operations of soul and body together' that embarrass the Platonists' identification of the human being with the human soul.

In the first place, what Aquinas has already observed regarding sensation may be observed as well, and more fundamentally, regarding life: 'living and sensing are attributed to the soul *and* the body, for we use "living" and "sensing" in respect of soul and body, but in respect of the soul as the *principle* of life[71] and of sensation'. Now, in the case of any m–f composite, the *principle*, or ultimate intrinsic source, of its being and its activity is not its matter but, rather, its form. 'Therefore, the soul' considered as the

---

[69] In ch. 68, Aquinas concludes his summary review of the negative results achieved in chs. 57–67 by saying that it is as a consequence of *all* those negative results that 'we are left with this: that the human soul is an intellective substance united with the body as a form' (1449). See sect. 10 below.

[70] 'That by means of which something is made an actual being from a being in potentiality is its form and *actus*. But it is by means of the soul that the body is made an actual being from what is existent in potentiality. For the being of a living thing is its *living*, but the semen before being animated is living only potentially and is made an actually living thing by means of the soul. Therefore, the soul is the form of the animated body' (1339). Cf. Aristotle, *Generation of Animals* II 3, 736b8–15. The allusion to human development in this argument is only a prefiguring of the much more detailed treatment Aquinas provides in chs. 86–9 (see Ch. Ten below, sects. 2–6).

[71] See sect. 7 above.

principle of human life and sensation 'is the form of the body' (1340).

In the second place, 'the whole sensory soul is related to the whole body as a part of it is related to a part of the body'. Aquinas here is thinking of the various senses as parts (or powers) of the sensory soul,[72] and of the various sense-organs as the relevant parts of the body. And therefore, he observes, as the sense of 'sight is the form and *actus* of the eye', so the whole sensory 'soul is the form and *actus* of the body' (1341).

9. Body and souls?

Once we've seen what sorts of grounds those two arguments offer in support of their conclusions, we can't any longer think of the conclusions as abbreviated versions of claim E in hypothesis SFB. Whatever precisely Aquinas will turn out to mean by his claim that the human soul is the substantial form of the human body, it surely won't be reducible to a claim about a *sensory* soul, the possession of which doesn't distinguish a human being from other animals, and so cannot give the human being its species. The purpose of these arguments at this juncture is solely to provide a transition to the next and last phase of Aquinas's critical analysis of the Platonist theory, which he has undertaken as a means of developing several features of his own theory.

In broad outline, the analysis so far has passed through the following five stages. First, Aquinas represents Platonists as having explained the union of the soul with the body in terms of power contact only, in order to avoid what they see as the unreasonable claim E in hypothesis SFB. Second, he points to the being-*per-accidens* account of a human being as an absurd consequence of their union-by-power-contact-only theory. Third, he portrays them as having attempted to avoid that absurdity by identifying the human being as simply the soul itself (using a body). Fourth, he presents sensing as an undoubted human activity that must be ascribed to soul and body together, thereby falsifying their soul-itself theory. Fifth, he uses the necessarily co-operative activity of sensing as a basis for inferring that the (sensory) soul is the form of

---

[72] See n. 65 above.

the body, thereby at least weakening the Platonist rejection of claim E.

The sixth stage is what Aquinas describes as the Platonists' way of resisting that inference. It begins with the observation that 'even if the *sensory* soul *is* the form of the body' (1342), the Platonists' fundamental thesis is, after all, only 'that the *intellective* soul is not united with the body as a form is united with matter' (1327).[73] And, since 'Plato claims that in us it is *not* one and the same soul that is intellective, nutritive, and sensory',[74] a Platonist could concede everything Aquinas has said about, and inferred from, sensation without thereby committing himself 'to say that *some intellective substance* can be the form of the body' (1342). If this pluralism regarding the soul(s) of an individual human being is defensible, the Platonist can again identify a human being as a soul—but just an *intellective* soul—that is merely using a body—a body that may itself have to be described now as having a nutritive soul and a sensory soul as its own intrinsic principles of life and sensation.

Not surprisingly, Aquinas considers this Platonist pluralism utterly indefensible: 'But that this [view regarding the souls of a human being] is impossible must be shown in the following way' (1343). The eight arguments in which he argues against it constitute the seventh and final stage of his critical analysis of the Platonist account of human nature, a stage that can and should be construed affirmatively as his arguing in defence of his own theory of the unicity of substantial form, here applied to human beings specifically.[75] Although several of the eight arguments (58.1344–51) have special strengths or interesting

---

[73] See sect. 8 above.   [74] See *Timaeus* 69C–71D.

[75] On Aquinas's theory of the unicity of substantial form, see e.g. Wippel 1993: 112–13: 'Aquinas's view that there is only one substantial form in each substance, including human beings, was ... much contested during his lifetime and after his death. One of his major reasons for defending this view is this: if substantial form communicates substantial existence to matter and the matter–form composite, a plurality of substantial forms would result in a plurality of substantial existences and would, therefore, undermine the composite's substantial unity. If the first substantial form gave substantial existence, all other forms could contribute only accidental *esse*. As Aquinas reasons in ST Ia.76, if a human being derived the fact that it lives from one form, the fact that it is an animal from another, and the fact that it is human from still another, it would not be one in the unqualified sense. ([note:] See ST Ia.76.3 (first argument against plurality of souls in human beings); and 76.4. Cf. QDSC 1, ad 9; 3; QDA 9; 11.)'

features,[76] the fourth and fifth of them are most pertinent to topics we've been considering.

In the fourth argument Aquinas shows that the Platonist doctrine of the plurality of souls revives 'the absurdity discussed earlier—viz. that from the intellective soul and the body is made not something unconditionally one, but something that is one only accidentally. For whatever comes to anything after [it has] complete being comes to it as an accidental form, since it is over and above the thing's essence. But any and every substantial form produces a being that is complete in the category of substance. . . . [And] the *nutritive* soul is a substantial form', since a biologically living being of absolutely any sort is defined as a body with a nutritive soul. Furthermore, '*living being* is predicated substantially of a human being and of an animal. [So] it will follow that the *sensory* soul comes to [the living human body] as an accidental form, and the *intellective* soul likewise. And in that case neither "animal" nor "human being" signifies [something that is] unconditionally one, or any genus or species in the category of substance'— which is absurd (1347). The strength of this argument is the case it makes for Aquinas's theory of the unicity of substantial form.[77] But it fails as an attempt to reduce the Platonist account once more to the previously recognized absurdity of treating the human being as one only *per accidens*. After all, Aquinas himself portrayed the Platonists as having initially side-stepped that absurdity by identifying the human being as not an unconditional union of soul and body, but as simply the soul itself (using a body), and the rest of his critical analysis of the Platonist account is directed against the results of that very move. The subsequent introduction of the Platonist plurality-of-souls doctrine leads only to a more precise version of that move: the human being is simply the *intellective* soul itself (using an *otherwise* ensouled body). So no Platonist with the courage of his convictions is going to be shaken by Aquinas's pointing out, correctly, that the Platonist human being couldn't be located on the branch of the Porphyrian Tree where Aristotelianism and common sense would lead us to look for the

---

[76] Such as the second argument's reliance on human development (see also n. 70 above), or the sixth argument's observation that the doctrine of the plurality of souls undermines the definition of soul as first principle of life (see also sect. 7 above).

[77] See n. 75 above.

human being, but off somewhere in the other half of the Tree, perched among the *in*corporeal substances.

However, in his fifth argument here against the plurality-of-souls doctrine, Aquinas does succeed in reducing the Platonist position to an absurdity, at least in the sense of a laughing-stock. He succeeds this time in part because he begins by acknowledging that 'on Plato's view a human being is not anything composed of soul and body but, rather, a soul using a body'. The trouble is that the introduction of the Platonist plurality-of-souls doctrine infects that radical dualism with galloping ambiguity, since now the claim that the human being is a soul using a body must be 'meant either as regards the intellective soul alone, or as regards the three souls (if there *are* three of them), or as regards two of them'. The attentive, fair-minded reader may want to protest that, according to Aquinas's own telling of it, the Platonist position clearly is identified with just the first of those three alternatives. Of course, Aquinas knows that, but he's ridiculing, not just criticizing, the position. 'Now if the claim is meant as regards [all] three, or [even just] two, it follows that a human being is not one [being] but, rather, two—or three. For [in that case] the human being *is* three souls—or at least two.' Having given the back of his hand to these recognizably irrelevant alternatives, Aquinas, in the same spirit, turns to what he knows is the intended interpretation of the claim. 'On the other hand, if this claim is meant as regards the intellective soul only—in the sense that we are to understand that the sensory soul is the form of the body, and that the human being *is* the intellective soul that uses that animate, sentient body, then further absurdities follow. I mean that [in that case] a human being *is* not an animal but, rather, *uses* an animal (since it's in virtue of a sensory soul that anything is an animal); and that [in that case] a human being *does* not sense but, rather, *uses* a sentient thing'— somewhat as a blind person uses a seeing-eye dog. 'Since these are absurdities, it is impossible that in us there are three substantially different souls: intellective, sensory, and nutritive' (1348).

Probably no one now could take the doctrine of the plurality of souls seriously even for the purpose of refuting it. But Aquinas's refutation of it here is an important step toward achieving his principal aim in the long argument of chapters 56–69. He has already shown that even the radical Platonist dualism must take seriously the thesis that *some* soul is the form of the living human body. If he has now shown also that there can't be a plurality of souls in the human being, then he has gone a long way toward dispelling the reader's natural scepticism regarding the unreasonable-looking hypothesis SFB.

In the course of his arguments against the plurality of souls, Aquinas infers that the single embodied intellective soul itself is not simply the human mind: 'It is by one and the same principle, therefore'—viz. by the intellective soul—'that someone is a human being, an animal, and a living thing' (1344). In other words, the distinctively human intellective soul alone, as the form of the right sort of body, is enough to constitute that matter into the living, breathing, sensing, thinking human being. In keeping with his doctrine of the unicity of substantial form, Aquinas thinks of the human soul not as three nested, co-operating forms of the body, but as the single form that gives a human being its specifically human mode of existence, from its genetic constitution on up to its most creative talents.[78] In the single human soul, 'the ordering of what is sensory to what is intellective, and of what is nutritive to what is sensory, is a kind of ordering of potentiality to actuality' (1345).[79] It's the human being's distinctive intellectivity that makes human sensation, and even human physiology, what it is.[80] Accordingly, Aquinas can refer to even the sensory (and, I should think, also the nutritive) aspect of the human soul as intellective.[81] 'There is no other substantial form in a human being but the intellective soul alone. And, just as it contains a sensory and nutritive soul in respect of its power (*virtute*), so does it contain *all* lower forms in respect of its power; and it alone brings about whatever is brought about in other [living] things by more imperfect forms. (We have to say the same sort of thing also regarding the sensory soul in non-human animals, the nutritive soul in plants, and, universally, of all more perfect forms in respect of those that are less perfect.)' (ST Ia.76.4c). The general principle at work here appears to be

[78] Among Aquinas's statements of the doctrine of the unicity of substantial form, In DA II.1: L2.224 is perhaps his fullest succinct presentation. For his application of the doctrine to the specific case of the human soul, see esp. ST Ia.76.3, 76.4, 77.6.

[79] Aquinas illustrates this ordering here by another allusion to human development: 'For as far as generation is concerned, the intellective is posterior to the sensory, and the sensory to the nutritive; for in [the process of] generation, [the embryo] becomes an animal before it becomes a human being.'

[80] Cf. ST Ia.76.3c: 'In this way, then, the intellective soul contains within its power (*in sua virtute*) whatever the sensory soul of non-human animals and the nutritive soul of plants possesses.'   [81] See e.g. ST Ia.76.3, ad 1.

something like this: if substantial form F_1 in matter M entails potentialities and activities that would ordinarily be associated with substantial form F_2,[82] then F_1 itself contains F_2 *virtute*—i.e. F_1 alone will
provide for M whatever F_2 would have provided (and then some).
An intellective soul in the matter that is flesh and bone (and the
rest) entails sensing, which entails life. So an intellective soul contains sensation and life *virtute*. And the sorts of sensation and life
entailed by intellectivity will be just the sorts that are appropriate
for intellectivity, the sorts without which intellectivity itself could
not occur.

We've now seen how Aquinas's criticism of the Platonist account
of the nature of a human being contributes to an understanding of
his own position, and helps to prepare the ground on which he will
establish it. His critical reviews of other opposing accounts contribute less to an understanding of his hypothesis SFB, because all the
rest of them are even more fundamentally unlike his own than
Plato's is. But Averroës' and Alexander's accounts are closely
related to Aquinas's in some important details. All three share a
commitment to Aristotle's fundamental division of human intellective powers and to his conception of intellect's connection with the
senses. That is, they distinguish the human intellect fundamentally
into two powers: 'the *agent* [i.e. essentially active or productive]
intellect', which acts on 'the *phantasms*'—i.e. the processed sensory
data that are indispensable for intellect's use—in a way that
produces 'intelligible species', which constitute intellect's primary
contents, stored in 'the *possible* [i.e. essentially receptive]
intellect'.[83]

But Averroës, on what he himself supposes to be Aristotelian
grounds, rejects not only claim E but also claim C, insisting that for
all human beings there is *just one* 'possible intellect, by which
[every individual] soul has intellective cognition', and that that one,
universally shared possible intellect 'is *separated from* the [indi-
vidual human] body in respect of its being', but 'conjoined with
us by means of the phantasm' (59.1359).[84] Whatever precisely

---

[82] It won't do to say simply that F_1 entails F_2, because an intellective soul, the F_1
we're interested in here, is a subsistent entity, capable of existing also *without*
matter.

[83] On Aquinas's distinction of intellective powers, see e.g. QDV 10.6c and ad 7.
These elements of his philosophy of mind are examined in Ch. Nine below.

[84] Technical terms belonging to Aquinas's philosophy of mind, such as 'possible
intellect' and 'phantasm', are explained in Ch. Nine below. The uniqueness of the

Aquinas turns out to mean by characterizing the intellective soul as a substance (in claim B), Averroës' version of that claim plainly does present the possible intellect, an aspect of the intellective soul, as a primary substance.[85] So it's especially interesting that Aquinas condemns this Averroistic monopsychism with special vehemence as 'silly and impossible' (59.1361), as 'false and involving a misuse of language' (60.1371), and as 'fiction' (61.1402). I'm inclined to think that the vehemence may have something to do with the fact that Averroës' position, for all its bizarre distinguishing characteristics, is in some other respects very much like what Aquinas himself maintains about the intellective soul.[86]

I've already said that, among the opponents confronted in these chapters, only Plato fully accepts the identification of the human soul as an intellective *substance* (claim B).[87] And, as we've just seen, Averroës accepts that identification for the separated possible intellect. Aquinas reports Alexander as having, on the contrary, characterized the possible intellect as 'a power in us . . . that is not founded in any intellective substance but is the result of the mixing together of elements in the human body' (62.1403); so Alexander needs no further account of the mode of its union with the body. In those respects Alexander's view is not unattractive, despite Aquinas's strictures against mixtures.[88] But Alexander went on to insist that there is only one *agent* intellect for all human beings, a separated primary substance like Averroës' single possible intellect, and that each individual's 'possible intellect is the very preparedness in human nature to receive the influence of the [single, separated] agent intellect' (1405).

10. The peculiar character of the human soul

The climax of the long argument that begins in chapter 56 occurs in chapters 68 and 69.[89] Before Aquinas offers his rejoinders to 'the

separated possible intellect is unmistakably implied by the things Aquinas says about Averroës' account in II.59–61; but in these chapters Aquinas is expressly concerned only with its separatedness. Its uniqueness becomes the issue in II.73–5, discussed in Ch. Nine below, sect. 3.

[85] See sect. 4 above.

[86] In the six long chapters (59–61 and 73–5) which Aquinas devotes to his refutation of Averroës, he introduces pieces of his own Aristotelian philosophy of mind in ways that I'll draw on in Ch. Nine below.

[87] See sect. 8 above.   [88] See sect. 2 above.   [89] See sect. 5 above.

objections'—arguments N1–N5—in chapter 69, he turns, in chapter 68, to face directly the difficulty at the heart of his own account of the human soul, to try to dispel the appearance of unreasonableness in his hypothesis SFB. At the outset, he summarizes the results of his ground-clearing critical reviews of eight opposing theories. On that basis, he says, 'we are left with this: that the human soul is an intellective substance united with the body as a form' (1449). His clearing of the ground has established that this specified version of SFB is the only remaining account worth considering; but he's still not drawing it as a conclusion, since he goes on at once to say, 'This can indeed be made manifest in the following way' (ibid.). Making it manifest that the human soul is both the substantial form of the human body and an intellective substance is a tall order, one that Aquinas fills more fully in the first article of his *Disputed Question on the Soul* (QDA), written just after SCG,[90] than he does in the remainder of chapter 68. The principal reason why that slightly later treatment is more successful is that in it Aquinas carefully makes explicit a distinction between two aspects of his concept of substance that he leaves implicit in these chapters of SCG II.[91] However, in our study of SCG II it's more instructive to stay with this earlier, less fully developed treatment.

To make it manifest that the human soul is an intellective substance united with the body as a form, Aquinas begins in chapter 68 by laying down two conditions that are necessary in order that something—some form—be the substantial form of something else (1450*a*). First, the form must be a principle or cause of this thing's existing as a substance. And he clarifies this first condition by explaining that this form is not the *efficient* principle or cause of this thing's existing as a substance. Rather, it is, of course, the *formal* principle or cause of the thing's existing as a substance. That is, the substantial form is not the principle by which the thing comes into existence, but the principle by which the thing subsists, and on the basis of which it is properly called a *being* and, as we've seen, a being of this or that *species*.

The second of these two necessary conditions (which, as he says, follows from the first) is that the thing's form and matter must come together in one single existence, the existence of the resultant hylomorphic composite substance—something that couldn't be

---

[90] See App. I.   [91] See Kretzmann 1993.

said 'of the *efficient* principle together with that to which it gives
existence' (ibid.). So far, then, he has given us necessary (and,
I think, also sufficient) conditions for some form's being the substantial form, the formal cause, of some hylomorphic composite
substance.

The next question is whether the human soul can meet those
specifications and thus qualify as the substantial form of the
hylomorphic composite substance that is the human being. As
we've been seeing, what makes that a hard question is the fact that
Aquinas has been insisting that the human soul is itself an intellective substance. He proceeds by confronting that difficulty directly:
'Now the fact that an intellective substance is subsistent (as has
been proved) does not prevent its being the formal principle of
existence for [some] matter, in the sense of sharing its existence
with the matter. For there is no logical difficulty in the fact that the
existence in which the composite subsists and the form itself subsists is one and the same, since the composite exists only through
the form, and neither of them subsists separately' (1450*b*). I agree
that the arrangement described in that second sentence poses no
logical difficulty. But the crucial connection between the second
sentence and the first has been left unclear, because Aquinas hasn't
yet told us how a subsistent intellective substance can *also* be a
substantial form that fills the bill he has just drawn up.

To the extent to which he deals with that issue here, he takes it
up in the form of an objection that some similarly unsatisfied
reader might raise at this point: 'an intellective substance can't
share its existence with corporeal matter in such a way that the
intellective substance and the corporeal matter have a single existence. For different genera have different modes of existence, and a
higher-ranking sort of substance has a higher-ranking sort of existence' (1451).

Aquinas accepts the general principle with which this objection
ends and on which it's based. But, he says, that principle doesn't
apply in this case, because here we're confronted by only *one* mode
of existence, the single existence of the composite, which 'belongs
to the intellective substance as to its principle and is in keeping with
the very nature of the intellective substance'. The body that is the
matter of the composite shares that one mode of existence, but in
a different respect, 'as a recipient and a subject raised up to something higher' (1452).

On this basis Aquinas could not be said to have shown that the intellective substance that is the human soul *is* the human body's substantial form, but he himself claims only to have shown that nothing *prevents* it. As he says in the chapter's first sentence, 'we can conclude that an intellective substance *can* be united with a body as a form' (68.1448). That much, I think, he really has shown here, and that much may be just enough to show that his SFB hypothesis is, after all, *not* unreasonable. For the rest of the story, we have to look to chapter 69, where he offers his rejoinders to the five objections put forward in chapter 56, and to chapter 70, where he develops Aristotelian arguments to show that 'it is necessary to say that intellect in respect of its substance is united with some body as its form' (70.1471). (And for a more convincing version of the story, we have to wait for QDA, and ST Ia.76.)

In chapter 69, when Aquinas finally offers his rejoinders to 'the objections' N1–N5 with which he ended chapter 56, he says that it's not hard to resolve them, 'now that these things have been considered' (1460). By 'these things' he must mean at least his attempts to show, in chapter 68, that the soul's being a substance and the soul's being a form are, after all, compatible; but it seems more likely that he means *all* the complex considerations developed in chapters 57–68. In any event, his rejoinders in chapter 69 are indeed simple, and sometimes too simple, even in the light of everything we've looked at in the intervening chapters.

N1: 'Nothing [that is unconditionally] one can be made from two actually existing substances, since the actuality (*actus*) of anything is that by which it is distinguished from something else. But an intellective substance is an actually existing substance (as is apparent from things put forward earlier [in II.46–55]); and, similarly, so is a body. Therefore, it seems, nothing that is [unconditionally] one can be made of an intellective substance and a body' (56.1321)

Although all five N-arguments are aimed against hypothesis SFB in its general form, regarding intellective substances and bodies, Aquinas's rejoinders treat most of them as applied specifically to the union of the human soul and body—which is only natural, 'now that these things have been considered'. Viewed in this way, N1 simply and effectively says that Aquinas's starting-points seem to require a radical substance dualism of soul and body, which N1 says is impossible—just as we've seen Aquinas himself arguing in the intervening chapters. For all its plainness, N1 raises a powerful challenge which we haven't seen Aquinas address directly as regards his own account. But his rejoinder to N1, though it moves in a promising direction, leaves too much unexplained: 'In the first argument something false is assumed, for a body and a soul are *not* two actually existing substances. Instead, out of those two is made one actually existing substance. For a human being's body is not the same in actuality when the soul is present and when it is absent. Instead, the soul makes the [human] body exist in actuality' (69.1461). If they're '*not* two actually existing substances', then what *are* 'those two' out of which 'is made one actually existing substance'? The third sentence might seem to be an allusion to the by now familiar point about a corpse, but we'll find that Aquinas here is almost certainly alluding instead to the foetal body after and before 'animation' (as the fourth and final sentence may suggest).[92] In any event, this rejoinder is too compressed to deal adequately with the challenge posed by N1, especially because in Book II he comes to his treatment of the human soul against the background of chapters 46–55, in which he certainly is discussing intellective substances that are also separated, 'actually existing' substances.[93]

N2: 'A form and [its] matter are contained in the same genus; for every genus is divided by actuality and potentiality. But *intellective substance* and *body* are different genera. Therefore, it does not seem possible for the one to be the form of the other' (56.1322).

As N2 is a technical objection, so Aquinas's rejoinder to it consists in a technical correction, but one that side-steps the fundamental issue. In fact, in order to make his correction, he simply assumes that we're considering an m–f composite that *is* the union of an intellective substance with a body—the very thing that N2 argues is impossible. 'What is objected in the second place, however—that a form and [its] matter are contained in the same genus—is *true*: not in the sense that each is a species of one and the same genus, but

---

[92] See Ch. Ten below, sects. 2–6.

[93] His rejoinder to a similar objection in QDA 2 is a little more forthcoming: 'Nothing that is [unconditionally] one is made of two actually existing substances that are complete in their own species and genus. But soul and body are not things of that sort, since they are [only] the parts of human nature. And so nothing prevents their being made into something that is [unconditionally] one' (ad 2).

because they are principles of one and the same species. In this way, therefore, an intellective substance and a body—which, if they existed separately, *would be* species of different genera—*as united* belong to a single genus as [its] principles' (69.1462). The 'principles' of a species or a genus are its metaphysical elements, as *life* and *body* might be said to be principles of the genus *plant*. But inanimate bodies and incorporeal life are species of different genera. So, yes, *if* an intellective substance and a body are united as Aquinas says they are united in the human being, then they do belong to the single species *human being* or *rational animal* as its principles. But in his rejoinder he seems to have begged the question raised by N2.

N3: 'Everything the being of which is in matter must be material. But if an intellective substance is the form of a body, its being must be in corporeal matter; for the being of the form is not over and above the being of the matter. It will follow, therefore, that an intellective substance is *not* immaterial, [the contrary of] which was shown above [in II. 50]' (56.1323).

   That 'the being of the form is not over and above the being of the matter' is N3's crucial premiss, and a principle that Aquinas subscribes to as regards all m–f composites except the one that is the human being. His rejoinder to N3 consists in no more than registering that exception and referring to his argument in support of it: 'But an intellective substance need not be a material form (as the third argument claimed), even though its being is in matter. For it is in matter not as *immersed* in matter, or *totally contained* by matter, but in another way, as was said' (69.1463). His argument based on the special character of intellective cognition is the place where that was said,[94] and the complexity of that argument of his justifies his simply referring to it here.

N4: 'It is impossible for anything the being of which is in a body to be separate from that body. However, philosophers have shown that intellect is separate from body, and that it is neither a body nor a power in a body. Therefore, an intellective substance is not the form of a body; for in that case its being would be in a body' (56.1324).

---

[94] See 68.1459.

As we've seen, Averroës and Alexander seem to be especially conspicuous members of the group of philosophers to which N4 alludes, since each of them maintains that one or another aspect of the intellect ordinarily thought of as human is a separated substance, existing altogether apart from every human body. But, as Aquinas points out at the outset of his detailed criticism of Averroës' position, such radical accounts stem from what he sees as misinterpretations of Aristotle, 'who, speaking of the possible intellect, says that it is separate, not mixed together with the body, simple, and impassible' (59.1354; cf. *De anima* III 4).[95] In his rejoinder to N4, Aquinas ignores the far-fetched misinterpretations he has already rejected, and tries to formulate a sense of 'separate' that suits his own account (and is what he thinks Aristotle must have had in mind).[96] 'All the same,[97] the fact that an intellective substance is united with a body as a form does not negate what philosophers say—that intellect is separate from body. For where the soul is concerned, we have to consider both its essence and its power. In respect of its essence, of course, it gives being to such a body.' So, in respect of its *essence*, in respect of its defining characteristic as the intrinsic first principle of life for a human body, soul is *not* separate from body. 'In respect of its power, on the other hand, it brings about the activities that are proper to it. Therefore, if an activity of the soul is carried out by means of a bodily organ, then the soul's power that is the source of that activity must be the *actus* of that part of the body through which its activity is carried out—as sight is the *actus* of an eye.' So, again, in respect of the power which the human soul manifests in sensing, in deliberate bodily movement, or in any other human activity directly dependent on the body, soul is *not* separate from body. 'However, if an activity of the soul is *not* carried out by means of a bodily organ, the power associated with that activity will not be the *actus* of any body. And it is on *that* account that intellect is said to be separate—but not in such a way that the substance of the soul to which the power of intellect belongs, or the intellective soul, is not the body's

---

[95] 'However, some people, misled by the fortuitous character of these words, have supposed that the possible intellect is separated from the body, like one of the separated substances—which is completely impossible, of course' (In DA III: L7.689).

[96] See SCG II.61.

[97] An appropriate beginning, in view of his emphasis in the immediately preceding rejoinder on the soul's status as form.

actus, as the form that gives being to such a body' (69.1464). As we've come to expect, it is what Aquinas sees as the organlessness of intellective cognition that requires and gives the only appropriate sense to the separateness of the intellective soul.[98] But, if the nutritive and sensory aspects of the human soul are clearly aspects of the substantial form of the human body, then, in accordance with the doctrine of the unicity of substantial form, even the (separate) intellective aspect of the soul belongs to 'the body's *actus*', to 'the form that gives being to such a body'.

N5: 'Anything the being of which is in common with a body must also have its activity in common with a body, since any thing acts in the respect in which it is a being. Moreover, the operative power of a thing cannot be more exalted than its essence, since its power is a consequence of principles that belong to its essence. However, if an intellective substance is the form of a body, its being must be common to it and to the body. For something that is unconditionally one, one as regards its being, is made of a form and matter. Therefore, the activity of an intellective substance will also be common to a body, and its power will be a power in a body. [But,] on the basis of things set out earlier [in II.49–55], this is clearly impossible' (56.1325).

Aquinas's rejoinder to N5, the last of the 'objections', draws on points already made in these rejoinders, especially in the ones responding to N4 and N3. In fact, the crux of this last rejoinder is, as in N3's, a reference to his argument in chapter 68 (and QDA 1c) for the uniqueness of the status of the soul as form of the body: 'But [even] if the soul as regards its substance *is* the form of the body', as Aquinas has just claimed in his rejoinder to N4, 'it is *not* necessary for every one of its operations to be brought about through the body and, consequently, for every one of its powers to be the *actus* of some body (as the fifth argument claimed). For it has already been shown that the human soul is not the sort of form that is totally immersed in matter; instead, of all forms [of bodies] it is the one that is most elevated above matter. That's why it can also produce an activity without the body—i.e. as independent of the body in its acting—since it does not depend on the body for its being, either' (69.1465).

[98] For further explanation and appraisal of the organlessness of intellective cognition, see Ch. Nine below, sect. 8.

Aquinas concludes chapter 69 by replying to Averroistic arguments he first presented in 59.1354–8. He then adds a chapter that has the look of an appendix to this long critical review. 'And because Averroës tries especially to confirm his view on the basis of Aristotle's words and demonstration, we still have to show that on Aristotle's view it is necessary to say that an intellect in respect of its substance is united with some body as a form' (70.1471). Apparently, then, what we still have to show is that Aquinas's unreasonable-seeming SFB hypothesis, radically incompatible with Averroës' view, is a proposition Aristotle himself put forward as *necessary*. So much for Averroës' appeals to Aristotelian authority! But what is actually presented in chapter 70 is, in more than one respect, not exactly what that introduction promises.

For one thing, in the Aristotelian version of SFB the expression 'with *some* body (*alicui corpori*)', although odd, is appropriate, because the evidence which Aquinas offers here has to do with his interpretation of Aristotle's line regarding the union of an intellective soul not with a *human* body but with a *heavenly* body. The heart of this evidence is Aristotle's thesis that 'the primary movable thing'—the outermost sphere of the heavens, the *primum mobile*—'is a self-mover'. Like every other self-mover, this heavenly body 'must be composed of two parts, one of which is the mover, and the other that which is moved.[99] But every thing of that sort is animate. Therefore, on Aristotle's view the primary movable thing—the heaven—is animate' (1472).

But, Aquinas asks (1473), what kind of soul does Aristotle think animates the *primum mobile*? Briefly, 'the heaven, according to Aristotle, is composed of an *intellective* soul and a body' (1474), an intellective soul that, unlike ours, has no *sensory* part, or involves no *sensory* soul (1475). 'Therefore, no one could say that intellect is made continuous with *heavenly* bodies through phantasms', which depend on sensory powers of the soul.[100] 'Instead, one will have to say that an intellect in respect of its substance is united with a heavenly body *as a form*' (1476). That's obviously not the only

[99] See Ch. Seven above, sect. 5; also TMOT, 74–6.

[100] As we've seen, Aquinas presents Averroës as having proposed that phantasms link the separated possible intellect with individual human beings (59.1359); see sect. 9 above. But unless Averroës intended to be making a perfectly general point about all intellective souls and the bodies they animate, this observation of Aquinas's shows only that that proposal couldn't even be entertained regarding this special Aristotelian case. On phantasms generally, see Ch. Nine below, esp. sect. 6.

alternative to a connection via phantasms. In the context of chapter 70, the only conceivable warrant for this immediate inference appears to be the characterization of the *primum mobile* as a *self-mover*, whose parts, the moving and the moved, must therefore be aspects of one and the same thing, involving real, unconditional unity. Consequently, mere power contact won't do.

Or so it might seem. And perhaps it did seem so to Aquinas when he was writing SCG II.70. But later, in ST Ia.70.3c, he says that 'in order that a soul move [a heavenly body], it need *not* be united with it as its form, but through power contact, as a mover is united with what is movable by it'.[101]

Of course, it's been a long, long time since anyone could take seriously an explanation of the movements of heavenly bodies in terms of souls, and Aquinas himself was not committed to any such explanation (as can be seen in 70.1478).[102] But any such explanation along the lines of SFB and involving an intellective soul is even less attractive than one in terms of power contact and a soul that need be no more than an intrinsic principle of movement. In view of these difficulties in chapter 70, I think we have to reject this attempt of Aquinas's to infer, from his interpretation of Aristotle's account of animated heavenly bodies, that an intellective substance is united 'in that way'—i.e. as its form—'also with the *human* body' (1477).

For all its length and complexity, the investigation in SCG II.56–70 develops only part of Aquinas's philosophy of mind, which will continue to be our topic in the next chapter.

---

[101] See also ad 5: 'the heaven is said to move itself in so far as it is composed of a mover and what is movable by that mover—*not* composed as of form and matter, but in virtue of power contact'.

[102] One reason for taking it seriously on the basis of a consideration of nature alone is offered by Aquinas in ST Ia.70.3c. In ordinary, terrestrial processes, such as the natural movement of 'heavy and light bodies', 'nature moves to just one [end] and, when that has been attained, it rests. This is just what does *not* appear in the movement of the heavenly bodies', which appear to be involved in a perpetual process of movement without rest. 'And that's why one is left with the conclusion that they are moved by some substance with a capacity for cognition (*aliqua substantia apprehendente*)'—i.e. a soul. In any case, 'it's clear that heavenly bodies are not animate in the way plants and animals are, but equivocally. For that reason, between those who claim that they are animate and those who claim that they are inanimate there is little or no real difference, but just a verbal difference.'

NINE

THE SOUL'S ANATOMY

1. Aquinas's philosophy of mind in SCG II

Aquinas begins to write about human beings specifically in chapter 57,[1] in the context of his consideration of intellective creatures generally, which begins in chapter 46. So the aspect of human nature that most concerns him in the series of chapters beginning with II.57 is the one that makes human beings a species of intellective creatures: rationality, the proper functioning of the human mind (or intellective soul) in the human body.[2] We've already seen that he's intensely interested in the nature of the intellective soul itself and in the nature of its union with the body. These topics make up the subject-matter of the metaphysical side of his philosophy of mind. But chapters 57–70 also contain some signs of his equally strong interest in the various powers and operations of the human soul, and there's more of that sort of evidence in chapters 71–8. In the present chapter I examine this psychological side of his philosophy of mind, along with some further details on the metaphysical side, regarding the nature of the soul's union with the body.

In other works, written just after he had finished SCG, Aquinas develops systematic presentations of his philosophy of mind.[3] However, the considerable amount of relevant material to be found in SCG II itself is incorporated in, and made to serve the purposes of, detailed attacks on theories of the soul that are opposed to his own SFB hypothesis (viz. his claim that an intellective substance, such as the human soul, can be appropriately united with a body only by being the substantial form of that body[4]). As a consequence of that

---

[1] See Ch. Eight above, sect. 6.

[2] 'Intellect, therefore, is the soul of a human being and, consequently, its form' (59.1367).

[3] Especially in QDA and ST Ia.75–88 (the 'Treatise on Man'), both begun very soon after he had finished SCG (see App. I below). See also Kenny 1993 and Kretzmann 1993. [4] See Ch. Eight above, esp. sect. 5.

special agenda and the dialectical framework in which he carries it out, the elements of his philosophy of mind that appear in SCG II are not systematically developed in it. Instead, they occur in no particular order almost anywhere throughout the polemic, but especially where they're needed as premises in arguments intended to refute rival theories. When he was writing these chapters, Aquinas hadn't yet given these elements of his philosophy of mind a full, systematic treatment from which he could extract them in order to make these scattered, *ad hoc* applications.[5] None the less, since these bits and pieces cohere well with one another and could easily be fitted into his later, systematic presentations, he seems to have been extracting them from a remarkably clear mental picture of a complete philosophy of mind. The clarity and completeness of that picture naturally owe a great deal to the fact that it was, in Aquinas's own view, largely a picture of Aristotle's philosophy of mind.[6] In fact, propositions that Aquinas uses in showing that an opponent has misinterpreted Aristotle can often be included among the elements of Aquinas's own philosophy of mind to be found here. And because he takes Aristotle to have successfully argued for many—perhaps all—of these elements (as he sometimes expressly says[7]), he often affirms them without offering explicit support for them here.

After examining the final details of Aquinas's development of SFB (in chs. 71–2) and providing an overview of chapters 73–8, I'll try to construct an orderly presentation of Aquinas's philosophy of mind in Book II by sorting and rearranging many of the pieces of it that lie scattered mainly in chapters 57–78, especially those that have to do with the powers and operations of the soul, which I didn't discuss in Chapter Eight.

[5] However, there is a great deal of relevant material in the earlier works In Sent., QQ (VII.1, VIII.2.1, X.3–4, XI.5), In BDT, and QDV (qq. 1, 2, 8, 9, and esp. 10).

[6] For an excellent, concise, critical account of Aristotle's philosophy of mind, see Irwin 1991. Aquinas's special focus on Aristotle in these chapters of Book II is partly explained by the facts that two of his opponents, Averroës and Alexander, make use of Aristotelian elements in their theories, each of which is incompatible in a different way with Aquinas's SFB account (which he takes to be Aristotle's view as well), and that both Averroës and Alexander claim to be interpreting Aristotle correctly. Aquinas's commentary on *De anima*, the first of his Aristotelian commentaries, was written soon after he completed SCG (see App. I below).

[7] See e.g. 57.1333; 59.1368; 60.1371, 1372, 1373, 1378, 1385, 1387, 1391; 62.1404, 1409; 67.1445; 73.1498, 1504, 1506, 1523a, 1524, 1526; 74.1538, 1541, 1542; 75.1558; 76.1569, 1570, 1578.

2. Special features of the soul's union with the body

Aquinas's (mainly polemical) concern with the metaphysical and psychological aspects of philosophy of mind is continuous from chapter 57 through at least chapter 78, but chapter 70 marks an important transition. There, as we've seen, he tries to show that his hypothesis SFB, which he has been defending against several older theories, was also Aristotle's general account of the relation between intellect and body: 'on Aristotle's view it is necessary to say that an intellect in respect of its substance is united with some body as its form' (70.1471). More precisely, according to Aristotle, 'one will have to say that an intellect in respect of its substance is united with a *heavenly* body as its form' (70.1476). On that rather remote basis Aquinas considers himself entitled to infer that 'an intellective substance is also united in that way not by means of any phantasms but as its very form—with the *human* body' (70.1477).[8] For all its shortcomings, this attempt on Aquinas's part to support his own position with Aristotelian authority (and thereby to block Averroës' appeal to it) is pretty clearly meant to put the finishing touch on his long dialectical development and defence of SFB as applied to the human soul and body.[9] But before he resumes the rebuttal of Averroës and others, he elaborates the basic SFB hypothesis, arguing for some important special features of the soul's union with the body.

a. Intermediaries in the soul's union with the body

To begin with, 'it can be concluded from things that have already been presented that the soul is united with the body without any intermediary (*immediate*)' (71.1479).[10] The relevant 'things that have already been presented' are those that touch on Aquinas's doctrine of the unicity of substantial form,[11] since this rejection of any intermediary between soul and body depends on SFB's identification of the soul as the substantial form of the body: 'the soul is united with the body as its form. But a form is united with matter

---

[8] See Ch. Eight above, sect. 10.

[9] As he says just after ch. 70, in ch. 71, '*it has been shown* that the soul is united with the body as its form' (1480).

[10] For a thorough study of Aquinas on the immediacy of the soul–body union see White 1995.

[11] See e.g. 58.1347–8; also Ch. Eight above, sect. 9.

without any intermediary (*absque omni medio*), since a form is suited to be the *actus* of such a body on its own, and not through anything else' (1480).

The apparently thoroughgoing rejection of intermediaries at the beginning of the chapter doesn't merely *depend* on the form–matter relationship of soul to body; it turns out also to be *restricted* to it: 'All the same, something *can* be said to be an intermediary between soul and body—although *not* as regards *being*' (1481*a*). Two other relationships of soul to body do involve special intermediaries, in very different ways.

In the first place, although the metaphysical union of soul as form with body as proximate (or 'proper') matter is the core of Aquinas's account of human nature, his account of human *activity* requires thinking of the human being also as a self-mover in which the soul is the part that does the moving, primarily internal and often also external, and the body is the part that gets moved by it.[12] And it turns out that intermediaries do have to be taken into account in a more detailed analysis of that intrinsic mover–moved relationship, 'because in connection with the movement with which the soul moves the body, there is a kind of ordering of the things that can be moved and the things that move them, since the soul brings about all its operations *through* its *powers*'—e.g. its cognitive, appetitive, and external motive powers (1481*b*). A power of the soul may not strike us as different enough from the soul itself to count as an intermediary between the soul and the body it moves, but Aquinas is bound to recognize those powers as genuine intermediaries, just because his conception of the soul as a substance and as the body's *actus* requires him to deny that the soul can be identified with any of its powers in the body, or even with all of them taken together.[13]

More concretely, in some cases the soul 'moves . . . one organ by

---

[12] See e.g. 46.1239. See also Ch. Eight above, sect. 10; and TMOT, 74–6. Some parts of the soul are also moved by other parts of the soul (as we'll see). But the question of intermediaries in the soul–body relationship of course concerns only the soul's moving of the body.

[13] See e.g. 55.1304: 'intellective substances are neither bodies nor powers or forms dependent on a body'. Also 56.1313, 1324, 1325; and QQ X.3.1. Cf. QDV 13.4c: 'The soul is united with the body as a form not through the intermediaries (*mediantibus*) that are its powers, but through its essence'; and ST Ia.77.1c, relying on the contrast between *potentia* and *actus*: 'it is impossible to say that the essence of the soul is its power (*potentia*), . . . since in respect of its essence the soul is an *actus*'.

means of another organ' (1481b).[14] In QDA 9c Aquinas provides a
fuller, generally plausible picture of this natural sequence in the
operations of some organs: 'But since there must be an ordering of
instruments corresponding to an ordering of operations, and since
one of the various operations that stem from the soul naturally
precedes another, one part of the body, in order to carry out its
operation, must be moved by another part. . . . For instance, by
means of the heart the soul moves other bodily members to carry
out vital operations. . . . This is the reason why many people say
that as a *form* the soul is united with the body *without* any intermediary, but that as a *mover* it is united with the body *through* an
intermediary.'[15] And in Book II itself we've already been given a
more detailed analysis of cases of this sort: 'if the soul's operation
is completed through a bodily organ, the power of the soul that is
the source of that operation must be the act or actualization (*actus*)
of that part of the body through which its operation is completed—
as seeing is the act or actualization of an eye' (69.1464). The ability
to see is a power of the soul that is exercised through an organ of
the body, and so a defect in the organ can hamper the exercise of
that power. The eyes of a near-sighted person are fully human, fully
living eyes, because the soul, as the body's substantial form, 'gives
substantial, specifying being to all the body's parts' (QDA 9c). But
although the near-sighted person's soul is unqualifiedly the substantial form of her eyes, and although 'eyes' is not at all equivocal
in the expression 'near-sighted eyes',[16] perhaps it does make sense
to say that the *power contact* between her soul and her eyes has
been weakened by the physical defect, and that it would be broken
if she were to become blind. In ST Ia.76.6 an objector who opposes

[14] In this same sentence Aquinas, relying on ancient medical theory, describes the
soul as moving the body's 'members by means of *spiritus*'. See also In Sent.
IV.49.3.2c, where he describes *spiritus animalis* as 'the soul's proximate instrument
in respect of operations that are carried out through the body'; also In Sent.
I.10.1.4c, where he describes *spiritus* as 'extremely fine vapours by means of which
the soul's powers are diffused into the parts of the body'. See also SCG IV.23.3592a.
It doesn't seem far-fetched to think of these *spiritus* as antique counterparts of the
electrical impulses in the nervous system.
[15] See also In DA II: L1.234: 'And so just as the body has being through the soul
as through a form, so, too, it is united with the soul without any intermediary in so
far as the soul is the form of the body. But nothing prevents there being an
intermediary in so far as the soul is [the body's] mover, just as the soul moves one
part by means of another.'
[16] See Ch. Eight above, sect. 8; also 72.1484: 'a dead person's eye and flesh are
called an eye and flesh only equivocally'; and n. 25 below.

Aquinas's very strong thesis of soul–body union claims that 'what is spiritual is joined to what is corporeal through power contact', and thereby suggests that this must be the only sort of union there is between the soul and the body (obj. 3). In his rejoinder, Aquinas concedes that 'a spiritual substance that is united with a body *only* as its mover is united with it [only] through power (*potentiam vel virtutem*). The intellective soul, however, is united with the body as a form, through its being. All the same, it does direct and move the body through its power (*potentiam et virtutem*)' (ad 3).[17] If we make a few allowances for antique science, Aquinas provides a succinct and not altogether implausible account of the intermediaries between the soul considered as the human being's internal mover and the body as the part of the human being that gets moved externally.

The account of intermediaries in the soul's moving of the body and its parts is quite general, but the other relationship of soul to body that does involve intermediaries has to do with the origin of an individual human being, the beginning of the union of an intellective soul with a particular, developing foetal body. Aquinas takes up the beginning (and the end) of a human being's life in more detail in II.79–90, which we'll be considering in Chapter Ten below. But we should also take into account the little he says about it here in identifying intermediaries that occur between an intellective soul and the body whose substantial form it begins to be. 'As regards the process of [human] generation (*via generationis*), however, dispositions for the form precede the form in the matter, even though they are posterior to the form as regards being. That's why the dispositions of the body by which the body is made something proper to be completed by such a form can in that respect be called intermediaries between the soul and the body' (71.1481c). These preparatory 'dispositions' must be features of the foetal body that suit it to become fully human at a certain stage in its development, features that are temporally prior to the foetus's becoming fully human but metaphysically subordinate (or 'posterior . . . as regards being') to the intellective soul as the human being's substantial form, in the sense that they couldn't be features of anything that wasn't on its way to being

---

[17] See also ST Ia.70.3c and ad 5, quoted in Ch. Eight above, sect. 10, where Aquinas says that souls functioning only as movers—if there are any—need be united only in power contact with the bodies they move.

human.[18] And of course, these dispositions must be some sort of forms of the foetal body. But what sort?

Aquinas regularly claims that the developing foetus has as its substantial form first a nutritive soul, and then not a nutritive but a sensory soul (with a nutritive aspect of its own), before being wholly reconstituted by an intellective soul (which of course has its own nutritive and sensory aspects, or 'parts').[19] So, could these preparatory dispositions be identified as those two preliminary, successive substantial forms of the foetus that are superseded by the intellective soul? After all, it's the development of the foetal body in the uterus that makes it the proper, proximate matter to be finally constituted by the intellective soul, and Aquinas thinks of that development in terms of one substantial form's superseding another.[20]

Speculations along this line might seem to be encouraged by a passage like the following, from the slightly later *Disputed Question on the Soul*: 'the variety of natural forms, through which matter is constituted in various species, must be understood in this way— viz. that one [of those forms] adds a [specifying] perfection over and above another. For instance, one form constitutes matter in *corporeal* being only, since this must be the lowest level of material forms . . . But another, higher-level (*perfectior*) form constitutes matter in corporeal being *and*, further, gives it *living* being. And, further, another form gives it corporeal being and living being *and* adds *sensory* being to all that. And so on as regards other forms'— such as an intellective soul, which gives it corporeal being and living being and sensory being *and* adds *rational* being to all that (QDA 9c).

None the less, the 'dispositions' mentioned in 71.1481c are pretty clearly not to be identified as the antecedent substantial forms of

---

[18] See Ch. Ten below, sect. 6.

[19] See e.g. 58.1345: 'the ordering of what is sensory to what is intellective, and of what is nutritive to what is sensory, is a kind of ordering of potentiality to actuality. For as far as generation is concerned, the intellective is posterior to the sensory, and the sensory to the nutritive; for in [the process of] generation, [the embryo] becomes an animal before it becomes a human being.' Also 21.975: 'the more common anything is, the more prior it is in the process of generation—as animal is prior to human being in the generation of a human being (as the Philosopher says in *Generation of Animals* [II 3, 736b2])'.

[20] 'And so we have to say that the soul does pre-exist [i.e. exist before birth] in the embryo: a nutritive soul from the beginning, of course, but afterwards a sensory soul, and finally an intellective soul' (ST Ia.118.2, ad 2).

the foetal body. Instead, the dispositions are accidental forms—'proper accidents'—that might be thought of as aspects of a foetal body, such as its organs, that develop while it is still at the stage of having a nutritive soul as its substantial form.

The accidental dispositions that make matter proper for some form are not intermediaries between the form and the matter considered just as such (*totaliter*), but rather between the form in so far as it provides [the thing's] *final* [specifying] perfection and the matter in so far as it has already been perfected by a lower-level [specifying] perfection. For matter considered just as such [i.e. prime matter] is proper in respect of the lowest-level perfection [i.e. the form of corporeality], because matter considered just as such is in a state of potentiality for substantial corporeal being, for which no disposition is required. But if we presuppose *that* [specifying] perfection in matter, then dispositions *are* required for *further* perfecting. Still, it's important to know that the soul's powers are proper accidents of the soul, which do not exist without it. And so they do not have the nature of dispositions relative to the soul in so far as they are powers of that soul, except in so far as powers of a lower part of the soul are called dispositions relative to a higher part—e.g. a power of the nutritive soul relative to the sensory soul. (QDA 9, ad 5)[21]

For instance, the nutritive soul's powers of circulating the blood and developing bodily organs are dispositions that eventually make possible the sensory soul's power of responding to stimuli.

Of course, the sensory soul ceases to be the substantial form of the foetal body immediately before the intellective soul supersedes it.[22] At that instant of change the foetal body loses what was its essence, yet it loses nothing that could then or afterwards be of any value to it, metaphysically or practically. 'Since the generation of one thing always is the corruption of another, we have to say, as regards both human beings and other animals, that when a

[21] See also QDA 9, obj. 5, to which the passage just quoted is the rejoinder: 'It seems that a soul is united with a body through an intermediary [not only as a mover but] also as a form, since a form is united with not just any matter but [only] with matter proper to it. But matter is made proper for this or that form through proper dispositions, which are proper accidents of a thing (as hot and dry are proper accidents of fire). Therefore, a form is united with matter through the intermediaries of proper accidents. But the proper accidents of things with souls are the powers of the soul. Therefore, the soul is united with the body through the intermediaries of the [soul's] powers.'

[22] That is, in such a way that there is absolutely no time in the transformation at which or during which the foetal body lacks a substantial form or has more than one substantial form. (On the medieval analysis of the instant of change, see Kretzmann 1976.)

higher-level [substantial] form takes over (*advenit*), the corruption of the preceding form occurs.[23] This happens in such a way, however, that the next form has whatever the first form had, and more besides. And it is in that way that the final substantial form is arrived at, as regards both human beings and other animals' (ST Ia.118.2, ad 2).[24]

b. The extent of the soul's union with the body

As we've just been seeing, the more interesting parts of chapter 71 are its second and third theses, which deal, respectively, with the soul considered as the body's internal mover, and with the place of an intellective soul in the development of an individual human being—i.e. with the *exceptions* to the chapter's general denial of intermediaries between a soul and the body in which it is. Now chapter 72's opening sentence indicates a close logical relationship with chapter 71, claiming that it is 'on the basis of the *same* considerations that it can be shown [1] that the whole soul is in the whole body and [2] that the whole soul is in [each of] the body's individual parts' (72.1482). But this logical connection is only with chapter 71's less interesting first thesis: that no intermediaries can be

---

[23] Aquinas sometimes writes in a way that might make this instantaneous transformation seem impossible—e.g. 'If there is a form [F_2] that does not give being to matter unconditionally but instead comes to matter that already exists in actuality through another form [F_1], then it [F_2] will not be a substantial form' (QDA 9c). But in this passage he's plainly intending to support his doctrine of the unicity of substantial form, which requires interpreting 'already exists (*iam existenti*) in actuality through another form' as 'already exists *and continues to exist* in actuality through another form'. See also e.g. 58.1347, where Aquinas is attacking Plato's doctrine of a plurality of human souls: 'Again, the absurdity mentioned earlier [57.1328] will still return—viz. that what is made from the intellective soul and the body is not something unconditionally one but something that is only accidentally one. For everything that comes to anything after [it has acquired] complete being comes to it as an accidental form, since it is outside the thing's essence. But each substantial form produces a being complete in the category of substance, since it produces a being in actuality and a *hoc aliquid*. Therefore, whatever comes to a thing after its first substantial form will come to it as an accidental form. Therefore, since the nutritive soul is a substantial form—for *living being* is predicated substantially of a human being and of an animal—it will follow that the sensory soul comes to [the developing human being] as an accidental form, and the intellective soul likewise. And in that case neither "animal" nor "human being" signifies [something that is] unconditionally one, or any genus or species in the category of substance'— which is absurd.

[24] See ST Ia.76.6 for more material on several aspects of this account of intermediaries between soul and body.

involved in the union of the soul as substantial form with the body as its proximate, proper matter. By contrast, your being able to see involves a particular power of your intellective soul that must be exercised through particular organs of your body. Both that power and those organs are to be thought of as intermediaries between your intellective soul and your actual seeing. However, your being human involves simply the presence of your intellective soul itself, and the predicate *human* applies fully not only to you but also to every organ and every cell of your body. No particular power of your soul, no particular organs of your body, could be intermediaries between your intellective soul as a substantial form and your body, which is made alive, and animal, and human by the presence of that form. 'The soul, in so far as it is the form of the body, is not united with the whole body through the intermediary of some part of the body, but rather with the whole body without any intermediary, since it is the form both of the whole body and of each and every part of it' (QDA 10c).[25] It is in that respect that the thesis of chapter 72 is a corollary of the first thesis of chapter 71.

Part of what this corollary means is that the soul in its role as substantial form can't be located exclusively in any one part of the body.[26] For in that role 'the soul is the *actus* of a body that has organs (*corporis organici*),[27] not the *actus* of just one organ. As regards its essence, in accordance with which it is the form of the body, the soul is, therefore, in the whole body and not in one part only' (72.1483). As we've seen, Aquinas elsewhere introduces

[25] See also 72.1484: 'when the soul is gone, neither the whole nor a part continues to belong to the same species. For a dead person's eye and flesh are called an eye and flesh only equivocally'; and QDSC 4c: 'The soul is united with the body not only as its mover, but [also] as its form. But . . . the soul [as form] does not presuppose in the matter other substantial forms that give substantial being to the body or its parts. Instead, both the whole body and all its parts have substantial, specifying being through the soul. When it is gone, then just as there remains neither a human being nor an animal nor a living thing, so neither does a hand or an eye or flesh or bone remain—except equivocally, as in a painting or a statue.'

[26] In this respect it differs somewhat from the soul considered as the internal mover, as Aquinas points out in 72.1487. On another sort of obstacle to assigning specific bodily locations see 58.1350b: 'it's obvious that operations belonging to various parts of the soul manifest themselves in the same part of the body. This is clear in the case of animals that go on living when they're cut in two, because one and the same part has movement, sensation, and appetite (by which it is moved). Similarly, one and the same part of a plant that has been cut in two takes nourishment, grows, and germinates. On this basis it is apparent that various parts of the soul are in one and the same part of the body.'

[27] This is Aristotle's well-known formulation of 'something common to every soul' in *De anima* II 1, 412b5–6.

his general account of the soul by presupposing that ' "soul" is what we call the first principle of life in things that live among us; for we call living things "animate" [or "ensouled"]' (ST Ia.75.1c).[28] That broad initial characterization of soul must continue to apply to it along with any others that are more precise; and it does seem intuitively clear that whatever it is that justifies our calling a corporeal thing alive, or animate, has got to permeate that body completely.

But the soul considered as the first principle of life or the substantial form permeates the body completely in such a way that it permeates each individual part as well, since each part, too, is living, and since each part, too, is specified as human as long as it is living. 'Therefore, if the soul is the *actus* of the individual parts, and an *actus* is in that of which it is the *actus*, we are left with the conclusion that the soul as regards its essence is in each and every part of the body' (72.1484). This conclusion has to do with the soul as regards its *essence*, because the point here is that it's the constant presence in the human body of the soul as form, as animator and specifier, that makes each and every part of the body continuously alive, animal, and human during the person's lifetime—not the more psychological point that the soul as internal mover is at various moments in various kinds of power contact with these or those parts of the body.

Aquinas's way of supporting the first half of chapter 72's opening claim—'[1] that the whole soul is in the whole body'—can leave the soul's permeation of the body resembling purple's permeation of an amethyst: the whole stone has all of the purple, and the purple is everywhere in it, so that each cubic millimetre of it has just that much of the whole stone's purple. But the kind of permeation he's arguing for here is radically more thorough than that, as can be seen in the second half of the chapter's opening claim: '[2] that the whole soul is in [each of] the body's individual parts'. He seems to be prepared to argue that your intellective soul is, for instance, wholly in your right eye, which is a part of your body, and also wholly in its retina, which is a part of your right eye and so a part of your body—and that seems absurd.[29]

---

[28] See Ch. Eight above, sect. 7.

[29] As is suggested in QDA 10, obj. 3: 'Nothing [belonging to a whole] can be found outside the whole. Therefore, if the soul as a whole is in any one part of the body, then nothing of the soul is outside that part. Therefore, it is impossible for the soul as a whole to be in each and every part of the body.'

The only way to try to mount a defence of such a claim must begin with sorting out senses of 'whole' and 'part', as Aquinas does in 72.1485 and more fully in QDA 10c, on which I'll draw in explaining this apparently implausible claim. He distinguishes senses of 'whole' that might apply to a form on the basis of the various ways in which something can correctly be described as having parts.

In the first and most familiar of those ways, a thing is divided *quantitatively*, so that, for example, the top and bottom halves of Anita's amethyst (which need not be separated physically) are parts of it. In this sense, the whole accidental form *purple* is in the whole stone, and is divided *per accidens* by any quantitative division of the stone, so that half of the purple (or half of the form) may correctly be said to be in half of the stone. 'But "whole" and "part" used quantitatively are suitably applied to forms only *per accidens*—I mean, in so far as forms are divided by the division of a subject that is quantitative' (1485*a*).

'In the second way, something is called a whole relative to the parts that are *essential to its specific nature*, both [1] in the sense in which the matter and the form are called the parts of a composite entity, and [2] in the sense in which the genus and the differentia are, in a way, the parts of a species' (QDA 10c). Elsewhere (QDSC 4c) he calls the first of these two part–whole relationships [1] 'physical' (or metaphysical) and the second [2] 'logical'. Of course, it's in just that first, metaphysical way that the soul as a substantial form is a part of the composite entity that is a human being: '"whole" or "part" used as regards completeness of essence is found in forms *per se*' (1485*a*). But if we consider that substantial form itself as a whole, then, for reasons that are by now familiar, it is wholly in each and every part of the body, animating and specifying everything everywhere in it: 'when we're speaking of the kind of wholeness that is suited to forms *per se*, it's apparent as regards each and every form that the whole [form] is in the whole [subject] and in each and every part of it' (1485*b*). By way of analogy, Aquinas suggests considering not the *extent* of the purple in the amethyst but its *intensity*, for the purple is, let's suppose, as intense in any part of the stone as it is in the whole (QDA 10c).[30] It's in this sense, and only in this sense, that one might correctly

[30] Aquinas's example uses whiteness in a surface rather than purple in an amethyst.

say (but presumably wouldn't say, except perhaps for pedagogical purposes) that your intellective soul is wholly in your body, wholly in your right eye, and wholly also in your right eye's retina.

Some substantial forms can also be thought of in terms of quantitative wholes and parts, but only *per accidens*. For instance, the substantial form *amethyst* would, like the accidental form *purple*, also be divided *per accidens* by the division of the stone into two halves, but *not* in such a way that each half would have only half of the whole substantial form. Even if the top and bottom halves of Anita's amethyst were cut apart, each resultant new whole (and former half) would be wholly informed by *amethyst*, just as the original whole stone had been. Aquinas accepts Aristotelian evidence that the souls of some plants and lower animals are substantial forms of this sort, since some plants can be propagated by cuttings, and since cutting an earthworm in half is a way of making two earthworms where there was only one.[31] But not even this sort of quantitative division *per accidens* is applicable to the substantial forms that are the souls of human beings and other higher animals, since, as Aquinas drily observes, the higher animals don't remain alive—animate—if they're cut in half (QDA 10c).

Aquinas also recognizes a third sense of 'whole' and 'part', less familiar than the first two, but very useful for his purposes here.[32] He suggests that we can legitimately think of a whole form in respect of the whole *power* of the form. This sense of 'whole' is appropriate, just because understanding the soul's obviously different operations (such as digesting, hearing, and choosing) entails the concept of quite different powers belonging to it, all of which are to be understood as parts of the power essentially associated with the form that is the soul.[33] Like the second sense of 'whole', this one

[31] See e.g. 58.1350*b* (quoted in n. 26 above); QDA 10, obj. 15 and ad 15; also QDP 3.12, obj. 5 and ad 5. Such passages draw on *De anima* II 2, 413b16–23.

[32] He recognizes this third sense in QDA 10, ST Ia.76.8, and QDSC 4, but not in SCG II.72.

[33] 72.1486: 'Now there is no incongruity in the fact that the soul, although it is a kind of simple form, is the *actus* of parts that are so different from one another. For matter is adapted to each and every form in keeping with what is suited to the form: the nobler and simpler the form, the greater the power associated with the form. That's why the soul, which is the noblest of earthly forms, is manifold in its power and has many operations, even though it is simple in its substance. And for that reason it needs various organs for carrying out its activities, organs of which the soul's various powers are said to be the proper *actus*—e.g. sight as the *actus* of the

obviously does apply to the soul *per se*. But, as we've already seen, in this sense of 'whole' Aquinas would *deny* that the whole soul is in each and every part of the body. (If we think of an amethyst's power to reflect light, then any part of the surface of the stone has only a part of that power.[34]) The part of the soul's power that is most noticeably in the ears is the power of hearing, although they are also a locus of the sense of touch and of various powers of the nutritive part of the soul; but there is no sense at all in which, say, the power of digesting is also in that part of the body. 'If "wholeness" is taken in the sense in which it pertains to power (*virtutem et potestatem*), then the whole soul is *not* in each and every part of the body in that sense. . . . As regards the operations that the soul exercises through bodily organs, its whole power is in the *whole* body but not in each and every *part* of the body, since different parts of the body are suited to different operations of the soul. For that reason, the soul as regards this or that power is only in the part that has to do with the operation that is carried out through that part of the body' (QDA 10c).[35]

eye, hearing of the ear, and so on as regards the others. As a result, the higher (*perfecta*) animals have the greatest variety among their organs, while plants have the least.'

[34] Aquinas's own example here strongly suggests something like this, but strikes me as a little puzzling: 'in respect of power the form is *not* wholly in each and every part. For the whiteness that is in a part of a surface does not have the same capacity for scattering (*non tantum potest in disgregando*) as does the whiteness that is in the whole surface, just as the heat in a little fire can't heat as much as the heat in a big fire' (QDA 10c). On this combination of whiteness and scattering, see also ST IaIIae.30.4c. The corresponding analogy in ST Ia.76.8c is clearer, and suggests that 'scattering' is, not surprisingly, to be interpreted as reflecting: 'For the whiteness that is in the whole surface can affect (*movere*) the sense of sight more than can the whiteness that is in some small part of the surface.'

[35] As we've seen (in Ch. Eight above, sect. 10), Aquinas takes the distinctively human powers of the human soul—intellect and will—to be 'separate' in the sense that their operations involve no bodily organ at all. And he uses this discussion of wholeness in respect of power to bring out another aspect of intellect's organlessness (in the passage whose omission is indicated in the quotation just above): 'Nor, if we're speaking of the soul of a human being, is the whole soul [in that sense even] in the *whole* body. For it was shown on the basis of earlier questions that a human soul, because it exceeds the capacity of the body, retains powers for carrying out certain operations without sharing them with the body—e.g. intellection and volition. That's why intellection and volition are not the acts of any bodily organ.' See also sect. 8 below.

3. Aquinas's agenda in SCG II.73–78

Aquinas's long argument in chapters 56–70 for his hypothesis SFB consists mainly in attacks on other theories of the soul that are incompatible with SFB in one way or another. But all his opponents agree with him that the human being has an intellective soul that is closely connected with the human body. Moreover, Plato and Averroës, his most formidable opponents in those chapters, agree with him further that the soul is a substance. Consequently, his strategy in the long argument for SFB is to uncover the inadequacies in other accounts of the soul–body relationship, especially Plato's and Averroës', and to show that the only way an intellective substance can be closely connected with the body in all the respects required by human nature is for it to be unconditionally united with the body as its substantial form. It's on that basis that Aquinas can say, after chapter 70, that SFB—'the soul is united with the body as its form'—'has been shown' (71.1480). As we've just been seeing, he then brings out further details of SFB in chapters 71 and 72, arguing for important aspects of the soul–body union that couldn't have been conveniently introduced in his polemical argument for the hypothesis, where they weren't at issue. It's no exaggeration, then, to say that chapters 56–72 contain Aquinas's whole argument for, and finishing touches to, his central thesis regarding the soul and its roles in human nature and human activity.

So it should come as a surprise to find him returning in chapters 73–8 to detailed criticisms of other theories of the soul, especially because his first target in these chapters is, again, Averroës' desperately implausible theory of the possible intellect, which Aquinas has already criticized, effectively and at length, in II.59–61.[36] The nature of the possible intellect and its place in Aquinas's own philosophy of mind will become clearer as we go on in this chapter. But at this stage it will help to have some broad indications of its role in Aristotelian philosophies of mind such as Aquinas's (and Averroës', too, in a different way), since its central importance in such theories is one reason why it warrants special attention.

---

[36] See Ch. Eight above, sect. 9. It's only Aquinas's presentation of Averroës' theory that's relevant to my present purposes. For the theory itself, which may not be as implausible as Aquinas's presentation makes it seem, see Crawford 1953 and Taylor, forthcoming.

Aquinas and Aristotelians like him assign to the possible intellect, 'a power of the soul' (75.1549), almost all the activity that we
would ordinarily think of as mental, and they retain that peculiar,
traditional name for it because the soul's distinctively intellective
capacities and potentialities are grouped under that designation,
especially its capacity for acquiring concepts.[37] But 'when the possible intellect has been actualized through an acquired intelligible
species [or concept], it can act on its own, as Aristotle says in De
anima III [4, 429b7]' (73.1526). And it has an impressive array of
activities of its own. More than once Aquinas cites Aristotle's
sweeping generalizations that 'the possible intellect is that by which
the soul engages in intellection (quo intelligit anima),[38] as is said in
De anima III' (60.1391), or that it is 'the supreme cognitive power
in us; for Aristotle says (in De anima III) that the possible intellect
is that by which the soul has cognition and engages in intellection'
(62.1409), or that, as 'Aristotle says in De anima III, the possible
intellect is that by which the soul thinks (opinatur) and engages in
intellection' (62.1411).[39] 'Intellectively considering, which is the
activity associated with having knowledge at one's disposal . . . belongs to the possible intellect itself' (60.1381).[40] And 'the possible
intellect not only acquires [concepts, or intelligible species], but
also preserves what it acquires. That's why in De anima III [4,
429a27–8] it's called the locus of [intelligible] species' (73.1517).[41]
What's more, it is the possible intellect actualized—i.e. having
acquired and making use of intelligible species—that is the source
of deliberate human action, since Aquinas identifies it as the aspect

---

[37] See e.g. 60.1375: 'since a child [even before birth] is in a state of potentiality as
regards intellective activity (potentia intelligens) although it is not actually engaging
in it, there must be some power in the child in virtue of which it is capable of
intellective activity. Now that power is the possible intellect.' Also 62.1408, 1412b;
78.1593c, 1594a, 1595.

[38] The traditional translation of intelligere as 'understand' is too narrow for the
range of activities Aquinas intends to convey by that term, though it's sometimes apt
in a context where understanding in our sense is the activity being talked about.
'Engage in intellection' is appropriately general, and awkward enough to signal that
a technical term is being used; but in other contexts I translate intelligere variously
as e.g. 'cognize intellectively', 'carry on intellective activity', or even 'understand'.
See e.g. n. 37 above and my translation of 66.1441 in sect. 6 below.

[39] See also e.g. 73.1493, 1504, 1522, 1524. The relevant passages in De anima III
are in 4, 429a10–11, 13–14, and 23.

[40] Sed considerare intelligendo, quod est actus huius habitus qui est
scientiae, . . . est ipsius intellectus possibilis.

[41] See also 73.1519; 74.1538; and n. 47 below.

of intellect that 'moves the will' (76.1579). It's no wonder that he describes the possible intellect as 'the worthiest aspect of the human being, and the one most closely associated with its form (*dignissimum et formalissimum in ipso*)', the one 'from which the human being gets its species' (60.1373). Nor is it any wonder, then, that he should be concerned with dismissing Averroës' theory, since Averroës maintains, on what he takes to be Aristotelian grounds, that the possible intellect is an independently existing entity that is itself not human. On his view it is, instead, a unique, sempiternal intellective substance, separated in its existence from every body, human or otherwise.

Obviously such a view must be set aside, not only by Aquinas, but by anyone engaging in a recognizable form of philosophy of mind. But it seems to deserve outright, blunt dismissal, and hardly to warrant the finely detailed refutation of it Aquinas develops here. Whatever medieval circumstances may have led him to take this fantastic theory so seriously as he was writing Book II have long since vanished,[42] so I won't take it seriously here, except in so far as some of its features may affect the way in which Aquinas presents pieces of his own philosophy of mind in opposing it. The explanation for his dividing his refutation of Averroës into two separated halves, however, lies not in Averroës' theory itself so much as in Aquinas's artificial division of it into two main theses for purposes of his own.[43]

Some things Aquinas says while repudiating Averroës' theory earlier, in chapters 59–61, unmistakably *imply* the uniqueness of Averroës' separated possible intellect. But in those chapters Aquinas is expressly concerned only with its alleged *separatedness*, and never mentions its uniqueness. Nor does he ever announce that he is sharply dividing Averroës' theory into two theses. But because it is precisely the altogether separated existence of the possible intellect that is expressly and unquestionably incompatible with SFB (in which, as we've just been seeing, the possible intellect is the single most important aspect of the substantial form of the human body), it is only that separatedness thesis of Averroës' theory that

---

[42] Especially because he was writing these chapters in Italy sometime between 1260 and 1265, before we have hard evidence of the intellectual excitement over Averroism that developed in the arts faculty at Paris and occasioned Aquinas's later treatise *On the Uniqueness of the Intellect: Against the Averroists* (*De unitate intellectus, contra Averroistas*) (see App. I below).

[43] I'm grateful to Eleonore Stump for an illuminating discussion of this division.

concerns Aquinas while he is working to establish SFB by eliminating its most prominent competitors. Having established and then elaborated his own theory, he now returns to complete his criticism of Averroës' theory by attacking what Aquinas chooses to recognize as its second thesis, that the possible intellect is unique (and sempiternal). That's why he begins chapter 73 with this announcement: 'Now, on the basis of things already set out, one shows clearly that there is not a *unique* possible intellect belonging to *all* the human beings who do exist, who will exist, and who have existed—as Averroës imagines in [his commentary on] *De anima* III [5]' (1488). And he ends that long chapter by declaring the success of his attack on this second thesis: 'Therefore, there is not a unique and eternal [i.e. sempiternal] possible intellect' (1526).[44] If there were just one possible intellect for the use of all human beings, past, present, and future, then, given Averroës' commitment to the beginninglessness of the world (and, as Aquinas suggests in 73.1521, the beginningless existence of human beings), that intellective substance would have to be also sempiternal; its uniqueness would imply its sempiternality. And, as long as Averroës' theory is not made even more grotesque than Aquinas's presentation of it makes it seem, as long as that unique intellective substance is not taken to be sempiternally, inhumanly *embodied* somehow, its sempiternal uniqueness would also imply its separatedness. So it looks as if Aquinas could have criticized Averroës' theory of the possible intellect thoroughly and much more economically if he had begun by focusing on the uniqueness thesis.[45] I've already said why I think he takes up only separatedness in the chapters in which he's arguing for SFB. If he's motivated by more than a desire for thoroughness in going on here to attack the uniqueness thesis as well, he may be led to it in part because in chapter 71 he's just been considering intermediaries in the soul–body relationship as seen in SFB. And, as his attacks on both the separatedness thesis and the uniqueness thesis often show, he sees Averroës' efforts to identify the needed intermediary be-

---

[44] On Aquinas's occasional use of 'eternal' for 'sempiternal' (and vice versa), see TMOT, 96.

[45] Aquinas's very first argument against the uniqueness thesis in ch. 73 claims that it, too, is incompatible with SFB: 'It has been shown that an intellective substance is united with the human body as a form. But a single form is necessarily the form of a single matter, since an actuality that is proper for something is brought about in a potentiality that is proper for it, because they are proportioned to each other. Therefore, there is not a unique intellect belonging to all human beings' (1489).

tween the sempiternal, unique, separated possible intellect and each individual human being as one of the most obviously vulnerable features of the theory.[46]

The main thrust of Aquinas's attack on the uniqueness thesis itself is contained in chapter 73, a long, dialectically complex series of arguments, counter-arguments, objections, and replies. It reads like an imagined scholastic disputation between Aquinas and Averroës. But although Aquinas ends the chapter by drawing the conclusion that there is no such thing as Averroës' unique, sempiternal possible intellect, that's not yet the end of the attack. In chapter 73's arguments Aquinas sometimes alludes to the Aristotelian view of the possible intellect as the soul's power for (among many other things) *preserving* the concepts, or intelligible species, it receives.[47] But because Avicenna (whom Aquinas typically takes even more seriously than Averroës) argues that the possible intellect could not have any such memorative function, Aquinas devotes chapter 74 to a careful critical examination of Avicenna's objection, which only then can be set aside. After chapter 74, which has the character of an extended footnote, Aquinas returns to Averroës' uniqueness thesis or, more precisely, to arguments that seem to support it. In chapter 75 he presents three arguments in support of the uniqueness of the possible intellect (1545–7), announcing that although the thesis itself was proved false in chapter 73, its apparent support has yet to be demolished (75.1548), and finally developing detailed refutations of the three supporting arguments (75.1549–59).

In chapter 74's respectful criticism of Avicenna's denial of the possible intellect's power to preserve concepts, Aquinas's presentation of Avicenna's position reveals that, according to Avicenna, 'whenever we actually engage in intellective activity, intelligible species flow into our possible intellect from the agent intellect, which he claims is some sort of separated substance' (74.1528e). (For the moment it will be enough to identify the agent intellect in Aquinas's terms as the soul's conceptualizing faculty, abstracting intelligible species for the possible intellect from materials acquired through sensation.) Aquinas is no friendlier to the notion of

---

[46] He usually discusses this problem in terms of the separated possible intellect's being made 'continuous' with the individual human beings who use it. See e.g. 59.1360, 1362, 1365, 1369; 60.1375, 1376, 1379, 1380, 1392, 1393; 68.1449; 73.1494, 1495, 1496, 1500, 1503, 1525; 76.1578.

[47] See e.g. 1514, 1517 (quoted above in this section), 1518–21, 1523a.

a unique, separated agent intellect than he has shown himself to be to Averroës' unique, separated possible intellect, but he offers only an implied criticism of it in chapter 74,[48] where he has a different issue in view, and is still bent on demolishing Averroës' theory. However, having at last achieved that aim in chapter 75, he begins chapter 76 with the claim that 'on the basis of these considerations one can conclude as well that there is not just one *agent* intellect for all people, as is claimed by Alexander and Avicenna, who do *not* claim that there is just one *possible* intellect for all' (76.1560). And he ends the chapter with the conclusion that 'the agent intellect is not a substance separated from the human being' (1579).

As if these distinct considerations of the possible intellect and the agent intellect had led him to think of reasons why their different characters might raise doubts about their union with each other in the intellective soul (and, consequently, about the intellective soul's union with the body), Aquinas devotes chapter 77 to an illuminating, detailed account of the nature and activities of intellect. On that basis he justifies another aspect of SFB: there can be no principled objection to identifying both an agent intellect and a possible intellect as aspects of each individual intellective soul within each individual human being.

Finally, since, he says, 'several people agree with the opinion set out above [about the need for a separated agent intellect], believing that it was Aristotle's view, we have to show on the basis of Aristotle's own words that he did *not* maintain regarding the agent intellect that it is a separated substance' (78.1585). And he devotes chapter 78 to doing so, frequently illuminating his own position in the process.

4. Parts of the soul

Because SCG II is a treatise on creation, it's only natural that Aquinas begins his general account of intellective creatures (in ch. 46) with an ample explanation of their existence and nature in terms of the will and nature of their creator.[49] But, after beginning in those terms, he says very little more of that sort. It's not surprising that in the chapters (56–78) that contain most of the elements of

[48] See esp. 74.1531.   [49] See Ch. Seven above, esp. sects. 1–3.

Aquinas's philosophy of mind that we're now concerned with he says nothing in his own voice about the divine origin of the human soul specifically, since that will be his topic in chapter 87.[50] But he also has nothing to say about implications of that origin that might be pertinent to philosophy of mind in the context of a treatise on creation—e.g. about manifestations of divine providence in the soul's having the powers and activities it has.[51]

In assessing this or any other feature of Aquinas's philosophy of mind that can (or can't) be found in this context, it's essential to remember that his primary aim here is to eradicate what he takes to be importantly mistaken views, rather than expound his own systematically.[52] Thus the little he says in these chapters about the source of the human soul—or, indeed, of souls generally—simply has the effect of ruling out an exclusively natural origin for life, rather than developing implications of its divine origin. Even the most primitive forms of life, he claims, cannot be explained as nothing more than combinations of the elements, since the elements are inanimate themselves. Of course, many of the qualities and events associated with living bodies are simply corporeal qualities and events, which can and should be explained in terms of natural philosophy. But any distinctively living activity, even one associated with an entity that is alive solely in virtue of having a *nutritive* soul, 'exceeds the power of the elemental qualities'. And 'if any activity's [proximate] source'—in this case, a nutritive soul—'does arise from several causes [such as the elemental qualities], then that activity must not exceed those causes, since a secondary

---

[50] See Ch. Ten below, sect. 4.

[51] I've identified only three explicit allusions to God or anything divine in chs. 56–78: 68.1453a (quoting Dionysius on human nature as representing the divine wisdom's conjoining of the highest level of corporeal being with the lowest level of intellective being), 75.1558c (reporting that 'theologians say that a human being teaches through outward ministration, while God teaches by acting inwardly'), and 76.1576 (observing that 'an activity that a human being carries out solely by the power of some supernatural substance is a supernatural activity—e.g. performing miracles, prophesying, and other things of that sort, which human beings do by divine favour', and distinguishing such activities from ordinary intellective activities).

[52] In order to provide a survey of his philosophy of mind in SCG II, I've resisted the temptation to bring in material from other works of his to connect and fill out the pieces that can be found here, although I have, once or twice, cited passages from Book I or from chapters of Book II later than ch. 78. For more inclusive expositions, see e.g. Pegis 1934; Bagnall 1982; Kenny 1993; Kretzmann 1991c and 1993; Stump 1997, 1998, forthcoming *a* and *b*.

cause acts in virtue of the primary cause'. But any distinctively living activity, such as reproduction, does exceed the explanatory power of the elements and their qualities taken together. 'Therefore, the vegetative [or nutritive] soul cannot arise from a mixture of elements. Much less, then, can the senses and the possible intellect arise in that way' (62.1410).[53]

As we've seen, the human soul is the intellective (or rational) soul, the culminating substantial form in pre-natal human development, superseding a merely sensory soul, which supersedes a merely nutritive soul.[54] And the distinctively human soul, even though Aquinas sometimes calls it simply 'intellect', includes a 'nutritive part' and a 'sensory part', versions of the powers that are otherwise associated with nutritive souls and sensory souls, but modified specifically to serve the needs of intellect.[55]

Wherever we find a higher activity belonging to a living thing, we also find a higher species of life, corresponding to that activity. For in plants we find only nutritive activity, while in animals we find higher activity—viz. sensation and local motion—as a consequence of which an animal lives in a higher species of life. In the human being, however, we find a still higher activity pertaining to life—viz. intellective activity. Therefore, the human being will have a higher species of life. But life is based on soul. Therefore, the human being will have a soul, on the basis of which it is alive, that is higher than a sensory soul. But there is none higher than intellect. Intellect, therefore, is the soul of the human being and, consequently, its form. (59.1367)[56]

Intellect as the form of the human being, as the soul on the basis of which the corporeal human being is alive, is 'intellect' in a broad, technical sense. Intellect in that sense includes versions of sub-intellective powers—sensation and growth,[57] for instance—especially adapted to accommodate the activities of the distinctively intellective powers.

---

[53] See also 63.1417.

[54] See e.g. 58.1345, quoted in n. 19 above.

[55] In this respect, as we've seen, Aquinas distinguishes his position from Plato's (58.1342, quoted in Ch. Eight above, sect. 9).

[56] See also 60.1372.

[57] One aspect of the sub-intellective status of the powers of the nutritive, or vegetative, soul is their naturally functioning below the level of direct human control. See e.g. 23.997: 'in the human being, intellect, which acts through will, is superior to the vegetative soul, which acts through the necessity of [its] nature'.

5. The sensory part

It's in virtue of having a nutritive soul, or a nutritive part of its soul, that any corporeal thing is alive, and it's in virtue of having a sensory soul (which must include a nutritive part), or a sensory part of its soul, that any living being counts as an animal.[58] The powers and activities of the nutritive part of the human soul are of course indispensable to every other feature of human life. But, as they were understood in the Middle Ages, their contributions to distinctively human aspects of existence were philosophically less interesting and less controversial than those associated with the sensory part. Aquinas therefore has little to say about them in these chapters, and they can be left out of account in what follows.

A sensory soul, or the sensory part of an intellective soul, has two principal parts of its own, cognitive and appetitive. The cognitive part is itself divided into the external senses (sight, hearing, smell, taste, and touch) and several less uncontroversial internal 'senses', about which more will be said in what follows: the common sense, phantasia (or, somewhat misleadingly, 'imagination'), sensory memory (or 'the memorative power'), and the cogitative power (which is sometimes confusingly called 'the passive intellect'[59]). The appetitive part consists of all the animal drives and desires, which acquire their particular objects as a result of sensory cognition. Aquinas sorts those basic urges into two complementary sets of powers. First, and more fundamental, are the *concupiscible*—the natural inclinations of an animal (non-human or human) to seek things or situations that it senses or imagines as being good for it, and to avoid what its external or internal senses react to negatively: the pursuit/avoidance instincts. The others, dependent on the reactions of the concupiscible powers, are the *irascible* powers—an animal's natural inclinations to resist and to overcome whatever it senses or imagines as deterring its access to what it takes to be good for it or as promoting what is bad for it: the competition/aggression/defence instincts.[60]

---

[58] See 58.1347 and 1348; also 1344: 'it is in virtue of the intellective soul that we are called human beings, in virtue of the sensory that we are called animals, and in virtue of the nutritive that we are called living beings'. For a very helpful critical study of Aquinas on sensory cognition, see Stump, forthcoming a.

[59] See e.g. 60.1371 and 1373; also 1382, quoted in n. 76 below.

[60] See e.g. 46.1237; also 60.1374, quoted in n. 65 below.

All the behaviour of non-human animals is explained by the natures and the naturally necessitated interrelations of the cognitive and appetitive parts of the sensory soul. 'Anything that cannot initiate the activity proper to it unless it is moved by an external source is acted upon in order to operate, rather than acting itself. Thus non-rational animals are moved to act rather than acting themselves, since their entire operation depends on an external source that moves them. For sensation, which is moved by some external sensible thing, leaves an imprint in phantasia,[61] and there is an orderly [necessitated] process of that sort in all the powers [of the soul] up to the motive powers' in non-human animals (76.1579).[62]

In the case of non-human animals, the sensed or imagined forms that move them are not [actively] discovered by the animals themselves.[63] Instead, they are [passively] received in them from external sensible things that act on a sense and are [then] evaluated through the animals' natural estimative power.[64] So, even though there is a way in which non-human animals are

---

[61] For the occurrence of phantasia in non-human animals, see e.g. 67.1443, quoted in n. 63 below. Aquinas sometimes calls this internal sense *imaginatio*, but it has more functions than those associated with what we call imagination, and some of them are absolutely essential to cognition. Consequently, I'll more often refer to it under its unmistakably technical name 'phantasia', which Aquinas takes over from Aristotle's Greek. See sect. 6 below.

[62] Relations between cognitive and appetitive faculties have explanatory power even where, as in human beings, they're not all naturally necessitated: 'in beings that have cognition, the apprehending power is related to the appetitive power as mover to movable. For what is apprehended through sense, imagination, or intellect moves the intellective or the animal appetite' (47.1240). See also e.g. 60.1373: 'in a human being the first mover is intellect; for intellect moves will on the basis of what is intelligible to it.'

[63] The forms mentioned here are the 'sensible species' (*species sensibiles*), the data taken in by the external senses and stored and processed by the internal senses—encodings or 'likenesses' that are in some respects the sensory counterparts of the intelligible species. See e.g. 46.1234: 'A likeness of one thing is found in another in two ways. In one way, it is found in respect of natural existence (*esse naturae*)—for instance, the way the likeness of a fire's heat is in a thing that is heated by the fire. In the other way, a likeness is found in accordance with cognition—for instance, the way the likeness of the fire is in the sense of sight or of touch.' They are described as sensed *or imagined* because 'there is imagination also in other animals. There is evidence of this in the fact that they flee or pursue sensible objects when those objects are absent—which wouldn't happen unless an imaginative apprehension of them remained' (67.1443).

[64] The estimative power is an internal sense in non-human animals that is in some respects the counterpart of the human cogitative power. On the cogitative power, which is discussed below, see e.g. 73.1501*b*; for the parallel, see 60.1370. As for the estimative power itself, see e.g. 48.1246: 'Some things lack freedom of judgement either because they have no judgement at all—as in the case of those that lack

said to move themselves—[i.e.] in so far as one part of the animal does the moving and another part is moved [by it]—this self-moving is not theirs on their own (*non est eis ex seipsis*), but is partly from external sensed things and partly from [the animals'] nature. For they are said to move themselves in so far as their appetite moves their bodily parts—[and this is] something they have over and above inanimate things and plants. But in so far as their very wanting (*appetere*) follows necessarily from forms they have acquired through sensation and through the 'judgement' of their natural estimative power, they themselves are not the cause of their moving (*non sibi sunt causa quod moveant*). It's for that reason that they are not fully in control (*non habent dominium*) of their actions. (46.1239c)[65]

Philosophy of mind is directly relevant to epistemology in its account of cognitive powers, and just as directly relevant to ethics in its account of appetitive powers—which include not only the distinctively human will (or 'rational appetite'), but also the concupiscible and irascible powers of the sensory part, as well as the passions associated with them. Aquinas tends to develop his account of human appetitive powers within his ethics rather than in his broader treatments of the soul.[66] The fact that he has little to say

cognition, such as stones and plants—or because they have judgement that is determined by [their] nature to one outcome—as in the case of non-rational animals. For it is by the natural estimative power that the sheep "judges" the wolf to be harmful to it, and it is on the basis of that "judgement" that the sheep runs away from the wolf. (Likewise in other cases.)'

[65] See also 60.1374: 'will is in reason, while the irascible and the concupiscible [powers] are in the sensory part. That's why the acts of the concupiscible and the irascible occur along with passion, but not an act of will, which instead occurs along with choice. A human being's will is not extrinsic to the human being, however, as if it were based in some sort of [Averroistic] separated substance, but is in the human being itself. Otherwise the human being would not be fully in control of its actions, since in that case it would be acted on by the will of some sort of separated substance, and in the human being itself there would be only the appetitive powers that operate together with passions—viz. the irascible and the concupiscible, which are in the sensory part [of the human soul], just as they are in other animals that are acted upon more than they act.' On animal and natural appetites, see also 55.1309. On will and control, see also 23.995. On the passions of the sensory soul, see e.g. 55.1308; 63.1416b, 1421; also 63.1420: 'the [intellective] soul rules the body and resists the passions, which are consequences of temperament. For it is on the basis of temperament that some people are more inclined than others to sexual desire, or to anger, and yet refrain more from them because of something that reins them in, as is clear in the case of those who are continent' as regards their passions. (Aquinas occasionally also calls certain passive cognitive powers of the sensory soul 'passions'; see e.g. 60.1372, quoted below.)

[66] See e.g. ST IaIIae.6–21. In QDA, one of his most detailed developments of philosophy of mind, there is no discussion of will.

about appetitive powers in SCG II.56–78 isn't surprising, then, especially given his special purposes there.[67] On the other hand, the cognitive powers, sensory as well as intellective, are naturally important to him in that context, at least in part because he's out to discredit other theories of the intellective cognitive powers (powers that in his view depend on sensory cognition).

Among the differences between intellective and sensory powers of cognition,[68] the most fundamental for purposes of understanding their interrelations is the fact that the intellective powers are active in some respects, while the sensory powers on their own are completely passive. Aquinas holds a causal theory of sensory cognition. 'For, as the Philosopher proves in *De anima* II [5, 416b33–4; 417b20–1], sensation occurs in connection with being moved by external sensible things. For that reason, a human being cannot sense in the absence of an external sensible thing, just as nothing can be moved in the absence of a mover. Therefore, a sense-organ is moved and is acted on in sensing, but by an external sensible thing. . . . Therefore, in connection with sensing the sensory soul does not play the role of the mover and agent, but is rather that by means of which what is acted on is acted on' (57.1333). Not only the external senses, but the internal senses as well are passive powers. 'Phantasia and the sort of powers that are dependent on it—[such internal senses as] the memorative power and the like—are passions of the sensory part (as the Philosopher proves in *De memoria* [1, 450a22–5])' (60.1372).[69]

Of course, passivity to some degree is one necessary condition of reliability in the cognitive faculties that are in touch with external reality, whether as receivers or as preservers. And since external, mind-independent, physical reality is made up entirely of determinate, particular things, qualities, events, and states of affairs, the requisite passivity of sensory cognition entails that all its objects

---

[67] However, as we've seen, there's a good deal of material relevant to human volition in his earlier discussions of the role of God's will in creation (see II.23, 24, 27, 29–32, and 35; also Ch. Four above, sect. 6), and of the necessity for will and free judgement in intellective creatures generally (see II.47 and 48; also Ch. Seven above, sects. 4 and 5).

[68] See also sect. 6 below.

[69] See also 76.1575. Some of the special character and importance of phantasia are implied in this passage, where, for reasons that have yet to be brought out, it is assigned a central role among the internal senses. And one crucial difference between phantasia and 'imagination' in our sense is implied in Aquinas's referring to (sensory) memory as dependent on phantasia.

must be determinate and particular, too. Only intellective cognition is active in some respects, and has universals rather than
particulars as its proper objects. The reason why Aristotle locates
even a kind of memory in the sensory part[70] is that 'it has to do with
something as covered by a determinate time, since it has to do only
with what is past. And so, since it does not abstract from individual
conditions, it does not pertain to the intellective part, which has to
do with universals' (74.1543). Intellective cognition wouldn't be
worthy of the name if it had no preserving power of its own, which
might be called intellective memory. But your ability to recall the
mathematical meaning of 'π' depends on a sort of non-sensory
retention that's quite different from an ability to remember the first
time you ever heard of it; and many people have the former sort
without the latter in many such cases. 'Various things that pertain
to various powers in a lower order of powers pertain to just one
power in a higher order.[71] . . . Therefore, apprehending and preserving, which in the sensory part of the soul[72] pertain to various
powers [such as the external senses and memory], must be united in
the highest power—viz. in intellect' (74.1536), where, as we've
already seen, the possible intellect both apprehends and preserves
the intelligible species.

Aquinas takes what he believes to be an Aristotelian line in
considering sensory cognition to be the basis of intellective cognition and thereby of all intellective achievement.[73] He brings this

---

[70] 'Aristotle shows that [sensory] memory is not in the intellective part but in the
sensory part of the soul (in *De memoria* [1, 450a9–14])' (74.1530). Among the
internal senses, phantasia also has a retentive function: 'some of the sensory powers—e.g. the senses—only receive, while others—e.g. imagination and memory—
also retain. (That's why they're called storehouses.)' (73.1519). See also 74.1528b.

[71] As Aquinas observes in the sentence omitted from this quotation, the ordering
of powers applies also within a single part of the soul: 'For instance, the common
sense'—the internal sense that combines and compares data from various external
senses—'apprehends the objects of all the proper senses.' The external senses are
here called proper in virtue of the fact that they typically can't have objects in
common. It's the common sense that combines the visual, auditory, and tactile
sensations I'm now having, enabling me to recognize that they stem from one and
the same physical object. Out of the colours, sounds, and textures that are the
proper objects of my external senses now, the common sense reconstructs a particular corporeal thing as an object of my sensory cognition—an object which intellect,
but not sense, recognizes as a computer.

[72] Reading *sensitiva* for *sensitivae*.

[73] See e.g. 44.1206: 'the human intellect, in the way it naturally engages in intellective activity, . . . needs sensation and phantasia'; also 37.1130: 'since all our cognition
begins from sensation, which has to do with individual things, human reflection

out, for instance, in rejecting Avicenna's theory of a unique, separated agent intellect because (among many other reasons) 'on that
view phantasms (and consequently the senses) would not be necessary *per se* for intellective activity, but only *per accidens*—as things
that somehow stimulate and prepare the possible intellect to receive' what that supposed separated agent intellect is said to de-
liver. 'This is a piece of Platonism, and it runs counter to the order
in which art and science develop, as Aristotle puts it in *Metaphysics*
I [1, 980b25–981a12] and at the end of *Posterior Analytics* [II 19,
100a3–8], where he says that memory stems from sensation: one
experience from many memories, and from many experiences a
universal comprehending, which is the starting-point of science and
of art' (76.1570). For some understanding of the ways in which
Aquinas thinks that sensory cognition makes its indispensable contributions to intellection, we have to look more closely at what he
says about those powers and their activities.

6. Sense in intellect's service

Some of the differences between sensory and intellective cognition
have already emerged in this survey. Because the operations of the
sensory part of the human soul are often affected by intellect and
will, the passivity and necessitation that wholly characterize sensory cognition are less evident in human beings than they are in
non-human animals, which 'do not engage in disparate and opposed activities, as if they had intellect. Instead, as moved by [their]
nature, they engage in certain determined activities that are uniform within the same species—e.g. every swallow builds its nest in
the same way' (66.1437).

But our concern now is with human sensory cognition in particu-

(*consideratio*) has progressed from particular to universal considerations'; also
74.1531, where Aquinas argues that if Plato's theory of Forms or Avicenna's theory
of the agent intellect is correct, 'it will follow that our knowledge is not caused by
sensible things. The contrary of this is apparent from the fact that a person who lacks
one of the senses lacks knowledge of the sensible things that are cognized through
that sense'; also 77.1584, where Plato's theory of Forms is again under attack: 'things
that are closer to our senses, things that are in themselves less intelligible, are more
intelligible to us. That's what led Aristotle to declare that things that are intelligible
to us are not certain things that are intelligible *per se*, but rather that they are made
intelligible on the basis of sensible things.'

lar, which differs from intellection also in ways that can't be obscured in human beings. For instance, intellect is capable of reflexive knowledge of itself and its activities, as sense is not (66.1440). And 'a sense is damaged by an abnormally strong sensible object', such as a very bright light or a very loud noise, 'while intellect is not damaged by that sort of abnormality in an intelligible object. On the contrary, a person who understands greater things can afterwards understand lesser things *better*' (66.1441).[74]

More to the epistemological point, the two kinds of human cognition differ in the ranges of objects to which they have access. 'Intellect . . . has cognition of universals, as is clear from experience', and also of individual things, as we'll see; while 'sense has cognition of individual things only' (66.1438). That limitation on the range of sensory cognition is a consequence not only of the fact that all the things in the external world are individual and none universal, but also of the way sensation works: 'For every sensory power has cognition through individual species, since it receives the species of things in bodily organs' (ibid.). The individual sensible species received in the organs of the external senses are e.g. colours, shapes, sounds, smells, flavours, textures, and temperatures—cognitive instances (or 'likenesses') of external qualities of individual things. Those individual species are the starting-points of sensory (and intellective) cognition, and the first step in their cognitive processing is the common sense's reconstruction of them into cognitive instances of individual things,[75] which provide the basis for the fundamental, familiar claim that 'sense has cognition of individual things (*singularium*)'. In the passage just quoted Aquinas explains the non-universal character of the sensible species on the basis of the recipient's nature rather than the object's, but it's fundamentally the same explanation: whatever is corporeal

---

[74] See also 55.1306 and 62.1407.

[75] See n. 71 above. See also II.100.1855 and I.61.510: 'The higher any cognitive power is, the more universal its proper object is, subsuming more things under it. That's why that which the sense of sight cognizes *per accidens*'—such as the three-dimensionality or the separateness of colours—'is apprehended by the common sense or the imagination as subsumed under *their* proper object'—e.g. under the corporeal thing that has the colours. The unifying of disparate sensible species is continued and enhanced intellectively: 'the one intellect exercises judgement over the various kinds of sensible objects that pertain to the various sensory powers. From this we can gather that the operations pertaining to the various sensory powers are united in the one intellect' (73.1519).

is individual.[76] And, of course, 'sensory cognition extends only to corporeal things. This is clear from the facts that sensible qualities, which are the proper objects of the senses, occur only in corporeal things, and that without them the senses cognize nothing. Intellect, on the other hand, has cognition of incorporeal things, such as wisdom, and truth, and relations among things' (66.1439).[77]

Aquinas is an epistemological realist. Sensible qualities are accidental forms in external objects, and those forms occur also as sensible species in the senses, external and internal.[78] Naturally there are differences between the two occurrences, and some of the differences are trivial: 'a colour species is *actually* sensed not in so far as it is in the stone', where it is just *potentially* sensed, 'but only in so far as it is in the pupil of the eye' (59.1365). It can be sensed by means of that bodily organ because 'the pupil of the eye, which receives colour species, lacks every colour. For if it had any colour of its own, that colour would prevent other colours from being seen—indeed, it would see nothing except under that colour' (59.1355). And, of course, unseen 'colours existing outside the soul in the presence of light are actually visible in respect of having the power to move the sense of sight, but not in respect of being actually sensed' (59.1366). 'In the senses there is a kind of preparedness for receiving sensible things in actualization' (62.1407)—i.e. for converting the sensible into the actually sensed.

But for a proper sense object to be actually sensed is for it to be made 'one with the sense in actuality' (59.1366). The external sensible quality and the actually sensed quality are two very different instantiations of one and the same form, and so the relationship between the external object and the actually cognizing faculty is formal identity in that particular respect. More of what's meant by calling this identity formal is brought out in Aquinas's saying that a

---

[76] See also 75.1533: 'the sensory powers cannot cognize universals; for they cannot receive an immaterial form, because they always receive in a bodily organ'; also 60.1382: 'universal species cannot be in the passive intellect [or cogitative power], because it is a power that makes use of a bodily organ, but only in the possible intellect'.

[77] One respect in which intellect cognizes individuals is simply a consequence of its cognizing incorporeally and universally: 'the forms of sensible things have being more perfectly in intellect than in the sensible things, for [in intellect] they are simpler and extended over more things, since [for instance] intellect cognizes all human beings through the one intelligible form *human being*' (50.1263).

[78] Consequently, Aquinas occasionally refers to qualities in the senses, and to species in external objects.

sense, which considered just as such is a power, capacity, or potentiality, 'is actualized in virtue of the fact that it is [made] actually the same as the thing sensed [*De anima* III 2, 425b25–6]'—'*actually* the same' because all actualization is a consequence of a potentiality's acquiring a form appropriate to it. 'Apprehending through sense takes place actually . . . whenever a sense . . . has been made one with the thing sensed . . . in so far as it has the thing's form' (74.1528*a*).[79]

As we've seen, Aquinas often explains cognition in terms of the soul's acquiring 'likenesses' of external cognized objects,[80] and that way of putting it can seem incompatible with the formal identity that is at the heart of his cognitive theory, or at least suggest a weakening of it. For instance, 'colours that are made actually visible by light unfailingly impress their likeness on a transparent medium' such as air, 'and, consequently, on the sense of sight', in case there's an observer in the vicinity (76.1569). But what he means by 'their likeness' in such expressions regarding sensory cognition is simply a new instantiation of those originally external material forms in a different medium: 'every cognitive power, considered just as such, is immaterial'—not the sense-organ, of course, but the power itself. 'That's why Aristotle says even of sensation (the lowest-ranking cognitive power) that it is receptive of sensible species without matter (*De anima* II [12, 424a17–19])' (62.1409).[81] The sensible qualities of external corporeal things make physical impressions on the bodily organs of the external senses. Those impressions internalized are the sensible species properly so-called. The species are transmitted from the external senses to the common sense and to other internal senses for preservation and further processing— most importantly to phantasia: 'sensation, moved by some external thing that is sensible, leaves an impression in phantasia' (76.1579).[82]

[79] See also 59.1365: 'a sense actualized and its sensible object actualized are one [*De anima* III 2, 425b25–6], but not . . . a sense in a state of potentiality and its sensible object in a state of potentiality'. Also 30.1076*d*: 'when a sense has been actualized through a sensible species, it is necessary that it sense'.

[80] See e.g. 77.1581: 'all cognition is produced in accordance with a likeness of the thing cognized in the one who has the cognition'.

[81] For a helpful discussion, see Cohen 1982, Haldane 1983, Hoffman 1990, and esp. Stump, forthcoming *a*, where the dispute among the three earlier authors is adjudicated.

[82] See also 59.1368 and 67.1444: 'imagination has to do only with corporeal and individual things, since phantasia is a movement brought about by actualized sensation (as is said in *De anima* [III 7, 431a14–15])'.

Even though the species themselves are initially realized in the anatomical matter of the animal's external and internal sensory apparatus, their sensory reception involves the reproduction of the sensible forms of external things apart from their original matter. The species are likenesses in so far as they are instantiations of certain material forms (sensible qualities) of external objects in different matter, likenesses that initially omit none of the details present in the external senses (which of course vary in sensitivity among individuals and from one time to another in the same individual).

Phantasia, 'the storehouse of forms apprehended through sensation' (73.1528b),[83] is especially important for its production and preservation of the sensory data that constitute the proximate raw material for the abstraction of intelligible species.[84] Those data are the phantasms: 'the intellective soul itself remains in a state of potentiality to determinate likenesses of the things of which we can have [intellective] cognition—which are the natures of sensible things.[85] And, of course, it is the phantasms that present to us the determinate natures of sensible things.' The phantasms themselves are not to be confused with the intelligible species, however, because they 'have not yet arrived at intelligible being, since they are likenesses of sensible things even in respect of their material conditions, which are proper to individuals'—i.e. all the individuating details picked up by the external senses. 'And, besides, the phantasms occur in material organs.[86] Therefore, they are not *actually* intelligible. None the less, since in connection with this or that human being, a likeness of whom the phantasms represent, we can receive a universal nature stripped of all the individuating conditions, the phantasms *are* intelligible *potentially*. In this way, therefore, they have intelligibility in potentiality, but in actuality the determinateness of the likeness of things. . . . There is a power in

---

[83] See also 74.1538: 'Aristotle says, in *De anima* III [4, 428a27–8], that the possible intellect is the locus of species, which is the same as saying that it is the storehouse of intelligible species, to use Avicenna's words.'

[84] See e.g. 68.1459 and 73.1514: 'the senses and phantasia are needed for nothing that contributes to intellective activity if intelligible species are not acquired from them'.

[85] On the natures, or quiddities, of sensible things as proper objects of intellective cognition, see Kretzmann 1991c and Stump 1998.

[86] See 73.1526, 77.1581, and 67.1446: 'the imagination has a determinate bodily organ'. Also 68.1459b: 'a human soul's intellective activity needs powers—viz. imagination and sensation—that operate through certain bodily organs'.

the intellective soul that is active on the phantasms, making them intelligible in actuality.[87] And that power of the soul is called the agent intellect' (77.1581).

Phantasms are cognitive likenesses of particular external things reinstantiated in physical configurations of the organ of phantasia (which Aquinas elsewhere reports as having been identified as the brain).[88] Phantasms do 'present to us the *determinate* natures of sensible things', and the proper objects of intellective cognition are the *universal* 'natures of sensible things', abstracted by the agent intellect from those determinate natures.[89] But because phantasms still include the 'material conditions' of external things, the likenesses in the phantasms are not themselves universal. Still, phantasms, which occur outside the distinctively intellective part of the soul as the raw material for intellective cognition, are related to an intelligible species that is actually cognized in the possible intellect much as a coloured thing outside the soul is related to an actually sensed colour species (59.1362).[90] 'The species of a thing, considered as it occurs *in* phantasms, is not *actually* intelligible. For it is not in *that* condition that it is one with intellect actualized, but [only] in so far as it has been abstracted *from* phantasms—just as a colour species is actually sensed not in so far as it is in a stone, but only in so far as it is in the pupil of the eye' (59.1365).

Aquinas's presentation of intellective cognition as structurally analogous to sensory cognition is intended not as mere illumination, but as the key to understanding intellective cognition. For instance, the reason why the unaided human intellect can have no full-fledged cognition of separated substances is just that they *are*

---

[87] All the internal senses, but especially phantasia itself and the cogitative power, are supposed to contribute to preparing the phantasms for the operation of the agent intellect. See e.g. 60.1370: 'by this [cogitative] power, along with the imaginative and memorative powers, the phantasms are prepared to receive the action of the agent intellect, by which they are made actually intelligible, just as there are various arts that prepare the material for the principal artificer'; also 73.1501*a*, 1503, 1513; and 76.1567, 1572. But Aquinas says nothing in SCG II about the nature of that preparation.

[88] See e.g. In Met. V: L14.69.

[89] See 77.1581, quoted more fully in the preceding paragraph. Anything that is linguistically expressible is already at the level of intellective cognition, but *glowing-grey-angular-hard-clicking-beeping-thing* seems to be a rough approximation of the determinate nature of the sensible thing I'm now experiencing, the sensible thing whose universal nature is *computer*.

[90] See also 73.1496. Kenny 1969 is helpful on the relations between phantasia and intellect. See also Stump 1998 and forthcoming *a*.

'altogether separated from matter', and so 'there are no phantasms of such things. But this intellect never engages in intellective cognition without a phantasm (as Aristotle says in *De anima* III [7, 431a16–17]), because phantasms are to it as sensible things are to a sense; and a sense does not sense without them' (60.1387). And if the analogy suggests a fundamental passivity in intellective cognition, that, too, is part of what Aquinas intends: 'phantasms move the possible intellect as sensible things move a sense (as Aristotle says in *De anima* III [4, 429a24–7])' (67.1445); 'in a way, phantasms are related to the possible intellect as the active to the passive— according to Aristotle's remark in *De anima* III [4, 429a13–14] that intellective cognizing is a kind of undergoing (*intelligere quoddam pati est*)' (73.1506).[91]

Still, it has already become clear that the cognitive passivity of intellect is not so thoroughgoing as the passivity of sensory cognition. For there is an agent intellect—an essentially active power of intellect—to which there is no corresponding agent sense.[92] And even though there is a respect in which it is the phantasms that 'move the possible intellect', and 'a way' in which they themselves are active, it is 'the agent intellect that has the function of making the phantasms, which are *potentially* objects of intellection, objects of intellection *in actuality* (*intellecta in actu*)' (78.1591).[93] And, in fact, that way of putting it is overly compressed. Fully actualized intellective cognition, like fully actualized sensory cognition, consists in the cognitive faculty's having been made one with its proper object. But the immediate effect of the agent intellect—the production of intelligible species—falls short of that cognitive unifying: 'phantasms are made actually *intelligible* through the light of the agent intellect, so that they *can* move the possible intellect, but not

---

[91] See also 74.1541: 'Aristotle also says, in *De anima* III [7, 431a15; 8, 432a9], that phantasms are related to the possible intellect as sensible things are related to a sense. From this it is clear that intelligible species are in the possible intellect from phantasms'; also 60.1375 and 1384: 'the perfecting of the possible intellect depends on the activity of a human being, since it depends on phantasms, which move the possible intellect'; and 76.1569: 'if the very phantasms illuminated by the agent intellect do not impress their likenesses on the possible intellect but only dispose it to receive them, the relationship of the phantasms to the possible intellect will not be like that of colour to sight, as Aristotle claims it is [*De anima* III 5, 430a16–17]'.

[92] However, some of the operations assigned to some of the internal senses, especially phantasia and the common sense, make them look like agent senses in all but official nomenclature.

[93] See also 73.1521.

so that they are objects of intellection in actuality in the sense that they are one with the actualized possible intellect' (59.1366).

The intellective soul is not in potentiality to the likenesses of things that are in phantasms *in the way* in which they are in the phantasms, but rather in so far as those likenesses are raised to a higher status—I mean, in so far as they are abstracted from the individuating material conditions [that are still associated with them in the phantasms]—as a result of which [abstraction] they are made actually intelligible. And so the agent intellect's action on the phantasm precedes the possible intellect's reception. In this way primacy (*principalitas*) of action is ascribed not to the phantasms but to the agent intellect. It's for that reason that Aristotle says that the agent intellect is related to the possible intellect as an art is related to its material [*De anima* III 5, 430a12–13]. (77.1582)[94]

7. Intellective cognition

'The activity proper to the human being is intellective activity' (76.1579), and 'a human being can have intellective cognition only by virtue of the agent intellect' (76.1576). This is because 'the primary source of intellective activity is the agent intellect, which produces intelligible species by which the possible intellect is passively affected in a certain way' (76.1579). Consequently, 'it's obvious that our knowledge (*scientia*)'—i.e. our intellective cognition—'depends on the agent intellect as its primary source' (76.1564). 'The agent intellect makes things intelligible only on the basis of phantasms' (60.1388), which are themselves the final cognitive production of the sensory part of the soul and the proximate raw material for the agent intellect's production of intelligible species for the possible intellect.[95] Aquinas describes that production either as making the potentially intelligible phantasms *actually* intelligible,[96] or as abstracting the intelligible species *from* the

[94] See also 76.1565 and 1574: 'the effect that consists in abstracting the universal forms from the phantasms is in our intention . . . Therefore, we must posit some proximate source of such an effect in us. But that is the agent intellect.'

[95] See e.g. 76.1562: 'The agent intellect produces actually intelligible species not so that *it* may have intellective cognition by means of them . . . but rather so that by means of them the possible intellect may have intellective cognition.' This is one respect in which intellective cognition is active, unlike sensory cognition; see 77.1583 for a helpful comparison.

[96] See e.g. 59.1365, 1366; 60.1370; 73.1503, 1513, 1517, 1521; 76.1565; 77.1581.

phantasms.[97] Two of Aquinas's favourite Aristotelian similes help to show how he understands this process.

First, 'Aristotle says that the agent intellect is related to the possible intellect as an art is related to its material [*De anima* III 5, 430a11–13]' (77.1582). Offhand, the relationship of the agent intellect to the possible intellect certainly seems more nearly like the relationship of the *artisan* to her material. The artisan is, paradigmatically, the product's efficient cause, as her art is its formal cause. Sometimes Aquinas presents this relation of an art to its material as if it were a straightforward instance of the agent–patient (or donor–recipient) relationship.[98] A relationship of that sort does seem to be just what's wanted, but not what's provided in the Aristotelian simile. None the less, even when Aquinas expressly characterizes the agent intellect as an efficient cause, he continues to characterize it as the art and not as the artisan.[99]

He comes closest to making this simile plausible and illuminating when he adds details that correspond to the intelligible species: 'the agent intellect is related to the intelligible species that are received

---

[97] See e.g. 75.1551*b*: 'The fact that the [possible] intellect cognizes the [universal] nature associated with a genus or a species, stripped of individuating principles, is a consequence of the condition of the intelligible species received in it, which is made immaterial by the agent intellect in virtue of being abstracted from matter and the conditions of matter, by which something is individuated.' Also 50.1261; 59.1365; 60.1388; 73.1496; 75.1551, 1553; 76.1574. In 77.1582 (quoted more fully at the end of sect. 6 above) he explains one of these two descriptions in terms of the other: the likenesses or determinate natures in phantasms 'are abstracted from the individuating material conditions [that are still associated with them in the phantasms], as a result of which [abstraction] they are made actually intelligible'.

[98] See e.g. 76.1561: 'the possible intellect is related to the agent intellect as its proper patient or recipient, since the agent intellect is related to it as an art is related to its matter (as is said in *De anima* III)'. Also 60.1383: 'the effects of the agent intellect are things that are actually intelligible, and the proper recipient of such things is the possible intellect, to which the agent intellect is related as an art is related to its material (as Aristotle says in *De anima* III)'.

[99] See e.g. 78.1588*a*: 'in every nature in which potentiality and actuality are found, there is something that has the role of matter, which is in a state of potentiality relative to things that belong to the genus, and something that has the role of the agent, which brings the potentiality to actuality (as in connection with an art's productions there is the art and the material). But the intellective soul is a sort of nature in which one finds potentiality and actuality, since it is sometimes actually and other times potentially engaged in intellection. Therefore, in the nature of the intellective soul there is something that plays the role of matter, which is in a state of potentiality relative to all intelligible things, which is called the possible intellect; and also something that plays the role of efficient cause, something that brings all [intelligible] things into actuality. And this is called the agent intellect.' On the agent intellect as an efficient cause, see also 78.1592*b*.

in the possible intellect as an art is related to the artificial forms that
are imposed on the material through the art, as is clear from Aristotle's example in *De anima* III. Now the forms associated with an
art do not attain to (*consequuntur*) the action associated with the
art, but only to formal likeness. For that reason the subject of those
forms'—viz. the art's material (analogous to the possible intellect[100])—'cannot carry out the action of the artisan through such
forms' (76.1578*b*). Perhaps this simile is most helpful, then, if we
think of the artisan, considered just as such, as an efficient cause
with an internalized formal cause—the art as the artisan's programme of action.[101] The agent intellect may then be thought of as
programmed to impose intelligible species on the possible intellect
somewhat as a bookbinder, considered just as such, has a programme of stamping letters on to leather—something the leather
couldn't do to itself. (In the midst of all this talk suggesting that the
agent and possible intellects are discrete entities, it's important to
remember that the distinction between them is only a conceptual
device for clarifying the intellective process, not the introduction of
really distinct parts within the intellective soul: 'the intellect in an
actualized state . . . [is] the part of the soul with which we are
actually engaging in intellective activity, comprising both the possible intellect and the agent intellect' (78.1596).[102])

In the second of these Aristotelian similes, the phantasms are
said to be related to the possible intellect as colours in external
objects are related to the sense of sight.[103] In total darkness, those
colours are invisible actually, but visible potentially. The action of

[100] See also 62.1412*b* and 1408: 'Aristotle says of the possible intellect that it is
passive relative to what is intelligible [and] receptive of intelligible species, being in
a state of potentiality to them [*De anima* III 4, 429a14–16]. He also compares it to
a tablet on which nothing has been written [429b31–430a2].' In 60.1370*b* Aquinas
also compares the phantasms to the art's material: 'by this [cogitative] power, along
with the imaginative and memorative powers, the phantasms are prepared to receive the action of the agent intellect, by which they are made actually intelligible,
just as there are various arts that prepare the material for the principal artisan'.

[101] See e.g. 47.1239*d*: 'a form associated with an art, which the artisan conceives
and thinks out, and through which he acts'.

[102] See also 77.1581; also 76.1577: 'Both actions—that of the possible intellect and
that of the agent intellect—belong to the human being. For the human being
abstracts from the phantasms and mentally receives (*recipit mente*) the actually
intelligible things; for we would not have come to know about these actions if we
had not experienced them in ourselves. Therefore, the sources to which these
actions are attributed—viz. the possible intellect and the agent intellect—must be
certain powers formally existing in us.'

[103] See e.g. 76.1569, quoted in sect. 6 above.

the agent intellect on the potentially intelligible aspects of the phantasms is like the effect of light on the external colours, which are the potentially visible aspects of the external physical objects. That's how Aquinas interprets Aristotle's saying (in *De anima* III 5, 430a10–17) that the agent intellect is like light. 'For, in a way, light makes potential colours to be colours actually—I mean, in so far as it makes them be actually visible. But where intelligible things are concerned, this [sort of effect] is attributed to the agent intellect' (78.1586). External colours that have been lighted have been made actually visible, which is of course not the same as being actually seen. Analogously, 'phantasms are made actually intelligible through the light of the agent intellect, so that they can move the possible intellect, but not so that they are objects of intellection in actuality (*ut sint intellecta actu*) in the sense that they are one with the actualized possible intellect' (59.1366).

The condition described as the possible intellect's having been actualized is at the core of Aquinas's conception of intellective cognition. As we've been seeing, he thinks of all cognition as the actualizing of one or another of the soul's cognitive powers. 'When a sense has been actualized through a sensible species, it is necessary that it sense; and, likewise, when intellect is actualized through an intelligible species', it must be actually engaging in an activity for which intellect is a capacity (30.1076*d*). The actualizing of the possible intellect is the culmination of the cognitive process that begins in sensation. 'The operation proper and natural to the human being is intellection, which is not completed without a kind of passivity, in so far as intellect is passive to what is intelligible. Nor is it completed without action, in so far as intellect makes things that are potentially intelligible be actually intelligible. Therefore, in the nature of the human being there must be a source proper to both of these—viz. the agent intellect and the possible intellect' (76.1575).[104] Actualizing (or exercising) a power consists in fulfilling (or completing, or perfecting) a potentiality (or capacity).[105] And, since a passive cognitive power is actualized in the respect in

---

[104] See also 76.1577 and 73.1526: 'any human being engages in intellective activity through the possible intellect in so far as it is brought to actuality through intelligible species'.

[105] See e.g. 55.1305, 1307; 76.1563: 'The possible intellect is perfected through forms that are actually received in intellect (*formas intellectas in actu*), just as prime matter is perfected through natural forms, which are outside the soul.'

which it takes on a form of its object,[106] Aquinas often describes
the actualizing of the possible intellect as its being *assimilated
to* its object,[107] or as its *becoming one with* its object,[108] or even
as its simply *becoming* its object.[109] These claims of cognitive
unification are all the more striking because they aren't merely
claims about the possible intellect and the intelligible species.
Aquinas clearly and emphatically distinguishes between intellective cognition's *object* (*id quod intelligitur*) and its *instrument* (*id
quo intelligitur*), and he assigns only the latter role to the intelligible
species.

The species received in the possible intellect does *not* have the role of that
which is intellectively cognized. For since all the arts and sciences have to
do with objects of intellective cognition, it would follow that all the sciences have to do with species existing in the possible intellect. That is
clearly false, since no science except the rational science [i.e. logic] and
metaphysics [including philosophy of mind] considers anything having to
do with intelligible species. Whatever things are included in any of the
sciences are cognized *through* those species, however. Therefore, the intelligible species received in the possible intellect in the process of intellection play the role of the *instrument* of intellective cognition, not the role of
its *object*.[110] (Analogously, the species of colour in the eye is not that which
is seen but that by means of which we see.) (75.1550)

Now it's already become clear that Aquinas takes the proper objects of intellective cognition to be the real universal natures of
sensible things,[111] and those natures are not to be confused with
their representations in intelligible species. 'The object of intellective cognition is the very nature (*ratio*) of things existing outside

---

[106] See e.g. 59.1362; 75.1553; 76.1563 (quoted in n. 105 above). On this aspect of
intellective cognition see Stump 1998.

[107] See e.g. 77.1581; also 60.1382: 'The assimilation associated with knowledge is
an assimilation of the knower to the thing known. But a knower is assimilated to a
known thing, in so far as it is known, only in accordance with universal species; for
knowledge has to do with things of that sort.'

[108] See e.g. 59.1366; 50.1261; 55.1307: 'The intelligible is the perfection proper to
intellect; that's why the intellect actualized and the intelligible actualized are one
[*De anima* III 4, 430a3–4].'

[109] This is Aristotle's doctrine that actual knowledge is identical with its object
(see *De anima* III 5, 430a19–20, and 7, 431a1), which Aquinas often alludes to. See
e.g. 46.1235; 47.1240; 74.1528, 1542; 78.1593*a, b, c, d, e,* 1595.

[110] See also e.g. 59.1361: 'The object of intellective cognition is something the
intelligible species of which is united with intellect (*Intelligitur autem id cuius species
intelligibilis intellectui unitur*).'

[111] See 77.1581, quoted in sect. 6 above.

the soul (just as it is things existing outside the soul that are seen by bodily vision). For the arts and sciences have been devised in such a way that things may be cognized as they exist in their own natures' (ibid.). Is Aquinas then committed to the claim that in intellective cognition your possible intellect is identical with the very nature of an external object?

Yes, but the claim is a good deal less drastic than it looks. I'm aware that there's a grey cat on my desk. My awareness obviously has sensory components. But it's unmistakably an instance of intellective cognition, because it involves my awareness of the (universal) nature of the grey thing on my desk. (Actual individual occurrences of the cognitive process that begins in sensation and culminates in intellective cognition are typically so fast that the transition goes altogether unnoticed or seems instantaneous.) Such sensible species as that colour and that shape are unified into a phantasm: my visual sensation of this particular thing here and now that looks like *that*. From that phantasm my agent intellect abstracts an intelligible species: a non-eidetic, universal concept of cats that might (and in this case does) actualize my possible intellect in that respect.[112] The concept's actualizing my possible intellect in this case is its becoming a feature of my consciousness with reference to that phantasm. 'The possible intellect is related in one way to the phantasm it needs before [it receives] the intelligible species, and it is related to it in another way after it receives the intelligible species. For *before* it receives the intelligible species, it needs the phantasm as that from which it acquires the intelligible species; consequently, the phantasm is [then] related to the possible intellect as the object that moves it. But *after* the species has been received in it, it needs the phantasm as an instrument or basis (*fundamento*) of the species it has; consequently, the possible intellect is [then] related to the phantasms as an efficient [moving] cause' (73.1523c).[113] 'When the possible intellect has been actualized through the received intelligible species, it can act on its own, as Aristotle says in *De anima* III [4, 429b7]' (73.1526). And in this case its action consists in my recognizing that the received intelligi-

---

[112] 'The possible intellect ... does indeed cognize immaterial things, but it observes (*inspicit*) them in something material. (The fact that in teaching universal truths we use particular examples in which what we say may be observed is a sign of this.)' (73.1523b).

[113] On this second, instrumental use of phantasms, see also 73.1526.

ble species represents the nature of the external object that is represented in that phantasm. I recognize that thing as a natural, material instantiation of the substantial form *cat*. Because my awareness includes a universal nature among its objects, it must be an instance of intellective cognition, an actualization of my possible intellect in just that respect. Like any other sort of actualization, the actualization of my possible intellect consists in its taking on a form.[114] And in this case, of course, the form it takes on is the form *cat*. That form is delivered to my possible intellect as a concept, but in my example the concept itself is not the object of my awareness; the cat is.[115] The crucial difference between the external and the internal instantiations of the form *cat* is that my intellect's instantiation of it is what Aquinas sometimes calls a 'spiritual', immaterial (rather than a natural, material) instantiation. (As we've been seeing, he takes immateriality to be essential to intellectivity: 'what is incompatible with intelligibility is materiality' (75.1553).[116]) What is instantiated on my desk and in my intellect is just the same, but the two modes of instantiation are radically distinct.[117] If seeing the cat on my desk started me thinking about cats in general, I would of course drop this cat's individuating conditions from my

---

[114] See e.g. 55.1299: 'each and every thing has being in so far as it has form'; also 59.1362: 'An intelligible species that is actually taken in (*intellecta in actu*) is a form of the possible intellect just as a species that is actually seen (*visa/visibilis*) is a form of the visual power, or of the eye itself'; and 1364: 'nothing is in actuality except through that which is its form'.

[115] Of course, in this *discussion* of my example it's not the cat but the concept (along with other elements and operations of intellective cognition) that I'm concerned with. 'Although we've said [in 75.1550] that an intelligible species that has been received in the possible intellect is not that which is intellectively cognized but that by which it is cognized, that doesn't prevent intellect from cognizing itself, its cognizing, and the species by which it cognizes. But it cognizes its own cognizing in two ways. In one way, it cognizes it particularly, for it cognizes itself cognizing at this instant. In the other way, it cognizes it universally, in so far as it thinks about the nature of its own activity. On this basis it likewise cognizes both intellect and the intelligible species in two ways: first, by perceiving itself existing and having an intelligible species—which is to cognize particularly—and, second, by considering its own nature and the nature of an intelligible species—which is to cognize universally. (And it is on this latter basis that intellect and what is intelligible are treated in the sciences.)' (75.1556).

[116] See also e.g. 50.1261; 62.1413; 75.1551*b*; 77.1581.

[117] See e.g. 16.940: 'the receiving that occurs in spiritual things is intelligible: intellect receives the species of intelligible things not in accordance with material being'. Also 46.1234, 1235; 50.1261, 1263; 51.1271; 55.1305; 59.1357; 62.1413; 69.1469. Geach 1963: 94–6 provides a helpful analysis of this formal identity. See also Stump 1998.

consideration: 'although the nature of a genus and of a species never exists except in these or those individuals, intellect cognizes the nature of species and of genus by not cognizing individuating principles. That's what it is to cognize universals. And so these two claims are not incompatible—that universals do not subsist outside the soul, and that intellect in cognizing universals cognizes things that are outside the soul'—i.e. the particulars subsumed under those universals (75.1551a).

8. Organlessness

Since Aquinas thinks that all intellective creatures other than human beings are incorporeal, it's only natural that he should think that no bodily organ could be a necessary condition for the existence and activity of intellect *generally*.[118] But he also claims, repeatedly, that the human intellect in particular uses no organ of the human body in its distinctively intellective activity.[119] Of all the Aristotelian elements in Aquinas's philosophy of mind, this is probably the one most flagrantly at odds with what we now know to be the case. He believed that metaphysical considerations required him to affirm and defend the thesis of intellect's organlessness, and we'll be looking at some of them in the remainder of this chapter. But I want first to suggest that in the thirteenth century there were also some empirical considerations that may have made that thesis seem not only theoretically required but also plausible in its own right.

Aquinas and his contemporaries of course knew very little about even the more accessible aspects of human anatomy and physiology, and they could have had no inkling of the sorts of neurophysiological discoveries that have recently begun to show us in some detail how the brain is intellect's organ. Some medievals did think that the brain is an organ that somehow contributes to sensory cognition, a view to which Aquinas doesn't commit himself in SCG II.[120] It's not hard to see why he might have hesitated. He's

---

[118] See Ch. Seven above, sect. 6.
[119] See n. 35 above. See also e.g. 58.1350, 1351; 60.1374, 1382; 62.1411, 1413; 67.1446; 68.1459; 69.1464, 1467, 1468b, 1469; 73.1502; 74.1528c, e; 78.1592c, 1596.
[120] See n. 88 above.

convinced that all the senses, external and internal, have organs. No one could have any difficulty in broadly identifying the external organs of the external senses. For Aquinas those organs—eyes, ears, and the others—are the paradigms of organs of cognition. But those paradigms are the narrowly dedicated instruments of the 'proper' senses,[121] and, in Aquinas's unavoidably superficial knowledge of them, they must have seemed to be simply mechanical in their structure and operations—on the order of a medieval artisan's tools. He probably thinks of the organs of the internal senses as another, covert set of dedicated, mechanical instruments, though he has no way of identifying, much less inspecting, any of them. Against that conceptual and experiential background, no medieval examination of a human brain would provide any compelling reason to recognize it as the organ of this or that internal sense. As for intellect, Aquinas's philosophical reasons for his thesis of organlessness would simply preclude a serious consideration of the brain in that connection. The concept he's likely to have had of an organ of cognition would make the brain seem a very unlikely candidate in any case. How could that lump of superficially homogeneous stuff have then been thought to be to thought as an eye is to sight?[122]

Given Aquinas's account of the relationship between intellective and sensory cognition, his thesis of organlessness can't be considered a broad rejection of any essential cognitive dependence of the human intellect on the human body. However, he sometimes says things that suggest it, as when he describes 'that part of the soul by which we engage in intellective activity, a part that comprises both the possible intellect and the agent intellect' as 'independent of the body' (78.1596).[123] But, of course, 'the activity of the possible intellect needs the body. For the Philosopher says (in *De anima* III [4, 429b5–10]) that intellect can act on its own—viz. have intellective cognition—when it has been actualized by means of a species abstracted from phantasms, which do not occur without the body. Therefore, the possible intellect is not altogether separated from the body' (60.1385). And because 'the activity of the possible intellect is completed by means of the bodily organs in which phantasms have to occur . . ., nature has united the possible intellect with bodily organs; and so it is not separated from the body *in respect of*

---

[121] See n. 71 above.　　[122] See 69.1464.　　[123] See also e.g. 78.1592c.

being' (60.1386).[124] The mode of existence that gives the intellective soul its capacity for ordinary human cognition is its status as the substantial form of the human body.[125] In that respect intellect is essentially dependent on the whole body and all its organs.[126] Organlessness, the essential independence of intellect from body, is associated strictly with those aspects of intellect's activity that are distinctively intellective, such as the cognition of universals: 'intellect has no *activity* in common with the body' (69.1468*a*).[127] 'The intellective power ... is not the act of any organ in the sense of carrying out its activity by means of it ... [e.g.] the intellective activity by which it intellectively cognizes all things' (69.1467).[128] Even the possible intellect's reception of intelligible species entails its immateriality, since 'the species of intellectively cognized things are made actually intelligible by being abstracted from individual matter. But in so far as they are actually intelligible, they become one with intellect. And so intellect, too, must be devoid of individual matter' (50.1261).[129]

The possible intellect's capacity for 'cognizing all sensible forms universally' (60.1374) of course cannot be fulfilled by any individual possible intellect, but there seems to be no good reason to deny it as a general human capacity, especially in the light of the spectacular development of the natural sciences since Aquinas's day. And that theoretically universal capacity of intellective cognition is part of his central argument for the organlessness of intellect. For to be a cognitive faculty is to be in a state of receptive *potentiality* relative to certain types of things, the faculty's proper objects—such as sounds, for the faculty of hearing. So, if the faculty itself has that type of thing in it *actually*—such as a ringing in the ears—it forfeits at least some of the natural receptive potentiality that made it a cognitive faculty in the first place. Therefore, 'since

---

[124] See also e.g. 68.1459*b*.

[125] See e.g. 68.1459*b*; 69.1464, 1465, 1467, 1468*b*.

[126] See e.g. 72.1483.

[127] See also e.g. 66.1438; 69.1465; 73.1502.

[128] See also 60.1374: 'One proves that the possible intellect is not the *actus* of any body in virtue of the fact that it is capable of cognizing all sensible forms universally. Therefore, no power whose activity can extend to the universals of all sensible forms can be the *actus* of any body.' On this claim of universality for human intellective cognition, see Kretzmann 1991c and 1993.

[129] See also e.g. 62.1411, 1413; 75.1551*b*; and 58.1351: 'there is an action in which the body does not share—viz. intellectively cognizing'.

the possible intellect receives all species of sensible things, existing in a state of potentiality relative to them, it must lack them all. In just the same way, the pupil of the eye, which receives all species of colours, lacks every colour. For if it had any colour of its own, that colour would prevent other colours from being seen—indeed, it would see nothing except under that colour.[130] And something similar would happen regarding the possible intellect if on its own it had any form or nature belonging to sensible things. But that would have to be the case if it were mixed together with any body' (59.1355).[131] So, Aquinas argues, since every normal bodily organ of an external sense must, simply in virtue of its corporeality, be incapable of cognizing certain sorts of corporeal objects, it follows, given the universal capacity of intellective cognition, that intellect cannot directly use any bodily organ, which will necessarily have some corporeal nature of its own. Of course, our cognition of any particular body itself is sensory, and so our cognition of anything associated with bodies, including their universal natures, depends ultimately on sensory cognition. So one's intellect does depend for its data on the operations of the bodily organs of one's other cognitive faculties.[132] But, as far as Aquinas could see, in intellectively processing those data it does not use any body at all or any part of the human body in the direct, essential way in which visual cognition uses the eye.

This treatment of the elements of philosophical psychology in

---

[130] Of course, the pupil of the eye as the organ of vision is receptive of shapes as well as of colours, despite its having a precise shape of its own. Similarly, the skin lacks neither texture nor temperature, and yet textures and temperatures are among the proper objects of the sense of touch, the external organ of which is the skin.

[131] See also 69.1468, Aquinas's rejoinder to the argument which Averroës bases on these Aristotelian considerations.

[132] In at least one passage Aquinas might seem to be suggesting that variations among human bodies and their sensory apparatus provide a basis for distinguishing types of human intellects and thus types of human beings: 'Any and every mover must have its proper instruments; for the piper's instruments are different from the architect's. Now intellect is related to the body as its mover, as Aristotle establishes in *De anima* III [10, 433a9–15]. Therefore, just as an architect cannot use a piper's instruments, so one human being's intellect cannot be another's intellect' (73.1490). See also 73.1491. But it seems to me that these considerations are most likely to have to do with Aquinas's views on the resurrection of the body, not with the introduction of an individual soul in the process of human generation. Cf. 44.1209.

SCG II is only a survey. Even an exhaustive catalogue of those elements wouldn't include all there is to Aquinas's philosophy of mind in its mature, systematic development. None the less, the pieces of it that are, almost accidentally, to be found here could all be easily integrated into his later, fuller discussions of these topics.

TEN

SOULS BEFORE BIRTH
AND AT DEATH

1. The rest of Book II

We've seen that Aquinas thinks of his natural theology of creation in Book II as the continuing development of Book I's reasoned inquiry into the existence and nature of God.[1] That's why he examines creation from the top down, beginning not with creatures but with God's activity of creating. For the same reason, when he does turn from the activity itself to considering its uncountably many kinds of products, he confines his attention to those that are most recognizably God-like: creatures that have (or simply are) intellects (and wills). Within that genus of intellective creatures, which Aquinas sees as vast, including innumerable species of its own, he focuses primarily on the human species. It is of course the one that is bound to matter most to him, not only because he's a human being, but also because he has a theologian's special interest in human beings and their relationship with God.[2]

There are also unique methodological advantages in his focusing on just our species. An investigation of the species to which the investigator himself belongs is the one in which first-hand experience (including introspection) is most likely to provide grounds for a plausible, detailed account—perhaps especially in a pre-scientific age. And even the place which Aquinas assigns to the human species within the grand scheme of things enhances its appropriateness as the focal point for his consideration of creation. As he sees it, the human species is at the very bottom of the metaphysical hierarchy of species of intellective creatures, because all the rest are permanently and totally independent of bodies, which are

---

[1] See Ch. One above, sect. 3.

[2] See Ch. One above, esp. sect. 9, and Ch. Seven above, sect. 1. Aquinas develops this special interest in SCG III, devoted to providence, or God's governance of creation.

necessarily corruptible. No other kind of intellective creature is also a corporeal creature in any respect. Since the human soul is the sole intellective substance that is naturally united with a body, human beings are the only metaphysical hybrids within the two immense, exhaustive genera of creatures, intellective and corporeal. So even a consideration of creatures that goes no further than the human species must take some account of both great genera of creatures as no consideration limited to any other single species could do.

As a consequence of that unique amalgam at the core of human nature, and because Aquinas sees intellectivity considered just in itself as essentially independent of everything corporeal, much of his consideration of the human being so far has understandably been concerned with the difficult intrinsic relationship that in his view distinguishes us from everything else: the human soul's union with the human body. In chapters 56–70 Aquinas investigates that union as part of the essential nature of the human being, and in chapters 71–8 he considers the effect it has on the powers and activities of the human soul. In the rest of Book II he undertakes two final investigations of the union of a soul with a body, attempting to explain both how the union is brought about (II.83–90) and how it is dissolved (II.79–82). He then concludes his natural-theological investigation of creation with a necessarily sketchy account of the nature of *super*human, utterly separated intellective substances (II.91–101).

Several factors combine to limit Aquinas's discussion of such beings in those last eleven chapters of Book II. He's already argued at length on a priori grounds that any universe created by God would have to include intellective substances,[3] but since he's been discussing only human souls for so many chapters, he devotes chapter 91 to arguing that there must also be intellective substances that are never united with bodies. His account of their natures (in the remaining chapters) is bound to lack detail, not only because he argues (in II.92–3) that they must exist in uncountably many species, but also because he denies that there can be any natural, direct human experience or understanding of any of them. In defence of his account of the possible intellect, the primary faculty of human intellective cognition, he's already argued that since human intellection depends on phantasms, derived from sensation, and

---

[3] See Ch. Seven above, sect. 3.

since only corporeal things can be sensed, in natural circumstances 'the possible intellect cannot have cognition of separated sub- stances' (60.1388); 'we are to them as the owl's eye is to the sun' (60.1391).[4] And, of course, the nature of his project in SCG I–III precludes his drawing on any authoritative accounts of separated substances, such as Scriptural lore about angels and demons. Con- sequently, demons go altogether unmentioned in chapters 91–101, and the only explicit references to angels occur in the by now familiar sort of citations of authoritative (or at least respected) texts, usually at the ends of chapters.[5] Aquinas's systematic discus- sion in those chapters is confined to abstract considerations.

However, since chapters 91–101 immediately follow his very long investigation of the soul, and since the general topic of those con- cluding chapters is intellective substances that exist apart from bodies, we might expect to find him referring there to human souls existing apart from their former bodies. But he says nothing at all in those chapters about the nature of a soul's existence after death.[6] Why not? Questions about a human soul's disembodied state have always been at least as important to theologians as any other topic in the range covered by considerations of separated intellective substances, and you don't have to be a theologian to be interested in such questions. I think Aquinas must have recognized that with- out recourse to revelation he has virtually nothing to say about the state of a soul after death. So he postpones his consideration of details of human immortality to Book IV, where he allows himself to consider propositions to which reason would have no access without the revelation he accepts, intending to show that even those propositions 'are *not opposed* to natural reason' (IV.1.3348).[7] He does, however, think that he has good, natural-theological

---

[4] See also 60.1389 and 1395; also SCG III.41–5.

[5] See e.g. 91.1781, 1782*d*; 92.1794*b*; 95.1809*c*; 98.1836. Aquinas does mention demons at the very end of ch. 90 (1771*b*) with a reference to certain mistaken views that grow out of a failure to understand that neither they nor angels can be naturally embodied. See also n. 14 below.

[6] In the earlier chs. 83 and 84 Aquinas does discuss at length, and reject utterly, the hypothesis that human souls exist apart from bodies *before* embodiment. See n. 13 below.

[7] See TMOT, 44 and 47–8; also SCG IV.79–95, where the nature of the soul's existence after death is considered along with the doctrine of the resurrection of the body. As we'll see (in sect. 8 below), in II.81 Aquinas uses his rejoinder to an important opposing argument as an occasion for speculating about the cognitive condition of a human soul after death.

arguments to show at least that at death a human soul is not corrupted along with the human body with which it has been united, and we'll be looking at those arguments.[8]

Only one broadly identifiable sort of extraterrestrial intellective being is not excluded from Aquinas's consideration by the methodology of his natural theology. Aristotle, after all, *argued for* the necessity of some such beings in his explanation of the movements of the heavens, so Aquinas is within his rights to mention those movers as examples of such beings, as he does in chapters 91–101.[9] But he's already shown some ambivalence about the explanatory need for those Aristotelian movers of the celestial spheres,[10] and he reveals different sorts of doubts about them in these concluding chapters.[11] Consequently, he has no admissible, indisputably real examples on which to focus in his chapters about separated intellective substances.

The one reliable, methodologically accessible source from which Aquinas can draw some content for this account of exotic superhuman creatures is the account of the human soul that he's been developing and arguing for since chapter 56. From conclusions he has established regarding the nature and activity of the intellective soul, he's entitled to extrapolate to certain general propositions about the natures and activities of beings that are themselves intellective, albeit superior to souls.[12] Naturally, his comparisons of them with the nature and activities of human beings contain material that illuminates his account of the human soul. I've already drawn on that material, and I make further use of it in this chapter. However, for all the reasons brought out in these introductory remarks, I won't deal directly with the topics of Aquinas's chapters 91–101, but will continue to concentrate on his account of *human* nature and existence.

As I've said, the two remaining topics belonging to that account are the making and the breaking of the soul–body union, the beginning and the end of a human being's ordinary existence. Aquinas

---

[8] In sects. 7 and 8 below.
[9] And in II.90, the immediately preceding chapter. See e.g. 90.1759, 1767; 91.1780. See also n. 14 below.
[10] See 70.1478 and 90.1759; also Ch. Eight above, sect. 10.
[11] See e.g. 92.1785.
[12] This sort of extrapolation bears some resemblance to the 'relational method' Aquinas uses in reasoning from creaturely characteristics to divine attributes. See TMOT, 140 ff.

takes them up in the unnatural, reverse order. His discernible reasons for doing so aren't strong enough to require us to follow his lead. He begins with the end of this life because the grounds on which he then argues for the soul's incorruptibility are all to be found in the immediately preceding discussions of its nature. And he takes up the soul's origin last rather than first because one mistaken view about it might be thought to stem directly from his just-established thesis that the soul is everlasting. My treatment of these topics will, instead, begin with conception, and end with death.

2. Reproduction, embryology, science, and metaphysics

In his investigation of the beginning of a human being's existence, Aquinas develops careful refutations of some medieval and ancient views that no one now would or should consider worth discrediting in detail. For instance, in chapters 83–4 he argues at length against the position that individual human souls exist beginninglessly, or at least before being united with bodies;[13] in chapter 85, against the thesis that each human soul 'belongs to the divine nature' (1704b)—i.e. that 'a human being is something belonging to the divine substance' (1705); and in chapter 90, against the view that an intellective substance could be united as a form with any *non-human* 'body composed of the elements'[14]—i.e. any terrestrial body

---

[13] Aquinas's refutation of this linked pair of views is especially elaborate, no doubt because he believed that at least the second of them—that all human souls have existed 'from the foundation of the world' (1657)—was still held by certain heretics of his own day (83.1656c). He presents four arguments: two for souls' existence 'from eternity' in 1651–2 and two for the creation of all human souls 'in the beginning' in 1653–4. In 1657–84 he offers many considerations and arguments on the basis of which, he says, 'one can easily show that the positions just presented [in the four arguments and a few informal descriptions] are not founded in truth' (1657); and he follows that elaborate general attack in ch. 84 with particular rejoinders to the four arguments (1686–90). It may be worth noting that in his attack on the foundations of these two mistaken views he uses passages from Scripture as premisses in three of his arguments (1670b, 1671, 1672). But since in them he is arguing against the foundation of the position taken on pre-existent souls by Origen, a fellow Christian, such a use contributes to an *ad hominem* refutation that is legitimate, even for a scrupulous natural theologian.

[14] The amount of trouble Aquinas takes over this view is probably explained in ch. 90's concluding paragraphs (1771a–b), where he says that 'on this basis we rule out the opinion of Apuleius and some Platonists, who said that demons are animals with an airy body, endowed with reason, passive in soul, everlasting in time . . . The

other than a human body.[15] Aquinas's refutations naturally provide further insights into his own position, and I draw on them for that purpose. But I won't consider those views themselves or assess his refutations of them here.

If those views opposed by Aquinas don't deserve our serious consideration because they're bizarre or outmoded, then what about the account of human reproduction and pre-natal development that makes up much of his attempt to explain the beginning of the soul–body union?[16] All that medieval philosophers and theologians knew or believed about embryology they owed to Aristotle and Galen, whose achievements in embryology, impressive as they are, have of course been thoroughly supplanted and partly repudiated by the development of the science since the middle of the seventeenth century. As regards reproduction and pre-natal development, Aristotle and Galen have nothing to teach us, and so neither does Aquinas. What's more, some of what Aquinas believes about human reproduction is just false, or at least so imprecise that it must count as false. For instance, he often describes the female contribution to conception as blood.[17] Blatant as it is, this mistake is not absurd. Once the ancients (and the medievals) had identified semen as the male contribution to conception, it made some sense for them to think that the blood discharged in men-

opinion maintaining that angels and demons have bodies of the nature of the higher or lower elements naturally united with them is also ruled out.' Consequently, he must intend to be arguing against the view that *any* intellective substance could be united as a form with any non-human terrestrial body. None the less, he sometimes seems to be arguing only against the hypothesis that an intellective *soul* might be united with some non-human body as its form. See e.g. 90.1760, where he claims that any non-human body with which an intellective substance could be united as its form would have to be an animal body equipped with organs like those we have.

[15] Like every other educated person in the thirteenth century, Aquinas takes it for granted that the heavenly bodies are made of something not found on earth—a fifth essence (the quintessence, or the ether), quite different from the four familiar elements. And so for purposes of this chapter he expressly sets aside 'what Aristotle thought about *heavenly* bodies—that they are [each] animated by an intellective soul'—something that 'Augustine left in doubt' (90.1759). (See also II.70 and Ch. Eight above, sect. 10.)

[16] I have little knowledge of, and not much interest in, the sources from which Aquinas draws his embryological lore, so when I refer to his account, I don't mean to suggest that anything in it originates with him.

[17] See e.g. 89.1743 (quoted in sect. 6 below); QDV 3.9, ad 9(F) (quoted in n. 26 below).

struation (but evidently retained after conception) must be the female contribution. And since they had no more idea of spermatozoa than of ova, their understandings of the female and the male principles were almost equally wrong (and right). Although the fluids they had identified in both cases turn out not to *be* the starting-points of conception, they do *contain* the single cells that are those starting-points.

A further mistake is hidden in the terminology Aquinas uses. The English word 'semen' is specific as the Latin word *semen* is not: it means seed of any kind. So Aquinas can say that 'from the activity of things of nature nothing can be produced other than the things that actually do come about—e.g. a human being from a human being's semen (*semen*), an olive-tree from an olive-tree's seed (*semen*)' (ST Ia.25.5c). This terminological sameness is technically appropriate from the medieval point of view. It conveys part of the theory of reproduction which Aquinas accepts: formally considered, the male's semen *is* the seed from which the embryo begins to grow; the female contributes the medium required for the seed's transformation into the embryo. As we'll see, he thinks of the maternal medium in human reproduction as much more complex, much more specified, and much more seed-like in itself than is the medium for growing olive-trees from seed; and the human (male) seed conveys less of the new individual in potentiality than does the olive seed. Of course, this mistake is also flagrant, even if understandable. None the less, although Aquinas thinks that 'semen is the starting-point (*principium*) of an animal generated out of semen'[18] (ST Ia.4.1, ad 2), even an up-to-date account would recognize radical differences between the male and female contributions to human conception, and would describe it as taking place when and only when the dynamic (active) spermatozoon penetrates the static (passive) ovum.

With a little good will and a little imagination, I think that we can in principle 'translate' along such lines all of Aquinas's thirteenth-century Aristotelian embryological observations into their

[18] See also 43.1198: 'Certain animals, for instance, are made only out of semen.' Aquinas follows Aristotle in believing that some lower animals—e.g. the maggots that become flies—are generated without semen in the process of putrefaction; see e.g. ST Ia.71.1, ad 1; 91.2, ad 2; 92.1c; 118.1, sc. And, of course, some lower animals about which Aristotle and Aquinas could not have known—e.g. amoebas—really are generated asexually.

corrected modern equivalents.[19] In the conviction that replacing his observations with their more precise counterparts would make no substantive difference to the points he's intent on establishing, I'll almost always deal with his observations as they stand, rather than trying to recast them in modern terms. Of course, such an approach makes sense only because Aquinas's principal concern here is not to *provide* an account of human reproduction and pre-natal development, but simply to use the best embryology available to him as the context in which to develop his own metaphysical account of the uniting of the human soul with the foetal body. As his account develops, we'll see that the embryological propositions on which he bases it are all general enough to be readily interpreted in modern terms without damaging that basis. I think that we'll also see that his account of the origin of an individual human being saves the embryological appearances, and that any genuine difficulties in his account are philosophical rather than scientific.

3. Aquinas's basic argument regarding the origin of an individual human being

Having successfully argued against various theories maintaining that individual human souls exist before they are united with bodies, Aquinas turns to investigate, in chapters 86–9, the one remaining alternative, which really was the only plausible hypothesis to begin with: that they begin to exist for the first time during the natural process of human generation. He's still developing the details of his account of the human soul (which began in ch. 56), so he naturally thinks of this part of his investigation as concerned with the origin of an individual human *soul*. But since he argues that it begins to exist only at the instant at which it becomes the substantial form of an individual body, and since only a composite entity with just those components counts as a full-fledged human being, it's quite correct, and sometimes illuminating, to recognize that his more general concern in these chapters is to explain the origin of an individual human being.

For instance, it's easier to appreciate the general line of argu-

---

[19] I certainly don't know enough to make all the translations into contemporary embryological terms myself, but I also don't know of anything in Aquinas's account for which there isn't any currently recognized counterpart.

ment which Aquinas develops in support of his own explanation of this origin if we cast it in those broader terms to begin with. He can then be described as observing that the explanation of the origin of an individual human being is largely the same as the explanation of the origin of an individual member of one of the species of higher animals, although he argues that it can't be entirely the same (II.86). The distinctively human aspect of each human being, he thinks, can be explained only as the result of a special divine contribution to the process of human generation (II.87). Acknowledging that this simple basic argument leaves many *purely* naturalistic explanations of human generation unexamined, he then turns (in ch. 88) to review arguments supporting such explanations, finally developing general and particular rejoinders to those arguments (II.89). Still, for purposes of expounding and evaluating the position he develops in those four chapters, I'll ordinarily follow his lead and carry on the discussion more narrowly in terms of the origin of a human being's distinctively human aspect, its intellective soul.

Aquinas begins chapter 86 by announcing that 'on the basis of things that have already been established, it can be shown that the human soul is not transmitted with the semen, as if sown by means of sexual intercourse' (1706). From his point of view a human soul is, broadly speaking, whatever it is that makes a living human being of what would be a post-human corpse or a pre-human embryo without it. So, if the human soul *were* transmitted with the semen, then the new individual's human soul—the humanness of the new individual—would be the exclusive contribution of the father. Aquinas could argue against that absurdity and still grant what may at first seem plausible: that an individual human soul begins to exist at the instant of human conception, when both parents' contributions are united. However, as we'll see, he means to argue not only that it is not contributed by the father, but also that it does not begin to exist at conception (or for some time thereafter).

Since the new thing that does begin to exist at conception also begins to grow then, and not just as an integral part of the mother's body, it must begin to be alive in its own right at the instant of conception, at least in the sense of having a nutritive/vegetative soul of its own. Now 'a nutritive (and [eventually] a sensory) soul is generated through the generation of the body', and 'the transmission of semen is directed to the generation of the body',[20] so that it is correct to say that 'the nutritive (and [eventually] the sensory) soul begins to exist through the transmission of the semen' (86.1707). All the same, even that most primitive sort of soul is not transmitted from the male in the semen because, Aquinas insists, there is no soul in the semen itself.[21] That denial leaves him with at least two questions to answer.

First, isn't the semen itself living (and thus animate, or en-souled)?[22] As we've seen, Aquinas understands every cell of a living creature's body to be living, considered just as such, because the creature's single substantial form or soul informs absolutely all of its body.[23] Consequently, the semen, while it is still part of the father's body, is in that way living, informed by the father's human soul. But, of course, in order to contribute to conception, it must leave the father's body, and that physical separation makes a big theoretical difference in Aquinas's account. His word for emission is not the expected *emissio*, but *divisio* or, most often, *decisio* (separation, loss, or fission).[24] Those unexpected words help to emphasize the metaphysical distinction between the semen as a living part of the father's body and the semen on its own, before conception occurs. In the interval between having been animated

---

[20] See also the apparently stronger claim in 86.1712: 'the transmission of the semen is the proper cause of the generation of the body'.

[21] See e.g. QDV 3.9, ad 9(F): 'from the beginning of its separation (*decisionis*) [from the male] there is no soul in the semen, but rather a power of soul (*virtus animae*) . . . Now that power of soul acts by arranging matter and forming it for taking on [a human] soul.'

[22] See e.g. the following argument, which Aquinas attributes to Gregory of Nyssa (88.1733): 'Anything is living only in virtue of a soul, and the semen is living. This is clear on the basis of three considerations. First, of course, because it is fissioned off (*deciditur*) from a living being. Second, because vital heat and the operation of life appear in the semen, and they are signs of a living thing. Third, because if plants' seeds (*semina*) that are dropped to the ground did not have life in themselves, they could not get the heat they need to live from the soil, which is soulless. Therefore, there is soul in the semen. And so the soul takes its origin from the fissioning off (*decisione*) of the semen.'

[23] See Ch. Nine above, sect. 2b, where this passage from QDA 10c is quoted: 'The soul, in so far as it is the form of the body, is not united with the whole body through the intermediary of some part of the body, but rather with the whole body without any intermediary, since it is the form both of the whole body and of each and every part of it.'

[24] See n. 22 above. See also e.g. 65.1432: 'a child is generated by a father through bodily fission (*decisionem*)'; 80.1618, quoted in sect. 8 below; 88.1726, 1728*b*, 1731, 1732, and 1734, all quoted in sect. 5 below; also 89.1738, 1739, and 1740*a*, the last of which is quoted in sect. 6 below.

by the father's soul and 'before being animated' by the nutritive soul of the new living being, 'the [emitted] semen is living only potentially, and it is [later] made actually living by means of the soul' (57.1339).[25] Between emission and conception the semen is only potentially a living thing, and, despite the way Aquinas expresses himself here, the semen itself never again becomes actually living. Something else is animated and actually living as soon as the semen is united with the mother's blood (or the ovum is fertilized), but the *semen* is not actually living at that point, because it has been corrupted in the union.[26]

Still, there is some sense in describing both the emitted semen and the mother's contribution to conception as potentially living, as can be seen by looking at what Aquinas would say in answer to this second question: If the semen doesn't transmit a bit of the father's soul, and isn't in any other way the direct source of the new individual's soul, then what *is* the source of the first, nutritive soul in the newly conceived embryo? I think that Aquinas's most promising answer to that question may be the one he gives in ST Ia.118.1, ad 4: 'In the higher animals, which are generated by means of sexual intercourse, there is an active power in the semen of the male (according to the Philosopher in *Generation of Animals* [II 3–4: 736a24 ff.]), while the *matter* of the foetus is what is contributed by the female. Indeed, in that matter there is, right from the beginning (*statim a principio*), a vegetative soul—not of course in *second* actuality, but in *first* actuality, the way the sensory soul is in animals that are asleep.[27] But when it begins to take in

---

[25] See Ch. Eight above, n. 70. See also 83.1658: 'actuality (*actus*), although it is naturally prior to potentiality, is temporally posterior to potentiality in one and the same thing; for something is moved from potentiality to actuality. Therefore, the semen, which is potentially alive, existed before there was a soul, which is the *actus* of life.'

[26] See e.g. QDV 3.9, ad 9(F): 'In the generation of an animal, however, various substantial forms appear, since first the sperm (*sperma*) appears, and then the blood, and so on until there is the form of a human being or an animal. So this sort of generation is not simple, but includes in itself several generations and corruptions.' Also ST Ia.118.2, ad 2: 'since the generation of one thing is always the corruption of another, it is necessary to say, both in the case of a human being and in the case of other animals, that when a more perfect form arrives, the corruption of the earlier form occurs, but in such a way that the next form has whatever the first one had and more besides. In that way, through many generations and corruptions, the final substantial form is arrived at, in the case of a human being as in the case of other animals.'

[27] On first and second actuality, see Ch. Two above, sect. 3. As the analogy here shows, a soul in first actuality *is* a *soul*: a sleeping animal continues to have an *actual*

nourishment'—or, for that matter, when it begins to grow—'then it is already in actual operation', and therefore in second actuality. 'Therefore, that sort of matter is transmuted by the power that is in the male's semen.' From Aquinas's point of view, then, the first effect of the union of the male and female contributions to conception is the beginning of a new life at the most primitive level, the level at which a pre-human nutritive soul is the newly living thing's substantial form. That's a point of view most of us share, whether or not we'd express it in those terms. What's more, the already formed, proximate matter supplied by the female is described as involving an actual, but inert, nutritive soul that begins actual operation as soon as it is 'transmuted by the power that is in the male's semen'—a description that translates easily into a correct account of the fertilization of an ovum by a spermatozoon. Aquinas's more detailed understanding of human reproduction, then, would be misleadingly summarized as the male's supplying the form of the new individual while the female supplies only its matter. Far from supplying the form of the new human being (its intellective soul), the male doesn't supply even the form—the nutritive soul—of the not yet fully human, not yet even fully animal, entity that begins to live at the instant of conception. Instead, a power in the semen brings into second actuality a nutritive soul latent in the female contribution.[28]

The second, most elaborate of Aquinas's six arguments in support of his main thesis (that the human soul of the new individual is not transmitted with the semen) is also the most instructive as regards his position generally. 'If a human soul did begin to exist

---

sensory soul, just not an *actually operating* sensory soul. So the nutritive soul in first actuality that he attributes to the maternal material is already an actual soul, and the active power of the semen is what makes it operative for the first time. And it seems to fit the rest of Aquinas's account to say that this nutritive soul begins to *animate*, to make something begin to live, only when it is transmuted by the active power in the semen. (In this passage Aquinas appears to be disagreeing with Aristotle, who claims that 'While the body is from the female, it is the soul that is from the male, for the soul is the substance of a particular body' (*Generation of Animals* II 4, 738b25). See also II 3, 737a28: 'the menstrual fluids are semen, only not pure; for there is only one thing they do not have in them, the principle of soul'.)

[28] See also ST Ia.118.2, ad 2: 'Some people have said that the vital operations that appear in the embryo are not from its soul but rather from the mother's soul, or from the formative power that is in the semen. Each of those views is false. For vital operations such as sensing, taking nourishment, and growing cannot be from an external source. So we have to say that a nutritive soul pre-exists in the embryo from the beginning, but afterwards a sensory soul, and eventually an intellective soul.'

through the transmission of the semen, that could happen in one of only two ways. First, in such a way that a human soul would be understood to exist in the semen actually, as if divided *per accidens* from the *soul* of the generator as the semen is divided from his *body*. We do observe something of this sort in the case of earth-worms, which go on living when they have been separated (*decisa*); in them there is one soul in actuality and many in potentiality. When the body of such an animal has been divided, a soul begins to exist in actuality in each living part' (86.1708*a–b*). Aquinas says that a (sensory) soul *begins* to exist in actuality in *each* of the two animals resulting from the division of the original earthworm, pre-sumably because he thinks of this division as borrowing from the soul that had been animating the original, uncut worm, so that where we have a new plurality of living bodies we also have a plurality of new souls. So he claims that anyone maintaining this first opposing view must be prepared to understand the emission of the semen as involving the fissioning of the generator's soul, which would have to result in at least one new human soul.[29] In that respect, dividing the semen from the living body of which it was an integral part would have to be seen as instructively like dividing one worm into two.

Since it is only the intellective soul whose transmission is at issue here, and 'since the intellective soul is the most perfect of souls and has the most power', Aquinas has a ready argument against this first opposing view. 'What is properly perfectible by such a soul is a body that has great diversity in its organs, through which it can carry out such a soul's many different operations. So an intellective soul cannot be produced in actuality in the separated semen, be-cause not even the souls of the higher non-human animals are pluralized through fission (as does happen in the case of earth-worms)' (1708*d*). The view he's rejecting is untenable just because the semen, to all appearances, is corporeally much too uncompli-cated, too unorganized to take on an intellective soul as its substan-tial form. The line taken in this refutation already shows that anything properly perfectible by a human soul before birth could only be a foetal body at an advanced stage of development.

---

[29] I find it hard to believe that Aquinas would want to maintain that in the human case, too, 'the soul of the generator' would be so altered by this fission as to count as new. This first opposing view has enough genuine troubles without any such implausible additions.

'In the other way' in which it could happen that a human soul did begin to exist through the transmission of the semen, 'a power productive of an intellective soul would be understood to exist in the semen, so that in this way an intellective soul would be supposed to exist in the semen virtually, but not actually [as in the first opposing view]' (1708c). For this second, less radical opposing view Aquinas offers no example like the poor earthworm(s), but I think that the (nutritive) soul of a new olive-tree could be said to exist 'virtually, but not actually' in the seed dropped by a mature olive-tree.[30] Certainly the dirt, water, air, and light required to start the seed growing make nothing like so specific a contribution to the existence of the new individual as does the nutritive soul that Aquinas says pre-exists in first actuality in the human female.

But this second opposing view, Aquinas argues, 'is also impossible':

For the active power that is in the semen contributes actively (*agit*) to the generation of an animal by transmuting matter,[31] since a power that exists in matter [in this case, in the matter of the semen] cannot act in any other way. But every form that begins to exist through the transmuting of matter has an existence that is dependent on matter,   5
for the transmuting of matter brings it from potentiality to actuality and so has its terminus in the matter's *actual* existence, which occurs through its union with the form. So if the form's existence also begins by this means, then the form's existence will occur only in its being united with matter, and in that way it will be dependent on matter for   10
its existence. Therefore, if a human soul is brought into existence

---

[30] See also this beginning of an argument that Aquinas attributes to Gregory of Nyssa (88.1730): 'In all things that are generated from seed, all the parts of the generated thing are contained together in the seed virtually, even though they do not appear actually. For example, we observe that in a grain of wheat (or in any other seed) the plant together with stem, joints, fruit, and tassels are contained in the primitive seed, and that afterwards the seed is opened up and revealed on the way to completion by a sort of natural consequence, without taking into account anything extrinsic.' For the end of this argument, see n. 44 below.

[31] Both the Leonine and the Marietti edns. have *transmutando corpus* (by transmuting a body), and no variants are cited in the Leonine edn. For two reasons, I'm reading *materiam* in place of *corpus*. First, there is no obviously identifiable body for the semen to transmute in the generation of an animal. I suppose that the blood contributed by the female might qualify, but not so obviously as to require no special identification. Second, the rest of Aquinas's rejoinder refers more than once to a transmutation of matter, never to a transmutation of a body (see lines 4–5).

through the active power that is in the semen, it follows that its existence is dependent on matter, like the existence of other, material forms. The contrary of this was shown earlier.[32]

The description of the generative process in lines 1–11 is one that Aquinas thoroughly subscribes to, on the basis of considerations some of which we've already seen. Here he puts it in terms of the generation of a non-human animal, because that sort of generation is *entirely* accounted for in terms of the transmuting of matter by powers that exist in matter. But everything in this description applies also to the early stages of the generation of a human being, as we've begun to see. The *nutritive* soul that animates the new living thing is a form that begins to exist fully (i.e. in second actuality) through the semen's transmuting of the matter contributed by the human female, and it has an existence that is dependent on matter (lines 4–5). And, as we'll see, the sensory soul in the not yet fully human embryo, which supersedes the nutritive soul as its single substantial form, is also a *material* form, and its development is also explained in purely material terms. So the only obstacle to Aquinas's subscribing to this view as a *complete* account of the origin of a human being is intellect's organlessness, presented tersely here in line 14's reference to earlier results.[33] Having rebutted both of what he takes to be the only possible opposing views, Aquinas is entitled to conclude, 'Therefore, in *no* way is an

[32] In such passages as 68.1459a–b: 'However, above all those forms is found a form that is like the higher substances even as regards its kind of cognition, which is intellection; and in that respect it is capable of an operation that is carried out entirely without a bodily organ. That form is the intellective soul; for intellection is not carried out through any bodily organ. So the principle by which a human being intellectively cognizes—which is the intellective soul, which also surpasses the condition of a material body—is not totally contained by matter or immersed in it, as are other, material forms. This is shown by its intellective operation, in which corporeal matter does not share. None the less, since a human soul's intellection needs powers that operate through certain bodily organs—viz. imagination and sensation—that very fact shows that it is naturally united with the body in order to complete the human species'—i.e. in order to complete the specification of the foetus as human.

[33] Intellect's organlessness also plays a pivotal role in three other of the six arguments in support of ch. 86's thesis: (1707) 'the operation of the intellective soul is not carried out through a bodily organ (as was established earlier)'; (1709) 'the intellective soul transcends the entire capacity of matter, because it has an operation without matter (as was shown earlier)'; (1710) 'the intellective soul surpasses the whole genus of bodies, since it has an operation elevated above all bodies—viz. intellection'.

intellective soul brought into being through the transmission of the semen' (1708*e*).

4. Particular creation as the source of a human soul's existence

Aquinas begins chapter 87 with the familiar sort of claim that the new chapter's thesis 'can be shown on the basis of things that have been said' (1714). Of course, this sort of claim is familiar in SCG just because it's the precisely appropriate formula with which to introduce each succeeding thesis in Aquinas's systematically developed natural theology. But in this case I want to review the relevant things that have been said, partly because I haven't discussed all of them in detail here, and partly because the thesis of chapter 87 is important and disputable. The thesis is that 'God alone brings a human soul into existence' (1714).

Among the things already said from which Aquinas claims to be able to prove this thesis, the most generally relevant is that 'everything whose substance is not its existence has an originator of its existence (as was shown above [in II.15]). But the human soul is not its own existence, since that [status] belongs to God alone (as was shown above [in I.22 and II.15]).[34] Therefore, it has an active cause of its existence' (87.1716). So a human soul is the sort of thing that must be brought into existence at some time by something else. For, as Aquinas has already argued in detail, it 'does begin to exist for the first time, since it is not eternal . . . as was shown earlier' (1715), in chapters 83 and 84.[35]

Next, 'everything that is brought into existence is either [1] generated ([a] *per se* or [b] *per accidens*) or [2] created' (1715). On the plausible supposition that those alternatives exhaust the possibilities, the next and largest step, which Aquinas promptly takes, is to show that everything other than (2) has already been ruled out as regards souls. It's easier to take that step with him if we first glance back at things he's already said about generation generally—e.g. that 'generation is a way into existence', and that 'the terminus of generation is a form . . . only because a form brings about exist-

---

[34] See TMOT, Ch. Four, sect. 4.   [35] See sect. 2 above, esp. n. 13.

ence' for a material entity when it is taken on by matter (I.26.242), since 'nothing is generated from what is entirely non-existent' (55.1300), and 'all generation is from a contrary and is based on matter' (42.1189).

Now, since a human soul is a form, and since typically 'forms . . . are made *per accidens* when composites are made' (1716), it makes sense to ask first about possibility (1b), that a human soul is generated *per accidens*. In that case it would 'not have existence *per se*, but only along with something else'—i.e. *per accidens*—and so it would be 'made not *per se*, but when that other thing is made, as the form of a fire is made when a fire is generated' (ibid.), or as the form of an olive-tree is made *per accidens* when an olive-tree is generated *per se*. (That material forms are generated *per accidens* in this way follows from Aquinas's Aristotelian view of forms as having real existence only in so far as they inform real substances.) However, a human soul is the form of a human body, and so if it is generated *per accidens* as all other forms of composites are, 'it would be generated through the generation of the body, which stems from the active power of the semen' (1715). And that is just what Aquinas has been arguing is impossible (in II.86).

What precludes *per accidens* generation of the form that is a human soul is, of course, implied in Aquinas's hypothesis SFB, which maintains not only that a human soul can be appropriately united with a body only by being the substantial form of that body, but also that the soul is an intellective substance.[36] As Aquinas puts it here, 'among [all] other forms, the human soul has this proprium,[37] that it is subsistent in its own existence' (1716). Rather than deriving its existence from the body whose form it is, the human soul 'shares with the body the existence that it has proper to itself' (ibid.), as he has already argued.[38] 'Therefore, a soul has its

[36] On hypothesis SFB, see Ch. Eight above, sect. 5; also Ch. Nine above, sect. 2.

[37] A proprium is a characteristic that is symptomatic of the essence of the thing that has it without being itself a component of the essence. The paradigm is the rational animal's capacity for laughter.

[38] See e.g. 68.1452: 'existence belongs to corporeal matter as to a recipient and to a subject raised up to something higher; but existence belongs to an intellective substance as to its principle and is in keeping with the very nature of intellective substance. Therefore, nothing prevents an intellective substance from being a human body's form, which is the human soul.'

being-made *per se*, contrary to the manner of other forms, which are made *per accidens* when composites are made' (ibid.).

However, although a human soul can be *made per se*, it can't be *generated per se*. *Per se* generation is the way a primary substance (such as an olive-tree) is brought into existence, as the result of some matter's taking on a substantial form contrary to the one it had up to the instant of transformation. The soul can't be generated in that way because it is a subsistent form itself.[39] 'A human soul is not [1a] generated *per se*, since it is not composed of matter and form (as was shown above)' (1715). That the human soul is not an m–f composite was shown generally in chapter 50 ('Intellective substances are immaterial'), and more particularly in chapter 65 ('The soul is not a body').

'But, since a human soul does not have matter as part of itself, it cannot be made *out of* anything, as out of matter. Therefore, we are left with its *being made out of nothing*. So it is created. Therefore, since creating is a work proper to God (as was shown above [in II.21]), it follows that a human soul is created by God, without any intermediaries' (1716). Aquinas may be most concerned here with ruling out the view that angels are intermediary creators of souls (1721), but it's more important to recognize that this denial of his also rules out all natural processes as intermediaries in the making of human souls. That need not mean that each human soul is the result of God's miraculously interrupting the course of nature, but only that the very familiar process of the development of a new human being involves one essential transition that can't be fully explained in purely natural terms—which may, indeed, continue to be true.

---

[39] See also 87.1718: 'Whatever is brought into existence by some agent acquires from it either [1] something that is the principle of existing in such and such a species or [2] absolute existence itself. Now a soul cannot be brought into existence as if [1] it acquired something that is for it a principle of existing—the sort of thing that happens in connection with things composed of matter and form, which are generated in virtue of the fact that they acquire a form in actuality. For a soul has nothing in itself that is for it a principle of existing, since it is a simple substance [i.e. not an m–f composite] (as was shown above [in II.50 and 65]). Therefore, we are left with the conclusion that [2] it is brought into existence only by an agent from which it receives existence absolutely. But existence itself is the proper effect of the first and universal agent. For secondary agents act by impressing on the things made by them likenesses of their own forms, which are [then] the forms of the things that are made. Therefore, a [human] soul can be brought into existence only by the first, universal agent, which is God.'

5. *Other naturalistic explanations of the origin of a human soul*

Aquinas claims that there can't be a thoroughly naturalistic explanation for the origin of new human souls, or human beings, and that, consequently, only particular creation can account for the human reproduction that occurs thousands of times every day all over the world.[40] But the naturalistic explanations which he rules out in chapter 86 in order to prepare the ground for the thesis of particular creation in chapter 87 emphasize the *transmission* of a new soul via the semen, and no such explanation could be translated into an account of human conception that would strike us as worth taking seriously. As a result, Aquinas can seem to have set up his thesis of particular creation and presented it as the only viable alternative before he has completely cleared the ground of attractive rivals. But the way he introduces chapter 88, immediately following the chapter arguing for particular creation, suggests that he acknowledges the problem: 'However, there are certain arguments that are evidently opposed to the claims made earlier' (1722).[41]

In chapter 88 he presents twelve such arguments in support of naturalistic explanations or at least opposed to particular creation. The first four are anonymous. Aquinas attributes the fifth to Apollinaris (of Laodicea), and the final seven to Gregory of Nyssa. Since all these arguments are intended to support views that are prima facie easier to accept than Aquinas's particular-creation thesis, it would be a tactical mistake to pick out only the ones that

[40] One of the arguments Aquinas presents in support of the opposing thesis that all individual human souls have existed from the beginning of creation depends on the apparently embarrassing circumstance of such unremitting, piecemeal creation in a world that Scripture seems to present as completed on the seventh day. See 82.1653 and Aquinas's rejoinder to it in 83.1689.

[41] Even allowing for the focus on transmission in ch. 86, I'm not sure why he introduces this much more thorough survey only *after* he's already argued that the human soul *must* be brought into existence directly by God. Establishing the gist of his own position before even introducing the most formidable opposing arguments runs counter to his usual pattern of the disputed question (see Ch. Eight above, sect. 6). But, as we'll see, he also does something very much like this in chs. 79–81, where he first argues for incorruptibility (79), and only then introduces opposing arguments (80) and rebuts them (81). And the first part of ch. 82 (1630–7) looks like a complete standard-form chapter in its own right, presenting arguments in support of the thesis stated in 1630 and ending, in 1635–7, with a review of religious and philosophical authorities. But then the second part of the chapter (1638–49) consists of an argument for the contrary thesis followed by a detailed refutation of it.

I think (or that Aquinas thinks) are the most formidable, ignoring all the others. So I will at least briefly describe each of them, beginning with those that are most unlikely to offer attractive alternatives.

In the fifth argument (88.1727), Apollinaris reportedly argues against particular creation because it would involve God's occasionally co-operating with illicit sexual intercourse.[42] The eleventh argument (1733) is one I quoted earlier as an example of grounds on which someone might (or actually did) argue that the semen is animate,[43] and I've already quoted the first part of the eighth argument (1730) as a good example of the medieval understanding of a plant's being incorporated in a seed virtually.[44] The sixth argument (1728b) reasons that since 'from a soul and a body is made one thing—i.e. one human being', and since 'the body begins to be made in connection with the separation of the semen', it follows that 'the soul, too, is brought into existence through the separation of the semen'. Otherwise, 'one and the same thing would be both before and after itself, which is evidently impossible'. The seventh argument (1729) also relies on the unity of the human being and on the semen as the source of the body: 'The operation of an agent that brings into existence not a whole thing but only one or another part of it is evidently imperfect. Therefore, if God were to bring the soul into existence while the body was formed by the power of the semen', God would be performing an imperfect operation. 'This is clearly absurd. Therefore, the soul and body of a human being is produced by one and the same cause. But it is certain that a human being's body is produced by the power of the semen. Therefore, the soul also.'

Aquinas offers particular rejoinders to each of these five arguments,[45] along with all the others. But none of these five strikes me

---

[42] But, as Aquinas points out in his rejoinder (89.1751), all that is illicit in such cases is the volition of at least one of the participants. The special-creation thesis requires God's co-operation only with the occasionally resultant natural process of reproduction, which is itself good.   [43] See n. 22 above.

[44] See n. 30 above. The remainder of the eighth argument aims at establishing a naturalistic origin for the human soul by assuming an essential likeness between plant seeds and human semen: 'But it is certain that the soul is a part of a human being. Therefore, the human soul is contained virtually in the semen of a human being and does not get its start from any external cause.'

[45] For the rejoinders, see 89.1751 (rejoinder to 88.1727; cf. ST Ia.118.2, ad 5), 89.1757 (rejoinder to 88.1733), 89.1754 (rejoinder to 88.1730), 89.1752 (rejoinder to 88.1728b), and 89.1753 (rejoinder to 88.1729).

as offering formidable opposition to his particular-creation thesis or an interesting naturalistic explanation as an alternative. The remaining seven arguments do deserve a closer look, however, especially because they tend to support, or are at least compatible with, accounts of pre-natal human development that are bound to look more plausible to late twentieth-century readers. I'll review the remaining three arguments attributed to Gregory of Nyssa before turning to the four anonymous arguments.

The twelfth argument (88.1734) acquires strength by beginning with parts of the account which Aquinas endorses: 'If the soul does not exist before the body (as was shown [in II.83]) and does not begin to exist along with the separation of the semen [as was argued in II.86], it follows that the body is formed first, and the newly created soul is infused into it later'—just what Aquinas himself maintains. 'But if that's true, then it follows further that the soul exists for the sake of (*propter*) the body, since we find that what exists for the sake of something else is later than it—like clothes that are made for someone. But that's false, since the body exists, rather, for the sake of the soul', as Aquinas would agree. 'Therefore, it must be said that the soul originated simultaneously with the separation of the semen.' Aquinas's rejoinder (89.1758) rests on a distinction between two ways in which X is properly said to be for the sake of Y: 'In one way, for the sake of its operation, its preservation, or anything of that sort that *depends on* its being.' If X is for the sake of Y in this first way, then X is posterior to Y both temporally and naturally, 'just like clothes, for the sake of a person, and tools, for the sake of an artisan' are temporally and naturally posterior to those for whom they are made. And, he points out, the soul *would* be for the sake of the body in this first way if the soul only *used* the body (as the Platonists suppose) and were not also its *form*: 'if it were not the case that from the soul and body was made *one thing as regards being*'.[46] X is for the sake of Y in the second way if X is not merely for the sake of Y's operation, or preservation, but for the sake of Y's very *being*. Having argued at length that the soul is the form of the body, Aquinas is entitled to adopt this second sense. 'What is for the sake of something else in *this* way is *temporally prior* and naturally posterior to it. It is in this way that the body is for the sake of the soul—in the way that all matter is for

[46] See Ch. Eight above, esp. sects. 8 and 9.

the sake of form.' The distinction he relies on is reasonable and recognizable, although his assimilation of the body–soul relationship to the *standard* matter–form relationship here seems misleadingly strong, given other things he needs to claim regarding the soul.

The tenth argument (88.1732) is like the twelfth in depending on a vague but broadly relevant ordering relationship: 'Whatever is configured to something is constituted by the action of that to which it is configured, as the wax that is configured to a seal takes on that configuration from the impression of the seal. But it's obvious that the body of a human being, and of any animal, is configured to its own soul, since the disposition of the [body's] organs is such as is suited to the operations of the soul that are to be carried out through them. Therefore, the body is formed by the action of the soul.' And anyone who understands that the soul—the form or nature of the human being—must in that way govern the foetal body's development can also understand 'why Aristotle says in *De anima* II [4, 415b21–2] that the soul is the efficient cause of the body.[47] But it wouldn't be so unless the soul was in the semen, since the body is constituted through the power that is in the semen. Therefore, a human soul is in a human being's semen, and so it originates from the separation of the semen.'

Of course Aquinas rejects that conclusion, but, as in his rejoinder to the twelfth argument, he distinguishes two senses of the ordering relationship, in one of which the premises of this argument are true (89.1756):

That the [foetal] body is configured to the soul and that the soul therefore prepares a body like itself is indeed partly true, but also partly false. For if that claim is understood as regards the soul of the *generator*, then what it says is true; but it's false if it is understood as regards the soul of what is *generated*. For the body, as far as its first and principal parts are concerned, is formed not by the power (*virtute*) of the soul of what is generated but by the power of the soul of the generator (as was proved above [in 89.1742]). For all matter is also likewise configured to its form. Still, this configuration is effected not by the action of what is generated but by the action of the generator's form.

The forming of the body even 'as far as its first and principal parts

---

[47] What Aristotle actually says in this passage is that 'the soul is also the cause of the living body as the original source of local motion'.

are concerned' is ascribed to the human nature of the generator because that embryonic body must be, from its very beginning, of such a sort that its natural development eventuates in the only kind of body that can be the proper subject of an intellective soul, a pre-human body that counts as fully human only when an intellective soul has become its substantial form. The human soul of the generator is in that way what sets the newly generated body on the developmental track that leads to its specification as fully human, presumably because the semen produced by a generator with a human soul could not contribute to the conception of a body susceptible to any other culminating development. And it is in just that uniquely orientating, preparatory way that the newly developing pre-human body is configured to the generator's soul.[48] If it had been generated by something that had a non-human soul, it would be impossible for it to develop to the stage of being susceptible of taking on a human soul of its own, and thereby to acquire fully human status in its own right. And since the merely nutritive soul of what is newly generated could not itself supply specification in this way, it is false to say that the embryonic body is configured to the soul of what is generated, or that that soul prepares a body like itself.[49] 'Therefore, we are left with the conclusion that the formation of the body, especially as far as its first and principal parts are concerned, is not from the soul of what is generated, or from a formative power acting out of the force of what is generated, but from a formative power acting out of the force of the father's generative soul—a power whose operation is to make something that is [eventually] like the generator in its species' (89.1742c). None the less, as we'll see, the pre-human souls that are, successively, the first and second substantial forms of the foetus do make essential contributions to preparing the body for its final, human soul.

[48] What Aquinas means here by 'the generator' is clearly the father alone. See e.g. 89.1742a: the formative power that is in the semen 'is responsible for the formation of the body in so far as it acts by the power of the soul of the father (to whom generation is attributed as to the principal agent), and not by the power of the soul of what is conceived, even after a soul exists in it; for what is conceived does not generate itself, but is generated by the father'. (See also 89.1742c, quoted below.) But, of course, what he has to say about the generator's contribution makes good sense only if both parents are thought of as the generator. And some of what he says elsewhere, especially in ST Ia.118.1, ad 4 (see sect. 3 above), strongly suggests that thinking along that line would not run counter to everything else he thinks about these topics.

[49] Aquinas dispels this hypothesis in detail in 89.1742b.

The ninth opposing argument (88.1731) draws on those contributions in ways that seem at first to conform to Aquinas's own view of
the stages of pre-natal development:

> Things that are found to have the same development and the same termi-
> nus [of development] must have the same originating source (*originis
> principium*). But in the generation of a human being we do find the same
> development of body and soul, and the same terminus. For the operations
> of the soul are manifested more and more as the shaping and growth of the
> [bodily] members proceeds, since the operation of a nutritive soul appears
> first, the operation of a sensory soul afterwards, and finally, when the
> [foetal] body has been completed, the operation of an intellective soul.
> Therefore, the source of the body and of the soul is one and the same. But
> the originating source of the body is through the separation of the semen,
> and therefore so is the originating source of the soul.

The fact that this argument assigns various stages of foetal development to various souls rather than emphasizing the continuity of
that development seems to play into Aquinas's hand, but he takes
no advantage of it in his rejoinder (89.1755). Instead, he quite
properly rejects the general principle on which the argument is
founded, observing that 'the fact that the operations of the soul
seem to develop in the process of human generation just as the
parts of the body develop does *not* show that the human soul and
the [foetal] body have the same source'.[50] What that fact *does* show,
he says, is 'that a disposition of the parts of the body is necessary for
the soul's operation'. And, of course, that is just what his thesis
maintains: that the human soul is infused by particular creation as
soon as the necessary disposition of parts has been achieved in the
natural course of pre-human foetal development.

Aquinas may have thought of the first four (anonymous) opposing arguments he presents in chapter 88 as especially important,
since he later uses versions of them as objections in ST Ia.118.2
('Is the intellective soul caused by the semen?').[51] Like the ninth
argument, which we've just examined, the third of these arguments
(1725) rests on a dubious general principle: 'Since the soul is the

---

[50] Aquinas's rejection of this principle has been recently confirmed. Two sheep
may have 'the same development and the same terminus [of development]' even
though one has been reproduced in the ordinary way and the other has been cloned.

[51] The ST article includes five objections. Obj. 1 is based on a biblical passage; obj.
2 parallels the first two arguments (1723 and 1724) in SCG II.88; obj. 3 parallels the
third (1725); obj. 4, the fourth (1726). Obj. 5 is a version of the fifth (Apollinarian)
argument (1727).

form of the body, it is united with the body in accordance with the soul's own being. But things that are one in being are the terminus of a single action of a single agent. For if the agents are distinct, and their actions are consequently distinct, it will follow that the things that are made [by them] are distinct in being. Therefore, the being of the soul and body must be the terminus of a single agent's single action. But it is certain that the body is made through an action of the power that is in the semen. Therefore, the soul that is its form is from that same power, and not from a separate agent.'[52] A correct understanding of sexual reproduction would provide a precisely relevant counter-instance to the principle that 'things that are one in being are the terminus of a single action of a single agent'. But, of course, that is not Aquinas's counter-instance. The principle 'that the actions of distinct agents do not terminate in one single thing's having been made must be understood as regards distinct agents that are *not* in an ordered relationship, since distinct agents *must* have a single effect if they *are* in an ordered relationship to one another' (89.1749).[53] Shakespeare and his pen are distinct agents in an ordered relationship. If the word 'live' appears in his manuscript where he thought he was writing 'love', the ordinary ordered relationship between him and his pen has been momentarily disrupted. 'For the primary agent cause [in an ordered series of causes] acts on the effect of a secondary agent cause more powerfully (*vehementius*) than even that secondary cause itself. (That's why we observe that an effect that is brought about by a principal agent through an instrument is attributed more properly to the principal agent than to the instrument.) It sometimes happens, however, that the principal agent's action pertains to something in what is done to which the action of the instrument does not pertain' (ibid.). The words Shakespeare writes, attributed more properly to him than to the pen with which he writes them, are, none the less, also written by his pen. But the action of his pen pertains not at all to the fact that he gives those words the form of a sonnet.[54] Now

[52] Cf. ST Ia.118.2, obj. 3: 'It is one and the same agent the action of which is terminated in the form and matter; otherwise something unconditionally one would not be made out of form and matter. But an intellective soul is the form of a human body, which is formed through the power of the semen. Therefore, the intellective soul, too, is caused through the power of the semen.'

[53] On ordered series of efficient (or agent) causes, see Ch. Two above, sect. 8.

[54] Aquinas's own example at this point in his rejoinder is drawn from antiquated natural science.

'every active power of nature', including the power of the semen, 'is related to God as an instrument is related to a primary and principal agent . . . Therefore, a human being's body is formed at once both by the power of God as the principal and primary agent and also by the power of the semen as a secondary agent. However, God's [direct] action produces the human soul, which the power of the semen cannot produce. Instead, the power of the semen disposes [matter] for it' (ibid.).[55] And, as we've seen, this disposition of matter for the human soul includes the natural generation of first a (pre-human) nutritive and then a (pre-human) sensory soul as succeeding substantial forms of the developing foetal body.[56]

The fourth opposing argument (88.1726) resembles the tenth (1732, considered above) in focusing on the specification of the newly generated thing. 'A human being generates something like itself through the power that is in the separated semen. But every univocal agent generates something like itself in species in virtue of the fact that it causes the form of what is generated, the form from which the generated thing gets its species. Therefore, the human soul, the source of a human being's species, is produced by the power that is in the semen.'[57] This simple argument gains strength from its dependence on a concept of univocal agent causation to which Aquinas himself subscribes and for which he uses biological reproduction as his paradigm.[58] A univocal agent cause C produces an effect E that is, for all its individuating distinctions, the same as C essentially—i.e. the same as C in species. The same form, f, is antecedently in C and consequently in E; f is associated with the same defining characteristic in both C and E; and f is essentially

[55] Cf. ST Ia.118.2, ad 3: 'That argument has its place in connection with distinct agents that are not ordered relative to one another. But if there are many agents that are so ordered, nothing prevents the power of a higher agent from extending all the way to the last form [produced by the combined operation of the ordered series of causes] while the powers of agents lower [in the causal series] extend only to some disposition of the matter. For instance, in the generation of an animal, the power of the semen disposes the matter, but the power of a soul provides the form. But from things already set out [in Ia.105.5 and 110.1] it's clear that the whole of corporeal nature acts as an instrument of a spiritual power, and especially of God's power. And so nothing prevents the [foetal] body's formation being from some corporeal power while the intellective soul is from God alone.'

[56] See 86.1707, quoted in sect. 3 above.

[57] Cf. ST Ia.118.2, obj. 4: 'A human being generates something like itself in species. But the human species is constituted through the rational soul. Therefore, the rational soul is from the generator.'

[58] See e.g. In Met. VII: L8.1444.

realized in the same way and (eventually and for the most part) to the same degree in E as in C.[59] As Aquinas points out, his rejoinder to the third argument (which we've just looked at) prefigures his succinct rejoinder to this fourth one (89.1750): 'A human being generates something like itself in species in so far as the power of its semen operates in such a way as to dispose (*dispositive operatur*) [matter] for the final form, from which a human being gets its species.'[60] There is an important sense, then, in which Aquinas's account of *human* biological reproduction makes it uniquely *not* an instance of univocal agent causation, since particular creation is required to complete the inchoately specifying contribution of the human generator.

The final phrase of 89.1750 (quoted just above)—*ex qua homo speciem sortitur*—suggests that the foetus can correctly be called human for the first time only when it acquires an intellective soul.[61] As we'll see, that suggestion is borne out by many other things Aquinas says in this connection. In some respects it appears to be just what's required by the rest of his account of pre-natal human development, and it's what leads me to characterize the earlier stages of that development as pre-human. But Aquinas sometimes says other things that suggest that the acquisition of an intellective soul is simply the *completion* of the specification process, which begins with conception, as when he describes the infusion of an intellective soul as 'naturally united with the body in order to *complete (ad complendam)* the human species'[62]—i.e. in order to complete the specification of the foetus as finally *fully* human. I'm inclined to think that these two suggestions are simply two aspects—strict and broad—of Aquinas's single account. The development of anything that is pre-human—i.e. not yet human—can culminate or be completed only in what is human—i.e. *fully* human. But, as we'll see, Aquinas has technical reasons for being especially concerned to stress the first, strict aspect of this account.

[59] See also TMOT, 148–50.
[60] Cf. ST Ia.118.2, ad 4: 'A human being generates something like itself in so far as through the power of its semen the matter is disposed to take on a form of that sort.'
[61] See also 88.1726, quoted earlier in the previous paragraph: 'the human soul, the source of a human being's species (*Anima . . . humana, a qua est species hominis*)'.
[62] 68.1459*b*, quoted more fully in n. 32 above. See also e.g. 89.1744*a*, quoted in sect. 6 below, and QDV 3.9, ad 10, quoted in n. 73 below. But see also nn. 77, 79, and 81 below.

6. *The argument from the substantial unity of the human soul*

Of all the arguments for naturalistic explanations that Aquinas presents in opposition to his own particular-creation thesis, the most instructive, and perhaps the most formidable, is fundamentally quite simple. In SCG II this argument occurs in two closely related versions as the first two of the twelve opposing arguments in chapter 88 (1723 and 1724). The corresponding single objection in ST Ia.118.2 is even simpler than either of the SCG versions, but Aquinas provides it with a very elaborate, very informative rejoinder (ad 2). A schematic presentation is the most convenient way to introduce what I take to be the gist of all three versions of this opposing argument.

In the pre-natal development of a human being:

1   There is a sensory (animal) soul before there is an intellective soul.[63]

2   The sensory soul is generated from the semen.[64]

3   The sensory soul is the same as the intellective soul in respect of substance.[65]

∴ 4   Even the intellective soul is generated from the semen.[66]

[63] 'As Aristotle teaches in *Generation of Animals* [II 3, 736b2–4], the foetus is an animal for a period of time before it is a human being' (88.1724); 'the Philosopher says in *Generation of Animals* [II 3, 736b2–4] that the animal [that becomes the human being] and the human being are not made simultaneously, but the animal, having a sensory soul, is made earlier' (118.2, obj. 2). The first version in SCG II (88.1723) has no premiss that parallels the schema's premiss 1 precisely, but this one comes close: 'Since a human being is an animal in so far as it has a sensory soul, and the defining characteristic of animal is univocally suited to a human being and to other animals, a human being's sensory soul evidently belongs to the same genus as the souls of other animals.'

[64] 'A human being's sensory soul, like that of other animals, is brought into existence through a power that is in the semen' (88.1723); 'while the foetus is an animal and not a human being, it has a sensory soul and not an intellective one—a sensory soul that is, no doubt, produced by the active power of the semen, as happens in connection with other animals' (88.1724); 'the sensory soul in a human being, as in other animals, is generated from the semen' (118.2, obj. 2).

[65] 'In a human being the intellective and sensory soul is the same in respect of substance (as was shown above [in II.58])' (88.1723); '[b]ut that same sensory soul is in a state of potentiality for being intellective, just as that animal is in a state of potentiality for being a rational animal—unless, perhaps, one might say that the supervening intellective soul is substantially different from that sensory soul, which has already been disproved [in II.58]' (88.1724); '[a]s was shown above [in Ia.76.3], in a human being there is one and the same soul in respect of substance: intellective, sensory, and nutritive' (118.2, obj. 2).

[66] 'It seems, therefore, that even the intellective soul is produced through the power of the semen' (88.1723); '[i]t seems, therefore, that the substance of

This argument from the substantial unity of the human soul isn't clearly valid on the face of it, but assumptions that would bridge the gap between the premisses and the conclusion aren't hard to grant, and Aquinas doesn't challenge its validity in his rejoinders to it. I will focus on its premisses without questioning its validity. There seems to be no good reason to worry about premiss 1 or premiss 2. Each of them is an integral part of Aquinas's account, and each of them can be readily translated into terms of correct embryology. As for premiss 3, there certainly is a sense in which it, too, is an integral part of Aquinas's account. We've seen him arguing at length in chapter 58 against the Platonist claim that 'in us it is *not* one and the same soul that is intellective, nutritive, and sensory' (1342).[67] If premiss 3 means only that in a human being there is no sensory soul in addition to an intellective soul, then there's no good reason to worry about premiss 3, either. Fully developed human foetuses do of course have sensory faculties, and we know that Aquinas understands them to be included within the intellective soul, as the 'sensory part' of that single human soul. This feature of his account also seems generally unobjectionable.

The difficulty in premiss 3, and in the argument generally, emerges when we ask what accounts for the fact that the faculties included in the developing foetus's earlier, sensory soul are eventually included in its final, intellective soul. One broadly attractive hypothesis is that this inclusion results from the continuous development of the new individual's single soul, paralleling the continuous development of its animated body, and that in the course of that process there comes a time at which the single soul that animates the foetal body beginning with conception can no longer be correctly described as merely sensory but must then and thereafter be characterized as also intellective, or fully human. It's easy to see that this hypothesis of a single soul's continuous development provides the most obvious support for step 4, the conclusion of this argument. So it's not surprising to find that Aquinas is aware of the hypothesis and of its significance for his position.[68] For instance, in

the intellective soul is from the power that is in the semen' (88.1724); '[t]herefore, the intellective soul, too, is caused by the semen' (118.2, obj. 2).

[67] See Ch. Eight above, sect. 9.

[68] This hypothesis of a single soul's continuous development may seem closer to what I'm calling the broad aspect of Aquinas's account, but the two are fundamentally incompatible. Even in its broad aspect Aquinas's account requires three successive souls in pre-natal development.

his rejoinder to the version of this argument in ST Ia.118.2 he reports that 'other people say that that same soul that was at first only vegetative is later developed, through the action of the power that is in the semen, to such a state that it becomes sensory as well, and is at length developed to such a state that it itself becomes intellective as well' (ad 2).[69]

Other people adopt the hypothesis of a single soul's continuous development, but not, of course, Aquinas himself. This hypothesis is contrary to his own theory of the foetus's acquisition of a human soul, as he shows succinctly but clearly in his rejoinder to the second version of this argument in chapter 88 (1724). The argument, he claims, 'does *not* show that the rational soul is propagated along with the semen'. And it fails just because 'the sensory soul in virtue of which what was conceived was an animal *does not remain*. Instead, it is *succeeded* by a soul that is at once sensory and intellective, on the basis of which what was conceived is an animal and a human being at once' (89.1748). He adds that this is clear from things that have been said. But before looking at relevant things he has already said, it will be helpful to consider one or two generally accessible reasons why Aquinas or anyone else might find his radical-replacement hypothesis more plausible than the hypothesis of a single soul's continuous development.

---

[69] See also 89.1740a: 'Other people say that even though the soul is not in the semen actually from the beginning of its separation but [only] potentially (*virtute*) (because of its lack of organs), yet this very power of the semen—the semen being a body that is capable of the development of organs (*organizabile*) although not yet equipped with them—is, proportionally to the semen, a soul in potentiality but not in actuality. And because plant life requires fewer organs than animal life, as soon as the development of organs in the semen is sufficient for plant life, the [seminal] power mentioned above becomes a vegetative soul. Later, when the organs have been more developed and multiplied, the same power is developed so that it is a sensory soul. And finally, when the form of the organs has been perfected, that same soul is made rational.' In both these passages Aquinas is concerned with only one particular version of the hypothesis of a single soul's continuous growth, the distinguishing details of which needn't concern us. The passage from ST Ia.118.2, ad 2, goes on in this way: '—not, indeed, through the active power of the semen, but through the power of a higher agent: viz. the power of God, illuminating it from outside. And it is for this reason that the Philosopher says [*Generation of Animals* II 3, 736b27–8] that intellect comes from what is extrinsic.' And 89.1740a concludes in these words: '—not, indeed, through the action of the seminal power, but by the influence of an external agent. They suppose that it is for this reason that Aristotle said, in *Generation of Animals* [II 3, 736b27–8], that intellect is from something extrinsic.' (In that passage Aristotle says: 'It remains, then, for the reason alone so to enter [the developing foetus] and alone to be divine, for no bodily activity has any connection with the activity of reason.')

Two versions of the argument we're considering cite Aristotle's claim that 'the foetus is an animal for a period of time before it is a human being',[70] a claim that Aquinas certainly accepts.[71] In the setting established by that claim he would have some reason to think that radical replacement is the only appropriate way for the foetus to become human if he thought either (a) that the foetus belongs to *a non-human species* within the genus animal during that second pre-human stage of its development, or (b) that, even if the foetus belongs to the genus animal, it is a full-fledged member of *no species at all* until it acquires a human soul. Alternative (a) is extremely unlikely because, as we've seen, Aquinas works at ascribing to the 'formative power' of 'the generator' a kind of inchoate, orientating, preliminary specification of the embryo during the two pre-human stages of its development.[72] Besides, there certainly are no otherwise recognized (vegetable or) non-human animal species to which the eventually fully human foetus could be assigned during either of those two stages.

None the less, in at least one of the relevant things he has already said, Aquinas might be read as adopting some form of alternative (a). Having claimed that the formative power of the generator continues to function 'from the beginning of the [pre-natal] formation until its end', Aquinas adds this: 'And yet the species of what is formed does not remain the same. For first it has the form of the semen, then of the blood, and so on until it arrives at its final fulfilment' (89.1743). But he doesn't mean that the form of the semen or the form of the blood count as different species to which the developing embryo can be assigned at successive stages. The reason why the species of the developing embryo does not remain the same throughout its development is just that those 'intermediate stages [through which it passes] do not have a *complete* species but are, so to speak, *on the way to* a species.[73] So those stages are

---

[70] See n. 63 above.

[71] See e.g. 21.975: 'The more common anything is, the more prior it is in the process of generation—as animal is prior to human being in the generation of a human being (as the Philosopher says in *Generation of Animals* [II 3, 736b2–4])'; also 58.1345: 'The ordering of the sensory to the intellective, and of the nutritive to the sensory, is a kind of ordering of potentiality to actuality. For as far as generation is concerned, the intellective is posterior to the sensory, and the sensory to the nutritive, since in [the process of] generation, [the foetus] becomes an animal before it becomes a human being.'

[72] See the discussion of the tenth argument (88.1732) in sect. 5 above.

[73] See n. 62 above; also QDV 3.9, ad 10: 'Before the embryo has a rational soul,

generated not so as to remain permanently, but in order that the final stage of generation (*ultimum generatum*) may be arrived at through them' (89.1744*a*). That final stage of generation is the *completion* of the foetus's acquisition of its one and only species: human.[74] Even this passage turns out to support alternative (b), which really is Aquinas's account.

Until it acquires a human soul, the foetus itself is not a full-fledged member of any species at all.[75] However, since the human species is the only one it can become a full-fledged member of, and the one it will become a full-fledged member of in the course of normal development, to classify the foetus as non-human would be misleadingly terse. In its earlier stages of development the foetus is more accurately classified as pre-human. Still, Aquinas's radical-replacement hypothesis seems called for by his view that being a full-fledged member of a species or having a substantial form[76] is an all-or-nothing state of affairs—like being precisely six

it is not a complete being, but is on the way to completion. That's why it is not in a genus or a species, except in virtue of being traced back [to the generator], as anything incomplete is traced back to the genus or species of something that is complete.'

[74] 'A child is in the human species even before it leaves the womb' (59.1369).

[75] Does it fully belong to a *genus* before it acquires full membership in a species? Aquinas's view seems to vary. In QDV 3.9, ad 10 (quoted in n. 73 above) he says that 'the embryo . . . is not in a genus or a species'. However, all three versions of premiss 1 in the argument we're considering classify the less-than-fully-human foetus as an animal (see n. 63 above), and Aquinas agrees (see n. 71 above; also 89.1745, quoted below). More ambiguously, in his rejoinder to the first version of the argument in II.88 (1723) he says: 'Even though the sensory soul in a human being and in a non-human animal agree in respect of the defining characteristic of the genus, they differ in species, as do the beings of which they are the forms. For just as an animal that is a human being differs in species from other animals in virtue of the fact that it is rational, so the sensory soul of a human being differs in species from the sensory soul of a non-human animal in virtue of the fact that it is also intellective. . . . For that reason one cannot conclude a diversity of genus, but only a diversity of species' (89.1747). It's certainly odd to find him saying that 'the sensory soul of a human being . . . is also intellective'. He obviously couldn't say that about the pre-human sensory soul that antedates the intellective soul in the development of a foetus, but that one isn't the sensory soul *of a human being*. I suppose his reasoning may go something like this: it makes at least superficial sense to agree that a fully developed human foetus's single soul is sensory. But if you do say that, then you have to describe that single (sensory) soul itself in the odd way he adopts here—viz. as being also intellective and not just sensory.

[76] For any individual to have full membership in a species is for it to have the substantial form that determines membership in that species; but not every substantial form confers membership in a species, as can be seen in the cases of the pre-human souls that are successively the substantial forms of the developing foetus before it has any complete species at all.

feet tall, and unlike being thin. If that's the case, then any substantial form must be acquired instantaneously, all at once. 'No substantial form takes on more and less. Instead, adding a greater
perfection to it makes another species, just as adding a unit makes
another species in the case of numbers. But it is not possible that
numerically one and the same [substantial] form be associated with
distinct species' (ST Ia.118.2, ad 2).[77] Given also Aquinas's doctrine
of the unicity of substantial form,[78] it follows that the acquisition of
any new substantial form entails the loss of the preceding substantial form.

In the generating of an animal and of a human being, in connection
with both of which there is a most perfect form, there are several intermediate forms and instances of generation. Consequently, there are also
several instances of corruption, since the generating of one thing is the
corrupting of another. Therefore, the vegetative soul, which is the first one
in the embryo (when the embryo lives the life of a plant), is corrupted,
and a more perfect soul succeeds it, one that is both nutritive and sensory
at once; and then the embryo lives an animal life. But when that
soul is corrupted, it is succeeded by a rational soul, introduced from
outside, even though the preceding souls existed by the power of the
semen. (89.1745)[79]

---

[77] See also e.g. Ia.76.4, ad 4 and Ia.93.3, ad 3: 'one and the same individual does
not belong to its species more at one time and less at another'. (It's hard to imagine
a clearer expression of the strict aspect of Aquinas's account.) 'Nor do even distinct
individuals belong more and less to species of substance.'

[78] See Ch. Eight above, sect. 9.

[79] See also 89.1740b–d: 'According to this position [i.e. the hypothesis of a single
soul's continuous development] it would follow that some power, numerically
one and the same, would at one time be only a vegetative soul, and afterwards a
sensory soul, and that in this way the substantial form itself would be more and
more perfected continuously. And it would follow, further, that the substantial
form would be brought from potentiality to actuality not all at once but successively.
And it would follow, further, that generating would be a continuous movement, just
like alteration. All these things are impossible in nature.' Also ST Ia.118.2, ad 2: 'if
there is a vegetative soul in the foetus from the beginning, and it is afterwards
developed little by little into what is perfect, there will always be the addition of the
next perfection without the corruption of the preceding perfection—which is contrary to the nature of generation considered unconditionally.... Since the generating of one thing is always the corrupting of another, it is necessary, both in the case
of a human being and in the case of other animals, to say that when a more perfect
form arrives, the corrupting of the earlier form occurs, but in such a way that the
next form has whatever the first one had and more besides. And in that way, through
many instances of generation and corruption, the ultimate substantial form is
arrived at, in the case of a human being as in the case of other animals.' See also
n. 26 above.

Aquinas thinks that this radical-replacement hypothesis—applicable to all generation, not just human[80]—means that 'the entire
transmutation associated with generation is not continuous; instead, there are many intermediate instances of generation'
(89.1744b). Perhaps that's an effective way of emphasizing the big
difference between his own position and the one he's opposing
here, but it seems misleadingly strong. There's no more discontinu-
ity in the pre-natal succession of substantial forms as he explains it
than there is in the fact that the foetus first attains a weight of three
pounds at some instant before which it always weighed less than
three pounds. Weighing precisely three pounds is an all-or-nothing
state of affairs that is, none the less, arrived at gradually.[81]
Aquinas's radical-replacement hypothesis is more plausibly read as
his analysis of the metaphysical details underlying the continuous
pre-natal development of the individual's soul. The real difference
between his hypothesis and the hypothesis of a single soul's continuous development has to do not with the continuity of the development, but with the singleness of the soul.

Since all these elements of Aquinas's radical-replacement hypothesis of human pre-natal development are simply particular
instances of his account of generation generally, there's nothing in
this part of his theory of the origin of the human soul that argues
for particular creation. The radical-replacement hypothesis applies
to the generating of cats and of olive-trees just as well as to the
generating of human beings.[82] Aquinas's additional arguments on

[80] See e.g. QDV 3.9, ad 9(F): 'The generating of air [from water in evaporation]
is simple, since in the entire generating of the air only two substantial forms appear—one that is thrown off and another that is taken on—and the whole is
accomplished simultaneously at a single instant. Thus before the introduction of the
form of air, the form of water remains there at all times, nor are there any dispositions in it to the form of air.' For a fuller general survey of the process of generation
see SCG III.22.2030.

[81] Aquinas may not see it this way. In fact, he sometimes goes so far, following
Aristotle, as to deny continuity to all sorts of change other than local motion. See
89.1744b, where he cites *Physics* VII (7, 261a28–b27) in support of his position. But
cf. ST Ia.118.2, ad 2, where he rejects the hypothesis of a single soul's continuous
development, in part 'because in that case it would follow that the generation of an
animal would be a continuous movement [or change], proceeding little by little from
what is imperfect to what is perfect, as does happen in the case of alteration'. (On
alteration in this connection see also 89.1740d, quoted in n. 79 above; but cf. In Sent.
II.13.1.1c, discussed in Ch. Six above, sect. 6, esp. n. 38, where generation and
corruption are characterized as occurring 'in accordance with' alteration.)

[82] Except for the fact that there are fewer instances of intermediate generating
and corrupting in the cases of non-human animals and plants. See 89.1745: 'the

behalf of particular creation were reviewed in section 4 above. In his rejoinders to the two versions of the argument from substantial unity in chapter 88 (1723 and 1724), Aquinas says nothing further about particular creation (89.1747 and 1748). In his rejoinder to the version in ST Ia.118.2 (obj. 2) he tries to show that combining particular creation with the hypothesis of a single soul's continuous development leads inevitably to intolerable consequences: 'Either [1] that [intellective soul] which is caused by God's action [in particular creation] is something subsistent (in which case it is something essentially other than the pre-existing form [i.e. the sensory soul], which was not subsistent), and so the view of those who posit more than one soul in the body will return; or [2] it is not anything subsistent, but rather a kind of perfecting of the pre-existing soul (in which case it follows necessarily that the intellective soul is corrupted when the body is corrupted, which is impossible)' (ad 2). I turn now to Aquinas's arguments to show that this is impossible.

7. Arguing for the incorruptibility of intellective souls

Aquinas's consideration of souls at death (in II.79–82) concludes with a chapter in which he argues in detail against the view that the (sensory) soul of a non-human animal might survive the animal's death. Chapter 82 includes observations on animal appetite (1633–4, 1647–8), as well as comparisons of sensation with intellection (1641–3) and analyses of self-movers that are by now familiar (1638–9, 1645–6).[83] The importance of chapter 82 for my purposes now, however, is limited to the very simple inference at the core of Aquinas's rejection of the hypothesis that animal souls are incorruptible: 'There is no operation of the soul of non-human animals that can occur without a body. Therefore, . . . the soul of a non-human animal will be incapable of existing without a body. Therefore, when the [animal's] body perishes, its soul perishes' (82.1631).

nobler any form is, and the farther it is from the form of an element, the more intermediate forms (and, consequently, the more instances of intermediate generating) there must be by which the final form is gradually arrived at'. (The continuation of this passage is quoted in the immediately preceding paragraph.)

[83] See n. 41 above on the structure of II.82. In the Marietti edn. the clause *et per se habet operationem* in lines 33–4 of 82.1646 is a typesetter's error, and should be omitted.

Or, even more simply, 'no operation of a non-human animal soul can occur without a body. From this it can be concluded with necessity that a non-human animal soul dies with the [animal's] body' (82.1649). This line of reasoning shows what we might have expected on other grounds as well: Aquinas's arguments for the incorruptibility of the human, intellective soul will depend on its having an operation that *can* occur without a body. In his view, then, the organlessness of intellection is the key to arguing for the intellective soul's survival of death.[84]

In chapter 79 Aquinas offers nine arguments on the basis of which, he claims, 'it can be clearly shown that a human soul is not corrupted when the body [with which it was united] is corrupted' (1597), and he follows those arguments with a survey of relevant passages from philosophical, ecclesiastical, and Scriptural authorities (1609–12). Given the theological importance of the topic, it's not surprising that his canvass of authorities is unusually elaborate, or that he provides a good number of arguments in support of his thesis. What is surprising is the arguments' poor quality.

Chapter 79 begins, like many others, with the assertion that the chapter's arguments are based on things that have already been established. In this case, the most precisely relevant preceding things would seem to be the thirteen arguments which Aquinas has already provided (in II.55) in support of the general thesis that 'intellective substances are incorruptible'.[85] We might expect, then, that this chapter will simply draw on chapter 55. There are some clear connections between these arguments and some of those in chapter 55, as we'll see. But it's only in his first argument in chapter 79 that Aquinas explicitly alludes to the earlier chapter, using its thesis as one premiss and adding only the required premiss that 'the human soul is a kind of intellective substance, as has been shown' (1598).[86] The reason why he can't simply recycle all the earlier arguments with the addition of that premiss is, pretty clearly, that human souls are the only intellective substances that are unconditionally united with corruptible bodies.[87] Even someone convinced

---

[84] On organlessness see n. 33 above; also Ch. Eight above, sect. 9; also Ch. Nine above, n. 117.

[85] See Ch. Seven above, sect. 9.

[86] For the explicit identification of the human soul as an intellective substance, see Ch. Eight above, sects. 6 and 8.

[87] On this unconditional union, see Ch. Eight above, sect. 4.

that intellective substances in general are incorruptible would be
entitled to wonder whether an intellective substance that begins its
existence in an unconditional union with something that is corruptible might not thereby have compromised or simply surrendered
the incorruptibility that would otherwise go with being an intellective substance. And the undoubted corruptibility with which
human souls are intimately associated isn't confined to the bodies
with which they are united. Every human being considered as a
whole is a matter–form (m–f) composite, and every such composite
is itself corruptible.[88] What's more, every terrestrial m–f composite
except the human being must involve a *material* form, and every
material form is itself corrupted in the corruption of the composite
of which it was a part.[89] In these circumstances, Aquinas clearly
does need new arguments for the incorruptibility of the intellective
substances that are human souls.

The second of the chapter's arguments is the first new argument
he offers, and it comes with some indications that it is to be taken
especially seriously, since it's the only one of the nine to be accompanied by an objection and a rejoinder. The argument itself reads
as follows:

No thing is corrupted as a result of that in which its perfecting consists,
since the changes leading to [a thing's] perfection and to [its] corruption are contrary to each other. Now the perfecting of the human soul
consists in a sort of abstraction (*abstractione quadam*) from the body.
For the soul is perfected by knowledge and by virtue; but it is the more   5
perfected as regards knowledge the more it considers immaterial
things, while the perfection of virtue consists in a person's not following the passions of the body but tempering and bridling them.

---

[88] See e.g. 54.1296: 'being generated and being corrupted ... are propria of
material substances' (quoted more fully in Ch. Seven above, sect. 8); and 54.1298:
'All corruption occurs through a separation of form from matter' (quoted more fully
in Ch. Seven above, sect. 9).

[89] A material form is corrupted *per accidens* when the composite of which it was
the substantial form is corrupted. See e.g. 55.1304: 'everything that is corrupted must
be a body, if it is corrupted *per se*. Or, if it is corrupted *per accidens*, it must be some
form or power belonging to a body. But intellective substances are not bodies, nor
are they powers or forms dependent on a body. Therefore, they are corrupted
neither *per se* nor *per accidens*. They are, therefore, altogether incorruptible.' See
also ch. 51, 'An intellective substance is not a material form'; 51.1268: 'intellective
natures are *subsistent* forms rather than forms existing in matter as if their being
depended on matter' (quoted also in Ch. Seven above, sect. 6). And see 79.1606,
partially quoted below.

Therefore, the corruption of the soul does not consist in its being
separated (*separetur*) from the body. (79.1599)[90]   10

This argument is of course intended to support the thesis of
chapter 79: that the soul is not corrupted when the body is corrupted. The body is corrupted when it is no longer animated, when
it and its soul have been separated in the separation that constitutes
the human being's death. The corpse that remains is, strictly speaking, post-human: no longer a human body, much less a human
being.[91] And the conclusion of this argument (in lines 9–10) is that
a soul's being separated from its body doesn't also constitute the
corruption of the *soul*. Why not? Because, according to this argument, in life a soul is (or ought to be) often separated from its
body in ways that, far from bringing about the soul's *corruption*,
are essential to its achieving its proper intellectual and moral
perfections.

As for a soul's moral perfection, we can agree that its moving in
that direction involves 'not following the passions of the body but
tempering and bridling them' (lines 7–8). But only a soul that is
not separated from its body could become aware of a need for that
sort of activity, or engage in it. It's easy to grant that such activity
involves what might be described as a soul's recognition of some
sort of distinction between it and its body;[92] but a distinction is not
yet a separation. And nothing less than a real separation will do, if
Aquinas's examples of knowledge and virtue are to support a conclusion that's relevant to considerations of the soul's status when
the body is corrupted. He introduces those examples (in line 4)
by talking cautiously about 'a sort of abstraction from the body',
rather than referring forthrightly to separation. But the description
he uses there is weak in a way that suits the examples better than
it could suit the case that's really at issue in the argument; and if
the premises can plausibly refer only to a sort of abstraction, while
the conclusion must refer to real separation, the argument is
broken-backed.

We've seen that Aquinas's cautious description, 'a sort of abstraction from the body', seems badly suited even to one of his two

---

[90] This argument bears some resemblance to the argument for incorruptibility in
55.1308, but not enough to count as just another version of it.

[91] See Ch. Eight above, sect. 8; also Ch. Nine, nn. 16 and 25.

[92] The sort of distinction famously and vividly depicted by St Paul in Rom. 7: 15–
25. For Aquinas's account of that passage, see Kretzmann 1988.

examples. But if, as we already have reason to think, organlessness is at the heart of Aquinas's arguments for incorruptibility, then, since organlessness is argued for more fully as a feature of intellection than as a feature of volition, we might simply discount the example of moral virtue and focus on the argument's example of knowledge. We might agree that the soul is perfected in knowledge to the extent to which it considers immaterial things—e.g. universals—and that those immaterial objects are themselves abstracted from phantasms, and thus ultimately from bodies (as we've seen Aquinas maintaining).[93] But why should the soul's consideration of things that have been abstracted from bodies involve *its* being abstracted from *its* body? Granting that the possible intellect is immaterial in virtue of the immateriality of its objects[94] doesn't commit one to agreeing that it is abstracted from its body in any sense that would approximate real separation, especially because Aquinas insists that intellection involves intellect's recourse to phantasms,[95] which depend on bodily senses. What's more, we've seen that Aquinas argues at great length (against Averroës) that it is impossible for the human intellect to be separated from the human body in carrying out intellection.[96] Aquinas's example of knowledge in this argument is at least as inapplicable as his example of virtue is to death's real separation of soul and body.

And so there would be no need to evaluate this argument further if it weren't for the fact that Aquinas himself goes on to consider a possible objection to it. 'But suppose someone were to say that the *perfection* of the soul consists in its separation from the body as regards [its] *operating*, while its *corruption* consists in its separation from the body as regards [its] *being*' (1600a). This objection is on the right track in so far as it questions the legitimacy of assuming that any soul–body relationship that obtains in operations associated with knowledge or virtue can be simply assimilated to the

---

[93] See e.g. 50.1261 (quoted more fully in Ch. Nine above, sect. 8): 'the species of intellectively cognized things are made actually intelligible by being abstracted from individual matter'.

[94] See e.g. 62.1409: 'every cognitive power, considered just as such, is immaterial' (quoted more fully in Ch. Nine above, sect. 6).

[95] See e.g. 60.1387 (quoted more fully in Ch. Nine above, sect. 6): the possible intellect 'never engages in intellective cognition without a phantasm (as Aristotle says in *De anima* III [7, 431a16–17]), because phantasms are to it as sensible things are to a sense; and a sense does not sense without them'.

[96] See Ch. Eight above, sect. 9.

soul–body relationship that constitutes death. But the objection is also too generous, especially in its use of 'separation from the body' for the first case (where not even the argument itself was so bold) as well as for the second, where it really does belong.

In his rejoinder Aquinas says that such an objection would miss its mark because 'a thing's operation reveals (*demonstrat*) its substance and its being, since anything whatever operates in the respect in which it is a being, and the operation that is proper to a thing follows that thing's proper nature. Therefore, no thing's operation can be perfected except in accordance with that which perfects its substance. Therefore, if as regards its *operating* the soul is perfected in leaving the body behind (*reliquendo corpus*), then its incorporeal substance will not fail in its *being* as a result of being separated from the body' (1600*a*–*b*). Someone who grants everything in this rejoinder before the final conditional sentence should none the less recognize that Aquinas has provided no basis on which to affirm that conditional's antecedent. On the contrary, our examination of the argument and objection has turned up reasons to deny that the soul's operations in connection with knowledge and virtue involve anything that might reasonably be described as the soul's leaving the body behind. So we're left in the position of having to withhold our assent to that conditional's consequent, which is the real conclusion of this rejoinder. Escalating terminology is the fatal flaw that runs through the argument, the objection, and the rejoinder—from 'a sort of abstraction from the body' through 'separation from the body' to 'leaving the body behind'.

Only the last of chapter 79's arguments for the incorruptibility of the human soul warrants an appraisal as detailed as this one has been, and some of the others can safely be left unexamined.[97] The fourth argument may be worth a little consideration, if only to raise some questions about its basic premises: '[1] It is impossible that a natural appetite be in vain (*frustra*), but [2] a human being has a

---

[97] e.g. the third argument (in 1601), which argues for the incorruptibility of the intellective soul on the basis of the incorruptibility of its proper objects (cf. 55.1307); also the fifth argument (in 1603), which takes a similar line (cf. 55.1305); also the sixth argument (in 1604), which argues that because prime matter, the primary recipient in the case of sensible things, 'is incorruptible in respect of its substance ... the possible intellect, which is receptive of intelligible forms, is much more so' just because 'intelligible being is more lasting than sensible being'.

natural appetite to remain for ever' (1602).[98] Unless the version
of an Aristotelian principle that is premiss 1[99] is taken to mean
that every natural appetite is necessarily *satisfied*, this argument
won't yield the conclusion it's aimed at: 'a human being attains
(*consequitur*) perpetuity in respect of the soul'. But, since natural
appetites include a stone's tendency toward the centre of the earth,
premiss 1 can't reasonably be given that interpretation. And if we
confine our attention to human beings, don't we have natural appetites that are, for the most part, manifestly in vain (or frustrated)?
Take, for instance, our natural appetite for remaining healthy. As
for premiss 2, it is famously open to question whether remaining for
ever really is the object of a natural human appetite.[100]

In the same vein we can look at the heart of the seventh argument, which depends on the Aristotelian principle that 'the maker
is superior (*honorabilius*) to that which is made'.[101] 'But the agent
intellect makes things actually intelligible . . . Therefore, since actually intelligible things, considered just as such, are incorruptible,
all the more will the agent intellect be incorruptible' (1605). The
principle is obviously unacceptable unless the superiority is understood not unconditionally but only in certain respects. A potter is
superior to her pots only in certain respects; in other respects—e.g.
fire resistance—the pots are superior to the potter. So the principle
doesn't warrant simply choosing any property of the thing made
and concluding that the maker is superior in that respect or even
shares that property.

The eighth argument opens with what is intended to be an exhaustive survey of ways in which a form is subject to *per accidens*
corruption: 'No form is corrupted except as a result of the action of
its contrary, the corruption of its subject, or the failure of its cause'
(1606). To serve its purpose, then, this argument must show that
every one of those kinds of corruption is ruled out in the case of
the substantial form that is the human soul. I want to examine
Aquinas's handling of just the first kind. His paradigm of this kind
of corruption where material forms are concerned is the corruption

---

[98] A much fuller version of this argument appears in 55.1309. See also Ch. Five
above, n. 48.

[99] See *De caelo* I 4, 271a33; also *Politics* I 2, 1253a9.

[100] 'To die: to sleep; / No more; . . . 'tis a consummation / Devoutly to be wish'd'
(*Hamlet*, III. i. 60–1, 63–4).

[101] *De anima* III 5, 430a18–19.

of the form of heat 'through the action of cold'. 'But', he says, 'the human soul [considered as a form] cannot be corrupted through the action of a contrary because there is nothing that is contrary to it.' The claim that there is nothing contrary to a human soul implies that there is no thing, event, or state of affairs whose presence in a human being's body would be incompatible with the presence of an intellective soul in that body. But why shouldn't an irreversible coma be considered a form that is contrary to an intellective soul? Where is there a mistake in thinking that permanent unconsciousness is to an intellective soul as cold is to heat? The living comatose body would presumably be animated by a nutritive soul only. Aquinas's evidence that there is nothing that is contrary to (incompatible with) the continuing existence of the human soul is simply that 'through the possible intellect the soul is cognizant of and receptive of all contraries'. But, of course, the fact that a sheet of clear plastic can take on all colours, even contrary colours at once (in different areas), provides no evidence that there is no thing, event, or state of affairs whose presence is incompatible with the continuing existence of the plastic sheet.

In some respects, the ninth and final argument of the chapter (79.1607) is the boldest one Aquinas offers here, and it deserves a closer look. He begins with a premiss that seems to invite trouble for his position: 'If the soul is corrupted through the corruption of the body, then it must be the case that its being is weakened through a weakness of the body.' In order to build the sort of argument he needs here, he must deny that consequent. But, offhand, it seems very easy to provide plenty of examples in which a person's intellect is weakened permanently through disease, injury, or ageing. Why shouldn't such cases count as instances of the weakening of the intellective soul's being? Aquinas's answer to that question seems to be implied in his next, even bolder move, in which he offers a very strong claim about the being of the soul's powers *in general*: 'However, if any power of the soul is weakened when the body is weakened, that is only *per accidens*—I mean, in so far as that power of the soul needs a bodily organ. For example, sight is weakened when its organ is weakened, but [only] *per accidens*.' He's claiming that a person's visual power itself, its *being*, is unimpaired as the person's vision deteriorates, even to the point of blindness. The bodily weakening that constitutes the *per accidens* corrupting of the visual power involves absolutely no *per se* corrupting of the power. 'This is clear in virtue of the fact that if some weakness were to affect the power itself, it would never be restored when the organ was repaired. We observe, however, that no matter how weakened the visual power *seems* to be, if the organ is repaired, the visual power is restored. That's why Aristotle says, in *De anima* I [4, 408b21–2], that if an old man were to get the eye of a young man, he would see as a young man sees.' Of course, we in the late twentieth century really do observe the kind of organ repair and replacement that Aristotle and Aquinas could only have been imagining, so we might be ready to agree (on much stronger empirical grounds) that the restorative effect of such interventions does provide evidence that a soul's powers are not to be *identified* with its body's organs.

None the less, the fact that an eye injury corrupts a person's visual power *per accidens* shows that the visual power needs a bodily organ for its operation, if not for its being. To make the case Aquinas needs to make for the utterly organless intellective power, however, he has to show that a bodily weakness can't adversely affect even intellect's *operation*, can't corrupt (or weaken) intellect even *per accidens*. Here is how he tries to do so in this ninth argument: 'Therefore, since intellect is a power of the soul that does not need an organ (as is clear from things established earlier[102]), it is not weakened either *per se* or *per accidens*, through old age or through any other weakness of the body.' That's certainly what he needs to claim, but how can he support a claim so implausible on the face of it? Only by acknowledging the undoubted appearances to the contrary and explaining them away. 'However, if in connection with the operation of intellect there is fatigue, or an impediment arising from a bodily infirmity, that's not because of a weakness of intellect itself, but rather because of a weakness of powers that intellect needs—I mean, of the imagination, or of the memorative and cogitative powers.'[103]

If for the sake of the argument we grant intellect's organlessness, then we do have to agree that when a person's intellective activity is adversely affected by getting tired, or old, or sick, or getting hit on the head, the explanatory causal connection can't directly link the body with intellect itself. As Aquinas spells out the explanation,

---

[102] e.g. in 68.1459, quoted in n. 32 above.
[103] On intellect's need for such powers, see also 68.1459*b*, quoted in n. 32 above.

a bodily weakness or injury may affect the organ needed by one or another internal sensory power, and in that way a bodily weakness or injury can bring about a *per accidens* corruption of one or another of those powers of the soul: the imagination (or phantasia), the memorative power, or the cogitative power (or passive intellect).[104] But, Aquinas admits, organless intellect *needs* those powers in its operation, so a weakness in one or more of them may look like a *per accidens* weakness in intellect itself. Following the line which Aquinas himself has laid down in this argument, it seems that such a state of affairs must simply *be* a *per accidens* weakness in (or corruption of) intellect itself. If, as he says, intellect needs those powers, and those powers need bodily organs, why isn't it right to say that intellect needs the organs those powers need—for all intellective activity, if not for its very being as a power?

In light of this examination of the ninth argument, perhaps its most surprising feature is the fact that, on the basis of no more than we've been looking at, Aquinas feels entitled to conclude that a *per se* corruption of the human soul is impossible: 'Therefore, it is clear that intellect is incorruptible. Therefore, the human soul, which is a kind of intellective substance, is also incorruptible.'

8. Arguing against arguments for the corruptibility of intellective souls

After presenting the nine arguments of chapter 79, designed to show that the intellective soul is not corrupted when the body is corrupted, Aquinas turns, in the conjoined chapters 80&81, to the consideration of arguments by which 'it seems that it could be proved that human souls could not remain after the body' (1613). Chapter 80 proper contains five such opposing arguments, and chapter 81 provides a refutation for each of those five. Three of the opposing arguments are narrowly technical. The first and second of them (1614 and 1615) take off from Aquinas's account of individuation, which runs into difficulties where disembodied indi-

---

[104] For discussions of these powers, see Ch. Nine above. For their dependence on bodily organs, see e.g. 66.1438: 'every sensory power has cognition through individual species, since it receives the species of things in bodily organs' (quoted more fully in Ch. Nine above, sect. 6). See also 68.1459*b*, quoted in n. 32 above; also Ch. Nine, nn. 86 and 87, and sect. 8.

vidual souls are concerned; and the third opposing argument (1616) is effective only for 'those who posit the eternity of the world'.[105] The fourth opposing argument (1617) begins with a sly and not altogether straightforward application of distorted Porphyrian authority: 'Whatever comes to something and goes from it without its corruption comes to it accidentally—for that is the definition of accident.[106] Therefore, if the soul is not corrupted by leaving the body, it will follow that the soul is united with the body accidentally.'[107] The complete argument isn't formidable as an attack on the soul's incorruptibility, but Aquinas makes good use of his rejoinder (1623) as an occasion for reviewing some of the metaphysical fundamentals underlying his account of the human being as an m–f composite.

The fifth and last opposing argument in chapter 80 (1618) offers much the strongest challenge to Aquinas's thesis of incorruptibility, besides contributing to an understanding of issues raised in our discussion of chapter 79's final argument (at the end of sect. 7 above). The case for intellect's bodily dependence is pressed so hard here that it's easy to forget that Aquinas himself devised this opposing argument.

The argument opens with a presentation of its case in a nutshell: 'It is impossible that there be any substance that has no operation, but every operation of the [human] soul is bounded by (*finitur cum*) the body.' Since Aquinas accepts the principle expressed in the first clause, if the argument can establish the general claim in the second clause, then a human soul without a body will have been shown to be a substance that has no operation, and thus a substance that cannot exist. The general claim is to be established 'by induction' on the various operations of the soul, beginning with the unproblematic cases of the operations of the nutritive and sensory parts of the human soul, here called the nutritive and sensory souls. 'For the powers of the *nutritive* soul operate through bodily qualities and through a bodily instrument [that operates] on the very body that is perfected through the soul, that is nourished and grows [through the soul], and from which the semen is separated for

---

[105] See Ch. Five above.

[106] Porphyry's definition in his *Isagoge* reads this way: 'An accident is what is present [to a subject] and absent [from it] without the corruption of the subject.'

[107] See also his earlier repudiation of the subject–accident analysis of the body–soul union in 56.1319c, discussed in Ch. Eight above, sect. 4.

generation. Also, all the powers that pertain to the *sensory* soul are carried out through bodily organs. And some of them are carried out along with a bodily change—e.g. those that are called passions of the soul, such as love, joy, and the like.' Since Aquinas himself subscribes to all these claims of the soul's dependence on the body, there's no apparent reason to examine them.

The crucial stage of the argument's induction is of course its attempt to show that the operations of the *intellective* part of a human soul also depend on the body with which the soul is united. 'Now although intellection is not an operation exercised through any bodily organ, its objects are phantasms, which are related to it as colours are related to sight. Thus, just as sight cannot see without colours, so the intellective soul cannot carry on intellective activity without phantasms', which can be produced only in phantasia, which depends on the body. 'Also, for intellection the soul needs powers that prepare the phantasms for being made actually intelligible, such as the cogitative and the memorative power. As for them, since they are acts of certain organs of the body through which they operate, it's certain that they cannot remain after the body.' This argument's focusing on phantasms and on certain sensory powers in order to show intellect's dependence on the body for its operations is what our examination of chapter 79's ninth argument might have led us to expect. And this crucial stage of the argument is greatly strengthened by the fact that everything said in it appears to echo Aquinas's own claims.

The argument then bolsters and extends its claims about intellect and body with references to Aristotle: 'It's for this reason, too, that Aristotle says that the soul never engages in intellection without a phantasm [*De anima* III 7, 431a16–17], and that it has intellective cognition of nothing without the passive intellect (which he calls the cogitative power) [5, 430a24–5], which is corruptible. It's also for this reason that he says, in *De anima* I [4, 408b24–5], that a human being's intellection is corrupted when something is corrupted internally—a phantasm, that is, or the passive intellect. And in *De anima* III [5, 430a23–4] he says that after death we do not remember the things that we knew in life'—thereby confirming the argument's earlier claim that the requisite memorative power, too, is corrupted when the body is corrupted. 'In this way, therefore, it is clear that *no* operation of the soul can remain after death.

Therefore, neither does its substance remain, since there can be no substance without any operation.'

Aquinas's rejoinder to this formidable opposing argument is appropriately long and complicated (81.1624–8), but it begins disappointingly: 'We say that the claim made in the fifth argument—that no operation can remain in the soul if it is separated from the body—is false; for the operations that are not exercised through organs do remain. Intellection and volition are of that sort. However, those that are exercised through organs, such as the operations of the nutritive and sensory powers, do not remain' (1624). This summary rejection seems simply to bypass the argument, which of course acknowledges that 'intellection is not an operation exercised through any bodily organ' before offering evidence that it does, all the same, depend on bodily products and powers.

However, in the next part of his rejoinder (1625a) Aquinas grants everything the opposing argument claims regarding intellect's dependence on the body:

Of course, while the human soul is united with the body, even though its absolute being is not dependent on the body, the body is a kind of substrate of it, none the less, and the subject that receives it. For that reason, too, and consequently, the soul's proper operation, which is intellection, has its object, the phantasms, in the body, even though it does not depend on the body in the sense of being exercised through a bodily organ. And that's why the soul, as long as it is in the body, cannot carry on intellective activity without a phantasm or even remember except through the cogitative and the memorative power through which the phantasms are prepared (as is clear from things already said). And for that reason intellective activity, as regards this mode of it, and memory likewise, is destroyed when the body is destroyed.

If it weren't for its escape clause—'as regards this mode of it'—that last sentence would simply concede what the opposing argument claims. The escape clause alludes to the first sentence of 1625a: 'Still, it is important to know that the soul separated from the body carries on intellective activity differently from the soul united with the body, just as it also exists in a different way; for each thing acts in accordance with the way it is.'

In nothing we have looked at so far has Aquinas made any claims about the nature of a separated soul's existence or activity. Does he have any warrant for making these claims here? Well, if an intellective soul is not corrupted when its body is corrupted, if it goes on existing after having been separated from the body, it surely must exist then 'in a different way'. And if it is still an intellective soul then, it surely must carry on intellective activity, but 'differently from the soul united with the body'. Aquinas might be warranted in making such conditional claims here, but the claims he does make aren't conditional, and they seem simply to ignore the conclusion of the opposing argument—an argument he does not refute, either before or after making those claims. The escape clause in the last sentence of 1625a is ineffectual, because no other mode of intellective activity has been established.[108] However, in the remainder of his rejoinder Aquinas seems uncharacteristically ready to speculate about modes of existence and of activity for which he hasn't argued.[109] 'But the being of the *separated* soul belongs to it alone, without the body. That's why its operation, which is intellective activity, will not be fulfilled on the basis of a relation to objects existing in bodily organs, which the phantasms are. Instead, it carries on intellective activity on its own, in the manner of [intellective] substances that are totally separated from bodies in their being. (They will be taken up [in this respect] below [in II.96–101].) And from those substances, as from things superior to it, it will be able to receive a more fruitful influence in order to understand more perfectly' (1625b).[110]

There is some indication of this even in young people. For the more a soul is prevented from being preoccupied with the body that is its own, the more capable it becomes of understanding some higher things. That's why the virtue of temperance, which pulls the soul back from bodily pleasures, makes people especially apt to understand. What's more, people who are asleep, when they aren't using their bodily senses and no disturbance of the humours or vapours impedes them, do, under the influence of higher

[108] As William Alston pointed out to me, in criticizing this opposing argument Aquinas is under no obligation to show, or even to make plausible, that there are modes of intellection open to human souls in separation from the body that don't require sensory input. For purposes of criticism it's enough that he point out that the argument doesn't show that there couldn't be such modes of intellection. That's right. But in this rejoinder Aquinas does more than would have been enough.

[109] Aquinas discusses an intellective soul's cognition after death in several other places where there are no such dialectical restrictions on the topic. See e.g. QDV 19.1–2; QDA 15 and 17–20; QQ III.9.1; ST Ia.89.1–8.

[110] Although Aquinas very often alludes to creaturely intellective cognition in his earlier *general* discussion of intellective substances (in II.46–55), he doesn't argue there for detailed claims of this sort.

beings, have some perception of future things, which lie beyond the mode of human reasoning. And this happens much more in connection with people in trances or in states of ecstasy, since a greater withdrawal from the bodily senses is effected in them. Nor does this happen undeservedly. For, since the human soul is on the borderline between bodies and incorporeal substances, as if on the horizon between eternity and time (as was shown above [68.1453]), in withdrawing from the lowest it approaches the highest. And so, too, when a soul has been entirely separated from its body, it will be perfectly assimilated to separated substances as regards its mode of intellective activity and will receive their influence abundantly. (1625c–g)

'In that way, therefore, even though our intellective activity in the mode of our present life is corrupted when the body is corrupted, another, higher mode of intellective activity will follow it' (1626). In the first clause of this crucial sentence Aquinas fully concedes the opposing argument's conclusion that '*no* operation of the soul'—no operation of the soul that we have any experience of—'can remain after death'. His reassuring claim in the second clause has no basis here other than speculation of the sort he offers in 1625b–g and carries on in the remainder of this rejoinder. And this attempt at reassurance is undercut by the fact that he later uses 'altogether different' modes of intellective activity to differentiate our species of intellective substance from all others. 'The species of a thing is perceived on the basis of its proper operation, since an operation reveals a power, which indicates an essence. Now the operation proper to a separated substance and to an intellective soul is intellective activity. However, the mode of intellective activity belonging to a separated substance is altogether different from that belonging to a soul, because a soul carries on intellective activity by receiving from phantasms while a separated substance doesn't, since it does not have bodily organs, in which phantasms must be.[111] Therefore, a human soul and a separated substance do not belong to a single species' (94.1805). If a human soul after death 'carries on intellective activity on its own, in the manner of [intellective] substances that are totally separated from bodies in their being', as Aquinas claims (in 1625b, quoted above), how is this differentiation of species supposed to be maintained?

Aquinas's rejoinder, with its catalogue of powers of the soul lost or retained at death, concludes with the following items.

---

[111] See also e.g. 96.1812–20.

Remembering, however, since it is an act exercised through a bodily organ (as Aristotle proves in *De memoria* [1, 451a14–17]), cannot remain in the soul after [its separation from] the body, unless 'remembering' is taken equivocally for the intellective cognition of things one knew before. For the separated soul must have present to it an intellective cognition even of the things it knew in life, since intelligible species are received in the possible intellect indelibly (as was shown above [in II.74]). But as regards other operations of the soul, such as loving, rejoicing, and the like, we have to watch out for an equivocation. For sometimes they are understood as passions of the soul, and in that case they are acts of the sensory appetite suited to the concupiscible and irascible powers and accompanied by some bodily change. Understood in that way they cannot remain in the soul after death (as Aristotle proves in *De anima* [I 4, 408b5–9, 18–31]). But they are at other times understood as a simple act of will, which is devoid of passion.[112] That's why Aristotle says in *Ethics* VII [15, 1154b26] that God rejoices in one simple activity, and in X [7, 1177a25] that there is marvellous delight in the contemplation of wisdom; and in VIII [7, 1157b28–9] he distinguishes the love that belongs to friendship from the kind of loving that is passion. But since will is a power that does not make use of an organ any more than intellect does, it is plain that things of this sort remain in the separated soul in so far as they are acts of will. (1627–1628a–c)

Because I think so well of almost everything else Aquinas does in his natural-theological account of creation, I'm left wondering whether he might not have done better to consign the whole topic of immortality to Book IV, where the data of revelation are admitted into the enterprise. In that case he might have concluded a much shorter version of the account here in the way he writes of the life everlasting in his exposition of the Apostles' Creed: 'No one can fulfil his desire in this life, nor can any created thing satisfy his desire. God alone satisfies, and infinitely surpasses, a person's desire—which for that reason is at rest only in God: "Thou hast made us for thyself, O Lord, and our heart is restless until it rests in thee." '[113]

[112] See TMOT, Ch. Eight, sects. 1 and 2.
[113] *In symbolum apostolorum expositio*, art. 12 (1012), quoting Augustine, *Confessions* I 1.

APPENDIX I

A Chronology of Aquinas's Life and Works

(based mainly on Torrell 1993 and Tugwell 1988)

1224/5	Born at Roccasecca
1231–9	Benedictine oblate at Monte Cassino
1239, spring–summer	Home at Roccasecca
1239, autumn, to 1244, spring	Student at University of Naples
	Joins Dominicans at Naples (1244)
1244	Sent by Dominicans to Paris
	Abducted by his family *en route* to Paris, taken to Roccasecca (1244)
1244–5	Kept at home by mother, Theodora
	Attempted seduction (1245)
	Allowed to return to Dominicans in Naples (1245)
1245–8	At University of Paris; studies with Albert the Great
	Offered abbacy of Monte Cassino by Innocent IV (1248)
1248–52	At University of Cologne; studies with Albert
	Ordained priest at Cologne (1250/1)
	De principiis naturae, ad fratrem Sylvestrum (On the Principles of Nature, for Brother Sylvester) (Cologne, 1248–52, or Paris, 1252–6?)
	Expositio super Isaiam ad litteram (Literal Commentary on Isaiah) (Cologne, 1251/2)
	Postilla super Ieremiam (Commentary on Jeremiah) (Cologne, 1251/2)
	Postilla super Threnos (Commentary on Lamentations) (Cologne, 1251/2)
1252–3	*Cursor biblicus* at Paris
	Postilla super Psalmos (Commentary on Psalms; incomplete: 1–54) (Paris, 1252–3, or Naples, 1273?)

	De ente et essentia, ad fratres et socios suos (On Being and Essence, for his Brothers and Companions) (Paris, 1252–6)
1253–6, spring	*Sententiarius* at Paris
	Scriptum super libros Sententiarum (Commentary on the *Sentences*) (Paris, 1253–6)
1256, spring	Inception as master in theology at Paris
	Principia: 'Hic est liber mandatorum Dei' et 'Rigans montes de superioribus suis' (Inaugural Lectures: 'This is the Book of God's Commandments' and 'Watering the Hills from his Places Above') (Paris, 1256)
1256–9	Regent master in theology at Paris, occupying the second Dominican chair ('for foreigners') at the university
	Contra impugnantes Dei cultum et religionem (Against those who Assail the Worship of God and Religion (a refutation of William of Saint-Amour's *De periculis novissimorum temporum*)) (Paris, 1256)
	Quaestiones disputatae de veritate (Disputed Questions on Truth) (Paris, 1256–9)
	Quaestiones quodlibetales [VII–XI] (Quodlibetal Questions; Quodlibets VII–XI) (Paris, 1256–9)
	Expositio super librum Boethii De trinitate (Commentary on Boethius's *De trinitate*; incomplete) (Paris, 1257/8–9)
	Expositio super librum Boethii De hebdomadibus (Commentary on Boethius's *De hebdomadibus*; incomplete) (Paris, 1259?)
	Summa contra gentiles [through I.53] (Synopsis (of Christian Doctrine) Directed Against Unbelievers) (Paris, 1259)
1259, end of academic year	Leaves Paris for Naples
1260–1	In Naples, at priory of San Domenico (?), writing SCG
	Designated a preacher general in his province (1260)
	Summa contra gentiles [from I.54] (Naples, 1260–1)

| 1261/2–5 | In Orvieto, as lector at the Dominican priory |

Contra errores Graecorum, ad Urbanem IV Pontificem Maximum (Against Mistakes of the Greek (Fathers of the Church), for Pope Urban IV (on an anonymous treatise *De fide sanctae trinitatis contra errores Graecorum*)) (Orvieto, 1263/4)

Summa contra gentiles [through Bk. IV] (Orvieto, 1261/2–5)

De rationibus fidei contra Saracenos, Graecos, et Armenos, ad cantorem Antiochiae (On Arguments for the Faith Directed against Muhammadans, Greek Orthodox Christians, and Armenians, for the Cantor of Antioch) (Orvieto, 1264)

Expositio super Iob ad litteram (Literal Commentary on Job) (Orvieto, 1261–5)

Glossa continua super Evangelia (Catena aurea) (A Continuous Gloss on the Four Gospels (The Golden Chain)) (Orvieto, Rome, 1262/ 3–8)

Officium de festo Corporis Christi, ad mandatum Urbanae Papae IV (Liturgy for the Feast of Corpus Christi, at the command of Pope Urban IV) (Orvieto, 1264)

De emptione et venditione ad tempus (A Letter on Buying and Selling on Credit) (Orvieto, c.1262)

Expositio super primum et secundum Decretalem, ad Archidiaconum Tudertinum (A Letter Explaining the First and Second Decretals, to the Archdeacon of Todi) (Orvieto, 1261–5?)

De articulis fidei et Ecclesiae sacramentis, ad archiepiscopum Panormitanum (A Letter on the Articles of Faith and the Church's Sacraments, to the Archbishop of Palermo) (Orvieto, 1261–5?)

| 1265–8 | In Rome, appointed to establish a studium for Dominicans at Santa Sabina and to serve as regent master there |

Expositio super librum Dionysii De divinis nominibus (Commentary on Dionysius's *De divinis nominibus*) (Orvieto, 1261–5, or Rome, 1265–8?)

Quaestiones disputatae de potentia (Disputed Questions on Power) (Rome, 1265–6)

Quaestio disputata de anima (Disputed Question on the Soul (21 articles)) (Rome, 1265–6)

Responsio ad fr. Ioannem Vercellensem de articulis 108 sumptis ex opere Petri de Tarentasia (Reply to Brother John of Vercelli Regarding 108 Articles Drawn from the Work of Peter of Tarentaise (on the *Sentences*)) (Rome, 1265–7)

Compendium theologiae, ad fratrem Reginaldum socium suum (A Compendium of Theology, for Brother Reginald, his Companion; incomplete) (Rome, 1265–7)

De regno (or *De regimine principum*), *ad regem Cypri* (On Kingship (or: On the Governance of Rulers), for the King of Cyprus (authentic only through Bk. II, ch. 4)) (Rome, 1267)

Summa theologiae Ia (Synopsis of Theology, First Part) (Rome, 1266–8)

Sententia super De anima (Commentary on Aristotle's *De anima*) (Rome, 1267–8)

Quaestio disputata de spiritualibus creaturis (Disputed Question on Spiritual Creatures (Angels) (11 articles)) (Rome, 1267–8)

1268	Leaves Rome for Paris assigned to occupy the second Dominican chair at the university again
1268, Sept., to 1272, Apr.	Second regency at Paris

Quaestiones disputatae de malo (Disputed Questions on Evil) (Rome, Paris, 1266–72)

Sententia super De sensu et sensato (Commentary on Aristotle's *De sensu et sensato*) (Rome, Paris, 1268–70)

Sententia super Physicam (Commentary on Aristotle's *Physics*) (Paris, 1268–9)

Sententia super Meteora (Commentary on Aristotle's *Meteora*; incomplete) (Paris, 1268–9)

Summa theologiae IaIIae (Synopsis of Theology, First Part of the Second Part) (Rome, Paris, 1268–71)

De forma absolutionis sacramentalis, ad generalem magistrum Ordinis (On the Form of Sacramental Absolution, for the Master General of the Order (John Vercelli)) (Paris, 1269)

De secreto (On Secret Testimony (a committee report in which Aquinas is the lone dissenter, supporting the right of a religious superior to compel a subject to reveal a secret even under the seal of confession)) (Paris, 1269)

Lectura super Matthaeum (Lectures on the Gospel of Matthew) (Paris, 1269–70)

De perfectione spiritualis vitae (On the Perfecting of the Spiritual Life (directed against Gérard d'Abbeville's *Contra adversarium perfectionis christianae*)) (Paris, 1269–70)

Sententia super De memoria et reminiscentia (Commentary on Aristotle's *De memoria et reminiscentia*) (Paris?, 1270?)

Tabula libri Ethicorum (An Analytical Table of Aristotle's *Ethics*; incomplete) (Paris, 1270)

De unitate intellectus, contra Averroistas (On the Unicity of Intellect, Against the Averroists) (Paris, 1270)

Sententia super Peri hermenias (Commentary on Aristotle's *De interpretatione*; incomplete) (Paris, 1270–1)

De aeternitate mundi, contra murmurantes (On the Eternity of the World, Against Grumblers) (Paris, 1271)

Responsio ad lectorem Venetum de articulis XXX (A Letter to the Lector at Venice on Thirty Articles) (Paris, 1271)

Responsio ad lectorem Venetum de articulis XXXVI (A Letter to the Lector at Venice on Thirty-Six Articles (this and the immediately preceding item are two preliminary versions of the next item)) (Paris, 1271)

Responsio ad magistrum Ioannem de Vercellis de articulis XLII (Reply to Master John Vercelli

Regarding Forty-Two Articles (Aquinas's answers to doctrinal questions which Vercelli submitted also to Albert the Great and Robert Kilwardby)) (Paris, 1271)

Quaestiones quodlibetales [I–VI, XII] (Quodlibetal Questions; Quodlibets I–VI and XII) (Paris, 1268–72)

Sententia libri Politicorum (Commentary on Aristotle's *Politics*; incomplete) (prob. Paris, 1269–72)

Contra doctrinam retrahentium a religione (Against the Teaching of those who Dissuade (Boys) from Entering the Religious Life (opposing Gérard d'Abbeville)) (Paris, 1271/2)

Quaestio disputata de unione verbi incarnati (Disputed Question on the Unity of the Incarnate Word (5 articles)) (Paris, 1272)

Expositio super librum De causis (Commentary on the *Liber de causis*) (Paris, 1272)

Lectura super Ioannem (Lectures on the Gospel of John) (Paris, 1270–2)

Sententia libri Ethicorum (Commentary on Aristotle's *Nicomachean Ethics*) (Paris, 1271–2)

Sententia super Posteriora analytica (Commentary on Aristotle's *Posterior Analytics*) (Paris, 1271–2)

Quaestio disputata de virtutibus in communi (Disputed Question on the Virtues in General (13 articles)) (Paris, 1271–2)

Quaestio disputata de caritate (Disputed Question on Charity (13 articles)) (Paris, 1271–2)

Quaestio disputata de correctione fraterna (Disputed Question on Fraternal Correction (2 articles)) (Paris, 1271–2)

Quaestio disputata de spe (Disputed Question on Hope (4 articles)) (Paris, 1271–2)

Quaestio disputata de virtutibus cardinalibus (Disputed Question on the Cardinal Virtues (4 articles)) (Paris, 1271–2)

Summa theologiae IIaIIae (Synopsis of Theology, Second Part of the Second Part) (Paris, 1271–2)

	De operationibus occultis naturae, ad quendam militem ultramontanum (A Letter on Natural Events that may seem to have no Natural Origin, to a Certain Italian Knight) (Paris, 1268–72?)
	De iudiciis astrorum, ad quendam militem ultramontanum (A Letter on Astrology, to a Certain Italian Knight) (Paris, 1268–72?)
	De mixtione elementorum, ad magistrum Philippum de Castro Caeli (A Letter on the Mixture of Elements (in Compounds), to Master Philip of Castrocaeli) (prob. Paris, 1270–1)
	Epistola ad ducissam Brabantiae (A Letter to the Duchess of Brabant (on the Treatment of the Jews)) (Paris, 1271)
	De sortibus, ad Dominum Iacobum de Tonengo (A Letter on Deciding by Casting Lots, to Lord James of Tonengo) (Paris, 1270/1)
	De motu cordis, ad magistrum Philippum de Castro Caeli (A Letter on the Motion of the Heart, to Master Philip of Castrocaeli) (Paris, 1270–1, or Naples, 1273?)
	Responsio ad lectorem Bisuntinum de articulis VI (A Letter to the Lector at Besançon on Six Articles (Regarding Subjects Admissible in Sermons)) (Paris, 1271?)
1272, June	Leaves Paris for Naples
1272–3	In Naples, assigned to establish a studium generale for Dominicans and to serve as regent master there
	Sententia super Metaphysicam (Commentary on Aristotle's *Metaphysics*) (Paris, 1270/1, and Naples, 1273?)
	Expositio et lectura super Epistolas Pauli Apostoli (Commentary and Lectures on the Epistles of Paul the Apostle) (Paris, Naples, 1270–3)
	De substantiis separatis, ad fratrem Reginaldum socium suum (On Separated Substances (Angels), for Brother Reginald, his Companion; incomplete) (Paris or Naples, 1271–3)

Sententia super libros De caelo et mundo (Commentary on Aristotle's *De caelo et mundo*; incomplete) (Naples, 1272–3)

Sententia super libros De generatione et corruptione (Commentary on Aristotle's *De generatione et corruptione*; incomplete) (Naples, 1272–3)

Collationes in decem praecepta (Sermon Commentaries on the Ten Commandments) (Naples, 1273, or Orvieto, Rome, 1261–8?)

Collationes super Ave Maria (Sermon Commentaries on the Ave Maria) (Naples, 1273, or Paris, 1268–72?)

Collationes super Credo in Deum (Sermon Commentaries on the Apostles' Creed) (Naples, 1273)

Collationes super Pater Noster (Sermon Commentaries on the Lord's Prayer) (Naples, 1273)

Summa theologiae IIIa (Synopsis of Theology, Third Part; incomplete) (Paris, Naples, 1272–Dec. 1273)

1273, 6 Dec.	Religious experience; stops writing
1274, Feb.	Sets out for Council of Lyons
	Responsio ad Bernardum abbatem casinensem (A Letter to Bernard, Abbot of Monte Cassino (on Gregory the Great on Predestination)) (perhaps *en route* to Lyons, 1274)
1274, mid-Feb.	Injures head near Borgonuovo, *en route* to Lyons
1274, 7 Mar.	Dies at Fossanuova

APPENDIX II

A Table Indicating the Correspondence between Sections of Chapters of SCG II in the Pera (Marietti) Edition and the Anderson Translation

Edn.	Trans.	Edn.	Trans.	Edn.	Trans.
1.851	passage	6.878	6.1	11.905	11.1
1.852	1.1	6.879	6.2	11.906	11.2
1.853	1.2	6.880	6.3	11.907	11.3
1.854	1.3	6.881	6.4	11.908	11.4
1.855	1.4	6.882	6.5	11.909	11.5
1.856	1.5	6.883	6.6	11.910	11.6
1.857	1.6	6.884	6.7	11.911	11.7
		6.885	6.8		
2.858	2.1				
2.859	2.2			12.912	12.1
2.860	2.3	7.886	7.1	12.913	12.2
2.861	2.4	7.887	7.2	12.914	12.3
2.862	2.5	7.888	7.3	12.915	12.4
2.863	2.6	7.889	7.4	12.916	12.5
		7.890	7.5		
3.864	3.1	7.891	7.6		
3.865	3.2			13&14.917	13&14.1
3.866	3.3			13&14.918	13&14.2
3.867	3.4	8.892	8.1	13&14.919a	13&14.3
3.868	3.5	8.893	8.2	13&14.919b	13&14.4
3.869	3.6	8.894	8.3	13&14.920	13&14.5
3.870	3.7	8.895	8.4	13&14.921	13&14.6
		8.896	8.5		
4.871	4.1	8.897	8.6		
4.872a	4.2			15.922	15.1
4.872b	4.3	9.898	9.1	15.923	15.2
4.873	4.4	9.899	9.2	15.924	15.3
4.874	4.4	9.900	9.3	15.925	15.4
4.875	4.4	9.901	9.4	15.926	15.5
4.876a–b	4.5	9.902	9.5	15.927	15.6
4.876c	4.6			15.928	15.7
				15.929	15.8
5.877	5.1	10.903	10.1	15.930	15.9
		10.904	10.2	15.931	15.10

Edn.	Trans.	Edn.	Trans.	Edn.	Trans.
16.932	16.1	21.976	21.8	25.1017	25.9
16.933	16.2	21.977	21.9	25.1018	25.10
16.934	16.3	21.978	21.10	25.1019	25.11
16.935	16.4	21.979	21.11	25.1020	25.12
16.936	16.5	21.980	21.12	25.1021	25.13
16.937	16.6			25.1022	25.14
16.938	16.7	22.981	22.1	25.1023	25.15
16.939	16.8	22.982	22.2	25.1024	25.16
16.940	16.9	22.983	22.3	25.1025	25.17
16.941	16.10	22.984	22.4	25.1026	25.18
16.942	16.11	22.985	22.5	25.1027	25.19
16.943	16.12	22.986a–c	22.6	25.1028	25.20
16.944	16.13	22.986d	22.7	25.1029	25.21
16.945	16.14	22.986e	22.8	25.1030	25.22
		22.987	22.9	25.1031	25.23
17.946	17.1	22.988	22.10	25.1032	25.24
17.947	17.2			25.1033	25.25
17.948	17.3	23.989	23.1		
17.949	17.4	23.990	23.2	26.1034	26.1
17.950	17.5	23.991	23.3	26.1035	26.2
		23.992	23.4	26.1036	26.3
18.951	18.1	23.993	23.5	26.1037	26.4
18.952	18.2	23.994	23.6	26.1038	26.5
18.953	18.3	23.995	23.7	26.1039	26.6
18.954	18.4	23.996	23.8	26.1040	26.7
		23.997	23.9	26.1041	26.8
19.955	19.1	23.998	23.10	26.1042	26.9
19.956	19.2	23.999	23.11		
19.957	19.3	23.1000	23.12	27.1043	27.1
19.958	19.4	23.1001	23.12	27.1044	27.2
19.959	19.5			27.1045	27.3
19.960	19.6	24.1002	24.1		
19.961	19.7	24.1003	24.2	28&29.1046	28&29.1
		24.1004	24.3	28&29.1047	28&29.2
20.962	20.1	24.1005	24.4	28&29.1048	28&29.3
20.963	20.2	24.1006	24.5	28&29.1049	28&29.4
20.964	20.3	24.1007	24.6	28&29.1050	28&29.5
20.965	20.4	24.1008	24.7	28&29.1051	28&29.6
20.966	20.5			28&29.1052	28&29.7
20.967	20.6			28&29.1053a–c	28&29.8
20.968	20.7	25.1009a	25.1	28&29.1053d–f	28&29.9
		25.1009b–c	25.2	28&29.1054	28&29.10
21.969	21.1	25.1010	25.3	28&29.1055	28&29.11
21.970	21.2	25.1011	25.4	28&29.1056a	28&29.12
21.971	21.3	25.1012	25.4	28&29.1056b	28&29.13
21.972	21.4	25.1013	25.5	28&29.1057	28&29.14
21.973	21.5	25.1014	25.6	28&29.1058	28&29.15
21.974	21.6	25.1015	25.7	28&29.1059	28&29.16
21.975	21.7	25.1016	25.8	28&29.1060	28&29.17

Edn.	Trans.	Edn.	Trans.	Edn.	Trans.
28&29.1061*a–d*	28&29.18	33.1104	33.9	38.1147	38.13
28&29.1061*e*	28&29.19			38.1148	38.14
28&29.1062	28&29.20	34.1105	34.1	38.1149	38.15
		34.1106	34.2	38.1150	38.16
30.1063	30.1	34.1107	34.3		
30.1064	30.2	34.1108	34.4	39.1151	39.1
30.1065	30.3	34.1109	34.5	39.1152	39.2
30.1066	30.4	34.1110	34.6	39.1153	39.3
30.1067	30.5			39.1154	39.4
30.1068	30.6	35.1111	35.1	39.1155	39.5
30.1069	30.7	35.1112	35.2	39.1156	39.6
30.1070	30.8	35.1113	35.3	39.1157	39.7
30.1071	30.9	35.1114	35.4	39.1158	39.8
30.1072	30.9	35.1115	35.5	39.1159	39.9
30.1073	30.9	35.1116	35.6		
30.1074	30.10	35.1117	35.7	40.1160	40.1
30.1075	30.11	35.1118	35.8	40.1161	40.2
30.1076	30.12	35.1119	35.9	40.1162	40.3
30.1077	30.13			40.1163	40.4
30.1078	30.14	36.1120	36.1	40.1164	40.5
30.1079	30.15	36.1121	36.2	40.1165	40.6
		36.1122	36.3	40.1166	40.7
31.1080	31.1	36.1123	36.4		
31.1081*a–b*	31.2	36.1124	36.5	41.1167	41.1
31.1081*c–e*	31.3	36.1125	36.6	41.1168	41.2
31.1082	31.4	36.1126	36.7	41.1169	41.3
31.1083	31.5	36.1127	36.8	41.1170	41.4
31.1084	31.6	36.1128	36.9	41.1171	41.5
31.1085	31.7			41.1172	41.6
		37.1129	37.1	41.1173	41.7
32.1086	32.1	37.1130*a–d*	37.2	41.1174	41.8
32.1087	32.2	37.1130*e–f*	37.3	41.1175	41.9
32.1088	32.3	37.1131	37.4	41.1176	41.10
32.1089	32.4	37.1132	37.5	41.1177	41.11
32.1090	32.5	37.1133	37.6	41.1178*a*	41.12
32.1091	32.6	37.1134	37.7	41.1178*b–c*	41.13
32.1092	32.7			41.1179*a–b*	41.14
32.1093	32.8	38.1135	38.1	41.1179*c*	41.15
32.1094	32.9	38.1136	38.2	41.1180	41.16
32.1095	32.10	38.1137	38.3		
		38.1138	38.4	42.1181	42.1
33.1096	33.1	38.1139	38.5	42.1182	42.2
33.1097	33.2	38.1140	38.6	42.1183	42.3
33.1098	33.3	38.1141	38.7	42.1184	42.4
33.1099	33.4	38.1142	38.8	42.1185	42.5
33.1100	33.5	38.1143	38.9	42.1186	42.6
33.1101	33.6	38.1144	38.10	42.1187	42.7
33.1102	33.7	38.1145	38.11	42.1188	42.8
33.1103	33.8	38.1146	38.12	42.1189	42.9

Edn.	Trans.	Edn.	Trans.	Edn.	Trans.
42.1190	42.10	46.1235	46.7	52.1278	52.6
42.1191	42.11			52.1279	52.7
42.1192	42.12	47.1236	47.1	52.1280	52.8
		47.1237	47.2	52.1281	52.9
43.1193	43.1	47.1238	47.3		
43.1194	43.2	47.1239	47.4	53.1282	53.1
43.1195	43.3	47.1240	47.5	53.1283	53.2
43.1196	43.4			53.1284	53.3
43.1197	43.5	48.1241	48.1	53.1285	53.4
43.1198	43.6	48.1242	48.2	53.1286	53.5
43.1199	43.7	48.1243	48.3		
43.1200	43.8	48.1244	48.4	54.1287	54.1
43.1201	43.9	48.1245	48.5	54.1288	54.2
43.1202	43.10	48.1246	48.6	54.1289	54.3
				54.1290	54.4
44.1203	44.1	49.1247	49.1	54.1291	54.5
44.1204	44.2	49.1248	49.2	54.1292	54.6
44.1205	44.3	49.1249	49.3	54.1293	54.7
44.1206	44.4	49.1250	49.4	54.1294	54.8
44.1207	44.5	49.1251	49.5	54.1295	54.9
44.1208	44.6	49.1252	49.6	54.1296	54.10
44.1209	44.7	49.1253	49.7		
44.1210	44.8	49.1254	49.8	55.1297	55.1
44.1211	44.9	49.1255	49.9	55.1298	55.2
44.1212	44.10	49.1256	49.10	55.1299	55.3
44.1213	44.11	49.1257	49.11	55.1300	55.4
44.1214	44.12	49.1258	49.11	55.1301	55.5
44.1215	44.13			55.1302	55.6
44.1216	44.14	50.1259	50.1	55.1303	55.7
44.1217	44.15	50.1260	50.2	55.1304	55.8
44.1218	44.16	50.1261	50.3	55.1305	55.9
		50.1262	50.4	55.1306	55.10
45.1219	45.1	50.1263	50.5	55.1307	55.11
45.1220	45.2	50.1264	50.6	55.1308	55.12
45.1221	45.3	50.1265	50.7	55.1309	55.13
45.1222	45.4	50.1266	50.8	55.1310	55.14
45.1223	45.5	50.1267	50.9	55.1311	55.15
45.1224	45.6			55.1312	55.16
45.1225	45.7	51.1268	51.1		
45.1226	45.8	51.1269	51.2	56.1313	56.1
45.1227	45.9	51.1270	51.3	56.1314a	56.2
45.1228	45.10	51.1271	51.4	56.1314b	56.3
		51.1272	51.5	56.1314c	56.4
46.1229	46.1			56.1314d	56.5
46.1230	46.2	52.1273	52.1	56.1315	56.6
46.1231	46.3	52.1274	52.2	56.1316	56.7
46.1232	46.4	52.1275	52.3	56.1317	56.8
46.1233	46.5	52.1276	52.4	56.1318	56.9
46.1234	46.6	52.1277	52.5	56.1319a	56.10

Edn.	Trans.	Edn.	Trans.	Edn.	Trans.
56.1319*b*	56.11	59.1364	59.12	62.1409	62.7
56.1319*c–d*	56.12	59.1365	59.13	62.1410	62.8
56.1320	56.13	59.1366	59.14	62.1411	62.9
56.1321	56.14	59.1367	59.15	62.1412	62.10
56.1322	56.15	59.1368	59.16	62.1413	62.11
56.1323	56.16	59.1369	59.17	62.1414	62.12
56.1324	56.17			62.1415	62.13
56.1325	56.18	60.1370	60.1		
		60.1371	60.2	63.1416	63.1
57.1326	57.1	60.1372	60.3	63.1417	63.2
57.1327	57.2	60.1373	60.4	63.1418	63.3
57.1328	57.3	60.1374	60.5	63.1419	63.4
57.1329	57.4	60.1375	60.6	63.1420	63.5
57.1330	57.5	60.1376	60.7	63.1421	63.6
57.1331	57.6	60.1377	60.8		
57.1332	57.7	60.1378	60.9	64.1422	64.1
57.1333	57.8	60.1379	60.10	64.1423	64.2
57.1334	57.9	60.1380	60.11	64.1424	64.3
57.1335	57.10	60.1381	60.12	64.1425	64.4
57.1336	57.11	60.1382	60.13		
57.1337	57.12	60.1383	60.14	65.1426	65.1
57.1338	57.13	60.1384	60.15	65.1427	65.2
57.1339	57.14	60.1385	60.16	65.1428	65.3
57.1340	57.15	60.1386	60.17	65.1429	65.4
57.1341	57.16	60.1387	60.18	65.1430	65.5
		60.1388	60.19	65.1431	65.6
58.1342	58.1	60.1389	60.20	65.1432	65.7
58.1343	58.2	60.1390	60.21	65.1433	65.8
58.1344	58.3	60.1391	60.22	65.1434	65.9
58.1345	58.4	60.1392	60.23	65.1435	65.9
58.1346	58.5	60.1393	60.24		
58.1347	58.6	60.1394	60.25	66.1436	66.1
58.1348	58.7	60.1395	60.26	66.1437	66.2
58.1349	58.8			66.1438	66.3
58.1350	58.9	61.1396	61.1	66.1439	66.4
58.1351	58.10	61.1397	61.2	66.1440	66.5
58.1352	58.11	61.1398*a*	61.3	66.1441	66.6
		61.1398*b–d*	61.4		
59.1353	59.1	61.1399	61.5	67.1442	67.1
59.1354	59.2	61.1400	61.6	67.1443	67.2
59.1355	59.3	61.1401	61.7	67.1444	67.3
59.1356	59.4	61.1402	61.8	67.1445	67.4
59.1357	59.5			67.1446	67.5
59.1358	59.6	62.1403	62.1	67.1447	67.6
59.1359	59.7	62.1404	62.2		
59.1360	59.8	62.1405	62.3	68.1448	68.1
59.1361	59.9	62.1406	62.4	68.1449	68.2
59.1362	59.10	62.1407	62.5	68.1450	68.3
59.1363	59.11	62.1408	62.6	68.1451	68.4

Edn.	Trans.	Edn.	Trans.	Edn.	Trans.
68.1452	68.5	73.1495	73.8	74.1541	74.15
68.1453	68.6	73.1496	73.9	74.1542	74.16
68.1454	68.7	73.1497	73.10	74.1543	74.17
68.1455	68.8	73.1498	73.11		
68.1456	68.9	73.1499	73.12	75.1544	75.1
68.1457	68.10	73.1500	73.13	75.1545	75.2
68.1458	68.11	73.1501	73.14	75.1546	75.3
68.1459	68.12	73.1502	73.15	75.1547	75.4
		73.1503	73.16	75.1548	75.5
69.1460	69.1	73.1504	73.17	75.1549	75.6
69.1461	69.2	73.1505	73.18	75.1550	75.7
69.1462	69.3	73.1506	73.19	75.1551	75.8
69.1463	69.4	73.1507	73.20	75.1552	75.9
69.1464	69.5	73.1508	73.21	75.1553	75.10
69.1465	69.6	73.1509a	73.22	75.1554	75.11
69.1466	69.7	73.1509b	73.23	75.1555	75.12
69.1467	69.8	73.1510	73.24	75.1556	75.13
69.1468a	69.9	73.1511	73.25	75.1557	75.14
69.1468b	69.10	73.1512a	73.26	75.1558	75.15
69.1469	69.11	73.1512b	73.27	75.1559	75.16
69.1470	69.12	73.1513	73.28		
		73.1514	73.29	76.1560	76.1
70.1471	70.1	73.1515	73.30	76.1561	76.2
70.1472	70.2	73.1516	73.31	76.1562	76.3
70.1473	70.2	73.1517	73.32	76.1563	76.4
70.1474	70.3	73.1518	73.33	76.1564	76.5
70.1475	70.4	73.1519	73.34	76.1565	76.6
70.1476	70.5	73.1520	73.35	76.1566	76.7
70.1477	70.6	73.1521	73.36	76.1567	76.8
70.1478	70.7	73.1522	73.37	76.1568	76.9
		73.1523	73.38	76.1569	76.10
71.1479	71.1	73.1524	73.39	76.1570	76.11
71.1480	71.2	73.1525	73.40	76.1571	76.11
71.1481	71.3	73.1526	73.41	76.1572	76.12
				76.1573	76.13
72.1482	72.1	74.1527	74.1	76.1574	76.14
72.1483	72.2	74.1528	74.2	76.1575	76.15
72.1484	72.3	74.1529	74.3	76.1576	76.16
72.1485	72.4	74.1530	74.4	76.1577	76.17
72.1486	72.5	74.1531	74.5	76.1578	76.18
72.1487	72.6	74.1532	74.6	76.1579	76.19
		74.1533	74.7		
73.1488	73.1	74.1534	74.8	77.1580	77.1
73.1489	73.2	74.1535	74.9	77.1581	77.2
73.1490	73.3	74.1536	74.10	77.1582	77.3
73.1491	73.4	74.1537	74.11	77.1583	77.4
73.1492	73.5	74.1538	74.12	77.1584	77.5
73.1493	73.6	74.1539	74.13		
73.1494	73.7	74.1540	74.14	78.1585	78.1

Edn.	Trans.	Edn.	Trans.	Edn.	Trans.
78.1586	78.2	82.1631	82.2	83.1677	83.30
78.1587	78.3	82.1632	82.3	83.1678	83.31
78.1588	78.4	82.1633	82.4	83.1679	83.32
78.1589	78.5	82.1634	82.5	83.1680*a–c*	83.33
78.1590	78.6	82.1635	82.6	83.1680*d*	83.34
78.1591	78.7	82.1636	82.7	83.1681	83.35
78.1592	78.8	82.1637	82.8	83.1682	83.36
78.1593	78.9	82.1638	82.9	83.1683	83.37
78.1594	78.10	82.1639	82.10	83.1684	83.38
78.1595	78.11	82.1640	82.11		
78.1596	78.12	82.1641	82.12	84.1685	84.1
		82.1642	82.13	84.1686	84.2
79.1597	79.1	82.1643	82.14	84.1687	84.3
79.1598	79.2	82.1644	82.15	84.1688	84.4
79.1599	79.3	82.1645	82.16	84.1689	84.5
79.1600	79.4	82.1646	82.17	84.1690	84.6
79.1601	79.5	82.1647	82.18	84.1691	84.7
79.1602	79.6	82.1648	82.19		
79.1603	79.7	82.1649	82.20	85.1692	85.1
79.1604	79.8			85.1693	85.2
79.1605	79.9	83.1650	83.1	85.1694	85.3
79.1606	79.10	83.1651	83.2	85.1695	85.4
79.1607	79.11	83.1652	83.3	85.1696	85.5
79.1608	79.12	83.1653	83.4	85.1697	85.6
79.1609	79.13	83.1654	83.5	85.1698	85.7
79.1610	79.14	83.1655	83.6	85.1699	85.8
79.1611	79.15	83.1656	83.7	85.1700	85.9
79.1612*a*	79.16	83.1657	83.8	85.1701*a–b*	85.9
79.1612*b*	79.17	83.1658	83.9	85.1701*c*	85.10
		83.1659	83.10	85.1702*a–c*	85.11
80&81.1613	80&81.1	83.1660	83.11	85.1702*d*	85.12
80&81.1614	80&81.2	83.1661*a–c*	83.12	85.1703	85.13
80&81.1615	80&81.3	83.1661*d*	83.13	85.1704	85.14
80&81.1616	80&81.4	83.1662	83.14	85.1705	85.15
80&81.1617	80&81.5	83.1663	83.15		
80&81.1618	80&81.6	83.1664	83.16	86.1706	86.1
80&81.1619	80&81.7	83.1665	83.17	86.1707	86.2
80&81.1620	80&81.7	83.1666	83.18	86.1708*a–c*	86.3
80&81.1621	80&81.8	83.1667	83.19	86.1708*d*	86.4
80&81.1622	80&81.9	83.1668	83.20	86.1708*e*	86.5
80&81.1623	80&81.10	83.1669	83.21	86.1709	86.6
80&81.1624	80&81.11	83.1670	83.22	86.1710	86.7
80&81.1625	80&81.12	83.1671	83.23	86.1711	86.8
80&81.1626	80&81.13	83.1672	83.24	86.1712	86.9
80&81.1627	80&81.14	83.1673	83.25	86.1713	86.10
80&81.1628	80&81.15	83.1674*a–c*	83.26		
80&81.1629	80&81.16	83.1674*d–e*	83.27	87.1714	87.1
		83.1675	83.28	87.1715	87.2
82.1630	82.1	83.1676	83.29	87.1716	87.3

Edn.	Trans.	Edn.	Trans.	Edn.	Trans.
87.1717	87.4	90.1763	90.5	95.1807	95.2
87.1718	87.5	90.1764	90.6	95.1808	95.2
87.1719	87.6	90.1765	90.7	95.1809*a*	95.3
87.1720	87.7	90.1766	90.8	95.1809*b*	95.4
87.1721	87.8	90.1767	90.9	95.1809*c*	95.5
		90.1768	90.10	95.1810	95.6
88.1722	88.1	90.1769	90.11		
88.1723	88.2	90.1770	90.12	96.1811	96.1
88.1724	88.3	90.1771	90.13	96.1812	96.2
88.1725	88.4			96.1813	96.3
88.1726	88.5	91.1772	91.1	96.1814	96.4
88.1727	88.6	91.1773	91.2	96.1815	96.5
88.1728	88.7	91.1774	91.3	96.1816	96.6
88.1729	88.8	91.1775	91.4	96.1817	96.7
88.1730	88.9	91.1776	91.5	96.1818	96.8
88.1731	88.10	91.1777	91.6	96.1819	96.9
88.1732	88.11	91.1778	91.7	96.1820	96.10
88.1733	88.12	91.1779	91.8		
88.1734	88.13	91.1780	91.9	97.1821	97.1
		91.1781	91.10	97.1822	97.2
89.1735	89.1	91.1782	91.11	97.1823	97.3
89.1736	89.2			97.1824	97.4
89.1737	89.3	92.1783	92.1	97.1825	97.5
89.1738	89.4	92.1784	92.2	97.1826	97.6
89.1739	89.5	92.1785	92.3		
89.1740	89.6	92.1786	92.4	98.1827	98.1
89.1741	89.7	92.1787	92.5	98.1828	98.2
89.1742	89.8	92.1788	92.6	98.1829	98.3
89.1743	89.9	92.1789	92.7	98.1830	98.4
89.1744	89.10	92.1790	92.8	98.1831	98.5
89.1745	89.11	92.1791	92.9	98.1832	98.6
89.1746	89.12	92.1792	92.10	98.1833	98.7
89.1747	89.12	92.1793	92.11	98.1834	98.8
89.1748	89.13	92.1794	92.12	98.1835	98.9
89.1749	89.14			98.1836	98.10
89.1750	89.15	93.1795	93.1	98.1837	98.11
89.1751	89.16	93.1796	93.2	98.1838	98.12
89.1752	89.17	93.1797	93.3	98.1839	98.13
89.1753	89.18	93.1798	93.4	98.1840	98.14
89.1754	89.19	93.1799	93.5	98.1841	98.15
89.1755	89.20	93.1800	93.6	98.1842	98.16
89.1756	89.21			98.1843	98.17
89.1757	89.22	94.1801	94.1	98.1844	98.18
89.1758	89.23	94.1802	94.2	98.1845*a*	98.19
		94.1803	94.3	98.1845*b*	98.20
90.1759	90.1	94.1804	94.4		
90.1760	90.2	94.1805	94.5	99.1846	99.1
90.1761	90.3			99.1847	99.2
90.1762	90.4	95.1806	95.1	99.1848	99.3

Edn.	Trans.	Edn.	Trans.	Edn.	Trans.
99.1849	99.4	100.1854	100.2	101.1859*a–b*	101.2
99.1850	99.5	100.1855	100.3	101.1859*c*	101.3
99.1851	99.6	100.1856	100.4	101.1860*a*	101.4
99.1852	99.7	100.1857	100.5	101.1860*b*	101.5
100.1853	100.1	101.1858	101.1		

APPENDIX III

In Sent. I.44.1.2: Could God Make a Better Universe?

We proceed to the second article in this way.

It seems that God could not make a better universe.

Obj. 1: For, according to Augustine [*Enchiridion* X], the things God established are good—even the individual things. However, all of them taken together are *very* good. But nothing can be better than   5
that which is superlatively good. Therefore, nothing can be better than the universe.

Obj. 2: Furthermore, the universe includes every good. But nothing can be better than every good. Therefore, God could not make a better universe.   10

Obj. 3: Furthermore, according to Dionysius [*De divinis nominibus* IV], what is good and what is better are found among things to the extent to which some participate in more divine goodnesses than others do. For instance, those that are alive are ranked ahead of those that merely exist, and so on. But all divine perfections that can be   15
passed on (*communicabiles*) to a created thing have been passed on to some created things. Therefore, it seems that the universe cannot be better.

Obj. 4: Furthermore, the more ordered anything is, the better it is— which is why even what is bad is defined by Augustine in terms of a   20
privation of order [*De natura boni* IV]. But in the universe nothing is disordered, since even evil itself is ordered by God (as was said above [in I.36.1.2]). Therefore, it seems that the universe cannot be better.

But, on the contrary:

Obj. 5: According to the Philosopher, what is whiter is what is more   25
unmixed with black [*Topics* III 5, 119a28]. Therefore, what is better is also what is more unmixed with what is bad. But God could make a universe in which there would be nothing bad. Therefore, since in this universe there are many bad things, it seems that God could make a better universe.   30

Obj. 6: Furthermore, if what is equal is added to what is larger, the

whole will be made larger. Therefore, too, if what is better is added to
what is better, the whole will be made better. But an angel is better
than a stone. Therefore, two angels are something better than an
angel and a stone. Therefore, too, if each part of the universe were an   35
angel, the universe would be much better. But God could make that.
Therefore, etc.

c: I reply that we have to say that the good of the universe
consists in two orders (according to the Philosopher in *Metaphysics*
XI [10, 1075a12–24])—viz. {1} in the order of the parts of the universe   40
to one another, and {2} in the order of the whole universe toward
its end, which is God himself. Similarly, in an army, too, there is an
order of the parts of the army to one another in accordance with
their various duties, and there is the order [of the whole army]
to the leader's good, which is victory. And the latter order {2} is   45
the principal one, the one for the sake of which the former order {1}
exists.

Therefore, if we take up the good of {1} the order that there is in the
parts of the universe to one another, it can be considered either {1.1}
as regards the parts themselves or {1.2} as regards the order of the   50
parts.

If {1.1} as regards the parts themselves, then the universe can be
understood to be made better [in either of two ways. First,] {1.11}
through the addition of more parts in such a way that many other
species would be created and the many levels of goodness there can be   55
would be increased (for between even the highest created thing and
God there is an infinite gap). And in this way God could have made
and could make a better universe. But that universe would be related
to this one as whole to part, so it would be neither entirely the same
nor entirely different. And this addition of goodness would be by way   60
of discrete quantity.

Alternatively, {1.12} [the universe] can be understood to be made
better intensively, so to speak, as {1.122} in case all its parts were
changed for the better. For if {1.121} some parts were improved while
others were not improved, there would not be as much goodness of   65
order—as is clear in the case of a harp. If {1.122} all its strings are
tuned, the harmony is made sweeter; but when {1.121} only some have
been tuned, the result is disharmony.

Now this improvement of all the parts can be understood either
{1.1221} as regards accidental goodness—in which case there could be   70
such an improvement by God while the parts remained the same and
the universe remained the same—or {1.1222} as regards essential
goodness. And in that case, too, it would be possible for God, who can
establish infinitely many other species. In that case the parts would

not be the same, however; and, consequently, neither would it be the   75
same universe, as is clear from things already said.

However, if {1.2} one takes the order of the parts itself, {1.21} it
cannot be better by way of discrete quantity unless an addition were
made to the parts of the universe, because in the universe there is
nothing that has not been ordered. But {1.22} while the parts remained   80
the same, {1.221} the universe could be intensively better as regards
the order that is consequent on accidental goodness. For the more
anything progresses into a greater good, the better the order is. On the
other hand, {1.222} the order that is consequent on essential goodness
could not be better unless other parts and [thus] another universe   85
were made.

Similarly, {2} the order that is directed toward the end can be
considered either {2.1} as regards the end itself—in which case {2.11}
it could not be better in the sense that the universe would be ordered
toward another end, since (*sicut*) there can be nothing better than   90
God—or {2.2} as regards the order itself. And in that latter case {2.21}
the order directed toward the end could be improved in so far as the
[accidental] goodness of the parts of the universe and their order to
one another prospered (*cresceret*), because the more closely they were
related to the end, the more they would approximate a likeness to the   95
divine goodness, which is the end of all things.

ad 1: In reply to the first, then, we have to say that Augustine is
speaking of the order of the universe, on the supposition that the
nature of such parts is the same. For in that case the order could not
be better (as was said in the body of the article).   100

ad 2: In reply to the second we have to say that we are talking
about the universe not as regards that *name*, but as regards this
thing that is now called the universe. Although it contains everything
that is good in actuality, it does not contain every good that God can
make.   105

ad 3: In reply to the third we have to say that there are many ways
of participating in the same divine perfection. For instance, there is
one way of participating in divine wisdom for intellective substances
[i.e. angels] and another for rational substances—viz. human beings.
And this extends even to non-human animals, which have sensory 110
cognition. Therefore, although it may be that all the [divine] perfections that can be passed on to a created thing have been passed on to
a created thing, they have not been passed on *in every way* they can be
participated in by a created thing.

ad 4: In reply to the fourth we have to say that although the order 115
of the universe cannot be better in the sense that more parts of this
universe are ordered, it could be better if it were ordered to a better

good as its *proximate* end—which could happen if the parts of the universe were made better (as was said).

ad 5: In reply to the fifth we have to say that a universe in which 120
there was nothing bad would not be as good as this universe, because there would not be as many good natures in that one as there are in this one, in which there are some good natures with which nothing bad is associated and others with which something bad is associated. And it is better that there be both kinds of natures than that there be only 125
one or the other.

ad 6: In reply to the sixth we have to say that although an angel is better than a stone absolutely, the two natures [together] are better than either one alone. And so the universe in which there are angels and other things is better than one in which there would be only 130
angels, because the perfection of the universe depends essentially on the diversity of natures by which the various levels of goodness are fulfilled, rather than on the multiplying of individuals within one nature.

REFERENCES

(For references to ancient and medieval authors, see *Index locorum*.)

Adams, M. M., and Adams, R. M. (1991) (eds.), *The Problem of Evil* (Oxford: Oxford University Press).

Adams, R. M. (1972), 'Must God Create the Best?', *Philosophical Review*, 81: 317–32.

Aertsen, Jan A. (1996), *Medieval Philosophy and the Transcendentals: The Case of Thomas Aquinas* (Leiden, New York, and Cologne: E. J. Brill).

Alston, William (1991), *Perceiving God: The Epistemology of Religious Experience* (Ithaca, NY, and London: Cornell University Press).

Anderson, James F. (1975) (trans.), *Saint Thomas Aquinas. Summa Contra Gentiles. Book Two: Creation*, with an introduction and notes (Notre Dame, Ind.: University of Notre Dame Press; repr. of 1956 edn.).

Antweiler, Anton (1961), *Die Anfangslosigkeit der Welt nach Thomas von Aquin und Kant* (Trier: Paulinus Verlag).

Bagnall, Jeffrey J. (1982), 'Aquinas' Theory of the Rational Soul in the *Summa contra Gentiles*' (unpub. M.Phil. thesis, University of London).

Baldner, Steven E. (1989), 'St. Bonaventure on the Temporal Beginning of the World', *New Scholasticism*, 63: 206–28.

——and Carroll, William E. (1997) (trans.), *Aquinas on Creation: Writings on the 'Sentences' of Peter Lombard, 2.1.1*, with an introduction and notes (Toronto: Pontifical Institute of Mediaeval Studies).

Barnes, Jonathan (1975), 'Introduction', in *Aristotle's Posterior Analytics*, trans. with notes. Clarendon Aristotle Series, ed. J. L. Ackrill (Oxford: Clarendon Press).

Behler, Ernst (1965), *Die Ewigkeit der Welt: Problemgeschichtliche Untersuchungen zu den Kontroversen um Weltanfang und Weltunendlichkeit im Mittelalter, Erster Teil: Die Problemstellung in der arabischen und jüdischen Philosophie des Mittelalters* (Munich, Paderborn, and Vienna: Verlag Ferdinand Schöningh).

Bonansea, Bernardino M. (1974*a*), 'The Impossibility of Creation from Eternity According to St. Bonaventure', *Proceedings of the American Catholic Philosophical Association*, 48: 121–35.

——(1974*b*), 'The Question of an Eternal World in the Teaching of St. Bonaventure', *Franciscan Studies*, 34: 7–33.

Brady, Ignatius (1974), 'John Pecham and the Background of Aquinas's *De aeternitate mundi*', in Maurer (1974), ii. 141–78.

Braine, David (1988), *The Reality of Time and the Existence of God* (Oxford: Clarendon Press).

Brown, Patterson (1964), 'St. Thomas' Doctrine of Necessary Being', *Philosophical Review*, 73: 76–90.

Brown, S. F. (1991), 'The Eternity of the World Discussion at Early Oxford', in A. Zimmermann and A. Speer (eds.), *Mensch und Natur im Mittelalter* (Berlin and New York: de Gruyter), 259–80.

Bukowski, Thomas (1979), 'J. Peckham, T. Aquinas et al., on the Eternity of the World', *Recherches de théologie ancienne et médiévale*, 46: 216–21.

——(1991), 'Understanding St. Thomas on the Eternity of the World: Help from Giles of Rome?', *Recherches de théologie ancienne et médiévale*, 58: 113–25.

Burrell, David B. (1993), *Freedom and Creation in Three Traditions* (Notre Dame, Ind.: University of Notre Dame Press).

Cartwright, Richard L. (1996), 'The Second Way', *Medieval Philosophy and Theology*, 5: 189–204.

——(1997), 'Aquinas on Infinite Multitudes', *Medieval Philosophy and Theology*, 6: 183–201.

Chenu, M.-D. (1950), *Introduction à l'étude de saint Thomas d'Aquin* (Paris: J. Vrin).

Cohen, Sheldon M. (1982), 'St. Thomas Aquinas on the Immaterial Reception of Sensible Forms', *Philosophical Review*, 91: 193–209.

Craig, William Lane, and Smith, Quentin (1993), *Theism, Atheism and Big Bang Cosmology* (Oxford: Clarendon Press).

Crawford, F. (1953) (ed.), *Averrois Cordubensis Commentarium magnum in Aristotelis De anima libros* (Cambridge, Mass.: Mediaeval Academy of America).

Dales, Richard C. (1990), *Medieval Discussions of the Eternity of the World* (Leiden: E. J. Brill).

——and Argerami, Omar (1991) (eds.), *Medieval Latin Texts on the Eternity of the World* (Leiden: E. J. Brill).

Davidson, H. A. (1987), *Proofs for Eternity, Creation and the Existence of God in Medieval Islamic and Jewish Philosophy* (New York and Oxford: Oxford University Press).

Davies, Paul (1983), *God and the New Physics* (New York: Simon and Schuster).

Descartes, René (1988), *Selected Philosophical Writings*, trans. J. Cottingham, R. Stoothoff, and D. Murdoch (Cambridge: Cambridge University Press).

Dewan, Lawrence (1991), 'St. Thomas, Aristotle, and Creation', *Dionysius*, 15: 81–90.

Dumont, Stephen (forthcoming), 'Aquinas, Henry of Ghent, and Duns Scotus on the Eternity of the World'.

English Dominican Fathers (1923) (trans.), *The Summa Contra Gentiles of Saint Thomas Aquinas: The Second Book*, literally translated by the English Dominican Fathers from the latest Leonine edition (London: Burns, Oates & Washbourne, Ltd.).

Frankfurt, Harry G. (1993), 'On God's Creation', in Stump (1993), 128–41.

Gallagher, David (1991), 'Thomas Aquinas on the Will as Rational Appetite', *Journal of the History of Philosophy*, 29: 31–66.

——(1994), 'Free Choice and Free Judgment in Thomas Aquinas', *Archiv für Geschichte der Philosophie*, 76: 247–77.

Garcia, Laura L. (1992), 'Divine Freedom and Creation', *Philosophical Quarterly*, 42: 191–213.

Gauthier, René-Antoine (1961), 'Introduction', in *Saint Thomas d'Aquin: Contra Gentiles, Livre Premier*, text of the Leonine edition; introduction by A. Gauthier; translation by R. Bernier and M. Corvez (Lyons: P. Lethielleux), 7–123.

——(1993), *Saint Thomas d'Aquin: Somme contre les gentils. Introduction*. European Philosophy Series, ed. Henri Hude (Paris: Éditions Universitaires).

Geach, P. T. (1963), 'Aquinas', in G. E. M. Anscombe and P. T. Geach, *Three Philosophers* (Oxford: Basil Blackwell), 65–125.

Gerson, Lloyd P. (1990), *God and Greek Philosophy: Studies in the Early History of Natural Theology* (London and New York: Routledge).

Grover, Stephen (1988), 'Why Only the Best Is Good Enough', *Analysis*, 48: 224.

Haldane, John J. (1983), 'Aquinas on Sense-Perception', *Philosophical Review*, 92: 233–9.

Hause, Jeffrey (forthcoming), 'Thomas Aquinas and the Voluntarists', *Medieval Philosophy and Theology*.

Hayes, Zachary (1964), *The General Doctrine of Creation in the Thirteenth Century (with special emphasis on Matthew of Aquasparta)* (Munich, Paderborn, and Vienna: Verlag Ferdinand Schöningh).

Hibbs, Thomas S. (1995), *Dialectic and Narrative in Aquinas: An Interpretation of the Summa Contra Gentiles* (Notre Dame, Ind.: University of Notre Dame Press).

Hodge, M. J. S. (1991), *Origins and Species: A Study of the Historical Sources of Darwinism and the Contexts of Some Other Accounts of Organic Diversity from Plato and Aristotle On* (New York and London: Garland Publishing, Inc.).

Hoenen, M. J. F. M. (1990), 'The Literary Reception of Thomas Aquinas' View on the Provability of the Eternity of the World', in Wissink (1990), 39–68.

——(1992), 'The Eternity of the World According to Marsilius of Inghen . . .', in H. A. G. Braakhuis and M. J. F. M. Hoenen (eds.), *Marsilius of Inghen* (Nijmegen: Ingenium), 117–43.

Hoffman, Paul (1990), 'St. Thomas Aquinas on the Halfway State of Sensible Being', *Philosophical Review*, 99: 73–92

Howard-Snyder, Daniel (1995) (ed.), *The Evidential Argument from Evil* (Bloomington, Ind.: Indiana University Press).

—— and Howard-Snyder, Frances (1994), 'How an Unsurpassable Being Can Create a Surpassable World', *Faith and Philosophy*, 11: 260–8.

Huby, Pamela (1971 & 1973), 'Kant or Cantor? That the Universe, if Real, must be Finite in both Space and Time', *Philosophy*, 46: 121–32; 48: 186–7.

Inwagen, Peter van (1993), 'Genesis and Evolution', in Stump (1993), 93–127.

—— (1995), 'The Place of Chance in a World Sustained by God,' in van Inwagen (ed.), *God, Knowledge, and Mystery* (Ithaca, NY, and London: Cornell University Press), 42–65.

Irwin, T. H. (1991), 'Aristotle's Philosophy of Mind', in S. Everson (ed.), *Psychology*. Companions to Ancient Thought, 2 (Cambridge: Cambridge University Press), 56–83.

Johnson, Mark F. (1989), 'Did St. Thomas Attribute a Doctrine of Creation to Aristotle?', *New Scholasticism*, 63: 129–55.

Kaufman, Gordon D. (1989), '"Evidentialism": A Theologian's Response', *Faith and Philosophy*, 6: 35–46.

Kenny, Anthony (1964), 'The Use of Logical Analysis in Theology', in Kenny (1987*b*), 3–20.

—— (1969), 'Intellect and Imagination in Aquinas', in Kenny (ed.), *Aquinas: A Collection of Critical Essays* (Garden City, NY: Doubleday), 273–96.

—— (1987*a*), 'Form, Essence and Existence in Aquinas', in Kenny (ed.), *The Heritage of Wisdom: Essays in the History of Philosophy* (Oxford: Basil Blackwell), 22–33.

—— (1987*b*), *Reason and Religion: Essays in Philosophical Theology* (Oxford: Basil Blackwell).

—— (1993), *Aquinas on Mind* (London and New York: Routledge).

Klima, Gyula (1997), 'Man = Body + Soul: Aquinas's Arithmetic of Human Nature', in T. Koistinen and T. Lehtonen (eds.), *Philosophical Studies in Religion, Metaphysics, and Ethics* (Helsinki: Luther–Agricola Society), 179–97.

Knuuttila, Simo (1982), 'Modal Logic', in Kretzmann *et al.* (1982), ch. 17.

—— (1993), *Modalities in Medieval Philosophy* (London: Routledge).

Kovach, Francis J. (1974), 'The Question of the Eternity of the World in St. Bonaventure and St. Thomas—A Critical Analysis', in R. W. Shahan and F. J. Kovach (eds.), *Bonaventure and Aquinas: Enduring Philosophers* (Norman, Okla.: University of Oklahoma Press), 155–86.

Kremer, Klaus (1965), 'Das "Warum" der Schöpfung: "quia bonus" vel/et "quia voluit"? Ein Beitrag zum Verhältnis von Neuplatonismus und Christentum an Hand des Prinzips "bonum est diffusivum sui"', in K. Flasch (ed.), *Parusia: Studien zur Philosophie Platons und zur Problemsgeschichte des Platonismus* (Frankfurt-on-Main: Minerva), 241–54.

Kretzmann, Norman (1976), 'Incipit/Desinit', in P. Machamer and R. Turnbull (eds.), *Motion and Time, Space and Matter* (Columbus, Oh.: Ohio State University Press), 101–36.

——(1981), '*Sensus Compositus, Sensus Divisus,* and Propositional Attitudes', *Medioevo*, 7: 195–229.

——(1983), 'Goodness, Knowledge, and Indeterminacy in the Philosophy of Thomas Aquinas', *Journal of Philosophy*, 80: 631–49.

——(1985), 'Ockham and the Creation of the Beginningless World', *Franciscan Studies*, 45: 1–31.

——(1988), 'Warring Against the Law of My Mind: Aquinas on Romans 7', in T. V. Morris (ed.), *Philosophy and the Christian Faith* (Notre Dame, Ind.: University of Notre Dame Press), 172–95.

——(1990), 'Faith Seeks, Understanding Finds: Augustine's Charter for Christian Philosophy', in T. Flint (ed.), *Christian Philosophy* (Notre Dame, Ind.: University of Notre Dame Press), 1–36.

——(1991*a*), 'A General Problem of Creation: Why Would God Create Anything at All?', in MacDonald (1991), 208–28.

——(1991*b*), 'A Particular Problem of Creation: Why Would God Create This World?', in MacDonald (1991), 229–49.

——(1991*c*), 'Infallibility, Error, and Ignorance', in R. Bosley and M. Tweedale (eds.), *Aristotle and his Medieval Interpreters*, Canadian Journal of Philosophy suppl. vol. 17: 159–94.

——(1992), 'Evidence Against Anti-Evidentialism', in K. J. Clark (ed.), *Our Knowledge of God: Essays on Natural and Philosophical Theology* (Dordrecht, Boston, and London: Kluwer Academic Publishers), 17–38.

——(1993), 'Philosophy of Mind', in Kretzmann and Stump (1993), 128–59.

——(1994), 'Mystical Perception: St Theresa, William Alston, and the Broadminded Atheist', in A. G. Padgett (ed.), *Reason and the Christian Religion: Essays in Honour of Richard Swinburne* (Oxford: Clarendon Press), 65–90.

——(1997), *The Metaphysics of Theism: Aquinas's Natural Theology in Summa contra gentiles I* (Oxford: Clarendon Press).

——and Pasnau, Robert (1992), review of Dales (1990), *Speculum*, 67: 654–6.

——and Stump, E. (1993) (eds.), *The Cambridge Companion to Aquinas* (Cambridge: Cambridge University Press).

——Kenny, Anthony, and Pinborg, Jan (1982) (eds.), *The Cambridge*

History of Later Medieval Philosophy (Cambridge: Cambridge University Press).

McCabe, Herbert (1969), 'The Immortality of the Soul: The Traditional Argument', in A. Kenny (ed.), *Aquinas: A Collection of Critical Essays* (Garden City, NY: Doubleday), 297–307.

MacDonald, Scott (1984), 'The *Esse/Essentia* Argument in Aquinas's *De ente et essentia*', *Journal of the History of Philosophy*, 22: 157–72.

——(1991) (ed.), *Being and Goodness* (Ithaca, NY, and London: Cornell University Press).

——(1993), 'Theory of Knowledge', in Kretzmann and Stump (1993), 160–95.

——(1996), 'What is Philosophical Theology?', in Peter McEnhill and George B. Hall (eds.), *The Presumption of Presence* (Edinburgh: Scottish Academic Press), 61–81.

——(1998), 'Aquinas's Libertarian Account of Free Choice', *Revue Internationale de Philosophie*, 21: 309–28.

McInerny, Ralph (1991), 'St. Thomas on *De hebdomadibus*', in MacDonald (1991), 74–97.

MacIntosh, J. J. (1994), 'St. Thomas and the Traversal of the Infinite', *American Catholic Philosophical Quarterly*, 68: 157–77.

McMullin, Ernan (1985*a*), 'Introduction: Evolution and Creation', in McMullin (1985*b*), 1–56.

——(1985*b*) (ed.), *Evolution and Creation* (Notre Dame, Ind.: University of Notre Dame Press).

Maurer, Armand A. (1974) (ed.), *St. Thomas Aquinas 1274–1974: Commemorative Studies* (2 vols., Toronto: Pontifical Institute of Mediaeval Studies).

Menssen, Sandra, and Sullivan, Thomas (1995), 'Must God Create?', *Faith and Philosophy*, 12: 321–41.

Pasnau, Robert (1997), *Theories of Cognition in the Later Middle Ages* (Cambridge: Cambridge University Press).

Peghaire, Julien (1932), 'L'Axiome "Bonum est diffusivum sui" dans le néo-platonisme et le thomisme', *Revue de l'Université d'Ottawa* (special section), 1: 5*–30*.

Pegis, Anton C. (1934), *St. Thomas and the Problem of the Soul in the Thirteenth Century* (Toronto: Pontifical Institute of Mediaeval Studies).

——(1964), 'Qu'est-ce que la Summa Contra Gentiles?', in *L'Homme devant Dieu: Mélanges offerts au Père Henri de Lubac* (3 vols., Paris: Aubier), ii. 169–82.

——(1974), 'The Separated Soul and its Nature in St. Thomas', in Maurer (1974), i. 131–58.

Peterson, M. L. (1992) (ed.), *The Problem of Evil* (Notre Dame, Ind.: University of Notre Dame Press).

Plantinga, Alvin (1974), *God, Freedom, and Evil* (New York: Harper and Row).

——(1983), 'Reason and Belief in God', in Plantinga and Wolterstorff (1983), 16–93.

——and Wolterstorff, N. (1983) (eds.), *Faith and Rationality* (Notre Dame, Ind.: University of Notre Dame Press).

Popper, Karl (1978), 'On the Possibility of an Infinite Past: A Reply to Whitrow', *British Journal for the Philosophy of Science*, 29: 47–8.

Quinn, Philip L. (1982), 'God, Moral Perfection, and Possible Worlds', in Frederick Sontag and M. Darrol Bryant (eds.), *God: The Contemporary Discussion* (New York: Rose of Sharon Press), 197–215.

Rickaby, Joseph (1905), *Of God and his Creatures: An Annotated Translation (with some Abridgement), of the* Summa Contra Gentiles *of Saint Thomas Aquinas* (repr. Westminster, Md.: Carroll Press, 1950).

Riet, S. van (1980) (ed.), *Avicenna Latinus: Liber de philosophia prima sive scientia divina* V–X (Louvain: E. Peeters, and Leiden: E. J. Brill).

Robb, James H. (1968) (ed.), *St. Thomas Aquinas: Quaestiones de Anima* (Toronto: Pontifical Institute of Mediaeval Studies).

Rowe, William L. (1975*a*), *The Cosmological Argument* (Princeton: Princeton University Press).

——(1975*b*), 'The Cosmological Argument and the Principle of Sufficient Reason', in Rowe (1975*a*), 60–114.

——(1975*c*), 'Two Criticisms of the Cosmological Argument', in Rowe (1975*a*), 115–67.

——(1994), 'The Problem of No Best World', *Faith and Philosophy*, 11: 269–71.

Sagan, Carl (1977), *The Dragons of Eden* (New York: Random House).

Scriven, Michael (1954–5), 'The Age of the Universe', *British Journal for the Philosophy of Science*, 5: 181–90.

Smith, Q. (1987), 'Infinity and the Past', *Philosophy of Science*, 54: 63–75.

Snyder, Steven C. (1991), 'Albert the Great: Creation and the Eternity of the World', in R. James Long (ed.), *Philosophy and the God of Abraham* (Toronto: Pontifical Institute of Mediaeval Studies), 191–202.

Sorabji, Richard (1983), *Time, Creation, and the Continuum: Theories in Antiquity and the Middle Ages* (Ithaca, NY, and London: Cornell University Press).

——(1987), 'The contra Aristotelem: Purpose, Context and Significance', in Wildberg (1987), 18–24.

Steenberghen, Fernand van (1974), *Introduction à l'étude de la philosophie médiévale* (Louvain: Publications universitaires).

——(1977), *Maître Siger de Brabant* (Louvain: Publications universitaires).

——(1980), *Thomas Aquinas and Radical Aristotelianism* (Washington: Catholic University of America Press).

Stump, Eleonore (1985), 'The Problem of Evil', *Faith and Philosophy*, 2: 392–423.

——(1993) (ed.), *Reasoned Faith* (Ithaca, NY, and London: Cornell University Press).

——(1995), 'Non-Cartesian Substance Dualism and Materialism without Reductionism', *Faith and Philosophy*, 12: 505–31.

——(1997), 'Aquinas's Account of Freedom: Intellect and Will', *Monist*, 80: 576–97.

——(1998), 'Aquinas's Account of the Mechanisms of Intellective Cognition', *Revue Internationale de Philosophie*, 21: 287–307.

——(forthcoming *a*), 'Aquinas's Account of the Mechanisms of Cognition: Sense and Phantasia'.

——(forthcoming *b*), 'Wisdom: Will, Belief, and Moral Goodness', in S. MacDonald and E. Stump (eds.), *Aquinas's Moral Theory* (Ithaca, NY, and London: Cornell University Press).

——and Kretzmann, Norman (1981), 'Eternity', *Journal of Philosophy*, 78: 429–58.

————(1982), 'Absolute Simplicity', *Faith and Philosophy*, 2: 353–82.

————(1987), 'Atemporal Duration: A Reply to Fitzgerald', *Journal of Philosophy*, 84: 214–19.

————(1988), 'Being and Goodness', in T. V. Morris (ed.), *Divine and Human Action: Essays in the Metaphysics of Theism* (Ithaca, NY, and London: Cornell University Press), 281–312; repr. in MacDonald (1991), 98–128.

————(1990), 'Theologically Unfashionable Philosophy' (a reply to Kaufman 1989), *Faith and Philosophy*, 7: 329–39.

————(1991), 'Prophecy, Past Truth, and Eternity', in J. W. Tomberlin (ed.), *Philosophical Perspectives*, 5, Philosophy of Religion, 395–424.

————(1992), 'Eternity, Awareness, and Action', *Faith and Philosophy*, 9: 463–82.

————(1995), 'God's Knowledge and its Causal Efficacy', in T. D. Senor (ed.), *The Rationality of Belief and the Plurality of Faith* (Ithaca, NY, and London: Cornell University Press), 94–124.

Swinburne, Richard (1979), *The Existence of God* (Oxford: Clarendon Press).

Taylor, J. H. (1982) (trans.), *St. Augustine: The Literal Meaning of Genesis* (2 vols., New York: Newman Press).

Taylor, Richard C. (forthcoming), translation of Crawford (1953) (New Haven: Yale University Press).

Thijssen, J. M. M. H. (1990), 'The Response to Thomas Aquinas in the Early Fourteenth Century: Eternity and Infinity in the Works of Henry of Harclay, Thomas of Wilton and William of Alnwick O.F.M.', in Wissink (1990), 82–100.

Torrell, J.-P. (1993), *Initiation à Saint Thomas d'Aquin: sa personne et son œuvre* (Fribourg and Paris: Éditions universitaires and Cerf).

Tugwell, Simon (1988), *Albert & Thomas: Selected Writings* (Mahwah, NJ: Paulist Press).

Velde, Rudi A. te (1995), *Participation and Substantiality in Thomas Aquinas* (Leiden, New York, and Cologne: E. J. Brill).

Veldhuijsen, Peter van (1990*a*), 'The Question on the Possibility of an Eternally Created World: Bonaventura and Thomas Aquinas', in Wissink (1990), 20–38.

——(1990*b*), 'Richard of Middleton contra Thomas Aquinas on the Question whether the Created World could have been Eternally Produced by God', in Wissink (1990), 69–81.

Vollert, Cyril, Kendzierski, Lottie H., and Byrne, Paul M. (1964) (trans.), *St. Thomas Aquinas, Siger of Brabant, St. Bonaventure: On the Eternity of the World* (Milwaukee: Marquette University Press).

Wallace, James D. (1968), 'The Beginning of the World', *Dialogue*, 6: 521–6.

Wallace, William A. (1974), 'Aquinas on Creation: Science, Theology, and Matters of Fact', *Thomist*, 38: 485–523.

Webb, Clement C. J. (1915), *Studies in the History of Natural Theology* (Oxford: Clarendon Press).

Weisheipl, James A. (1983), 'The Date and Context of Aquinas' "*De aeternitate mundi*"', in L. P. Gerson (ed.), *Graceful Reason* (Toronto: Pontifical Institute of Mediaeval Studies), 239–71.

White, Kevin (1995), 'Aquinas on the Immediacy of the Union of Soul and Body', in P. Lockey (ed.), *Studies in Thomistic Theology* (Houston: Center for Thomistic Studies), 209–80.

Whitrow, G. J. (1954–5), 'The Age of the Universe', *British Journal for the Philosophy of Science*, 5: 215–25.

——(1978), 'On the Impossibility of an Infinite Past', *British Journal for the Philosophy of Science*, 29: 39–45.

Wildberg, Christian (1987) (trans.), *Philoponus: Against Aristotle, on the Eternity of the World* (London: Duckworth).

Wippel, John F. (1980), *The Metaphysical Thought of Godfrey of Fontaines* (Washington: Catholic University of America Press).

——(1984), *Metaphysical Themes in Thomas Aquinas* (Washington: Catholic University of America Press).

——(1987) (trans.), *Boethius of Dacia: On the Supreme Good, On the Eternity of the World, On Dreams* (Toronto: Pontifical Institute of Mediaeval Studies).

——(1992), 'Thomas Aquinas on What Philosophers Can Know about God', *American Catholic Philosophical Quarterly*, 66: 279–97.

——(1993), 'Metaphysics', in Kretzmann and Stump (1993), 83–127.

Wissink, J. B. M. (1990) (ed.), *The Eternity of the World in the Thought of Thomas Aquinas and his Contemporaries* (Leiden: E. J. Brill).

Wolfson, H. A. (1943), 'The Kalam Arguments for Creation in Saadia, Averroës, Maimonides and St. Thomas', in *Saadia Anniversary Volume, American Academy of Jewish Research, Texts and Studies*, 2 (New York: American Academy of Jewish Research), 197–245.

INDEX LOCORUM

Anselm
De veritate 1: 168 n.
Monologion 18: 168 n.

Thomas Aquinas
Collationes super Credo in Deum
preface: 14 n.
1.880: 142 n.
12.1012: 418 n.
CT *Compendium theologiae*
I.11.20: 258 n.
I.68.116: 56 n.
I.68.117: 56 n.
I.71–4: 186 n.
I.71: 213 n.
I.74.128: 252 n.
I.98–9: 142 n.
I.98: 161 n.
I.99: 173 n., 174 n.
I.102: 186 n.
I.102.199: 215 n.
I.161.323: 186 n.
I.170.336: 186 n., 188 n.
DAM *De aeternitate mundi, contra*
murmurantes: 142 n.
298: 144 n.
310: 181 n.
DEE *De ente et essentia*
4.27: 35 n., 46 n., 56 n.
DSS *De substantiis separatis*
9.99–100: 142 n., 150 n.
10.100: 159
DUI *De unitate intellectus, contra*
Averroistas: 339 n.
In BDH *Expositio super librum*
Boethii De hebdomadibus
L2.22: 265 n.
L2.34: 266 n.
In BDT *Expositio super librum Boethii*
De trinitate: 324 n.
In DA *Sentential super De anima*:
324 n.
I: L1.15: 14 n.
II: L1.234: 327 n.
II.1: L2.224: 311 n.
III: L7.689: 319 n.

In DDN *Expositio super librum*
Dionysii De divinis nominibus
4: L3.318: 240 n.
In Met. *Sentential super Metaphysicam*
V: L7: 278 n.
V: L14.69: 355 n.
VII: L8.1444: 394 n.
XII: L2.2438: 213 n.
XII: L2.2439: 214 n.
XII: L2.2440: 214 n.
XII: L5.2495–9: 145 n.
XII: L5.2496–7: 142 n.
In PA *Sentential super Posteriora*
analytica
I: L4.43: 14 n.
II: L13.533: 14 n.
In Phys. *Sentential super Physicam*
I: L12.102: 288 n.
V: L5.694: 282 n.
VIII: L2: 168 n.
VIII: L2.986: 142 n., 145 n.
In Sent. *Scriptum super libros*
Sententiarum: 324 n.
I.2.1.4, sc: 135 n.
I.10.1.4c: 327 n.
I.13.1.2c: 195 n.
I.13.2.1c: 205 n.
I.26.2.2c: 195 n.
I.29.1.3c: 195 n.
I.42.2.2c: 104 n., 118 n.
I.43.2.1, ad 2: 121 n., 127 n.
I.43.2.1, ad 3: 121 n.
I.44.1.2: 219–27, 238 n., App. III
II.1.1.2: 54 n.
II.1.1.2c: 56 n., 75
II.1.1.2, ad 3: 94 n.
II.1.1.5: 142 n., 160, 176 n.
II.1.1.5c: 144 n.
II.1.1.5, obj. 1: 173 n.
II.1.1.5, objs. 2, 3, 8, 9: 169 n.
II.1.1.5, objs. 2, 3: 167 n.
II.1.1.5, objs. 5, 6: 170 n.
II.1.1.5, obj. 5: 171 n.
II.1.1.5, obj. 8: 174 n.
II.1.1.5, obj. 11: 160 n., 161 n.
II.1.1.5, objs. 12–14: 160 n., 161 n.

Thomas Aquinas
In Sent. *Scriptum super libros*
  Sententiarum (*cont.*):
II.1.1.5, sc 1–6, 9: 176 n.
II.1.1.5, sc 3: 177 n.
II.1.1.5, sc 4: 180
II.1.1.5, sc 5 & ad sc 5: 151 n.
II.1.1.5, ad sc 1: 176
II.1.1.5, ad sc 2: 76 n., 177 n.
II.1.1.5, ad sc 3: 178
II.1.1.5, ad sc 4: 180
II.1.1.5, ad sc 7: 142 n.
II.12.1.2: 191–3, 201 n.
II.12.1.2c: 191 n.
II.13.1.1: 186 n., 189, 198
II.13.1.1c: 199–202, 402 n.
II.13.1.1c, ad 3: 201
II.13.1.1, obj. 1 & ad 1: 198–9
II.13.1.1, obj. 3: 198 n.
II.13.1.1, obj. 5 & ad 5: 189–90, 194 n.,
  198, 200
II.13.1.1, ad 2: 199–200
II.14.1.5: 186 n.
II.14.5, obj. 6: 188 n.
II.15.1.1: 186 n.
II.15.2.2: 186 n.
II.17.2.2, obj. 3, ad 3: 186 n.
II.37.1.1: 56 n.
II.37.1.2: 54 n., 56 n.
II.37.1.2, sc 2: 56 n.
III.27.1.1, ad 5: 278 n.
IV.5.2.2.3c: 115 n.
IV.49.3.2c: 327 n.
QDA *Quaestio disputata de anima*:
  314, 316, 323 n., 347 n.
1: 314
1c: 234 n., 296 n., 320
2, ad 2: 317 n.
9: 308 n.
9c: 293 n., 327, 329, 331 n.
9, obj. 5: 330 n.
9, ad 5: 330
9, ad 10: 276 n.
10: 335 n.
10c: 298 n., 332, 334–6, 378 n.
10, obj. 3: 333 n.
10, obj. 15 & ad 15: 335 n.
11: 308 n.
15: 416 n.
17–20: 416 n.
QDP *Quaestiones disputatae de*
  potentia
1.1c: 40 n., 42, 43 n., 45, 47 n.

1.1, ad 1: 49 n.
1.5: 124 n.
1.7c: 104, 114, 119 n.
1.7, ad 4: 119 n.
3.1c: 75
3.3c: 53 n.
3.5: 56 n.
3.5, obj. 3 & ad 3: 79
3.6, ad 6: 115 n.
3.11, ad 8: 111 n.
3.12, obj. 5 & ad 5: 335 n.
3.14: 142 n.
3.14, obj. 7 & ad 7: 150 n.
3.14, ad sc 1: 142 n.
3.14, ad sc 3: 142 n.
3.14, ad 8: 150
3.15c: 122 n., 124 n.
3.15, ad 11: 124 n.
3.15, ad 18: 121 n.
3.16: 197 n.
3.16c: 215 n.
3.17: 142 n.
3.17, objs. 1, 7, 8, 14: 166 n.
3.17, objs. 2, 3: 169 n.
3.17, objs. 4, 6, 9, 12, 13, 26: 161 n.
3.17, objs. 10, 11: 174 n.
3.17, objs. 15–18, 24, 25: 170 n.
3.17, obj. 20: 169 n., 171 n.
3.17, objs. 27, 28: 168 n.
9.7c: 194
QDSC *Quaestio disputata de*
  spiritualibus creaturis
1c: 79 n.
1, obj. 8 & ad 8: 258 n., 266 n.
1, ad 9: 308 n.
3: 308 n.
4: 335 n.
4c: 332 n., 334
11, ad 3: 14 n.
QDV *Quaestiones disputatae de*
  veritate
1: 324 n.
1.1: 285 n.
2: 324 n.
2.12, ad 4: 129 n.
3.9, ad 9: 374 n., 378 n., 379 n., 402 n.
3.9, ad 10: 395 n., 399 n., 400 n.
4.1, ad 8: 14 n.
4.5c: 52 n.
6.1, ad 8: 14 n.
8: 324 n.
9: 324 n.
10: 324 n.

10.1*c*: 14 n.
10.1, ad 6: 14 n.
10.6*c*: 312 n.
10.6*c*, ad 7: 312 n.
13.4*c*: 326 n.
19.1–2: 416 n.
23.1*c*. 240 n.
23.1, sc 4: 250 n.
23.4: 125 n.
23.4*c*: 125
24.1: 244 n.
24.3*c*: 217
QQ *Quaestiones quodlibetales*
III.9.1: 416 n.
III.14.2: 142 n
VII.1: 324 n.
VIII.2.1: 324 n.
X.3–4: 324 n.
X.3.1: 326 n.
XI.5: 324 n.
XII.6.1: 142 n.
SCG *Summa contra gentiles*
I-III: 1, 2 n., 6–9, 11–12, 20, 25, 30,
    31 n., 37, 93, 186, 232, 270, 281,
    371
I-II: 14, 16, 17 n., 18, 24, 31, 33, 54 n.,
    161, 184, 203–4, 231, 253, 256, 369
I: 1–4, 5 n., 8, 13, 16, 18–19, 28, 30, 35,
    50, 56, 70, 122, 125–6, 229
I.1.2: 27
I.1.3: 26–7
I.1.5: 27
I.1.6: 19
I.1.7: 13 n., 19
I.2.9: 11, 19, 27
I.2.10–11: 1 n.
I.2.11: 6
I.2.12: 7
I.3.14: 12–13
I.3.18: 14 n.
I.4.21: 12 n., 13 n.
I.9.51: 13
I.9.52: 12
I.9.55–6: 11
I.9.55: 7, 14
I.9.57: 3, 5, 9, 183
I.10–11: 14 n.
I.13: 28 n., 31 n., 34 n., 161 n., 163, 170–1
I.13.95: 63
I.13.113: 33 n., 34, 37 n., 56 n.
I.14–102: 14
I.14.117–19: 259 n.
I.14.117: 15

I.14.118: 9 n.
I.15: 28 n., 39, 51, 154, 161 n., 162, 196
I.15.121: 154
I.15.122: 149, 155 n.
I.15.123: 154
I.15.124: 50, 57
I.15.125: 154
I.16: 16, 37, 51, 128, 161 n.
I.16.128: 39 n.
I.16.130: 259 n.
I.16.131: 37, 40 n.
I.16.132: 40 n., 42 n.
I.16.133: 40 n.
I.17: 172
I.17.140*b*: 195
I.18: 12, 13 n.
I.18.141*b*: 285 n.
I.20: 257 n.
I.20.183: 5 n.
I.20.188: 6
I.21–2: 257
I.22: 384
I.22.207: 46 n.
I.22.211: 258 n.
I.23: 44
I.24: 12
I.25: 12, 197
I.25.235–6: 259 n.
I.26.239: 194, 197 n.
I.26.242: 385
I.28–102: 9 n.
I.28: 15, 21, 31 n., 219
I.28.264: 38
I.28.265: 40 n.
I.28.268: 38 n.
I.29.270: 40 n.
I.30.278: 9 n., 15
I.31: 257
I.37–102: 15
I.37–41: 16, 161 n.
I.37.306: 241
I.37.307: 40 n., 134
I.38: 31 n.
I.38.310: 135 n.
I.40: 21, 31 n.
I.42: 57, 68 n., 101 n., 197
I.43: 98 n., 103, 206
I.43.368: 103, 150 n.
I.44–96: 31 n.
I.44–71: 16 n., 69, 255
I.44–61: 231 n.
I.44.376: 256 n.
I.45.385: 40

Thomas Aquinas
SCG *Summa contra gentiles* (*cont.*):
I.46–9: 127 n.
I.46: 127
I.47.397: 256 n.
I.49 ff.: 22, 31 n.
I.50.420: 40 n.
I.50.421: 185 n.
I.53.443: 256 n.
I.54.446: 197 n.
I.54.451: 230
I.61.510: 351 n.
I.62–102: 231 n.
I.62: 168
I.62.515–18: 13
I.62.519: 13
I.63.521: 256 n.
I.67.565: 158
I.71.605: 185
I.72–96: 16 n.
I.72.624: 244
I.73.630: 40 n.
I.74 ff.: 239
I.74–84: 154
I.74.637–8: 125
I.75: 78 n.
I.75.643: 126 n.
I.75.644: 135 n.
I.76: 78 n.
I.76.647: 126 n.
I.80: 125 n.
I.80.676: 125
I.81–3: 128
I.81: 102, 152–3
I.81.682: 126 n.
I.82: 128
I.83.701–2: 128 n.
I.83.705: 133 n.
I.86: 103
I.87.727: 126
I.88: 102
I.88.732: 102 n.
I.90–1: 16
I.93.784: 133 n.
I.94.792: 127 n.
I.95: 105 n.
II–III: 4, 8 n., 9, 13, 70, 232
II: 1, 3 n., 5, 6 n., 8, 18–20, 27, 40 n., 71,
        74–5, 102–3, 108–13, 120–2, 128,
        183, 185–6, 189, 258 n., 314, 323–4,
        343 n., 364, 368–9
II.1–30: 160
II.1–16: 71

II.1–5: 8, 30, 71, 229
II.1–4: 29
II.1: 13–14, 84
II.1.851: 228
II.1.852: 14, 36, 231
II.1.853: 16–17, 77
II.1.854: 16–18, 232 n.
II.1.854–5: 17
II.1.856: 9, 13, 18, 31 n., 33, 70, 122,
        232 n.
II.1.857: 20, 84, 228
II.2–3: 21
II.2: 103 n.
II.2.858: 20, 23
II.2.859: 21, 232 n.
II.2.860: 21
II.2.861: 21, 31 n.
II.2.862: 22–3, 31 n., 232 n.
II.2.863: 23, 25 n.
II.3.864: 20 n., 23, 229
II.3.865: 24, 98
II.3.866: 24
II.3.867: 24, 120
II.3.868: 25, 232
II.4: 10 n., 25
II.4.871: 5 n., 21 n., 25 n., 229, 231
II.4.871–2*a*: 228
II.4.872: 26, 34
II.4.872*a*: 71 n.
II.4.872*b*: 228
II.4.873: 25
II.4.874: 27
II.4.875: 28
II.4.876: 23 n., 28, 232 n.
II.5.877: 28–9, 32, 54 n., 183, 228, 230,
        271 n.
II.6–38: 28–9, 53, 183, 228
II.6–15: 29, 31–2, 36, 54, 70–1, 101
II.6: 30–2, 34 n., 35–6, 41–2, 48, 54–5
II.6.878: 30–1, 33, 35
II.6.879–84: 30
II.6.879–80: 34
II.6.879: 34–6, 55, 56 n.
II.6.880: 36, 55
II.6.881–4: 34
II.6.881: 36, 40 n., 55
II.6.882: 36, 55
II.6.883: 36, 55
II.6.884: 36–41, 55, 115 n.
II.6.885: 30
II.7–10: 33, 36, 48, 54, 103
II.7: 41–2
II.7.886: 41

II.7.887: 42, 55 n.
II.7.890: 42
II.8–14: 30 n.
II.8: 43–4
II.8.893: 38 n.
II.8.896: 44
II.9: 43, 45, 123, 125
II.9.902: 44
II.10: 45–6
II.10.903: 43 n., 45–8, 123
II.11–14: 33, 36, 49 n., 54
II.11.905: 48
II.11.906: 48, 55 n.
II.11.907: 48
II.11.908: 48
II.11.909: 48
II.12.913: 49–51
II.12.914: 51–2
II.12.915: 51–2
II.12.916: 51
II.13&14: 52
II.13&14.917: 52 n.
II.13&14.918: 52 n.
II.13&14.919*b*: 52
II.13&14.920: 52 n., 53
II.13&14.921: 52 n., 53 n.
II.15: 23, 30 n., 36, 54, 56, 58, 71, 73–4,
        78, 80–1, 101, 129 n., 161 n., 214,
        384
II.15.922: 54
II.15.923–6: 73 n.
II.15.923: 56 n.
II.15.924: 56 n.
II.15.925: 56 n., 115 n.
II.15.926: 56 n.
II.15.927–9: 73 n.
II.15.927: 57, 204
II.15.929: 56 n.
II.16–38: 36
II.16–21: 32, 70
II.16–17: 90, 172
II.16: 71, 73–6, 78–9, 82, 84, 87–8, 90,
        101
II.16.932: 74
II.16.933–43: 75 n.
II.16.935: 81
II.16.936: 81, 87
II.16.940: 363 n.
II.16.941: 78 n.
II.16.943: 80, 173 n.
II.16.944: 85
II.16.945: 85, 173
II.17–21: 87

II.17–19: 71, 87, 101, 175–6
II.17: 87–91, 150, 173, 257 n.
II.17.946: 87, 91
II.17.949: 90–1
II.17.950: 89, 91 n., 92
II.18–28: 87 n.
II.18: 87
II.18.951: 90
II.18.952: 91, 150
II.18.953: 90, 172
II.19: 91, 92 n., 94
II.19.956: 91–2
II.19.957: 82 n.
II.19.958: 92 n.
II.19.959: 94
II.19.960: 92 n., 94 n.
II.19.961: 93, 112 n.
II.20–1: 71, 101
II.20: 98
II.20.968: 99
II.21: 99–100, 107, 116, 138, 386
II.21.969: 99
II.21.971: 99, 115 n.
II.21.972: 116 n.
II.21.973: 100 n.
II.21.974: 100
II.21.975: 100 n., 329 n., 399 n.
II.21.978: 116
II.21.979: 99
II.21.979*a*: 95
II.21.980: 99
II.22–38: 32
II.22–4: 129 n.
II.22: 103–4, 118, 121–2, 124, 149,
        175 n., 197
II.22.981: 105, 113
II.22.982: 83 n., 107–13
II.22.983: 114–19
II.22.986*b*: 109 n.
II.22.986*e*: 104 n.
II.22.988: 106
II.23–9: 103
II.23–4: 206, 238
II.23: 44 n., 106 n., 120–7, 138, 152,
        348 n.
II.23.989: 120, 125
II.23.990: 121
II.23.991: 124–5
II.23.992: 122, 126
II.23.993: 123, 125
II.23.995: 125, 347 n.
II.23.997: 344 n.
II.23.1001: 121

Thomas Aquinas
SCG *Summa contra gentiles* (*cont.*):
II.24: 126, 128, 348 n.
II.24.1002: 127
II.24.1003: 127
II.24.1006: 122 n., 127
II.24.1008: 126
II.25–7: 44 n.
II.25: 105 n., 127, 226
II.25.1009*a*: 104 n., 127
II.25.1009*b*: 128
II.25.1010: 128 n.
II.25.1017: 128 n.
II.25.1018–21: 117 n.
II.25.1022–3: 118 n.
II.25.1026: 101 n.
II.25.1027: 18 n.
II.25.1028: 105 n., 128 n.
II.25.1030: 105 n.
II.25.1031–2*a*: 128, 132
II.25.1032*b–c*: 128
II.25.1033: 128
II.26–7: 129, 131
II.26.1039: 129 n.
II.27: 153 n., 257 n., 348 n.
II.27.1044: 129
II.28–30: 103
II.28&29: 126, 130, 138, 154–5, 157, 161 n.
II.28&29.1046–62: 130
II.28&29.1046–52: 130, 132
II.28&29.1046–50: 136
II.28&29.1046: 130
II.28&29.1048: 131
II.28&29.1053–7: 131
II.28&29.1053: 130, 136
II.28&29.1053*a–f*: 131–3, 135, 138 n., 164 n.
II.28&29.1055: 136
II.28&29.1056*a*: 132, 133 n., 136
II.28&29.1057: 137
II.28&29.1057*a–b*: 132
II.28&29.1058–60: 137
II.28&29.1060–1: 158 n.
II.28&29.1060*a–e*: 137
II.28&29.1061*a–d*: 138, 153, 156–7
II.29–32: 348 n.
II.30: 130, 149, 153, 156–7, 169
II.30.1063*a–b*: 139, 157
II.30.1064: 139
II.30.1066: 139 n., 157
II.30.1069: 139 n.
II.30.1070: 139, 153

II.30.1071–3: 140
II.30.1073*a*: 139 n.
II.30.1074: 140
II.30.1075: 140
II.30.1076–8: 140
II.30.1076*c–e*: 18 n., 353 n., 360
II.30.1078*a–c*: 140
II.30.1079*b*: 141
II.31–8: 59, 87, 142, 151–2, 160 n., 196
II.31: 148–50, 154, 156, 160, 169
II.31.1080: 149
II.31.1081: 148
II.31.1081*b–e*: 152–4, 156 n.
II.31.1082: 152, 156 n.
II.31.1083: 153, 156 n.
II.31.1084: 154
II.31.1085: 156
II.32: 159 n., 160–1, 162 n.
II.32.1086: 152
II.32.1088: 160 n., 161 n.
II.32.1089: 160 n., 161 n.
II.32.1090: 161 n.
II.32.1091: 160 n., 161 n.
II.32.1092: 161 n., 162 n., 163
II.32.1093: 161 n., 165
II.32.1094: 161 n., 166
II.33: 167
II.33.1097: 167 n., 169
II.33.1098: 167 n., 169
II.33.1099: 167 n., 169
II.33.1100: 167 n., 196 n.
II.33.1101: 163 n., 167 n., 170
II.33.1102: 163 n., 168, 171
II.33.1103: 168
II.34.1106: 172
II.34.1107: 173
II.34.1108: 174
II.34.1109: 175
II.35: 161, 348 n.
II.35.1113–15: 159 n.
II.35.1113: 162
II.35.1114: 115 n., 162
II.35.1115: 162
II.35.1116: 163
II.35.1117: 165
II.35.1118: 166, 182 n., 196 n.
II.36.1121: 169
II.36.1122: 169
II.36.1123: 170
II.36.1124: 167 n., 196 n.
II.36.1125: 170
II.36.1126: 171
II.36.1127: 168

II.37.1130: 173, 349 n.
II.37.1130*d–f*: 86, 173
II.37.1131: 173
II.37.1132: 174
II.37.1133: 175
II.38: 32, 151, 175–6, 177 n.
II.38.1135–41: 152 n.
II.38.1135: 152
II.38.1136: 176
II.38.1137: 176
II.38.1138: 177
II.38.1139: 179
II.38.1140: 180
II.38.1141: 181
II.38.1142–8: 152 n.
II.38.1142: 175, 182
II.38.1143: 150, 176
II.38.1144: 176
II.38.1145: 178
II.38.1146: 179
II.38.1147: 180
II.38.1148: 181
II.38.1149: 167 n., 182, 196
II.39–45: 29, 80, 183–6, 190, 193, 196 n., 198, 202, 203 n., 228
II.39–40: 211, 216
II.39.1151: 32 n., 183, 189 n., 203
II.39.1152: 207 n.
II.39.1153: 207–8, 209 n.
II.39.1154: 208, 209 n.
II.39.1155: 208
II.39.1156: 205–6, 209 n.
II.39.1157: 206
II.39.1158: 210–11
II.39.1159: 210
II.40: 211–14
II.40.1160: 213
II.40.1161: 215 n.
II.40.1162: 216
II.40.1163: 215 n.
II.40.1164: 214
II.40.1165: 213 n.
II.40.1166: 214 n.
II.41–3: 216
II.41: 203 n.
II.41.1168: 203 n.
II.41.1170: 214 n.
II.41.1171: 215 n.
II.41.1174: 205 n.
II.41.1176: 215 n.
II.42: 203 n.
II.42.1181: 197 n.
II.42.1182: 203 n.

II.42.1183: 206 n.
II.42.1184: 206 n.
II.42.1185: 206 n.
II.42.1189: 83 n., 110 n., 385
II.42.1191: 197 n.
II.43: 203 n.
II.43.1195: 207 n.
II.43.1196–7: 212 n.
II.43.1197: 293 n.
II.43.1198: 375 n.
II.43.1200: 115 n.
II.44: 203 n., 216
II.44.1203: 203 n., 216
II.44.1204: 206 n.
II.44.1205: 203 n.
II.44.1206: 234 n., 235, 349 n.
II.44.1209: 367 n.
II.44.1211: 195 n.
II.45: 202–3, 216–17
II.45.1220: 218, 230 n.
II.45.1221: 218 n., 230 n.
II.45.1222: 218 n., 230 n.
II.45.1223: 226
II.45.1224: 218 n., 230 n.
II.45.1226: 218 n., 230 n.
II.46–101: 29, 54 n., 228–32
II.46–56: 302
II.46–55: 232, 234 n., 253 n., 254 n., 270, 272, 281 n., 316–17, 416 n.
II.46–8: 251
II.46: 109, 235–6, 255, 323, 342
II.46.1229: 230, 233 n., 236–7
II.46.1230: 233 n., 236 n., 237
II.46.1231: 233 n., 236 n., 237
II.46.1232: 233 n., 236 n., 237, 256
II.46.1233: 233 n., 234 n., 236 n., 237–8, 254 n., 295 n.
II.46.1234: 233 n., 236 n., 239, 256 n., 346 n., 363 n.
II.46.1235: 233 n., 236 n., 361 n., 363 n.
II.46.1237: 345 n.
II.46.1239: 326 n.
II.46.1239*c*: 347
II.47–8: 236, 348 n.
II.47.1236: 233 n., 240
II.47.1237: 233 n., 240
II.47.1238: 231 n., 233 n., 245–6, 256
II.47.1239: 233 n.
II.47.1239*d*: 359 n.
II.47.1240: 233 n., 243, 254 n., 346 n., 361 n.
II.48: 244, 249
II.48.1241: 244

Thomas Aquinas
SCG *Summa contra gentiles* (*cont.*):
II.48.1242: 245
II.48.1243: 233 n., 246
II.48.1244: 233 n., 248 n., 256 n.
II.48.1245: 233 n., 249
II.48.1246: 233 n., 248, 256 n., 346 n.
II.49–55: 236, 270, 302 n., 320
II.49–51: 251, 254–7, 259, 263
II.49: 251, 271, 272 n.
II.49.1247: 233 n., 254
II.49.1248: 233 n., 255 n.
II.49.1249: 233 n., 255 n., 281 n.
II.49.1250: 233 n., 255 n., 281 n.
II.49.1251: 233 n., 255 n., 256, 281 n.
II.49.1252: 233 n., 243 n., 254 n., 255 n.,
    271, 272 n.
II.49.1253: 233 n., 255 n., 256 n.
II.49.1254: 233 n., 248 n., 255 n.
II.49.1255: 233 n., 248 n., 255 n.
II.49.1256: 233 n., 253 n.
II.49.1257: 234 n., 252 n., 295 n.
II.49.1258: 234 n., 295 n.
II.50–1: 266
II.50: 252, 268, 318, 386
II.50.1259: 233 n., 254 n.
II.50.1260: 233 n., 251 n.
II.50.1261: 233 n., 255 n., 256, 358 n.,
    361 n., 363 n., 366, 407 n.
II.50.1262: 233 n., 255 n.
II.50.1263: 233 n., 234 n., 255 n., 295 n.,
    352 n., 363 n.
II.50.1264: 233 n., 234 n., 254 n., 255 n.,
    295 n.
II.50.1265: 233 n., 255 n.
II.50.1266: 233 n., 255 n.
II.51: 252, 293
II.51.1268: 233 n., 252, 254 n., 405 n.
II.51.1269: 233 n.
II.51.1270: 233 n.
II.51.1271: 233 n., 363 n.
II.51.1272: 233 n.
II.52–4: 257, 278
II.52: 259–63
II.52.1273: 233 n., 257, 293 n.
II.52.1274: 259
II.52.1277: 259
II.52.1278: 259–60, 262–3
II.52.1281: 258 n., 259 n.
II.53: 260–3, 269
II.53.1282: 233 n., 261
II.53.1283: 233 n., 261
II.53.1284: 262 n.

II.53.1285: 262 n.
II.53.1286: 262 n.
II.54: 263
II.54.1287: 263, 289 n.
II.54.1288: 263
II.54.1289: 212, 264
II.54.1290: 265
II.54.1291: 265
II.54.1292: 266
II.54.1293–4: 266
II.54.1293: 233 n.
II.54.1294: 258 n.
II.54.1295: 258 n., 265
II.54.1296: 267, 405 n.
II.54.1298: 405 n.
II.55: 268, 270, 276, 404
II.55.1297: 233 n., 268
II.55.1298: 233 n., 268
II.55.1299: 233 n., 363 n.
II.55.1300: 233 n., 269, 385
II.55.1301: 233 n., 269 n.
II.55.1302: 233 n.
II.55.1303: 233 n.
II.55.1304: 233 n., 270 n., 272 n., 326 n.,
    405 n.
II.55.1305: 233 n., 360 n., 363 n., 408 n.
II.55.1306: 233 n., 351 n.
II.55.1307: 233 n., 360 n., 361 n., 408 n.
II.55.1308: 233 n., 234 n., 295 n., 347 n.,
    406 n.
II.55.1309: 233 n., 347 n., 409 n.
II.55.1310: 233 n.
II.55.1311: 234 n.
II.55.1312: 233 n.
II.56–90: 254 n.
II.56–78: 342, 343 n., 348
II.56–72: 337
II.56–70: 322, 337, 370
II.56–69: 271, 292, 294–6, 310, 313
II.56–60: 273 n.
II.56: 271, 272 n., 273, 299 n., 316, 372,
    376
II.56.1313: 234, 271, 272 n., 273, 293 n.,
    326 n.
II.56.1314*a–d*: 274–7
II.56.1315: 277
II.56.1316: 278
II.56.1317: 279–81
II.56.1318: 282
II.56.1318*a–c*: 282–4
II.56.1319*a–d*: 284–90, 294, 413 n.
II.56.1320: 291
II.56.1321: 292, 316

II.56.1322: 293, 317
II.56.1323: 293, 318
II.56.1324: 293, 318, 326 n.
II.56.1325: 293, 320, 326 n.
II.57–78: 324–5
II.57–70: 323
II.57–68: 292, 294, 300–1, 316
II.57–67: 294, 306 n.
II.57–8: 286
II.57: 299, 323
II.57.1326*a–b*: 294–5
II.57.1327: 301, 308
II.57.1328: 301, 331 n.
II.57.1329: 301
II.57.1330: 302
II.57.1331: 303
II.57.1332: 304
II.57.1333–8: 304
II.57.1333: 304, 324 n., 348
II.57.1335: 305
II.57.1336: 305 n.
II.57.1339–41: 305
II.57.1339: 306 n., 379
II.57.1340: 307
II.57.1341: 307
II.58: 396 n.
II.58.1342: 306, 308, 344 n., 397
II.58.1343: 308
II.58.1344–51: 308
II.58.1344: 311, 345 n.
II.58.1345: 309 n., 311, 329 n., 344 n., 399 n.
II.58.1347–8: 325 n., 345 n.
II.58.1347: 309, 331 n., 345 n.
II.58.1348: 310, 345 n.
II.58.1349: 309 n.
II.58.1350*b*: 332 n., 335 n., 364 n.
II.58.1351: 364 n., 366 n.
II.59–61: 312 n., 313 n., 337, 339
II.59.1354–8: 321
II.59.1354: 319
II.59.1355: 352, 367
II.59.1357: 363 n.
II.59.1359: 312, 321 n.
II.59.1360: 341 n.
II.59.1361: 313, 361 n.
II.59.1362: 341 n., 355, 361 n., 363 n.
II.59.1364: 363 n.
II.59.1365: 341 n., 352, 353 n., 355, 357 n., 358 n.
II.59.1366: 352, 357, 360, 361 n.
II.59.1367: 323 n., 344
II.59.1368: 324 n., 353 n.

II.59.1369: 341 n., 400 n.
II.60.1370: 346 n., 355 n., 357 n.
II.60.1370*b*: 359 n.
II.60.1371: 313, 324 n., 345 n.
II.60.1372: 324 n., 344 n., 347 n., 348
II.60.1373: 324 n., 339, 345 n., 346 n.
II.60.1374: 345 n., 347 n., 364 n., 366
II.60.1375: 338 n., 341 n., 356 n.
II.60.1376: 341 n.
II.60.1378: 324 n.
II.60.1379: 341 n.
II.60.1380: 341 n.
II.60.1381: 338
II.60.1382: 345 n., 352 n., 361 n., 364 n.
II.60.1383: 358 n.
II.60.1384: 356 n.
II.60.1385: 324 n., 365
II.60.1386: 366
II.60.1387: 324 n., 356, 407 n.
II.60.1388: 357, 358 n., 371
II.60.1389: 371 n.
II.60.1391: 324 n., 338, 371
II.60.1392: 341 n.
II.60.1393: 341 n.
II.60.1395: 371 n.
II.61-III.43: 273 n.
II.61: 319 n.
II.61.1402: 313
II.62.1403: 313
II.62.1404: 324 n.
II.62.1405: 313
II.62.1407: 351 n., 352
II.62.1408: 338 n., 359 n.
II.62.1409: 324 n., 338, 353, 407 n.
II.62.1410: 344
II.62.1411: 338, 364 n., 366 n.
II.62.1412*b*: 338 n., 359 n.
II.62.1413: 363 n., 364 n., 366 n.
II.63: 300 n.
II.63.1416*b*: 347 n.
II.63.1417: 344 n.
II.63.1420: 347 n.
II.63.1421: 347 n.
II.64.1422: 300 n.
II.65: 297, 300 n., 386
II.65.1432: 378 n.
II.66: 300 n.
II.66.1437: 350
II.66.1438: 351, 366 n., 412 n.
II.66.1439: 352
II.66.1440: 351
II.66.1441: 338 n., 351
II.67: 300 n.

Thomas Aquinas
SCG *Summa contra gentiles* (*cont.*):
II.67.1443: 346 n.
II.67.1444: 353 n.
II.67.1445: 324 n., 356
II.67.1446: 354 n., 364 n.
II.68: 294, 306 n., 313–16, 320
II.68.1448: 316
II.68.1449: 295, 300 n., 306 n., 314,
    341 n.
II.68.1450a–b: 314–15
II.68.1451: 315
II.68.1452: 315, 385 n.
II.68.1453: 417
II.68.1453a: 343 n.
II.68.1453b: 296 n.
II.68.1459: 318 n., 354 n., 364 n., 411 n.
II.68.1459a–b: 383 n.
II.68.1459b: 354 n., 366 n., 395 n., 411 n.,
    412 n.
II.69: 292, 294, 313–16, 321
II.69.1460: 292, 316
II.69.1461: 317
II.69.1462: 318
II.69.1463: 318
II.69.1464: 320, 327, 364 n., 365 n.,
    366 n.
II.69.1465: 320, 366 n.
II.69.1467: 364 n., 366
II.69.1468: 367 n.
II.69.1468a: 366
II.69.1468b: 364 n., 366 n.
II.69.1469: 363 n., 364 n.
II.70: 272 n., 316, 321–2, 325, 337, 374 n.
II.70.1471: 316, 321, 325
II.70.1472: 321
II.70.1473: 321
II.70.1474: 321
II.70.1475: 321
II.70.1476: 321, 325
II.70.1477: 322, 325
II.70.1478: 322, 372 n.
II.71–8: 323, 370
II.71–2: 324, 337
II.71: 331–2, 340
II.71.1479: 325
II.71.1480: 325 n., 326–7
II.71.1481a–c: 326–30
II.72: 331–6
II.72.1482: 331–3
II.72.1483: 332, 366 n.
II.72.1484: 327 n., 332 n., 333
II.72.1485: 298 n., 334

II.72.1485a–b: 334
II.72.1486: 335 n.
II.72.1487: 332 n.
II.73–8: 324, 337
II.73–5: 312 n., 313 n.
II.73: 341
II.73.1488: 340
II.73.1489: 340 n.
II.73.1490: 367 n.
II.73.1491: 367 n.
II.73.1493: 338 n.
II.73.1494: 341 n.
II.73.1495: 341 n.
II.73.1496: 341 n., 355 n., 358 n.
II.73.1498: 324 n.
II.73.1500: 341 n.
II.73.1501a: 355 n.
II.73.1501b: 346 n.
II.73.1502: 364 n., 366 n.
II.73.1503: 341 n., 355 n., 357 n.
II.73.1504: 324 n., 338 n.
II.73.1506: 324 n., 356
II.73.1513: 355 n., 357 n.
II.73.1514: 341 n., 354 n.
II.73.1517: 338, 341 n., 357 n.
II.73.1518–21: 341 n.
II.73.1519: 338 n., 349 n., 351 n.
II.73.1521: 340, 356 n., 357 n.
II.73.1522: 338 n.
II.73.1523a: 324 n., 341 n.
II.73.1523b: 362 n.
II.73.1523c: 362
II.73.1524: 324 n., 338 n.
II.73.1525: 341 n.
II.73.1526: 324 n., 338, 340, 354 n.,
    360 n., 362
II.73.1528a–b: 353–4
II.74: 341–2, 418
II.74.1528: 361 n.
II.74.1528b: 349 n.
II.74.1528c: 364 n.
II.74.1528e: 341, 364 n.
II.74.1530: 349 n.
II.74.1531: 342 n., 349 n.
II.74.1536: 349
II.74.1538: 324 n., 338 n., 354 n.
II.74.1541: 324 n., 356 n.
II.74.1542: 324 n., 361 n.
II.74.1543: 349
II.75: 341–2
II.75.1533: 352 n.
II.75.1545–7: 341
II.75.1548: 341

II.75.1549–59: 341
II.75.1549: 338
II.75.1550: 361, 363 n.
II.75.1551: 358 n.
II.75.1551a: 364
II.75.1551b: 358 n., 363 n., 366 n.
II.75.1553: 358 n., 361 n., 363
II.75.1556: 363 n.
II.75.1558: 324 n.
II.75.1558c: 343 n.
II.76.1560: 342
II.76.1561: 358 n.
II.76.1562: 357 n.
II.76.1563: 360 n., 361 n.
II.76.1564: 357
II.76.1565: 357 n.
II.76.1567: 355 n.
II.76.1569: 324 n., 353, 356 n., 359 n.
II.76.1570: 324 n., 350
II.76.1572: 355 n.
II.76.1574: 357 n., 358 n.
II.76.1575: 348 n., 360
II.76.1576: 343 n., 357
II.76.1577: 359 n., 360 n.
II.76.1578: 324 n., 341 n.
II.76.1578b: 359
II.76.1579: 339, 342, 346, 353, 357
II.77: 342
II.77.1581: 353 n., 354 n., 355, 357 n.,
    359 n., 361 n., 363 n.
II.77.1582: 357–8
II.77.1583: 357 n.
II.77.1584: 349 n.
II.78: 342
II.78.1585: 342
II.78.1586: 360
II.78.1588a: 358 n.
II.78.1591: 356
II.78.1592b: 358 n.
II.78.1592c: 364 n., 365 n.
II.78.1593a–e: 361 n.
II.78.1593c: 338 n.
II.78.1594a: 338 n.
II.78.1595: 338 n., 361 n.
II.78.1596: 359, 364 n., 365
II.79–90: 328
II.79–82: 370, 403
II.79–81: 268, 387 n.
II.79: 387 n., 404, 413–14
II.79.1597: 404
II.79.1598: 234, 295 n., 404
II.79.1599: 406–8
II.79.1600a–b: 407–8

II.79.1601: 408 n.
II.79.1602: 409
II.79.1603: 408 n.
II.79.1604: 408 n.
II.79.1605: 409
II.79.1606: 405 n., 409
II.79.1607: 410–12
II.79.1609–12: 404
II.80: 387 n., 412
II.80.1613: 412
II.80.1614–15: 412
II.80.1616: 413
II.80.1617: 413
II.80.1618: 378 n., 413–15
II.81: 371 n., 387 n., 412
II.81.1622: 181 n.
II.81.1623: 413
II.81.1624–8: 415–18
II.81.1624: 415
II.81.1625a–g: 415–17
II.81.1626: 417
II.81.1627–8a–c: 418
II.82: 403 n.
II.82.1630–7: 387 n.
II.82.1630: 387 n.
II.82.1631: 403
II.82.1633–4: 403
II.82.1635–7: 387 n.
II.82.1638–49: 387 n.
II.82.1638–9: 403
II.82.1641–3: 403
II.82.1645–6: 403
II.82.1646: 403 n.
II.82.1647–8: 403
II.82.1649: 404
II.82.1653: 387 n.
II.83–90: 370
II.83–4: 371 n., 373, 384
II.83: 389
II.83.1651–2: 373 n.
II.83.1653–4: 373 n.
II.83.1656c: 373 n.
II.83.1657–84: 373 n.
II.83.1657: 373 n.
II.83.1658: 379 n.
II.83.1670b: 373 n.
II.83.1671: 373 n.
II.83.1672: 373 n.
II.83.1689: 387 n.
II.84.1686–90: 373 n.
II.85.1704b: 373
II.85.1705: 373
II.86–9: 306 n., 376

Thomas Aquinas
SCG *Summa contra gentiles* (*cont.*):
II.86: 377, 385, 387, 389
II.86.1706: 377
II.86.1707: 378, 383 n., 394 n.
II.86.1708*a–e*: 381–4
II.86.1709: 383 n.
II.86.1710: 383 n.
II.86.1712: 378 n.
II.87: 343, 377, 387
II.87.1714: 384
II.87.1715: 384–6
II.87.1716: 384–6
II.87.1718: 386 n.
II.87.1721: 386
II.88: 377, 387, 392
II.88.1722: 387
II.88.1723–6: 392
II.88.1723: 392 n., 396, 400 n., 403
II.88.1724: 392 n., 396, 398, 403
II.88.1725: 392
II.88.1726: 378 n., 392 n., 394, 395 n.
II.88.1727: 388, 392 n.
II.88.1728*b*: 378 n., 388
II.88.1729: 388
II.88.1730: 382 n., 388
II.88.1731: 378 n., 392
II.88.1732: 378 n., 390, 394, 399 n.
II.88.1733: 378 n., 388
II.88.1734: 378 n., 389
II.89: 377
II.89.1738: 378 n.
II.89.1739: 378 n.
II.89.1740*a*: 378 n., 398 n.
II.89.1740*b–d*: 401 n., 402 n.
II.89.1742: 390
II.89.1742*a–c*: 391 n.
II.89.1742*c*: 391
II.89.1743: 374 n., 399
II.89.1744*a*: 395 n., 400 n.
II.89.1744*b*: 402
II.89.1745: 400 n., 401, 402 n.
II.89.1747: 400 n., 403
II.89.1748: 398, 403
II.89.1749: 393
II.89.1750: 395
II.89.1751: 388 n.
II.89.1752: 388 n.
II.89.1753: 388 n.
II.89.1754: 388 n.
II.89.1755: 392
II.89.1756: 390
II.89.1757: 388 n.

II.89.1758: 389
II.90: 272 n., 372 n., 373
II.90.1759: 372 n., 374 n.
II.90.1760: 373 n.
II.90.1767: 372 n.
II.90.1771*a–b*: 371 n., 373 n.
II.91–101: 234, 370–3
II.91: 370
II.91.1780: 372 n.
II.91.1781: 371 n.
II.91.1782*d*: 371 n.
II.92–3: 252 n., 370
II.92: 6 n.
II.92.1785: 372 n.
II.92.1794: 6 n.
II.92.1794*b*: 371 n.
II.94.1805: 235, 417
II.95.1809*c*: 371 n.
II.96–101: 416
II.96.1812–20: 417 n.
II.98.1836: 371 n.
II.100.1855: 351 n.
III: 1, 5, 70, 232 n., 249, 369 n.
III.3.1886: 205, 209 n.
III.22.2030: 402 n.
III.41–5: 371 n.
III.75: 249 n.
III.85: 249 n.
III.87–90: 249 n.
III.102.2771: 111 n.
IV: 1 n., 11–12, 371, 418
IV.1.3348: 1 n., 371
IV.19.3558: 243 n.
IV.23.3592: 253 n.
IV.23.3592*a*: 327 n.
IV.24: 195 n.
IV.79–95: 371 n.
ST *Summa theologiae*
Ia.1.1*c*: 13
Ia.1.7, sc: 9
Ia.1.7*c*: 10
Ia.2, intro: 10
Ia.2.2, ad 1: 12
Ia.4.1, ad 2: 375
Ia.5.1: 241 n.
Ia.5.1*c*: 38 n.
Ia.5.3, sc: 71
Ia.7.2, sc: 73
Ia.7.2, ad 3: 79
Ia.10: 154 n.
Ia.11.1: 285 n.
Ia.12.11*c*: 111
Ia.13.2: 15 n.

Ia.19.1c: 243 n.
Ia.19.2c: 135
Ia.19.3: 119 n., 125 n.
Ia.19.4c: 120 n., 121 n., 122 n.
Ia.21.1: 130 n.
Ia.21.1, ad 3: 135 n.
Ia.23.5, ad 3: 200 n., 227 n., 250
Ia.25.1: 47 n.
Ia.25.1, ad 3: 45, 123 n.
Ia.25.3c: 104, 114, 118–19
Ia.25.3, ad 2: 104–5
Ia.25.5: 124 n.
Ia.25.5c: 375
Ia.25.6, ad 3: 220
Ia.27.1c: 231 n., 257
Ia.31.2, ad 2: 195
Ia.36.2c: 195 n.
Ia.44.1: 54 n.
Ia.44.1c: 56 n.
Ia.44.2c: 80, 115 n.
Ia.45.1c: 77
Ia.45.2: 54 n.
Ia.45.2, obj. 1: 85 n.
Ia.45.2, ad 3: 94 n.
Ia.46.1: 142 n.
Ia.46.1c: 144 n., 145 n.
Ia.46.1, obj. 1: 173 n., 174 n.
Ia.46.1, obj. 2: 169 n.
Ia.46.1, obj. 5: 169 n.
Ia.46.1, objs. 6, 9, 10: 161 n.
Ia.46.1, obj. 7: 170 n., 171 n.
Ia.46.2: 142 n.
Ia.46.2, obj. 1: 176 n.
Ia.46.2, obj. 2: 176 n.
Ia.46.2, obj. 6: 177 n.
Ia.46.2, obj. 7: 180 n.
Ia.46.2, obj. 8: 181 n.
Ia.46.2, ad 7: 59, 63, 151 n.
Ia.46.3c: 93 n., 111
Ia.47, preface: 189 n.
Ia.47.1c: 214 n.
Ia.47.2c: 195, 208 n., 276 n.
Ia.47.3: 108 n.
Ia.48: 189 n.
Ia.48.5c: 39, 200 n.
Ia.50.1c: 238 n.
Ia.50.2, ad 3: 258 n., 265 n.
Ia.50.3c: 109 n., 195 n.
Ia.50.5c: 212 n.
Ia.59.1c: 242 n.
Ia.59.2, ad 2: 195 n.
Ia.59.4c: 242 n.
Ia.65–74: 94, 185–6, 188–9

Ia.65, preface: 186
Ia.65.3, sc: 96 n.
Ia.65.3c: 96
Ia.66.1c: 96 n., 188 n.
Ia.66.1, sc: 96
Ia.66.1, ad 2: 96
Ia.66.4, ad 4: 93 n.
Ia.67, preface: 95 n.
Ia.67.2c: 94 n.
Ia.68.1c: 96 n., 97, 112 n.
Ia.68.1, ad 1: 96 n.
Ia.69.2: 188
Ia.69.2c: 188 n.
Ia.69.2, ad 1: 189 n.
Ia.70, preface: 95 n.
Ia.70.1c: 95 n.
Ia.70.3c: 322, 328 n.
Ia.70.3, ad 5: 322 n., 328 n.
Ia.71.1, ad 1: 375 n.
Ia.73.1, ad 3: 96 n.
Ia.74.1, ad 1: 93 n., 96 n.
Ia.74.2, ad 1: 96 n.
Ia.74.2, ad 2: 96 n.
Ia.74.2, ad 4: 96 n.
Ia.75–88: 323 n.
Ia.75.1c: 296–9, 333
Ia.75.1, ad 3: 282 n.
Ia.75.2c: 233 n.
Ia.75.5, ad 1: 40 n.
Ia.75.7c: 195 n.
Ia.76: 308 n., 316
Ia.76.1c: 298 n.
Ia.76.3: 308 n., 311 n., 396 n.
Ia.76.3c: 311 n.
Ia.76.3, ad 1: 311 n.
Ia.76.4: 308 n., 311 n.
Ia.76.4c: 311
Ia.76.4, ad 4: 276 n., 401 n.
Ia.76.6: 331 n.
Ia.76.6c: 212 n.
Ia.76.6, obj. 3 & ad 3: 327–8
Ia.76.8: 335 n.
Ia.76.8c: 336 n.
Ia.77.1c: 326 n.
Ia.77.2c: 234 n., 296 n.
Ia.77.6: 311 n.
Ia.77.6c: 200 n.
Ia.80.2c: 250 n.
Ia.82.1: 133 n.
Ia.82.1c: 120 n.
Ia.82.1, ad 3: 246 n.
Ia.82.3, ad 2: 250 n.
Ia.83.1c: 244 n.

Thomas Aquinas
SCG *Summa contra gentiles* (*cont.*):
Ia.83.3, ad 2: 250
Ia.83.4c: 245, 250n.
Ia.84.3, ad 2: 79n.
Ia.85.1, ad 2: 111
Ia.89.1–8: 416n.
Ia.91.2, ad 2: 375n.
Ia.92.1c: 375n.
Ia.93.3, ad 3: 401n.
Ia.105.2, ad 1: 282n.
Ia.105.5: 394n.
Ia.108.5c: 234n.
Ia.110.1: 394n.
Ia.115.1, ad 2: 79n.
Ia.118.1, sc: 375n.
Ia.118.1, ad 4: 379, 391n.
Ia.118.2: 392
Ia.118.2, obj. 1: 392n.
Ia.118.2, obj. 2: 392n., 396n., 403
Ia.118.2, obj. 3: 392n., 393n.
Ia.118.2, obj. 4: 392n., 394n.
Ia.118.2, obj. 5: 392n.
Ia.118.2, ad 2: 329n., 331, 379n., 380n., 396–8, 401, 402n., 403
Ia.118.2, ad 3: 394n.
Ia.118.2, ad 4: 395n.
Ia.118.2, ad 5: 388n.
IaIIae.1.1c: 250n.
IaIIae.6–21: 347n.
IaIIae.6.2c: 247n.
IaIIae.7.2, ad 3: 10
IaIIae.8.1c: 241
IaIIae.8.2c: 242n.
IaIIae.13.3c: 250n.
IaIIae.17.1, ad 2: 251
IaIIae.18.2, ad 3: 81n.
IaIIae.30.4c: 336n.
IaIIae.57.2: 127n.
IaIIae.57.4c: 105
IaIIae.85.5c: 115n.
IaIIae.111.1, ad 2: 134–5, 155
IIaIIae.8.1c: 14n.
IIaIIae.64.8c: 205n.
IIaIIae.107.1, ad 3: 133n.
IIIa.2.1c: 276n.
IIIa.14.2: 120n.

Aristotle
Categories
5, 3b33–4: 94
7, 6a36–7, b6–8: 49n.
8, 9a14–27: 44n.

9, 11b1–14: 44n.
De anima
I 4, 408b5–9; 18–31: 418
I 4, 408b21–2: 411
I 4, 408b24–5: 414
II 1, 412b5–6: 332n.
II 1, 413a8–9: 301n.
II 2, 413b16–23: 335n.
II 4, 415a26-b2: 196n.
II 4, 415b21–2: 390
II 5, 416b33–4: 348
II 5, 417b20–1: 348
II 12, 424a17–19: 353
III 2, 425b25–6: 353
III 4: 319
III 4, 428a27–8: 354n.
III 4, 429a10–11, 23: 338n.
III 4, 429a13–14: 338n., 356
III 4, 429a14–16: 359n.
III 4, 429a24–7: 356
III 4, 429a27–8: 338
III 4, 429b5–10: 365
III 4, 429b7: 338, 362
III 4, 429b31–430a2: 359n.
III 4, 430a3–4: 361n.
III 5, 430a10–17: 360
III 5, 430a11–13: 358
III 5, 430a12–13: 357
III 5, 430a14–15: 243
III 5, 430a16–17: 356n.
III 5, 430a18–19: 409n.
III 5, 430a19–20: 361n.
III 5, 430a23–4: 414
III 5, 430a24–5: 414
III 7, 431a1: 361n.
III 7, 431a3: 40n.
III 7, 431a14–15: 353n.
III 7, 431a15: 356n.
III 7, 431a16–17: 356, 407n., 414
III 8, 432a9: 356n.
III 10, 433a9–15: 367n.
De caelo et mundo
I 3, 270a12–22: 143n., 167n.
I 4, 271a33: 409n.
I 12, 281b18–282a4: 167n.
I 12, 282a21-b1: 143n.
II 1, 283b26–284a2: 143n.
De generatione et corruptione
I 6, 323a32–3: 280n.
I 7, 324a9–12: 196n.
I 10, 328a1 ff.: 276n.
I 10, 328b20: 275

De memoria
1, 450a9–14: 349 n.
1, 450a22–5: 348
1, 451a14–17: 418
Generation of Animals
II 3–4, 736a24 ff.: 379
II 3, 736b2–4: 396 n., 399 n.
II 3, 736b2: 329 n.
II 3, 736b8–15: 306 n.
II 3, 736b27–8: 398 n.
II 3, 737a28: 380 n.
II 4, 738b25: 380 n.
II 6, 743a23: 40 n.
Metaphysics
I 1, 980b25–981a12: 350
I 2, 982b9–10: 127 n.
I 2, 982b26: 246
I 2, 982b28–30: 127 n.
I 2, 983a5–10: 127 n.
II 2, 994a1–19: 34 n.
II 2, 994a1–8: 151 n.
V 12, 1019a15–20: 43 n.
V 12, 1019b12, 21–7: 174
V 12, 1020a1–2, 5–6: 43 n.
V 15, 1021a29–30: 51 n.
VII: 167 n.
VII 2: 174
VII 7, 1032a12: 174
VII 8, 1033b29–32: 196 n.
VIII 8, 1050a23-b2: 16 n.
IX 3: 40 n.
IX 6: 40 n.
IX 9, 1051a4–17: 241
XI 10, 1066a35-b1: 177 n.
XI 10, 1066b11–12: 181 n.
XI 10, 1075a12–24: App. III
XII: 145 n.
XII 6: 40 n.
XII 6, 1071b3–11: 143 n.
XII 7, 1072a21–6: 143 n.
Nicomachean Ethics
I 1, 1094a2–3: 241
III 4, 1111b20–4: 243
III 5, 1113a9–12: 250
V 11, 1138a4–5, b4–14: 132
VII 15, 1154b26: 418
VIII 7, 1157b28–9: 418
IX 7, 1168a5–9: 43 n.
X 7, 1177a25: 418
Physics
I 4, 187a26–9: 85 n., 86 n.
I 7, 190a9–13: 288 n.
I 9, 192a25–34: 143 n., 173 n.

II 3, 195b28: 40 n.
III 1, 201a10: 174
III 2, 202a15: 170
III 5, 204b7–10: 177 n.
III 6, 206b24–5: 172
IV 11: 142 n.
IV 11, 219a12–13, 17–19: 171
IV 11, 219b1: 163 n., 170
IV 11, 220a25: 171
IV 13, 222b1: 170
V 3, 227a21 ff.: 277 n.
VI 3, 233b33–5: 93
VII 3, 247b8 ff.: 255 n.
VII 7, 261a28-b27: 402 n.
VIII: 145 n., 151 n.
VIII 1, 251a8–28: 160 n.
VIII 1, 251a9-b28: 143 n.
VIII 1, 251a28-b5: 160 n.
VIII 1, 251b5–10: 167 n., 174 n.
VIII 1, 251b10–28: 167 n.
VIII 1, 251b19–28: 160 n.
VIII 1, 252a5-b6: 160 n.
VIII 5, 256a21-b3: 63 n.
VIII 8, 263b3–6: 177 n.
Politics
I 2, 1253a9: 409 n.
Posterior Analytics
I: 7 n.
II 19, 100a3–8: 350
Topics
I 11, 104b12–17: 144 n.
III 5, 119a28: App. III

Augustine
Confessions
I 1: 418 n.
De doctrina christiana
I.32: 131
De Genesi ad litteram
I.18, 19, 21: 97
I.18.37: 97 n., 193 n.
I.19: 193 n.
I.19.39: 97 n.
II.13.26–7: 187 n.
II.15.30: 191 n.
III.12.18–19: 191 n.
IV.33.51–2: 191 n.
V.4.7–11: 191 n.
V.23.44–6: 191 n.
VI.1.1–2: 191 n.
VI.4.5–6.11: 191 n.
VI.10.17–11.19: 191 n.
VI.14.25–16.27: 191 n.

Augustine
De Genesi ad litteram (*cont.*):
VII.24.35: 191 n.
IX.17.32: 191 n.
Soliloquies
II.11.2: 168 n.

Avicenna
Liber de philosophia prima
    (Metaphysics)
VI.i–ii: 177 n.
IX.i: 160 n.
IX.iv: 177 n.
IX.iv, 479.4–6: 106 n., 197 n.
IX.iv, 479.92–4: 106 n., 121, 197 n.

The Bible
Daniel 7:10: 6 n.
Deuteronomy 4:6: 27 n.
Ecclesiasticus 42:15: 23
Exodus 3:14: 258 n.
Genesis 1: 94, 185 n., 186–93
Genesis 1:1: 84–5, 93, 112, 146, 186,
    211
Genesis 1:2–13: 186, 211
Genesis 1:2: 188 n.
Genesis 1:4: 95, 211
Genesis 1:6–7: 211 n.
Genesis 1:7: 95
Genesis 1:9–13: 188
Genesis 1:14–31: 186
Genesis 1:14: 95
Genesis 1:15: 187 n.
Genesis 1:31: 211
Genesis 2:5: 96 n.
John 4:24: 6
1 Peter 3:15: 20 n.
Proverbs 8:7: 18–19
Psalms 19:1: 239
Psalms 142/3:5: 18, 84, 228

Psalms 148:1–6: 234 n.
Romans 1:20: 8, 21
Romans 7:15–25: 406 n.

Boethius
De hebdomadibus: 258 n.
The Consolation of Philosophy
V, pr. 6: 142 n.

Bonaventure
Commentary on the Sentences
I.44.1.4c: 149 n.
II.1.1.1.2: 178 n.
II.1.1.1.2.6c: 149 n.

Giles of Rome
In secundum librum Sententiarum
1.1.4.2: 146 n.

Gregory the Great
Moralia in Iob
XVI, 37: 177 n.

Hugh of St Victor
De sacramentis
I.1.24–5: 187 n.

Peter Lombard
Sententiae
II.12.5.4: 189
II.12.6: 189
II.14.9: 187 n.
II.15: 187 n.

Plato
Timaeus
29E–30B: 143 n., 218 n.
69C–71D: 308 n.

Porphyry
Isagoge: 413 n.

Index Locorum compiled by Barbara E. Kretzmann and Julia A. Kretzmann

GENERAL INDEX

abstraction 255 n., 256, 341, 354–9, 362, 365–6, 405–7
accident 5 n., 44, 49, 59, 137, 140, 163 n., 171, 175, 330, 413; Porphyry's definition of 413 n.; *see also* category
action, *see* activity
activity (*operatio*) 14, 16, 24, 36; and passivity 199, 201; as category of accident 44; as second actuality 39, 40, 42, 46, 200 n.; characteristic 297, 298 n.; deliberate 338; extrinsic 14, 16, 123; free 244–8; immanent 14–19, 31 n., 37, 40, 43, 46–7, 70, 77–8, 122–3, 231; intellective (*see* cognition, intellective); intrinsic 14, 16; mental 338; paradigm of 16–17; perfect 104; transeunt 14–20, 29, 33–7, 40–3, 46, 47, 55, 70, 77–8, 82–3, 87–8, 120, 122–3, 228, 231–2; vital 297, 327; volitional (*see* volition); voluntary 247 n.; *see also* God's activity
actuality: as naturally prior/temporally posterior to potentiality 379 n.; as object of appetite 241; as source of action 37, 40, 78; as terminus of action 78–9; complete (or full) 38; contrasting (or mixing together) with potentiality 37–41, 260–9, 276, 285 n., 289 n., 311; first 39–43, 200, 379, 380 n., 382; from form 207 n., 212 n., 243 n.; infinite 40 n.; pure (*actus purus*) 36–47, 79 n., 115 n.; second 39–47, 200, 379–80, 383; two levels of 39, 42; *see also* being
actus 298 n., 305–7, 316–19, 320, 326 n., 366 n., 379 n.
actus purus argument 36–41, 43, 55, 115 n.
Adams, M. M. 205 n.
Adams, R. M. 205 n., 224 n.
Aertsen, Jan A. 241 n.
affirmation 15

agency, causal 202–3; *see also* cause, agent
agent 16–18, 40, 43, 46, 71–2, 77, 85–9, 95, 101, 123, 125, 127, 140, 150, 167 n., 176, 214–19, 230 n., 237, 280, 304, 348, 388, 393; first (primary) 37 n., 100, 116 n., 203 n., 391–4; free 124 n.; instrumental 99; intellective 17, 162, 166, 206, 210, 216, 237, 251; natural 140; nature of 36; –patient relationship 358; perfect 218; omniscient 209; omnipotent 79, 134, 136, 209; power of 36, 43–4, 105, 174–5, 182; secondary 197 n., 203 n.; substance of 44; universal 173, 386 n.; volitional 17, 140, 154–5, 166, 206, 210, 216, 251; *see also* cause, agent
Albert the Great 148 n.
Alexander of Aphrodisias 299 n., 300, 312–13, 319, 324, 342
Alexander of Hales 147 n.
Alnwick, William 148 n.
Alston, William 3, 4, 7, 12 n., 14 n., 416 n.
alteration 72, 81 n., 94, 139, 201, 208, 274, 276, 279–80, 402 n.; *see also* change; motion
Ambrose 193
Anaximines 210 n.
Anaxagoras 214 n.
Anderson, James F. 4 n., 6 n., 88 n., 226 n., 287 n.
angels 25, 203 n., 234–5, 240 n., 253, 272 n., 289 n., 296 n., 371, 374 n., 386; *see also* demons; substances, separate
animal 53 n., 73, 119, 137, 151 n., 184, 186–9, 191–2, 201 n., 209, 230, 232 n., 234 n., 240 n., 245–6, 248, 296–7, 302, 307–11, 322 n., 329–32, 335–6, 344–7, 350, 373 n., 379–81, 383, 398–403; rational 39, 140, 234 n., 251, 318
Anselm 14 n., 147 n., 168 n.

Antweiler, Anton 142 n.
Apollinaris of Laodicea 387–8, 392 n.
appetite 105, 123, 168 n., 240 n., 241 n.,
  242 n., 243, 247, 250–1, 326, 332 n.,
  345–8; animal 240, 242–4, 346 n.,
  403; for good 240, 241, 242,
  244 n.; intellective 240, 242–3,
  247, 346 n. (see also will);
  natural 240, 244 n., 347 n., 408–9;
  rational 240, 347 (see also will);
  sensory 242, 247, 418;
  universal 241–2; see also power,
  concupiscible/irascible
apprehension, see cognition
Apuleius 373 n.
Argerami, Omar 142 n.
argument: E/U (eternality/
  universality) 56–69, 76, 83, 91,
  204; G6 50 n., 57–8, 63, 65, 67; MC
  (movement and change) 81–2,
  87–8, 91; MT (movements and
  their termini) 89–92; NB (not-
  being) 114–19, 129; PM (prime
  matter) 79–80; SE (single
  effect) 107–13
arguments/argumentation: a priori 12,
  14 n., 113, 295, 370; a posteriori
  17 n., 28 n., 113, 295; appealing to
  revelation (or scripture) 6 n., 11 n.
  (see also authority); authoritative
  11, 20, 146 (see also authority);
  characteristic of philosophy 11 n.;
  demonstrative 11–12, 144 n.,
  145 n., 146, 151, 182; natural-
  theological 20, 22; ontological 15;
  probable 11, 144 n., 151, 181–2;
  purely natural 6 n.; sophistical
  144 n.; see also existence,
  arguments for God's
Aristotelian: account of heavenly
  bodies 322; arguments for the
  eternity of the world 144, 167–70,
  173; astronomy 112 n., 139;
  authority 325; demonstration 7 n.;
  categories (see categories);
  change 81 n.; commentaries 324 n.;
  embryology 375; evidence 335,
  339; examples 77, 358–9; first
  principles 6 n., 40 n.; metaphysics
  6 n., 27, 78 n., 79, 252; movers
  of the spheres 372; natural
  philosophy 27, 67, 144 n.;
  philosophy of mind 313 n., 324,

325, 337, 364; principle of
  universal appetite 241–2;
  principles 254, 409; science 7 n.,
  31; version of SFB 321
Aristotelianism 309
Aristotelians 338
Aristotle 5 n., 6 n., 7 n., 10 n., 16 n.,
  27–8, 34, 40 n., 43 n., 44 n., 49, 51,
  63, 86, 109 n., 143, 144–5, 148 n.,
  149, 159–60, 167–9, 171, 173,
  177 n., 181, 196 n., 241, 246 n., 247,
  274, 276 n., 280 n., 297, 299 n., 301,
  306 n., 312, 316, 319, 321, 324–5,
  332 n., 335, 338, 342, 349–50, 353,
  354 n., 356–62, 367 n., 372, 374–5,
  390, 396 n., 398, 402 n., 407 n., 411,
  414, 418
Aristotle's: first philosophy 10 n.;
  Greek 346 n.; metaphysics 28 n.;
  philosophy 28 n.
arithmetic 118 n.
art 4, 21, 105, 122 n., 350, 357–9
artisan 19, 20, 49, 50, 84, 105, 122, 127,
  129, 200 n., 228, 230 n., 250, 358,
  359, 365, 389
arts 10, 355 n., 359 n., 362
assimilation, see God, likeness of
  things to; likeness
astrology 25
astronomy 26
audacious assessment (of arguments
  for eternity of the world) 145–8,
  178
augmentation/diminution 81 n., 94
Augustine 97, 131, 168, 187 n., 190–3,
  199, 200 n., 374 n., 418 n.
Augustinian maxim 21 n.
authority: Aristotelian 325;
  ecclesiastical 11 n., 404; divine 6;
  philosophical 254, 387 n., 404;
  religious/doctrinal 3, 151, 387 n.;
  scriptural 1 n., 6–7, 11 n., 30, 93,
  96, 130, 151, 182, 197, 211, 371,
  404
Averroës 144 n., 160, 168 n., 299 n.,
  300, 312–13, 319, 321, 324–5, 337,
  339–42, 347 n., 367 n., 407; see also
  Commentator
Averroism 339 n.
Averroists, Latin 148 n.
Avicenna 106 n., 121, 144 n., 160,
  177 n., 197, 299 n., 341–2, 350,
  354 n.

bad 241; *see also* evil
Bacon, Roger 147 n.
Bagnall, Jeffrey J. 343 n.
Baldner, Steven E. 94 n., 142 n., 145 n., 147 n., 151 n.
Barnes, Jonathan 7 n.
Basil 93
beauty 188 n.
beginning/ceasing 91, 201 n.
Behler, Ernst 142 n.
being 27, 241–2, 257–67, 272, 278, 289 n., 384; -absolutely 200 n.; absolutely perfect 29, 101–4, 125–6, 136, 154, 217, 221 n.; absolutely simple 29; as *per se* effect of God's power 115–17; caused 57; complete 309, 331 n.; contingent 57–60, 66, 157, 258, 267; dependent 59–68, 91, 218; explanatory 58–61; first 116 n., 173; formal 197 n.; in actuality 79 n., 212 n., 331 n.; in general 267; in potentiality 79 n., 80, 96, 200 n., 306; intellective (*see* substances, intellective); intelligible (*see* thing, intelligible); itself 218, 262, 266 n.; modes of 159, 218, 237, 251; necessary 15, 50, 57, 65–7, 157 (dependent 66–7; *per se* 67–9, 101 n., 154, 156–8); of things other than God 32–3, 35 n., 56 n., 71, 80, 99; *per accidens* 301, 307; *qua* being 10 n.; *qua* divine 10 n.; rational (*see* substances, rational); separate 339 (*see also* substances, separate); substantial 79 n., 94, 332 n. (*see also* substance); temporal 39, 218, 242; terrestrial 296 n.; ultimately explanatory 15, 57; universal 77, 86, 94, 173, 176; volitional 16; *see also* actuality; existence; substance; substances; thing
belief, religious 3, 7
believer 25–6
Bible: old Latin 187 n.; vulgate 93, 187 n., 211
biblical passages, *see* Scripture
big bang 147, 184 n.
body 24, 98, 137, 203 n., 207 n., 210, 231 n., 235, 251, 254–7, 271–322, 325, 326 n., 347 n., 366–7; *actus* of 298, 319–20, 326–7, 332–3,

335 n., 366 n.; animal 298, 333, 374, 403; animated 300 n., 305, 306 n., 310, 397; as proximate matter 326, 329, 332; corruptibility of 369, 404; foetal 317, 328–30, 376, 381, 390, 392, 394, 397 (*see also* foetus); heavenly 99, 139, 169, 186, 189, 191, 235, 280 n., 321–2, 322 n., 325, 374 n.; inanimate 318; individual 376; internal mover of 331–3; living 297, 299, 332–3, 343, 378, 381, 410; natural 279; parts of (*see* parts, of body); passions of 405–6; pre-human 391; resurrection of (*see* resurrection of the body); sentient 310; terrestrial 373–4; vegetable 298; *see also* substances, corporeal; thing, corporeal; union of soul with body
Boethius 142–3, 148 n., 258 n.
Boethius of Dacia 148 n.
Bonansea, Bernardino M. 147 n.
Bonaventure 147, 149 n., 178, 179 n.
Brady, Ignatius 142 n.
brain 283 n., 355, 364–5
Brown, S. F. 142 n.
Bukowski, Thomas 142 n., 146 n.

capacities, *see* potentialities
Caramello, P. 4 n.
Carroll, William E. 94 n., 142 n., 145 n., 151 n.
Cartwright, Richard L. 181 n.
category: of accident 44; of quality 44; of quantity 282; of relation 91; of substance 259 n., 288, 292 n., 309, 331 n.; *see also* accident; substance
causation: efficient 10, 56 n., 120 n., 131, 138–40, 153, 157; final 10, 131–2, 139, 153; formal 120 n., 131, 138–9; material 120 n., 138–9; sustaining 62; univocal 166 n.
cause: agent 107, 180, 214, 215 n., 237, 393–5; beginningless series of 59–3, 67–8; dependent 67–8; efficient 34, 35, 59, 63, 151 n., 153, 180, 265–6, 314–15, 358, 359, 390; extrinsic 153; final 35 n., 122, 140–1, 238, 242 (*see also* end, good); first (primary) 15, 25, 34 n., 56 n., 60, 63–9, 100, 106 n., 156–9, 197, 203 n., 206 n., 211–18, 344; first

cause (*cont.*):
  efficient 34–6, 55; formal 35 n.,
    86 n., 104, 140, 153, 265, 314–15,
    358–9 (*see also* form); generative
    150; highest 26–7, 127;
    independent 66–9; instrumental
    63–4, 68, 99, 100 (*see also*
    instrument); intermediate 34 n.,
    63–4, 107, 113; intrinsic 153;
    material 35 n., 86 n., 153, 210,
    212 (*see also* matter); of being
    56–61, 72–3; ordered series
    of 34 n., 58–67, 87, 156–8, 203,
    208, 215, 393 n., 394 n.
    (accidentally [*per accidens*] 59,
    150, 180; essentially [*per se*] 63–8,
    151 n.); originating 67; *per
    se* 72 n., 116–17, 151 n., 205 n.,
    215 n.; *per accidens* 72 n., 116,
    151 n., 205 n., 208, 210; productive
    35 n., 60–3, 67–8; proper 25;
    secondary 206 n., 343–4; sufficient
    162; sustaining 35 n., 58, 61, 63–4,
    67–9, 76; universal 77, 80–2, 88,
    99, 116 n.; univocal 394–5
chance 203–11, 215–16
change 81 n., 82, 87–92, 95, 96 n., 99,
    101, 150, 172–4, 296 n., 402 n.;
    bodily 414, 418; instant of 90 n.,
    330, 331 n.; natural 68, 83; real 51;
    see also alteration; augmentation/
    diminution; generation/corruption;
    motion
chaos 96
choice (*electio*) 102 n., 103, 124–6, 133,
    217, 246 n., 250, 347 n.
Christian: Aristotelian 144; doctrine
    (*see* doctrine, Christian);
    orthodoxy 145, 148 n.; truths 12
Christians 11
clarification 11, 27
coercion 247
cognition 14, 120–6, 237 n., 239, 242 n.,
    243–51, 254 n., 255, 256 n., 281 n.,
    322 n., 326, 338, 345–8, 351, 353,
    360, 365–6; complete 14, 36;
    immateriality of 353; imperfect
    23; incorporeality of 352 n.;
    intellective 16–19, 22, 37, 40–1,
    46–7, 78, 119 n., 122–3, 126–7,
    229–30, 232–6, 239 n., 240, 242–5,
    251 n., 255 n., 256, 281 n., 303, 312,
    318, 320, 336 n., 338, 341, 343 n.,

344, 349–67, 370–1, 383 n., 403,
    407, 411, 414–18; of created
    things 23, 35–6; of God 9 n., 10,
    13, 23, 28, 127, 229; of truth about
    God 13; passivity in 350, 356;
    particular 363 n.; *per accidens*
    351 n.; reflexive 248 n., 255 n.,
    363 n.; sensory 239 n., 240, 242–3,
    246 n., 248, 345, 348–57, 364–7;
    theoretical 127; of universals 350,
    352 n., 363 n., 366
Cohen, Sheldon M. 353 n.
Commentator 151 n., 160 n., 167 n.; *see
    also* Averroës
composition; essence-existence 257–61;
    matter-form (m-f) 257, 260 n.,
    262–9, 272, 275, 289, 292–3, 295 n.,
    298, 306, 308 n., 314–18, 334, 386,
    405, 413; potentiality-actuality
    (p-a) 260–9, 285 n., 289 n.; *quod
    est-quo est* 266; substance-being
    (s-b) 260–7, 272, 278, 289 n.,
    384
compounded/divided sense 128–9, 158
concept 338, 341, 362–3
conception 373–80, 387, 397; female/
    male contribution to 374–5, 379–
    80
conditions: individual/
    individuating 354, 357, 358 n.,
    363–4, 349; material 354–5, 357,
    358 n.
conservation 18, 91
contingency: divine 18; in created
    things 103, 207
contradiction 92, 114, 117, 118 n., 124,
    129, 149
control 245–7, 347
corruption, *see* generation/corruption
Craig, William Lane 177 n.
Crawford, F. 337 n.
creating 24, 29, 95
creation 8–9, 17 n., 18, 23, 28 n., 29,
    54 n., 55 n., 66 n., 69–71, 74, 79, 82,
    85–91; and beginning of time (*see*
    world, eternity of); as God's
    willing something's existence 78,
    89, 155; as universal production
    (*see* production, universal); by
    angels 25, 99; con- 79; considered
    from the top down 34, 231, 256,
    271, 369; days of 93–7, 185–93,
    211; definition of 85; differentia

for 75, 85, 87, 90–1; doctrine
of 146; *ex nihilo* 74–7, 83, 85–6,
96, 98 n., 106, 108–9, 122–3, 149 n.,
168 n., 172, 176, 177 n., 195, 202,
204, 208 (three senses of 75);
explanations of 101–3
(necessitarian accounts of 24, 102,
121–2, 124 n., 126, 130–41, 156;
non-necessitarian accounts of 24,
102, 120–1, 124 n., 126, 138 n.,
139 n., 153, 156, 157); in category
of relation 91; meditating on (*see*
meditating); particular 384, 387–9,
392, 395–6, 402–3; relation of
distinguishing to 198; single-effect
account of 106, 107–14, 121, 197;
under a form 79
creator, *see* God: as creator
creatures 21, 71, 79, 83, 148; as
dependent on creator 53 n., 84, 91,
99; as emerging from God 5, 9,
183; as ordered toward God 5,
9–10 (*see also* God, likeness of
things to); as related to God
28, 34, 48–53, 55 n., 71, 228;
cognitive 248; in their own
right 28, 228; intellective (*see*
substances, intellective); mistaken
views about 24–5, 232; possible
44 n.; rational 1 n., 10, 203 n.;
spiritual 111, 203 n., 234 n., 296;
see also substances; thing
creed 11; Apostles' 418

Dales, Richard C. 142 n., 144 n.
Damascene, John 99
Darwinism 203, 209
Davidson, H. A. 142 n.
decision (*arbitrium*) 102, 203 n., 245 n.,
246, 249; free 244–51
de dicto/de re sense 129, 158
definition: of a species 195 n.; of terms
applied to God 45; signifying the
essence 258 n.; real 70
deliberation 250
Democritus 210
demons 234–5, 253, 371, 373 n., 374 n.;
see also angels; substances,
separated
demonstration 7; a priori 12
dependence/independence 49–50,
77; causal 50, 59–60; conceptual
50, 52 n.; ontological 51, 58, 150,

152; metaphysical 51; real 50,
52 n.
Descartes, René 19, 271, 283 n., 302
desire, *see* appetite
Dionysius 40 n., 240 n., 343 n.; *see*
principle, Dionysian
distinction: conceptual 46; logical 128;
real 44, 46, 302 n.; *see also*
composition; distinguishing;
division
distinguishing 95–6, 108 n., 183–217,
218 n., 227 n., 228–9, 232, 271 n.;
determinate 208; formal 195, 199,
206, 209–10, 213, 215; material
195, 199, 209; of individuals 209–
10; of species 183–210, 230; on the
basis of difference of power 190,
198, 200; Origen's account
of 203 n., 216, 235; pre-Socratic
accounts of 210; taken
generally 193–8; taken
narrowly 198–202
division: *per accidens* 334–5, 381;
qualitative 94; quantitative 94,
195 n., 334–5
doctrine, Christian 11, 12 n., 151
dualism, substance 271, 288, 292,
299 n., 301–2, 316 (Cartesian 271,
283 n., 302; Platonist 301–10)
Dumont, Stephen 148 n.
Duns Scotus, John 148 n.

effect: contingent 139, 153, 157;
determined 129; extrinsic 123–4;
per accidens 115–16, 215 n.; *per
se* 114–17, 215 n.; proper 114–15;
single immediate 83; *see also*
cause
element 36, 59, 61, 71, 78–9, 87, 96, 99,
140, 186 n., 191–2, 199–202, 210 n.,
213, 280 n., 313, 318, 323, 342–4,
363 n., 364, 367, 373–4, 403 n.
emanation(ism) 77, 99, 106 n., 120,
121 n., 197, 203 n., 303
embryo 375, 377, 379, 383, 399, 400 n.,
401
embryology 373–6, 397
Empedocles 295 n.
end: natural 217 n.; ultimate 206 n.,
207; *see also* cause, final; appetite,
for good; will, object of
entity, *see* being; substance; thing
epistemology 5, 347, 351–2

equivocation 305, 322 n., 332 n., 418
Eriugena, John Scotus 148 n.
error 19
eternity 39, 142–3, 155, 163, 172, 417;
    of the world 59, 142–82; *see also*
    God's eternality; world, eternity
    of
ethics 5, 347
evil 217; argument from 119 n., 205 n.,
    218 n.; problem of 205 n., 217 n.
evolution 60, 73, 184–5, 190, 203–5,
    210
exegesis, scriptural 5
existence: absolute 386 n.; of God (*see*
    God, existence of); of intellects 29;
    of things 15, 18, 33; of world 3,
    14 n.; arguments for God's 4,
    14 n., 15, 28 n., 31 n., 34, 50, 56 n.,
    57 (a posteriori 17 n., 28 n.; a
    priori 12, 14 n.; cosmological
    117 n.; g2 34 n.; g6 50 n., 57;
    ontological 15); atemporal 142–3;
    beginningless 58 n., 59, 142–82
    (*see also* world, eternity of);
    conceptual 265; contingent 58 n.,
    63, 157; dependent 58, 60, 64, 67,
    76 n., 150, 152; eternal 39 (*see also*
    God's eternality); independent
    339; infinite 143; instantaneous
    18 n., 61; necessary 67–8, 101 n.,
    152–3, 157, 169; natural 45, 346 n.;
    per accidens/per se 385; real 265;
    successive 61; temporal 39, 143,
    154; *see also* actuality; being
experience: human 86 n.; religious 5
explanation 344, 351, 372;
    metaphysical 65, 194, 205; natural/
    naturalistic 98, 377, 387, 389, 396;
    of origin of individual human
    being 377, 387; partial 297;
    scientific 187, 211; theistic 185,
    203–5, 216; ultimate 9–10, 15,
    24, 61, 65 n., 73, 102, 127, 216,
    297

faculty: appetitive (*see* appetite; will);
    cognitive (*see* cognition; intellect)
faith 7, 11–12, 20–3, 29, 97 n., 145 n.,
    147, 191, 193, 228–31, 271 n.;
    articles of 11 n., 12; catholic 175,
    182; mysteries of 12; substance
    of 191; teaching of 25–8; *see also*
    belief, religious; truth of faith

Faith and Philosophy 3 n.
Fathers of the English Dominican
    Province 97 n., 226 n., 287 n.
first-efficient-cause argument 55
flesh and bone 305, 312
foetus 379, 383 n., 391, 395, 396 n.,
    397–9, 400, 402; *see also* body,
    foetal
form 78 n., 79 n., 83 n., 106 n., 107–12,
    116–17, 120 n., 138–40, 153, 194–8,
    203 n., 206–8, 212, 214 n., 215 n.,
    216, 219, 237–8, 248, 251 n., 252,
    255 n., 257, 260–9, 279–81, 306–7,
    335 n., 354, 359 n.; accidental 42,
    72, 78 n., 80, 115 n., 263 n., 268,
    289, 291, 309, 330–1, 334–5, 352;
    Aristotelian view of 385; as first
    actuality 39, 42, 200 n.; as
    terminus of generation 384;
    dependent on body 326 n.;
    dispositions for 328–30;
    elemental 213 n.; immaterial
    252, 257, 267, 270, 290, 352 n.;
    immaterial instantiation of
    363; imposition of 96, 96 n.;
    incorporeal 252, 270; intelligible
    237, 243 n., 244 n., 255 n., 352 n.,
    354, 361, 408; material 252, 254,
    257, 261, 265, 267, 293, 318, 329,
    353, 383, 385, 405, 409; material
    instantiation of 363; –matter
    composition (*see* composition,
    matter–form); natural 243 n.,
    244 n., 293 n., 329, 360 n.; of
    corporeality 330; of sensible
    things 352 n.; Plato's theory
    of 109 n., 350 n.; received
    intelligibly 237, 256 n., 281 n.,
    360 n.; received materiallly 237;
    sensible 346, 347, 354, 366;
    simple 335 n.; subsistent 252–3,
    257, 270, 291, 386, 405 n.;
    substantial 35 n., 78 n., 80, 115 n.,
    199–200, 202, 212, 263 n., 268,
    288–95, 298–9, 305–12, 316, 320,
    331 n., 332 n., 335, 363, 378–83,
    400–1 (plurality of 308–11,
    331 n.; unicity of 308–11, 325,
    331 n., 397, 401); universal (*see*
    universals); *see also* cause, formal;
    identity, formal; union of soul
    with body
freedom 125–6, 244–51; root of 250;

subject of 250; cause of 250; *see also* activity, free; decision, free; judgement, free

furnishing 95–6, 186–90, 202

Galen 300 n., 374
Galileo 141 n.
Gallagher, David 251 n.
Gauthier, René-Antoine 1 n., 8 n., 27 n.
Geach, P. T. 363 n.
generation/corruption 67, 81, 83–4, 110 n., 139, 151 n., 167 n., 180, 196 n., 201 n., 208–9, 213 n., 252 n., 267–9, 276, 279, 286, 311, 330–1, 367 n., 375–9, 382–4, 391–7, 400–2, 414; *per accidens/per se* 384, 386, 405 n., 409, 412
geometry 26, 53 n., 118 n.
Gerson, Lloyd P. 1 n.
Giles of Rome 146 n., 148 n.
God: as actual being (*ens actu*) 36; as being itself 218; as cause of being 23, 33–5, 37, 54–60, 73–7, 80, 84, 88, 99, 101 n., 102, 107, 114, 115 n., 116 n., 204; as creator 23–4, 50, 53 n., 55 n., 122, 138, 149–50, 196; as first actuality 40 n.; as first agent 37 n., 394; as first cause 15, 34–6, 56 n., 76, 138, 216; as first mover 36, 160; as first principle 5, 10, 296 n.; as formal being of things 197 n.; as goal 5, 9, 10, 27; as highest good 15, 226; as pure actuality 36–46, 79 n.; as second actuality 43–6; as source of all things 10, 15, 27, 33–5, 42, 53–7, 60, 73, 81, 120, 129 n., 150 n., 156, 176; as spirit 6; as subject of theology 10; as three and one 12 (*see also* trinity); attributes of 3, 14 n., 15, 21, 28 n., 48, 122 n., 229, 372 n.; communication from 3; concept of 3, 10, 14 n.; considered in himself 3, 5, 8, 9, 33, 70, 122, 229, 231; considered in his works 229; existence of 1 n., 3–5, 12, 14–17, 31 n., 33–5, 50–1, 184, 369 (*see* existence, arguments for God's); experience of 3; in himself 10, 23, 34; incorporeality of 6; knowledge of 9 n., 231 (*see also* cognition, of God); likeness of things to 21 n., 22, 40 n., 48, 55,

122, 135, 166, 197 n., 218 n., 223, 229, 230 n., 231, 236–9, 256–7, 369; mistaken views about 21, 23, 25; nature of 4–5, 14, 15, 17 n., 20, 24, 33–6, 41, 43–4, 51, 54, 103, 120–2, 131, 135, 160–1, 166, 184, 195–7, 202, 218, 224, 229, 231, 258, 342, 369; negative characterizations of 12 n.; no accidents in 44, 49; no imperfection in 15; no passive potentiality in 37 n., 40 n., 41, 42 n., 51, 124, 128; no real distinction in 46; not composite 12, 44, 257, 259; not specified by differentiae 12; not subject of a priori demonstration 12; relation of things to 5, 55 n.; relations in 48–50, 51–4
God's: activity 14–19, 29, 31 n., 34–6, 41–7, 55, 70, 77–8, 82–3, 87–8, 96 n., 99, 103–6, 115 n., 121 n., 122–6, 160, 162, 228–9, 231, 369; actuality 39; atemporality (*see* God's eternality); cognition 28, 33, 55, 123, 127, 157–8, 159, 256; eternality 15, 39 n., 51, 56–7, 89 n., 122 n., 150 n., 154–5, 159, 161–5, 173, 175, 196, 218, 225, 238; free choice 24, 102 n., 103, 120, 125, 217–18; free decision 102, 120–5; freedom in creating 101–3, 120, 122 n., 126, 153, 155, 156–7, 217–18, 226; goodness 15, 16 n., 21–2, 125–6, 130–41, 153–6, 158, 161 n., 164–7, 182, 196, 203 n., 205, 207, 217, 224–7, 230, 237 n., 238–40; governance 18, 33, 70, 122, 204, 232 n., 369; ideas 86 n., 119 n.; immateriality 257 n.; immovability 161, 163 n., 170–1; immutability 38 n., 51, 89–90, 128; inability to do things 127–8; independence 49–50, 218; infinity 15, 103–4; influence 176; intellect 16, 69, 86, 122, 125, 127–31, 168, 204, 229, 238, 255–6; intellection 17, 19, 41, 55, 70, 78, 119 n., 124–7, 159; intention 209, 238 n.; joy 16; justice 130, 133 n., 203 n., 216; knowing 48; knowledge 51, 52, 86 n., 122 n., 129 n., 131, 176; love 16; moving 48; name 258 n.;

God's: activity (*cont.*):
obligations 103; omnipotence
44 n., 101 n., 103–5, 113–19, 127–8,
149–50, 175, 177 n., 204–5, 217,
224–6; omniscience 13, 22 n.,
204–5, 217, 224–6, 239;
perfection 15, 17, 21–2, 36, 38, 55,
71, 77, 87, 104, 119 n.; perfections
15–16; plan 130–41, 232 n., 236;
power 21–2, 24, 36, 40 n., 41–8, 52,
54–5, 85 n., 96, 98 n., 103–8,
112–25, 128–9, 150 n., 159, 166,
182, 196, 206, 226, 394 n.;
production of things (*see*
production); providence (*see*
providence); simplicity 13, 43–4,
53 n., 121 n., 154 n., 196–7,
218, 225, 238, 257; sinning 104–5;
substance 9 n., 43–5, 49–50, 123,
125, 259, 373; transcendence 166;
uniqueness/unity 12, 101 n., 197;
volition 18–19, 24, 33, 41, 70, 78,
102 n., 103, 120, 122–6, 128, 131,
135, 139, 152–64, 176, 200 n.;
will 16, 24, 36, 55, 78, 86, 105,
121–34, 137–9, 156 n., 157, 161,
165–6, 170, 182, 204, 217, 231, 342,
348 n.; wisdom 21–2, 28, 121 n.,
122 n., 127, 343 n.; works 20–3, 84,
228, 239 (*see also* six days, work
of)
Godfrey of Fontaines 148 n.
good: apprehended 127, 248 n., 250 n.,
251, 345; as object of appetite/
will 122, 127, 242 n., 244 n.;
essential nature of 249; highest
15, 226; particular 243 n.;
universal 243 n., 249; *see also*
cause, final; end
goodness 21, 126, 130–41, 166, 206 n.,
217, 241–2; accidental 221, 223;
diffusiveness of 134–5, 156 (*see*
principle, Dionysian); essential
221–2; itself 243 n., 249; levels
of 222, 224 n., 225; manifestation
of (*see* manifestation, of God's
goodness); perfect 16, 126, 131–5,
154 n., 155–8, 165, 205, 217, 224–6,
238
Grandest Unified Theory 9, 10
Gregory of Nyssa 177 n., 378 n., 382 n.,
387, 389
Grosseteste, Robert 147 n.

Grover, Stephen 224 n.
growth 297, 332 n., 344

Haldane, John J. 353 n.
handiwork, *see* God's works
happiness 217 n.
Hause, Jeffrey 251 n.
Hayes, Zachary 90 n., 197 n., 203 n.
heaven and earth 20, 84–5, 93, 95–6,
108, 111–12, 211, 228
Henry of Ghent 147 n.
Henry of Harclay 148 n.
heretics 373 n.
historian 7 n.
hoc aliquid 331 n.
Hoenen, M. J. F. M. 142 n., 148 n.
Hoffman, Paul 353 n.
Holy Spirit 191, 193
hope 20 n.
Howard-Snyder, Daniel 205 n., 224 n.
Howard-Snyder, Frances 224 n.
Huby, Pamela 177 n.
Hugh of St Victor 187 n.
human: activity 326, 337, 360;
body 109 n., 111, 270–2, 281,
283 n., 287, 295, 299 n., 300–25,
332–3, 337, 364–5, 367 n., 372,
374, 387, 394 (*see also* union of
soul with body); cognition
(*see* cognition); dignity 232;
development 306, 309 n., 311 n.,
328–9, 331, 344, 374, 376, 381, 386,
389–402 (single soul's continuous
398; by succession of souls 402);
essence 302; existence 39
(beginning of 372–3, 380, 382;
end of 372–3); experience
86 n.; generation 328, 329 n. (*see
also* generation/corruption);
ideas 86 n.; intellect 5 n., 72,
232 n., 246 n., 253, 255, 267, 270,
319 (*see also* intellect); life 4, 328;
mind 270–2, 281, 311, 323;
morality 1 n.; nature and
behaviour 5, 39, 134–5, 155, 286,
299 n., 304, 308, 317 n., 323, 337,
343, 360, 370, 372, 391 (Platonist
account of 286, 312); philosophy
(*see* philosophy, human);
reason 12–13; soul 25, 233–5, 268,
272 n., 283 n., 287, 295 n., 296,
299–307, 311–17, 320, 323, 325,
336 n., 343–5, 350, 354 n., 370–2,

377, 380–8, 391, 394, 412–13, 417
(*see also* soul); well-being 13;
will 25, 72, 120 (*see also* will)
human beings 13, 22, 25, 137, 140, 153,
155, 187 n., 192, 201 n., 209, 223,
232–4, 240 n., 242, 244 n., 251,
255 n., 270–3, 283 n., 287, 294–5,
299–323, 328–60, 364, 367 n.; as
metaphysical hybrids 270, 273,
285, 370; as related to God 10,
232, 369; individual 328, 331, 341,
341 n.
hylomorphism 251 n.
hypothesis SFB, *see* union of soul with
body: as substantial form of the
body

identity, formal 352–3, 362, 363 n.; *see
also* union, cognitive
imagination 172, 243, 246–7, 300 n.,
345–56, 359 n., 383 n., 410, 412; as
storehouse of forms 354
immortality 269, 371, 418
impossibility, logical (absolute) 117–
19, 253
improvement 222–5; additive 221–2,
225; evolutionary 221 n.;
intensive 221–3
Incarntion 1 n., 12 n.
incorruptibility 268–9
individual 72–3, 96, 195, 208–10, 215,
218 n., 224 n., 230 n., 243 n., 259,
288, 302 n., 312, 321, 349 n., 351,
352 n., 353 n., 354, 364, 377, 379–
80, 400 n., 401 n.; *see also*
particular
individuation 195, 208–9, 213 n., 252 n.,
255 n., 358 n., 394, 412
induction 413–14
infinity 177; actual 177 n., 181; of past
time 147, 164, 177 n., 178–80; *see
also* world, eternity of
instrument 327, 361, 362 n., 365, 367 n.,
393–4, 413
intellect 13, 15–16, 24–5, 46, 126–7,
129, 134, 153, 204, 206, 214 n., 228–
69, 271, 281 n., 285, 293, 295 n.,
312, 316, 318–19, 321, 323 n., 325,
336 n., 339, 344, 346 n., 349–52,
355–6, 359–67, 369, 407, 410, 418;
agent 181, 312–13, 341–2, 350,
355–62, 365, 409 (Aristotelian
view of 342; Avicenna's theory

of 350); as self-reflective (*see*
cognition, reflexive); existence
of 235, 237; immateriality of
366; incorporeality of 5 n., 6 n.;
passive 345, 352 n., 412, 414;
possible 181, 243, 312–13, 319,
321 n., 337–44, 349–66, 370–1,
407, 408 n., 410, 418 (Aristotelian
view of 341; Averroistic view
of 347 n.); sempiternal 340–1;
separated 313, 321 n., 339–42,
350; substance of 325; *see also*
God's intellect; soul, intellective;
substances, intellective
intellection, *see* cognition, intellective
intelligences 227, 234 n.; *see also*
substances, separated
intention 140, 205–6, 209–10, 214–16,
218, 230 n., 357 n.; *see also* God's
intention
Inwagen, Peter van 190 n., 193 n.,
203 n., 205 n.
Irwin, T. H. 40 n., 324 n.

joy 16, 414, 418
judgement 246–50, 347, 351 n.;
free 246–8, 251, 346 n., 348 n.;
intellective 245, 247, 250 n.; self-
reflective 248
judicious assessment (of arguments for
the eternity of the world) 146–8
jumble 276–7
justice 130–41

Kant, Immanuel 142–3, 177
Kenny, Anthony 10 n., 11 n., 81 n.,
191 n., 258 n., 296 n., 302 n., 323 n.,
343 n., 355 n.
kinds, natural, *see* species
knowledge 296 n., 338, 350 n., 357,
361 n., 405–6, 408; as relation 51–
3; notion of 134; of what God is
in himself 9 n.; reflexive 351; *see
also* cognition
Knuuttila, Simo 129 n.
Kovach, Francis J. 147 n.
Kremer, Klaus 102 n.
Kretzmann, Norman 13 n., 16 n., 21 n.,
22 n., 39 n., 43 n., 52 n., 89 n., 90 n.,
91 n., 102 n., 124 n., 129 n., 135 n.,
142 n., 158 n., 162 n., 167 n., 179 n.,
215 n., 217 n., 232 n., 238 n., 240 n.,
241 n., 256 n., 288 n., 296 n., 314 n.,

Kretzmann, Norman (*cont.*):
 323 n., 330 n., 343 n., 354 n., 366 n.,
 406 n.

language, emotive 22
laws: mathematical 138; natural 62,
 66, 68–9, 73, 84, 138, 184, 200 n.,
 201
Leibniz, Gottfried Wilhelm 218 n.
Leonine edition 31 n., 32 n., 54, 78 n.,
 88 n., 97 n., 106 n., 121, 130, 155 n.,
 382 n.
Leucippus 210
life 4, 142–3, 155, 188–9, 229, 296–9,
 305–8, 312, 318–19, 333, 343, 378 n.
likeness 173, 197 n., 218–19, 223,
 230 n., 237, 239–40, 279, 346 n.,
 351, 353–8, 361, 386 n., 388 n., 394–
 5; *see also* God, likeness of things
 to; manifestion
logic 118 n., 361
logicians, medieval 91–3
Lombard, Peter 144 n., 186, 189
love 16, 414, 418

MacDonald, Scott 11 n., 35 n., 105 n.,
 241 n., 251 n., 258 n.
McInerny, Ralph 258 n.
MacIntosh, J. J. 142 n., 178 n.
McMullin, Ernan 190 n.
making (*facere*) 17, 134, 172–5; *see
 also* production
Manichaeism 203 n., 216
manifestation 17, 40 n., 167 n., 182,
 196, 207, 216–17, 224–7, 231 n.,
 238–40; of God's goodness 126,
 134, 136, 153–4, 165–7, 182, 230,
 238–9; of God's providence 343
Marc, P. 4 n.
Marietti edition 31 n., 32 n., 52 n., 56 n.,
 78 n., 88 n., 93 n., 97 n., 107 n., 130,
 196 n., 234 n., 246 n., 382 n., 403 n.
materialism 298
materialists 253, 296–300
mathematics 4
matter 83 n., 85, 88, 96, 99, 106 n., 107–
 13, 116, 120 n., 138–42, 153, 172,
 197–8, 200 n., 203 n., 207–16, 251–
 7, 261–9, 274, 306, 318, 329, 335 n.,
 353–4, 358 n.; antecedent (pre-
 existing) 73, 75 n., 76–8, 80–91,
 95, 101, 110, 174, 215 n., 331 n.;
 beginningless 87; conditions of

(*see* conditions, material);
 considered relatively/absolutely
 78 n.; corporeal 107–12, 251, 293,
 315, 318; elemental 213;
 formed 251; –form analysis
 212–13; –form composition (*see*
 composition, matter–form);
 individual 255 n., 256, 366, 407 n.;
 metaphysical 212–15, 251 n.;
 organic 268; potential 261, 262 n.;
 physical 212–13 (two varieties
 213); prime 78–80, 82, 110–11,
 173, 200, 207, 212–14, 252, 330,
 360 n., 408 n.; proximate/proper
 326, 329–32, 380; self-existent
 215 n.; sensible 111; spiritual
 252 n.; transmuting of 382–3;
 see also cause, material; stuff,
 pre-existing
Matthew of Aquasparta 148 n.
mechanics 26
medicine, ancient 327 n.
meditating 18–24, 84, 103 n., 228
memory 349 n., 350, 415, 418;
 intellective 349; sensory 345,
 348 n., 349; *see also* power,
 memoritive
Menssen, Sandra 224 n.
menstrual blood 374, 379, 399
merit 216, 235
metaphysician 86
metaphysics 5, 6 n., 27, 58, 361, 373;
 Aristotelian 6 n.; of theism 27; of
 creation 27, 29, 37, 69; of
 providence 27; theistic 2 n., 4
method: disputational 294, 341;
 eliminative 15; relational 15–16,
 21 n., 45, 48, 70, 77, 372 n.;
 scholastic 294 n., 341
Migne edition 97 n.
mind 204–5, 233 n., 253, 295 n.;
 human 231, 233–4, 254; *see also*
 intellect; mind–body relationship;
 reason; soul
mind–body relationship 271–2, 288; *see
 also* union of soul with body
miracles 24, 82–3, 208, 343 n., 386
monopsychism 313
morality 4; human 1 n.; *see also* ethics
Moses 96, 193
motion 63, 72, 76, 81–95, 99, 101,
 143 n., 150, 163, 170–6, 210, 280 n.,
 332 n.; local 81 n., 91–4, 168, 189,

198, 201, 276, 344, 402 n.; of the
heavens 372; perpetuity of 145 n.,
168 n., 169–71; terminus of 89–92;
see also change
movement, *see* motion
Muhammadans 1 n.

natural theologian 77
natural theology 1–22, 25–6, 29–36, 45,
49 n., 56, 75, 83, 93, 98 n., 135 n.,
138, 160, 170, 183–6, 194, 196, 198,
202–3, 228–32, 254, 256–7, 260,
369–72, 384, 418; Alston's view
of 3–4, 14 n.; as arguing for (or
against) God's existence 3, 5; as
branch of philosophy 3, 5; as
expository 7; as integrating
theology with philosophy 3, 5; as
investigating God's nature 3–5,
14; as making restricted use of
revealed propositions 6; as
science 6 n.; as subordinate to
metaphysics 6 n.; as supporting
religious beliefs 3, 7; broad
conception of 3–4, 9; classical 4;
explanatory capacity of 4, 9;
history of 1 n.; methods for (*see*
method; theology, methods in);
nature and status of 3; Plantinga's
discussion of 3 n.; starting-points
of 3, 4, 14 n.; subject-matter of
3–4
nature 1, 14, 24, 26, 27 n., 29, 67, 78–9,
85–7, 96, 106, 112, 120, 192, 194,
199, 201 n., 204, 207–8, 224 n., 228,
230, 232, 234 n., 236, 237 n., 241–5,
258, 285, 295, 322 n., 351, 354 n.,
355, 361–5; angelic 111–12, 124;
human (*see* human nature);
intellective (*see* substances,
intellective); specifying seminal
(see *rationes seminales*); universal
(*see* universals)
necessity: absolute 103, 124 n., 128 n.,
137–40, 152, 155–8, 169; associated
with sensory cognition 350;
causal 157; cause of 67–8;
conditional 103, 137;
contingent 66; *de dicto/de re* 129,
158; divine 18; *ex hypothesi* 128,
132, 137–8; in created things 103,
130–41; logical 66, 157, 168;
moral 129–31, 133, 136, 156;

metaphysical 131, 133–6, 155–6;
natural 24, 120–6, 138, 217 n.,
346 n.; *per accidens* 350; *per se*
158, 350; of coercion 120 n., 125;
of the consequence 158; of the
consequent 158; of the end 133,
138, 154, 165; of God's plan 132,
137; of matter 215 n.; of one's own
nature 68, 120–6, 152, 182, 344 n.;
of an ordered relationship 169; *see
also* obligation
necessity argument 156–8
negation 15
not-being (non-being) 75–7, 82 n., 114,
117–18, 213 n., 215 n., 269;
absolute 81–3, 88; natural priority
of 75–6; temporal priority of 75–
6, 171–2; nothing is made out of
nothing (*ex nihilo nihil fit*) 85–7
nourishment 332 n., 380
number 180 n.

obligation (*debitum*) 130–41, 154–5;
moral 133; of gratitude 133; of
justice 130–6; of necessity 132,
135; of right 133; to possible
created things 131; to divine
goodness 136, 156
Ockham, William 148 n., 179 n.
omnipotence, *see* God's omnipotence
omniscience, *see* God's omniscience
ontology 10 n.
operation, *see* activity
order: cosmic 221; natural 192–3; of
actual world 220; of parts (*see*
universe, ordering of parts of);
pedagogical 192–3; purely
rational 6 n.; teleological 3, 14 n.;
temporal 192–3; two kinds of
219
ordering relationship 169, 390, 393
organ 326–7, 330, 332, 335–6, 348, 351–
5, 364–7, 374, 381, 390, 398 n., 410–
11, 415–18; -lessness 383, 404, 407,
411, 415
Origen 203 n., 216, 235, 373 n.
orthodoxy, *see* Christian orthodoxy

pagans 1 n.
Paris 148 n., 339 n.
part(s) 39, 48, 85 n., 137, 140, 206 n.,
219, 236, 239–40, 255 n., 263,
268, 283 n., 285 n., 317, 326;

part(s) (*cont.*):
    metaphysical 298 n.; of an
    animal 347; of a body 297–307,
    319, 327, 331–6, 347, 390–1; of a
    human being 328; of motion 171;
    of the soul (*see* soul, parts of);
    of the universe (*see* universe,
    ordering of parts of); quantitative
    287; really distinct 359; temporal
    163–4, 172
participation 37, 37 n., 165–6, 234 n.
particulars 72, 77, 83–5, 117 n., 164,
    249–50, 255 n., 348–9, 349 n.,
    350 n., 364
Pasnau, Robert 142 n., 256 n.
patient 140
Pecham, John 148 n.
Peghaire, Julien 102 n., 134 n.
Pegis, Anton C. 252 n., 343 n.
Pera, C. 4 n.
perfection (completeness) 21–2, 36–9,
    77, 87, 101, 105, 119 n., 133–7,
    218 n., 223–4, 230 n., 236–8, 244 n.,
    329–30, 361 n., 405–7; *see also*
    God's perfection; God's
    perfections
Peterson, M. L. 205 n.
phantasia, see imagination
phantasms 246 n., 312, 321–2, 325, 350,
    354–65, 370, 407, 414–17
Philoponus, John 148 n., 177 n.
Philosopher 7 n., 43 n., 85 n., 127 n.,
    132, 143 n., 144 n., 160 n., 167 n.,
    174, 241, 243, 250, 329 n., 348, 365,
    396 n., 398 n., 399 n.; *see also*
    Aristotle
philosopher-theologians, Christian 143
philosophers 11, 25, 75, 76 n., 90 n.,
    106, 121, 177 n., 180, 240, 251, 293,
    299, 319; ancient 85–6, 98, 173,
    210, 252 n., 263 n., 297, 300 n.;
    Christian 145; medieval 93 n., 146,
    374; natural 86, 210, 252 n., 263 n.;
    neoplatonist 106 n.; of
    religion 11 n.; pre-twentieth-
    century 2; twentieth-century 2,
    26; *see also* pre-Socratics
philosophical psychology 367
philosophical theology 11, 45, 135 n.
philosophy 25, 28; arguments
    characteristic of 11 n.;
    Aristotelian 5, 144; branches of
    5; history of 86, 271; human 5 n.,

28; first 10 n.; late-twentieth-
    century 5; natural 26–7, 87, 201,
    228, 343; naturally evident
    starting-points 5; of creation 6 n.;
    of mind 5, 254 n., 312 n., 313 n.,
    322–5, 337, 339, 343, 347, 361, 364,
    368; of religion 253; starting-
    points 28; subject-matter of 2–3;
    theistic 28 n.
plan, *see* God's plan
plant 72–3, 96 n., 137, 184, 186 n., 188,
    189 n., 191–2, 201 n., 205 n., 209,
    230, 241, 245, 248, 296–7, 311 n.,
    318, 322 n., 335, 336 n., 344, 347,
    378 n., 398 n., 402 n.
Plantinga, Alvin 3 n., 119 n.
Plato 109 n., 143 n., 218 n., 300–3, 310,
    312–13, 337, 344 n., 397
Platonism 350
Platonists 148 n., 150 n., 301–3, 305,
    307–8, 310, 312, 373 n., 389
Popper, Karl 177 n.
Porphyrian tree 292 n., 309
Porphyry 150 n., 413
possibility 113; absolute 118–19;
    logical 118–19, 124, 174, 281;
    real 207, 284, 286, 291
potentialities: intellective 338;
    natural 39, 79, 184, 192, 200 n.,
    298; nutritive 297; specifying 38 n.,
    200, 241, 242–3; unactualized 39,
    124, 241; vegetative 297
potentiality: for not-being 139, 168–9;
    passive 37 n., 42, 51, 124 n., 128,
    174; pure 78 n., 79, 111, 207,
    213 n., 252; receptive 366; to
    another form 139
power: active 40 n., 41–4, 47, 109 n.,
    111, 124 n., 199–202, 210, 212–13,
    215; appetitive (*see* appetite); as
    implying as relation 118 n.; as
    source of activity 43, 45–7, 105,
    123; as source of effect 45–8,
    53 n., 123; associated with
    form 141; cogitative 345, 346 n.,
    352 n., 355 n., 359 n., 411–12, 414–
    15; cognitive (*see* cognition);
    concupiscible 240, 243 n., 345, 347,
    418; creative 103–14, 116–17;
    defining characteristic of 45, 48,
    123 n.; dependent on body 271,
    274, 293, 326 n.; estimative 248,
    346–7; in action 43; infinite 98 n.,

103–4, 114; intellective (*see* intellect); irascible 240, 243 n., 345, 347, 418; memoritive 341, 345, 348, 355 n., 359 n., 411–12, 414–15; motive 326, 346; natural 44 n.; passive 42–4, 199–202, 210, 212–13, 215, 250 n., 304, 347 n., 348, 360; perfect 114–15; productive 114–17, 119 n.; separate 336 n.

powers 14, 16, 35–6, 40 n., 44, 47, 199, 200 n., 210 n., 234 n., 236, 349, 353

preambles to the articles of faith 12

predications: affirmative 15; relational 48; two-place 48

pre-Socratics 23 n., 210, 215 n., 295 n., 297

principle: agent's-likeness 218, 219, 230 n., 237; Dionysian 126, 134, 135 n., 136, 154, 156, 165–6; ENNF (*ex nihilo nihil fieri*) 85–7, 172–3; first 5, 10, 19, 24, 27, 85–7, 98, 296–9, 305, 319, 333; of action 122 n.; of life (*see* soul: as first principle of life); of movement 322; of non-contradiction 92, 117, 168, 226; of sufficient reason 65–8; of universal appetite 241–2

principles 5 n., 120; derived from Aristotle 5 n., 6 n., 196, 254; essential 14 n., 117 n., 137, 139, 140, 153; explanatory 24; extrinsic 35 n.; first 6 n., 85 n., 127; formal 118 n.; individuating (*see* conditions, individuating); intrinsic 120 n., 322; material 210, 214 n.; motive 210 n.; of a thing's nature 35 n.; philosophically authoritative 254; self-evidently true 5 n., 40 n., 127

privation 79 n., 195 n.

production: artificial 72, 81, 85, 106–11; by moving and altering pre-existing stuff 72, 76, 81–5, 87–8, 107, 110; of things 32–6, 61–2, 66, 70, 77, 84, 87, 90, 122, 188, 195, 206 n., 271 n.; God's 18, 32, 35 n., 36–7, 41, 43, 44 n., 46, 50, 53, 54–6, 70, 74, 76–84, 96, 102, 106–8, 119–20, 122 n., 127, 132, 135, 155, 182, 228–9, 232, 239; holistic interpretation of 83–4, 107 n.; in being 28, 32, 53, 55 n., 58–9, 76,

81, 85, 96, 131–2, 135–7, 183, 199, 204; natural 73, 83, 85, 106–11; out of nothing (*see* creation *ex nihilo*); source of 32–4, 66, 70, 101, 123; terminus of 32–3, 70, 78, 101; universal 56–7, 70–1, 79, 81–4, 87, 131, 154–5, 173 (distributively 71, 73, 76–8, 80, 82–4, 95, 101 n.; intrinsically 73, 76–7, 80, 82–4, 86, 94–5, 101 n.); *see also* creation

propositions: accessible only via revelation 8, 12; as objects of faith 20; categorical 158; Christian doctrinal 1 n., 12; conditional 5 n., 158; divinely revealed 6, 11 n., 12; doctrinal 20; non-metaphorical 45; theoretical 12

proprium 140, 267, 385, 405 n.

providence 9, 18, 24, 201, 232 n., 249, 343, 369

prudence 296 n.

quality 44, 94, 201, 228, 238, 343, 344, 348, 351; corporeal 343, 413; elemental 201, 343; sensible 111, 352–4

quantity 94, 172, 195 n., 255 n., 266 n., 282, 287

quiddity 35 n., 354 n.

Quinn, Philip. L. 224 n.

radical-replacement hypothesis 400, 402

rationality 323

rationes seminales 191–2, 199, 200 n., 201 n.

realism, epistemological 352

reality 14, 112, 252–3, 348

reason 11–12, 20 n., 28 n., 97, 250 n., 251, 347 n.; as guided by revelation 7; for existence 65–6, 68; natural 1 n., 6, 12, 371; unaided 6–7, 9, 12–13, 20, 30

reasoning, *see* arguments; reason

redemption 18 n.

reduction 297, 299

regress, infinite 57–65, 87, 150–1, 173–5, 180; *see also* causes, ordered series of

relations 15; as externally existent 52 n., 53 n.; attributed to

relations (*cont.*):
    God 47, 49–53; category of 91;
        cognition of 352; conceptual 52–
        3; real 49 n., 50–3; *see also*
        category
relatives, Aristotle's definition of 49
religion 7, 190
representation, *see* manifestation
reproduction 297, 344, 373–6, 380, 387,
        393–5
result, external (*factum*) 17, 37, 41,
        45–8
resurrection of the body 1 n., 367 n., 371
revelation 1 n., 5–6, 11–13, 22–3, 25,
        28 n., 83, 93, 98, 135 n., 145, 371,
        418; as guide for reason 7
Richard of Middleton 148 n.
Richard of St Victor 147 n.
Riet, S. van 106 n.
Robb, James H. 293 n.
Rowe, William L. 61 n., 64, 65, 224 n.

sacra doctrina 10
Sagan, Carl 147 n.
Saint Paul 406 n.
saints 11, 191
salvation history 12 n.
scholarship: philosophical 1; medieval
        philosophical 2
science 4, 10, 118 n., 127, 190, 213, 231,
        242, 350, 361–3, 373–4;
        ancient 328; Aristotelian 7 n., 31;
        history of 65; natural 4, 26, 58, 73,
        138, 184, 199 n., 201, 280 n., 366,
        393 n.; of being *qua* being 10 n.;
        of being *qua* divine 10 n.; of
        truth 27; rational 361; subordinate
        6 n.
scientist 7 n., 22, 252
Scripture 1 n., 6–7, 11 n., 18, 21–3,
        30 n., 84–5, 93, 95 n., 96–8, 130,
        151, 182, 188, 190–1, 193, 197,
        210–11, 253 n., 373 n., 387 n., 392 n.
Scriven, Michael 177 n.
selection, natural 203, 209–10
self-mover 246, 247 n., 321–2, 326, 403
self-mover argument 247
self-reflection 248, 255 n., 363 n.
semen 374–85, 388–401, 413
sempiternity 61, 152, 154–5, 159, 165,
        168, 170–5, 340 n.; *see also* world,
        eternity of; existence,
        beginningless

sempiternity argument 154–5
sensation 189 n., 194, 234 n., 244 n.,
        303–4, 306–8, 310–12, 319
sense 111, 239, 242–3, 246–7, 280–1,
        300 n., 304, 307, 312, 332 n., 341,
        344–56, 360, 416–17; common 345,
        349 n., 351, 353, 356 n.; internal
        246 n., 345–9, 351–6, 365; external
        246 n., 304, 345–54, 365, 367
Shakespeare, William 147, 204, 393
Siger of Brabant 148 n.
simplicity: absolute 13, 154 n., 161,
        196–7, 257–8, 266 n., 278; *see*
        composition
sin 56 n., 104
six days, work of 93–7, 185–93, 211;
        Augustinian interpretation of 191
Smith, Q. 177 n.
Snyder, Steven C. 148 n.
Society of Christian Philosophers 3 n.
Sorabji, Richard 142 n., 143 n., 177 n.
soul(s) 25, 109 n., 111, 137, 153, 243,
        298–9, 302 n., 303–4, 306 n., 310,
        317, 319 n., 343; accidents of
        330; activities of 324, 326, 336,
        343, 350, 370, 390, 392, 413;
        animal 403–4; as efficient cause of
        body 390; as first principle of
        life 296–9, 305–9, 319, 333; as
        form (*see* union of soul with
        body); as harmony 300 n.; as
        power (*see* union of soul with
        body); as separated from
        body 406–18; as temperament
        300 n.; at death 372, 403, 406,
        407–8; –body relationship 299 n.,
        326, 337, 390, 407–8 (*see also*
        union of soul with body);
        corruption of 372–3; disembodied
        413; Empedocles' view about
        295 n.; essence of 319, 326 n., 333;
        existence after death 287 n., 371,
        414, 417–18; existence before
        birth 329 n., 373 n.; existence
        before embodiment 371, 376;
        heretical doctrine of 295 n.;
        human (*see* human soul);
        immortality of 181, 232, 371, 373;
        incorruptibility of 403–4, 407–8;
        individual 367 n.; intellective
        234 n., 235, 243 n., 270–2, 295–6,
        300, 302 n., 305, 308–13, 321, 323,
        328–31, 337, 344–9, 354–9, 366,

372, 374, 380–4, 391–400, 403–4,
410, 412, 414, 417; nutritive 297,
302 n., 308–11, 320, 329–31, 343–5,
377–83, 391–2, 394, 396 n., 397,
401, 410, 413, 415; of heavenly
bodies 235; of living things 305;
operations of (*see* soul, activities
of); origin of 232, 343, 373, 387,
402; parts of 332 n., 342–9, 365,
413–14; passions of 296 n., 347,
414, 418; plurality of (*see* form,
substantial: plurality of); powers
of 307, 319, 324, 326–7, 330, 332,
335–6, 338, 343–7, 349 n., 352–5,
362, 410, 412–13, 417 (*see also*
power); pre-human 391; pre-
Socratic views about 295 n.;
rational 233–4, 253 n., 293 n., 344,
394 n., 398, 401; sensory 253 n.,
297, 302 n., 304, 307–11, 320–1,
329–31, 344–52, 357, 367 n.,
377–83, 392–403, 412–13, 415;
subsistent 385, 403; vegetative
377, 379, 398, 401
species 16–17, 29 n., 44, 53 n., 63, 70,
74 n., 76–7, 79 n., 96, 108, 109 n.,
119, 167 n., 177 n., 180, 183–216,
218, 221 n., 222–5, 227 n., 229–30,
240 n., 241, 243 n., 244 n., 255 n.,
256, 260–1, 263, 269–70, 285, 304,
307, 309, 314, 317, 317 n., 323, 329,
332 n., 334, 339, 344, 350–4, 358 n.,
361–6, 369, 377, 386 n., 394–5, 399–
401, 417; individual 351, 412 n.;
intelligible 255 n., 256, 312, 337,
341, 346 n., 349, 354–63, 407 n.,
418; origin of 184, 186, 188–9, 190,
192, 194, 201, 204, 210 n.; sensible
346 n., 351–3, 355, 360, 362, 367;
universal 352 n., 361 n.
spirits 347 n.; *see also* substances,
spiritual
state: instantaneous 92; successive 91–
2
Steenberghen, Fernand van 142 n.,
178 n.
stuff: pre-existing 74, 76–7, 80, 110,
173; primordial 73, 79, 83, 210; *see
also* matter
Stump, Eleonore 13 n., 16 n., 22 n.,
39 n., 43 n., 52 n., 89 n., 127 n.,
142 n., 152, 153, 162 n., 205 n.,
215 n., 232 n., 241 n., 246 n., 251 n.,

256 n., 271 n., 296 n., 299 n., 304 n.,
339 n., 343 n., 345 n., 353 n., 355 n.,
361 n., 363 n.
subject 71 n., 74, 83 n., 89, 109–11, 119,
159, 163 n., 171, 175, 200 n., 268,
289–90, 315, 383 n., 409, 413, 415;
first 99, 174–5
substance 5 n., 44, 49, 56 n., 79 n., 94,
96 n., 212, 241, 252 n., 259–60, 263,
266, 288, 292 n., 309, 314, 385, 408,
413, 415
substances: corporeal 252 n., 267 n.,
270–2, 278–9, 281 n., 288–92, 296,
329, 370; corruptible 268–9;
extraterrestrial 372; formal 267;
immaterial 252–3, 257, 259, 260–3,
266–8, 276, 281, 289 n., 293, 302,
318; incorporeal 257, 271, 273,
277, 289 n., 290, 292, 296, 296 n.,
302, 310, 417; incorruptible 270,
276; intellective 16, 109, 169,
228–326, 339, 342, 348 n., 364,
369–73, 377, 385, 404, 416;
material 254, 260, 262 n., 264,
267, 405 n.; natural 267, 288–9,
301, 313; primary 288–9, 301,
313, 386; rational 234 n., 235,
240 n., 329; sempiternal 339;
sensory 329; separated 6 n.,
107–12, 139, 234–5, 296 n., 319,
339–42, 347 n., 355, 370–2,
416–17; spiritual 191, 203 n.,
234 n., 253, 296, 328;
subsistent 266–7, 270, 312 n., 315;
superhuman 370, 372;
supernatural 343; volitional 240,
244–5, 249; *see also* things
substratum 212, 415
successiveness 91–5, 101, 175
Sullivan, Thomas 224 n.
Sylvester, Francis 32 n.

Taylor, J. H. 192 n., 193 n.
Taylor, Richard C. 337 n.
teaching 20–8
theism 7, 25, 26, 203, 205 n.; Christian
8, 25; mono- 5; perfect-being 8,
12; *see also* explanation, theistic
theists 22
theologians 343 n., 369, 371;
Christian 145; late-twentieth-
century 3; medieval 11 n., 90 n.,
146, 374

theology 185 n.; aim of 10; as
    continuous with philosophy 2;
    Christian 148 n.; dogmatic 11,
    187; God as subject of 9; natural
    (*see* natural theology); methods
    in 15 n.; philosophical (*see*
    philosophical theology);
    physical 23 n.; revealed (or
    dogmatic) 5, 7, 9, 15 n., 56, 93,
    94 n., 97; as science 9–10; subject-
    matter of 2–3, 10; (see also *sacra
    doctrina*)
Theory of Everything 66, 253
Thijssen, J. M. M. H. 148 n.
thing: actually existent 34;
    animate 296–7, 333; artificial 72;
    contingent 57, 58 n., 60–3, 139,
    259; corporeal 24, 95–8, 208, 298,
    333, 343 n., 349 n., 351–3, 371;
    created (*see* creatures);
    dependent 24, 58, 60–2, 84, 218;
    extended 302 n.; existence of 33,
    45; generable and corruptible 57,
    67, 168 n.; immaterial 405, 407;
    inanimate 296, 347; incorporeal
    24, 282 n., 352, 364; independently
    existing 339; individual (*see*
    individuals); intellective 343 n.;
    intelligible 238, 350 n., 351, 360,
    408–9; invisible 8, 21;
    living 277 n., 296, 298–9, 329,
    331 n., 332 n., 333, 344–5, 378 n.,
    379, 383; material 78 n., 363 n.;
    nature of 33, 36, 49, 54 n., 69, 120;
    natural 5 n., 33, 54, 58, 60–3, 68,
    71–2, 83–4, 121, 138, 140–1, 167–8,
    194, 195, 200 n., 228, 243 n., 259,
    277 n., 302; necessary 57, 65–6,
    139; permanent 288, 290;
    possible 118; real 297;
    sensible 109 n., 255 n., 302, 346,
    348, 350 n., 351–6, 361, 367, 407 n.,
    408; separately existing;
    spiritual 363 n.; successive 288;
    thinking 302 n.; volitional 121; *see
    also* creatures; substances
Thomas of Wilton 148 n.
Thomas of York 147 n.
time 39, 93, 111–12, 150 n., 163–4, 166,
    168, 170–2, 178–9, 349, 417;
    beginning/beginninglessness of 93,
    111–12, 145 n., 147, 149 n., 180
TMOP 1

TMOT 1–4, 6 n., 9, 10 n., 12 n., 14 n.,
    15 n., 16 n., 18 n., 23 n., 31 n., 34 n.,
    38 n., 39 n., 43 n., 50 n., 57, 57 n.,
    60 n., 66 n., 68 n., 69 n., 70 n., 78 n.,
    98 n., 102 n., 103 n., 120 n., 122 n.,
    124 n., 125, 126 n., 127 n., 150 n.,
    155 n., 166 n., 205 n., 217 n., 229 n.,
    230 n., 231 n., 232 n., 233 n., 241 n.,
    243 n., 244 n., 246 n., 247 n., 254 n.,
    256 n., 257 n., 258 n., 321 n., 326 n.,
    340 n., 371 n., 372 n., 384 n., 395 n.,
    418 n.
transcendentals 241 n., 285 n.
Trinity 1 n., 12 n., 49 n., 135 n., 191
truth: about everything 10; about
    God 9–13, 19, 28 n.; all-
    inclusive 13; as identical with
    God 13; as subject-matter of
    SCG 11; Christian 12;
    clarification of 11; demonstrative
    7; divine 9–13, 18–19, 33, 70, 122;
    existence of 168; explanatory 27;
    highest 27; incorporeal 352;
    investigated by reason 7, 11–13;
    meditating on 19 (*see also*
    meditating); of faith 29, 228–31,
    271 n.; professed by faith 7, 11–12,
    14, 27; revealed 6, 11, 30;
    surpassing reason 11–12; teaching
    of 20 n., 23, 193; two modes
    of 11–13

understanding 21, 27 n., 338 n., 351,
    416
unicity of substantial form: *see* form,
    substantial: unicity of
union: of two actually existing
    substances 292, 316–17; by
    composition 278; by contact
    (taken literally) 277–90; by
    continuity 277–8, 286–90, 341; by
    fastening 277–8, 285 n.; by
    indivisibility 282, 286–7; by mixed
    together 274–9, 286, 290, 313, 319;
    by power contact 278, 281–6, 290,
    301–7, 322, 327–8, 333; by
    touching (*see* by contact [taken
    literally]); cognitive 361, 361 n.,
    362
union of soul with body 271–4, 295,
    302, 323, 325, 370, 372, 374, 376;
    accidental 413; Aristotelian
    account of 299, 325; Averroës'

account of 337, 339–40; as active
and passive relative to one
another 274–5; as an agent with its
patient 282, 285 n.; as power and
what it depends on 271, 274, 293;
as form and matter 278 n., 289–96,
300, 308, 326, 335 n., 390 (*see also*
as substantial form of the body); as
mover and what is movable 300,
304, 321–2, 328, 367 n.; as subject
and accident 289–90, 413 n.; as
substantial form of the body
(hypothesis SFB) 289–96, 299–
301, 305–8, 311–12, 314, 316, 319–
42, 366, 374, 376, 385, 389, 393;
Greek and Muslim views about
299; identity 271 n., 274, 293;
intermediaries in 325–32, 340,
378 n.; Platonist account of 286,
303, 312, 337 (*see also* dualism:
Platonist)
unity: accidental 309, 331 n.; as
regards being 389; in respect of
acting and being acted on 285; in
respect of defining characteristic
286–90, 295, 319; unconditional
278 n., 285–8, 290 n., 292, 301,
303, 308 n., 309, 316, 317 n.,
320, 322, 331 n., 337, 393, 404;
(*see also* union; union of soul with
body)
universals 249–50, 255 n., 349–58,
361–4, 366 n., 407
universe 64, 66, 73, 83–4, 86, 90–1, 95,
98, 101, 106, 108–12, 117, 137,
142–4, 147–8, 159, 161 n., 162,
177 n., 184, 186 n., 187 n., 194–5,
199 n., 206, 210, 215 n., 216, 218,
220, 221 n., 222–4, 230 n., 235–6,
238, 370; form of 207 n.; good
of 219; ordering of parts of 206,
207 n., 219, 220–5; perfection
of 206 n., 224, 236 n., 237–8; *see
also* world
Ussher, Archbishop 147

Veldhuijsen, Peter van 147 n., 148 n.,
150 n.

virtue 135 n., 405–6, 408;
intellectual 127
volition 16–19, 37, 41, 46–7, 78, 105,
122–3, 126, 134, 160, 162, 232,
237 n., 247 n., 336 n., 348 n., 388 n.,
407, 415; simple 250, 418
Vollert, Cyril 142 n., 147 n.
voluntarism 126
vulgate, *see* Bible, vulgate

Wallace, James D. 177 n., 178 n.
Wallace, William A. 142 n.
Webb, Clement C. J. 1 n.
Weisheipl, James A. 142 n.
Wetherbee, Winthrop 97 n.
White, Kevin 325 n.
Whitrow, G. J. 177 n.
whole–part relationship 85 n., 206 n.,
334; quantitative 334–5; with
respect to body 332; with respect
to form's power 335–6; with
respect to soul 333–4; with
respect to specific nature 334;
why–then? argument 162–4;
wickedness, human 4; *see also* evil
Wildberg, Christian 148 n.
will 24–5, 36, 47, 120 n., 122, 126–9,
204, 206, 231–3, 240, 242 n., 243–7,
250–1, 256, 336 n., 339, 344 n.,
346 n., 347, 348 n., 350, 369, 418;
freedom of 247; *see also* God's
will
Wippel, John F. 15 n., 142 n., 145 n.,
146 n., 148 n., 258 n.
wisdom 19, 21–2, 27, 127, 352, 418
wise person 19, 26–7
Wissink, J. B. M. 142 n.
word of God 6 n.
world, 27 n., 29; actual 220, 227 n.,
236; best of all possible 101,
217–19, 225; end of 186 n.;
eternity (sempiternity) of 59–61,
75, 142–84, 196, 340, 413; existence
of 3; material 253; natural 185;
possible 102, 217, 223, 225–6;
teleological order of 3
worship 22
worshippers 24

General Index compiled by Scott MacDonald

Printed in the United Kingdom
by Lightning Source UK Ltd.
131460UK00001B/67/A